Learning MySQL

Learning MySQL

Seyed M.M. "Saied" Tahaghoghi and Hugh E. Williams

O'REILLY®

Beijing · Cambridge · Farnham · Köln · Sebastopol · Taipei · Tokyo

Learning MySQL

by Seyed M.M. "Saied" Tahaghoghi and Hugh E. Williams

Published by O'Reilly Media, Inc., 1005 Gravenstein Highway North, Sebastopol, CA 95472.

O'Reilly books may be purchased for educational, business, or sales promotional use. Online editions are also available for most titles (*http://safari.oreilly.com*). For more information, contact our corporate/institutional sales department: (800) 998-9938 or *corporate@oreilly.com*.

Editor: Andy Oram	**Indexer:** Julie Hawks
Production Editor: Sanders Kleinfeld	**Cover Designer:** Karen Montgomery
Copyeditor: Sanders Kleinfeld	**Interior Designer:** David Futato
Proofreader: Colleen Gorman	**Illustrators:** Robert Romano and Jessamyn Read

Printing History:

November 2006: First Edition.

This book uses RepKover™, a durable and flexible lay-flat binding.

ISBN: 978-0-596-00864-2

[M]   [01/09]

1229018475

Table of Contents

Part II. Using MySQL

Part III.   Advanced Topics

Part IV.   Web Database Applications with PHP

Part VI.   Appendix

Preface

Database management systems are the electronic filing cabinets that help individuals and organizations to manage the mass of information they process each day. With a well-designed database, information can be easily stored, updated, accessed, and collated. For example, a freight company can use a database to record data associated with each shipment, such as the sender and recipient, origin and destination, dispatch and delivery time, current location, and shipping fee. Some of this information needs to be updated as the shipment progresses. The current status of a shipment can be read off the database at any time, and data on all shipments can also be summarized into regular reports.

The Web has inspired a new generation of database use. It's now very easy to develop and publish multi-user applications that don't require any custom software to be installed on each user's computer. Adding a database to a web application allows information to be automatically collected and used. For example, a customer can visit an online shopping site, see what's in stock, place an order, submit payment information, and track the order until the goods are delivered. He can also place advance orders for goods that aren't available, and submit reviews and participate in discussions on items he has purchased. If all goes well, the site's staff doesn't need to intervene in any of these actions; the less staff intervention required during normal operation, the more scalable the application is to large numbers of users. The staff are then free to do more productive tasks, such as monitoring sales and stock in real time, and designing special promotions based on product sales.

Both authors of this book have always been interested in using computers as a tool to make things faster, more efficient, and more effective. Over the past few years we've repeatedly found that the MySQL database management system—and the PHP and Perl programming languages—provide a perfect platform for serious applications such as managing research records and marking student assignments, and not-so-serious ones like running the office sweepstakes. On the way, we've learned a lot of lessons that we'd like to pass on; this book contains the tips that we think most readers will find useful on a daily basis.

Who This Book Is for

This book is primarily for people who don't know much about deploying and using an actual database-management system, or about developing applications that use a database. We provide a readable introduction to relational databases, the MySQL database management system, the Structured Query Language (SQL), and the PHP and Perl programming languages. We also cover some quite advanced material that will be of interest even to experienced database users. Readers with some exposure to these topics should be able to use this book to expand their repertoire and deepen their understanding of MySQL in particular, and database techniques in general.

What's in the Book

The book is divided into six main parts:

1. Introduction
2. Using MySQL
3. Advanced Topics
4. Web Database Applications with PHP
5. Interacting with MySQL using Perl
6. Appendix

Let's look at how the individual chapters are laid out.

Introduction

We first provide some context for the book in Chapter 1, where we describe how MySQL and web database applications fit into the domain of information management tools and technologies.

In Chapter 2, we explain how you can configure the software required for this book on different operating systems. This chapter provides far more detail than most books because we know that it's hard to learn MySQL if you can't first get it up and running.

Chapter 3 introduces the standard text-based interface to the MySQL server. Through this interface, you can control almost every aspect of the database server and the databases on it.

Using MySQL

Before we dive into creating and using databases, we look at proper database design in Chapter 4. You'll learn how to determine the features that your database must have, and how the information items in your database relate to each other.

In Chapter 5, we explore how to read data from an existing MySQL database and how to store data in it.

In Chapter 6, we explain how to create a new MySQL database and how to modify an existing one.

Chapter 7 covers more advanced operations such as using nested queries and using different MySQL database engines.

Chapter 8 continues the advanced operations theme; in this chapter, you'll find a discussion of importing and exporting data, and peeking under the hood to see how the MySQL server processes a given query.

In any serious application, you'll need to prevent unauthorized data access and manipulation. In Chapter 9, we look at how MySQL authenticates users and how you can allow or disallow access to data or database operations.

Advanced Topics

Data stored on a computer can be lost due to hardware failure, theft, or other incidents such as fire or flood. If you need your database, you'll save yourself a lot of hair-pulling by setting up regular and complete backups of your database structure and data. In Chapter 10, we introduce techniques that can help you easily recover from a data loss or corrupted database.

MySQL is highly configurable; in Chapter 11, we describe how you can use configuration files to modify the behavior of the MySQL server and associated programs.

In Chapter 12, we introduce several ways to customize your MySQL server and your application database for improved performance. Small speedups for frequently used queries can markedly improve the overall performance of your system.

Web Database Applications with PHP

In Chapter 13, we examine how web database applications work.

Chapter 14 follows with an introduction to the PHP programming language and a discussion of how PHP can be used to access and manipulate data in a MySQL database.

In Chapter 15, we walk through the design of a wedding gift registry to illustrate the process of developing a full-fledged web database application.

Interacting with MySQL Using Perl

In Chapter 16, we present an easy-to-follow introduction to the powerful Perl programming language.

We continue in Chapter 17 by using the Perl DBI module to connect to a MySQL database to store and read information, and to import and export data.

We conclude this part in Chapter 18 by using the Perl CGI module to create dynamic web pages that can interact with a MySQL database.

Appendix

The Appendix contains all the source code for the wedding gift registry developed in Chapter 15. You can download this source code, and much more, from the book's web site.

Conventions Used in This Book

This book uses the following typographical conventions:

Italic

> Indicates nomenclature that we've not previously used. Also used for emphasis and to indicate files and directories.

`Constant Width`

> Indicates commands and command options, usernames, and hostnames. Also used to show the command output, and the contents of text and program files.

`Constant Width Bold`

> Used in examples to indicate commands or other text that should be typed literally by the user.

`Constant Width Italic`

> Indicates text that you should replace with your own values—for example, your own name or password. When this appears as part of text that you should type in, it is shown as ***`Constant Width Italic Bold`***.

`#, $`

> Used in some examples as the root shell prompt (#) and as the user prompt ($) under the Bourne or `bash` shell. Unless stated otherwise, instructions in such examples can be used with little modification from the Windows command prompt.

`C:\>`

> Used in some examples as the Windows command prompt.

 Signifies a tip, suggestion, or general note.

 Indicates a warning or caution.

Resources

Each chapter finishes with a list of books and web sites that contain further information on the topics covered. The book also has a companion web site at *http://www.learning mysql.com* that contains links to useful resources, frequently asked questions (FAQs), and the example code and data used in this book. It's probably a good idea to have a quick look at the web site now so that you know what's there; it could save you a lot of searching and typing!

Using Code Examples

This book is here to help you get your job done. In general, you may use the code in this book in your programs and documentation. You do not need to contact us for permission unless you're reproducing a significant portion of the code. For example, writing a program that uses several chunks of code from this book does not require permission. Selling or distributing a CD-ROM of examples from O'Reilly books does require permission. Answering a question by citing this book and quoting example code does not require permission. Incorporating a significant amount of example code from this book into your product's documentation does require permission.

We appreciate, but do not require, attribution. An attribution usually includes the title, author, publisher, and ISBN. For example: "*Learning MySQL* by Seyed M.M. Tahaghoghi and Hugh E. Williams. Copyright 2007 O'Reilly Media, Inc., 978-0-596-00864-2."

If you feel your use of code examples falls outside fair use or the permission given above, feel free to contact us at *permissions@oreilly.com*.

Safari® Enabled

Safari ⁑⃗ When you see a Safari® Enabled icon on the cover of your favorite tech-
Books Online nology book, that means the book is available online through the O'Reilly Network Safari Bookshelf.

Safari offers a solution that's better than e-books. It's a virtual library that lets you easily search thousands of top tech books, cut and paste code samples, download chapters, and find quick answers when you need the most accurate, current information. Try it for free at http://safari.oreilly.com. (*http://safari.oreilly.com*)

How to Contact Us

Please address comments and questions concerning this book to the publisher:

    O'Reilly Media, Inc.
    1005 Gravenstein Highway North

Sebastopol, CA 95472
800-998-9938 (in the United States or Canada)
707-829-0515 (international/local)
707-829-0104 (fax)

We have a web page for this book, where we list errata, examples, or any additional information. You can access this page at:

http://www.oreilly.com/catalog/learnmysql

To comment or ask technical questions about this book, send email to:

bookquestions@oreilly.com

For more information about books, conferences, Resource Centers, and the O'Reilly Network, see the O'Reilly web site at:

http://www.oreilly.com

We've spent a lot of effort trying to ensure that the material in this book is correct and that the instructions and examples will work in your environment. However, there is always room for improvement, and we're keen to know your thoughts on how we can make things better. Please send your thoughts by email to *saied@tahaghoghi.com*, or use the online feedback form at *http://www.learningmysql.com/feedback*.

Acknowledgments

First of all, we thank all the people around the world who have contributed to the MySQL, PHP, and Perl projects, and related open source initiatives such as Linux. These have been an important part of our lives, and of course, this wouldn't be much of a book without them!

Writing a technical book is an incredibly time-consuming process, and only an editor as patient and steady-handed as Andy Oram could have coaxed and cajoled us into getting the book done and out of the door. Thanks Andy!

We also thank our technical reviewers, Paul Kinzelman, Falk Scholer, and Omkhar Arasaratnam, for pointing out many ways in which the content could be improved, and the team at O'Reilly for converting our material into a professionally produced book.

Saied Tahaghoghi

I thank Hugh for inviting me to collaborate on this project (and for the countless other ways he's made my life more interesting); Santha Sumanasekara for helping me to set up my first ever Linux box and introducing me to MySQL and PHP so many years ago; my various teachers and mentors for painstakingly showing me the way; and my friends and colleagues for helping me maintain an appearance of sanity. Most of all, I thank all my family for their constant kindness, support, and prayers; I'm especially indebted to my wife, Somayyeh, for patiently enduring for so long my claims that, "The book's almost done!"

Hugh Williams

I thank Selina Williams for being always patient, even-tempered, encouraging, and ready to listen while I slaved away on yet another (and maybe my last?) book project. Thanks also to Lucy and Rose for letting Dad work upstairs day after day, and to Mum and Dad for the lend of the Winnebago in the paddock while I bashed out a few of the more technical chapters. But most of all, thanks Saied for agreeing to take up the reins and finish the book after I moved to Microsoft: you're one of the best men I know. Last, another thank you to Andy Oram; you're a very patient guy whom I've learnt a lot from.

PART I

Introduction

## CHAPTER 1

Introduction

MySQL (pronounced "My Ess Cue Ell") is more than just "the world's most popular open source database," as the developers at the MySQL AB corporation (*http://www .mysql.com*) claim. This modest-sized database has introduced millions of everyday computer users and amateur researchers to the world of powerful information systems.

MySQL is a relatively recent entrant into the well-established area of *relational database management systems* (RDBMs), a concept invented by IBM researcher Edgar Frank Codd in 1970. Despite the arrival of newer types of data repositories over the past 35 years, relational databases remain the workhorses of the information world. They permit users to represent sophisticated relationships between items of data and to calculate these relationships with the speed needed to make decisions in modern organizations. It's impressive how you can go from design to implementation in just a few hours, and how easily you can develop web applications to access terabytes of data and serve thousands of web users per second.

Whether you're offering products on a web site, conducting a scientific survey, or simply trying to provide useful data to your classroom, bike club, or religious organization, MySQL gets you started quickly and lets you scale up your services comfortably over time. Its ease of installation and use led media analyst Clay Shirky to credit MySQL with driving a whole new type of information system he calls "situated software"— custom software that can be easily designed and built for niche applications.

In this book, we provide detailed instructions to help you set up MySQL and related software. We'll teach you Structured Query Language (SQL), which is used to insert, retrieve, and manipulate data. We'll also provide a tutorial on database design, explain how to configure MySQL for improved security, and offer you advanced hints on getting even more out of your data. In the last five chapters, we show how to interact with the database using the PHP and Perl programming languages, and how to allow interaction with your data over the medium most people prefer these days: the Web.

Why Is MySQL so Popular?

The MySQL development process focuses on offering a very efficient implementation of the features most people need. This means that MySQL still has fewer features than its chief open source competitor, PostgreSQL, or the commercial database engines. Nevertheless, the skills you get from this book will serve you well on any platform.

Many database management systems—even open source ones—preceded MySQL. Why has MySQL been the choice for so many beginners and small sites, and now for some heavyweight database users in government and industry? We can suggest a few factors:

Size and speed
> MySQL can run on very modest hardware and puts very little strain on system resources; many small users serve up information to their organizations by running MySQL on modest desktop systems. The speed with which it can retrieve information has made it a longstanding favorite of web administrators.
>
> Over the past few years, MySQL AB has addressed the need of larger sites by adding features that necessarily slow down retrieval, but its modular design lets you ignore the advanced features and maintain the suppleness and speed for which MySQL is famous.

Ease of installation
> Partly because MySQL is small and fast, it works the way most people want straight "out of the box." It can be installed without a lot of difficult and sophisticated configuration. Now that many Linux distributions include MySQL, installation can be almost automatic.
>
> This doesn't mean MySQL is free of administrative tasks. In particular, we'll cover a few things you need to do at the start to tighten security. Very little configuration is shown in this book, however, which is a tribute to the database engine's convenience and natural qualities.

Attention to standards
> As we'll explain in the "Structured Query Language" section later in this chapter, multiple standards exist in the relational database world, and it's impossible to claim total conformance. But learning MySQL certainly prepares you for moving to other database engines. Moving code from one database engine to another is never trivial, but MySQL does a reasonable job of providing a standard environment, and gets better as it develops more features.

Responsiveness to community
> With a few hundred employees scattered around the globe, MySQL AB is a very flexible organization that keeps constant tabs on user needs. At its conferences, lead developers get out in front and make themselves available to everyone with a gripe or a new idea. There are also local MySQL user groups in almost every major city. This responsiveness is helped by the fact that MySQL is open and free; any

sufficiently skilled programmer can look at the program code to find and perhaps help in fixing problems.

MySQL actually has a dual-license approach: if you want to build your own product around it, you pay MySQL AB a license fee. If you just want to use MySQL to serve your own data, you don't have to pay the license fee. MySQL also offers technical support, as do numerous other companies and consultants, some of them probably near you.

Easy interface to other software

It is easy to use MySQL as part of a larger software system. For example, you can write programs that can interact directly with a MySQL database. Most major programming languages have libraries of functions for use with MySQL; these include C, PHP, Perl, Python, Ruby, and the Microsoft .NET languages. MySQL also supports the Open Database Connectivity (ODBC) standard, making it accessible even when MySQL-specific functionality isn't available.

Elements of MySQL and Its Environment

You need to master several skills to run a database system. In this section, we'll lay out what goes into using MySQL and how we meet those needs in this book.

A MySQL installation has two components: a *server* that manages the data, and *clients* that ask the server to do things with the data, such as change entries or provide reports. The client that you'll probably use most often is the `mysql` "MySQL monitor" program, provided by the MySQL AB company and available in most MySQL installations. This allows you to connect to a MySQL server and run SQL queries. Other simple clients are included in a typical installation; for example, the `mysqladmin` program is a client that allows you to perform various server administration tasks.

In fact, any program that knows how to talk to the MySQL server is a client; a program for a web-based shopping site or an application to generate sales graphs for a marketing team can both be clients. In Chapter 3, you'll learn to use the MySQL monitor client to access the MySQL server. In Chapters 13 through 15, we'll look at how we can use PHP to write our own custom clients that run on a web server to present a web frontend to the database for this. We'll use the Apache web server (*http://httpd.apache.org*). Apache has a long history of reliable service and has been the most popular web server in the world for over 10 years. The Apache web server—or "HTTP server"— project is managed by the Apache Foundation (*http://www.apache.org*). Although the web server and MySQL server are separate programs and can run on separate computers, it's common to find small- to medium-scale implementations that have both running on a single computer. In Chapters 16 through 18, we'll explore how the Perl programming language can be used to build command-line and web interfaces to the MySQL server.

To follow the content in this book, you will need some software; fortunately, all the software we use is open source, free for noncommercial use, and easily downloaded from the Internet. To cover all parts of this book, you need a MySQL database server, Perl, and a web server that can talk to MySQL using the PHP and Perl programming languages. We'll explore four aspects of using MySQL:

MySQL server
> We explain how to create your own MySQL installation, and how to configure and administer it.

SQL
> This is the core of MySQL use, and the major topic in this book. It's introduced in "Structured Query Language."

Programming languages
> SQL is not a simple or intuitive language, and it can be tedious to repeatedly perform complex operations. You can instead use a general-purpose programming language such as PHP or Perl to automatically create and execute SQL queries on the MySQL server. You can also hide the details of the interaction with the database behind a user-friendly interface. We'll show you how to do this.

Web database applications
> We explain how you can use PHP or Perl to create dynamic, database-driven web applications that can publish information from the database to the Web, and capture information provided by users.

HTML is the lingua franca of the Web. Although learning HTML is not within the scope of this book, there are many great HTML guides available, including *HTML and XHTML: The Definitive Guide* by Chuck Musciano (O'Reilly). We recommend that you pick up the basics of HTML before reading Chapters 13, 14, 15, or 18.

The LAMP Platform

It's very common to find web database applications developed using the Linux operating system, the Apache web server, the MySQL database management system, and the Perl or PHP scripting language. This combination is often referred to by the acronym LAMP, a term invented at O'Reilly Media.

Linux is the most common development and deployment platform, but as we'll show in this book, you can run all the tools on other operating systems. In fact, we'll give directions for getting started on Linux, Windows, and Mac OS X. Most of the content in this book can be used for other operating systems with little modification.

The P in LAMP originally stood for Perl, but over the past decade, users have increasingly turned to PHP for developing dynamic web pages. PHP is very clean and efficient for retrieving data and displaying it with minimal processing. If you have to do heavy data crunching after the data is returned from MySQL, Perl may still be a better choice. We discuss PHP and Perl largely independently; you can pick up one without needing to learn the other, although we believe that you'll benefit from learning both languages. In fact, almost any modern language can be used to perform this task; most of them have the necessary interfaces to both web servers and database engines.

Structured Query Language

IBM is to be credited not only with inventing the relational database, but developing the language still used today to interact with such databases. SQL is a little odd, bearing the stylistic marks of its time and its developers. It's also gotten rather bloated over the years—a process made worse by its being standardized (multiple times)—but in this book we'll show you the essentials you really need and help you become fluent in them.

SQL shows many of the problems that are commonly attributed to computing standards: it tries to accomplish too much, it forces new features into old molds to maintain backward compatibility, and it reflects uneasy compromises and trade-offs among powerful vendors. As a result, there are several standards that database management systems can adhere to. SQL-92 dates back to 1992 and provides just about everything that you will need for beginning work. However, it lacks features demanded by some modern applications. SQL:1999 was standardized in 1999 and adds a huge number of new features, many of them considered overkill by some experts. There is also a more recent standard, SQL:2003, that was published in 2003 and adds support for XML data.

Each development team has to decide on the trade-offs between the features requested by users and the need to keep software fast and robust, and so database engines generally don't conform totally to any one standard. Furthermore, historical differences have stayed around in legacy database engines. That means that even if you use fairly simple, vanilla SQL, you may have to spend time when porting your skills and your code to another database engine.

In this book, we'll show you how to use MySQL's flavor of SQL to create databases and store and modify data. We'll also show you how to use this SQL variant to administer the MySQL server and its users.

MySQL Software Covered in This Book

You can be very productive with MySQL without dedicating a lot of time to configuration and administration. In Chapter 2, we'll look at several common ways of setting up the software you'll need for this book. While you can skip most of the instructions if you already have a working MySQL installation, we recommend you at least skim through the material for your operating system; we'll frequently refer to parts of this chapter later on. As part of this chapter, we explain how you can configure your MySQL server for good security.

MySQL provides many other tools for administration, including compile-time options, a large configuration file, and standalone utilities developed by both MySQL AB and external developers. We'll give you the basics that will keep you up and running in most environments, and will briefly describe even some relatively advanced topics.

We won't cover all the programs that come with the MySQL distribution, and we won't spend too long on each one; the MySQL reference manual does a good job of covering all the options. We'll instead look at the programs and options that you're most likely to use in practice; these are the ones we've used ourselves a reasonable number of times over several years of working with MySQL.

The Book's Web Site

We've set up the web site, *http://www.learningmysql.com*, which contains the sample databases, datafiles, and program code. We recommend you make good use of the web site while you read this book.

## CHAPTER 2

Installing MySQL

Learning MySQL is easiest if you have a database server installed on your computer. By administering your own server, you can go beyond querying and learn how to manage users and privileges, configure the server, and make the best use of its features. Importantly, you also learn the steps required to install and configure MySQL, which is useful when you need to deploy your applications elsewhere.

This chapter explains how to choose and configure a suitable environment for learning MySQL. We cover the following topics:

- What to install: how to decide between precompiled packages, an integrated web development environment, and compiling from the source code
- Where to install: Linux, Microsoft Windows, or Mac OS X?
- Why, when, and how to upgrade MySQL
- How MySQL has changed and how to migrate between versions
- How to configure the Apache web server and support for the PHP and Perl scripting languages.

MySQL is available in several forms and for many operating systems. In the next section, we examine the choices available and how you can decide what suits you.

Installation Choices and Platforms

As we mentioned before, you'll need MySQL, the Apache web server, PHP, and Perl for this book. How you choose to install these depends on what you want to do, how confident you are in using your operating system environment, and the level of privileges you have on your system. If you're planning to use the installation for learning and development only, and not for a production site, then you have greater choice, and you need not be so concerned about security and performance. We'll describe the most common ways to install the software you need.

You can find the ready-to-use MySQL programs (known as *binaries*) on the MySQL AB web site and on Linux installation CDs and web sites. You can also download the source code for MySQL from the MySQL AB web site and prepare, or *compile*, the executable programs yourself. By doing the compiling yourself, you ensure that you have the most up-to-date version of the software, and you can optimize the compiler output for your particular needs. The MySQL manual says that you can get a performance increase of up to 30 percent if you compile the code with the ideal settings for your environment. However, rolling your own installation from source code can also be a tedious and error-prone process, so we suggest that you stick with the ready-made binaries unless you're experienced and really need to squeeze every ounce of performance from your server. Compiling from source under Windows and Mac OS X is even more involved, so it's uncommon, and we don't discuss it in this book.

You can also install MySQL as part of an integrated package that includes the Apache, PHP, and Perl software that you'll need later in this book. Using an integrated package allows you to follow a step-by-step installation wizard. It's easier than integrating standalone packages, and many of the integrated packages include other tools that help you adjust configuration files, work with MySQL, or conveniently start and stop services. Unfortunately, many of the integrated packages are a couple of minor releases behind the current version and may not include all the PHP libraries that you require. Another disadvantage is that an integrated package doesn't always fit in with your current setup; for example, even if you already have a MySQL installation, you'll get another one as part of the integrated package, and you'll have to take care to avoid clashes. Despite the disadvantages, we recommend you follow this approach. There are several integrated packages available; we feel that XAMPP is probably the best produced of these, and we'll describe how to install and use this. XAMPP includes MySQL, the Apache web server with PHP and Perl support, and other useful software such as phpMyAdmin. We recommend that you start out by using XAMPP, and we won't spend time describing how to separately install and configure Apache, PHP, and Perl to work together on your system.

The software packages you need—MySQL, Apache, PHP, and Perl—are available ready to install on many operating systems and can be compiled to run on a large number of others. However, chances are that you're running one of three major operating systems: Linux, Windows, or Mac OS X, so we'll provide detailed instructions for only these three. Let's see how they compare as MySQL development and production platforms.

Linux

Linux is an open source operating system that is closely modeled on Unix, which is why it's often called a Unix clone. Even though it's free, Linux is very powerful and very secure, with versions available for a wide range of hardware.

You typically get Linux in the form of a *distribution*, such as Red Hat or Mandriva. A distribution packages the operating system together with a large range of useful software for things such as word processing, networking, web and database development, and even games. These distributions are free to download and distribute; you can also buy low-cost CD copies or more expensive shrink-wrapped packs with printed manuals. Many of the most popular web sites run on Linux, and it's an excellent choice for learning MySQL.

Live CDs

You can install Linux on its own, or alongside Windows on a single computer (this is known as *dual-booting*). If you want to try out Linux without installing it on your computer, you can use a bootable, or *live*, CD distribution. This allows you to boot your computer from a CD to get a fully-working Linux system without making any changes to your hard disk. When you remove a live CD and reboot, everything is back to what you had before; you don't have to worry about doing any damage while you learn how to use Linux. For example, the Knoppix (*http://www.knoppix.org*) live CD includes all the software—MySQL, the Apache web server, PHP, and Perl—that you need for this book. However, we recommend that you use a live CD only to become familiar with Linux. While it's possible to save files from a live CD onto the hard disk, a USB flash disk, or another computer through a network connection, this is tedious. For anything that involves using Linux for extended periods of time, you're better off with a full installation to hard disk.

Windows

Microsoft Windows is by far the most common commercial PC operating system today, and new PCs often come with Windows pre-installed. Windows XP, released in 2001, is available on most current PCs. Windows Vista is the latest version of Windows; at the time of writing, it's in "release candidate" (for testing) form and due to be published in the next few months.

We've tested the instructions in this book using both XP and Vista. While we wouldn't recommend using either version for a production server, they're quite appropriate for learning the material in this book. We assume you're using either XP or Vista; you can set up a suitable environment on older versions of Windows such as 98 and Me, but the process is less straightforward. When we say "Windows" in this book, we mean XP or Vista.

Mac OS X

All new Apple computers since 2001 have come with OS X; recent versions include 10.3 (Panther) and 10.4 (Tiger), with 10.5 (Leopard) due for release in the next few months. OS X has a nice graphical user interface over a Unix-like heart, which means it's not hard to use software originally designed for Unix or Linux. Most new Apple computers built from 2006 onward have an x86-type processor; older systems have a PowerPC processor. You can easily check which operating system version or processor your system has by clicking on the Apple menu and choosing the About This Mac entry.

It's not common to find a production MySQL server running on OS X, but it's a good environment for learning MySQL.

So, What Should I Do?

As we mentioned earlier, you can use almost any major operating system when practising the material covered in this book, but to keep things sensible, we'll assume you're using one of the big three just listed. Where the process varies between operating systems, we'll clearly explain the necessary steps. It shouldn't be too hard to interpret the instructions for other operating systems that we don't focus on in this book. For example, many of the Linux instructions can be used with little adaptation on Solaris or FreeBSD.

To install a MySQL server with the standard directories and settings for a system-wide installation, you'll generally need *superuser* (also known as the *system root user* or *administrator*) privileges on your system. Always be careful when using superuser access. The superuser can do anything on a system, so you might be tempted to always log in under the superuser account. However, "anything" means *anything*—including accidentally deleting vital system files and making the system unusable. There are also security risks associated with using this level of access by default, so we strongly suggest you stick to an ordinary, or *nonprivileged*, user account and switch to the privileged account only when necessary. We'll explain how to configure a MySQL server installed on a Linux or Mac OS X system to run as a less privileged user; any files and directories that the server creates are then owned by this account.

If you don't have superuser access—for example, you're using a shared university computer or want to experiment without touching the system-wide MySQL installation —you can generally install a local MySQL server using nonstandard settings; we'll also explain how you can do this. However, we recommend that you go with the default settings if you can, at least while you're still learning a lot about MySQL. You're far less likely to make mistakes, and less likely to run into difficulties with the software; programs are rarely tested as well on nonstandard configurations as they are on the default settings.

Finally, there are cases when the database server may already be set up for you. Many hosting companies, for example, allow you to administer your databases using only a web-based MySQL client such as phpMyAdmin. We'll take a brief look at phpMyAdmin in Chapter 13.

Using the Command-Line Interface

The three operating systems we use in this book all have graphical user interfaces; you can start programs by clicking on icons, you can select tasks from menus, and you can drag and drop files and folders. However, once you start to use more powerful aspects of the operating system and applications, you'll quickly find that some tasks are more easily done by typing in commands. For example, you can tell the operating system to list certain files in a folder or run a given program in a particular way.

Linux, Windows, and Mac OS X all have a command-line interface that allows you to do this. In Linux and Mac OS X, you use a Terminal program to show you the command-line interface, which is called the *shell*. In Windows, you use the Command Prompt Window program to show you the Command Prompt, sometimes called the DOS prompt.

In this section, we'll describe how each command-line interface works; you can skip the descriptions for the operating systems you don't use.

The Linux and Mac OS X Shell

To access the shell under Linux, open a terminal program, such as konsole, rxvt, or xterm; these are often listed in the main menu under the System or System Tools group, and may be simply labeled Terminal. To access the shell under Mac OS X, open a terminal window by double-clicking on the Terminal icon in the Utilities folder under the Applications group.

Under Linux, you'll see a prompt similar to this one:

    [adam@eden ~]$

while under Mac OS X, you'll see something like this:

    eden:~ adam$

This *shell prompt* indicates what user account you're logged in under, what computer you're logged in to, and what directory you're working from. You'll generally be first logged in as an ordinary user (we've shown the user adam here) on the computer (eden), and working from your home directory. The tilde (~) character is a shortcut symbol to a user's home directory on any Unix-like system, including Linux and Mac OS X; for example, a user's home directory could be /home/adam, but you can refer to it as ~adam, or, if you're logged in as adam, simply as ~. The sample prompt shows that the user adam is logged in to the computer eden and working from his home directory. To keep things simple, we'll just show a dollar sign to indicate the Linux or Mac OS X shell prompt, as below:

    $

From the shell, you can run many useful commands; we'll see some as we progress through this book. Two standard commands that are important to know for this book are:

cd

> Changes your working folder or directory on disk. For example, you can change to the /tmp directory by typing:

        $ cd /tmp

You can also change to your home directory by using the tilde shortcut:

```
$ cd ~
```

In fact, you can leave out the tilde: cd on its own means "change to my home directory."

ls

Lists the files and directories in your working folder. For example, you can list the files in your home directory by typing:

```
$ ls ~
```

Together, the cd and ls commands are the text equivalent of using a graphical file manager—such as Konqueror or Nautilus under Linux, or the Finder under Mac OS X—to go to different directories and view their contents.

Command completion and history

Command completion is a great time-saving feature; when you start to type the name of a command, file, or directory, pressing the Tab key cycles through names that could match. The best way to understand this is to try it. For example, when you type:

```
$ cd /t
```

and then repeatedly press the Tab key, you'll see items beginning with the letter "t" in the / (filesystem root) directory. If a name has spaces, a backslash character is added automatically before each space—for example My\ Important\ Notes.txt. Most Linux and Mac OS X systems are configured to use the bash shell, and we assume you're using this, too. If you're using a different shell variant, such as tcsh, you'll need to press the Ctrl-D key combination in place of the Tab key.

Pressing the up and down arrow keys will cycle through the last commands you typed; you can use the arrow keys to edit a previous command, and you can press the Enter key to run a displayed command. You can see a list of recently used commands with the history command, as below:

```
$ history
1  cd Photos/
2  lt
3  find . -name "*AMES*"
4  cfdisk /dev/hda
5  ssh ubuntu@192.168.1.1
```

You can quickly run a command again by typing the number preceded by an exclamation mark (!) character. For example, to run the command numbered 3 in the history list, you can type !3 and press the Enter key.

Performing restricted operations

Certain restricted operations on a Linux or Mac OS X system are allowed only if you have *superuser*, or *root*, privileges. On a Linux system, you can log in as the system root user by typing the su - (switch user) command. When prompted, type in the system root user's password and press the Enter key:

```
[adam@eden ~]$ su -
Password: the_system_root_password
[root@eden ~]#
```

This is almost identical to the case for Mac OS X:

```
eden:~ adam$ su -
Password: the_system_root_password
eden:~ root#
```

After you type in the password, you'll be logged in as the user root on the same computer (in this example, eden) and be working from that user's home directory (also indicated by a tilde).

Notice how the last character of the prompt is a dollar sign ($) when you're not the root user and the hash or pound (#) sign when you are. In this book, we'll use these symbols to indicate whether you should run a certain command as an ordinary user or as the root user. When you've finished doing the restricted operations, you can log out from the system root account by typing exit:

```
# exit
$
```

You can generally use the sudo command to perform actions with system superuser privileges, even though you're not actually logged in as root. You can also use the sudo -s command to log in as the root user (in place of su -). If you log in as the system root user, you can then omit the sudo keyword. Again, we emphasize that you can inadvertently do a great deal of damage if you use the root account, and we recommend that you log in as the system root user as infrequently as you can. Some configuration is necessary to allow ordinary Linux users to use the sudo command, but it's enabled by default under Mac OS X, and we'll use this approach when discussing installation for this operating system.

You can add the ampersand symbol (&) at the end of a command to start the command in the background, allowing you to use the shell for other work. It's better to avoid using this symbol in conjuction with the sudo command, since you won't see any system prompt for you to enter your password. When we want you to run a sudo job in the background, we'll ask you to start the job normally, then press the CTRL-Z key combination to suspend this new job. You can then type the command bg to send the suspended job to the background.

Restricting access to files and directories

Before we end our discussion of the Linux and Mac OS X shell, let's look at how access to files and directories is controlled under such Unix-like operating systems. Each file or directory can have read, write, and execute permissions set for the *user* who owns it, the *group* associated with it, and *every other user*.

When the operating system is asked to allow access to a file or directory, it looks to see who the user is and what groups this user belongs to. It then checks the user and the group associated with that file or directory, and allows access only if the permission settings are appropriate.

Your group on a Linux or Mac OS X system is typically the same as your username, so, for example, the username and group for the user adam would both be adam. The user and group associated with a file or directory can be changed by using the chown command and specifying the username and group as *username:group*. For example, you can set the owner of *myfile.txt* to be adam, and the associated group to be managers, by typing:

```
# chown adam:managers myfile.txt
```

Only the superuser is allowed to change the owner of a file or directory.

You can allocate permissions to a file or directory by using the chmod command. To allow the user who owns the file *myfile.txt* to read and write (modify) it but allow other users to only read it, you would write:

```
$ chmod u=rw,g=r,o=r myfile.txt
```

You can also ensure that only the user who owns the file can read and write to the file as follows:

```
$ chmod u=rw,g=,o= myfile.txt
```

Here, the group and other users have been assigned no permissions. Similarly, you can give everyone read, write, and execute permissions to the directory *mydir* by typing the command:

```
$ chmod u=rwx,g=rwx,o=rwx mydir
```

When reading other documentation, you'll probably also come across cases where an octal value (or *mask*) is used with the chmod command. In this notation, read access has the value 4, write access has the value 2, and execute access has the value 1. So, read-only access has the value 4, but read-and-write access has the value 4+2=6. Our previous two examples would be written as:

```
$ chmod 644 myfile.txt
```

and:

```
$ chmod 777 mydir
```

The chown or chmod operation can be applied to all files and directories under a specified directory by using the --recursive option (under Linux) or the -R option (under Mac OS X as well as Linux). We'll see examples of this later in this chapter.

The Windows Command Prompt

Under Windows, you can open a command-prompt window by clicking on the Command Prompt entry under the Accessories submenu. You can also type `cmd` in the Start menu search box (Vista) or in the Start menu "Run..." field (XP).

The command prompt typically shows you the current working disk and directory:

```
C:\Documents and Settings\Adam>
```

In this example, the current working directory is the home directory *Documents* and *Settings\Adam* on the `C:` disk. Under Vista, the location of the home directory is slightly different:

```
C:\Users\Adam>
```

From the command prompt, you can run many useful commands; we'll see some as we progress through this book. Two standard commands that are important to know for this book are:

cd
> Changes your working folder or directory on disk.

dir
> Lists the files and directories in your working folder.

Together, the `cd` and `dir` commands are the text equivalent of using a graphical file manager such as Windows Explorer to go to different directories and view their contents.

Windows uses the variable `%HOMEPATH%` to refer to your home directory, so you can always change to your home directory by typing:

```
C:\> cd %HOMEPATH%
C:\Documents and Settings\Adam>
```

Command completion and history

Command completion is a feature that can save you a lot of typing. When you start to type the name of a command, file, or directory, pressing the completion key sequence cycles through matches. The completion key varies between systems; it is generally the Tab key or the Ctrl-D or Ctrl-F key combination.

Under Windows, you can activate the command-completion feature if you start the command prompt with the `/f:on` option (command completion is active by default in Vista). If the `/f:on` switch doesn't work on your system, try calling the `cmd` program without the switch. You can also configure Windows XP to have command completion active by default, but we won't describe how to do this here.

The best way to understand command completion is to try it out. For example, when you type **cd c:\p**:

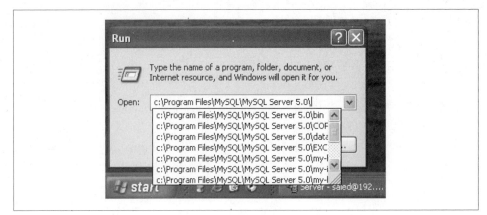

Figure 2-1. Starting a program from the Run menu item

```
C:\> cd c:\p
```

and then repeatedly press the completion key sequence, you'll see items beginning with the letter "p" in the `C:\` directory. Note that Windows doesn't mind whether you use uppercase or lowercase when referring to files and folders.

Quotes are added automatically around names with spaces—for example, `"C:\Program Files"`. To continue expansion, press the backspace key to delete the last quote and type a further hint. For example, to switch to the `C:\Program Files\MySQL` directory, you'd delete the quote, type a backslash (\), and then press the completion key sequence again.

Pressing the up and down arrow keys will cycle through the command history. You can see a list of recently used commands with the `doskey/history` command, as below:

```
C:\> doskey/history
dir C:\
doskey/history
```

There are many more tweaks for the command prompt; just do a search on the Web for "windows cmd".

You can also start other programs from the Start menu; under XP, you would use the Run menu item to browse to select the program you want. If you type in the command, you'll also get command completion, as shown in Figure 2-1. Under Vista, simply type the name of the program in the Start menu search box. However, this approach doesn't always keep the results of running a program on the screen, so we suggest you use the command-prompt window.

Using a Text Editor

As you read through this book, you'll frequently find references to using a text editor. This means a program that can edit and save files that contain only plain text. Word processors save additional formatting instructions that only other word processors understand. Word processing programs also tend to use proportional fonts, which makes it hard to read and write files of scripts and commands. It *is* possible to use a word processor to load and save plain-text files, but it's rather inconvenient and error-prone, and so we don't recommend you do this.

So, what should you use? There are hundreds of text editors available, and most people find one they prefer to use. You should try out several different programs and settle on one that you're comfortable with. Let's look at some options:

Linux
> Under Linux, popular text editors include `pico`, `gvim`, `vim`, `emacs`, `joe`, `kate`, `gedit`, and `xedit`. You can often find these listed under the Editors group in the main menu of most Linux distributions. If you're curious, you can also type the command `apropos "text editor"` at the shell to see a list of programs that have the phrase "text editor" in their description.

Windows
> Under Windows, use Notepad; you can also download and install free text editors such as `gvim`, or commercial editors such as `EditPad` and `TextPad`.

Mac OS X
> Under Mac OS X, you can use the included editors `pico`, `vim`, or `emacs`, configure the TextEdit program to behave as a text editor, or install and use other editors such as BBEdit or Smultron.

To start an editor from the command line, type in the name of the program followed by the name of the file you wish to edit; for example, you can open the file *myfile.txt* with the `pico` editor by typing:

```
$ pico myfile.txt
```

You can also open files from the graphical user interface; double-clicking on the text-file icon will generally open the file in a text editor. You can modify the program that's used to open text files by right-clicking on the text-file icon (in Windows, depress the Shift button while clicking) and work your way through the program options. We won't go into detail here.

Under Mac OS X, you can also configure the TextEdit program to act as a text editor. Start the TextEdit program, and then choose the Preferences option from the TextEdit menu. In the dialog box that appears, select Plain Text under the Format heading. To open a file with TextEdit from the command line, you should type:

```
$ open -a TextEdit myfile.txt
```

You can instead select the plain-text mode for individual files one at a time by selecting the Make Plain Text option from the Format menu, but this approach is likely to be tedious and error-prone over time.

Following the Instructions in This Book

Starting in the next section, we'll explain how to configure a MySQL server on the same system that you're logged in to (that is, `localhost`). We won't describe how to set up the MySQL server on one computer and the web server on a different computer; it shouldn't be too hard to modify our instructions to do this. If you modify any of the default settings, you'll need to remember to specify them where necessary.

We also assume that if you're using Windows, you use only the `C:` disk; we'll explain how and when to change your working directory. When we show only the Linux or Mac OS X prompt as below:

```
$
```

or the Windows Command Prompt as:

```
C:\>
```

the working disk and directory are unimportant, or you will be in the appropriate location after following the steps we describe.

When we use the hash or pound symbol (#) as the prompt:

```
#
```

you will need to type in the commands as the superuser. For a Linux or Mac OS X system, this means you should log in as the system superuser by typing **su -**, or use the **sudo** keyword before the command. For a Windows system, you must be logged in with a system account that has administrator privileges.

Most of our command-line examples outside this chapter are written in a form suitable for Linux and Mac OS X; to run these instructions under Windows, simply replace the forward slash character (/) with the backslash character (\). For example, you may see an example starting the MySQL monitor program (`mysql`) from the `bin` subdirectory as follows:

```
$ bin/mysql
```

On Windows, you'd type **bin\mysql** at the Windows Command Prompt. After this chapter, we'll mostly omit the path to programs and assume that you'll call them using the appropriate path described for your installation in this chapter.

The behavior of many of the programs that we describe in this book can be modified through options. For example, you can use the **user** and **password** options to specify the username and password you want to use. Options can be specified on the command line after the program name. Some programs can also read options from a file. We explain options files in Chapter 11.

When you list options on the command line, you identify them by two adjacent hyphens:

```
$ mysql --user=saleh --password=tomcat
```

Here, we've specified the username `saleh` and the password `tomcat`.

If specified in a configuration file, the leading dashes should be omitted. For example, you would write `--user=saleh` on the command line and `user=saleh` in an options file. We'll generally omit the leading dashes in our descriptions.

Many options also have a short form that can be used only from the command line. For example, instead of writing `--user=saleh` on the command line, you can write the short form `-u saleh`. To help you understand what each command does, we consistently use the long form of each option (where one exists).

Most of the command-line utilities we describe in this book have a `help` option that you can use to discover the command syntax, including any short forms. For example, to learn about the options to use for the `mysql` program, type:

```
$ mysql --help
mysql  Ver 14.12 Distrib 5.0.22, for pc-linux-gnu (i686) using readline 5.0
Copyright (C) 2002 MySQL AB
This software comes with ABSOLUTELY NO WARRANTY. This is free software,
and you are welcome to modify and redistribute it under the GPL license
Usage: mysql [OPTIONS] [database]
  -?, --help Display this help and exit.
...
  -p, --password[=name]
     Password to use when connecting to server. If password is
     not given it's asked from the tty.
  -u, --user=name User for login if not current user.
...
```

We've shown only part of the output here. You can see that you can use the short form `-?` instead of `--help`, `-u` in place of `--user=`, and `-p` in place of `--password=`. The brackets indicate that a clause is optional; for example, you can call the `mysql` program without any command-line options or database name.

Some options assume default values if you don't specify anything. To avoid surprises, you can always explicitly specify the values you want.

When a command gets too long for the page, we show it on multiple lines, with each line ending with a backslash (\) symbol. For example, we might show the previous command as:

```
$ mysql \
    --user=saleh \
    --password=tomcat
```

The backslash characters indicate that this is a single command that should be typed in all on one line. You can actually type in the backslash on a Linux or Mac OS X system to continue your command on a new line, but it's not necessary.

Downloading and Verifying Files from the MySQL AB Web Site

We'll now describe in detail the steps you need to follow to get MySQL up and running on Linux, Windows, and Mac OS X systems. We'll also describe how to start, stop, and configure your MySQL server.

If you install MySQL using the packages provided by MySQL AB, you still need Apache, PHP, and Perl for the later chapters in this book. You can instead follow the instructions to install the XAMPP integrated package to get everything you need. For Linux, you can also use packages provided by your distribution.

Downloading MySQL from the MySQL AB Web Site

The MySQL AB web site usually has the very latest versions of the MySQL software. To download from this web site, follow these steps:

1. Visit the MySQL AB downloads page at *http://dev.mysql.com/downloads*. Figure 2-2 shows what this page looks like.
2. Select the MySQL version that you want. You'll normally want the latest Generally Available (GA) release; this is 5.0.67 at the time of writing. However, you can also download the cutting-edge beta version to try out new features or to help identify problems before the new version becomes the general release.
3. You'll see a long list of packages for the MySQL version you selected; Figure 2-3 shows part of this downloads page. Select the appropriate package to download for your system. In the following sections, we'll tell you what this is for each operating system and installation approach.
4. Before the file download starts, you'll probably be asked to to pick a mirror server near you. Mirrors are servers that have identical copies of files for download, and are used to share the burden of many people downloading the packages. The MySQL site uses an IP-to-location database to guess where you are and will suggest some nearby servers you can download from. Selecting a mirror will start the file download.

Verifying Package Integrity with MD5

When downloading files from the Internet, it's a good idea to ensure that what you've got is what you wanted to get. For a production server, we recommend that you check the integrity of packages that you download. A simple way to do this is to compare checksums generated by a digest algorithm such as MD5.

A digest algorithm takes some data (for example, an RPM file) as input and calculates a 128-bit number, or *checksum*, from this data. With a good digest algorithm, it's practically impossible to change the data without changing the checksum, so if the checksums of two files match, you can be certain that the files are identical.

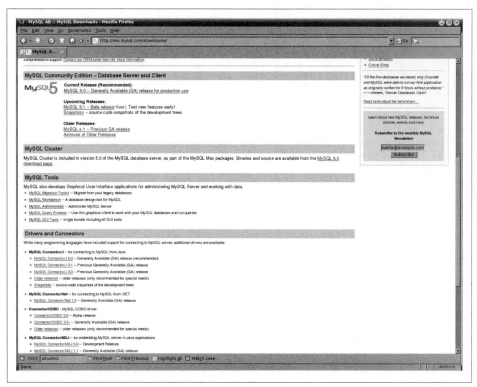

Figure 2-2. The MySQL AB downloads page

On the MySQL download page, you'll see a different string of characters such as:

```
MD5: 0d2a3b39e7bb4109b2f7b451b7768f34
```

next to each file. You should ensure that the checksum of the file you have downloaded matches the corresponding value on the downloads page.

On Linux, use the md5sum program on the downloaded file:

```
$ md5sum mysql-standard-5.0.22-linux-i686.tar.gz
0eaa7a8ec18699ce550db1713a27cda3 mysql-standard-5.0.22-linux-i686.tar.gz
```

 The filename is shown in italic in this example because the name is likely to change, and you'll have to type in the actual name of the file you download.

On Windows, you can download and use the free winMd5Sum program from *http://www.nullriver.com/winmd5sum*. This program is very easy to use; just install and start the program, press the "..." button to browse for and select the downloaded file, and

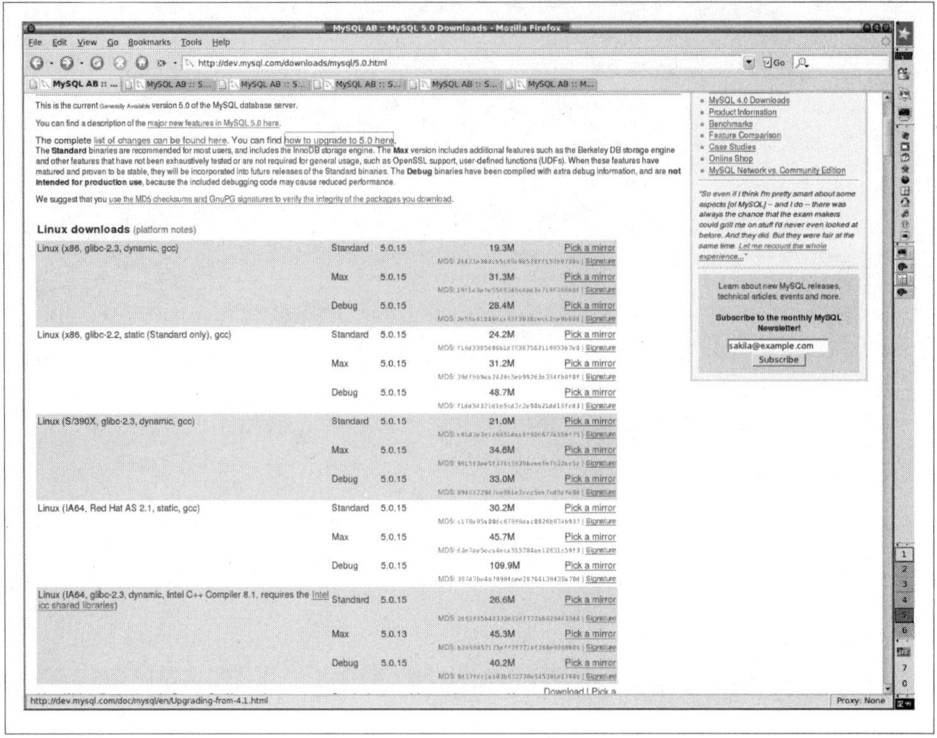

Figure 2-3. The Linux section of the MySQL downloads page

then read off the checksum value. Figure 2-4 shows what this program's dialog box looks like.

On Mac OS X, open a terminal window and use the `md5` program:

```
$ md5 mysql-standard-5.0.22-osx10.4-i686.dmg
MD5
(mysql-standard-5.0.22-osx10.4-i686.dmg) =
b7d7f0878503db504e1eaed5d2518f4e
```

Digitally signed packages offer a more secure way to ensure that files have not been tampered with; however, MD5 checksums should be sufficient for most readers of this book.

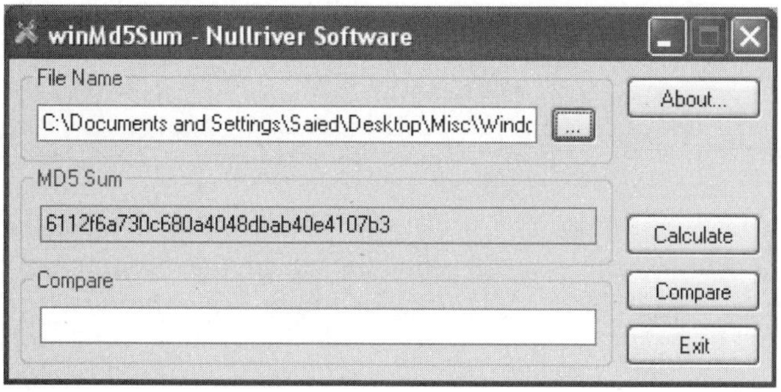

Figure 2-4. *Using winMd5Sum to verify the MD5 checksum of a downloaded file*

Open source projects such as MySQL, Apache, PHP, and Perl produce constantly evolving software, with new versions appearing regularly. The installation files typically include the version number in the filename—for example, *MySQL-server-<version>.i686.rpm*. The versions of the software that you will use are almost certainly newer than the ones used in our examples, so you should substitute the appropriate version number when handling them. Of course, installation details change over time—things generally become easier—so expect some variation from the steps we discuss here. You'll also probably find that the output we show for various programs will be slightly different from what you see on your own system.

Whenever you install software that can accept connections from other computers, you should take care to configure your computer firewall software to block connections from unauthorized systems. This is particularly important if your computer is easily accessible from the Internet, for example through your connection to your Internet Service Provider (ISP).

Installing Under Linux

There are five main ways to get MySQL up and running on a Linux system. You can:

- Install a system-wide server from packages downloaded from the MySQL AB web site. Using packages supplied by MySQL AB means that the MySQL-related files are located together in a consistent way.

  MySQL AB provides these packages in the RPM format: a collection of files that can be processed and installed by the `rpm` program. The name is a vestige of the program's origins as the Red Hat Package Manager. However, many Linux distributions other than Red Hat use RPMs for managing software installation; these include Fedora, Mandriva/Mandrake, and SUSE. The MySQL AB company also provides files for download in the format used by Debian-based distributions but recommends that the `apt-get` method be used instead; we describe the recommended approach in this chapter.

- Install a system-wide or local server using using a compressed directory (known as a gzipped tar archive) from the MySQL AB web site. This directory has all the necessary MySQL files ready to run in place; you don't need to run an installer program or place the files in a particular location on disk.

- Install a system-wide or local server by downloading the MySQL source code from the MySQL AB web site and compiling the executable programs yourself. This is the most time-consuming way of setting up Linux, but is the most flexible for power users.

- Install a system-wide server using packages created by your Linux distribution; you can download these from the Web or install them from your Linux CDs.

- Install a system-wide server by downloading the XAMPP integrated package. Note that XAMPP is not designed for use as a local server, and significant effort is required to get around this limitation.

We'll describe each of these approaches in detail. If you're not sure which approach is most suitable for you, we recommend you first try to use the packages provided by your Linux distribution.

Installing MySQL on Linux Using RPM Packages from MySQL AB

First, go to the MySQL AB downloads page following the instructions in the "Downloading MySQL from the MySQL AB Web Site" section, and scroll down the list to the part of the page with the label "Linux x86 RPM downloads." The x86 indicates the processor type; almost all PCs today use x86 processors. If you have a more advanced type, such as an AMD 64-bit processor, you should find the appropriate part of the downloads page.

Pick RPM packages for both the MySQL server and the client, taking care that you select the correct version for your Linux distribution and your processor. These will be called something like *MySQL-server-5.0.22-0.i386.rpm* and *MySQL-client-5.0.22-0.i386.rpm*. Packages with higher CPU numbers, such as i586 or i686, are better tuned for newer machines, but won't work on older machines.

If you intend to do server benchmarking and testing, you may need to download the benchmark and test suites package (with a name like *MySQL-bench-5.0.22-0.i386.rpm*); however, you won't need them for this book.

To install the RPM files, you'll need to log in as the system root user. Open a terminal program and use the `su -` command to log in as the root user:

```
$ su -
#
```

Change to the directory containing the MySQL RPM files you downloaded. This is typically your home directory or your desktop directory. To change to the home directory of the user adam, you'd type:

```
# cd ~adam
```

The location of the desktop directory depends on the Linux distribution you use, but is commonly the Desktop directory under the home directory. To change to the desktop directory of the user adam, you'd type:

```
# cd ~adam/Desktop
```

You can then install the MySQL server and MySQL client RPMs (or upgrade any existing versions) by typing:

```
# rpm --upgrade --verbose --hash \
    MySQL-server-5.0.22-0.i386.rpm MySQL-client-5.0.22-0.i386.rpm
```

If all goes well, your MySQL server should now be installed. We'll look at how to configure it in "Configuring a Newly Installed Server," later in this chapter.

Installing MySQL on Linux Using a gzipped Tar Archive from MySQL AB

Instead of using an installable package, you can download a compressed directory of the MySQL executable and support files. This process is slightly more involved than installation from a package.

Follow the instructions of "Downloading MySQL from the MySQL AB Web Site" and download the appropriate package from the "Linux (non RPM package) downloads" section of the MySQL AB downloads page. For this book, select the "standard" package, rather than the "Max" or "debug" versions.

If you're unsure what to choose, try picking the Linux download at the top of the list. This will be named something like *mysql-standard-5.0.22-linux-i686.tar.gz*.

For distribution, Linux software is often packaged using the tar program, and then this package is compressed using the gzip program, so the final file often has the file extension *.tar.gz* or *.tgz*. A *.tar* file, or its gzipped version, is often referred to as a *tarball*. You'll need to unpack, or *untar,* this package:

```
$ tar --gunzip --extract --file mysql-standard-5.0.22-linux-i686.tar.gz
```

The gunzip option asks the program to decompress the file first using the gunzip program. Some browsers automatically decompress files that have a *.gz* extension; if you get a message like "gzip: stdin: not in gzip format," this has probably happened in your case, and you can omit the gunzip option:

```
$ tar --extract --file mysql-standard-5.0.22-linux-i686.tar.gz
```

You should now have the directory: *mysql-standard-5.0.22-linux-i686*. To keep things simple, we'll call this the MySQL directory.

The MySQL directory is self-contained and has all the files you need to run and access the server. If you have superuser access on the Linux machine and want this MySQL server to be the system-wide instance on the machine, you should move it across to a the standard location under the /usr/local/ directory:

```
# mv mysql-standard-5.0.22-linux-i686 /usr/local/
```

and make a link /usr/local/mysql that points to this directory:

```
# ln --symbolic /usr/local/mysql-standard-5.0.22-linux-i686 /usr/local/mysql
```

Now you can simply refer to the MySQL directory as /usr/local/mysql. Using a symbolic link in this way allows you to have different versions of MySQL ready to run on the system, with /usr/local/mysql pointing to the directory containing the version you want to use.

If you want to have a local installation, you can leave the MySQL directory under your home directory. You'll probably find it helpful to create the link ~/mysql to point to the actual MySQL directory—for example:

```
$ ln --symbolic ~/mysql-standard-5.0.22-linux-i686 ~/mysql
```

With this link, you can use ~/mysql wherever you want to refer to the ~/mysql-standard-5.0.22-linux-i686 directory.

Installing MySQL on Linux by Compiling the Source Code from MySQL AB

Given the nature of this book, we won't go into detailed compile-time settings, but will just look at how you can quickly get the server up and running.

First, you need to download the source file package from the MySQL AB downloads page, following the directions in "Downloading MySQL from the MySQL AB Web Site." Go to the "Source downloads" section and download the "Tarball (tar.gz)" package.

After downloading, you should have a file with a name like *mysql-5.0.22.tar.gz*. Decompress this package using the following command:

```
$ tar --gunzip --extract --file mysql-5.0.22.tar.gz
```

This creates a new directory containing the MySQL source files; change your working directory to this by typing:

```
$ cd mysql-5.0.22
```

You must now compile the source code and install the resulting programs. After you've done this, you'll have a MySQL directory that has all the files you need to run and access the server. This is very similar to the tarball approach. Unlike the tarball approach, however, you need to first use the configure command to tell the compilation process where you want the MySQL directory to be located.

If you have superuser privileges and want your MySQL installation to be system-wide, it's best to install to a directory under the */usr/local* directory—for example, */usr/local/ mysql-5.0.22*. On the other hand, if you want to run a local server, you can have the MySQL directory wherever you wish—for example, under your own home directory at *~/mysql-5.0.22*.

To install MySQL to the directory */usr/local/mysql-5.0.22*, we call the `configure` command with the target as follows:

```
$ ./configure --prefix=/usr/local/mysql-5.0.22
```

If all is not well, you may see some error messages. Problems during configuration are generally due to Linux programs and libraries missing from your system; read the error messages carefully to identify the cause of the problem.

If the configuration is successful, you can use the `make` command to compile the files:

```
$ make
```

The compilation process may take a long time.

 You need to use the GNU variant of the `make` program (*http://www.gnu .org/software/make*). The `make` command on most Linux systems is in fact the GNU make program; if you run into problems when using `make`, it might not be GNU `make`, and the problem may be resolved by using the `gmake` (GNU make) command instead.

When it's done, you need to install the files to the directory you specified earlier. If you've chosen to install a local server, you can simply type:

```
$ make install
```

If—as in our example—you've specified a prefix path that you can't normally write to as an ordinary user, you'll need to first log in as root:

```
$ su -
```

and then run `make install` from the root prompt to copy the compiled files to the target installation directory:

```
# make install
```

If all goes well, the MySQL files will be installed in the correct directory. You'll often find it helpful to create a link to refer to this directory easily. For example, for a system-wide server, you can make the link `/usr/local/mysql` to point to the */usr/local/ mysql-5.0.22* directory:

```
# ln --symbolic /usr/local/mysql-5.0.22 /usr/local/mysql
```

Now you can simply refer to the MySQL directory as `/usr/local/mysql`. Similarly, if you specified the path */home/adam/mysql-5.0.22* for a local installation, you can make the link `~/mysql` to point to the *~/mysql-5.0.22* directory:

```
$ ln --symbolic ~/mysql-5.0.22 ~/mysql
```

and refer to the directory as ~/mysql.

Again, using a symbolic link in this way allows you to configure and use different versions of MySQL on a system, with the symbolic link pointing to the directory containing the version you want to use.

Note that the configuration process assumes default values for anything that you don't specify. For example, you can explicitly set the data directory, TCP port, and socket file (more about these later):

```
$
./configure \
  --prefix=/home/adam/mysql \
  --localstatedir=/home/adam/mysql/data \
  --with-unix-socket-path=/home/adam/mysql/mysql.sock \
  --with-tcp-port=53306
```

However, we recommend you compile only with the prefix directory specified. You can then modify other settings by passing options to MySQL from the command line; we explain how to do this in "Configuring a local server," later in this chapter. Even better, you can specify the options in an options file as described in Chapter 11.

Installing MySQL, Apache, PHP, and Perl on Linux Using Distribution Packages

Almost all distributions include packaged versions of the main pieces of software that you need to follow this book: MySQL, the Apache web server, and support for the PHP and Perl scripting languages. In this section, we'll explain how to install these if they're not already present on your Linux system.

The three main distributions we'll cover are Red Hat, Mandriva, and Debian, as well as distributions associated with these, including Fedora, Mandrake, Ubuntu, and Knoppix. These are very widely used, and are well supported by the distributors and by the general Linux community. Configured correctly, they can automatically fetch and install the required software from the installation media or from the Internet.

Most distributions have an easy-to-use graphical package-management tool that you can use, but the command-line tools are generally more reliable, and we feel you'll better understand how things fit together by carrying out the installation from the command line.

Installation on Red Hat and Fedora Core

Red Hat is probably the most famous Linux distribution, and Fedora Core is the cutting-edge version of Red Hat's Enterprise Linux distribution. If you're installing one of these two from scratch, select the Custom installation option and, when you see the package-selection list like that shown in Figure 2-5, select (put a checkmark) next to

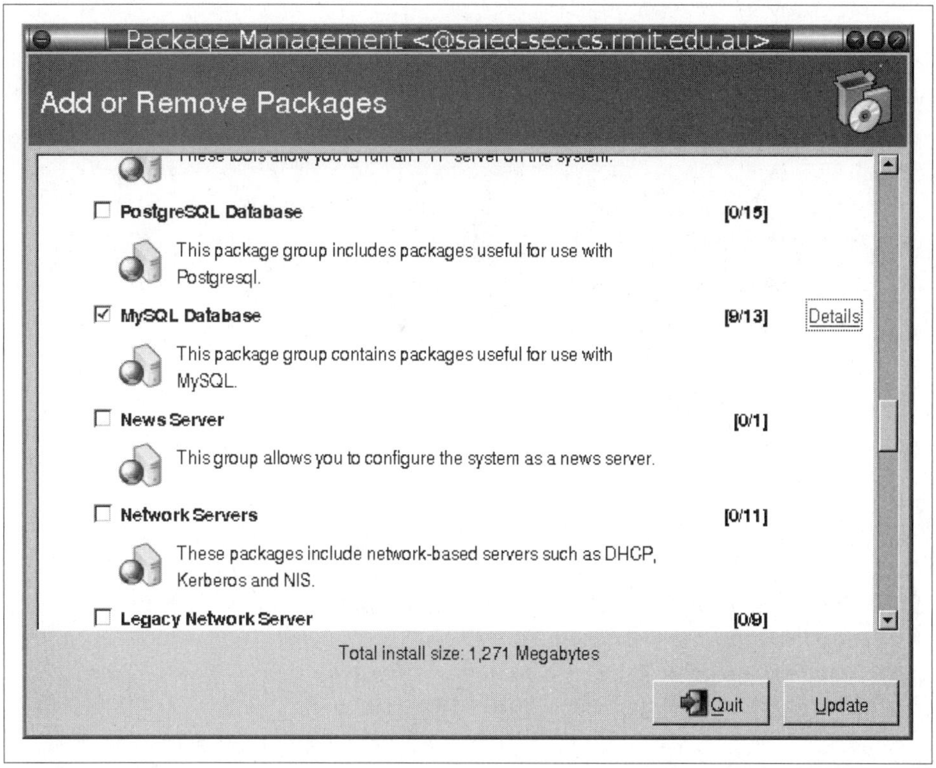

Figure 2-5. Red Hat and Fedora package options

the Web Server item. To add PHP support and PHP MySQL libraries, click on the Details link on the right and select the packages "php" and "php-mysql" from the list; you should see something similar to Figure 2-6. Once you've done this, return to the package-selection list and select (put a checkmark) next to the MySQL Database item. As before, click on the Details link and ensure the "php-mysql" package is selected.

If you already have a running Linux installation, you can use the rpm command to check whether MySQL, Apache (known as *httpd*), and PHP are already installed:

```
$ rpm --query --whatprovides mysql php php-mysql
mysql-5.0.22-1.FC5.1
mysql-server-5.0.22-1.FC5.1
httpd-2.2.0-5.1.2
php-5.1.4-1
php-mysql-5.1.4-1
```

If, as in this example, all the necessary packages are installed, you can simply skip to "Configuring a Newly Installed Server," later in this chapter.

If the packages aren't present, you'll see messages like this:

```
no package provides php
```

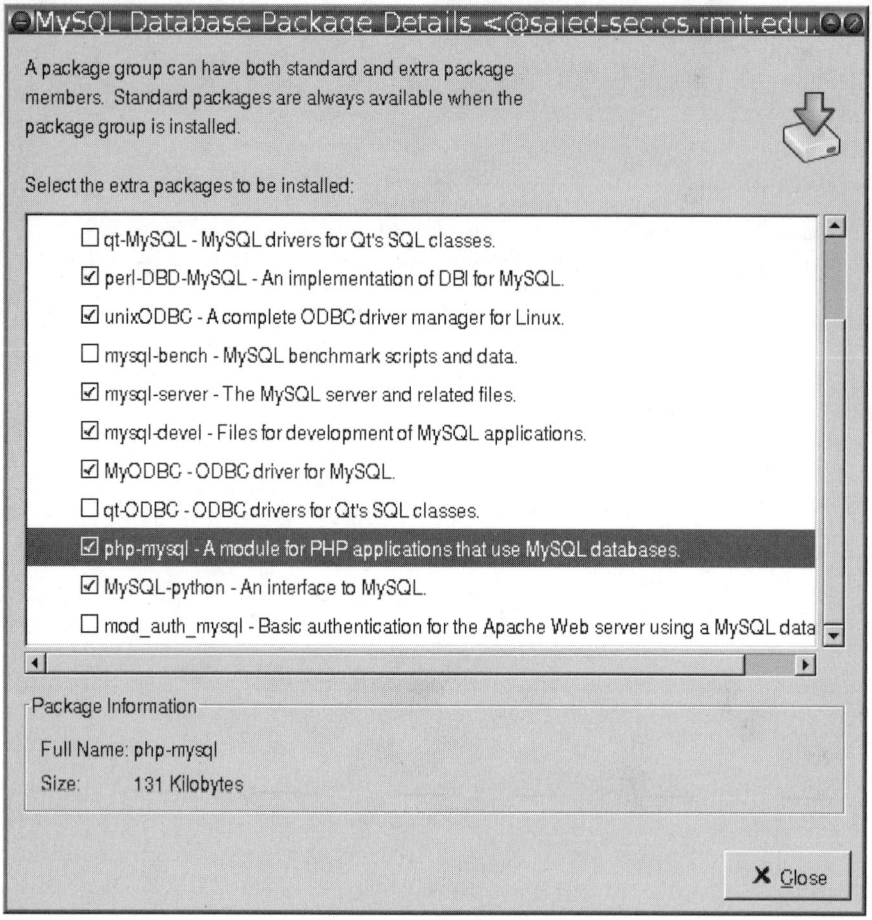

A package group can have both standard and extra package
members. Standard packages are always available when the
package group is installed.

Select the extra packages to be installed:

☐ qt-MySQL - MySQL drivers for Qt's SQL classes.

☑ perl-DBD-MySQL - An implementation of DBI for MySQL.

☑ unixODBC - A complete ODBC driver manager for Linux.

☐ mysql-bench - MySQL benchmark scripts and data.

☑ mysql-server - The MySQL server and related files.

☑ mysql-devel - Files for development of MySQL applications.

☑ MyODBC - ODBC driver for MySQL.

☐ qt-ODBC - ODBC drivers for Qt's SQL classes.

☑ php-mysql - A module for PHP applications that use MySQL databases.

☑ MySQL-python - An interface to MySQL.

☐ mod_auth_mysql - Basic authentication for the Apache Web server using a MySQL data

Package Information

Full Name: php-mysql

Size: 131 Kilobytes

✕ Close

Figure 2-6. Detailed Red Hat and Fedora package options

and you'll need to install any missing packages.

Run the Package Manager by selecting Add/Remove Software from the Fedora menu.
Alternatively, log in as root and type:

```
# pirut
```

You should see a window similar to the one shown in Figure 2-7. Select the List tab,
and choose any of these packages that don't already have a checkmark next to them:

httpd-2.2.0-5.1.2.i386
    Apache HTTP Server

mysql-5.0.22-1.FC5.1.i386
    MySQL client programs and shared libraries

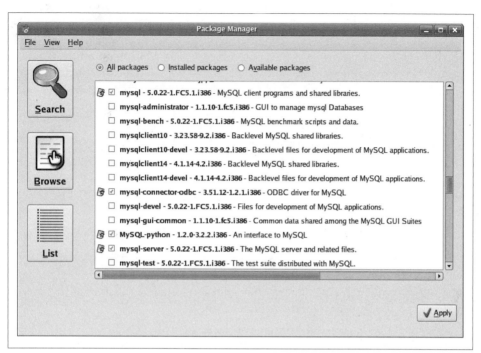

Figure 2-7. Red Hat and Fedora 5 package-management program

mysql-server-5.0.22-1.FC5.1.i386
> The MySQL server and related files

php-5.1.2-5.i386
> The PHP HTML-embedded scripting language (PHP Hypertext Preprocessor)

php-mysql-5.1.4-1.i386
> A module for PHP applications that use MySQL databases

The version numbers you see will probably be different from the ones we've listed. Once you've selected these, click the Apply button, and the software should be installed.

If you're using an older version of Red Hat or Fedora, the easiest way to install is to log in under the root user account (by typing **su -**) and launch the package-management program shown in Figure 2-5:

```
# system-config-packages
```

Place a checkmark next to the entry for MySQL Database, and click on the Details link. You'll see a window such as that in Figure 2-6. Select the "mysql-server" and "php-mysql" packages, and then click the Close button. You'll be prompted for the Red Hat or Fedora installation CDs, and the selected packages will be installed.

If you have a relatively recent version of Red Hat or Fedora, you can also use the yum (short for Yellowdog Updater Modified) program to automatically download and install the necessary packages from the Internet. This is very convenient because you don't have to spend time digging up your installation CDs. More importantly, the latest version of a package generally has patches for known bugs and security vulnerabilities. If you've never used yum before, you need to configure it first. First, type su - to log in as the system root user, and then update your /etc/yum.conf configuration file by typing:

```
# wget http://www.fedorafaq.org/samples/yum.conf
# /bin/mv /etc/yum.conf /etc/yum.conf.bak
# /bin/mv yum.conf /etc
```

Now, update the yum indexes that list packages and the locations that they can be downloaded from:

```
# rpm --upgrade --verbose --hash http://www.fedorafaq.org/yum
Retrieving http://www.fedorafaq.org/yum
Preparing...                 ########################################### [100%]
1:yum-fedorafaq               ########################################### [100%]
```

Once you've configured yum, you can download and install all the programs you need by simply specifying them from the command line:

```
# yum update mysql mysql-server httpd php php-mysql
[root@saiedpc ~]# yum update mysql mysql-server httpd php php-mysql
...

Could not find update match for php
Could not find update match for php-mysql
Could not find update match for mysql-server
Could not find update match for mysql
Resolving Dependencies

...

=============================================================================
Package                 Arch        Version          Repository        Size
=============================================================================
Updating:
httpd                   i386        2.2.2-1.2        updates           1.1 M
Updating for dependencies:
httpd-manual            i386        2.2.2-1.2        updates           846 k
mod_ssl                 i386        1:2.2.2-1.2      updates           99 k

Transaction Summary
=============================================================================
Install       0 Package(s)
Update        3 Package(s)
Remove        0 Package(s)
Total download size: 2.0 M
Is this ok [y/N]: y
Downloading Packages:
(1/3): mod_ssl-2.2.2-1.2. 100% |=========================|  99 kB    00:14
```

```
(2/3): httpd-2.2.2-1.2.i3 100% |=========================| 1.1 MB   03:14
(3/3): httpd-manual-2.2.2 100% |=========================| 846 kB   02:40
Running Transaction Test
Finished Transaction Test
Transaction Test Succeeded
Running Transaction
  Updating  : httpd                         ######################### [1/6]
  Updating  : mod_ssl                       ######################### [2/6]
  Updating  : httpd-manual                  ######################### [3/6]
  Cleanup   : mod_ssl                       ######################### [4/6]
  Cleanup   : httpd                         ######################### [5/6]
  Cleanup   : httpd-manual                  ######################### [6/6]

Updated: httpd.i386 0:2.2.2-1.2
Dependency Updated: httpd-manual.i386 0:2.2.2-1.2 mod_ssl.i386 1:2.2.2-1.2
Complete!
```

You'll see lots of interesting messages flash by; we haven't shown them all here. If all goes well, you should see the reassuring Complete status message at the end. If the latest version of a package is already installed, yum will tell you that it Could not find update match for that package. To learn more about Fedora and configuring yum, visit the Unofficial Fedora FAQ page (*http://www.fedorafaq.org*).

You can also download Red Hat or Fedora RPMs and install and upgrade them manually just as you would the MySQL AB ones. For example, you can visit the web site *http://rpm.pbone.net* and search for mysql; pick and download the RPM for Red Hat or Fedora with the highest version number. Once you've downloaded the files, log in under the root account by typing su -, and then install the RPM packages by typing in this command (all on one line):

```
# rpm --upgrade --verbose --hash \
    mysql-server-5.0.22-2.1.i386.rpm \
    mysql-5.0.22-2.1.i386.rpm \
    httpd-2.2.2-7.i386.rpm \
    php-5.1.4-8.1.i386.rpm
```

Installation on Mandriva

Mandriva, formerly known as Mandrake, is very easy to use for this book (we use it ourselves). MySQL, Apache, PHP, and Perl all come on the distribution CDs.

If you're installing Mandriva from scratch, choose the Expert installation option and select the MySQL server and client packages.

If you already have a running Mandriva installation, you can check whether Apache, PHP, and MySQL are already installed by typing:

```
$ rpm --query --whatprovides mysql mysql-client apache php php-mysql
MySQL-5.0.23-1mdv2007.0
MySQL-client-5.0.23-1mdv2007.0
apache-mpm-prefork-2.2.3-1mdv2007.0
apache-mod_php-5.1.4-1mdk
```

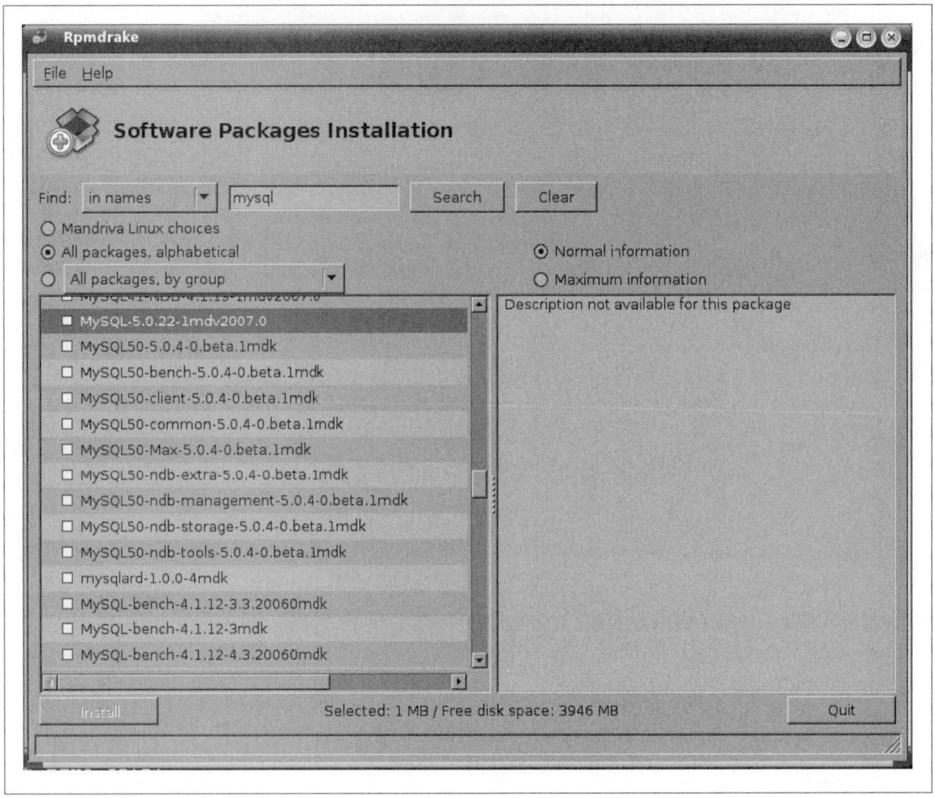

Figure 2-8. The Mandriva package-management program

```
php-cli-5.1.4-6mdv2007.0
php-mysql-5.1.4-3mdv2007.0
```

If, as in this example, all the necessary packages are installed, you can simply skip to "Configuring a Newly Installed Server," later in this chapter.

If the packages aren't present, you'll see messages like this:

```
no package provides php
```

and you'll need to install any missing packages.

The easiest way to install is to log in under the root account (by typing **su** -) and type:

```
# rpmdrake
```

This will launch the package-management program, shown in Figure 2-8. Place a checkmark next to the entries for the MySQL server and client, and click on the Install button. You'll be prompted to insert the Mandriva installation CDs, and the selected packages will be copied and installed.

If you prefer to use the command line, you can use the **urpmi** command to specify packages to install. This will prompt you to insert the appropriate installation CDs, and will install the packages. You may be prompted to install other related packages, depending on what's already available on your system, but in most cases, it should be painless.

If you have a fast Internet connection, you can also configure urpmi to download and install the very latest packages from the Internet. This is very convenient because you don't have to spend time digging up your installation CDs. More importantly, the latest version of a package generally has patches for known bugs and security vulnerabilities. To set up Internet downloads, you'll first need to tell urpmi where to find the packages. The easiest way to do this is to go to *http://easyurpmi.zarb.org*; this site will ask you a few questions and then provide you a list of commands you need to type in as the system root user to configure the sources (Figure 2-9 shows how this site looks.) From time to time, you should update the urpmi indexes by logging in as the system root user and typing:

```
# urpmi.update -a
```

Whichever approach—CDs or the Internet—you use, you just need to type **urpmi** *package_name* as the root user to fetch and install the required packages.

```
$ urpmi mysql mysql-client apache php php-mysql
One of the following packages is needed:
 1- MySQL-5.0.23-1mdv2007.0.i586 : MySQL: a very fast and reliable SQL database
    engine (to install)
 2- MySQL-Max-5.0.23-1mdv2007.0.i586 : MySQL - server with extended functionality
    (to install)
 3- MySQL-NDB-4.1.12-4.3.20060mdk.i586 : MySQL - server with Berkeley DB, Innodb
    and NDB Cluster support (to install)
What is your choice? (1-3) 1
To satisfy dependencies, the following packages are going to be installed:
MySQL-5.0.23-1mdv2007.0.i586
MySQL-client-5.0.23-1mdv2007.0.i586
MySQL-common-5.0.23-1mdv2007.0.i586
apache-mod_php-5.1.4-2mdv2007.0.i586
libmysql15-5.0.23-1mdv2007.0.i586
perl-DBD-mysql-3.0006-1mdv2007.0.i586
php-mysql-5.1.4-3mdv2007.0.i586
Proceed with the installation of the 7 packages? (39 MB) (Y/n) Y

    ftp://somehost.net/somedir/libmysql15-5.0.23-1mdv2007.0.i586.rpm
    ftp://somehost.net/somedir/perl-DBD-mysql-3.0006-1mdv2007.0.i586.rpm
    ftp://somehost.net/somedir/MySQL-common-5.0.23-1mdv2007.0.i586.rpm
    ftp://somehost.net/somedir/MySQL-client-5.0.23-1mdv2007.0.i586.rpm
    ftp://somehost.net/somedir/MySQL-5.0.23-1mdv2007.0.i586.rpm
    ftp://somehost.net/somedir/apache-mod_php-5.1.4-2mdv2007.0.i586.rpm
installing
    libmysql15-5.0.23-1mdv2007.0.i586.rpm
    MySQL-client-5.0.23-1mdv2007.0.i586.rpm
    MySQL-common-5.0.23-1mdv2007.0.i586.rpm
    perl-DBD-mysql-3.0006-1mdv2007.0.i586.rpm
    MySQL-5.0.23-1mdv2007.0.i586.rpm
    apache-mod_php-5.1.4-2mdv2007.0.i586.rpm
```

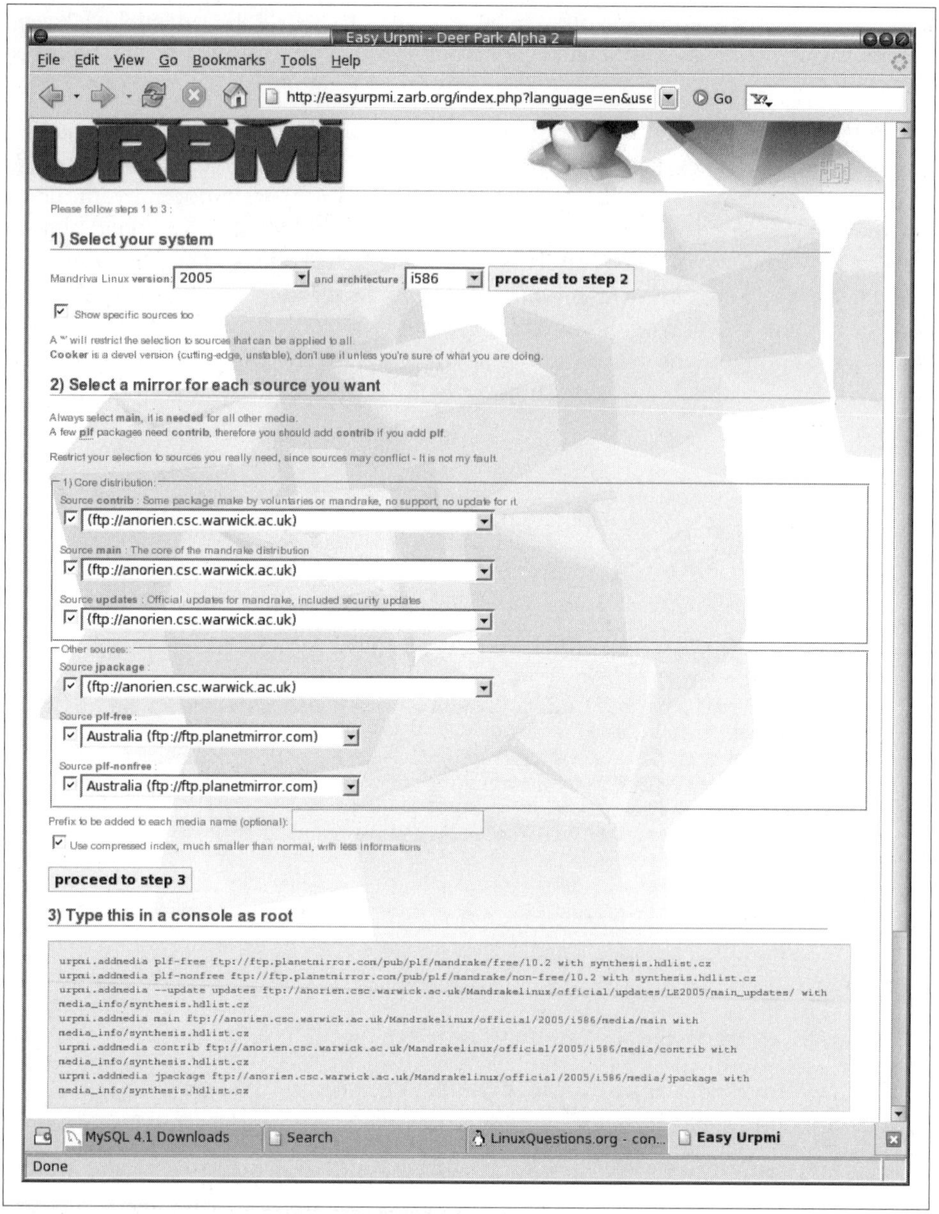

Figure 2-9. The easyURPMI configuration page

```
       php-mysql-5.1.4-3mdv2007.0.i586.rpm
from /var/cache/urpmi/rpms
Preparing...                   ######...######
     1/7: libmysql15           ######...######
     2/7: MySQL-client         ######...######
     3/7: perl-DBD-mysql       ######...######
```

```
  4/7: MySQL-common           ######...######
  5/7: MySQL                  ######...######
  6/7: apache-mod_php         ######...######
  7/7: php-mysql              ######...######
----------------------------------------------------------------------

More information on package MySQL-5.0.23-1mdv2007.0.i586

The initscript used to start mysql has been reverted to use the one shipped by
MySQL AB. This means the following changes:

 * The MYSQLD_OPTIONS="--skip-networking" option in the /etc/sysconfig/mysqld
   file has been removed, this is now set in the /etc/my.cnf file.

 * The MySQL Instance Manager is used by default, set use_mysqld_safe="1" in
   the /etc/sysconfig/mysqld file to use the old mysqld_safe script.

The extra MySQL-NDB server package has been merged into the MySQL-Max package
and ndb related pieces has been split into different sub packages as done by
MySQL AB. The MySQL libraries and the MySQL-common sub package uses the
MySQL-Max build so that no functionality required by for example the NDB parts
are lost.

The MySQL-common package now ships with a default /etc/my.cnf file that is
based on the my-medium.cnf file that comes with the source code. The
/etc/my.cnf file is constructed at build time of this package.

To connect to the Instance Manager you need to pass the correct command line
options like in the following examples:

 * mysql -u root --password=my_password --port=2273 --protocol=TCP
 * mysql -u root --password=my_password
                  --socket=/var/lib/mysql/mysqlmanager.sock

Please note you also need to add a user in the /etc/mysqlmanager.passwd file
and make sure the file is owned by the user under which the Instance Manager
service is running under.

----------------------------------------------------------------------
```

Here, `urpmi` has downloaded the latest versions of the programs from the Internet. During installation, some packages display messages that you should read; in our example, the MySQL package installation routine has described how the configuration has changed since older versions.

You can also download and install or upgrade the Mandriva RPMs without using `urpmi`. For example, you can visit *http://rpm.pbone.net* and search for `mysql`; pick and download the RPMs for Mandriva with the highest version number. Once you've downloaded the files, log in as the root user by typing `su -`, and then install the RPM packages by running this command (all on one line):

```
# rpm --upgrade --verbose --hash \
    MySQL-5.0.23-1mdv2007.0.i586.rpm \
    MySQL-client-5.0.23-1mdv2007.0.i586.rpm \
```

```
MySQL-common-5.0.23-1mdv2007.0.i586.rpm \
apache-mod_php-5.1.4-2mdv2007.0.i586.rpm \
libmysql15-5.0.23-1mdv2007.0.i586.rpm \
perl-DBD-mysql-3.0006-1mdv2007.0.i586.rpm \
php-mysql-5.1.4-3mdv2007.0.i586.rpm
```

Installing under Debian-based systems

Debian Linux and its derivatives use Debian *.deb* packages, rather than RPMs. The popular Ubuntu and Knoppix distributions are based on Debian.

To check whether Apache, PHP, and MySQL are already installed on a Debian-based Linux system, use the dpkg --list command. If any packages aren't present, the dpkg program will let you know:

```
$ dpkg --list mysql-common mysql-server mysql-client apache2 php5
No packages found matching mysql-client.
No packages found matching apache2.
No packages found matching php5.
Desired=Unknown/Install/Remove/Purge/Hold
| Status=Not/Installed/Config-files/Unpacked/Failed-config/Half-installed
|/ Err?=(none)/Hold/Reinst-required/X=both-problems (Status,Err: uppercase=bad)
||/ Name            Version         Description
+++-===============-===============-=============================================
ii  mysql-common    5.0.21-3ubuntu1 mysql database common files (e.g. /etc/mysql/my.cnf)
un  mysql-server    <none>          (no description available)
```

On some older distributions, you may need to specify php4 rather than php5.

To install MySQL, Apache, and PHP, you must first log in as the root user by typing su -, and then use the apt-get install command:

```
# apt-get --verbose-versions install mysql-common mysql-server mysql-client apache2 php5
Reading package lists... Done
Building dependency tree... Done
mysql-common is already the newest version.
The following extra packages will be installed:
apache2-common (2.0.55-4ubuntu2)
apache2-mpm-prefork (2.0.55-4ubuntu2)
apache2-utils (2.0.55-4ubuntu2)
libapache2-mod-php5 (5.1.2-1ubuntu3)
libapr0 (2.0.55-4ubuntu2)
libdbd-mysql-perl (3.0002-2build1)
libdbi-perl (1.50-1)
libnet-daemon-perl (0.38-1)
libplrpc-perl (0.2017-1)
mysql-client-5.0 (5.0.21-3ubuntu1)
mysql-server-5.0 (5.0.21-3ubuntu1)
php5-common (5.1.2-1ubuntu3)
ssl-cert (1.0.13)
Suggested packages:
apache2-doc (2.0.55-4ubuntu2)
lynx (2.8.5-2ubuntu1)
www-browser ()
php-pear (5.1.2-1ubuntu3)
```

```
dbishell ()
libcompress-zlib-perl (1.41-1)
Recommended packages:
mailx (8.1.2-0.20050715cvs-1ubuntu1)
The following NEW packages will be installed:
apache2 (2.0.55-4ubuntu2)
apache2-common (2.0.55-4ubuntu2)
apache2-mpm-prefork (2.0.55-4ubuntu2)
apache2-utils (2.0.55-4ubuntu2)
libapache2-mod-php5 (5.1.2-1ubuntu3)
libapr0 (2.0.55-4ubuntu2)
libdbd-mysql-perl (3.0002-2build1)
libdbi-perl (1.50-1)
libnet-daemon-perl (0.38-1)
libplrpc-perl (0.2017-1)
mysql-client (5.0.21-3ubuntu1)
mysql-client-5.0 (5.0.21-3ubuntu1)
mysql-server (5.0.21-3ubuntu1)
mysql-server-5.0 (5.0.21-3ubuntu1)
php5 (5.1.2-1ubuntu3)
php5-common (5.1.2-1ubuntu3)
ssl-cert (1.0.13)
0 upgraded, 17 newly installed, 0 to remove and 0 not upgraded.
Need to get 31.9MB/32.2MB of archives.
After unpacking 75.8MB of additional disk space will be used.
Do you want to continue [Y/n]? Y
...
```

The `--verbose-versions` option displays detailed information on the packages. Once you press the Y key, the required packages will be automatically downloaded and installed. We've left out most of the displayed messages to save space.

You can also download and install or upgrade the Debian packages without using apt-get; for example, you can visit the web page *http://www.debian.org/distrib/pack ages*, select your distribution, and search for "mysql." Pick and download the package with the highest version number for your distribution. Once you've downloaded the files, log in as the root user by typing su -, and then install the packages by using the dpkg --install command—for example:

```
# dpkg --install \
    mysql-common_5.0.22-4_all.deb \
    mysql-server_5.0.22-4_all.deb \
    mysql-client-5.0_5.0.22-4_i386.deb \
    libmysqlclient15off_5.0.22-4_i386.deb
```

However, it's quite likely that you'll need to download other associated packages before the installation can proceed, and we recommend that you use the apt-get approach to automate the process. As we mentioned earlier in "Installing Under Linux," you can also download packages in the *.deb* format from the MySQL AB downloads page.

Uninstalling MySQL

You can generally install a newer software package over an older one by using the `rpm --upgrade`, `urpmi`, `yum update`, or `apt-get install` commands described earlier. If, you actually want to remove a package altogether rather than upgrading it, you should first type `su -` to log in as the root user, and then execute the appropriate uninstall commands.

Note that the data directory that contains your database files is not actually installed but created after installation. This is typically the directory *data* under the MySQL base directory, or */var/lib/mysql* for a Linux distribution package installation. Uninstalling MySQL packages does not delete this directory, so the files containing your data should remain in place, unchanged.

For an RPM-based system such as Red Hat, Fedora, or Mandriva, use the `rpm --erase` command to uninstall specific packages. If you're unsure what the exact package names are, you can use the `rpm --query --all` command to list all the installed RPM packages, together with the `grep --ignore-case` command to show only those with "mysql" (in uppercase or lowercase letters) in their name:

```
$ rpm --query --all | grep --ignore-case mysql
perl-DBD-mysql-3.0004-1mdv2007.0
MySQL-5.0.23-1mdv2007.0
libmysql15-5.0.23-1mdv2007.0
MySQL-client-5.0.23-1mdv2007.0
php-mysql-5.1.4-3mdv2007.0
MySQL-common-5.0.23-1mdv2007.0
```

Note that the *.rpm* file extension is not considered to be part of the package name. To uninstall RPM packages, you use the `rpm` command with the `--erase` option, and list the packages to remove. For example, you'd type (all on one line):

```
# rpm --erase \
    perl-DBD-mysql-3.0004-1mdv2007.0 \
    MySQL-5.0.23-1mdv2007.0 \
    libmysql15-5.0.23-1mdv2007.0 \
    MySQL-client-5.0.23-1mdv2007.0 \
    php-mysql-5.1.4-3mdv2007.0 \
    MySQL-common-5.0.23-1mdv2007.0
```

You can query and remove the packages in one go by using the `xargs` command:

```
# rpm --query --all | grep --ignore-case mysql | xargs rpm --erase
warning: /etc/my.cnf saved as /etc/my.cnf.rpmsave
#
```

On a Red Hat or Fedora system with `yum`, you can also use the `yum remove` command:

```
# yum remove mysql
[root@saiedpc yum.repos.d]# yum remove mysql
...

Dependencies Resolved
```

```
===============================================================================
 Package              Arch        Version           Repository        Size
===============================================================================
Removing:
 mysql                i386        5.0.22-1.FC5.1     installed          5.5 M
Removing for dependencies:
 MySQL-python         i386        1.2.0-3.2.2        installed          2.3 M
 libdbi-dbd-mysql     i386        0.8.1a-1.2.1       installed           37 k
 mysql-connector-odbc i386        3.51.12-1.2.1      installed          387 k
 mysql-server         i386        5.0.22-1.FC5.1     installed           22 M
 perl-Class-DBI-mysql noarch      1.00-1.fc5         installed           38 k
 perl-DBD-MySQL       i386        3.0004-1.FC5       installed          324 k
 php-mysql            i386        5.1.4-1            installed          176 k

Transaction Summary
===============================================================================
Install      0 Package(s)
Update       0 Package(s)
Remove       8 Package(s)
Is this ok [y/N]: y
Downloading Packages:
Running Transaction Test
Finished Transaction Test
Transaction Test Succeeded
Running Transaction
  Removing   : mysql-connector-odbc         ######...###### [1/8]
  Removing   : perl-Class-DBI-mysql         ######...###### [2/8]
  Removing   : perl-DBD-MySQL               ######...###### [3/8]
  Removing   : php-mysql                    ######...###### [4/8]
  Removing   : mysql                        ######...###### [5/8]
  Removing   : libdbi-dbd-mysql             ######...###### [6/8]
  Removing   : MySQL-python                 ######...###### [7/8]
warning: /var/log/mysqld.log saved as /var/log/mysqld.log.rpmsave
  Removing   : mysql-server                 ######...###### [8/8]

Removed: mysql.i386 0:5.0.22-1.FC5.1
Dependency Removed:
  MySQL-python.i386 0:1.2.0-3.2.2
  libdbi-dbd-mysql.i386 0:0.8.1a-1.2.1
  mysql-connector-odbc.i386 0:3.51.12-1.2.1
  mysql-server.i386 0:5.0.22-1.FC5.1
  perl-Class-DBI-mysql.noarch 0:1.00-1.fc5
  perl-DBD-MySQL.i386 0:3.0004-1.FC5
  php-mysql.i386 0:5.1.4-1
Complete!
```

For Debian-based systems, you can uninstall the MySQL server and client by using the apt-get remove command:

```
# apt-get remove mysql-server mysql-client
Reading package lists... Done
Building dependency tree... Done
The following packages will be REMOVED:
  mysql-client mysql-server
0 upgraded, 0 newly installed, 2 to remove and 1 not upgraded.
Need to get 0B of archives.
```

```
After unpacking 31.3MB disk space will be freed.
Do you want to continue [Y/n]? Y
(Reading database ... 103699 files and directories currently installed.)
Removing mysql-client ...
Removing mysql-server ...
```

If you're unsure what to use for the package names, you can search for packages associated with MySQL using the following command:

```
# dpkg --search "*mysql*" | cut --fields=1 --delimiter=":" | sort --unique
```

Installing MySQL, Apache, PHP, and Perl on Linux Using the XAMPP Integrated Package

To install XAMPP on your Linux system, first visit the XAMPP home page (*http://www .apachefriends.org/en/xampp.html)*, follow the link to XAMPP for Linux, and download the gzipped tar package. Switch to the superuser account:

```
$ su -
```

and create the directory */opt*:

```
# mkdir --parents /opt
```

We're using the `--parents` option here to tell Linux not to complain if the directory already exists.

Now change to this directory and extract the files from the package:

```
# cd /opt
# tar --gunzip --extract --file ~adam/xampp-linux-1.5.3a.tar.gz
```

Here, we've assumed that the downloaded file is in *adam*'s home directory (~adam); use the appropriate location on your system.

You can now start XAMPP by typing:

```
# /opt/lampp/lampp start
Starting XAMPP for Linux 1.5.3a...
XAMPP: Starting Apache with SSL (and PHP5)...
XAMPP: Starting MySQL...
XAMPP: Starting ProFTPD...
XAMPP for Linux started.
```

If there is already a running MySQL or Apache server running on your system, XAMPP may complain during startup. If this happens, shut these down before trying to start XAMPP again. Stop any existing MySQL or Apache server before starting XAMPP.

Now that the server's running, tighten up the security settings by typing:

```
# /opt/lampp/lampp security
XAMPP: Quick security check...
XAMPP: Your XAMPP pages are NOT secured by a password.
XAMPP: Do you want to set a password? [yes] n
XAMPP: MySQL is accessible via network.
```

```
XAMPP: Normally that's not recommended. Do you want me to turn it off? [yes] y
XAMPP: Turned off.
XAMPP: Stopping MySQL...
XAMPP: Starting MySQL...
XAMPP: The MySQL/phpMyAdmin user pma has no password set!!!
XAMPP: Do you want to set a password? [yes] y
XAMPP: Password:
XAMPP: Password (again):
XAMPP: Setting new MySQL pma password.
XAMPP: Setting phpMyAdmin's pma password to the new one.
XAMPP: MySQL has no root password set!!!
XAMPP: Do you want to set a password? [yes] y
XAMPP: Write the password somewhere down to make sure you won't forget it!!!
XAMPP: Password:
XAMPP: Password (again):
XAMPP: Setting new MySQL root password.
XAMPP: Change phpMyAdmin's authentication method.
XAMPP: The FTP password is still set to 'lampp'.
XAMPP: Do you want to change the password? [yes] y
XAMPP: Password:
XAMPP: Password (again):
XAMPP: Reload ProFTPD...
XAMPP: Done.
```

This will allow you to set a password for the MySQL server and also to configure the server for improved security.

The XAMPP installation may have PHP configured with the `register_globals` setting turned on. You should disable this old, insecure feature. Open the file */opt/lampp/etc/php.ini* and look for the line `register_globals = On`. Change the value `On` to `Off`, save the file, and quit the editor. The new setting will be in effect after you restart your Apache server.

You can stop your XAMPP servers by typing:

```
# /opt/lampp/lampp stop
Stopping XAMPP for Linux 1.5.3a...
XAMPP: Stopping Apache with SSL...
XAMPP: Stopping MySQL...
XAMPP: Stopping ProFTPD...
XAMPP stopped.
```

The MySQL data directory is */opt/lampp/var/mysql*; the files are owned by the user **nobody**, and in the **root** group. Given the nature of the XAMPP installation as a development platform, we won't go into detailed modification of permissions.

Configuring a Newly Installed Server

Once you've installed the server, there are some steps you should take to initialize the database tables and configure the server for good security. One of the first things to do is to set a password for the database **root** account; this is not the same as the system root account but is similar in that it has all privileges on the MySQL server. Let's look at three situations:

- You've installed the server using RPM or Debian packages.
- You've installed a system-wide server using a tarball or by compiling source code.
- You've installed a local server to run under your own account using a tarball or by compiling source code.

As we explained earlier, the XAMPP package is tightly integrated and is not designed for easy modification, so we won't explore how to customize an XAMPP installation.

Configuring a server installed using RPM or Debian packages

The package installation process generally places the MySQL program files in the */usr/bin* directory, the datafiles in the */var/lib/mysql* directory, and the server logs in the */var/log/mysqld* directory or the */var/log/mysqld.log* file.

The installation typically configures the files and directories securely and also creates the */etc/init.d/mysql* or */etc/init.d/mysqld* (MySQL daemon) startup script for easy control of the server.

Check what this script is called on your system using the `ls` command:

```
$ ls /etc/init.d/mysql*
/etc/init.d/mysql
```

In the preceding example, the file is called `mysql`. Use the appropriate name (`mysql` or `mysqld`) where you see *mysql* in the commands below.

To start the server, run the following command:

```
# /etc/init.d/mysql start
```

Set a password for the database `root` account:

```
$ mysqladmin --user=root password the_new_mysql_root_password
```

You can stop the server by typing the command:

```
# /etc/init.d/mysql stop
```

The package-based installation process generally starts the MySQL server, and configures it to be started automatically each time the system is started. In "Configuring MySQL for automatic start," later in this chapter, we explain how to check and configure automatic startup.

Configuring a system-wide server installed from tarball or source

For security reasons, it's a good idea to have the system-wide MySQL server run under its own username and group, rather than the superuser account. First, log in as the root user with the `su -` command, and then create the `mysql` user group:

```
# groupadd mysql
```

and the `mysql` user account that's in the `mysql` user group:

```
# useradd --gid mysql mysql
```

It's all right if you get a message that the group or user already exists.

Now let's configure the MySQL files and directories. Change to the directory where you installed MySQL; here, we'll assume that MySQL is installed in the directory */usr/local/mysql*:

```
# cd /usr/local/mysql
```

To create the data directory and initialize the database for the user `mysql`, run the `mysql_install_db` script from the *scripts* directory under the MySQL directory:

```
# scripts/mysql_install_db --user=mysql
```

You should now change the files in the MySQL directory to be owned by `root` but be in the `mysql` group:

```
# chown --recursive root:mysql .
```

And change the database files in the data directory to be be owned by the `mysql` user and group:

```
# chown --recursive mysql:mysql data
```

We described this use of the `chown` command in "Restricting access to files and directories," earlier in this chapter.

You can now start the server to run under the `mysql` system account by running the `mysqld_safe` program from the MySQL `bin` directory:

```
# bin/mysqld_safe --user=mysql &
```

The ampersand (&) character tells Linux to run the server in the background so that you can use the shell to do other things. If you don't add the ampersand at the end, you won't see the shell prompt again until the MySQL server is stopped from another shell window.

The next thing to do is to set a password for the database `root` account:

```
$ bin/mysqladmin --user=root password the_new_mysql_root_password
```

You can stop the server by running the command:

```
$ bin/mysqladmin --user=root --password=the_mysql_root_password shutdown
```

Note that the user `root` on the Linux system is different from the user `root` on the MySQL server, and you don't need to be logged in as the Linux `root` user to shut down the server with `mysqladmin`.

You can also start and stop the server using the *mysql.server* script that comes in the *support-files* directory; start the server with:

```
$ support-files/mysql.server start
```

and stop the server with:

```
$ support-files/mysql.server stop
```

You can copy the *mysql.server* script and place it as the file *mysql* in the */etc/init.d* directory:

```
# cp support-files/mysql.server /etc/init.d/mysql
```

This allows you to control the server by typing:

```
# /etc/init.d/mysql start
```

and

```
# /etc/init.d/mysql stop
```

as with the package-based installation approaches. Importantly, this also allows you to configure the server to start on every boot; this is explained later in "Configuring MySQL for automatic start."

Configuring a local server

With a local installation, the MySQL files will be placed in a directory under your home directory, and the server will run under your username rather than `mysql`.

First, change to the directory containing the MySQL installation. If you followed our instructions in "Installing MySQL on Linux by Compiling the Source Code from MySQL AB," you can type:

```
$ cd ~/mysql
```

To configure the data directory and initialize the database, you must run the *mysql_in stall_db* script from the *scripts* directory:

```
$ scripts/mysql_install_db
```

If you want to use a data directory that's not under the MySQL installation directory, you can specify the path using the `datadir` option, as in:

```
$ mysql_install_db datadir=/home/adam/MySQL_Data
```

However, we'll assume you'll use the default data directory *~/mysql/data*.

Now you need to change the files in the MySQL directory to be owned by your username and your group. For the username and group `adam`, you would write:

```
$ chown --recursive adam:adam ~/mysql
```

Again, we described this use of the `chown` command earlier in "Restricting access to files and directories."

By default, MySQL listens for incoming client connections on port number 3306; if there's already another server running on the same computer, you should choose a different port number for this installation. It's best to avoid using port numbers that are typically used by other common programs. For instance, port 8080 is often used by web servers and proxies. A web search for "common ports" is a good way to learn about these. Note that only the root user can allocate port numbers below 1024. We'll use the port number 57777 for our example.

You also need to specify a custom location for the socket file; this is a special type of file used by clients to connect to a server on the same machine. A common choice for a socket file location is the server data directory; we'll use the file path ~/mysql/data/mysql.sock in the following example.

Now, start the server using the nonstandard port and socket file:

```
$ bin/mysqld_safe --port=57777 --socket=~/mysql/data/mysql.sock &
```

Note that if you're using a nonstandard MySQL installation directory and don't start the server from inside that directory, you have to specify the path to the `mysqld_safe` program and tell this program where the data directory is. For example, to run the program from the ~/mysql/bin directory with the data directory ~/mysql/data, you would type (all on one line):

```
$ ~/mysql/bin/mysqld_safe \
    --port=57777 \
    --socket=~/mysql/data/mysql.sock \
    --datadir=~/mysql/data &
```

Now that the server is running, set a password for the database root account by typing:

```
$ bin/mysqladmin \
    --port=57777 \
    --socket=~/mysql/data/mysql.sock \
    --user=root \
    password the_new_mysql_root_password
```

Once you've added a password for the database root user, you'll have to use it for all further client connections to the server for the root account.

You can stop the server using the `mysqladmin shutdown` command, with the necessary options added to identify the server. Type all on one line:

```
$ bin/mysqladmin \
    --port=57777 \
    --socket=~/mysql/data/mysql.sock \
    --user=root \
    --password=the_mysql_root_password \
    shutdown
```

Configuring MySQL for automatic start

If you're planning to use MySQL a lot, you'll probably want to have the server start automatically every time your computer is switched on. The typical way to do this is to call a script to start and stop the MySQL server when the computer is started and stopped.

If you used an RPM or Debian package to install MySQL, this script is generally already installed as */etc/init.d/mysql* or */etc/init.d/mysqld* (MySQL daemon). Check what this script is called on your system using the `ls` command:

```
$ ls /etc/init.d/mysql*
/etc/init.d/mysql
```

In the preceding example, the file is called *mysql*. Use the appropriate name (`mysql` or `mysqld`) where you see *mysql* in the commands below.

If you installed from a tarball or from source, you'll need to copy the file across yourself as discussed in the earlier section, "Configuring a system-wide server installed from tarball or source."

A Linux system can start in one of six *runlevels*; a system starting in runlevel 5 will typically boot straight into the graphical windowing environment such as KDE or GNOME, while a system starting in runlevels 2 or 3 will end up at a text-based login screen. There's an easy way to check what runlevel you're in; just use the `runlevel` program in the */sbin* directory:

```
$ /sbin/runlevel
N 5
```

Here, the system is in runlevel 5.

A program is started automatically for a particular runlevel if there's a startup entry for it in the corresponding */etc/rc<runlevel>.d* directory. You can list all the entries for MySQL by typing:

```
$ ls /etc/rc*.d/*mysql*
/etc/rc0.d/K90mysql  /etc/rc2.d/S11mysql  /etc/rc4.d/S11mysql  /etc/rc6.d/K90mysql
/etc/rc1.d/K90mysql  /etc/rc3.d/S11mysql  /etc/rc5.d/S11mysql
```

The entries starting with "S" start the program when the system is booted, and the entries starting with "K" stop (or kill) the program when the system is shut down. Here, MySQL is set to start and stop automatically in runlevels 2, 3, 4, and 5. On Red Hat or Mandriva systems, you can more conveniently determine this using the `chkconfig --list` command:

```
# chkconfig --list mysql
mysql           0:off   1:off   2:on    3:on    4:on    5:on    6:off
```

If your server shows "off" for the runlevel that you found using the `runlevel` command, the MySQL server is not started automatically.

If you don't see an entry for your preferred runlevel (normally 3 or 5), you'll need to add one yourself. Most Linux distributions have a graphical tool to configure startup services. For example, under Red Hat and Fedora, you can run the Service Configuration program by choosing the Services entry from the Administration submenu of the System menu; you can also run this program by typing **system-config-services** at the command line. Similarly, with Mandriva, you can use the Services program from the Mandriva Control Center (select Configure Your Computer from the Configuration submenu of the System menu); you can also run this program by typing **drakxservices** at the command line. We'll explain how to configure services without using these graphical tools.

On a Red Hat or Mandriva system, type:

```
# chkconfig --level 35 mysql on
```

to enable automatic startup in runlevels 3 and 5 (corresponding to normal console or graphical operation run levels), and:

```
# chkconfig --level 35 mysql off
```

to disable it.

In a Debian-based system, startup services are controlled using the `update-rc.d` command. Enable MySQL as follows:

```
# update-rc.d mysql defaults
Adding system startup for /etc/init.d/mysql ...
/etc/rc0.d/K20mysql -> ../init.d/mysql
/etc/rc1.d/K20mysql -> ../init.d/mysql
/etc/rc6.d/K20mysql -> ../init.d/mysql
/etc/rc2.d/S20mysql -> ../init.d/mysql
/etc/rc3.d/S20mysql -> ../init.d/mysql
/etc/rc4.d/S20mysql -> ../init.d/mysql
/etc/rc5.d/S20mysql -> ../init.d/mysql
```

and disable automatic startup as follows:

```
# update-rc.d -f mysql remove
update-rc.d: /etc/init.d/mysql exists during rc.d purge (continuing)
Removing any system startup links for /etc/init.d/mysql ...
/etc/rc0.d/K20mysql
/etc/rc1.d/K20mysql
/etc/rc2.d/S20mysql
/etc/rc3.d/S20mysql
/etc/rc4.d/S20mysql
/etc/rc5.d/S20mysql
/etc/rc6.d/K20mysql
```

If you have a standalone Apache web server installed, you can enable and disable its automatic startup by using `httpd` or `apache2` instead of `mysql` in the preceding commands.

Installing Under Windows

The MySQL installation process for Windows uses graphical installation programs and is relatively straightforward. You need to first decide whether you want to install only MySQL, or whether you'd like to install an integrated package including additional software that you're likely to need later. Both approaches are equally easy to follow. At various points during the installation process, you may be prompted to allow the installer program to run and modify your system, including unblocking server ports. Read these prompts carefully; in most cases, you'll want to allow the installer to do what it needs to do. Remember to follow the instructions of "Verifying Package Integrity with MD5," earlier in this chapter, to verify that you're running the correct installer program. You need to unblock ports only if you want to allow connections to your server from other hosts.

In this section, we'll look at three ways to install MySQL on a Windows system:

- System-wide, using a graphical installation package provided by MySQL AB
- Local, using a "no-install" package by MySQL AB
- System-wide, using the XAMPP integrated package

To install system-wide, you'll need to log in as a user with Windows administrator privileges. The MySQL AB "no-install" package does not need to be installed using a setup program and is handy for cases where you don't have administrator privileges on the computer.

Installing Only MySQL Using Packages from MySQL AB

First, follow the instructions of "Downloading MySQL from the MySQL AB Web Site," earlier in this chapter, and download the package you need. If you are using Windows XP and have administrator privileges, it's easiest if you download the "Windows Essentials (x86)" package. This is small and has all the MySQL programs you need. If you don't have administrator privileges on your Windows machine, or you need to have a complex server setup with nonstandard configuration, you should download the package labeled "Without installer (unzip in C:\)." We'll discuss how to install each of these packages in the following sections.

Windows installation using the installer

Start the installer program and go with the default (typical) settings. This will install MySQL in the *C:\Program Files\MySQL\MySQL Server 5.0* directory. Vista may ask you to confirm whether you want to allow the installer to access your computer; click Allow.

You might be prompted to sign up for a *mysql.com* account; you can skip this unless you want to subscribe to MySQL newsletters, add comments to the online manual, or file bug reports.

On the final screen of the installer program, you'll see the "Configure the MySQL Server now" option selected. When you click the Finish button to exit the installer, the MySQL Server Instance Configuration Wizard will start. Follow the prompts and select Standard Configuration to go with the default settings.

On the next screen, shown in Figure 2-10, select "Install as a Windows Service" (typically already selected by default) and "Include Bin Directory in Windows PATH" (typically not already selected by default).

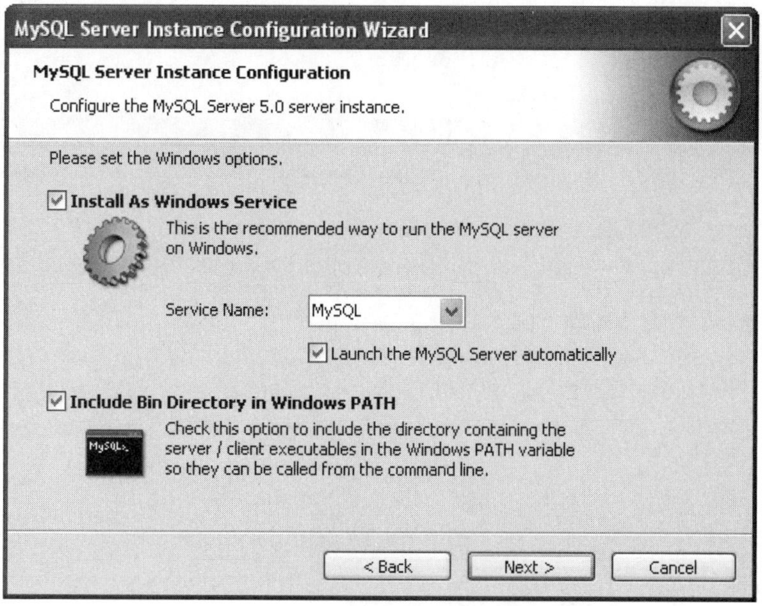

Figure 2-10. Specifying the server options during the Windows installation

Select a new root user password (there isn't one by default), and then follow the prompts until the installation process is completed. Unless you know what you're doing, don't select the option to enable root access from remote machines. Also, don't select the option to create an anonymous account; we'll discuss anonymous accounts and the security problems associated with them in Chapter 9.

You may find that the installation program fails to configure the service under Vista (you'll see an error message like "Could not connect to the Service Control Manager"). If this happens, click the Back button twice to return to the options dialog box, and then uncheck the "Install as a Windows Service" checkbox. Continue the installation process from this point.

You can run the configuration program again at any time by selecting the MySQL Server Instance Config Wizard entry from the MySQL Server 5.0 section of the MySQL submenu of the Windows Start menu.

Starting and stopping MySQL as a service

If the installation process successfully configures MySQL as a Windows service, you can use the Windows Services window at any time to check and control the server. On Windows XP, select the Performance and Maintenance entry from the Control Panel, and then choose Administrative Tools. If you have Classic View enabled, you can choose Administrative Tools directly from the Control Panel. Figure 2-11 shows the Windows Services window.

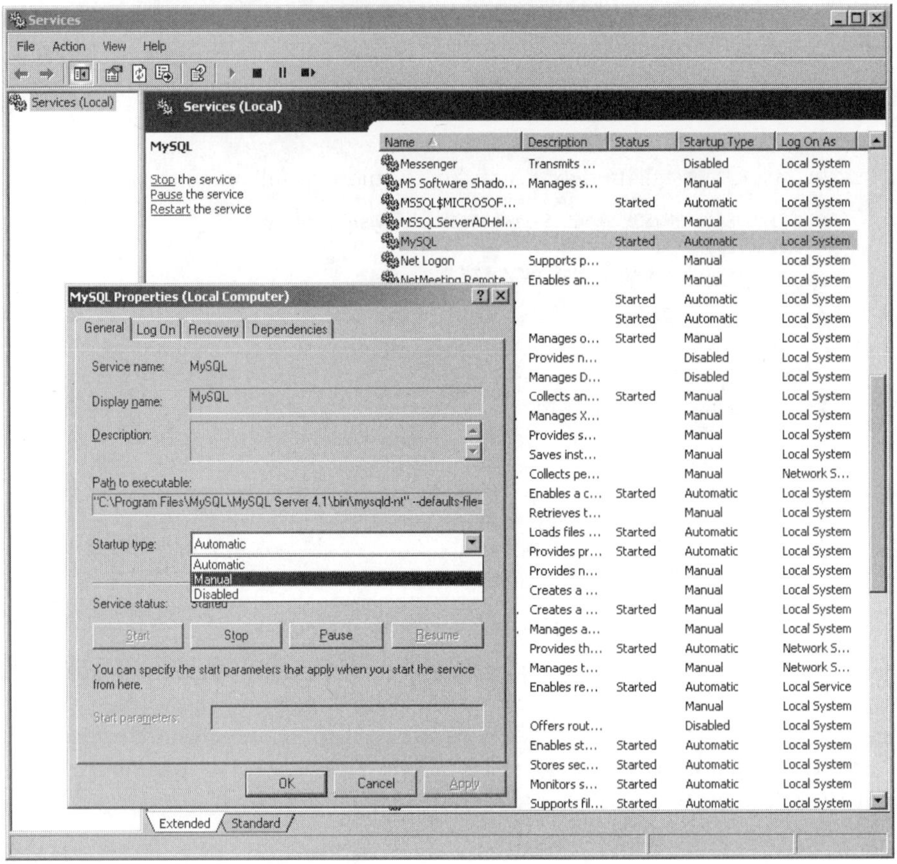

Figure 2-11. The Windows services window

Under Vista, open the Control Panel, and select the "System and Maintenance" entry. From here, select the Administrative Tools and then the Services entry. Windows may prompt you for authorization—click Continue.

Scroll down the list of services till you see an entry for MySQL, and select it. The installation process sets the service status to be Automatic—that is, the server is started automatically every time Windows is booted. If you'd prefer to start and stop the server manually, you can set the service status to Manual. You can also start and stop the server by clicking the Start or Stop link on the left of the Services window, or by opening a command-prompt window and typing:

```
C:\> net start mysql
```

or:

```
C:\> net stop mysql
```

You can run MySQL programs from the command window by first changing to the MySQL directory:

```
C:\> cd "C:\Program Files\MySQL\MySQL Server 5.0"
```

and then typing in the MySQL program name.

For example, you can stop the server directly by calling the `mysqladmin` program directly from the MySQL installation directory. You would type (all on one line):

```
C:\Program Files\MySQL\MySQL Server 5.0> bin\mysqladmin \
    --user=root \
    --password=the_mysql_root_password \
    shutdown
```

Never kill the MySQL server from the Windows task manager; you could lose data.

Starting and stopping MySQL from the command line

If the installation program could not install the service, you'll need to start and stop the server from the command line. To do this, open a command prompt window and change your working directory to the directory where the MySQL installation has been installed. This is typically *C:\Program Files\MySQL\MySQL Server 5.0*:

```
C:\> cd C:\Program Files\MySQL\MySQL Server 5.0\
```

To start the server, type:

```
C:\Program Files\MySQL\MySQL Server 5.0> bin\mysqld-nt
```

Under Windows, executable programs such as *mysqld-nt* have the extension *.exe*. You can include the full name and extension, as in *mysqld-nt.exe*; if you leave it out, Windows won't complain. If the program ends immediately, restart the server but add the option `no-defaults`:

```
C:\Program Files\MySQL\MySQL Server 5.0> bin\mysqld-nt --no-defaults
```

This tells the server not to expect an options file—we discuss this in further detail in Chapter 11. You may also be prompted by your firewall software to authorize the server to listen for incoming connections from the network; unless you need to allow connections from other computers, it's a good idea to keep blocking such connections.

Once the program's started, nothing exciting will happen—you'll just see a blinking cursor; this command window will remain open as long as the server is running, so to use any other MySQL command-line programs, you'll need to open another command-prompt window.

For example, to shut the server down, you should open another command-prompt window and change to the MySQL directory:

```
C:\> cd C:\Program Files\MySQL\MySQL Server 5.0\
```

and then stop the server by sending the `shutdown` command:

```
C:\Program Files\MySQL\MySQL Server 5.0> bin\mysqladmin \
    --user=root \
    --password=the_mysql_root_password \
    shutdown
```

Never kill the MySQL server from the Windows task manager; you could lose data.

Installation with the "no-install" .zip Archive

The "no-install" package is a ready-to-use collection of files bundled together and compressed using the popular ZIP compression method. All you need to do is extract the package to the desired directory. This is useful if you don't have administrator access on a Windows computer or if you want to avoid changes that the installer program might make to your Windows configuration.

Windows can handle ZIP files itself; if you've installed an archiving program such as *WinZip* or *PKZIP*, this application will normally process the file instead of the standard Windows decompression tool. In this book, we explain only the default Windows behavior and assume that you know how to use any extra utility programs on your system.

The icon for a compressed file often has a picture of a zipper on it, as shown in Figure 2-12. If you double-click on the icon, you'll be able to see inside the package, but this isn't useful right now. Instead, right-click on the icon, select "Extract All..." as shown in Figure 2-12, and follow the prompts. Ignore the Password button; the archive doesn't have one. When you see the message "Select a Destination," replace the existing text with the directory you want the MySQL directory to be located in. Figure 2-13 shows this window. The recommended directory for this package is C:\, so use this, and click the Next button. The files will be installed to the *mysql-5.0.22-win32* subdirectory.

When you use the ZIP archive, a Windows service isn't configured for MySQL; you'll need to start the server using the MySQL commands themselves. The MySQL executables directory isn't added to your Windows path either, so you'll need to always tell Windows where to find the MySQL programs you're trying to run. In the examples here, we assume you first change to the MySQL directory and then tell Windows to run the programs from the *bin* directory. Alternatively, you can add the directory to the search path manually following the steps outlined later in "Error Message About MySQL Executable Programs Not Being Found or Recognized."

To control and access the server, open a command-prompt window and change your working directory to the MySQL directory. For example, if you extracted the files to the C:\ directory, change to the MySQL directory under there:

```
C:\> cd C:\mysql-5.0.22-win32
```

To start the server, type:

```
C:\mysql-5.0.22-win32> bin\mysqld-nt
```

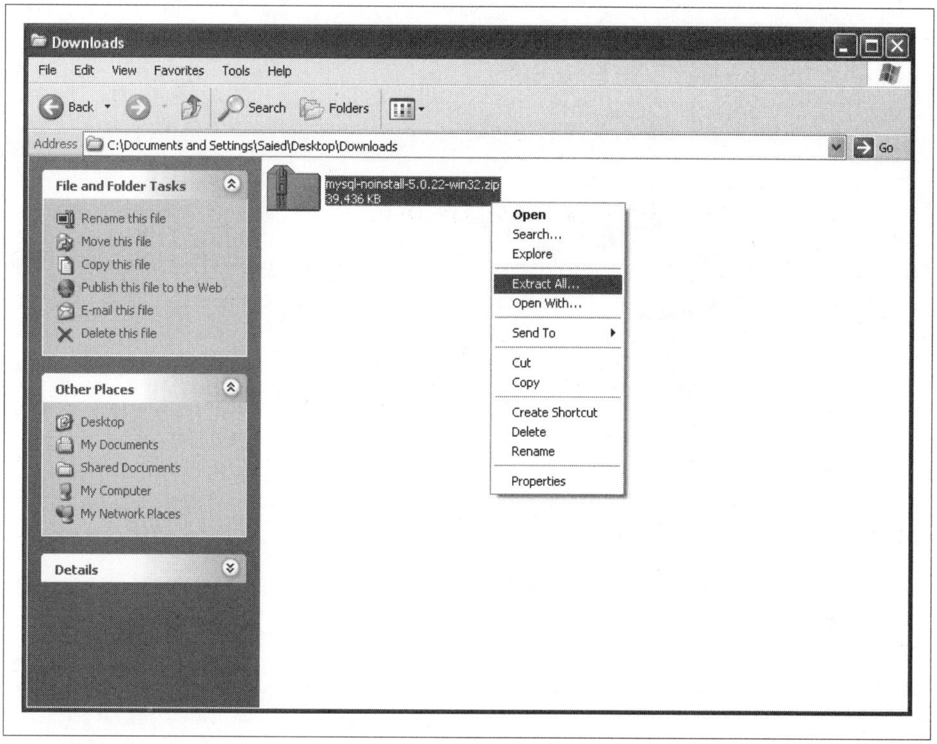

Figure 2-12. Decompressing the compressed package

as shown in Figure 2-14. Under Windows, executable programs such as `mysqld-nt` have the extension *.exe*. You can include the full name and extension, as in `mysqld-nt.exe`; if you leave it out, Windows won't complain. If the program ends immediately, restart it with the option `no-defaults`:

```
C:\mysql-5.0.22-win32>bin\mysql-nt --no-defaults
```

This tells the server not to expect an options file. We discuss options files in Chapter 11

You may also be prompted by your firewall software to authorize the server to listen for incoming connections from the network; unless you need to allow connections from other computers, it's a good idea to keep blocking such connections.

Once the program's started, nothing exciting will happen: you'll just see a blinking cursor; this command window will remain open as long as the server is running, so to use any other MySQL command-line programs, you'll need to open another command-prompt window.

Open another command-prompt window and change to the MySQL directory:

```
C:\> cd C:\mysql-5.0.22-win32
```

Now, set a password for the database root account (all on one line):

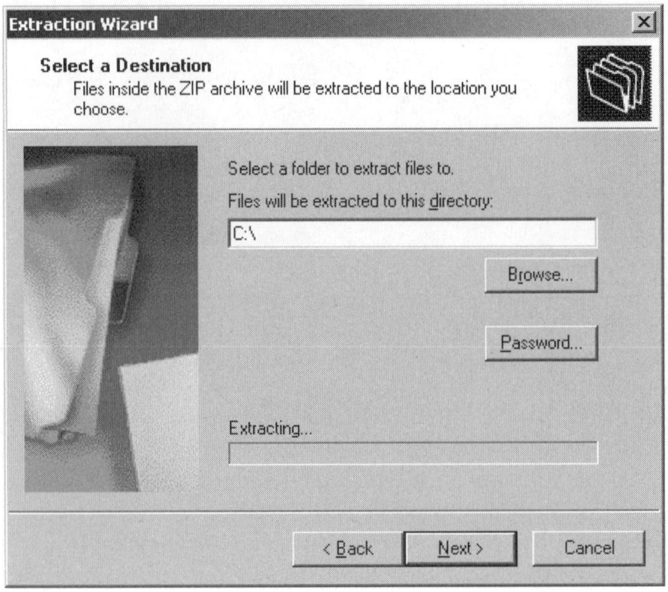

Figure 2-13. The Windows compressed-file-extraction dialog window

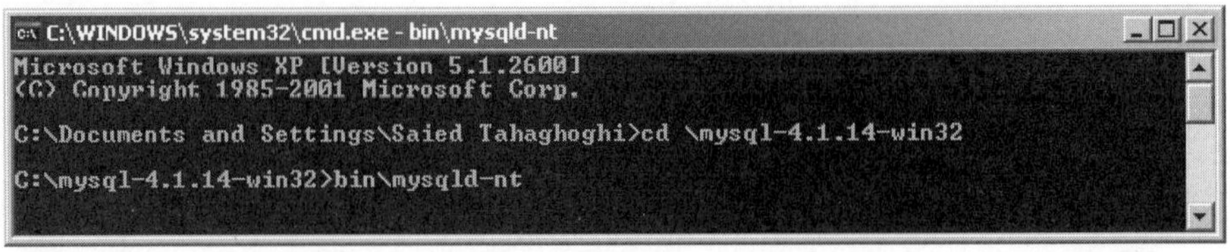

Figure 2-14. Starting the server in Windows

```
C:\mysql-5.0.22-win32> bin\mysqladmin --user=root \
    password the_new_mysql_root_password
```

Finally, stop the server by sending the `shutdown` command:

```
C:\mysql-5.0.22-win32> bin\mysqladmin --user=root \
    --password=the_mysql_root_password shutdown
```

Figure 2-15 shows the second command-prompt window and the `mysqladmin` commands we've just discussed. Here, we used the password `"new root password"` as an example; you should choose a password that's hard to guess. As we've got spaces in the password, we've enclosed it in quotes. Notice also how the command to shut down the server has wrapped to the next line; this is fine, but don't press the Enter key until you've finished typing the whole command.

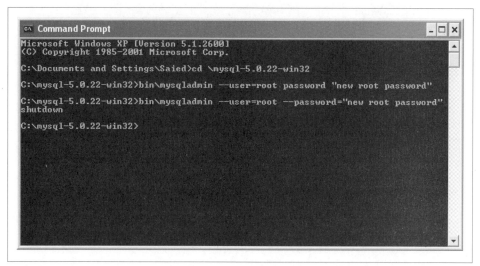

Figure 2-15. Running the mysqladmin program from the Windows command prompt

Installing MySQL, Apache, PHP, and Perl on Windows Using the XAMPP Integrated Package

To install XAMPP on your Windows system, first visit the XAMPP home page at *http://www.apachefriends.org/en/xampp.html*, follow the link to XAMPP for Windows, and download the installer package. The package will have a name like *xampp-win32-1.5.3a-installer.exe*.

Run the installer package once you've downloaded it; Vista may prompt you to confirm you want to do this. Accept *C:\Program Files* as the installation directory and click the Install button. XAMPP is installed to the *C:\Program Files\xampp* directory. Don't change this unless you really have to. We assume this is the directory you're using.

After XAMPP is installed, you'll be prompted to install XAMPP servers as a service; choose "yes". Also select "yes" when asked whether you want to install Apache2 as a service and whether you want to autostart the server. If you get a message about port 80 (the web server port) being blocked on your system, check whether you have another running web server, such as Microsoft IIS; this server could have been installed as part of Visual Studio .NET. You can also select "yes" to install the FileZilla FTP server as a service, "no" to autostart the service, "no" to start the service, and "no" to uninstall the server.

If your Windows Firewall is active, you may be told that Apache has been blocked from accepting incoming network connections. Unless you need to allow connections from other computers, this is a good setting to stick with, so choose to keep blocking the connections.

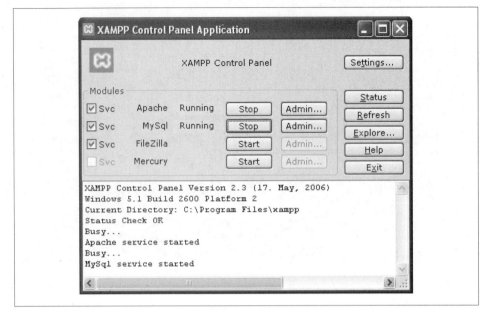

Figure 2-16. The XAMPP control panel

Finally, select "yes" when prompted to start the XAMPP control panel. The installation program places a shortcut to the XAMPP control panel on your desktop, but if it's not there, you can also start it from the XAMPP control panel from the "apachefriends" submenu of the Windows Start menu. Figure 2-16 shows what the XAMPP control panel looks like. Start the MySQL server by clicking the Start button next to the MySQL label. You need to be logged in as a user with Windows Administrator privileges to control XAMPP, although an unprivileged user is allowed to place files on the web server. Stop any existing MySQL or Apache server before starting XAMPP.

XAMPP does not modify the Windows path. If you need to run any MySQL programs from the command prompt, you'll need to run them from the MySQL *bin* directory. You can avoid this inconvenience by adding the *C:\Program Files\xampp\mysql\bin* directory to your Windows path as discussed in "Error Message About MySQL Executable Programs Not Being Found or Recognized," later in this chapter.

The first thing you should do once you've started the server is to set a password for the database root account. First, open a command window and change to the MySQL directory:

```
C:\> cd C:\Program Files\xampp\mysql
```

Then run the `mysqladmin` program from the `bin` directory:

```
C:\Program Files\xampp\mysql> bin\mysqladmin \
    --user=root \
    password the_new_mysql_root_password
```

You can also configure the server password, as well as other settings for better security, by loading *http://localhost* in your browser and clicking on the Security link on the left of the page. This takes you to a page that displays information on your server security configuration and allows you to add passwords to authenticate access to the MySQL and Apache servers.

The XAMPP installation has PHP configured, with the `register_globals` setting turned on. You should disable this old, insecure feature: open the file *C:\Program Files \xampp\php\php.ini* and look for the line `register_globals = On`. Change the value `On` to `Off`, save the file, and quit the editor. The new setting will be in effect after you restart your Apache server.

Finally, you can stop the MySQL server by pressing the Stop button next to the MySQL label in the XAMPP control panel.

Installing Under Mac OS X

In this section, we'll look at three ways to install MySQL on a Mac OS X system:

- System-wide, using an installation package provided by MySQL AB.
- Local, using an non-installation gzipped tar package provided by MySQL AB.
- System-wide, using the `XAMPP` integrated package.

To install system-wide, you should be able to access superuser privileges through the `sudo` command.

Installing only MySQL Using the Installer from MySQL AB

Following the instructions of "Downloading MySQL from the MySQL AB Web Site," earlier in this chapter, visit the MySQL AB downloads page and choose the package corresponding to the version of your operating system and your system processor.

Pick the Standard installer (rather than TAR) package. This is a small package that has everything you need. Once the file is downloaded, double-click on it to unpack the archive and view the package contents. You should see something similar to Figure 2-17.

Double-click on the package file with a name beginning with *mysql-standard-* to start the installation process.

Simply following the prompts will install to the */usr/local/mysql-<version>* directory, where *<version>* is the MySQL version number. It also creates the symbolic link (or alias) `/usr/local/mysql` that points to this installation directory. For example, the files could be installed in the */usr/local/mysql-5.0.22* directory, and the `/usr/local/mysql` link set to point to this directory.

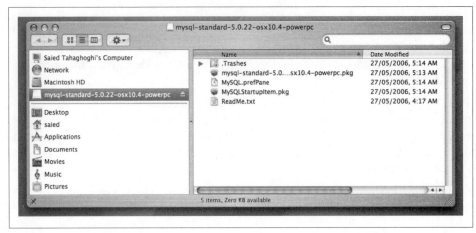

Figure 2-17. The contents of the MySQL AB Mac OS X installer package

Next, double-click on the MySQL.prefPane item and install it. This adds a MySQL configuration entry to the System Preferences; from the System Preferences window, you can manually start and stop the MySQL server, and also select whether you want the server to be automatically started each time the system boots.

Finally, if you want the MySQL server to be started and stopped automatically each time the computer is started or stopped, double-click on the MySQLStartupItem.pkg item and install this too.

Configuring the installed server

For security reasons, it's a good idea to have the MySQL server run under its own username and group, rather than under the superuser account. If something goes wrong with the server, or an attacker gains control of the server, the damage will be restricted to the MySQL user rather than the whole system. Mac OS X comes with a `mysql` user and group already defined. You can check this using the graphical NetInfo Manager tool, or from the shell prompt.

To check using the NetInfo Manager, double-click on the NetInfo Manager icon in the Utilities folder under the Applications group, as shown in Figure 2-18. Then, select "groups" and scroll down to make sure that there is an entry for the `mysql` group, as shown in Figure 2-19. Similarly, you can select "users" and scroll down to see that there is an entry for the `mysql` user there too.

You can instead check these settings from the shell prompt. To do this, open a terminal window and use the `grep` command to search for the word `mysql` in the system's list of users (the */etc/passwd* file) and groups (the */etc/group* file):

```
$ grep mysql /etc/passwd /etc/group
/etc/passwd:mysql:*:74:74:MySQL Server:/var/empty:/usr/bin/false
/etc/group:mysql:*:74:
```

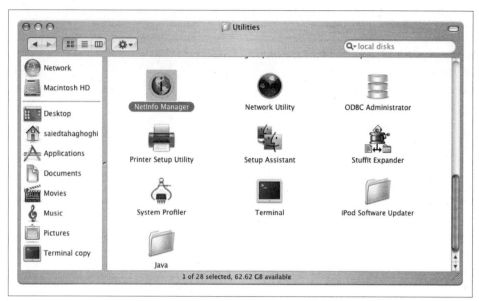

Figure 2-18. Starting the Mac OS X NetInfo Manager

You should see two lines similar to the ones above.

If, for some reason, the `mysql` user and group aren't configured on your system, you have to create them. You can add them in the NetInfo Manager by clicking on the lock icon at the bottom of the screen and selecting the Add entry from the Edit menu. However, it's probably faster to perform these steps from the command line.

First, create the user `mysql` (note that the first forward slash symbol (/) stands by itself on the line):

```
$ sudo niutil -create    / /users/mysql
```

and assign invalid (and therefore relatively secure) values for the home directory and login shell:

```
$ sudo niutil -createprop / /users/mysql home /var/empty
$ sudo niutil -createprop / /users/mysql shell /usr/bin/false
```

Next, create the group `mysql`:

```
$ sudo niutil -create    / /groups/mysql
```

Once you've done this, define a Group ID number (`gid`) for the `mysql` group and a User ID number (`uid`) for the `mysql` user. The Mac OS X default value for both these IDs is 74; you can choose this or any other value—for example, 674—that's not already allocated to a user or group. Let's use 74 in our example, and assign this value to the `mysql` group and user:

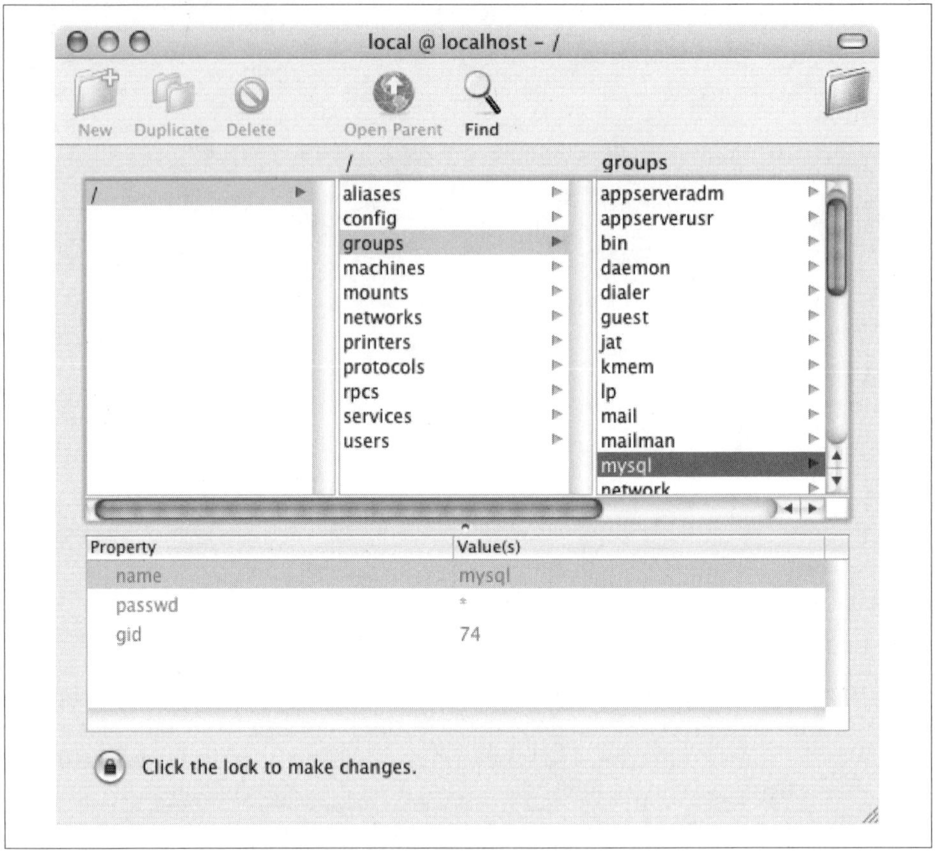

Figure 2-19. Verifying that the mysql group exists

```
$ sudo niutil -createprop / /groups/mysql gid 74
$ sudo niutil -createprop / /users/mysql   uid 74
```

Finally, associate the mysql user with the mysql group:

```
$ sudo niutil -createprop / /users/mysql   gid 74
```

When you're sure the correct user and group exist, you have to initialize the MySQL databases. First, change to the MySQL base directory:

```
$ cd /usr/local/mysql
```

Then run the mysql_install_db script from the scripts directory. The user option assigns ownership of the MySQL datafiles and folders to the specified user—here to the system mysql account:

```
$ sudo scripts/mysql_install_db --user=mysql
```

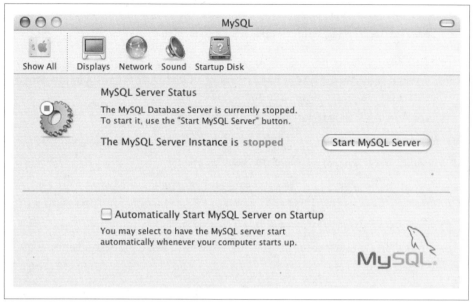

Figure 2-20. The MySQL preferences pane

You should now change the files in the MySQL directory to be owned by root but be in the mysql group:

```
$ sudo chown -RL root:mysql /usr/local/mysql
```

The -RL option tells the chown command to apply the ownership rule recursively (R) to everything under the /usr/local/mysql directory, following symbolic links (L) if necessary. You should also change the database files in the data directory to be owned by the mysql user and group:

```
$ sudo chown -RL mysql:mysql /usr/local/mysql/data
```

If you used the mysql_install_db script with the user=mysql option, this will already have been done for you.

You can now start the server and stop it in several ways; let's look at a few of these.

First, if you installed the MySQL.prefPane item, you can use the MySQL pane in the System Preferences window. To access this, click on the Apple logo at the top left of the screen menu, select the "System Preferences..." menu entry, and then click on the MySQL icon in the System Preferences window. This will bring up a window similar to Figure 2-20, with a button labeled Start MySQL Server when the server is not running and Stop MySQL Server when it is. Clicking on this button will start or stop the server. You may be asked to type in your password.

Second, you can use the *mysql.server* script in the MySQL directory:

```
$ sudo /usr/local/mysql/support-files/mysql.server start
```

to start the MySQL server, and:

```
$ sudo /usr/local/mysql/support-files/mysql.server stop
```

to stop it.

Third, if you installed the *MySQLStartupItem.pkg* file during the installation process, you can start the server from the command line by calling:

```
$ sudo /Library/StartupItems/MySQLCOM/MySQLCOM start
```

and stop it by calling:

```
$ sudo /Library/StartupItems/MySQLCOM/MySQLCOM start
```

Finally, you can use the generic `mysqld_safe` and `mysqladmin` programs from the command prompt. To start the server to run under the system `mysql` user account, type:

```
$ sudo /usr/local/mysql/bin/mysqld_safe --user=mysql
```

Then, press the Ctrl-Z key combination, and type **bg** to leave the server running in the background.

You can then stop the server by running the command:

```
$ /usr/local/mysql/bin/mysqladmin --user=root \
    --password=the_mysql_root_password shutdown
```

This approach is the most robust, and also the most flexible if you need to add custom options to your server.

The first thing you should do once you've started the server is to set a password for the database root account:

```
$ sudo /usr/local/mysql/bin/mysqladmin --user=root password \
    the_new_mysql_root_password
```

Once you've set the MySQL root password, you'll need to use this in all further accesses to the server. For example, to shut down the server using `mysqladmin`, you would type:

```
$ /usr/local/mysql/bin/mysqladmin --user=root \
    --password=the_mysql_root_password shutdown
```

Installing Only MySQL Using the no-installer Package from MySQL AB

Following the instructions in "Downloading MySQL from the MySQL AB Web Site," earlier in this chapter, visit the MySQL AB downloads page and download the "Without installer" package corresponding to the version of your operating system and processor type.

This will download a compressed package with a name like *mysql-standard-5.0.22-osx10.4-i686.tar.gz*. This is normally automatically decompressed and unpacked by the web browser to leave the directory *mysql-standard-5.0.22-osx10.4-i686* in the download directory. You may instead find that your browser decompresses the file but does not unpack it. If this is the case, you'll find the file *mysql-standard-5.0.22-osx10.4-*

i686.tar in your download directory. You can unpack this in any location by opening a terminal window, changing to the directory you want to run MySQL from, and calling the `tar` program from there to unpack the file. For example, if the file was downloaded to your Desktop directory, but you want to have the MySQL directory under your home directory, you can open a terminal window and type:

```
$ cd
```

to go to your home directory, and:

```
$ tar --extract --file ~/Desktop/mysql-standard-5.0.22-osx10.4-i686.tar
```

to unpack the file that's in your Desktop directory. If the browser does not decompress the file at all, you'll find the downloaded file still has a *.gz* extension. You can follow the same steps as for the decompressed file, but use the `gunzip` option to decompress the file before unpacking it:

```
$ tar --gunzip --extract --file \
    ~/Desktop/mysql-standard-5.0.22-osx10.4-i686.tar.gz
```

Once the package has been decompressed, you can move the resulting directory to the location you want. For example, you can move it to be under your home directory, either by dragging and dropping with the mouse, or by using the `mv` command from the shell:

```
$ mv ~/Desktop/mysql-standard-5.0.22-osx10.4-i686 ~
```

You can also create a symbolic link to the MySQL directory so that you can refer to it as simply ~/mysql:

```
$ ln -s ~/Desktop/mysql-standard-5.0.22-osx10.4-i686 ~/mysql
```

Once you have the extracted directory, you should change to that directory:

```
$ cd ~/mysql
```

and run the *mysql_install_db* program from the *scripts* directory to initialize the MySQL databases:

```
$ scripts/mysql_install_db
```

You can now start the server using the command:

```
$ bin/mysqld_safe &
```

Set a password for the MySQL server `root` account immediately:

```
$ bin/mysqladmin --user=root password the_new_mysql_root_password
```

Since we've set a password for the root user, you need to use this password in all further accesses to the server for the root account. You can now stop the server using the command:

```
$ bin/mysqladmin --user=root --password=the_mysql_root_password shutdown
```

Installing MySQL, Apache, PHP, and Perl on Mac OS X Using the XAMPP Integrated Package

To install XAMPP on Mac OS X, visit the XAMPP home page (*http://www.apachefriends.org/en/xampp.html*), follow the link to "XAMPP for Mac OS X," and download the installer package.

The installer package is in the StuffIt Expander (*.sitx*) format. If you get a screen of garbled text in your browser when trying to download it, press the "back" button to see the download link—for example, *http://easynews.dl.sourceforge.net/sourceforge/xampp/xampp-macosx-0.3.sitx*. Hold down the Ctrl key and click on the link. From the menu that appears, select the entry that says Download Linked File (for Safari), Save Link As (for Firefox), or Download Link to Disk (for Internet Explorer).

Once the StuffIt archive is downloaded, double-click on it to extract the installation package, and then double-click on the installation package to start the XAMPP installation program. When the decompression program finishes, you should find the installation program saved in the same directory as the downloaded file, or on your Desktop. This installation program has a name like *xampp-macosx-0.5.pkg*. Running this and accepting the default settings will install XAMPP to the */Applications/xampp/* directory, with the MySQL datafiles located in the */Applications/xampp/xamppfiles/var/mysql* directory.

If there is already a running MySQL or Apache server running on your system, XAMPP may complain during startup. If this happens, shut these down before trying to start XAMPP again. To switch off the default installation of Apache, go to the System Preferences Window and click on Sharing. If the Personal Web Sharing entry has a checkmark next to it, uncheck it to stop the Apache web server.

You can start XAMPP by typing:

```
$ sudo /Applications/xampp/xamppfiles/mampp start
```

Now that the server's running, tighten up the security settings by typing:

```
$ sudo /Applications/xampp/xamppfiles/mampp security
```

and follow the prompts to add a password to your MySQL server.

The XAMPP installation has PHP configured with the `register_globals` setting turned on. You should disable this old, insecure feature: open the file */Applications/xampp/etc/php.ini* and look for the line `register_globals = On`. Change the value `On` to `Off`, save the file, and quit the editor. The new setting will be in effect after you restart your Apache server.

You can also manually set the MySQL server root password as follows:

```
$ sudo /Applications/xampp/xamppfiles/bin/mysqladmin \
    --user root \
    password the_new_mysql_root_password
```

When the XAMPP web server is running, you can load pages from your own computer by starting a browser such as Safari and opening the web page *http://localhost*.

You can stop XAMPP by typing:

```
$ sudo /Applications/xampp/xamppfiles/mampp stop
```

If you're keen to access the MySQL executable files directly, you can start the server by typing:

```
$ sudo /Applications/xampp/xamppfiles/bin/mysqld_safe
```

Then, press the Ctrl-Z key combination, and type `bg` to leave the server running in the background.

Similarly, you can shut down the server by typing:

```
$ sudo /Applications/xampp/xamppfiles/bin/mysqladmin \
    --user root \
    --password=the_mysql_root_password \
    shutdown
```

Using a MySQL Installation Provided by an ISP

Most individuals and small- to medium-sized organizations don't have the time or resources to maintain a production web server that's available around the clock. Fortunately, there are countless Internet Service Providers (ISPs) that provide—usually for a fee—access to servers they maintain.

Since you're reading this book, we can assume you're interested in servers that can host dynamic web pages (for example, using PHP or Perl scripts) and provide a backend MySQL database that can be accessed by the web application. It's not hard to find an ISP that provides this; a web search for "php mysql hosting" turns up several million sites.

When selecting a hosting package, see whether you are given `ssh` or `telnet` access to the server to run the MySQL client, or whether you can use only web clients such as phpMyAdmin; using web clients is easy, but you could soon find them tedious to use over extended periods of time. On a different note, don't forget to also check how much data transfer is included when comparing costs of alternative web hosting deals. If your site becomes popular, it could end up costing you a lot of money!

Upgrading an Existing MySQL Server

If you've got a MySQL server that's running well and without problems, you may wonder whether it's necessary to upgrade it to the latest version. There are three main reasons to upgrade:

Fixes for bugs
> No complex software such as MySQL can be free of bugs; over time, people dis-
> cover unexpected behavior, or possible data corruption. As these problems come
> to light, they are fixed for the latest version. MySQL bugs are reported and analyzed
> at the *http://bugs.mysql.com* web site. You can use this web site to view the bug
> reports for your MySQL version and determine whether any are likely to affect your
> operations.

Fixes for security vulnerabilities
> Security vulnerabilities are an especially dangerous class of bug; by exploiting a
> vulnerability, an attacker could gain unauthorized access to data, or render your
> system unusable (cause a denial of service). If your server is connected to a network
> or otherwise accessible to people other than yourself, you need to take security
> issues very seriously.

Improved features
> As software matures, new features are added to make some tasks easier or to im-
> prove efficiency. For example, MySQL 5.0 introduced support for *views* (virtual
> tables), *stored procedures* (predefined queries that clients can call), *cursors* (pointers
> to the result of database operations), and *triggers* (predefined operations that are
> carried out automatically before or after a row is inserted, deleted, or updated).
> Similarly, subqueries (nested SELECT queries) were not possible in MySQL before
> version 4.1; neither were multiple concurrent character sets.

> Some new features could greatly simplify your application, allowing you to reduce
> development time by simply upgrading your MySQL server. On a related note,
> application software that you might want to use with your database server—for
> example, a free web portal system—might require you to have a minimum version
> of MySQL.

Newer versions of MySQL are generally backward-compatible with recent versions—
that is, older ways of doing things will continue to work. A new server can work with
old data, and even with older clients. For example, MySQL password management was
improved in version 4.1.0. The new server can correctly handle passwords stored in
the old format, and, if it's started with the old-passwords option, it can modify its
behavior to cater to older clients, such as a web server that uses the old mechanism.

However, software is generally not upward-compatible—that is, you're more likely to
have difficulty if moving from a newer version of MySQL to an older version, especially
if they are major versions apart (for example, moving from MySQL 5.0 to MySQL 4.1).
It's hard to find cases where downgrading is warranted.

You should assess your own needs and decide whether an upgrade is necessary or
worthwhile; if, for example, you have an online shopping application that's running
perfectly, you would only need to upgrade if you wanted to make changes that would
be easier done with a newer MySQL version or if you learn of bugs that could affect the
reliability or security of your site. Upgrading a MySQL server could require upgrades

to other associated software—for example, the version of PHP that the application uses; you must think carefully about the implications of an upgrade before diving in.

Before deciding to upgrade, read the release notes for the new version; in particular, note any changes marked as an "incompatible change." You can find a complete set of release notes under the "MySQL Change History" section of the MySQL manual (*http://dev.mysql.com/doc/refman/5.1/en/news.html*). For example, you may find that support for something that you need is no longer available in the new version, or that you need to carry out certain steps before you start the new server with your existing data. You should also read the "Upgrading MySQL" section of the MySQL manual (*http://dev.mysql.com/doc/refman/5.1/en/upgrade.html*). Note that these links point to the latest version of the manual (5.1) available at the time of writing.

In this book, we don't describe how to change over from a non-MySQL database server, such as Microsoft Access, Microsoft SQL Server, or Oracle. The MySQL Migration Toolkit is a graphical tool that helps you through the process of moving your data over to MySQL. You can download this program as as part of the MySQL GUI Tools Bundle from the MySQL AB downloads page at *http://dev.mysql.com/downloads*.

Should I Upgrade to MySQL 5.1?

At the time of writing, MySQL 5.1 is in beta testing; this means that it's available for easy use and testing, but that it's best to avoid using it for mission-critical production sites. You can download and install MySQL 5.1 using the same procedures discussed in this chapter for the Generally Available versions. Probably the most interesting new features in MySQL 5.1 are its powerful text search capabilities, improved support for XML data, and optimizations for applications where the server must handle very high loads with very high reliability. It's likely that you won't need these features for a considerable time after beginning to use MySQL, and you can complete all the examples in this book with any version of the MySQL server newer than 4.1.0 onwards.

How to Upgrade

We have seen in this chapter that different installation approaches place the MySQL program and datafiles in different locations. For example, a MySQL AB RPM installs the MySQL program files and the data directory under the */usr/local/mysql* directory, while a package provided by a Linux distribution typically places the MySQL program files in the */usr/bin* directory, and the datafiles in the */var/lib/mysql* directory. Upgrading a MySQL server installs new versions of the program files but will not affect your datafiles.

The best way to ensure a trouble-free upgrade is to use the same approach as that used to install the original server because the installation process can upgrade the existing program files, and the new server will know where to find your datafiles. Alternatively, you should isolate or remove the old version so that there is no confusion about which program version is called when you type in a command.

To be able to revert to the older version of the MySQL server if the migration runs into problems, you can install the new server to a different directory from the default. Under Linux and Mac OS X, you can also make a symbolic link to the directory containing the version you want to use. We discussed how to do this earlier in "Installing MySQL on Linux Using a gzipped Tar Archive from MySQL AB" and "Installing MySQL on Linux by Compiling the Source Code from MySQL AB" for the tarball and source installation methods under Linux, and in "Installing Only MySQL Using the no-installer Package from MySQL AB" for a local MySQL installation under Mac OS X. The MySQL AB installer for Mac OS X creates this symbolic link automatically for a system-wide installation. Under Windows, you can specify a different installation directory during the installation process. It isn't straightforward to have coexisting MySQL versions under Linux if you use RPM or Debian packages.

Steps to Upgrade an Existing MySQL Server

There are several ways to upgrade a server. Here, we look at a simple and reliable approach. We first save all the databases on the old server to a dump file. Next, we install the new server. Finally, we load the saved databases into the new server. This last step is not always necessary; you can often get the new server to use the datafiles from the old one.

1. To start, change directories to make the old MySQL installation directory your current working directory. Under Linux or Mac OS X, this is typically */usr/local/mysql* for a system-wide installation:

   ```
   $ cd /usr/local/mysql
   ```

   and *~/mysql* for a local installation:

   ```
   $ cd ~/mysql
   ```

   Under Windows, the MySQL server is typically installed under the MySQL directory —for example, *C:\Program Files\MySQL\MySQL Server 5.0*:

   ```
   C:\> cd C:\Program Files\MySQL\MySQL Server 5.0
   ```

   Again, we'll show the command-line instructions for Linux and Mac OS X; under Windows, simply replace the forward slash (/) with the backslash (\).

2. We discuss how to make a database dumps in detail in Chapter 10. You can dump all the databases on the old MySQL server to the file *dump_of_all_data bases_from_old_server.sql* by typing (all on one line):

   ```
   $ bin/mysqldump \
       --user=root \
       --password=the_mysql_root_password \
       --result-file=dump_of_all_databases_from_old_server.sql \
       --all-databases
   ```

It's a good idea to make a backup of this file on CD or copy it across to another computer.

3. Shut down the old server:

```
$ bin/mysqladmin --user root --password=the_mysql_root_password shutdown
```

4. Install the new server.

5. Configure and start the new server using the appropriate commands discussed earlier in this chapter.

6. At this point, you should have a fresh installation of the MySQL server and associated programs. If the new server version was installed using the same approach as the old version, it's likely to have the same data directory. To check that your databases are available on the new server, you can use the mysqlshow command to connect to it and list the databases:

```
$ bin/mysqlshow --user root --password=the_mysql_root_password
```

You can also use the SHOW DATABASES command in the MySQL monitor (described in Chapter 3).

If you used a different approach, or for some reason the new server doesn't know about your old databases, you should now change your working directory to the location of the new MySQL installation, and then load the databases from the dump file you created earlier:

```
$ bin/mysql \
    --user root \
    --password=the_mysql_root_password \
    < dump_of_all_databases_from_old_server.sql
```

Of course, you should use the password of the new MySQL server here.

7. Your new server should now have loaded all the databases from your old server. One of these, the mysql database, contains *grant tables* that specify user access levels. You should now check and upgrade these tables if necessary.

Under Linux, change to your MySQL base directory and type:

```
$scripts/mysql_fix_privilege_tables \
    --user=root \
    --password=the_mysql_root_password
```

For a Windows MySQL server version 4.0.15 or newer, type:

```
C:\Program Files\MySQL\MySQL Server 5.0> bin/mysql \
    --user=root \
    --password=the_mysql_root_password \
    --database=mysql \
    < scripts\mysql_fix_privilege_tables.sql
```

Finally, for Mac OS X, type:

```
$ sudo /usr/local/mysql/bin/mysql_fix_privilege_tables \
    --user=root \
    --password=the_mysql_root_password
```

Don't worry if you see warnings about duplicate column names. Once you've completed upgrading the tables, stop the server.

Configuring Access to the MySQL Server

By default, there is no password set for the MySQL server. You must set a root password as soon as possible. The MySQL AB Windows installer automatically prompts you to set one as part of the configuration process. For other cases, make sure you follow our installation instructions to set a root password.

A MySQL client connects to a server differently depending on where the server is running. When the client and server are on the same Linux or Mac OS X system, a local connection is made through a Unix socket file, typically */tmp/mysql.sock* or */var/lib/mysql/mysql.sock*. On a Windows system, the connection is made through the MYSQL named pipe if the server was started with the enable-named-pipe option. In other cases, clients send their requests through a TCP/IP network connection. Using a named pipe can actually be slower than using TCP/IP.

If you intend for your server to be accessed only from the host it is running on, you can disable network access to the server by starting the server with the skip-networking option. For a server running on Windows, remember to enable the enable-named-pipe option at the same time; otherwise you won't be able to connect to the server.

If you carry out the steps outlined in this chapter, the filesystem access permissions for the MySQL data directory and the server logs should be configured correctly. Keep in mind that users need access to the socket file to connect to the server; if the socket file is in the data directory (sometimes the case when using Linux distribution RPMs), take care that users can't access other files in that directory. We discussed permission settings in "Restricting access to files and directories," at the beginning of this chapter. Of course, securing the database server is only a small part of overall system security.

If you're running Linux or Mac OS X, you can use the *mysql_secure_installation* script from the MySQL bin directory to walk interactively through steps to improve the security of your server:

```
$ bin/mysql_secure_installation
...
Change the root password? [Y/n] n
...
Remove anonymous users? [Y/n] y
...
Disallow root login remotely? [Y/n] y
...
Remove test database and access to it? [Y/n] n
...
```

```
Reload privilege tables now? [Y/n] y
...
```

The ellipsis (...) symbols indicate where we've left out some of the program output.

What If Things Don't Work?

Hopefully, you'll have managed to get the server up and running without problems. Sadly, things don't always work perfectly. Here's how to get around some of the more common problems.

Can't Download Files from Behind a Proxy

If you have to use a proxy to connect to the Web, you'll need to ask web clients to use them. Web browsers typically allow you to configure proxies under the program connection preferences. For the Linux `wget`, `yum`, and `apt-get` programs, you can declare the HTTP and FTP proxy settings as shown below:

```
# export http_proxy=http://proxy_username:mypass@server_name:port
# export  ftp_proxy=http://proxy_username:mypass@server_name:port
```

For example, you might type:

```
# export http_proxy=http://adam:mypass@proxy.mycompany.com:8080
# export  ftp_proxy=http://adam:mypass@proxy.mycompany.com:8080
```

Your Internet service provider or company network administrator can provide the proxy settings that you should use. If for some reason the `rpm` command does not work through the proxy, you can download the file yourself using a browser or with `wget`. You can then install this downloaded file manually using the `rpm --upgrade` or `dpkg --install` commands.

Error Message About MySQL Executable Programs Not Being Found or Recognized

To use MySQL, you need to run MySQL executable programs, such as the server programs `mysqld_safe` and `mysqld-nt.exe` (described in Chapter 12), the monitor program `mysql` (described in Chapter 3), and the `mysqladmin` administration program that we use in this chapter and throughout this book. These programs are located together in a *bin* directory somewhere on the system; examples of these are:

Linux
  /usr/local/mysql/bin for a system-wide installation from a tarball or source files, *~/mysql-5.0.22/bin* for a local gzipped-tar installation, */usr/bin* directory for an installation from RPM or Debian packages, and */opt/lampp/bin* for an XAMPP installation.

Windows

> *C:\mysql-5.0.22-win32\bin* for a "no-install" (zip) installation; *C:\Program Files \MySQL\MySQL Server 5.0\bin* for a standard installation; and *C:\Program Files \xampp\mysql\bin* for an XAMPP installation.

Mac OS X

> */usr/local/mysql/bin* for a system-wide installation from a tarball or source files, *~/mysql-5.0.22/bin* for a local gzipped-tar installation, */Applications/xampp/xampp files/bin* for an XAMPP installation.

If you can't find the MySQL programs in one of these directories, try to remember where you installed the server files. On a Linux or Mac OS X system, use the `find` command as the root user to locate the `mysqld_safe` program:

```
# find / -name mysqld_safe
```

If you run this command as an ordinary user (not as **root**), you're likely to see lots of "permission denied" messages telling you that you can't look inside certain directories.

On a Windows system, use the search tool to look for files with the word "mysql" in their names. If your search doesn't turn anything up, it's likely that MySQL hasn't in fact been installed. Run the installation process again, note the directory in which the files will be installed, and ensure that all the steps complete successfully.

Once you know where the executable programs are located, you can run each executable program by specifying the full path to it—for example:

```
$ /usr/local/mysql/mysqladmin status
```

on a Linux or Mac OS X system, and:

```
C:\> "C:\Program Files\MySQL\MySQL Server 5.0\bin\mysqladmin status
```

on a Windows system.

If the MySQL `bin` directory is listed in your system PATH, you can simply type:

```
$ mysqladmin status
```

from your operating system command prompt. If you get a message such as:

```
command not found
```

under Linux or Mac OS X, or:

```
'mysqladmin' is not recognized as an internal or external command,
operable program or batch file.
```

under Windows, the directory containing the MySQL executable programs is not in the system path.

The convenient thing to do is to add the MySQL *bin* directory to your system path. You can see the list of directories in your system path by typing:

```
$ echo $PATH
```

at the command line. If the MySQL *bin* directory isn't listed there, take the following steps.

For a Linux or Mac system, open your *~/.bashrc* shell configuration file (start a new file if there isn't one already) in a text editor using the instructions in "Using a Text Editor" at the beginning of this chapter, and add this line to the bottom:

```
export PATH=$PATH:/usr/local/mysql/bin:
```

If you use a shell other than `bash`, you'll need to edit the appropriate shell configuration file. For example, if you use `tcsh`, you'll need to edit the *~/.tcshrc* or *~/.cshrc* file and add the line:

```
setenv PATH $PATH:/usr/local/mysql/bin
```

To activate the changes, type **$ source ~/.bashrc**, log out and log in again, or simply restart the computer.

For Windows, you can update the path in two ways. The first way is to run the MySQL server configuration program again by selecting MySQL Server Instance Config Wizard from the Windows Start menu and selecting the "Include Bin Directory in Windows PATH" checkbox as described earlier in this chapter.

The second way is to manually add the appropriate entry to your Windows path by following these steps:

1. Open the Windows control panel.
2. If you don't have the control panel Classic View enabled (it's disabled by default), you'll need to step through one additional window (if you have Classic View enabled, you can skip this step). Under XP, if you have Category View enabled, you'll see an icon for Performance and Maintenance; open this. Under Vista, the control panel window will open at the Control Panel Home view by default; click on the System and Maintenance entry.
3. Open the System entry. Under Vista, click on the Advanced System Settings link under the list of tasks.
4. Select the Advanced tab
5. Click on the Environment Variables button
6. In the bottom half of the window, you'll see the "System variables" pane. Scroll down this list until you see an entry for Path.
7. Double-click on this entry, or select it and press the Edit button.
8. In the dialog box that appears, go to the end of the Variable value field and add a semicolon followed by the path to the MySQL *bin* directory. For example, if you installed MySQL to the *C:\Program Files\MySQL\MySQL Server 5.0\bin* directory, you should add:

   ```
   ;C:\Program Files\MySQL\MySQL Server 5.0\bin
   ```

   The semicolon at the start is a delimiter used to separate entries in the system path.

9. Press the OK button to close the edit dialog box, and then press the OK button to close the Environment Variables dialog box. The new path should be active immediately.

Error Message Running mysql_install_db

If, on a Linux or Mac OS X system, you get messages like these when running mysql_install_db:

```
$ bin/mysql_install_db
Installing all prepared tables
/home/saied/mysql/libexec/mysqld: Can't read dir of '/root/tmp/' (Errcode: 13)
Fill help tables
/home/saied/mysql/libexec/mysqld: Can't read dir of '/root/tmp/' (Errcode: 13)
...
```

then the setting for your temporary files isn't set correctly. The solution is to declare the directory to use for temporary files as:

```
$ export TMPDIR=/tmp
```

On most systems, the directory */tmp* is present and accessible by all users. You can use any other directory you wish, but remember that it must exist, and you must have permission to create and delete files in that directory.

Server Doesn't Start

Possible questions to ask yourself include:

- Do you have filesystem access to the MySQL commands? Under Linux, try running mysqld_safe as the user root. Under Windows, ensure that you have administrator privileges. Under Mac OS X, check that you used the sudo keyword when calling mysqld_safe.

- Is the server already running? Try stopping the server first and then starting it again.

- Is there another server using port 3306? Try starting your server with a different port using the port option.

    If you're interested, you can list the open ports on a system using the open source nmap security scanner program that is available for Linux, Windows, and Mac OS X. To list the open ports on your own machine (localhost), you'd type:

    ```
    $ nmap localhost

    Starting Nmap 4.11 ( http://www.insecure.org/nmap/ ) at 2006-07-23 02:09 EST
    Interesting ports on saied-ltc.cs.rmit.edu.au (127.0.0.1):
    Not shown: 1669 closed ports
    PORT    STATE SERVICE
    22/tcp  open  ssh
    25/tcp  open  smtp
    80/tcp  open  http
    ```

```
143/tcp   open   imap
631/tcp   open   ipp
1494/tcp  open   citrix-ica
3306/tcp  open   mysql
6000/tcp  open   X11
8080/tcp  open   http-proxy
32770/tcp open   sometimes-rpc3

Nmap finished: 1 IP address (1 host up) scanned in 0.472 seconds
```

Here, you can see that there is a MySQL server listening on port 3306.

A good place to find clues to your problem is to look at the error logfile; this is normally in the data directory with the system host name and the extension *.err*. For example, the logfile for the host *eden.learningmysql.com* is generally called *eden.err* or *eden.lear ningmysql.com.err*. For a Linux host, this might be the file */var/lib/mysql/eden.err*, */usr/ local/mysql/eden.err*, or */opt/lampp/var/mysql/eden.err*, depending on the way MySQL was installed. Similarly, on a Windows system, possible locations for the error logfile include *C:\mysql-5.0.22-win32\data\eden.err*, *C:\Program Files\MySQL \MySQL Server 5.0\data\eden.err*, and *C:\Program Files\xampp\mysql\data\eden.err*. Finally, for a Mac OS X system, likely locations for the error logfile are */usr/local/mysql/ eden.err* and */Applications/xampp/xamppfiles/var/mysql/eden.err*.

You can use the more command to look inside this file:

```
$ more /var/lib/mysql/eden.err
050813 22:31:04  mysqld started
050813 22:31:04  InnoDB: Operating system error number 13 in a file operation.
InnoDB: The error means mysqld does not have the access rights to
InnoDB: the directory.
InnoDB: File name ./ibdata1
InnoDB: File operation call: 'create'.
InnoDB: Cannot continue operation.
050813 22:31:04  mysqld ended
```

This particular message indicates that the directory permissions may not be set correctly. Press Ctrl-C to exit the more program.

If you installed MySQL on a Linux system using packages provided by your Linux distribution, you may instead find the MySQL logs under a different name—for example, *mysqld.log*, in the */var/log/mysql* or */var/log/mysqld* directory.

Client Programs Can't Connect to the Server

Consider these questions:

1. Did you use the correct username and password? Since the default MySQL installation doesn't have a password set, it is easy to be confused when passwords are enabled. For the MySQL command-line tools, try using the user and password options. If you've forgotten your password, try resetting it by following the steps of "Resetting Forgotten MySQL Passwords" in Chapter 9.

2. Is the server running? Try running the command `mysqladmin status` from a terminal window or command prompt.

3. If connecting to a server on `localhost`, do you have filesystem access to the socket file? The socket file is normally created as */tmp/mysql.sock* but can be created in any location specified when the server was started. If it's created in a directory that some users can't access—for example, in the MySQL server's data directory—these users won't be able to connect to the server. For the MySQL command-line tools, use the `socket` option to specify a custom socket path.

4. If connecting to a server on a host other than `localhost`, is the server running on a port other than 3306? You should specify the same port to the client as the one you specified when starting your server; if you don't administer the server, ask the system administrator to tell you the correct port number. For the MySQL command-line tools, use the `port` option to specify a custom port number.

5. If connecting to a server on a host other than `localhost`, is it configured to accept network connections? Ensure that the server was not started with the `skip-net working` option on the command line or in an options file (we discuss options files in Chapter 11).

6. If connecting to a server on a host other than `localhost`, is a firewall preventing network connections? Firewall software or hardware may be preventing connections to the port on which MySQL listens for incoming connections (the default port is 3306). To fix this, you need to modify the firewall so that connections on this port are allowed. Firewalls vary between networks and platforms, and you'll need to refer to your documentation or discuss with your system administrator how to make these changes to your network or host-based firewall. Any firewall changes should be considered carefully to balance feature and security requirements.

Server Doesn't Stop

When you try to shut down the server, you may get a message like:

```
$ bin/mysqladmin shutdown
mysqladmin: shutdown failed; error: 'Access denied; you need the SHUTDOWN privilege
for this operation'
```

This indicates that you have to use a MySQL user account that has the privilege to shut down the server. If you're not logged in to your system under the **root** account, MySQL will use your own username and the password, if any, (for example, **adam**) when connecting to the MySQL server. (We discuss user privileges in detail in Chapter 9.) For now, it's enough to know that you should use the MySQL root account to shut down the server. You can do this by specifying the username from the command line:

```
$ bin/mysqladmin --user=root --password-che-root.passwordshutdown
STOPPING server from pid file /var/run/mysql.pid
060706 21:04:02  mysqld ended
```

The Contents of the MySQL Directory

A MySQL installation has several key files and directories, and several optional ones. In this section, we'll briefly cover the contents of the MySQL directory when you've downloaded and installed MySQL using a MySQL AB package.

First, there are some text files covering the licensing conditions and the installation process. It's a good idea to have a quick read through these:

- *COPYING*
- *README*
- *EXCEPTIONS-CLIENT*
- *INSTALL-BINARY*

The directory also contains the *configure* script to configure and start a freshly installed server; you shouldn't need to use this if you've followed the instructions in this chapter.

Then there are several subdirectories; the important ones are:

bin/

Contains the executable programs—*binaries*—such as `mysqld_safe` and `mysqladmin`. Compiled programs contain binary (0 and 1) code, rather than human-readable text, hence the name of this directory. However, you'll probably find some human-readable script files in this directory too.

data/

Contains a subdirectory holding the data and index files for each database on the server. A newly installed and configured MySQL server comes with the `mysql` and `test` databases, so you'll have at least these two subdirectories in your data directory. The `mysql` database contains information on user access privileges to different databases; as its name suggests, the `test` database can be used for testing.

docs/

Contains the MySQL manual. Under Linux and Mac OS X, the manual file is in an *info* file called *mysql.info*; you can view this by changing into the *docs* directory and typing:

```
$ info mysql.info
```

To see how to navigate in the `info` viewer, press the "?" key in the program.

Under Windows, the manual file is in the Microsoft HTML Help file called *manual.chm*; you can view this file by double-clicking on the file icon, or by changing to the *Docs* directory and typing:

```
C:\Program Files\MySQL\MySQL Server 5.0> hh manual.chm
```

In practice, you're more likely to find it more convenient to refer to the HTML version of the MySQL manual available from the MySQL AB web site.

include/

> Contains header files for use when developing programs that use MySQL libraries.

lib/

> Contains library files that can be used by third-party programs to access the MySQL server.

mysql-test/

> Contains detailed tests you can run to confirm that your server is working properly.

sql-bench/

> Contains detailed tests that can be used to measure database server performance.

scripts/

> Contains scripts, such as *mysql_install_db*, that may be needed for server administration. Under Windows, you can't run most of the scripts directly, but there are several files that contain SQL statements to do certain tasks, which can be run through the MySQL server.

share/

> Contains configuration files, such as translations of MySQL display messages for different languages.

Other directories that are typically present on a full installation include:

man/

> Contains information on some MySQL programs in the classic Unix manual format.
>
> If you installed MySQL using RPMs or an installer, you should be able to view the manual pages by typing man followed by the command name—for example:
>
> ```
> $ man mysqldump
> ```
>
> If you used a gzipped tar archive, you can add the MySQL *man* directory to the search path used by the manual page-viewer program. To do this, edit the file *.bashrc* in your home directory (*~/.bashrc*) and add this line to the end:
>
> ```
> export MANPATH=$MANPATH:/usr/local/mysql/man
> ```
>
> To activate the changes, type **$ source ~/.bashrc**, log out and log in again, or simply restart the computer.
>
> Finally, you can always view these files by typing a command such as the one below (using the *mysqldump* file as an example):
>
> ```
> $ man /usr/local/mysql/man/man1/mysqldump.1
> ```

support-files/

> Contains files and scripts used to configure the server, including ones you can use or modify for your system.

tests/
> Contains sample Perl programs to connect to the MySQL server and perform various simple database operations.

If you install MySQL using packages provided by your Linux distributions, the directory locations will vary from the standard layout. For example, the executable files—such as *mysqld_safe*, *mysql*, and *mysqladmin*—are typically installed in */usr/bin/*, and the data directory is located at */var/lib/mysql*. Similarly, the logfiles may be stored in the */var/log/mysqld* directory, or the main server log may be the file */var/log/mysql*. Clearly, there's a trade-off between easy installation using RPM packages and the disparate location of MySQL-related files when the server is installed in this way. The XAMPP web page has a section under "Basic Questions" named "Where is What?" which lists the locations of configuration files and components.

Configuring and Controlling the Apache Web Server

For all chapters up through Chapter 12, you will need access to only a MySQL server. To practice the examples in Chapters 13, 14, and 15, you'll need an Apache web server with support for the PHP language. In Chapter 18, you'll learn how to run Perl scripts on a Apache web server.

If you haven't installed Apache using XAMPP, you should check whether you have Apache installed and, if so, whether it supports PHP. You should also check whether your PHP engine supports your installation of MySQL.

If you've used the XAMPP package, you can relax, knowing that this has been done for you. You also know how to start and stop Apache using the */opt/lampp/lampp* script (Linux), the XAMPP control panel (Windows), or the */Applications/xampp/xamppfiles/ mampp* script (Mac OS X). If you're using Linux and aren't using XAMPP, you'll need to ensure that your web server can work with your database server.

Apache is installed as part of the standard Mac OS X configuration, where it's referred to as Personal Web Sharing. You can configure it from the Sharing section of the System Preferences window. However, we'll rely on the XAMPP installation in this book, so go to the Sharing settings and ensure that Personal Web Sharing is switched off.

In this section, we look at how to check that your web server is running, and how to find the directory from which it serves files to your browser. We also explain where to find the Apache configuration file and error log. Finally, we describe how you can control the Apache web server on a Linux system where you haven't used XAMPP, and how to check that your web server is correctly configured for the work that you'll do in this book.

You can test whether a web server is running on your machine by opening a browser (for example, Firefox, Internet Explorer, or Safari), and typing in the address *http:// localhost*. If your browser reports that it can't open this page, you can try to start the server by using the appropriate XAMPP startup command, or the `apachectl` or apache2ctl commands described later in this section in "Starting and Stopping Apache."

If you see some response when you try to load a page in your browser, you can try placing content in the server's document root. Let's see how to find this directory.

The Apache Document Root

The *document root* is the base or parent directory in which the web server stores web resources (such as HTML, PHP, or image files) and serves them to web browsers. For the Apache web server, common locations of the document root include:

Linux
> */var/www/html*, */var/www/htdocs*, or */var/www* for a distribution installation; */usr/ local/apache/htdocs* for a standalone installation, and */opt/lampp/htdocs* for an XAMPP installation.

Windows
> *C:\Program Files\xampp\htdocs* for an XAMPP installation, and *C:\Program Files \Apache Group\Apache2\htdocs* if Apache is installed independently

Mac OS X
> */Applications/xampp/htdocs* for an XAMPP installation, and */Library/WebServer/ Documents* for the installation of Apache that is part of the standard Mac OS X configuration

If you're using a Linux system and don't know where your server's document root is, search for it by following these instructions.

First, log in as the system superuser by typing **su -** in a terminal window. Then try to list the common document root directories that we listed previously:

```
# ls --directory /var/www/html /var/www/htdocs /var/www /usr/local/apache/htdocs
/bin/ls: /var/www/htdocs: No such file or directory
/bin/ls: /usr/local/apache/htdocs: No such file or directory
/var/www  /var/www/html
```

The `--directory` option asks the `ls` program to list only directory names, and not their contents.

If you get an error message for a directory, that directory doesn't exist. Where the directory name is listed, as for */var/www* and */var/www/html* above, the directory exists. One of these is likely to be the document root. If none of the directories exist, you can try searching your whole filesystem for a directory called `htdocs`:

```
# find / -type d -name htdocs
```

Be patient; this may take a few minutes. Any directory it finds is likely to be the directory root; if more than one is found, you'll need to experiment by creating files in each to determine which is the one used by your Apache installation.

The Apache Configuration File

The Apache configuration file is usually called *httpd.conf* and is found in one of several common locations:

Linux
> */etc/httpd/conf/httpd.conf* or */etc/apache/conf/httpd.conf* for an installation from Linux distribution files; */usr/local/apache/conf/httpd.conf* for an installation from Apache Foundation files; and */opt/lampp/etc/httpd.conf* for an XAMPP installation

Windows
> *C:\Program Files\xampp\apache\conf\httpd.conf* for an XAMPP installation

Mac OS X
> */Applications/xampp/etc/httpd.conf* for an XAMPP installation, and */etc/httpd/httpd.conf* for the installation of Apache that is part of the standard Mac OS X configuration

It's increasingly common to find servers configured in a modular way, with a main configuration file that reads in other files, for example under the directory */etc/httpd/modules.d* on a Linux system, or in the *apache\conf\extra* directory under the XAMPP install directory. For example, directives specific to PHP are often stored in the file */etc/httpd/modules.d/70_mod_php.conf*.

If you make changes to the Apache configuration file, you need to restart the web server to put the changes into effect.

The Apache Error Log

Common locations for the web server error log include:

Linux
> */usr/local/apache/logs/error.log* for Apache installed from Apache Foundation files, */var/log/httpd/error_log* or */var/log/apache/error.log* for an installation using distribution packages, and */opt/lampp/logs/error_log* for an XAMPP installation

Windows
> *C:\Program Files\xampp\apache\logs\error.log* for an XAMPP installation

Mac OS X
> */Applications/xampp/xamppfiles/logs/error_log* for an XAMPP installation, and */private/var/log/httpd/error_log* for the Apache installation that is part of the standard Mac OS X configuration

Starting and Stopping Apache

Apache web server installations usually include a control script called: `apachectl`that you can use to start or stop the server. On newer installations this is sometimes called apache2ctl; if the examples below don't work for you, try replacing `apachectl` with `apache2ctl`. You can generally start an installed Apache server by using the command:

```
# apachectl start
```

If this fails on a Linux or Mac OS X system because the command isn't found, use the `find` command to locate the *apachectl* script file:

```
# find / -type f -name apachectl
```

On a Windows system, use the built-in search instead of the `find` command. If it's reported as being in, say, */usr/local/apache/bin/apachectl*, try starting Apache using that full path:

```
# /usr/local/apache/bin/apachectl start
```

Apache should start, and you should be able to test it by loading the web page *http://localhost* in your browser.

You can stop the server by typing:

```
# apachectl stop
```

If you make a change to the web server configuration file, you can stop and start the server in one go by typing:

```
# apachectl restart
```

If you have an XAMPP installation, you can more easily start and stop the Apache web server using the XAMPP control scripts (Linux and Mac OS X) or control panel (Windows). Earlier, we described how to do this alongside our XAMPP installation instructions for each operating system.

Checking Whether Your Apache Installation Supports PHP

Once you've found your document root and have Apache running, you can check whether it can serve PHP requests, and whether its PHP engine has support for MySQL. Using a text editor, create the file *phpinfo.php* so that it has one line with the following contents:

```
<?php phpinfo(); ?>
```

Save this file with the name *phpinfo.php* in the document root directory. On a Linux or Mac OS X system, you can check the file permissions by listing the file, *<path_to_document_root>/phpinfo.php*, for example:

```
$ ls -al /var/www/html/phpinfo.php
-rw-------  1 saied saied 20 Jul 22 11:35 /var/www/html/phpinfo.php
```

Here, only the user who owns the file (`saied`) has permission to read and write the file. For the web server to read a file, the file should be readable by everyone. You can set the appropriate permissions as follows:

```
$ chmod u=rw,g=r,o=r path_to_document_root/phpinfo.php
```

If you check the permissions again, you should find that other users can access the file; we've granted the group read access as well, but that's not strictly necessary:

```
$ ls -al path_to_document_root/phpinfo.php
-rw-r--r--  1 saied saied 20 Jul 22 11:35 /var/www/html/phpinfo.php
```

A common cause of Access Denied problems is the file or directory not being readable. The web server also needs execute access to the directory containing the file, and all the directories above it. On some systems, only the superuser can write to the document root, so you may also need to allow write access to the document root. See "Restricting access to files and directories," at the beginning of this chapter, for more discussion of file and directory permissions.

After creating the file, run the script by requesting the address *http://localhost/phpinfo .php* with a web browser that is running on the same machine as the web server. If you see a readable web page—and not just what you typed into the file—then your web server has PHP support. Search this page for the word "mysql"; if you find a section labeled "mysql" (and perhaps another labeled "mysqli"), your PHP installation can talk to your MySQL server.

If you just see the contents of the *phpinfo.php* file, or your browser tries to download the file, your Apache server may not support PHP. However, there are three common problems that can cause this to happen even when your server does support PHP:

- Your PHP test files don't have the extension *.php*. If this is the case, your web server will deliver the source code and not run the scripts. Rename your scripts with a *.php* extension.

- Your web server isn't configured to run the PHP engine when a file with the *.php* extension is requested. In Apache, this is controlled by the Apache configuration file described earlier in "The Apache Configuration File." Open the configuration file and search for the following line:

    ```
    AddType application/x-httpd-php .php
    ```

    If this line is commented out—that is, there's a pound or hash symbol (#) before the text on the line—uncomment the line by removing this symbol, save the file, and restart the web server following the instructions listed earlier in "Starting and Stopping Apache." If the line isn't there at all, add it and restart the server.

- Your Apache PHP module isn't being loaded by Apache. Open the Apache configuration file and check whether one of the following lines appears in the file:

    ```
    LoadModule php4_module        libexec/libphp4.so
    LoadModule php5_module        libexec/libphp5.so
    ```

    Add one of these lines if they don't appear in the file. Try using the `php5_module` line first. If both lines have the pound or hash symbol before the text on the line, remove the comment symbol from one of the lines to activate the PHP module. If you change the Apache configuration file, restart the web server.

If you're sure that you have Apache but not PHP, or that your PHP installation does not support MySQL, the easiest solution is to reinstall by following the instructions earlier in this chapter.

Setting up Perl

Chapters 16, 17, and 18 require that you have a working installation of Perl. Perl is available as standard on almost all Linux and Mac OS X systems, and it is included in the XAMPP integrated package, so you don't need to install it separately. For Chapters 17 and 18, you'll need two Perl extension packages or *modules*. We'll use the Perl DBI (Database Interface) module in Chapter 17 to talk to a MySQL server, and the Perl CGI (Common Gateway Interface) module in Chapter 18 to write clean and readable scripts that can be run by a web server. If you're not planning to write complex Perl scripts for a web application, you can manage without the CGI module, but you'll definitely need the DBI module to use Perl for interaction with MySQL.

Checking Your Existing Setup

To run Perl scripts, you need to know where the Perl interpreter (called `perl`) is installed on your system. For Linux, we'll use the instance of Perl that comes with the distribution; to find where this is located, use the `which` command:

```
$ which perl
/usr/bin/perl
```

In this example, the Perl interpreter is the file */usr/bin/perl*.

For Windows and Mac OS X systems, we'll use the instance of Perl that comes with XAMPP. On a Windows system, the XAMPP Perl interpreter is *C:\Program Files \xampp\perl\bin\perl.exe*, while on a Mac OS X system, the XAMPP Perl interpreter is */Applications/xampp/xamppfiles/bin/perl*. You can also use the Mac OS X system default installation (*/usr/bin/perl*), but as we discuss later in "Installing Perl modules under Mac OS X," we recommend you stick with the XAMPP installation for consistency.

Let's start by examining what the version of this Perl installation is. On a Linux system, type:

```
$ perl --version
```

On a Windows or Mac OS X system, the XAMPP Perl interpreter is not in the system path, so you should specify the full path on a Windows system as:

```
C:\> C:\Program Files\xampp\perl\bin\perl --version
```

or on a Mac system as:

```
$ /Applications/xampp/xamppfiles/bin/perl --version
```

You should either add this *bin* directory to your system path following the instructions earlier in this chapter in "Error Message About MySQL Executable Programs Not Being Found or Recognized," or specify the full path to the Perl interpreter whenever you see `perl` for the remainder of this chapter.

If Perl is available, the command will display several lines of text describing the version and other configuration details. If Perl is not installed, you'll see an error message saying something like `command not found` (Linux or Mac OS X) or `'perl' is not recognized as an internal or external command, operable program or batch file` (Windows). You can find more information on obtaining and installing Perl at *http://www.perl.org/get.html*, and more information on installing modules at *http://www.cpan.org/modules/INSTALL.html*. For a Linux system, download and install the Perl package for your distribution according to the instructions in "Installing MySQL, Apache, PHP, and Perl on Linux Using Distribution Packages." For a Windows or Mac OS X system, check that you've installed XAMPP correctly.

Once you know that Perl is installed, you can test whether the DBI and CGI modules are installed by asking the Perl interpreter to use these modules to run an empty Perl script. To check whether the DBI module is installed, type:

```
$ perl -mDBI -e ''
```

If you see an error message that Perl "Can't locate" *DBI.pm*, you'll need to install the module yourself. Similarly, check whether the CGI module is installed by typing:

```
$ perl -mCGI -e ''
```

If the DBI module is installed, you should also check whether the MySQL database driver (DBD) is installed. An easy way to do this is to ask Perl to print out all the drivers that are available:

```
$ perl -e "use DBI; foreach $d (DBI->available_drivers()){print $d;}"
DBMExamplePFileSpongemysql
```

If you don't see the letters "mysql", you'll need to install the MySQL database driver.

Installing the Perl DBI and CGI Modules

If you found that you need to install the CGI or DBI module, or the MySQL DBD, then you need to follow the steps outlined in the following sections for each operating system.

Installing Perl modules under Linux

The standard way to install Perl modules is to get Perl to use the CPAN (Comprehensive Perl Archive Network) module to install new modules from the Internet. Log in as the system root user by typing `su -`, and then install the DBI module, the DBI MySQL Database Driver, and the CGI module by running the following commands in turn:

```
# perl -MCPAN -e 'install DBI'
# perl -MCPAN -e 'install DBD::mysql;'
# perl -MCPAN -e 'install CGI;'
```

If this is the first time you're installing Perl modules this way, you may be prompted to answer a few questions. It's generally safe to answer no to the question:

```
Are you ready for manual configuration? [yes]
```

and leave it to Perl to figure out how to fetch the required packages. If all goes well, you should see reassuring status messages as Perl downloads and installs everything.

Perl modules are also available for individual Linux distributions, and you can download and install them manually. For RPM-based systems, you should download and install the *perl-DBI* package for DBI, the *perl-DBD-mysql* package for the DBI MySQL driver, and the *perl-CGI* package for CGI. For example, on a Red Hat or Fedora system, type:

```
# yum update perl-DBI perl-DBD-mysql perl-CGI
```

For a Mandriva or Mandrake system, type:

```
# urpmi perl-DBI perl-DBD-mysql perl-CGI
```

For a Debian-based system, the package names are slightly different:

```
# apt-get install libdbi-perl libdbd-mysql-perl libcgi-pm-perl
```

Installing Perl modules under Windows

Windows does not have Perl support by default, so you need to install a Perl interpreter yourself. The XAMPP package you installed earlier in this chapter includes a minimal Perl setup. However, to include a reasonable set of Perl libraries, including the DBI and CGI modules and the MySQL DBD, you should also visit the web page *http://www.apachefriends.org/en/xampp.html* and download and install the Perl Addons installer. This will have a filename similar to *xampp-perl-addon-5.8.7-2.2.2-installer.exe*. Install this in the same directory in which your XAMPP installation is located; we assume this is *C:\Program Files\xampp*.

Many of the MySQL command-line programs in the *scripts* directory are in fact Perl scripts; if you want to use these scripts, you'll need to associate Perl files with the Perl interpreter. To do this, you tell Windows that all files with the standard Perl extension *.pl* must be run by the Perl interpreter. Open a command prompt window and type the following two lines:

```
C:\> ASSOC .pl=PerlScript
C:\> FTYPE PerlScript=C:\Program Files\xampp\perl\bin\perl.exe %1 %*
```

You can now run Perl scripts by double-clicking on the icon of the script file, or by typing in the name of the script file at the command prompt. You can find other tips for using Perl under Windows in the Perl Win32 FAQ (*http://www.perl.com/doc/FAQs/nt/perlwin32faq4.html*).

Installing Perl modules under Mac OS X

Mac OS X comes with a Perl interpreter already installed, so after installing XAMPP following the instructions earlier in this chapter, you'll have two Perl interpreters on your system: */usr/bin/perl* and */Applications/xampp/xamppfiles/bin/perl*. You'll need to configure the DBI and CGI modules for at least one of these.

Since we use XAMPP for other parts of this book, our instructions will focus on it. You can still configure the system default Perl interpreter by typing */usr/bin/perl* in place of */Applications/xampp/xamppfiles/bin/perl* in our instructions, but we feel that you'll have fewer difficulties if you work with the XAMPP installation.

For XAMPP, you need to do two things to ensure a hassle-free DBD MySQL driver installation. First, to allow the DBD installation process to test the installation process using the MySQL server, start XAMPP by typing:

```
$ sudo /Applications/xampp/xamppfiles/mampp start
```

Then create a symbolic link to the XAMPP MySQL socket file in the default MySQL socket file location */tmp/mysql.sock*, which is where Perl will expect to find it:

```
$ ln -s /Applications/xampp/xamppfiles/var/mysql/mysql.sock /tmp/mysql.sock
```

Some versions of XAMPP come with permission settings for the */Applications/xampp/xamppfiles/lib/perl5* directory that don't allow ordinary users to access it, causing modules to appear missing. To ensure that the permissions are correctly set, type:

```
$ sudo chmod u=rwx,g=rx,o=rx /Applications/xampp/xamppfiles/lib/perl5
```

We discussed permission settings in "Restricting access to files and directories," at the beginning of this chapter.

You can download and install the DBI module, the MySQL driver, and the CGI module for the XAMPP Perl installation by typing these commands in turn:

```
$ sudo /Applications/xampp/xamppfiles/bin/perl -MCPAN -e 'install DBI;'
$ sudo /Applications/xampp/xamppfiles/bin/perl -MCPAN -e 'install DBD::mysql;'
$ sudo /Applications/xampp/xamppfiles/bin/perl -MCPAN -e 'install CGI;'
```

You may be prompted for the system root user password. You may also be prompted to configure the download locations with the message:

```
Are you ready for manual configuration? [yes]
```

Unless you're very sure of what you're doing, just type **no** and press the Enter key to let Perl figure out how best to download the required files.

Problems installing the Perl modules

If, during the install process, you see an error message such as this one:

```
Error: Unable to locate installed Perl libraries or Perl source code.

It is recommended that you install perl in a standard location before
```

```
building extensions. Some precompiled versions of perl do not contain
these header files, so you cannot build extensions. In such a case,
please build and install your perl from a fresh perl distribution. It
usually solves this kind of problem.

(You get this message, because MakeMaker could not find
"/System/Library/Perl/5.8.1/darwin-thread-multi-2level/CORE/perl.h")
# Looks like your test died before it could output anything.
Running make test
Make had some problems, maybe interrupted? Won't test
Running make install
Make had some problems, maybe interrupted? Won't install
```

you'll need to install the Apple Developer Tools. These are available on the Mac OS X
install disk that came with your system. Double-click on the *XcodeTools.mpkg* icon on
the screen of disk contents and follow the prompts to install this package.

You can also get the latest version of the Developer Tools by visiting *http://developer
.apple.com* and registering as a developer (it's free). Once you've registered and logged
in to the site, click on the Downloads link, and then click on the Developer Tools link
on the downloads page. From the Developer Tools download page, click on the latest
release of the .Mac SDK; at the time of writing, this was 1.2, with version 2.0 available
for testing.

If you see a message similar to the one below:

```
Writing Makefile for DBD::mysql
-- NOT OK
Running make test
Can't test without successful make
Running make install
make had returned bad status, install seems impossible
```

you'll need to build the downloaded module manually. First, check the directories
containing the downloaded module source files:

```
$ ls ~/.cpan/build
DBD-mysql-3.0002        DBI-1.48
```

In this example, we have files for DBI version 1.48 and DBD MySQL driver version
3.0002. The versions you download may be different.

Now, build the module by changing to the corresponding directory (here we'll compile
the DBI module):

```
$ cd ~/.cpan/build/DBI-1.48
```

and using the make command:

```
$ make
```

Once the module has been successfully built, install it as the system root user:

```
$ sudo make install
```

Repeat this process for any other modules you need to compile.

Resources

You can find a detailed reference manual on MySQL and several sample databases on the MySQL AB web site at *http://dev.mysql.com/doc*, although we recommend you explore these after you've finished reading this book.

You can also participate in MySQL-related discussion forums and mailing lists. Some of these are run by MySQL AB. To learn more, visit the MySQL AB forums page at *http://forums.mysql.com* and the lists page at *http://lists.mysql.com*.

There's also a lot of helpful material on the MySQL community web site (*http://forge .mysql.com*). In particular, look at the collection of (mostly user-contributed) documentation by following the "Wiki" link near the top of the page. Don't worry if it all seems overwhelming at first; you'll be able to make sense of most of it by the time you reach the end of this book!

To learn more about installing the software described in this book, we recommend the following resources:

- For more on the Windows XP command prompt, visit the Microsoft XP command-line reference at *http://www.microsoft.com/resources/documentation/windows/xp/ all/proddocs/en-us/ntcmds_o.mspx*. Much of this information applies to Vista too.

- A useful list of frequently-asked questions about XAMPP, including discussion of common installation problems is available from the XAMPP web site (*http://www .apachefriends.org/en)*.

- For detailed information on setting up and configuring the Apache web server, including a list of all the configuration directives, visit *http://httpd.apache.org*.

To learn more about shell or command-prompt instructions, do a web search for "learn unix Linux" (for Linux), "learn unix mac os x" (for Mac OS X), or "Windows command prompt" (for Windows).

Throughout this book, we point out security aspects you should consider while installing, configuring, and running MySQL and associated web applications. To better understand security issues, we highly recommend these resources:

- *Security Engineering: A Guide to Building Dependable Distributed Systems* by Ross J. Anderson (Wiley). This book is also available online at *http://www.cl.cam.ac.uk/ ~rja14/book.html*.

- *Secrets and Lies: Digital Security in a Networked World* by Bruce Schneier (Wiley).

- The monthly Crypto-Gram Newsletter, written by Bruce Schneier, available at *http: //www.schneier.com/crypto-gram.html*.

Exercises

1. What is command completion?
2. What are the relative advantages of installing MySQL using the package, directory archive (tarball or "no-install"), or compiled methods?
3. How do you verify the integrity of downloaded packages?
4. How do you add the MySQL *bin* directory to the operating system path?

## CHAPTER 3

Using the MySQL Monitor

MySQL has a *client-server architecture*; clients connect to the server to perform database operations such as reading or storing data. There are many MySQL clients available, including some that have graphical interfaces. You can also develop your own clients. The standard MySQL command-line client or "monitor" program provided by MySQL AB is the client you'll probably use the most often. The monitor allows you to control almost all aspects of database creation and maintenance using SQL and the custom MySQL extensions to SQL.

In this chapter, we'll examine how to start the monitor and how to run commands through the monitor either interactively or in batch mode. We'll describe how you can access the inbuilt MySQL help functions, and how to test your MySQL setup using the sample databases from the book web site. We'll also take a quick look at a couple of graphical tools that you can use instead of the monitor.

Starting the Monitor

The monitor program is called simply `mysql` and is found in a directory with the other MySQL programs. The exact location depends on your operating system and how you chose to install MySQL; we considered some of these in "Error Message About MySQL Executable Programs Not Being Found or Recognized," in Chapter 2.

If your MySQL server isn't already running, start it using the appropriate procedure for your setup as discussed in Chapter 2. Now, follow these steps to start the monitor and connect to your MySQL server as the MySQL administrator (the MySQL **root** user) by typing this from the command line:

```
$ mysql --user=root
```

If you followed our instructions in Chapter 2, the MySQL **root** account is protected by the password you chose earlier, and so you'll get a message saying that you've been denied access to the server. If your server has a password, you should specify the password as follows:

```
$ mysql --user=root --password=the_mysql_root_password
```

If you get a message from the operating system saying that it can't find the MySQL program, you'll need to specify the full path to the `mysql` executable file as discussed in "Error Message About MySQL Executable Programs Not Being Found or Recognized."

If you used a nonstandard socket file when starting your server, you'll need to provide the details to any MySQL client programs you run, including `mysql`. For example, you might type:

```
$ mysql \
 --socket=server_socket \
 --user=root \
 --password=the_mysql_root_password
```

If you're trying to connect to a MySQL server on a different computer or a nonstandard port, you should specify these when starting the monitor:

```
$mysql \
 --host=server_host_name \
 --port=server_port \
 --user=root \
 --password=the_mysql_root_password
```

We list a few more options to the monitor program at the end of this chapter.

Most of the other MySQL programs we'll describe in this book take the same `port` and `socket` options to identify the server to connect to, and the same `user` and `password` options to identify and authenticate the MySQL user.

If all goes well, you'll get the monitor's `mysql>` prompt:

```
Welcome to the MySQL monitor.  Commands end with ; or \g.
Your MySQL connection id is 456 to server version: 5.0.22

Type 'help;' or '\h' for help. Type '\c' to clear the buffer.

mysql>
```

You can now type in commands that MySQL understands. To start things off, ask the server what version of MySQL it is:

```
mysql> SELECT VERSION();
+------------+
| VERSION()  |
+------------+
| 5.0.22 |
+------------+
1 row in set (0.03 sec)
```

You'll almost certainly be using a different version number from the one we're using. Now ask the server to list all the databases that it has:

```
mysql> SHOW DATABASES;
+----------+
| Database |
+----------+
```

```
| mysql  |
| test   |
+----------+
2 rows in set (0.00 sec)
```

You may see different results on your MySQL server. There are two databases here; the `mysql` database is used to store information about user access privileges, and the `test` database is an empty scratch space for experimentation. Not terribly exciting, but you'll remedy this situation as you progress through this book!

Style, Case, and Semicolons

When interacting with a MySQL server, you'll use a combination of SQL keywords, MySQL proprietary commands, and names of databases and database components. We follow common convention and use a style to make it easier to distinguish between components of an SQL query. We always show SQL statements and keywords in capitals, such as `SELECT` or `FROM`. We also show the MySQL monitor's proprietary SQL commands—such as `USE`—in uppercase. We always enter database components—such as database, table, and column names—in lowercase. This makes our SQL more readable and easier to follow in source code and books.

MySQL isn't fussy about whether you enter SQL or the monitor's proprietary statements in uppercase or lowercase. For example, `SELECT`, `select`, `Select`, and even `SeLeCt` are equivalent. However, depending on your platform, MySQL can be fussy about database and table names. For example, under Windows, MySQL isn't fussy at all (because Windows itself isn't fussy about the filenames that store those structures), while on Mac OS X its fussiness depends on what underlying filesystem you use to store disk files. Linux and Unix systems observe the difference between uppercase and lowercase strictly. A reliable approach is to adopt the convention of using lowercase for all database, table, and column names. You can control how MySQL manages different case behavior using an option when you start the MySQL server, `mysqld`, but we don't recommend you do this, and we don't discuss it further in this book.

There are some restrictions on what characters and words you can use in your database, table, and other names. For example, you can't have a column named `from` or `select` (in any mix of uppercase and lowercase). These restrictions are mostly obvious, since they apply to reserved keywords that confuse MySQL's parser. We discuss the characters that can and can't be used in Chapter 6.

You'll notice that we terminate all SQL statements with the semicolon character (`;`). This tells MySQL that we've finished entering a statement and that it should now parse and execute it. This gives you flexibility, allowing you to type in a statement over several lines. For example, the following statement works fine:

```
mysql> SELECT User,Host
    -> FROM user;
+------+--------------------------+
```

```
| User | Host                    |
+------+-------------------------+
|      | localhost               |
| root | localhost               |
|      | saied-ltc.cs.rmit.edu.au |
| root | saied-ltc.cs.rmit.edu.au |
+------+-------------------------+
4 rows in set (0.00 sec)
```

We often use this style in this book, because it helps long statements fit in the margins of a page. Notice that the monitor shows you a different prompt (->) to indicate that it's waiting for you to enter more of your SQL statement or to type in a semicolon.

In fact, you can add *whitespace*—such as space and tab characters—anywhere between the components of a statement to improve its formatting, and we often do this in our longer statements. Of course, because whitespace separates keywords and values, you can't add space within the keywords or values themselves; for example, if you type the keyword SELECT as SEL ECT, you'll get an error.

In contrast to SQL statements, you can't span the MySQL monitor's own commands over more than one line. This is because the semicolon isn't actually required for these, and just pressing the Enter key has the same effect. For example, the USE command tells MySQL that you want to use a particular database. The following works fine:

```
mysql> USE test
Database changed
```

However, if you try to span the command over more than one line, you won't get far:

```
mysql> USE
ERROR:
USE must be followed by a database name
```

The Monitor Help

The monitor has a handy HELP command that you can use to get more information on the monitor commands or SQL syntax. If you type HELP and press the Enter key, you'll get a list of commands the monitor understands:

```
mysql> HELP
For information about MySQL products and services, visit:
   http://www.mysql.com/
For developer information, including the MySQL Reference Manual, visit:
   http://dev.mysql.com/
To buy MySQL Network Support, training, or other products, visit:
   https://shop.mysql.com/

List of all MySQL commands:
Note that all text commands must be first on line and end with ';'
?         (\?) Synonym for `help'.
clear     (\c) Clear command.
connect   (\r) Reconnect to the server. Optional arguments are db and host.
delimiter (\d) Set statement delimiter. NOTE: Takes the rest of the line as new
```

```
                 delimiter.
edit        (\e) Edit command with $EDITOR.
ego         (\G) Send command to mysql server, display result vertically.
exit        (\q) Exit mysql. Same as quit.
go          (\g) Send command to mysql server.
help        (\h) Display this help.
nopager     (\n) Disable pager, print to stdout.
notee       (\t) Don't write into outfile.
pager       (\P) Set PAGER [to_pager]. Print the query results via PAGER.
print       (\p) Print current command.
prompt      (\R) Change your mysql prompt.
quit        (\q) Quit mysql.
rehash      (\#) Rebuild completion hash.
source      (\.) Execute an SQL script file. Takes a file name as an argument.
status      (\s) Get status information from the server.
system      (\!) Execute a system shell command.
tee         (\T) Set outfile [to_outfile]. Append everything into given outfile.
use         (\u) Use another database. Takes database name as argument.
charset     (\C) Switch to another charset. Might be needed for processing binlog with
                 multi-byte charsets.
warnings    (\W) Show warnings after every statement.
nowarning   (\w) Don't show warnings after every statement.

For server side help, type 'help contents'
```

Depending on the version of the monitor that you're using, you may see a different list. The characters in the parentheses indicate a shortcut for each command. You typed in the USE command earlier in this chapter to change to the **test** database. From the list, you can see a short description of this command and also see that you can type \u instead of USE.

Let's look at another entry on this list. The monitor has command completion, just like the Linux and Mac OS X shells, and like the Windows command prompt. You can press the Tab key to complete SQL statements and table and attribute names. If not all the options you expect are shown, you can update the internal list of expansions ("rebuild the completion hash") by typing rehash (or using the shortcut characters \#) and pressing the Enter key.

Using the help function of the monitor, you can also get help on how to interact with the MySQL server. To see a table of contents for the help documentation, type HELP Contents:

```
mysql> HELP Contents
You asked for help about help category: "Contents"
For more information, type 'help <item>', where <item> is one of the following
categories:
 Account Management
 Administration
 Data Definition
 Data Manipulation
 Data Types
 Functions
 Functions and Modifiers for Use with GROUP BY
```

```
Geographic Features
Language Structure
Storage Engines
Stored Routines
Table Maintenance
Transactions
Triggers
```

You may see more or less help content depending on the help files that have been installed with your server. You can get information on individual topics by typing in the HELP command followed by the topic name. For example, to get information on data manipulation, you would type:

```
mysql> HELP Data Manipulation
You asked for help about help category: "Data Manipulation"
For more information, type 'help <item>', where <item> is one of the following
topics:
CACHE INDEX
...
DELETE
...
EXPLAIN
...
INSERT
...
SELECT
...
SHOW
...
SHOW CREATE DATABASE
...
SHOW CREATE TABLE
...
SHOW DATABASES
...
SHOW GRANTS
...
SHOW STATUS
...
SHOW TABLES
...
UPDATE
```

We've omitted some items to keep the output short.

You can request further information on any of the items by typing HELP followed by the appropriate keywords. For example, for information on the SHOW DATABASES command, you'd type:

```
mysql> HELP SHOW DATABASES
Name: 'SHOW DATABASES'
Description:
Syntax:
SHOW {DATABASES | SCHEMAS} [LIKE 'pattern']
```

SHOW DATABASES lists the databases on the MySQL server host. You see only those databases for which you have some kind of privilege, unless you have the global SHOW DATABASES privilege. You can also get this list using the mysqlshow command.

If the server was started with the --skip-show-database option, you cannot use this statement at all unless you have the SHOW DATABASES privilege.

SHOW SCHEMAS can be used as of MySQL 5.0.2

Running the Monitor in Batch Mode

The MySQL monitor can be used in *interactive mode* or in *batch mode*. In interactive mode, you type in SQL queries or MySQL commands such as SHOW DATABASES at the MySQL prompt, and view the results.

In batch mode, you tell the monitor to read in and execute a list of commands from a file. This is useful when you need to run a large set of operations—for example, when you want to restore a database from a backup file. It's also useful when you need to run a particular sequence of operations frequently; you can save the commands in a file and then tell the monitor to read in the file whenever you need it.

The examples we've presented earlier in this chapter, and most of the examples in this book, show the monitor being used in interactive mode. Let's look at an example for batch mode. Say you have a text file called *count_users.sql* containing the SQL commands:

```
use mysql;
SELECT COUNT(*) FROM user;
```

This script tells MySQL that you want to use the mysql database, and that you want to count all the users who have accounts on the MySQL server (we'll explain the syntax of the SELECT command in Chapter 5).

You can run all the commands in this file using the SOURCE command:

```
mysql> SOURCE count_users.sql
Database changed
+----------+
| count(*) |
+----------+
| 4        |
+----------+
1 row in set (0.00 sec)
```

If the *count_users.sql* file isn't in the current directory, you should give the full path to the file—for example, */home/adam/Desktop/count_users.sql* or *C:\count_users.sql*. Alternatively, from the command line, you can use the less-than (<) redirection operator followed by the filename:

```
$ mysql --user=root --password=the_mysql_root_password < count_users.sql
count(*)
4
```

Loading the Sample Databases

To get a working sample database that you can play with, start by visiting the book's web site and downloading the music database file *music.sql* from the sample databases section.

To load the file into your server, you need to use the SOURCE command and specify where MySQL can find the `music.sql` file. For example, this might be *~/music.sql* or *~/Desktop/music.sql* on a Linux or Mac OS X system, or *C:\Documents and Settings \my_windows_login_name\Desktop\music.sql* on a Windows system.

Once you run the SOURCE command, you should see some reassuring messages flash by:

```
mysql> SOURCE path_to_music.sql_file;
Query OK, 1 row affected (0.00 sec)

Query OK, 1 row affected (0.01 sec)

Query OK, 1 row affected (0.00 sec)
...
```

You can now see if the database is there by using the SHOW DATABASES command:

```
mysql> SHOW DATABASES;
+----------+
| Database |
+----------+
| music    |
| mysql    |
| test     |
+----------+
3 rows in set (0.00 sec)

mysql>
```

We'll see how to use this database in future chapters.

Repeat this process for the two additional sample database files, *flight.sql* and *university.sql*, that are available from the book's web site. Finally, you can leave the MySQL monitor by typing **quit**:

```
mysql> quit
```

MySQL Monitor Program Options

The monitor program can take several parameters; the ones you'll need most frequently are:

---

host

> The host the server is running on; you can leave this out if the server is running on the same host as the client (`localhost`).

user

> The username to use when connecting to the MySQL server. This bears no relation to the username the server is running under, or to your Linux or Mac OS X username. If you don't provide a username with this option, the monitor uses a default value; this default username is your machine account name on a Linux or Mac OS X system, and `ODBC` on a Windows system.

password

> The password of this user. If you don't provide the `password` parameter, no password is supplied to the server. This is fine if there is no password stored for that user, but if the user does have a password, the connection will fail:

```
$ mysql --user=the_username
ERROR 1045 (28000): Access denied for user 'the_username'@'localhost'
  (using password: NO)
```

If you include the `password` option but don't specify a password, the client will prompt you for a password after you press the Enter key. If the user has no password, pressing the Enter key will work; otherwise, the connection will fail again:

```
$ mysql --user=the_username --password
Enter password:
ERROR 1045 (28000): Access denied for user 'the_username'@'localhost'
  (using password: NO)
```

If you provide an incorrect password, or you don't have permission to access a specified database, MySQL will note this in the error message:

```
$ mysql --user=the_username --password=wrong_password
Enter password:
ERROR 1045 (28000): Access denied for user 'the_username'@'localhost'
  (using password: YES)
```

If you specify the correct password at the `Enter password:` prompt, or if you specify the correct password on the command line when starting the monitor, the connection will succeed:

```
$ mysql --user=the_username --password=the_password
Welcome to the MySQL monitor.  Commands end with ; or \g.
Your MySQL connection id is 169 to server version: 5.0.22

Type 'help;' or '\h' for help. Type '\c' to clear the buffer.

mysql>
```

Some users prefer not to specify the password on the command line because suppressing the password guarantees the password won't be displayed in the operating system process table or command history. Under all operating systems we've tested, the password is hidden and can't be seen using operating system utilities to view running processes. However, the password may be stored in your command-line history, which other users may be able to access.

database

The database to use. This saves you from having to type USE ***the_database_name*** after the MySQL monitor starts. You can also simply omit the database option and just add the name of the database you want to use at the end of the mysql command.

safe-updates

Most experienced MySQL users can remember occasions where they've accidentally deleted all the data in a table by issuing a DELETE FROM *table_name* command, forgetting to add a limiting condition.

The safe-updates option prevents you from doing this by requiring you to provide a key constraint to DELETE and UPDATE, or to use a LIMIT clause. For example:

```
mysql> DELETE FROM user;
ERROR 1175 (HY000): You are using safe update mode and you tried to update
    a table without a WHERE that uses a KEY column
```

We'll explain these commands in later chapters.

Let's look at a couple of examples. First, let's say you want to connect to the server running on the same machine you're working on (localhost), as the MySQL user root, and with the password ***the_mysql_root_password***. You want to use the database music, so you would type:

```
$ mysql --user=root --password=the_mysql_root_password --database=music
```

Now for a more complex example: say you're working on the host *sadri.learning-mysql.com*, and wish to use the Moodle database on the MySQL server listening to port 57777 on the host *zahra.learningmysql.com*. For this MySQL server, you have the MySQL account name moodleuser and the password moodlepass. You would type the command (all on one line):

```
$ mysql \
    --host=zahra.learningmysql.com \
    --port=57777 \
    --user=moodleuser \
    --password=moodlepass \
    --database=Moodle
```

We'll look at how to create and manage users in Chapter 9.

Instead of specifying options on the command line, you can list them in the mysql section of an options file. You can also store your password in an options file to avoid typing it in every time you start the monitor. We discuss how to do this in Chapter 11.

Graphical Clients

Before we end this chapter, let's have a quick look at two graphical clients that you can use in place of the monitor.

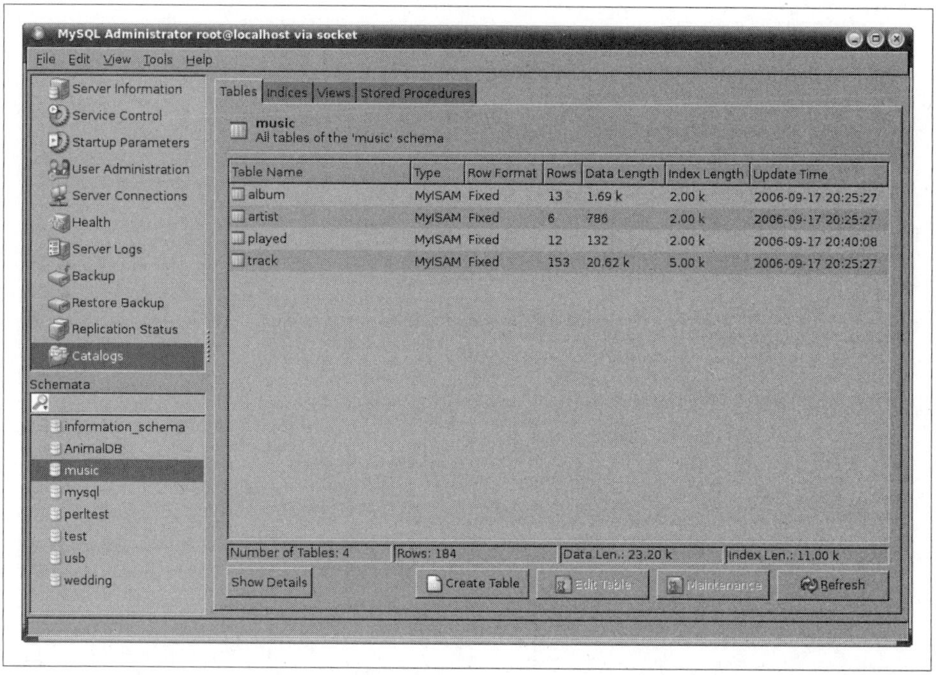

Figure 3-1. The MySQL Administrator graphical MySQL administration tool

The MySQL Administrator program is a graphical tool that you can download as part of the MySQL GUI Tools Bundle from the MySQL AB downloads page at *http://dev .mysql.com/downloads*. This program allows you to perform most database administration from within a graphical environment, as shown in Figure 3-1.

The MySQL Query Browser program is also available for download from the same web page. This allows you to run SQL queries from within a graphical environment, and view the results. A sample query is shown in Figure 3-2. Together, these tools replace an older program known as the MySQL Control Center `mysqlcc`. In this book, we focus on doing things using the monitor; once you understand the way MySQL works, you'll find it easy to use other clients such as these.

Exercises

1. What do we mean when we say that MySQL has a client-server architecture?
2. Use the monitor help to look up information on the `SELECT` statement. (We'll discuss `SELECT` in detail in Chapter 5.)
3. What is the difference between using the monitor in interactive mode and using the monitor in batch mode?
4. What do the monitor `user`, `password`, and `database` options do?

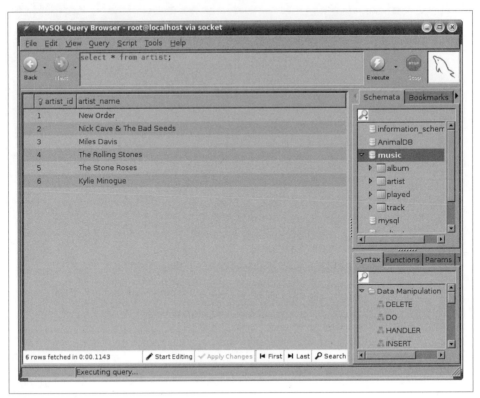

Figure 3-2. The MySQL Query Browser graphical MySQL client

## PART II

Using MySQL

## CHAPTER 4

Modeling and Designing Databases

When implementing a new database, it's easy to fall into the trap of trying to quickly get something up and running without dedicating adequate time and effort to the design. This carelessness frequently leads to costly redesigns and reimplementations down the track. Designing a database is similar to drafting the blueprints for a house; it's silly to start building without detailed plans. Importantly, good design allows you to extend the original building without having to pull everything down and start from scratch.

How Not to Develop a Database

Database design is probably not the most exciting task in the world, but it's still important. Before we describe how to go about the design process, let's look at an example of database design on the run.

Imagine we want to create a database to store student grades for a university computer science department. We could create a `Student_Grades` table to store grades for each student and each course. The table would have columns for the given names and the surname of each student as well as for each course they have taken, the course name, and the percentage result (shown as `Pctg`). We'd have a different row for each student for each of their courses:

```
+------------+---------+---------------------------+------+
| GivenNames | Surname | CourseName                | Pctg |
+------------+---------+---------------------------+------+
| John Paul  | Bloggs  | Web Database Applications |   72 |
| Sarah      | Doe     | Programming 1             |   87 |
| John Paul  | Bloggs  | Computing Mathematics     |   43 |
| John Paul  | Bloggs  | Computing Mathematics     |   65 |
| Sarah      | Doe     | Web Database Applications |   65 |
| Susan      | Smith   | Computing Mathematics     |   75 |
| Susan      | Smith   | Programming 1             |   55 |
| Susan      | Smith   | Computing Mathematics     |   80 |
+------------+---------+---------------------------+------+
```

This is nice and compact, and we can easily access grades for any student or any course. However, we could have more than one student called Susan Smith; in the sample data, there are two entries for Susan Smith and the Computing Mathematics course. Which Susan Smith got an 80? A common way to differentiate duplicate data entries is to assign a unique number to each entry. Here, we can assign a unique Student ID number to each student:

```
+------------+------------+----------+----------------------------+------+
| StudentID  | GivenNames | Surname  | CourseName                 | Pctg |
+------------+------------+----------+----------------------------+------+
| 12345678   | John Paul  | Bloggs   | Web Database Applications  |  72  |
| 12345121   | Sarah      | Doe      | Programming 1              |  87  |
| 12345678   | John Paul  | Bloggs   | Computing Mathematics      |  43  |
| 12345678   | John Paul  | Bloggs   | Computing Mathematics      |  65  |
| 12345121   | Sarah      | Doe      | Web Database Applications  |  65  |
| 12345876   | Susan      | Smith    | Computing Mathematics      |  75  |
| 12345876   | Susan      | Smith    | Programming 1              |  55  |
| 12345303   | Susan      | Smith    | Computing Mathematics      |  80  |
+------------+------------+----------+----------------------------+------+
```

So, the Susan Smith who got 80 is the one with the Student ID number 12345303.

There's another problem. In our table, John Paul Bloggs has failed the Computing Mathematics course once with 43 percent, and passed it with 65 percent in his second attempt. In a relational database, the rows form a set, and there is no implicit ordering between them; you might guess that the pass happened after the fail, but you can't actually be sure. There's no guarantee that the newer grade will appear after the older one, so we need to add information about *when* each grade was awarded, say by adding a year and semester (Sem):

```
+------------+------------+----------+----------------------------+------+-----+------+
| StudentID  | GivenNames | Surname  | CourseName                 | Year | Sem | Pctg |
+------------+------------+----------+----------------------------+------+-----+------+
| 12345678   | John Paul  | Bloggs   | Web Database Applications  | 2004 |  2  |  72  |
| 12345121   | Sarah      | Doe      | Programming 1              | 2006 |  1  |  87  |
| 12345678   | John Paul  | Bloggs   | Computing Mathematics      | 2005 |  2  |  43  |
| 12345678   | John Paul  | Bloggs   | Computing Mathematics      | 2006 |  1  |  65  |
| 12345121   | Sarah      | Doe      | Web Database Applications  | 2006 |  1  |  65  |
| 12345876   | Susan      | Smith    | Computing Mathematics      | 2005 |  1  |  75  |
| 12345876   | Susan      | Smith    | Programming 1              | 2005 |  2  |  55  |
| 12345303   | Susan      | Smith    | Computing Mathematics      | 2006 |  1  |  80  |
+------------+------------+----------+----------------------------+------+-----+------+
```

Notice that the Student_Grades table has become a bit bloated: the student ID, given names, and surname are repeated for every grade. We could split up the information and create a Student_Details table:

```
+------------+------------+----------+
| StudentID  | GivenNames | Surname  |
+------------+------------+----------+
| 12345121   | Sarah      | Doe      |
| 12345303   | Susan      | Smith    |
| 12345678   | John Paul  | Bloggs   |
```

```
| 12345876   | Susan      | Smith   |
+------------+------------+---------+
```

and keep less information in the `Student_Grades` table:

```
+------------+---------------------------+------+-----+------+
| StudentID  | CourseName                | Year | Sem | Pctg |
+------------+---------------------------+------+-----+------+
| 12345678   | Web Database Applications | 2004 |   2 |   72 |
| 12345121   | Programming 1             | 2006 |   1 |   87 |
| 12345678   | Computing Mathematics     | 2005 |   2 |   43 |
| 12345678   | Computing Mathematics     | 2006 |   1 |   65 |
| 12345121   | Web Database Applications | 2006 |   1 |   65 |
| 12345876   | Computing Mathematics     | 2005 |   1 |   75 |
| 12345876   | Programming 1             | 2005 |   2 |   55 |
| 12345303   | Computing Mathematics     | 2006 |   1 |   80 |
+------------+---------------------------+------+-----+------+
```

To look up a student's grades, we'd need to first look up her Student ID from the
`Student_Details` table and then read the grades for that Student ID from the `Stu
dent_Grades` table.

There are still issues we haven't considered. For example, should we keep information
on a student's enrollment date, postal and email addresses, fees, or attendance? Should
we store different types of postal address? How should we store addresses so that things
don't break when a student changes his address?

Implementing a database in this way is problematic; we keep running into things we
hadn't thought about and have to keep changing our database structure. Clearly, we
can save a lot of reworking by carefully documenting the requirements and then working through them to develop a coherent design.

The Database Design Process

There are three major stages in database design, each producing a progressively lower-
level description:

Requirements analysis
> First, we determine and write down what exactly the database is needed for, what
> data will be stored, and how the data items relate to each other. In practice, this
> might involve detailed study of the application requirements and talking to people
> in various roles that will interact with the database and application.

Conceptual design
> Once we know what the database requirements are, we distill them into a formal
> description of the database design. In this chapter, we'll see how to use modeling
> to produce the conceptual design.

Logical design
> Finally, we map the database design onto an actual database management system
> and database tables.

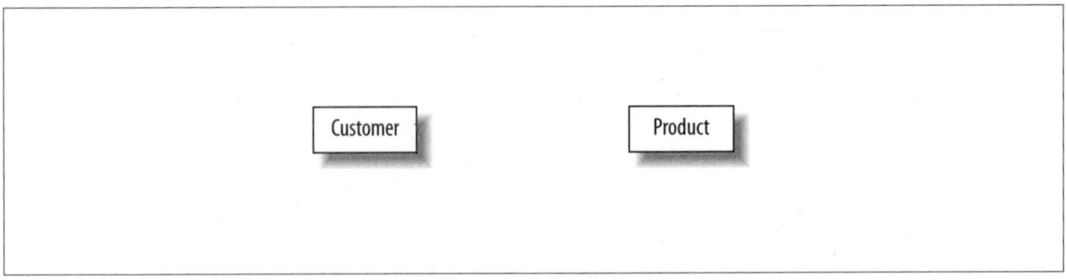

Figure 4-1. An entity set is represented by a named rectangle

At the end of the chapter, we'll look at how we can use the open source MySQL Work bench tool to automatically convert the conceptual design to a MySQL database schema.

The Entity Relationship Model

At a basic level, databases store information about distinct objects, or *entities*, and the associations, or *relationships*, between these entities. For example, a university database might store information about students, courses, and enrollment. A student and a course are entities, while an enrollment is a relationship between a student and a course. Similarly, an inventory and sales database might store information about products, customers, and sales. A product and a customer are entities, while a sale is a relationship between a customer and a product.

A popular approach to conceptual design uses the *Entity Relationship* (ER) model, which helps transform the requirements into a formal description of the entities and relationships that appear in the database. We'll start by looking at how the Entity Relationship modeling process itself works, then apply it in "Entity Relationship Mod eling Examples" for three sample databases.

Representing Entities

To help visualize the design, the Entity Relationship Modeling approach involves drawing an Entity Relationship (ER) diagram. In the ER diagram, an *entity set* is represented by a rectangle containing the entity name. For our sales database example, the product and customer entity sets would be shown as in Figure 4-1.

We typically use the database to store certain characteristics, or *attributes*, of the entities. In a sales database, we could store the name, email address, postal address, and telephone number for each customer. In a more elaborate customer relationship man agment (CRM) application, we could also store the names of the customer's spouse and children, the languages the customer speaks, the customer's history of interaction with our company, and so on. Attributes describe the entity they belong to.

An attribute may be formed from smaller parts; for example, a postal address is composed of a street number, city, ZIP code, and country. We classify attributes as *composite* if they're composed of smaller parts in this way, and as *simple* otherwise.

Some attributes can have multiple values for a given entity. For example, a customer could provide several telephone numbers, so the telephone number attribute is *multivalued*.

Attributes help distinguish one entity from other entities of the same type. We could use the name attribute to distinguish between customers, but this could be an inadequate solution because several customers could have identical names. To be able to tell them apart, we need an attribute (or a minimal combination of attributes) guaranteed to be unique to each individual customer. The identifying attribute or attributes form a *key*.

In our example, we can assume that no two customers have the same email address, so the email address can be the key. However, we need to think carefully about the implications of our choices. For example, if we decide to identify customers by their email address, it would be hard to allow a customer to have multiple email addresses. Any applications we build to use this database might treat each email address as a separate person, and it might be hard to adapt everything to allow people to have multiple email addresses. Using the email address as the key also means that every customer must have an email address; otherwise, we wouldn't be able to distinguish between customers who don't have one.

Looking at the other attributes for one that can serve as an alternative key, we see that while it's possible that two customers would have the same telephone number (and so we cannot use the telephone number as a key), it's likely that people who have the same telephone number never have the same name, so we can use the combination of the telephone number and the name as a composite key.

Clearly, there may be several possible keys that could be used to identify an entity; we choose one of the alternative, or *candidate*, keys to be our main, or *primary*, key. You usually make this choice based on how confident you are that the attribute will be non-empty and unique for each individual entity, and on how small the key is (shorter keys are faster to maintain and use).

In the ER diagram, attributes are represented as labeled ovals and are connected to their owning entity, as shown in Figure 4-2. Attributes comprising the primary key are shown underlined. The parts of any composite attributes are drawn connected to the oval of the composite attribute, and multivalued attributes are shown as double-lined ovals.

Attribute values are chosen from a *domain* of legal values; for example, we could specify that a customer's given names and surname attributes can each be a string of up to 100 characters, while a telephone number can be a string of up to 40 characters. Similarly, a product price could be a positive rational number.

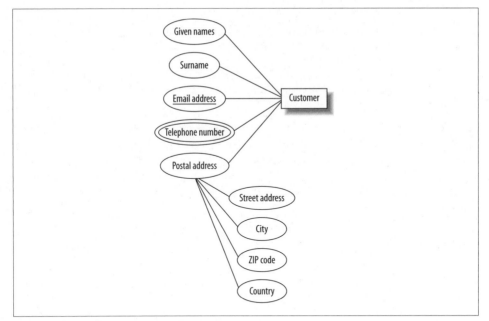

Figure 4-2. The ER diagram representation of the customer entity

Attributes can be empty; for example, some customers may not provide their telephone numbers. The primary key of an entity (including the components of a multiattribute primary key) must never be unknown (technically, it must be NOT NULL); for example, if it's possible for a customer to not provide an email address, we cannot use the email address as the key.

You should think carefully when classifying an attribute as multivalued: are all the values equivalent, or do they in fact represent different things? For example, when listing multiple telephone numbers for a customer, would they be more usefully labeled separately as the customer's business phone number, home phone number, cell phone number, and so on?

Let's look at another example. The sales database requirements may specify that a product has a name and a price. We can see that the product is an entity because it's a distinct object. However, the product's name and price aren't distinct objects; they're attributes that describe the product entity. Note that if we want to have different prices for different markets, then the price is no longer just related to the product entity, and we'd need to model it differently.

For some applications, no combination of attributes can uniquely identify an entity (or it would be too unwieldy to use a large composite key), so we create an artificial attribute that's defined to be unique and can therefore be used as a key: student numbers, Social Security numbers, driver's license numbers, and library card numbers are examples of unique attributes created for various applications. In our inventory and sales applica-

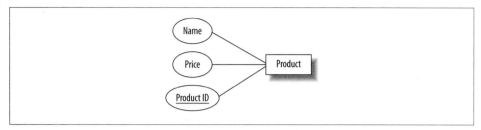

Figure 4-3. The ER diagram representation of the product entity

tion, it's possible that we could stock different products with the same name and price. For example, we could sell two models of "Four-port USB 2.0 Hub," both at $4.95 each. To distinguish between products, we can assign a unique product ID number to each item we stock; this would be the primary key. Each product entity would have name, price, and product ID attributes. This is shown in the ER diagram in Figure 4-3.

Representing Relationships

Entities can participate in relationships with other entities. For example, a customer can buy a product, a student can take a course, an artist can record an album, and so on.

Like entities, relationships can have attributes: we can define a sale to be a relationship between a customer entity (identified by the unique email address) and a given number of the product entity (identified by the unique product ID) that exists at a particular date and time (the timestamp).

Our database could then record each sale and tell us, for example, that at 3:13 p.m. on Wednesday, March 22, Ali Thomson bought one "Four-port USB 2.0 Hub," one "300 GB 16 MB Cache 7200 rpm SATA Serial ATA133 HDD Hard Disk," and two sets of "2000 Watt 5.1 Channel Sub-Woofer Speakers."

Different numbers of entities can appear on each side of a relationship. For example, each customer can buy any number of products, and each product can be bought by any number of customers. This is known as a *many-to-many* relationship. We can also have *one-to-many* relationships. For example, one person can have several credit cards, but each credit card belongs to just one person. Looking at it the other way, a *one-to-many* relationship becomes a *many-to-one* relationship; for example, many credit cards belong to a single person. Finally, the serial number on a car engine is an example of a *one-to-one* relationship; each engine has just one serial number, and each serial number belongs to just one engine. We often use the shorthand terms 1:1, 1:N, and M:N for one-to-one, one-to-many, and many-to-many relationships, respectively.

The number of entities on either side of a relationship (the *cardinality* of the relationship) define the *key constraints* of the relationship. It's important to think about the cardinality of relationships carefully. There are many relationships that may at first seem to be one-to-one, but turn out to be more complex. For example, people some-

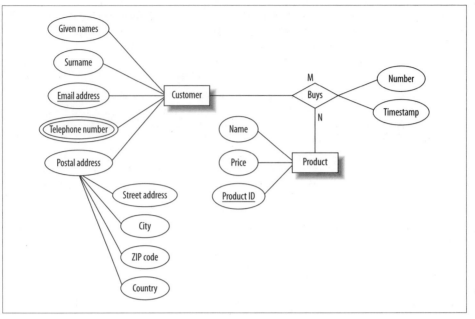

Figure 4-4. The ER diagram representation of the customer and product entities, and the sale relationship between them.

times change their names; in some applications, such as police databases, this is of particular interest, and so it may be necessary to model a many-to-many relationship between a person entity and a name entity. Redesigning a database can be time-consuming if you assume a relationship is simpler than it really is.

In an ER diagram, we represent a *relationship set* with a named diamond. The cardinality of the relationship is often indicated alongside the relationship diamond; this is the style we use in this book. (Another common style is to have an arrowhead on the line connecting the entity on the "1" side to the relationship diamond.) Figure 4-4 shows the relationship between the customer and product entities, along with the number and timestamp attributes of the sale relationship.

Partial and Total Participation

Relationships between entities can be optional or compulsory. In our example, we could decide that a person is considered to be a customer only if they have bought a product. On the other hand, we could say that a customer is a person whom we know about and whom we hope might buy something—that is, we can have people listed as customers in our database who never buy a product. In the first case, the customer entity has *total participation* in the bought relationship (all customers have bought a product, and we can't have a customer who hasn't bought a product), while in the second case it has *partial participation* (a customer can buy a product). These are referred to as the *participation constraints* of the relationship. In an ER diagram, we indicate total participation with a double line between the entity box and the relationship diamond.

Entity or Attribute?

From time to time, we encounter cases where we wonder whether an item should be an attribute or an entity on its own. For example, an email address could be modeled as an entity in its own right. When in doubt, consider these rules of thumb:

Is the item of direct interest to the database?
> Objects of direct interest should be entities, and information that describes them should be stored in attributes. Our inventory and sales database is really interested in customers, and not their email addresses, so the email address would be best modeled as an attribute of the `customer` entity.

Does the item have components of its own?
> If so, we must find a way of representing these components; a separate entity might be the best solution. In the student grades example at the start of the chapter, we stored the course name, year, and semester for each course that a student takes. It would be more compact to treat the course as a separate entity and to create a class ID number to identify each time a course is offered to students (the "offering").

Can the object have multiple instances?
> If so, we must find a way to store data on each instance. The cleanest way to do this is to represent the object as a separate entity. In our sales example, we must ask whether customers are allowed to have more than one email address; if they are, we should model the email address as a separate entity.

Is the object often nonexistent or unknown?
> If so, it is effectively an attribute of only some of the entities, and it would be better to model it as a separate entity rather than as an attribute that is often empty. Consider a simple example: to store student grades for different courses, we could have an attribute for the student's grade in every possible course; this is shown in Figure 4-5. Because most students will have grades for only a few of these courses, it's better to represent the grades as a separate entity set, as in Figure 4-6.

Entity or Relationship?

An easy way to decide whether an object should be an entity or a relationship is to map nouns in the requirements to entities, and to map the verbs to relations. For example, in the statement, "A degree program is made up of one or more courses," we can identify the entities "program" and "course," and the relationship "is made up of." Similarly, in the statement, "A student enrolls in one program," we can identify the entities "student" and "program," and the relationship "enrolls in." Of course, we can choose different terms for entities and relationships than those that appear in the relationships, but it's a good idea not to deviate too far from the naming conventions used in the

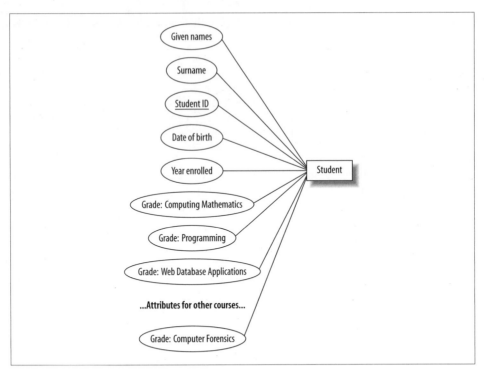

Figure 4-5. The ER diagram representation of student grades as attributes of the student entity

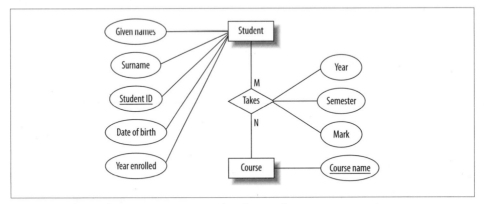

Figure 4-6. The ER diagram representation of student grades as a separate entity

requirements so that the design can be checked against the requirements. All else being equal, try to keep the design simple, and avoid introducing trivial entities where possible; i.e., there's no need to have a separate entity for the student's enrollment when we can model it as a relationship between the existing student and program entities.

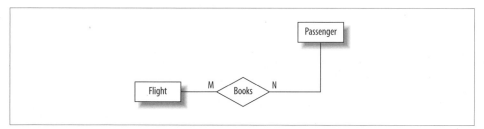

Figure 4-7. A passenger participates in an M:N relationship with flight

Intermediate Entities

It is often possible to conceptually simplify many-to-many relationships by replacing the many-to-many relationship with a new *intermediate entity* (sometimes called an *associate entity*) and connecting the original entities through a many-to-one and a one-to-many relationship.

Consider the statement: "A passenger can book a seat on a flight." This is a many-to-many relationship between the entities "passenger" and "flight." The related ER diagram fragment is shown in Figure 4-7.

However, let's look at this from both sides of the relationship:

- Any given flight can have many passengers with a booking.
- Any given passenger can have bookings on many flights.

Hence, we can consider the many-to-many relationship to be in fact two one-to-many relationships, one each way. This points us to the existence of a hidden intermediate entity, the booking, between the flight and the passenger entities. The requirement could be better worded as: "A passenger can make a booking for a seat on a flight." The related ER diagram fragment is shown in Figure 4-8.

Each passenger can be involved in multiple bookings, but each booking belongs to a single passenger, so the cardinality of this relationship is 1:N. Similarly, there can be many bookings for a given flight, but each booking is for a single flight, so this relationship also has cardinality 1:N. Since each booking must be associated with a particular passenger and flight, the booking entity participates totally in the relationships with these entities. This total participation could not be captured effectively in the representation in Figure 4-7. (We described partial and total participation earlier in "Partial and Total Participation.")

Weak and Strong Entities

Context is very important in our daily interactions; if we know the context, we can work with a much smaller amount of information. For example, we generally call family members by only their first name or nickname. Where ambiguity exists, we add further information such as the surname to clarify our intent. In database design, we can omit

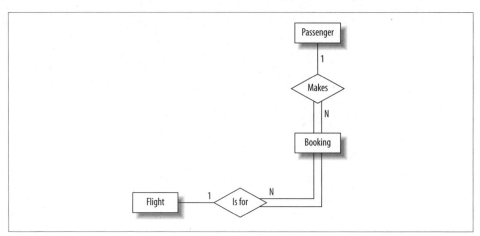

Figure 4-8. The intermediate booking entity between the passenger and flight entities

some key information for entities that are dependent on other entities. For example, if we wanted to store the names of our customers' children, we could create a child entity and store only enough key information to identify it in the context of its parent. We could simply list a child's first name on the assumption that a customer will never have several children with the same first name. Here, the child entity is a *weak* entity, and its relationship with the customer entity is called an *identifying relationship*. Weak entities participate totally in the identifying relationship, since they can't exist in the database independently of their owning entity.

In the ER diagram, we show weak entities and identifying relationships with double lines, and the partial key of a weak entity with a dashed underline, as in Figure 4-9. A weak entity is uniquely identified in the context of its regular (or *strong*) entity, and so the full key for a weak entity is the combination of its own (partial) key with the key of its owning entity. To uniquely identify a child in our example, we need the first name of the child and the email address of the child's parent.

Figure 4-10 shows a summary of the symbols we've explained for ER diagrams.

Entity Relationship Modeling Examples

Earlier in this chapter, we showed you how to design a database and understand an Entity Relationship (ER) diagram. This section explains the requirements for our three example databases—music, university, and flight—and shows you their Entity Relationship diagrams:

- The music database is designed to store details of a music collection, including the albums in the collection, the artists who made them, the tracks on the albums, and when each track was last played.

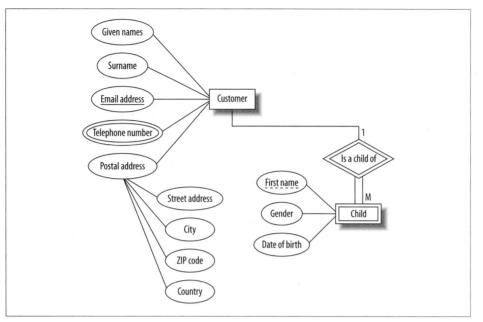

Figure 4-9. The ER diagram representation of a weak entity

- The `university` database captures the details of students, courses, and grades for a university.

- The `flight` database stores an airline timetable of flight routes, times, and the plane types.

The next section explains these databases, each with its ER diagram and an explanation of the motivation for its design. You'll find that understanding the ER diagrams and the explanations of the database designs is sufficient to work with the material in this chapter. We'll show you how to create the `music` database on your MySQL server in Chapter 5.

The Music Database

The `music` database stores details of a personal music library, and could be used to manage your MP3, CD, or vinyl collection. Because this database is for a personal collection, it's relatively simple and stores only the relationships between artists, albums, and tracks. It ignores the requirements of many music genres, making it most useful for storing popular music and less useful for storing jazz or classical music. (We discuss some shortcomings of these requirements at the end of the section in "What it doesn't do.")

We first draw up a clear list of requirements for our database:

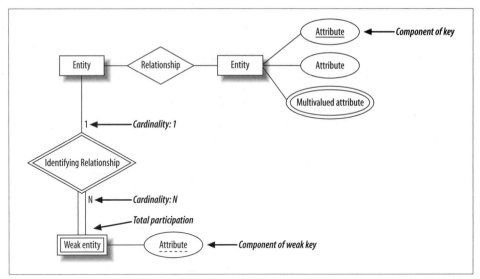

Figure 4-10. Quick summary of the ER diagram symbols

- The collection consists of albums.
- An album is made by exactly one artist.
- An artist makes one or more albums.
- An album contains one or more tracks
- Artists, albums, and tracks each have a name.
- Each track is on exactly one album.
- Each track has a time length, measured in seconds.
- When a track is played, the date and time the playback began (to the nearest second) should be recorded; this is used for reporting when a track was last played, as well as the number of times music by an artist, from an album, or a track has been played.

There's no requirement to capture composers, group members or sidemen, recording date or location, the source media, or any other details of artists, albums, or tracks.

The ER diagram derived from our requirements is shown in Figure 4-11. You'll notice that it consists of only one-to-many relationships: one artist can make many albums, one album can contain many tracks, and one track can be played many times. Conversely, each play is associated with one track, a track is on one album, and an album is by one artist. The attributes are straightforward: artists, albums, and tracks have names, as well as identifiers to uniquely identify each entity. The track entity has a time attribute to store the duration, and the played entity has a timestamp to store when the track was played.

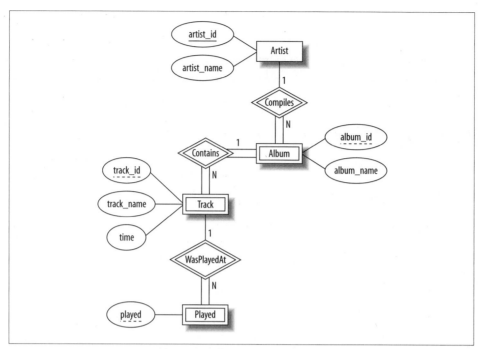

Figure 4-11. The ER diagram of the music database

The only strong entity in the database is `Artist`, which has an `artist_id` attribute that uniquely identifies it. Each `Album` entity is uniquely identified by its `album_id` combined with the `artist_id` of the corresponding `Artist` entity. A `Track` entity is similarly uniquely identified by its `track_id` combined with the related `album_id` and `artist_id` attributes. The `Played` entity is uniquely identified by a combination of its `played` time, and the related `track_id`, `album_id`, and `artist_id` attributes.

What it doesn't do

We've kept the `music` database simple because adding extra features doesn't help you learn anything new, it just makes the explanations longer. If you wanted to use the `music` database in practice, then you might consider adding the following features:

- Support for compilations or various-artists albums, where each track may be by a different artist and may then have its own associated album-like details such as a recording date and time. Under this model, the album would be a strong entity, with many-to-many relationships between artists and albums.
- Playlists, a user-controlled collection of tracks. For example, you might create a playlist of your favorite tracks from an artist.
- Track ratings, to record your opinion on how good a track is.

- Source details, such as when you bought an album, what media it came on, how much you paid, and so on.

- Album details, such as when and where it was recorded, the producer and label, the band members or sidemen who played on the album, and even its artwork.

- Smarter track management, such as modeling that allows the same track to appear on many albums.

The University Database

The university database stores details about university students, courses, the semester a student took a particular course (and his mark and grade if he completed it), and what degree program each student is enrolled in. The database is a long way from one that'd be suitable for a large tertiary institution, but it does illustrate relationships that are interesting to query, and it's easy to relate to when you're learning SQL. We explain the requirements next and discuss their shortcomings at the end of this section.

Consider the following requirements list:

- The university offers one or more programs.
- A program is made up of one or more courses.
- A student must enroll in a program.
- A student takes the courses that are part of her program.
- A program has a name, a program identifier, the total credit points required to graduate, and the year it commenced.
- A course has a name, a course identifier, a credit point value, and the year it commenced.
- Students have one or more given names, a surname, a student identifier, a date of birth, and the year they first enrolled. We can treat all given names as a single object —for example, "John Paul."
- When a student takes a course, the year and semester he attempted it are recorded. When he finishes the course, a grade (such as A or B) and a mark (such as 60 percent) are recorded.
- Each course in a program is sequenced into a year (for example, year 1) and a semester (for example, semester 1).

The ER diagram derived from our requirements is shown in Figure 4-12. Although it is compact, the diagram uses some advanced features, including relationships that have attributes and two many-to-many relationships.

In our design:

- Student is a strong entity, with an identifier, student_id, created to be the primary key used to distinguish between students (remember, we could have several students with the same name).

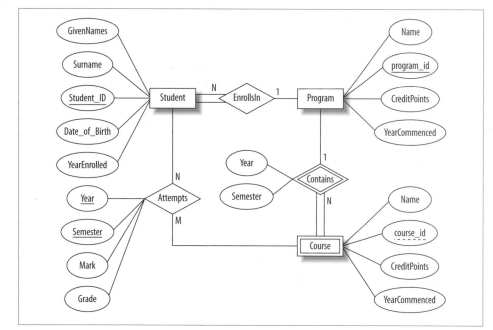

Figure 4-12. The ER diagram of the university database

- **Program** is a strong entity, with the identifier **program_id** as the primary key used to distinguish between programs.

- Each student must be enrolled in a program, so the **Student** entity participates totally in the many-to-one **EnrollsIn** relationship with **Program**. A program can exist without having any enrolled students, so it participates partially in this relationship.

- A **Course** has meaning only in the context of a **Program**, so it's a weak entity, with **course_id** as a weak key. This means that a **Course** is uniquely identified using its **course_id** and the **program_id** of its owning program.

- As a weak entity, **Course** participates totally in the many-to-one identifying relationship with its owning **Program**. This relationship has **Year** and **Semester** attributes that identify its sequence position.

- **Student** and **Course** are related through the many-to-many **Attempts** relationships; a course can exist without a student, and a student can be enrolled without attempting any courses, so the participation is not total.

- When a student attempts a course, there are attributes to capture the **Year** and **Semester**, and the **Mark** and **Grade**.

What it doesn't do

Our database design is rather simple, but this is because the requirements are simple. For a real university, many more aspects would need to be captured by the database. For example, the requirements don't mention anything about campus, study mode, course prerequisites, lecturers, timetabling details, address history, financials, or assessment details. The database also doesn't allow a student to be in more than one degree program, nor does it allow a course to appear as part of different programs.

The Flight Database

The `flight` database stores details about an airline's fleet, flights, and seat bookings. Again, it's a hugely simplified version of what a real airline would use, but the principles are the same.

Consider the following requirements list:

- The airline has one or more airplanes.
- An airplane has a model number, a unique registration number, and the capacity to take one or more passengers.
- An airplane flight has a unique flight number, a departure airport, a destination airport, a departure date and time, and an arrival date and time.
- Each flight is carried out by a single airplane.
- A passenger has given names, a surname, and a unique email address.
- A passenger can book a seat on a flight.

The ER diagram derived from our requirements is shown in Figure 4-13:

- An `Airplane` is uniquely identified by its `RegistrationNumber`, so we use this as the primary key.
- A `Flight` is uniquely identified by its `FlightNumber`, so we use the flight number as the primary key. The departure and destination airports are captured in the `From` and `To` attributes, and we have separate attributes for the departure and arrival date and time.
- Because no two passengers will share an email address, we can use the `EmailAddress` as the primary key for the `Passenger` entity.
- An airplane can be involved in any number of flights, while each flight uses exactly one airplane, so the `Flies` relationship between the `Airplane` and `Flight` relationships has cardinality 1:N; because a flight cannot exist without an airplane, the `Flight` entity participates totally in this relationship.
- A passenger can book any number of flights, while a flight can be booked by any number of passengers. As discussed earlier in "Intermediate Entities," we could specify an M:N `Books` relationship between the `Passenger` and `Flight` relationship,

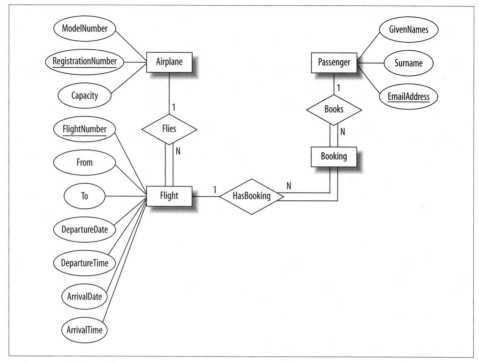

Figure 4-13. The ER diagram of the flight database

but considering the issue more carefully shows that there is a hidden entity here: the booking itself. We capture this by creating the intermediate entity `Booking` and 1:N relationships between it and the `Passenger` and `Flight` entities. Identifying such entities allows us to get a better picture of the requirements. Note that even if we didn't notice this hidden entity, it would come out as part of the ER-to-tables mapping process we'll describe next in "Using the Entity Relationship Model."

What it doesn't do

Again, this is a very simple flight database. There are no requirements to capture passenger details such as age, gender, or frequent-flier number.

We've treated the capacity of the airplane as an attribute of an individual airplane. If, instead, we assumed that the capacity is determined by the model number, we would have created a new `AirplaneModel` entity with the attributes `ModelNumber` and `Capacity`. The `Airplane` entity would then not have a `Capacity` attribute.

We've mapped a different flight number to each flight between two destinations. Airlines typically use a flight number to identify a given flight path and schedule, and they specify the date of the flight independently of the flight number. For example, there is one IR655 flight on April 1, another on April 2, and so on. Different airplanes can operate on the same flight number over time; our model would need to be extended to support this.

The system also assumes that each leg of a multihop flight has a different `FlightNumber`. This means that a flight from Dubai to Christchurch via Singapore and Melbourne would need a different `FlightNumber` for the Dubai-Singapore, Singapore-Melbourne, and Melbourne-Christchurch legs.

Our database also has limited ability to describe airports. In practice, each airport has a name, such as "Melbourne Regional Airport," "Mehrabad," or "Tullamarine." The name can be used to differentiate between airports, but most passengers will just use the name of the town or city. This can lead to confusion, when, for example, a passenger could book a flight to Melbourne, Florida, USA, instead of Melbourne, Victoria, Australia. To avoid such problems, the International Air Transport Association (IATA) assigns a unique airport code to each airport; the airport code for Melbourne, Florida, USA is MLB, while the code for Melbourne, Victoria, Australia is MEL. If we were to model the airport as a separate entity, we could use the IATA-assigned airport code as the primary key. Incidentally, there's an alternative set of airport codes assigned by the International Civil Aviation Organization (ICAO); under this code, Melbourne, Florida is KMLB, and Melbourne, Australia is YMML.

Using the Entity Relationship Model

In this section, we'll look at the steps required to manually translate an ER model into database tables. We'll then perform these steps using the `music` database as an example. In "Using Tools for Database Design," we'll see how we can automate this process with the MySQL Workbench tool.

Mapping Entities and Relationships to Database Tables

When converting an ER model to a database schema, we work through each entity and then through each relationship according to the following rules to end up with a set of database tables.

Map the entities to database tables

For each strong entity, create a table comprising its attributes and designate the primary key. The parts of any composite attributes are also included here.

For each weak entity, create a table comprising its attributes and including the primary key of its owning entity. The primary key of the owning entity is known as a *foreign key* here, because it's a key not of this table, but of another table. The primary key of the table for the weak entity is the combination of the foreign key and the partial key of the weak entity. If the relationship with the owning entity has any attributes, add them to this table.

For each multivalued attribute of an entity, create a table comprising the entity's primary key and the attribute.

Map the relationships to database tables

For each one-to-one relationship between two entities, include the primary key of one entity as a foreign key in the table belonging to the other. If one entity participates totally in the relationship, place the foreign key in its table. If both participate totally in the relationship, consider merging them into a single table.

For each nonidentifying one-to-many relationship between two entities, include the primary key of the entity on the "1" side as a foreign key in the table for the entity on the "N" side. Add any attributes of the relationship in the table alongside the foreign key. Note that identifying one-to-many relationships (between a weak entity and its owning entity) are captured as part of the entity-mapping stage.

For each many-to-many relationship between two entities, create a new table containing the primary key of each entity as the primary key, and add any attributes of the relationship. This step helps to identify intermediate entities.

For each relationship involving more than two entities, create a table with the primary keys of all the participating entities, and add any attributes of the relationship.

Converting the Music Database ER Model to a Database Schema

Following the mapping rules as just described, we first map entities to database tables:

- For the strong entity `Artist`, we create the table `artist` comprising the attributes `artist_id` and `artist_name`, and designate `artist_id` as the primary key.

- For the weak entity `Album`, we create the table `album` comprising the attributes `album_id` and `album_name`, and include the primary key `artist_id` of the owning `Artist` entity as a foreign key. The primary key of the `album` table is the combination {`artist_id`, `album_id`}.

- For the weak entity `Track`, we create the table `track` comprising the attributes `track_id`, `track_name`, and `time`, and include the primary key {`artist_id`, `album_id`} of the owning `Album` entity as a foreign key. The primary key of the `track` table is the combination {`artist_id`, `album_id`, `track_id`}.

- For the weak entity `Played`, we create the table `played` comprising the attribute `played`, and include the primary key {`artist_id`, `album_id`, `track_id`} of the owning `Track` entity as a foreign key. The primary key of the `played` table is the combination {`artist_id`, `album_id`, `track_id`, `played`}.

- There are no multivalued attributes in our design, nor are there any nonweak relationships between our entities, so our mapping is complete here.

You don't have to use consistent names across all tables; for example, you could have a column `musician` in the `album` table that contains the artist ID that you call

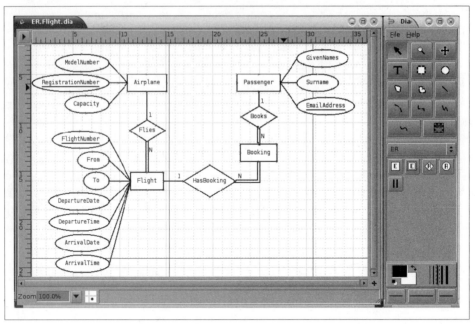

Figure 4-14. Using the Dia program to draw an ER diagram

`artist_id` in the `artist` table. Obviously, it's much better to use a consistent naming convention to avoid confusion. Some designers put `fk_` in front of columns that contain foreign keys; for example, in the `album` table, we could store the artist ID in the `fk_artist_id` column. We don't use this convention in this book.

Using Tools for Database Design

It's a good idea to use a tool to draw your ER diagrams; this way, you can easily edit diagrams as you refine your designs, and the final diagram is clear and unambiguous. There are a large number of programs that can be used for this purpose. A good free tool that is available for both Linux and Windows is Dia; you can download the latest version from *http://www.gnome.org/projects/dia*. Mac OS X users can use the Omni-Graffle program that comes bundled with the operating system. Windows users can also use Microsoft Visio.

A screenshot of Dia is shown in Figure 4-14. When you open the program, you should first select the ER "sheet" of shapes from the drop-down list in the middle of the control window (where the ER label appears at the right of the figure) and then select from the entity and relation shapes.

You can assign properties to shapes by double-clicking on them. For example, you can mark an attribute as being a key or a weak key, and you can mark an entity's participation in a relation as being total or partial.

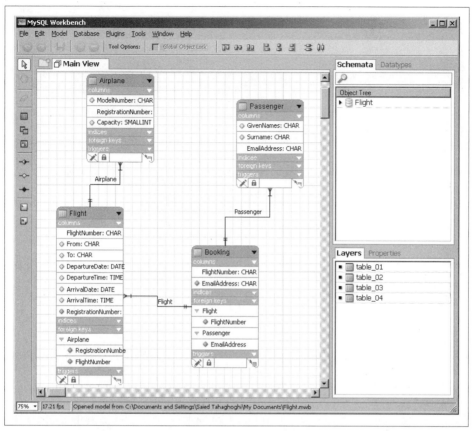

Figure 4-15. A screenshot of the MySQL Workbench program to design the Flight database

The open source MySQL Workbench program is a very powerful visual database design tool available as part of the MySQL GUI Tools Bundle from the MySQL AB downloads page at *http://dev.mysql.com/downloads*.

Figure 4-15 shows a screenshot of using MySQL Workbench to design the `flight` database. You can select tables and relations from the toolbar icons on the left of the screen, and double-click on each object to set properties such as attributes and relationship cardinality.

A very useful feature of MySQL Workbench is that it can export your design as SQL statements ready to use on a MySQL database. Even better, it can connect to a MySQL database to export a design directly. You can also reverse-engineer an ER model from an existing database, edit the model, and then export the modified design back to the MySQL database. Note that this program is currently in the beta testing phase, so you should use it with care.

Resources

To learn more about database fundamentals, including ER modeling, we recommend the following books:

- *Database Management Systems* by Raghu Ramakrishnan and Johannes Gehrke (McGraw-Hill).
- *Fundamentals of Database Systems* by Ramez Elmasri and Shamkant B. Navathe (Addison-Wesley).
- *Database Systems: A Practical Approach to Design, Implementation and Management* by Thomas M. Connolly and Carolyn E. Begg (Addison-Wesley).

Exercises

1. When would you use a weak entity?
2. Is it better to use entities instead of attributes?
3. Alter and extend the `music` database ER model so that it can store compilations, where a *compilation* is an album that contains tracks by two or more different artists.
4. Create an ER diagram for an online media store using the following requirements:
   - There are two types of product: music CDs and video DVDs.
   - Customers can buy any number of each product.
   - For each CD, store the title, the artist's name, the label (publisher), and the price. Also store the number, title, and length (in seconds) of each track on the CD.
   - For each video DVD, store the title the studio name, and the price.

   Tables 4-1 and 4-2 contain some sample data to help you better understand the requirements.

Table 4-1. Video DVDs

Title	Studio	Price
Leon—The Professional	Sony Pictures	$21.99
Chicken Run	Dreamworks Video	$19.99

Table 4-2. Music CDs

Title	Artist	Label	Price
Come Away With Me	Norah Jones	Blue Note Records	$11.99
Feels Like Home	Norah Jones	Blue Note Records	$11.99
The Joshua Tree	U2	Island	$10.99
Brothers in Arms	Dire Straits	Vertigo	$9.99

Table 4-3 contains a sample list of music CD track titles and length in seconds for the CD with the title "Come Away With Me" by the artist Norah Jones.

Table 4-3. Tracks

Number	Name	Length
1	Don't Know Why	186
2	Seven Years	145
3	Cold, Cold Heart	218
4	Feelin' the Same Way	177
5	Come Away with Me	198
6	Shoot the Moon	236
7	Turn Me On	154
8	Lonestar	186
9	I've Got to See You Again	253
10	Painter Song	162
11	One Flight Down	185
12	Nightingale	252
13	The Long Day Is Over	164
14	The Nearness of You	187

## CHAPTER 5

Basic SQL

SQL is the only database language in widespread use. Since it was first proposed in the early 1970s, it has been criticized, changed, extended, and finally adopted by all the players in the database market. The latest standard is SQL-2003—the 2003 denotes its release year—but the version supported by most database servers is more closely related to its predecessors, SQL-1999 and SQL-1992. MySQL supports most of the features of SQL-1992 and many from the newer SQL standards, but it also includes many non-standard features that give more control over the database server and how it evaluates queries and returns results.

This chapter introduces the basics of MySQL's implementation of SQL. We show you how to read data from a database with the `SELECT` statement, and how to choose what data is returned and the order it is displayed in. We also show you the basics of modifying your databases with the `INSERT` statement to add data, `UPDATE` to change, and `DELETE` to remove it. We also explain how to use the nonstandard `SHOW TABLES` and `SHOW COLUMNS` statements to explore your database.

Following our example-based approach, we use the `music` database designed in Chapter 4 to show you how to work with an existing database, and use basic SQL to read and write data. In Chapter 6, we'll explain how to create the `music` database on your MySQL server. We'll also show how you can create your own database and tables, and modify the structure of existing ones. In Chapters 7 and 8, you'll learn about some advanced features of the SQL variant used by MySQL.

Using the Music Database

In Chapter 4, we showed you how we understood the requirements for storing a music collection and how we designed the `music` ER model. We also introduced the steps you take to convert an ER model to a format that makes sense for constructing a relational database. For convenience, we've reproduced the `music` database ER diagram in Figure 5-1. In this section, we show you the structure of the MySQL database that we created after converting the ER model into SQL statements. We don't explain the SQL statements we used to create the database; that's the subject of Chapter 6.

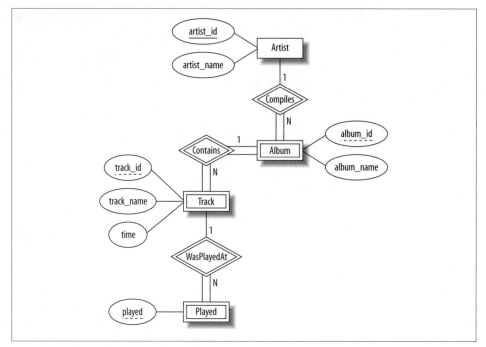

Figure 5-1. The ER diagram of the music database

To begin exploring the music database, connect to the MySQL monitor using the root MySQL account. For Mac OS X or Linux, run a terminal program, and in the terminal window type:

```
$ mysql --user=root --password=the_mysql_root_password
Welcome to the MySQL monitor.  Commands end with ; or \g.
Your MySQL connection id is 3 to server version: 5.0.22

Type 'help;' or '\h' for help. Type '\c' to clear the buffer.

mysql>
```

For Windows, click on the Start menu, then on the Run option, and then type **cmd** and press Enter. In the DOS or command window, type:

```
C:\> mysql --user=root --password=the_mysql_root_password
Welcome to the MySQL monitor.  Commands end with ; or \g.
Your MySQL connection id is 3 to server version: 5.0.22

Type 'help;' or '\h' for help. Type '\c' to clear the buffer.

mysql>
```

If you find that the monitor doesn't start, check the instructions in "Error Message About MySQL Executable Programs Not Being Found or Recognized" in Chapter 2 to see how to run it.

The structure of the `music` database is straightforward; it's the simplest of our three sample databases. Let's use the MySQL monitor to explore it. If you haven't already, start the monitor using the instructions in "Loading the Sample Databases" in Chapter 3. To choose the `music` database as your current database, type the following:

```
mysql> USE music;
Database changed
mysql>
```

You can check that this is the active database by typing in the `SELECT DATABASE( );` command:

```
mysql> SELECT DATABASE();
+------------+
| DATABASE() |
+------------+
| music      |
+------------+
1 row in set (0.00 sec)
mysql>
```

Now, let's explore what tables make up the `music` database using the `SHOW TABLES` statement:

```
mysql> SHOW TABLES;
+-----------------+
| Tables_in_music |
+-----------------+
| album           |
| artist          |
| played          |
| track           |
+-----------------+
4 rows in set (0.01 sec)
```

MySQL reports that there are four tables, which map exactly to the four entities in Figure 5-1. The `SHOW` statement is discussed in more detail later in "Exploring Databases and Tables with SHOW and mysqlshow."

So far, there have been no surprises. Let's find out more about each of the tables that make up the `music` database. First, let's use the `SHOW COLUMNS` statement to explore the `artist` table:

```
mysql> SHOW COLUMNS FROM artist;
+-------------+-------------+------+-----+---------+-------+
| Field       | Type        | Null | Key | Default | Extra |
+-------------+-------------+------+-----+---------+-------+
| artist_id   | smallint(5) | NO   | PRI | 0       |       |
| artist_name | char(128)   | NO   |     |         |       |
+-------------+-------------+------+-----+---------+-------+
2 rows in set (0.00 sec)
```

The `DESCRIBE` keyword is identical to `SHOW COLUMNS FROM`, and can be abbreviated to just `DESC`, so we can write the previous query as follows:

```
mysql> DESC artist;
+-------------+-------------+------+-----+---------+-------+
| Field       | Type        | Null | Key | Default | Extra |
+-------------+-------------+------+-----+---------+-------+
| artist_id   | smallint(5) | NO   | PRI | 0       |       |
| artist_name | char(128)   | NO   |     |         |       |
+-------------+-------------+------+-----+---------+-------+
2 rows in set (0.00 sec)
```

Let's examine the table structure more closely. As you'd expect from the ER model in Figure 5-1, the artist table contains two columns, artist_id and artist_name. The other information in the output shows the types of the columns—an integer of length 5 for artist_id and a character string of length 128 for artist_name—and whether the column is allowed to be NULL (empty), whether it's part of a key, and the default value for it. You'll notice that the artist_id has PRI in the Key column, meaning it's part of the primary key for the table. Don't worry about the details; all that's important right now is the column names, artist_id and artist_name.

We'll now explore the other three tables. Here are the SHOW COLUMNS statements you need to type:

```
mysql> SHOW COLUMNS FROM album;
+------------+-----------+------+-----+---------+-------+
| Field      | Type      | Null | Key | Default | Extra |
+------------+-----------+------+-----+---------+-------+
| artist_id  | int(5)    |      | PRI | 0       |       |
| album_id   | int(4)    |      | PRI | 0       |       |
| album_name | char(128) | YES  |     | NULL    |       |
+------------+-----------+------+-----+---------+-------+
3 rows in set (0.00 sec)

mysql> SHOW COLUMNS FROM track;
+------------+--------------+------+-----+---------+-------+
| Field      | Type         | Null | Key | Default | Extra |
+------------+--------------+------+-----+---------+-------+
| track_id   | int(3)       |      | PRI | 0       |       |
| track_name | char(128)    | YES  |     | NULL    |       |
| artist_id  | int(5)       |      | PRI | 0       |       |
| album_id   | int(4)       |      | PRI | 0       |       |
| time       | decimal(5,2) | YES  |     | NULL    |       |
+------------+--------------+------+-----+---------+-------+
5 rows in set (0.02 sec)

mysql> SHOW COLUMNS FROM played;
+-----------+-----------+------+-----+-------------------+-------+
| Field     | Type      | Null | Key | Default           | Extra |
+-----------+-----------+------+-----+-------------------+-------+
| artist_id | int(5)    |      | PRI | 0                 |       |
| album_id  | int(4)    |      | PRI | 0                 |       |
| track_id  | int(3)    |      | PRI | 0                 |       |
| played    | timestamp | YES  | PRI | CURRENT_TIMESTAMP |       |
+-----------+-----------+------+-----+-------------------+-------+
4 rows in set (0.00 sec)
```

Again, what's important is getting familiar with the columns in each table, as we'll make use of these frequently later when we're learning about querying. Notice also that because all of these three entities are weak, each table contains the primary key columns from the table it's related to. For example, the `track` table contains `artist_id`, `album_id`, and `track_id`, because the combination of all three is required to uniquely identify a track.

In the next section, we show you how to explore the data that's stored in the `music` database and its tables.

The SELECT Statement and Basic Querying Techniques

Up to this point, you've learned how to install and configure MySQL, and how to use the MySQL monitor. Now that you understand the `music` database, you're ready to start exploring its data and to learn the SQL language that's used by all MySQL clients. In this section, we introduce the most commonly used SQL keyword, and the only one that reads data from a database: the `SELECT` keyword. We also explain some basic elements of style and syntax, and the features of the `WHERE` clause, Boolean operators, and sorting (much of this also applies to our later discussions of `INSERT`, `UPDATE`, and `DELETE`). This isn't the end of our discussion of `SELECT`; you'll find more in Chapter 7, where we show you how to use its advanced features.

Single Table SELECTs

The most basic form of `SELECT` reads the data in all rows and columns from a table. Start the monitor and choose the `music` database:

```
mysql> use music;
Database changed
```

Let's retrieve all of the data in the `artist` table:

```
mysql> SELECT * FROM artist;
+-----------+---------------------------+
| artist_id | artist_name               |
+-----------+---------------------------+
|         1 | New Order                 |
|         2 | Nick Cave & The Bad Seeds |
|         3 | Miles Davis               |
|         4 | The Rolling Stones        |
|         5 | The Stone Roses           |
|         6 | Kylie Minogue             |
+-----------+---------------------------+
6 rows in set (0.08 sec)
```

The output has six rows, and each row contains the values for the `artist_id` and `artist_name` columns. We now know that there are six artists in our database and can see the names and identifiers for these artists.

A simple SELECT statement has four components:

1. The keyword SELECT.
2. The columns to be displayed. In our first example, we asked for all columns by using the asterisk (*) symbol as a wildcard character.
3. The keyword FROM.
4. The table name; in this example, the table name is artist.

Putting all this together, we've asked for all columns from the artist table, and that's what MySQL has returned to us.

Let's try another simple SELECT. This time, we'll retrieve all columns from the album table:

```
mysql> SELECT * FROM album;
+-----------+----------+----------------------------------------+
| artist_id | album_id | album_name                             |
+-----------+----------+----------------------------------------+
|         2 |        1 | Let Love In                            |
|         1 |        1 | Retro - John McCready FAN              |
|         1 |        2 | Substance (Disc 2)                     |
|         1 |        3 | Retro - Miranda Sawyer POP             |
|         1 |        4 | Retro - New Order / Bobby Gillespie LIVE |
|         3 |        1 | Live Around The World                  |
|         3 |        2 | In A Silent Way                        |
|         1 |        5 | Power, Corruption & Lies               |
|         4 |        1 | Exile On Main Street                   |
|         1 |        6 | Substance 1987 (Disc 1)                |
|         5 |        1 | Second Coming                          |
|         6 |        1 | Light Years                            |
|         1 |        7 | Brotherhood                            |
+-----------+----------+----------------------------------------+
13 rows in set (0.03 sec)
```

We have 13 albums in our database, and the output has the same basic structure as our first example.

The second example gives you an insight into how the relationships between the tables work. Consider the first row of the results—for the album "Let Love In," which is by the artist with the artist_id value of 2. If you inspect the output of our first example that retrieved data from the artist table, you'll note that the matching artist is "Nick Cave & The Bad Seeds." So, Nick Cave recorded *Let Love In*. You'll also notice that the albums we own for a given artist each have a number in the album_id column. You can see, for example, that we own seven albums by the artist with an artist_id of 1. We'll discuss how to write queries on relationships between tables later in this chapter in "Joining Two Tables."

Notice also that we have several different albums with the same album_id. This isn't a problem, since album_id is only a weak key; an album is uniquely identified by the combination of its `album_id` and the primary key of its owning entity, which is `artist_id`.

You should now feel comfortable about choosing a database, listing its tables, and retrieving all of the data from a table using the `SELECT` statement. To practice, you might want to experiment with the `university` or `flight` databases you loaded in Chapter 3 in "Loading the Sample Databases." Remember that you can use the `SHOW TABLES` statement to find out the table names in these databases.

Choosing Columns

You've so far used the * wildcard character to retrieve all columns in a table. If you don't want to display all the columns, it's easy to be more specific by listing the columns you want, in the order you want them, separated by commas. For example, if you want only the `artist_name` column from the `artist` table, you'd type:

```
mysql> SELECT artist_name FROM artist;
+--------------------------+
| artist_name              |
+--------------------------+
| New Order                |
| Nick Cave & The Bad Seeds |
| Miles Davis              |
| The Rolling Stones       |
| The Stone Roses          |
| Kylie Minogue            |
+--------------------------+
6 rows in set (0.01 sec)
```

If you want both the `artist_name` and the `artist_id`, in that order, you'd use:

```
mysql> SELECT artist_name,artist_id FROM artist;
+--------------------------+-----------+
| artist_name              | artist_id |
+--------------------------+-----------+
| New Order                |         1 |
| Nick Cave & The Bad Seeds |         2 |
| Miles Davis              |         3 |
| The Rolling Stones       |         4 |
| The Stone Roses          |         5 |
| Kylie Minogue            |         6 |
+--------------------------+-----------+
6 rows in set (0.00 sec)
```

You can even list columns more than once:

```
mysql> SELECT artist_id, artist_id FROM artist;
+-----------+-----------+
| artist_id | artist_id |
+-----------+-----------+
|         1 |         1 |
|         2 |         2 |
|         3 |         3 |
```

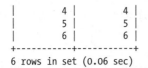

```
|           4 |          4 |
|           5 |          5 |
|           6 |          6 |
+-------------+------------+
6 rows in set (0.06 sec)
```

Even though this appears pointless, it can be useful when combined with *aliases* in more advanced queries, as we show in Chapter 7.

You can specify databases, tables, and column names in a SELECT statement. This allows you to avoid the USE command and work with any database and table directly with SELECT; it also helps resolve ambiguities, as we show later in "Joining Two Tables." Consider an example: suppose you want to retrieve the album_name column from the album table in the music database. You can do this with the following command:

```
mysql> SELECT album_name FROM music.album;
+------------------------------------------+
| album_name                               |
+------------------------------------------+
| Let Love In                              |
| Retro - John McCready FAN                |
| Substance (Disc 2)                       |
| Retro - Miranda Sawyer POP               |
| Retro - New Order / Bobby Gillespie LIVE |
| Live Around The World                    |
| In A Silent Way                          |
| Power, Corruption & Lies                 |
| Exile On Main Street                     |
| Substance 1987 (Disc 1)                  |
| Second Coming                            |
| Light Years                              |
| Brotherhood                              |
+------------------------------------------+
13 rows in set (0.01 sec)
```

The music.album component after the FROM keyword specifies the music database and its album table. There's no need to enter USE music before running this query. This syntax can also be used with other SQL statements, including the UPDATE, DELETE, INSERT, and SHOW statements we discuss later in this chapter.

Choosing Rows with the WHERE Clause

This section introduces the WHERE clause and explains how to use the Boolean operators to write expressions. You'll see these in most SELECT statements, and often in other statements such as UPDATE and DELETE; we'll show you examples later in this chapter.

WHERE basics

The WHERE clause is a powerful tool that allows you to choose which rows are returned from a SELECT statement. You use it to return rows that match a condition, such as having a column value that exactly matches a string, a number greater or less than a value, or a string that is a prefix of another. Almost all our examples in this and later chapters contain WHERE clauses, and you'll become very familiar with them.

The simplest WHERE clause is one that exactly matches a value. Consider an example where we want to find out the details of the artist with the name "New Order." Here's what you type:

```
mysql> SELECT * FROM artist WHERE artist_name = "New Order";
+-----------+-------------+
| artist_id | artist_name |
+-----------+-------------+
|         1 | New Order   |
+-----------+-------------+
1 row in set (0.00 sec)
```

MySQL returns all rows that match our search criteria—in this case, just the one row and all its columns. From this, you can see that the artist "New Order" has an artist_id of 1.

Let's try another exact-match example. Suppose you want to find out the name of the artist with an artist_id value of 4. You type:

```
mysql> SELECT artist_name FROM artist WHERE artist_id = 4;
+-------------------+
| artist_name       |
+-------------------+
| The Rolling Stones |
+-------------------+
1 row in set (0.00 sec)
```

In this example, we've chosen both a column and a row: we've included the column name artist_name after the SELECT keyword, as well as WHERE artist_id = 4.

If a value matches more than one row, the results will contain all matches. Suppose we ask for the names of all tracks with a track_id of 13; this retrieves the thirteenth song on every album that has at least that many songs. You type in:

```
mysql> SELECT track_name FROM track WHERE track_id = 13;
+-----------------------------------------+
| track_name                              |
+-----------------------------------------+
| Every Little Counts                     |
| Everyone Everywhere                     |
| Turn My Way [Olympia, Liverpool 18/7/01] |
| Let It Loose                            |
+-----------------------------------------+
4 rows in set (0.02 sec)
```

The results show the names of the thirteenth track of different albums, so there must be 4 albums that contain at least 13 tracks If we could join the information we get from the track table with information we get from the album table, we could display the names of these albums. We'll see how to perform this type of query later in "Joining Two Tables."

Now let's try retrieving values in a range. This is simplest for numeric ranges, so let's start by finding the names of all artists with an `artist_id` less than 5. To do this, type:

```
mysql> SELECT artist_name FROM artist WHERE artist_id < 5;
+--------------------------+
| artist_name              |
+--------------------------+
| New Order                |
| Nick Cave & The Bad Seeds |
| Miles Davis              |
| The Rolling Stones       |
+--------------------------+
4 rows in set (0.06 sec)
```

For numbers, the frequently used operators are equals (=), greater than (>), less than (<), less than or equal (<=), greater than or equal (>=), and not equal (<> or !=).

Consider one more example. If you want to find all albums that don't have an `album_id` of 2, you'd type:

```
mysql> SELECT album_name FROM album WHERE album_id <> 2;
+-----------------------------------------+
| album_name                              |
+-----------------------------------------+
| Let Love In                             |
| Retro - John McCready FAN               |
| Retro - Miranda Sawyer POP              |
| Retro - New Order / Bobby Gillespie LIVE |
| Live Around The World                   |
| Power, Corruption & Lies                |
| Exile On Main Street                    |
| Substance 1987 (Disc 1)                 |
| Second Coming                           |
| Light Years                             |
| Brotherhood                             |
+-----------------------------------------+
11 rows in set (0.01 sec)
```

This shows us the first, third, and all subsequent albums for all artists. Note that you can use either <> or != for not-equal.

You can use the same operators for strings. For example, if you want to list all artists whose name appears earlier alphabetically than (is less than) `'M'`, use:

```
mysql> SELECT artist_name FROM artist WHERE artist_name < 'M';
+----------------+
| artist_name    |
+----------------+
| Kylie Minogue  |
+----------------+
1 row in set (0.00 sec)
```

Since `Kylie Minogue` begins with a letter alphabetically less than `'M'`, she's reported as an answer; the names of our six other artists all come later in the alphabet. Note that by default MySQL doesn't care about case; we'll discuss this in more detail later in

"ORDER BY Clauses." Of course, we haven't stored the surname and the given names separately, and MySQL isn't smart enough to know that `Kylie Minogue` is a person's name that should ordinarily be sorted by surname (in phonebook order).

Another very common task you'll want to perform with strings is to find matches that begin with a prefix, contain a string, or end in a suffix. For example, you might want to find all album names beginning with the word "Retro." You can do this with the `LIKE` operator in a `WHERE` clause:

```
mysql> SELECT album_name FROM album WHERE album_name LIKE "Retro%";
+------------------------------------------+
| album_name                               |
+------------------------------------------+
| Retro - John McCready FAN                |
| Retro - Miranda Sawyer POP               |
| Retro - New Order / Bobby Gillespie LIVE |
+------------------------------------------+
3 rows in set (0.00 sec)
```

Let's discuss in detail how this works.

The `LIKE` clause is used only with strings and means that a match must meet the pattern in the string that follows. In our example, we've used `LIKE "Retro%"`, which means the string `Retro` followed by zero or more characters. Most strings used with `LIKE` contain the percentage character (`%`) as a wildcard character that matches all possible strings. You can also use it to define a string that ends in a suffix—such as `"%ing"`—or a string that contains a particular substring, such as `%Corruption%`.

For example, `"John%"` would match all strings starting with `"John"`, such as `John Smith` and `John Paul Getty`. The pattern `"%Paul"` matches all strings that have `"Paul"` at the end. Finally, the pattern `"%Paul%"` matches all strings that have `"Paul"` in them, including at the start or at the end.

If you want to match exactly one wildcard character in a `LIKE` clause, you use the underscore character (`_`). For example, if you want all tracks that begin with a three-letter word that starts with `'R'`, you use:

```
mysql> SELECT * FROM track WHERE track_name LIKE "R__ %";
+----------+----------------+-----------+----------+----------+
| track_id | track_name     | artist_id | album_id | time     |
+----------+----------------+-----------+----------+----------+
|        4 | Red Right Hand |         2 |        1 | 00:06:11 |
|       14 | Run Wild       |         1 |        1 | 00:03:57 |
|        1 | Rip This Joint |         4 |        1 | 00:02:23 |
+----------+----------------+-----------+----------+----------+
3 rows in set (0.00 sec)
```

The specification `"R__ %"` means a three-letter word beginning with `'R'`—for example `"Red"`, `"Run"` and `"Rip"`—followed by a space character, and then any string.

Combining conditions with AND, OR, NOT, and XOR

So far, we've used the WHERE clause to test one condition, returning all rows that meet it. You can combine two or more conditions using the Boolean operators AND, OR, NOT, and XOR.

Let's start with an example. Suppose you want to find all albums with a title that begins with a character greater than C but less than M. This is straightforward with the AND operator:

```
mysql> SELECT album_name FROM album WHERE
    -> album_name > "C" AND album_name < "M";
+----------------------+
| album_name           |
+----------------------+
| Let Love In          |
| Live Around The World |
| In A Silent Way      |
| Exile On Main Street |
| Light Years          |
+----------------------+
5 rows in set (0.06 sec)
```

The AND operation in the WHERE clause restricts the results to those rows that meet both conditions.

The OR operator is used to find rows that meet at least one of several conditions. To illustrate, imagine you want a list of all albums that have a title beginning with L, S, or P. You can do this with two OR and three LIKE clauses:

```
mysql> SELECT album_name FROM album WHERE
    -> album_name LIKE "L%" OR
    -> album_name LIKE "S%" OR
    -> album_name LIKE "P%";
+-------------------------+
| album_name              |
+-------------------------+
| Let Love In             |
| Substance (Disc 2)      |
| Live Around The World   |
| Power, Corruption & Lies |
| Substance 1987 (Disc 1) |
| Second Coming           |
| Light Years             |
+-------------------------+
7 rows in set (0.00 sec)
```

The OR operations in the WHERE clause restrict the answers to those that meet any of the three conditions. As an aside, it's particularly obvious in this example that the results are reported without sorting; in this case, they're reported in the order they were added to the database. We'll return to sorting output later in "ORDER BY Clauses."

You can combine AND and OR, but you need to make it clear whether you want to first AND the conditions or OR them. Consider an example where the function isn't obvious from the query:

```
mysql> SELECT album_name FROM album WHERE
    -> album_name LIKE "L%" OR
    -> album_name LIKE "S%" AND
    -> album_name LIKE "%g";
+-----------------------+
| album_name            |
+-----------------------+
| Let Love In           |
| Live Around The World |
| Second Coming         |
| Light Years           |
+-----------------------+
4 rows in set (0.00 sec)
```

When you inspect the results, it becomes clear what's happened: the answers either begin with L, or they have S at the beginning and g at the end. An alternative interpretation of the query would be that the answers must begin with L or S, and all end with g; this is clearly not how the MySQL server has handled the query, since one of the displayed answers, "Let Love In," doesn't end in a g. To make queries containing several Boolean conditions easier to read, group conditions within parentheses.

Parentheses cluster parts of a statement together and help make expressions readable; you can use them just as you would in basic math. Our previous example can be rewritten as follows:

```
mysql> SELECT album_name FROM album WHERE
    -> album_name LIKE "L%" OR
    -> (album_name LIKE "S%" AND album_name LIKE "%g");
+-----------------------+
| album_name            |
+-----------------------+
| Let Love In           |
| Live Around The World |
| Second Coming         |
| Light Years           |
+-----------------------+
4 rows in set (0.00 sec)
```

The parentheses make the evaluation order clear: we want albums beginning with 'L', or those beginning with 'S' and ending with 'g'. We've also typed the query over three lines instead of four, making the intention even clearer through careful layout; just as when writing program code, spacing, indentation, and careful layout help make readable queries.

You can also use parentheses to force a different evaluation order. If you did want albums having names with 'L' or 'S' at the beginning and 'g' at the end, you'd type:

```
mysql> SELECT album_name FROM album WHERE
    -> (album_name LIKE "L%" OR album_name LIKE "S%") AND
```

```
    -> album_name LIKE "%g";
+---------------+
| album_name    |
+---------------+
| Second Coming |
+---------------+
1 row in set (0.00 sec)
```

Both examples with parentheses are much easier to understand. We recommend that you use parentheses whenever there's a chance the intention could be misinterpreted; there's no good reason to rely on MySQL's implicit evaluation order.

The unary NOT operator negates a Boolean statement. Suppose you want a list of all albums except the ones having an album_id of 1 or 3. You'd write the query:

```
mysql> SELECT * FROM album WHERE NOT (album_id = 1 OR album_id = 3);
+-----------+----------+-----------------------------------------+
| artist_id | album_id | album_name                              |
+-----------+----------+-----------------------------------------+
|         1 |        2 | Substance (Disc 2)                      |
|         1 |        4 | Retro - New Order / Bobby Gillespie LIVE |
|         3 |        2 | In A Silent Way                         |
|         1 |        5 | Power, Corruption & Lies                |
|         1 |        6 | Substance 1987 (Disc 1)                 |
|         1 |        7 | Brotherhood                             |
+-----------+----------+-----------------------------------------+
6 rows in set (0.00 sec)
```

The expression in the parentheses says we want:

```
(album_id = 1 OR album_id = 3)
```

and the NOT operation negates it so we get everything but those that meet the condition in the parentheses. There are several other ways you can write a WHERE clause with the same function, and it really doesn't matter which you choose. For example the following three expressions have the same effect:

```
WHERE NOT (album_id = 1) AND NOT (album_id = 3)
```

```
WHERE album_id != 1 AND album_id != 3
```

```
WHERE album_id != 1 AND NOT (album_id = 3)
```

Consider another example using NOT and parentheses. Suppose you want to get a list of all albums with an album_id greater than 2, but not those numbered 4 or 6:

```
mysql> SELECT * FROM album WHERE album_id > 2
    -> AND NOT (album_id = 4 OR album_id = 6);
+-----------+----------+---------------------------+
| artist_id | album_id | album_name                |
+-----------+----------+---------------------------+
|         1 |        3 | Retro - Miranda Sawyer POP |
|         1 |        5 | Power, Corruption & Lies   |
|         1 |        7 | Brotherhood                |
+-----------+----------+---------------------------+
3 rows in set (0.01 sec)
```

Again, the expression in parentheses lists albums that meet a condition—those that are numbered 4 or 6—and the NOT operator negates it so that we get everything else.

The NOT operator's precedence can be a little tricky. Formally, if you apply it to any statement that evaluates to a Boolean FALSE or arithmetic zero, you'll get TRUE (and TRUE is defined as 1). If you apply it to a statement that is nonzero, you'll get FALSE (and FALSE is defined as 0). We've so far considered examples with clauses where the NOT is followed by a expression in parentheses, such as NOT (album_id = 4 OR album_id = 6). You should write your NOT expressions in this way, or you'll get unexpected results. For example, the previous expression isn't the same as this one:

```
mysql> SELECT * FROM album WHERE album_id > 2
    -> AND (NOT album_id) = 4 OR album_id = 6;
+-----------+----------+-------------------------+
| artist_id | album_id | album_name              |
+-----------+----------+-------------------------+
|         1 |        6 | Substance 1987 (Disc 1) |
+-----------+----------+-------------------------+
1 row in set (0.00 sec)
```

This returns unexpected results: just those albums with an album_id of 6. To understand what happened, try just the part of the statement with the NOT operator:

```
mysql> SELECT * FROM album WHERE (NOT album_id) = 4;
Empty set (0.00 sec)
```

What has happened is that MySQL has evaluated the expression NOT album_id, and then checked if it's equal to 4. Since the album_id is always nonzero, NOT album_id is always zero and, therefore, never equal to 4, and you get no results! Now, try this:

```
mysql> SELECT * FROM album WHERE (NOT album_id) != 4;
+-----------+----------+------------------------------------------+
| artist_id | album_id | album_name                               |
+-----------+----------+------------------------------------------+
|         2 |        1 | Let Love In                              |
|         1 |        1 | Retro - John McCready FAN                |
|         1 |        2 | Substance (Disc 2)                       |
|         1 |        3 | Retro - Miranda Sawyer POP               |
|         1 |        4 | Retro - New Order / Bobby Gillespie LIVE |
|         3 |        1 | Live Around The World                    |
|         3 |        2 | In A Silent Way                          |
|         1 |        5 | Power, Corruption & Lies                 |
|         4 |        1 | Exile On Main Street                     |
|         1 |        6 | Substance 1987 (Disc 1)                  |
|         5 |        1 | Second Coming                            |
|         6 |        1 | Light Years                              |
|         1 |        7 | Brotherhood                              |
+-----------+----------+------------------------------------------+
13 rows in set (0.00 sec)
```

Again album_id is always nonzero, and so NOT album_id is 0. Since 0 isn't equal to 4, we see all albums as answers. So be careful to use those parentheses: if you don't, NOT's high priority (or *precedence*) means it is applied to whatever immediately follows it, and not to the whole expression!

You can combine the `NOT` operator with `LIKE`. Suppose you want all albums that don't begin with an L. To do this, type:

```
mysql> SELECT album_name FROM album WHERE album_name NOT LIKE "L%";
+-------------------------------------------+
| album_name                                |
+-------------------------------------------+
| Retro - John McCready FAN                 |
| Substance (Disc 2)                        |
| Retro - Miranda Sawyer POP                |
| Retro - New Order / Bobby Gillespie LIVE  |
| In A Silent Way                           |
| Power, Corruption & Lies                  |
| Exile On Main Street                      |
| Substance 1987 (Disc 1)                   |
| Second Coming                             |
| Brotherhood                               |
+-------------------------------------------+
10 rows in set (0.01 sec)
```

The result is all albums, except those beginning with L.

You can combine `NOT LIKE` with `AND` and `OR`. Suppose you want albums beginning with S, but not those ending with a closing parenthesis, `')'`. You can do this with:

```
mysql> SELECT album_name FROM album WHERE
    -> album_name LIKE "S%" AND album_name NOT LIKE "%)";
+---------------+
| album_name    |
+---------------+
| Second Coming |
+---------------+
1 row in set (0.00 sec)
```

MySQL also supports the exclusive-OR operation through the `XOR` operator. An exclusive OR evaluates as true if only one—but not both—of the expressions is true. To be precise, a `XOR` b is equivalent to `(a AND (NOT b)) OR ((NOT a) AND b)`. For example, suppose you want to find artists whose names end in "es" or start with "The," but not both. You'd need to type:

```
mysql> SELECT artist_name FROM artist WHERE
    -> artist_name LIKE "The%" XOR
    -> artist_name LIKE "%es";
Empty set (0.00 sec)
```

There are no matching entries in the database, since both "The Stone Roses" and "The Rolling Stones" meet both criteria.

Before we move on to sorting, we'll discuss syntax alternatives. If you're familiar with a programming language such as PHP, C, Perl, or Java, you'll be used to using ! for NOT, || for OR, and && for AND. MySQL also supports these, and you can use them interchangeably with the word-based alternatives if you want to. However, we always use the word-based versions, as that's what you'll see used in most SQL statements.

ORDER BY Clauses

We've so far discussed how to choose the columns and rows that are returned as part of the query result, but not how to control how the result is displayed. In a relational database, the rows in a table form a set; there is no intrinsic order between the rows, and so we have to ask MySQL to sort the results if we want them in a particular order. In this section, we explain how to use the ORDER BY clause to do this. Sorting has no effect on *what* is returned, and only affects *what order* the results are returned.

Suppose you want to return a list of the artists in the music database, sorted in alphabetical order by the artist_name. Here's what you'd type:

```
mysql> SELECT * FROM artist ORDER BY artist_name;
+-----------+---------------------------+
| artist_id | artist_name               |
+-----------+---------------------------+
|         6 | Kylie Minogue             |
|         3 | Miles Davis               |
|         1 | New Order                 |
|         2 | Nick Cave & The Bad Seeds |
|         4 | The Rolling Stones        |
|         5 | The Stone Roses           |
+-----------+---------------------------+
6 rows in set (0.03 sec)
```

The ORDER BY clause indicates that sorting is required, followed by the column that should be used as the sort key. In this example, we're sorting by alphabetically-ascending artist_name. The default sort is case-insensitive and in ascending order, and MySQL automatically sorts alphabetically because the columns are character strings. The way strings are sorted is determined by the character set and collation order that are being used. We discuss these in "Collation and Character Sets." For most of this book, we assume that you're using the default settings.

Consider a second example. This time, let's sort the output from the track table by ascending track length—that is, by the time column. Since it's likely that two or more tracks have the same length, we'll add a second sort key to resolve collisions and determine how such ties should be broken. In this case, when the track times are the same, we'll sort the answers alphabetically by track_name. Here's what you type:

```
mysql> SELECT time, track_name FROM track ORDER BY time, track_name;
+------+-------------------------------------------------------+
| time | track_name                                            |
+------+-------------------------------------------------------+
| 1.34 | Intermission By Alan Wise [Olympia, Paris 12/11/01]   |
| 1.81 | In A Silent Way                                       |
| 2.38 | Rip This Joint                                        |
| 2.78 | Jangling Jack                                         |
| 2.81 | Full Nelson                                           |
```

```
| 2.90 | I Just Want To See His Face        |
| 2.97 | Sweet Black Angel                  |
| 2.99 | Your Star Will Shine               |
| 3.00 | Shake Your Hips                    |
| 3.08 | Happy                              |
| 3.20 | Dreams Never End                   |
| 3.26 | Straight To The Man                |
| 3.40 | Under The Influence Of Love        |
| 3.40 | Ventilator Blues                   |
| 3.42 | Cries And Whispers                 |
| 3.44 | Mesh                               |
...
```

We've shown only part of the 153-row output. Notice that there's a collision of track times where the length is 3.40. In this case, the second sort key, track_name, is used to resolve the collision so that "Under the Influence of Love" appears before "Ventilator Blues." You'll find you often use multiple columns in an ORDER BY clause when you're sorting people's names, where typically you'll use something like ORDER BY surname, firstname, secondname.

You can also sort in descending order, and you can control this behavior for each sort key. Suppose you want to sort the artists by descending alphabetical order. You type this:

```
mysql> SELECT artist_name FROM artist ORDER BY artist_name DESC;
+--------------------------+
| artist_name              |
+--------------------------+
| The Stone Roses          |
| The Rolling Stones       |
| Nick Cave & The Bad Seeds |
| New Order                |
| Miles Davis              |
| Kylie Minogue            |
+--------------------------+
6 rows in set (0.00 sec)
```

The DESC keyword specifies that the preceding sort key (in this case, artist_name) should be sorted in descending order. You can use a mixture of ascending and descending orders when multiple sort keys are used. For example, you can sort by descending time and alphabetically increasing track_name:

```
mysql> SELECT time, track_name FROM track
    -> WHERE time < 3.6
    -> ORDER BY time DESC, track_name ASC;
+------+-------------------------------------------------------+
| time | track_name                                            |
+------+-------------------------------------------------------+
| 3.57 | Casino Boogie                                         |
| 3.57 | Procession [Polytechnic of Central London, London 6/12/85] |
| 3.56 | Your Disco Needs You                                  |
| 3.55 | I'm So High                                           |
| 3.55 | On A Night Like This                                  |
| 3.54 | Mr. Pastorius                                         |
```

```
| 3.46 | Spinning Around                                     |
| 3.44 | Mesh                                                |
| 3.42 | Cries And Whispers                                  |
| 3.40 | Under The Influence Of Love                         |
| 3.40 | Ventilator Blues                                    |
| 3.26 | Straight To The Man                                 |
| 3.20 | Dreams Never End                                    |
| 3.08 | Happy                                               |
| 3.00 | Shake Your Hips                                     |
| 2.99 | Your Star Will Shine                                |
| 2.97 | Sweet Black Angel                                   |
| 2.90 | I Just Want To See His Face                         |
| 2.81 | Full Nelson                                         |
| 2.78 | Jangling Jack                                       |
| 2.38 | Rip This Joint                                      |
| 1.81 | In A Silent Way                                     |
| 1.34 | Intermission By Alan Wise [Olympia, Paris 12/11/01] |
+------+-----------------------------------------------------+
24 rows in set (0.06 sec)
```

In this example, the rows are sorted by descending `time` and, when there's a collision, by ascending `track_name`. We've used the optional keyword `ASC` to indicate an ascending sort key. Whenever we sort, ascending order is assumed if the `DESC` keyword isn't used. You don't need to explicitly include the `ASC` keyword, but including it does help to make the statement's behavior more obvious. Notice also that we've included a `WHERE` clause; using `WHERE` and `ORDER BY` together is very common, and `WHERE` always appears before `ORDER BY` in the `SELECT` statement.

If a collision of values occurs, and you don't specify another sort key, the sort order is undefined. This may not be important for you; you may not care about the order in which two customers with the identical name "John A. Smith" appear. A common source of collisions is string sorting, where MySQL ignores the case of characters. For example, the strings `john`, `John`, and `JOHN` are treated as identical in the `ORDER BY` process. If you do want sorting to behave like ASCII does (where uppercase comes before lowercase), then you can add a `BINARY` keyword to your sort as follows:

```
mysql> SELECT * FROM artist ORDER BY BINARY artist_name;
+-----------+---------------------------+
| artist_id | artist_name               |
+-----------+---------------------------+
|         6 | Kylie Minogue             |
|         3 | Miles Davis               |
|         1 | New Order                 |
|         2 | Nick Cave & The Bad Seeds |
|         4 | The Rolling Stones        |
|         5 | The Stone Roses           |
+-----------+---------------------------+
6 rows in set (0.01 sec)
```

Because there are no case collisions in the `music` database, this example doesn't do anything different from the example without the `BINARY` keyword.

Note you can use the `BINARY` keyword in many places; for example, you can use it in string comparisons. For example, searching for tracks with names alphabetically earlier than the letter b returns 12 tracks:

```
mysql> SELECT track_name FROM track WHERE track_name < 'b';
+-------------------------------------------------------+
| track_name                                            |
+-------------------------------------------------------+
| Ain't Gonna Rain Anymore                              |
| All Day Long                                          |
| 1963                                                  |
| Age Of Consent [Spectrum Arena, Warrington 1/3/86]    |
| As It Is When It Was [Reading Festival 29/8/93]       |
| Amandla                                               |
| Age Of Consent                                        |
| 5 8 6                                                 |
| All Down The Line                                     |
| Angel Dust                                            |
| All Day Long                                          |
| As It Is When It Was                                  |
+-------------------------------------------------------+
12 rows in set (0.00 sec)
```

However, if we specify that we want to perform the search in ASCII order, we get all 153 tracks, since they all start with an uppercase letter, and uppercase letters appear before lowercase letters in the ASCII table:

```
mysql> SELECT track_name FROM track WHERE track_name < BINARY 'b';
+------------------------------------------------------------------+
| track_name                                                       |
+------------------------------------------------------------------+
| Do You Love Me?                                                  |
| Nobody's Baby Now                                                |
| Loverman                                                         |
| Jangling Jack                                                    |
| Red Right Hand                                                   |
| I Let Love In                                                    |
...
| Broken Promise                                                   |
| As It Is When It Was                                             |
| Weirdo                                                           |
| Paradise                                                         |
+------------------------------------------------------------------+
153 rows in set (0.00 sec)
```

Sorting is performed as appropriate to the column type. For example, if you're sorting dates, it organizes the rows in ascending date order. You can force the sort to behave differently, using the `CAST( )` function and the `AS` keyword. Suppose, for example, you want to sort the `track` table by ascending `time`, but you want the times to be treated as strings. Here's how you do it:

```
mysql> SELECT time, track_name FROM track ORDER BY CAST(time AS CHAR);
+-------+-------------------------------------------------------+
| time  | track_name                                            |
```

```
+-------+---------------------------------------------------+
|  1.34 | Intermission By Alan Wise [Olympia, Paris 12/11/01] |
|  1.81 | In A Silent Way                                   |
| 11.37 | Breaking Into Heaven                              |
| 12.80 | Human Nature                                      |
| 16.67 | Shhh/Peaceful                                     |
| 16.67 | In A Silent Way/It's About That Time              |
|  2.38 | Rip This Joint                                    |
|  2.78 | Jangling Jack                                     |
|  2.81 | Full Nelson                                       |
  ...
```

The results are ordered alphabetically, so that, for example, numbers beginning with 1 appear before numbers beginning with 2. The CAST( ) function forces a column to be treated as a different type, in this example as a character string using the AS CHAR clause. You can specify:

- AS BINARY, to sort as binary, which has the same effect as ORDER BY BINARY
- AS SIGNED, to sort as a signed integer
- AS UNSIGNED, to sort as an unsigned integer
- AS CHAR, to sort as a character string
- AS DATE, to sort as a date
- AS DATETIME, to sort as a date and time
- AS TIME, to sort as a time

The types of columns are discussed in detail in "Column Types" in Chapter 6.

The LIMIT Clause

The LIMIT clause is a useful, nonstandard SQL tool that allows you to control which rows are output. Its basic form allows you to limit the number of rows returned from a SELECT statement, which is useful when you want to limit the amount of data communicated over a network or output to the screen. You might use it, for example, in a web database application, where you want to find the rows that match a condition but only want to show the user the first 10 rows in a web page. Here's an example:

```
mysql> SELECT track_name FROM track LIMIT 10;
+---------------------------+
| track_name                |
+---------------------------+
| Do You Love Me?           |
| Nobody's Baby Now         |
| Loverman                  |
| Jangling Jack             |
| Red Right Hand            |
| I Let Love In             |
| Thirsty Dog               |
| Ain't Gonna Rain Anymore  |
| Lay Me Low                |
```

```
| Do You Love Me? (Part Two) |
+----------------------------+
10 rows in set (0.00 sec)
```

The LIMIT clause in this example restricts the output to the first 10 rows, saving the cost of buffering, communicating, and displaying the remaining 143 tracks.

The LIMIT clause can be used to return a fixed number of rows beginning anywhere in the result set. Suppose you want five rows, but you want the first one displayed to be the sixth row of the answer set. You do this by starting from after the fifth answer:

```
mysql> SELECT track_name FROM track LIMIT 5,5;
+----------------------------+
| track_name                 |
+----------------------------+
| I Let Love In              |
| Thirsty Dog                |
| Ain't Gonna Rain Anymore   |
| Lay Me Low                 |
| Do You Love Me? (Part Two) |
+----------------------------+
5 rows in set (0.00 sec)
```

The output is rows 6 to 10 from the SELECT query.

If you want all rows after a start point, and you don't know how many rows are in the table, then you need to choose a large integer as the second parameter. Suppose you want all rows after row 150 in the track table. Use the following command:

```
mysql> SELECT track_name FROM track LIMIT 150,999999999;
+--------------------+
| track_name         |
+--------------------+
| As It Is When It Was |
| Weirdo             |
| Paradise           |
+--------------------+
3 rows in set (0.01 sec)
```

Since there are likely to be at most tens of thousands of rows in the track table, providing 999999999 as the second parameter guarantees all rows are returned. Technically, the largest number you can use is 18446744073709551615; this is the maximum value that can be stored in MySQL's unsigned BIGINT variable type. MySQL will complain if you try to use a larger value. We discuss variable types in "Other integer types" in Chapter 6.

There's an alternative syntax that you might see for the LIMIT keyword: instead of writing LIMIT 10,5, you can write LIMIT 10 OFFSET 5.

Joining Two Tables

We've so far worked with just one table in our SELECT queries. However, you know that a relational database is all about working with the relationships between tables to answer information needs. Indeed, as we've explored the tables in the music database, it's become obvious that by using these relationships, we can answer more interesting queries. For example, it'd be useful to know what tracks make up an album, what albums we own by each artist, or how long an album plays for. This section shows you how to answer these queries by *joining* two tables. We'll return to this issue as part of a longer, more advanced discussion of joins in Chapter 7.

We use only one join syntax in this chapter. There are several more, and each gives you a different way to bring together data from two or more tables. The syntax we use here is the INNER JOIN, which hides some of the detail and is the easiest to learn. Consider an example, and then we'll explain more about how it works:

```
mysql> SELECT artist_name, album_name FROM artist INNER JOIN album
    -> USING (artist_id);
+--------------------------+------------------------------------------+
| artist_name              | album_name                               |
+--------------------------+------------------------------------------+
| New Order                | Retro - John McCready FAN                |
| New Order                | Substance (Disc 2)                       |
| New Order                | Retro - Miranda Sawyer POP               |
| New Order                | Retro - New Order / Bobby Gillespie LIVE |
| New Order                | Power, Corruption & Lies                 |
| New Order                | Substance 1987 (Disc 1)                  |
| New Order                | Brotherhood                              |
| Nick Cave & The Bad Seeds | Let Love In                             |
| Miles Davis              | Live Around The World                    |
| Miles Davis              | In A Silent Way                          |
| The Rolling Stones       | Exile On Main Street                     |
| The Stone Roses          | Second Coming                            |
| Kylie Minogue            | Light Years                              |
+--------------------------+------------------------------------------+
13 rows in set (0.00 sec)
```

The output shows the artists and their albums. You can see for the first time how many albums we own by each artist and who made each one.

How does the INNER JOIN work? The statement has two parts: first, two table names separated by the INNER JOIN keywords; second, the USING keyword that indicates which column (or columns) holds the relationship between the two tables. In our first example, the two tables to be joined are artist and album, expressed as artist INNER JOIN album (for the basic INNER JOIN, it doesn't matter what order you list the tables in, and so using album INNER JOIN artist would have the same effect). The USING clause in the example is USING (artist_id), which tells MySQL that the column that holds the relationship between the tables is artist_id; you should recall this from our design and our previous discussion in "The Music Database," in Chapter 4.

The data comes from the artist table:

```
mysql> SELECT * FROM artist;
+-----------+---------------------------+
| artist_id | artist_name               |
+-----------+---------------------------+
| 1         | New Order                 |
```

```
| 2          | Nick Cave & The Bad Seeds |
| 3          | Miles Davis               |
| 4          | The Rolling Stones        |
| 5          | The Stone Roses           |
| 6          | Kylie Minogue             |
+-----------+---------------------------+
6 rows in set (0.01 sec)
```

and the album table:

```
mysql> SELECT * FROM album;
+-----------+----------+----------------------------------------------+
| artist_id | album_id | album_name                                   |
+-----------+----------+----------------------------------------------+
| 2         | 1        | Let Love In                                  |
| 1         | 1        | Retro - John McCready FAN                    |
| 1         | 2        | Substance (Disc 2)                           |
| 1         | 3        | Retro - Miranda Sawyer POP                   |
| 1         | 4        | Retro - New Order / Bobby Gillespie LIVE     |
| 3         | 1        | Live Around The World                        |
| 3         | 2        | In A Silent Way                              |
| 1         | 5        | Power, Corruption & Lies                     |
| 4         | 1        | Exile On Main Street                         |
| 1         | 6        | Substance 1987 (Disc 1)                      |
| 5         | 1        | Second Coming                                |
| 6         | 1        | Light Years                                  |
| 1         | 7        | Brotherhood                                  |
+-----------+----------+----------------------------------------------+
13 rows in set (0.00 sec)
```

In response to our query, MySQL finds the artist_name and album_name value pairs that have the same artist_id values. For each artist_id in the artist table (let's use 1 as an example):

```
+-----------+---------------------------+
| artist_id | artist_name               |
+-----------+---------------------------+
| 1         | New Order                 |
+-----------+---------------------------+
```

the server finds all the entries in the album table that have this value of artist_id:

```
+-----------+----------+----------------------------------------------+
| artist_id | album_id | album_name                                   |
+-----------+----------+----------------------------------------------+
| 1         | 1        | Retro - John McCready FAN                    |
| 1         | 2        | Substance (Disc 2)                           |
| 1         | 3        | Retro - Miranda Sawyer POP                   |
| 1         | 4        | Retro - New Order / Bobby Gillespie LIVE     |
| 1         | 5        | Power, Corruption & Lies                     |
| 1         | 6        | Substance 1987 (Disc 1)                      |
| 1         | 7        | Brotherhood                                  |
+-----------+----------+----------------------------------------------+
```

It can then form a new temporary table from these two sets:

```
+-----------+-------------+----------+-------------------------------------------+
| artist_id | artist_name | album_id | album_name                                |
+-----------+-------------+----------+-------------------------------------------+
| 1         | New Order   | 1        | Retro - John McCready FAN                 |
| 1         | New Order   | 2        | Substance (Disc 2)                        |
| 1         | New Order   | 3        | Retro - Miranda Sawyer POP                |
| 1         | New Order   | 4        | Retro - New Order / Bobby Gillespie LIVE  |
| 1         | New Order   | 5        | Power, Corruption & Lies                  |
| 1         | New Order   | 6        | Substance 1987 (Disc 1)                   |
| 1         | New Order   | 7        | Brotherhood                               |
+-----------+-------------+----------+-------------------------------------------+
```

Once it has processed all the different `artist_id` values, it selects the colums you asked for—`artist_name` and `album_name`—to display:

```
+-------------------------+-----------------------------------------+
| artist_name             | album_name                              |
+-------------------------+-----------------------------------------+
| New Order               | Retro - John McCready FAN               |
| New Order               | Substance (Disc 2)                      |
| New Order               | Retro - Miranda Sawyer POP              |
| New Order               | Retro - New Order / Bobby Gillespie LIVE |
| New Order               | Power, Corruption & Lies                |
| New Order               | Substance 1987 (Disc 1)                 |
| New Order               | Brotherhood                             |
| ...                                                               |
+-------------------------+-----------------------------------------+
```

There are a few important issues you need to know about when using the basic INNER JOIN syntax:

- It works only when two tables share a column with the same name that you can use as the join condition; otherwise, you must use an alternative syntax described in Chapter 7. Note that MySQL can't automatically determine the column you want to use for the join, (even if there are columns with the same name in the two tables), so you have to specify it explicitly.

- The result rows shown are those where the join column (or columns) match between the tables; rows from one table that don't have a match in the other table are ignored. In the previous example, any artist who had no albums would be ignored.

- With the exception of the join column or columns after the USING keyword, any columns you specify must be unambiguous. For example, if you want to SELECT the artist_name, you can use just artist_name because it exists only in the artist table. However, if you want artist_id, then you need to specify it explicitly as artist.artist_id or album.artist_id because both tables have a column of the same name.

- Don't forget the USING clause. MySQL won't complain if you omit it, but the results won't make sense because you'll get a *Cartesian product*. We discuss this further in Chapter 7.

- The column or columns following the USING clause must be surrounded by parentheses. If you want to join on more than one column, separate the column names with a comma. We'll show you an example in a moment.

If you remember these rules, you'll find joins with INNER JOIN are reasonably straightforward. Let's now consider a few more examples that illustrate these ideas.

Suppose you want to list the track names for all your albums. Examining the album and track tables, you identify that you would have to join two columns, artist_id and album_id. Let's try the join operation:

```
mysql> SELECT album_name, track_name FROM album INNER JOIN track
    -> USING (artist_id, album_id) LIMIT 15;
+------------------------------+------------------------------+
| album_name                   | track_name                   |
+------------------------------+------------------------------+
| Let Love In                  | Do You Love Me?              |
| Let Love In                  | Nobody's Baby Now            |
| Let Love In                  | Loverman                     |
| Let Love In                  | Jangling Jack                |
| Let Love In                  | Red Right Hand               |
| Let Love In                  | I Let Love In                |
| Let Love In                  | Thirsty Dog                  |
| Let Love In                  | Ain't Gonna Rain Anymore     |
| Let Love In                  | Lay Me Low                   |
| Let Love In                  | Do You Love Me? (Part Two)   |
| Retro - John McCready FAN    | Elegia                       |
| Retro - John McCready FAN    | In A Lonely Place            |
| Retro - John McCready FAN    | Procession                   |
| Retro - John McCready FAN    | Your Silent Face             |
| Retro - John McCready FAN    | Sunrise                      |
+------------------------------+------------------------------+
15 rows in set (0.00 sec)
```

We've specified the two join columns in the USING clause separated by commas as USING (artist_id, album_id). The results show the tracks for the album *Let Love In*, and the first few from *Retro - John McReady FAN*. To fit the results into the book, we've limited the output to 15 rows, using the LIMIT clause we discussed earlier in "The LIMIT Clause."

We can improve our previous example by adding an ORDER BY clause. It makes sense that we'd want to see the albums in alphabetical order, with the tracks shown in the order they occur on the album, so we could modify our previous query to be:

```
mysql> SELECT album_name, track_name FROM album INNER JOIN track
    -> USING (artist_id, album_id)
    -> ORDER BY album_name, track_id LIMIT 15;
+----------------------+------------------------+
| album_name           | track_name             |
+----------------------+------------------------+
| Brotherhood          | State of the Nation    |
| Brotherhood          | Every Little Counts    |
| Brotherhood          | Angel Dust             |
```

```
| Brotherhood          | All Day Long          |
| Brotherhood          | Bizarre Love Triangle |
| Brotherhood          | Way of Life           |
| Brotherhood          | Broken Promise        |
| Brotherhood          | As It Is When It Was  |
| Brotherhood          | Weirdo                |
| Brotherhood          | Paradise              |
| Exile On Main Street | Rocks Off             |
| Exile On Main Street | Rip This Joint        |
| Exile On Main Street | Shake Your Hips       |
| Exile On Main Street | Casino Boogie         |
| Exile On Main Street | Tumbling Dice         |
+----------------------+-----------------------+
15 rows in set (0.00 sec)
```

You can see that the ORDER BY clause sorts the albums and tracks in the required order, and that it's listed last in the query after the join condition.

Let's try a different query. Suppose you want to find out which tracks you've played. You can do this with a join between the track and played tables, using the artist_id, album_id, and track_id columns in the join condition. Here's the query:

```
mysql> SELECT played, track_name FROM
    -> track INNER JOIN played USING (artist_id, album_id, track_id)
    -> ORDER BY track.artist_id, track.album_id, track.track_id, played;
+---------------------+-----------------------+
| played              | track_name            |
+---------------------+-----------------------+
| 2006-08-14 10:21:03 | Fine Time             |
| 2006-08-14 10:25:22 | Temptation            |
| 2006-08-14 10:30:25 | True Faith            |
| 2006-08-14 10:36:54 | The Perfect Kiss      |
| 2006-08-14 10:41:43 | Ceremony              |
| 2006-08-14 10:43:37 | Regret                |
| 2006-08-14 10:47:21 | Crystal               |
| 2006-08-14 10:54:02 | Bizarre Love Triangle |
| 2006-08-15 14:00:03 | In A Silent Way       |
| 2006-08-15 14:26:12 | Intruder              |
| 2006-08-15 14:33:57 | New Blues             |
+---------------------+-----------------------+
11 rows in set (0.00 sec)
```

We've sorted the results by artist, then album, then track, and then the play date and time. Notice we've also had to unambiguously specify the columns in the ORDER BY clause using the table name, since the first three columns occur in both tables. In practice, if columns are used in the join condition, it doesn't matter whether you sort or select using the column from either table; for example, in this query, track.artist_id and played.artist_id are interchangeable because they're always the same for each row.

Before we leave SELECT, we'll give you a taste of one of the functions you can use to *aggregate* values. Suppose you want to find out how long New Order's *Brotherhood* album takes to play. You can do this by summing the times of the individual tracks with the SQL SUM( ) function. Here's how it works:

```
mysql> SELECT SUM(time) FROM
    -> album INNER JOIN track USING (artist_id, album_id)
    -> WHERE album.artist_id = 1 AND album.album_id = 7;
+-----------+
| SUM(time) |
+-----------+
|     43.78 |
+-----------+
1 row in set (0.00 sec)
```

You can see the album runs for just under 44 minutes. The SUM( ) function reports the sum of all values for the column enclosed in the parentheses—in this case, time—and not the individual values themselves. Because we've used a WHERE clause to choose only rows for the *Brotherhood* album, the sum of the time values is the total play time of the album. Of course, to run this query, we needed to know that New Order's artist_id is 1 and that the album_id of "Brotherhood" is 7. We discovered this by running two other SELECT queries beforehand:

```
mysql> SELECT artist_id FROM artist WHERE artist_name = "New Order";
+-----------+
| artist_id |
+-----------+
|         1 |
+-----------+
1 row in set (0.00 sec)

mysql> SELECT album_id FROM album
    -> WHERE artist_id = 1 AND album_name = "Brotherhood";
+----------+
| album_id |
+----------+
|        7 |
+----------+
1 row in set (0.00 sec)
```

We explain more features of SELECT and aggregate functions in Chapter 7.

The INSERT Statement

The INSERT statement is used to add new data to tables. In this section, we explain its basic syntax and show you simple examples that add new rows to the music database. In Chapter 6, we'll discuss how to load data from existing tables or from external data sources.

INSERT Basics

Inserting data typically occurs in two situations: when you *bulk-load* in a large batch as you create your database, and when you add data on an ad hoc basis as you use the database. In MySQL, there are different optimizations built into the server for each situation and, importantly, different SQL syntaxes available to make it easy for you to work with the server in both cases. We explain a basic INSERT syntax in this section, and show you examples of how to use it for bulk and single record insertion.

Let's start with the basic task of inserting one new row into the artist table. To do this, you need to understand the table's structure. As we explained in Chapter 4 in "The Music Database," you can discover this with the SHOW COLUMNS statement:

```
mysql> SHOW COLUMNS FROM artist;
+-------------+-------------+------+-----+---------+-------+
| Field       | Type        | Null | Key | Default | Extra |
+-------------+-------------+------+-----+---------+-------+
| artist_id   | smallint(5) | NO   | PRI | 0       |       |
| artist_name | char(128)   | NO   |     |         |       |
+-------------+-------------+------+-----+---------+-------+
2 rows in set (0.00 sec)
```

This tells you that the two columns occur in the order artist_id and then artist_name, and you need to know this for the basic syntax we're about to use.

Our new row is for a new artist, "Barry Adamson." But what artist_id value do we give him? You might recall that we already have six artists, so we should probably use 7. You can check this with:

```
mysql> SELECT MAX(artist_id) FROM artist;
+----------------+
| MAX(artist_id) |
+----------------+
|              6 |
+----------------+
1 row in set (0.04 sec)
```

The MAX( ) function is an aggregate function, and it tells you the maximum value for the column supplied as a parameter. This is a little cleaner than SELECT artist_id FROM artist, which prints out all rows and requires you to inspect the rows to find the maximum value; adding an ORDER BY makes it easier. Using MAX( ) is also much simpler than SELECT artist_id FROM artist ORDER BY artist_id DESC LIMIT 1, which also returns the correct answer. You'll learn more about the AUTO_INCREMENT shortcut to automatically assign the next available identifier in Chapter 6, and about aggregate functions in Chapter 7.

We're now ready to insert the row. Here's what you type:

```
mysql> INSERT INTO artist VALUES (7, "Barry Adamson");
Query OK, 1 row affected (0.00 sec)
```

A new row is created—MySQL reports that one row has been affected—and the value 7 is inserted as the `artist_id` and `Barry Adamson` as the `artist_name`. You can check with a query:

```
mysql> SELECT * FROM artist WHERE artist_id = 7;
+-----------+---------------+
| artist_id | artist_name   |
+-----------+---------------+
|         7 | Barry Adamson |
+-----------+---------------+
1 row in set (0.01 sec)
```

You might be tempted to try out something like this:

```
mysql> INSERT INTO artist
       VALUES((SELECT 1+MAX(artist_id) FROM artist), "Barry Adamson");
```

However, this won't work because you can't modify a table while you're reading from it. The query would work if you wanted to `INSERT INTO` a different table (here, a table other than `artist`).

To continue our example, and illustrate the bulk-loading approach, let's now insert Barry Adamson's album *The Taming of the Shrewd* and its tracks. First, check the structure of the `album` table:

```
mysql> SHOW COLUMNS FROM album;
+------------+----------+------+-----+---------+-------+
| Field      | Type     | Null | Key | Default | Extra |
+------------+----------+------+-----+---------+-------+
| artist_id  | int(5)   |      | PRI | 0       |       |
| album_id   | int(4)   |      | PRI | 0       |       |
| album_name | char(128)| YES  |     | NULL    |       |
+------------+----------+------+-----+---------+-------+
3 rows in set (0.00 sec)
```

Second, insert the album using the approach we used previously:

```
mysql> INSERT INTO album VALUES (7, 1, "The Taming of the Shrewd");
Query OK, 1 row affected (0.00 sec)
```

The first value is the `artist_id`, the value of which we know from creating the artist, and the second value is the `album_id`, which must be 1 because this is the first album we've added for Barry Adamson.

Third, check the `track` table structure:

```
mysql> SHOW COLUMNS FROM track;
+------------+-------------+------+-----+---------+-------+
| Field      | Type        | Null | Key | Default | Extra |
+------------+-------------+------+-----+---------+-------+
| track_id   | int(3)      |      | PRI | 0       |       |
| track_name | char(128)   | YES  |     | NULL    |       |
| artist_id  | int(5)      |      | PRI | 0       |       |
| album_id   | int(4)      |      | PRI | 0       |       |
| time       | decimal(5,2)| YES  |     | NULL    |       |
```

```
+------------+-------------+------+-----+---------+-------+
5 rows in set (0.01 sec)
```

Finally, insert the tracks:

```
mysql> INSERT INTO track VALUES (1, "Diamonds", 7, 1, 4.10),
    -> (2, "Boppin Out / Eternal Morning", 7, 1, 3.22),
    -> (3, "Splat Goes the Cat", 7, 1, 1.39),
    -> (4, "From Rusholme With Love", 7, 1, 3.59);
Query OK, 4 rows affected (0.00 sec)
Records: 4  Duplicates: 0  Warnings: 0
```

Here, we've used a different INSERT style to add all four tracks in a single SQL query. This style is recommended when you want to load more than one row. It has a similar format to the single-insertion style, except that the values for several rows are collected together in a comma-separated list. Giving MySQL all the data you want to insert in one statement helps it optimize the insertion process, allowing queries that use this syntax to be typically many times faster than repeated insertions of single rows. There are other ways to speed up insertion, and we discuss several in Chapter 6.

The single-row INSERT style is unforgiving: if it finds a duplicate, it'll stop as soon as it finds a duplicate key. For example, suppose we try to insert the same tracks again:

```
mysql> INSERT INTO track VALUES (1, "Diamonds", 7, 1, 4.10),
    -> (2, "Boppin Out / Eternal Morning", 7, 1, 3.22),
    -> (3, "Splat Goes the Cat", 7, 1, 1.39),
    -> (4, "From Rusholme With Love", 7, 1, 3.59);
ERROR 1062 (23000): Duplicate entry '7-1-1' for key 1
```

The INSERT operation stops on the first duplicate key. You can add an IGNORE clause to prevent the error if you want:

```
mysql> INSERT IGNORE INTO track VALUES (1, "Diamonds", 7, 1, 4.10),
    -> (2, "Boppin Out / Eternal Morning", 7, 1, 3.22),
    -> (3, "Splat Goes the Cat", 7, 1, 1.39),
    -> (4, "From Rusholme With Love", 7, 1, 3.59);
Query OK, 0 rows affected (0.01 sec)
Records: 4  Duplicates: 4  Warnings: 0
```

However, in most cases, you want to know about possible problems (after all, primary keys are supposed to be unique), and so this IGNORE syntax is rarely used.

You'll notice that MySQL reports the results of bulk insertion differently from single insertion. From our initial bulk insertion, it reports:

```
Query OK, 4 rows affected (0.00 sec)
Records: 4  Duplicates: 0  Warnings: 0
```

The first line tells you how many rows were inserted, while the first entry in the final line tells you how many rows (or records) were actually processed. If you use INSERT IGNORE and try to insert a duplicate record—for which the primary key matches that of an existing row—then MySQL will quietly skip inserting it and report it as a duplicate in the second entry on the final line:

```
Query OK, 0 rows affected (0.01 sec)
Records: 4  Duplicates: 4  Warnings: 0
```

We discuss causes of warnings—shown as the third entry on the final line—in Chapter 6.

Alternative Syntaxes

There are several alternatives to the **VALUES** syntax we've shown you so far. This section shows you these and explains the advantages and drawbacks of each. If you're happy with the basic syntax we've described so far, and want to move on to a new topic, feel free to skip ahead to "The DELETE Statement."

There are three disadvantages of the **VALUES** syntax we've shown you. First, you need to remember the order of the columns. Second, you need to provide a value for each column. Last, it's closely tied to the underlying table structure: if you change the table's structure, you need to change the **INSERT** statements, and the function of the **INSERT** statement isn't obvious unless you have the table structure at hand. However, the three advantages of the approach are that it works for both single and bulk inserts, you get an error message if you forget to supply values for all columns, and you don't have to type in column names. Fortunately, the disadvantages are easily avoided by varying the syntax.

Suppose you know that the `album` table has three columns and you recall their names, but you forget their order. You can insert using the following approach:

```
mysql> INSERT INTO album (artist_id, album_id, album_name)
    -> VALUES (7, 2, "Oedipus Schmoedipus");
Query OK, 1 row affected (0.00 sec)
```

The column names are included in parentheses after the table name, and the values stored in those columns are listed in parentheses after the **VALUES** keyword. So, in this example, a new row is created and the value 7 is stored as the `artist_id`, 2 is stored as the `album_id`, and `Oedipus Schmoedipus` is stored as the `album_name`. The advantages of this syntax are that it's readable and flexible (addressing the third disadvantage we described) and order-independent (addressing the first disadvantage). The disadvantage is that you need to know the column names and type them in.

This new syntax can also address the second disadvantage of the simpler approach—that is, it can allow you to insert values for only some columns. To understand how this might be useful, let's explore the `played` table:

```
mysql> SHOW COLUMNS FROM played;
+-----------+-----------+------+-----+-------------------+-------+
| Field     | Type      | Null | Key | Default           | Extra |
+-----------+-----------+------+-----+-------------------+-------+
| artist_id | int(5)    |      | PRI | 0                 |       |
| album_id  | int(4)    |      | PRI | 0                 |       |
| track_id  | int(3)    |      | PRI | 0                 |       |
| played    | timestamp | YES  | PRI | CURRENT_TIMESTAMP |       |
```

```
+-----------+-----------+------+-----+------------------+-------+
```
4 rows in set (0.00 sec)

Notice that the played column has a default value of CURRENT_TIMESTAMP. This means that if you don't insert a value for the played column, it'll insert the current date and time by default. This is just what we want: when we play a track, we don't want to bother checking the date and time and typing it in. Here's how you insert an incomplete played entry:

```
mysql> INSERT INTO played (artist_id, album_id, track_id)
    -> VALUES (7, 1, 1);
Query OK, 1 row affected (0.00 sec)
```

We didn't set the played column, so MySQL defaults it to the current date and time. You can check this with a query:

```
mysql> SELECT * FROM played WHERE artist_id = 7
    -> AND album_id = 1;
+-----------+----------+----------+---------------------+
| artist_id | album_id | track_id | played              |
+-----------+----------+----------+---------------------+
|         7 |        1 |        1 | 2006-08-09 12:03:00 |
+-----------+----------+----------+---------------------+
1 row in set (0.00 sec)
```

You can also use this approach for bulk insertion as follows:

```
mysql> INSERT INTO played (artist_id, album_id, track_id)
    -> VALUES (7,1,2),(7,1,3),(7,1,4);
Query OK, 3 rows affected (0.00 sec)
Records: 3  Duplicates: 0  Warnings: 0
```

The disadvantages of this approach are that you can accidentally omit values for columns, and you need to remember and type column names. The omitted columns will be set to the default values.

All columns in a MySQL table have a default value of NULL unless another default value is explicitly assigned when the table is created or modified. Because of this, defaults can often cause duplicate rows: if you add a row with the default primary key values and repeat the process, you'll get a duplicate error. However, the default isn't always sensible; for example, in the played table, the artist_id, album_id, and track_id columns all default to 0, which doesn't make sense in the context of our music collection. Let's try adding a row to played with only default values:

```
mysql> INSERT INTO played () VALUES ();
Query OK, 1 row affected (0.00 sec)
```

The ( ) syntax is used to represent that all columns and values are to be set to their defaults. Let's find our new row by asking for the most recent played time:

```
mysql> SELECT * FROM played ORDER BY played DESC LIMIT 1;
+-----------+----------+----------+---------------------+
| artist_id | album_id | track_id | played              |
+-----------+----------+----------+---------------------+
```

```
|          0 |         0 |         0 | 2006-08-09 12:20:40 |
+-----------+----------+----------+---------------------+
1 row in set (0.00 sec)
```

The process worked, but the row doesn't make any sense. We'll discuss default values further in Chapter 6.

You can set defaults and still use the original INSERT syntax with MySQL 4.0.3 or later by using the DEFAULT keyword. Here's an example that adds a played row:

```
mysql> INSERT INTO played VALUES (7, 1, 2, DEFAULT);
Query OK, 1 row affected (0.00 sec)
```

The keyword DEFAULT tells MySQL to use the default value for that column, and so the current date and time are inserted in our example. The advantages of this approach are that you can use the bulk-insert feature with default values, and you can never accidentally omit a column.

There's another alternative INSERT syntax. In this approach, you list the column name and value together, giving the advantage that you don't have to mentally map the list of values to the earlier list of columns. Here's an example that adds a new row to the played table:

```
mysql> INSERT INTO played
    -> SET artist_id = 7, album_id = 1, track_id = 1;
Query OK, 1 row affected (0.00 sec)
```

The syntax requires you list a table name, the keyword SET, and then column-equals-value pairs, separated by commas. Columns that aren't supplied are set to their default values. The disadvantages are again that you can accidentally omit values for columns, and that you need to remember and type in column names. A significant additional disadvantage is that you can't use this method for bulk insertion.

You can also insert using values returned from a query. We discuss this in Chapter 8.

The DELETE Statement

The DELETE statement is used to remove one or more rows from a database. We explain single-table deletes here, and discuss multi-table deletes—which remove data from two or more tables through one statement—in Chapter 8.

If you want to try out the steps in this section on your MySQL server, you'll need to reload your music database afterwards so that you can follow the examples in later sections. To do this, follow the steps you used in "Loading the Sample Databases" in Chapter 3 to load it in the first place.

DELETE Basics

The simplest use of DELETE is to remove all rows in a table. Suppose you want to empty your played table, perhaps because it's taking too much space or because you want to share your music database with someone else and they don't want your played data. You do this with:

```
mysql> DELETE FROM played;
Query OK, 19 rows affected (0.07 sec)
```

This removes all rows, including those we just added in "The INSERT Statement"; you can see that 19 rows have been affected.

The DELETE syntax doesn't include column names, since it's used to remove whole rows and not just values from a row. To reset or modify a value in a row, you use the UPDATE statement, described later in this chapter in "The UPDATE Statement." The DELETE statement doesn't remove the table itself. For example, having deleted all rows in the played table, you can still query the table:

```
mysql> SELECT * FROM played;
Empty set (0.00 sec)
```

Of course, you can also continue to explore its structure using DESCRIBE or SHOW CREATE TABLE, and insert new rows using INSERT. To remove a table, you use the DROP statement described in Chapter 6.

Using WHERE, ORDER BY, and LIMIT

If you've deleted rows in the previous section, reload your music database now. You need the rows in the played table restored for the examples in this section.

To remove one or more rows, but not all rows in a table, you use a WHERE clause. This works in the same way as it does for SELECT. For example, suppose you want to remove all rows from the played table with played dates and times earlier than August 15, 2006. You do this with:

```
mysql> DELETE FROM played WHERE played < "2006-08-15";
Query OK, 8 rows affected (0.00 sec)
```

The result is that the eight played rows that match the criteria are removed. Note that the date is enclosed in quotes and that the date format is *year*, *month*, *day*, separated by hyphens. MySQL supports several different ways of specifying times and dates but saves dates in this internationally friendly, easy-to-sort format (it's actually an ISO standard). MySQL can also reasonably interpret two-digit years, but we recommend against using them; remember all the work required to avoid the Y2K problem?

Suppose you want to remove an artist, his albums, and his album tracks. For example, let's remove everything by Miles Davis. Begin by finding out the artist_id from the artist table, which we'll use to remove data from all four tables:

```
mysql> SELECT artist_id FROM artist WHERE artist_name = "Miles Davis";
+-----------+
| artist_id |
+-----------+
|         3 |
```

```
+-----------+
1 row in set (0.00 sec)
```

Next, remove the row from the artist table:

```
mysql> DELETE FROM artist WHERE artist_id = 3;
Query OK, 1 row affected (0.00 sec)
```

Then, do the same thing for the album, track, and played tables:

```
mysql> DELETE FROM album WHERE artist_id = 3;
Query OK, 2 rows affected (0.01 sec)

mysql> DELETE FROM track WHERE artist_id = 3;
Query OK, 13 rows affected (0.01 sec)

mysql> DELETE FROM played WHERE artist_id = 3;
Query OK, 3 rows affected (0.00 sec)
```

Since all four tables can be joined using the artist_id column, you can accomplish this whole deletion process in a single DELETE statement; we show you how in Chapter 8.

You can use the ORDER BY and LIMIT clauses with DELETE. You usually do this when you want to limit the number of rows deleted, either so that the statement doesn't run for too long or because you want to keep a table to a specific size. Suppose your played table contains 10,528 rows, but you want to have at most 10,000 rows. In this situation, it may make sense to remove the 528 oldest rows, and you can do this with the following statement:

```
mysql> DELETE FROM played ORDER BY played LIMIT 528;
Query OK, 528 rows affected (0.23 sec)
```

The query sorts the rows by ascending play date and then deletes at most 528 rows, starting with the oldest. Typically, when you're deleting, you use LIMIT and ORDER BY together; it usually doesn't make sense to use them separately. Note that sorting large numbers of entries on a field that doesn't have an index can be quite slow. We discuss indexes in detail in "Keys and Indexes" in Chapter 6.

Removing All Rows with TRUNCATE

If you want to remove all rows in a table, there's a faster method than removing them with DELETE. By using the TRUNCATE TABLE statement, MySQL takes the shortcut of *dropping* the table—that is, removing the table structures and then re-creating them. When there are many rows in a table, this is much faster.

If you want to remove the data in the played table, you can write this:

```
mysql> TRUNCATE TABLE played;
Query OK, 0 rows affected (0.00 sec)
```

Notice that the number of rows affected is shown as zero: to quickly delete all the data in the table, MySQL doesn't count the number of rows that are deleted, so the number

---

shown (normally zero, but sometimes nonzero) does not reflect the actual number of rows deleted.

The `TRUNCATE TABLE` statement has two other limitations:

- It's actually identical to `DELETE` if you use InnoDB tables.
- It does not work with locking or transactions.

Table types, transactions, and locking are discussed in Chapter 7. In practice, none of these limitations affect most applications, and you can use `TRUNCATE TABLE` to speed up your processing. Of course, it's not common to delete whole tables during normal operation. An exception is temporary tables, which are used to temporarily store query results for a particular user session and can be deleted without losing the original data.

The UPDATE Statement

The `UPDATE` statement is used to change data. In this section, we show you how to update one or more rows in a single table. Multitable updates are discussed in Chapter 8.

If you've deleted rows from your `music` database, reload it by following the instructions in "Loading the Sample Databases" in Chapter 3. You need a copy of the unmodified `music` database to follow the examples in this section.

Examples

The simplest use of the `UPDATE` statement is to change all rows in a table. There isn't much need to change all rows from a table in the `music` database—any example is a little contrived—but let's do it anyway. To change the artist names to uppercase, you can use:

```
mysql> UPDATE artist SET artist_name = UPPER(artist_name);
Query OK, 6 rows affected (0.04 sec)
Rows matched: 6  Changed: 6  Warnings: 0
```

The function `UPPER( )` is a MySQL function that returns the uppercase version of the text passed as the parameter; for example, `New Order` is returned as `NEW ORDER`. You can see that all six artists are modified, since six rows are reported as affected. The function `LOWER( )` performs the reverse, converting all the text to lowercase.

The second row reported by an `UPDATE` statement shows the overall effect of the statement. In our example, you see:

```
Rows matched: 6  Changed: 6  Warnings: 0
```

The first column reports the number of rows that were retrieved as answers by the statement; in this case, since there's no `WHERE` or `LIMIT` clause, all six rows in the table match the query. The second column reports how many rows needed to be changed, and this is always equal to or less than the number of rows that match; in this example, since none of the strings are entirely in uppercase, all six rows are changed. If you repeat the statement, you'll see a different result:

```
mysql> UPDATE artist SET artist_name = UPPER(artist_name);
Query OK, 0 rows affected (0.00 sec)
Rows matched: 6  Changed: 0  Warnings: 0
```

This time, since all of the artists are already in uppercase, six rows still match the statement but none are changed. Note also the number of rows changed is always equal to the number of rows affected, as reported on the first line of the output.

Our previous example updates each value relative to its current value. You can also set columns to a single value. For example, if you want to set all played dates and times to the current date and time, you can use:

```
mysql> UPDATE played SET played = NULL;
Query OK, 11 rows affected (0.00 sec)
Rows matched: 11  Changed: 11  Warnings: 0
```

You'll recall from "Alternative Syntaxes" that since the default value of the played column is CURRENT_TIMESTAMP, passing a NULL value causes the current date and time to be stored instead. Since all rows match and all rows are changed (affected), you can see three 11s in the output.

Using WHERE, ORDER BY, and LIMIT

Often, you don't want to change all rows in a table. Instead, you want to update one or more rows that match a condition. As with SELECT and DELETE, the WHERE clause is used for the task. In addition, in the same way as with DELETE, you can use ORDER BY and LIMIT together to control how many rows are updated from an ordered list.

Let's try an example that modifies one row in a table. If you browse the album database, you'll notice an inconsistency for the two albums beginning with "Substance":

```
mysql> SELECT * FROM album WHERE album_name LIKE
    -> "Substance%";
+-----------+----------+------------------------+
| artist_id | album_id | album_name             |
+-----------+----------+------------------------+
|         1 |        2 | Substance (Disc 2)     |
|         1 |        6 | Substance 1987 (Disc 1) |
+-----------+----------+------------------------+
2 rows in set (0.00 sec)
```

They're actually part of the same two CD set, and the first-listed album is missing the year 1987, which is part of the title. To change it, you use an UPDATE command with a WHERE clause:

```
mysql> UPDATE album SET album_name = "Substance 1987 (Disc 2)"
    -> WHERE artist_id = 1 AND album_id = 2;
Query OK, 1 row affected (0.01 sec)
Rows matched: 1  Changed: 1  Warnings: 0
```

As expected, one row was matched, and one row was changed.

To control how many updates occur, you can use the combination of ORDER BY and LIMIT. As with DELETE, you would do this because you either want the statement to run for a controlled amount of time, or you want to modify only some rows. Suppose you want to set the 10 most recent played dates and times to the current date and time (the default). You do this with:

```
mysql> UPDATE played SET played = NULL ORDER BY played DESC LIMIT 10;
Query OK, 10 rows affected (0.00 sec)
Rows matched: 10  Changed: 10  Warnings: 0
```

You can see that 10 rows were matched and were changed.

The previous query also illustrates an important aspect of updates. As you've seen, updates have two phases: a matching phase—where rows are found that match the WHERE clause—and a modification phase, where the rows that need changing are updated. In our previous example, the ORDER BY played is used in the matching phase, to sort the data after it's read from the table. After that, the modification phase processes the first 10 rows, updating those that need to be changed. Since MySQL 4.0.13, the LIMIT clause controls the maximum number of rows that are matched. Prior to this, it controlled the maximum number of rows that were changed. The new implementation is better; under the old scheme, you had little control over the update processing time when many rows matched but few required changes.

Exploring Databases and Tables with SHOW and mysqlshow

We've already explained how you can use the SHOW command to obtain information on the structure of a database, its tables, and the table columns. In this section, we'll review the most common types of SHOW statement with brief examples using the music database. The mysqlshow command-line program performs the same function as several SHOW command variants, but without needing to start the monitor.

The SHOW DATABASES statement lists the databases you can access. If you've followed our sample database installation steps in Chapter 3 in "Loading the Sample Databases," your output should be as follows:

```
mysql> SHOW DATABASES;
+------------+
| Database   |
+------------+
| flight     |
| music      |
| mysql      |
| test       |
| university |
+------------+
5 rows in set (0.01 sec)
```

These are the databases that you can access with the USE command; as we explain in Chapter 9, you can't see databases for which you have no access privileges unless you have the global SHOW DATABASES privilege. You can get the same effect from the command line using the mysqlshow program:

```
$ mysqlshow --user=root --password=the_mysql_root_password
```

You can add a LIKE clause to SHOW DATABASES. This is useful only if you have many databases and want a short list as output. For example, to see databases beginning with m, type:

```
mysql> SHOW DATABASES LIKE "m%";
+----------------+
| Database (m%)  |
+----------------+
| music          |
| mysql          |
+----------------+
2 rows in set (0.00 sec)
```

The syntax of the LIKE statement is identical to that in its use in SELECT.

To see the statement used to create a database, you can use the SHOW CREATE DATABASE statement. For example, to see how music was created, type:

```
mysql> SHOW CREATE DATABASE music;
+----------+-----------------------------------------------------------------+
| Database | Create Database                                                 |
+----------+-----------------------------------------------------------------+
| music    | CREATE DATABASE music /*!40100 DEFAULT CHARACTER SET latin1 */   |
+----------+-----------------------------------------------------------------+
1 row in set (0.00 sec)
```

This is perhaps the least exciting SHOW statement; it only displays the statement:

```
CREATE DATABASE music
```

There are some additional keywords that are enclosed between the comment symbols /*! and */:

```
40100 DEFAULT CHARACTER SET latin1
```

These instructions contain MySQL-specific extensions to standard SQL that are unlikely to be understood by other database programs. A database server other than MySQL would ignore this comment text, and so the syntax is usable by both MySQL and other database server software. The optional number 40100 indicates the minimum version of MySQL that can process this particular instruction—in this case, version 4.01.00; older versions of MySQL ignore such instructions. You'll learn about creating databases in Chapter 6.

The SHOW TABLES statement lists the tables in a database. To check the tables in music, type:

```
mysql> SHOW TABLES FROM music;
+-----------------+
| Tables_in_music |
+-----------------+
| album           |
| artist          |
| played          |
| track           |
+-----------------+
4 rows in set (0.01 sec)
```

If you've already selected the music database with the USE music command, you can use the shortcut:

```
mysql> SHOW TABLES;
+-----------------+
| Tables_in_music |
+-----------------+
| album           |
| artist          |
| played          |
| track           |
+-----------------+
4 rows in set (0.01 sec)
```

You can get a similar result by specifying the database name to the mysqlshow program:

```
$ mysqlshow --user=root --password=the_mysql_root_password music
```

As with SHOW DATABASES, you can't see tables that you don't have privileges for. This means you can't see tables in a database you can't access, even if you have the SHOW DATABASES global privilege.

The SHOW COLUMNS statement lists the columns in a table. For example, to check the columns of track, type:

```
mysql> SHOW COLUMNS FROM track;
+------------+--------------+------+-----+---------+-------+
| Field      | Type         | Null | Key | Default | Extra |
+------------+--------------+------+-----+---------+-------+
| track_id   | int(3)       |      | PRI | 0       |       |
| track_name | char(128)    | YES  |     | NULL    |       |
| artist_id  | int(5)       |      | PRI | 0       |       |
| album_id   | int(4)       |      | PRI | 0       |       |
| time       | decimal(5,2) | YES  |     | NULL    |       |
+------------+--------------+------+-----+---------+-------+
5 rows in set (0.01 sec)
```

The output reports all column names, their types and sizes, whether they can be NULL, whether they are part of a key, their default value, and any extra information. Types, keys, NULL values, and defaults are discussed further in Chapter 6. If you haven't already chosen the music database with the USE command, then you can add the database name before the table name, as in music.track. Unlike the previous SHOW statements, you can always see all column names if you have access to a table; it doesn't matter that you don't have certain privileges for all columns. You can get a similar result by using mysqlshow with the database and table name:

```
$ mysqlshow --user=root --password=the_mysql_root_password music track
```

You can see the statement used to create a particular table using the SHOW CREATE TABLE statement; creating tables is a subject of Chapter 6. Some users prefer this output to that of SHOW COLUMNS, since it has the familiar format of a CREATE TABLE statement. Here's an example for the track table:

```
mysql> SHOW CREATE TABLE track;
+-------+------------------------------------------------------+
| Table | Create Table                                         |
+-------+------------------------------------------------------+
| track | CREATE TABLE `track` (                               |
|       |   `track_id` int(3) NOT NULL default '0',            |
|       |   `track_name` char(128) default NULL,               |
|       |   `artist_id` int(5) NOT NULL default '0',           |
|       |   `album_id` int(4) NOT NULL default '0',            |
|       |   `time` decimal(5,2) default NULL,                  |
|       |   PRIMARY KEY  (`artist_id`,`album_id`,`track_id`)   |
|       | ) ENGINE=MyISAM DEFAULT CHARSET=latin1               |
+-------+------------------------------------------------------+
```

We've reformatted the output slightly so it fits better in the book.

Exercises

All exercises here concern the music database. You'll find the table structures in "The Music Database" are a useful reference, or you can practice using the SHOW statement as you work your way through the tasks:

1. Use one or more SELECT statements to find out how many tracks are on New Order's *Brotherhood* album.

2. Using a join, list the albums that we own by the band New Order.

3. With INSERT statements, add the artist Leftfield to the database. For this new artist, add the album Leftism that has the following tracks:

    a. Release the Pressure (Time: 7.39)

    b. Afro-Melt (Time: 7.33)

    c. Melt (Time: 5.21)

    d. Song of Life (Time: 6.55)

    e. Original (Time: 6.00)

    f. Black Flute (Time: 3.46)

    g. Space Shanty (Time: 7.15)

    h. Inspection Check One (Time: 6.30)

    i. Storm 3000 (Time: 5.44)

    j. Open Up (Time: 6.52)

    k. 21st Century Poem (Time: 5.42)

    l. Bonus Track (Time: 1.22)

4. How long in minutes is the Leftism album you added in Question 3? Hint: use the SUM( ) aggregate function.

5. Change the time for the Original track on the Leftism album to 6.22.

6. Remove the Bonus Track from the Leftism album.

## CHAPTER 6

Working with Database Structures

This chapter shows you how to create your own databases, add and remove structures such as tables and indexes, and make choices about column types in your tables. It focuses on the syntax and features of SQL, and not the semantics of conceiving, specifying, and refining a database design; you'll find an introductory description of database design techniques in Chapter 4. To work through this chapter, you need to understand how to work with an existing database and its tables, as discussed in Chapter 5.

This chapter lists the structures in the sample music database used in this book; detail on how to load the database is presented in Chapter 2. If you've followed those instructions, you'll already have the database available and know how to restore the database after you've modified its structures.

When you finish this chapter, you'll have all the basics required to create, modify, and delete database structures. Together with the techniques you learned in Chapter 5, you'll have the skills to carry out a wide range of basic operations. Chapters 7, 8, and 9 cover skills that allow you to do more advanced operations with MySQL.

Creating and Using Databases

When you've finished designing a database, the first practical step to take with MySQL is to create it. You do this with the CREATE DATABASE statement. Suppose you want to create a database with the name lucy. Here's the statement you'd type in the monitor:

```
mysql> CREATE DATABASE lucy;
Query OK, 1 row affected (0.10 sec)
```

We assume here that you know how to connect to and use the monitor, as described in Chapter 3. We also assume that you're able to connect as the **root** user or as another user who can create, delete, and modify structures (you'll find a detailed discussion on user privileges in Chapter 9). Note that when you create the database, MySQL says that one row was affected. This isn't in fact a normal row in any specific database—but a new entry added to the list that you see with SHOW DATABASES.

Behind the scenes, MySQL creates a new directory under the data directory for the new database and stores the text file *db.opt* that lists the database options; for example, the file might contain:

```
default-character-set=latin1
default-collation=latin1_swedish_ci
```

These particular two lines specify the default character set and collation of the new database. We'll look at what these mean later, but you generally won't need to know much about the *db.opt* file or access it directly.

Once you've created the database, the next step is to use it—that is, choose it as the database you're working with. You do this with the MySQL command:

```
mysql> USE lucy;
Database changed
```

As discussed previously in Chapter 5, this command must be entered on one line and need not be terminated with a semicolon, though we usually do so automatically through habit. Once you've used the database, you can start creating tables, indexes, and other structures using the steps discussed next in "Creating Tables."

Before we move on to creating other structures, let's discuss a few features and limitations of creating databases. First, let's see what happens if you create a database that already exists:

```
mysql> CREATE DATABASE lucy;
ERROR 1007 (HY000): Can't create database 'lucy'; database exists
```

You can avoid this error by adding the IF NOT EXISTS keyword phrase to the statement:

```
mysql> CREATE DATABASE IF NOT EXISTS lucy;
Query OK, 0 rows affected (0.00 sec)
```

You can see that MySQL didn't complain, but it didn't do anything either: the 0 rows affected message indicates that no data was changed. This addition is useful when you're adding SQL statements to a script: it prevents the script from aborting on error.

Let's discuss how to choose database names and the use of character case. Database names define physical directory (or folder) names on disk. On some operating systems, directory names are case-sensitive; on others, case doesn't matter. For example, Unix-like systems such as Linux and Mac OS X are typically case-sensitive, while Windows isn't. The result is that database names have the same restrictions: when case matters to the operating system, it matters to MySQL. For example, on a Linux machine, LUCY, lucy, and Lucy are different database names; on Windows, they refer to just one database. Using incorrect capitalization under Linux or Mac OS X will cause MySQL to complain:

```
mysql> select artIst.Artist_id from ARTist;
ERROR 1146 (42S02): Table 'music.ARTist' doesn't exist
```

but under Windows, this will normally work. To make your SQL machine-independent, we recommend that you consistently use lowercase names for databases (and for tables, columns, aliases, and indexes).

There are other restrictions on database names. They can be at most 64 characters in length. You also shouldn't use MySQL reserved words—such as SELECT, FROM, and USE —as names for structures; these can confuse the MySQL parser, making it impossible to interpret the meaning of your statements. There's a way around this problem: you can enclose the reserved word with the backtick symbol (') on either side, but it's more trouble remembering to do so than it's worth. In addition, you can't use selected characters in the names: specifically, you can't use the forward slash, backward slash, semicolon, and period characters, and a database name can't end in whitespace. Again, the use of these characters confuses the MySQL parser and can result in unpredictable behavior. For example, here's what happens when you insert a semicolon into a database name:

```
mysql> CREATE DATABASE IF NOT EXISTS lu;cy;
Query OK, 1 row affected (0.00 sec)

ERROR 1064 (42000): You have an error in your SQL syntax.  Check the manual
that corresponds to your MySQL server version for the right syntax to use
near 'cy' at line 1
```

Since more than one SQL statement can be on a single line, the result is that a database lu is created, and then an error is generated by the very short, unexpected SQL statement cy;.

Creating Tables

This section covers topics on table structures. We show you how to:

- Create tables, through introductory examples
- Choose names for tables and table-related structures
- Understand and choose column types
- Understand and choose keys and indexes
- Use the proprietary MySQL AUTO_INCREMENT feature

When you finish this section, you'll have completed all of the basic material on creating database structures; the remainder of this chapter covers the sample music database used in the book, and how to alter and remove existing structures.

Basics

For our examples in this section, we'll assume that the database music hasn't been created. If you want to follow the examples, and you have already loaded the database, you can drop it for this section and reload it later; dropping it removes the database, tables, and all of the data, but the original is easy to restore by following the steps in Chapter 2. Here's how you drop it temporarily:

```
mysql> DROP DATABASE music;
Query OK, 4 rows affected (0.06 sec)
```

The DROP statement is discussed further at the end of this chapter in "Deleting Structures."

To begin, create the database music using the statement:

```
mysql> CREATE DATABASE music;
Query OK, 1 row affected (0.00 sec)
```

Then select the database with:

```
mysql> USE music;
Database changed
```

We're now ready to begin creating the tables that'll hold our data. Let's create a table to hold artist details. Here's the statement that we use:

```
mysql> CREATE TABLE artist (
    -> artist_id SMALLINT(5) NOT NULL DEFAULT 0,
    -> artist_name CHAR(128) DEFAULT NULL,
    -> PRIMARY KEY (artist_id)
    -> );


Query OK, 0 rows affected (0.06 sec)
```

Don't panic: even though MySQL reports that zero rows were affected, it's definitely created the table:

```
mysql> SHOW TABLES;
+-----------------+
| Tables_in_music |
+-----------------+
| artist          |
+-----------------+
1 row in set (0.00 sec)
```

Let's consider all this in detail. The CREATE TABLE statement has three major sections:

1. The CREATE TABLE statement, which is followed by the table name to create. In this example, it's artist.
2. A list of one or more columns to add to the table. In this example, we've added two: artist_id SMALLINT(5) NOT NULL DEFAULT 0 and artist_name CHAR(128) default NULL. We'll discuss these in a moment.
3. Optional key definitions. In this example, we've defined a single key: PRIMARY KEY (artist_id). We'll discuss keys and indexes in detail later in this section.

Notice that the CREATE TABLE component is followed by an opening parenthesis that's matched by a closing parenthesis at the end of the statement. Notice also that the other

---

components are separated by commas. There are other elements that you can add to a CREATE TABLE statement, and we'll discuss some in a moment.

Let's discuss the column specifications. The basic syntax is as follows: *name type* [NOT NULL | NULL] [DEFAULT *value*]. The *name* field is the column name, and it has the same limitations as database names, as discussed in the previous section. It can be at most 64 characters in length, backward and forward slashes aren't allowed, periods aren't allowed, it can't end in whitespace, and case sensitivity is dependent on the underlying operating system. The *type* defines how and what is stored in the column; for example, we've seen that it can be set to CHAR for strings, SMALLINT for numbers, or TIMESTAMP for a date and time.

If you specify NOT NULL, a row isn't valid without a value for the column; if you specify NULL or omit the clause, a row can exist without a value for the column. If you specify a *value* with the DEFAULT clause, it'll be used to populate the column when you don't otherwise provide data; this is particularly useful when you frequently reuse a default value such as a country name. The *value* must be a constant (such as 0, "cat", or 20060812045623), except if the column is of the type TIMESTAMP. Types are discussed in detail later in this section.

The NOT NULL and DEFAULT features can be used together. If you specify NOT NULL and add a DEFAULT value, the default is used when you don't provide a value for the column. Sometimes, this works fine:

```
mysql> INSERT INTO artist SET artist_name = "Duran Duran";
Query OK, 1 row affected (0.05 sec)
```

And sometimes it doesn't:

```
mysql> INSERT INTO artist SET artist_name = "Bob The Builder";
ERROR 1062 (23000): Duplicate entry '0' for key 1
```

Whether it works or not is dependent on the underlying constraints and conditions of the database: in this example, artist_id has a default value of 0, but it's also the primary key. Having two rows with the same primary-key value isn't permitted, and so the second attempt to insert a row with no values (and a resulting primary-key value of 0) fails. We discuss primary keys in detail later in this section.

Column names have fewer restrictions than database and table names. What's more, they're not dependent on the operating system: the names are case-insensitive and portable across all platforms. All characters are allowed in column names, though if you want terminate them with whitespace or include periods (or other special characters such as the semicolon), you'll need to enclose the name with a backtick symbol (`) on either side. We recommend that you consistently choose lowercase names for developer-driven choices (such as database, alias, and table names) and avoid characters that require you to remember to use backticks. We also recommend being descriptive with your choices: name doesn't mean much outside of the context of the artist table, but artist_name has universal meaning across the music database. We like using the underscore character to separate words, but that's just a matter of style and taste; you could use underscores or dashes, or omit the word-separating formatting altogether. As with database and table names, the longest column name is 64 characters in length.

Collation and Character Sets

Because not everyone wants to store English strings, it's important that a database server be able to manage non-English characters and different ways of sorting characters. When you're comparing or sorting strings, how MySQL evaluates the result depends on the *character set* and *collation* used. Character sets define what characters can be stored; for example, you may need to store non-English characters such as Î or ü. A collation defines how strings are ordered, and there are different collations for different languages: for example, the position of the character ü in the alphabet is different in two German orderings, and different again in Swedish and Finnish.

In our previous string-comparison examples, we ignored the collation and character-set issue, and just let MySQL use its defaults; the default character set is `latin1`, and the default collation is `latin1_swedish_ci`. MySQL can be configured to use different character sets and collation orders at the connection, database, table, and column levels.

You can list the character sets available on your server with the `SHOW CHARACTER SET` command. This shows a short description for each character set, its default collation, and the maximum number of bytes used for each character in that character set:

```
mysql> SHOW CHARACTER SET;
+----------+-----------------------------+---------------------+--------+
| Charset  | Description                 | Default collation   | Maxlen |
+----------+-----------------------------+---------------------+--------+
| big5     | Big5 Traditional Chinese    | big5_chinese_ci     | 2      |
| dec8     | DEC West European           | dec8_swedish_ci     | 1      |
| cp850    | DOS West European           | cp850_general_ci    | 1      |
| hp8      | HP West European            | hp8_english_ci      | 1      |
| koi8r    | KOI8-R Relcom Russian       | koi8r_general_ci    | 1      |
| latin1   | cp1252 West European        | latin1_swedish_ci   | 1      |
| latin2   | ISO 8859-2 Central European | latin2_general_ci   | 1      |
| swe7     | 7bit Swedish                | swe7_swedish_ci     | 1      |
| ascii    | US ASCII                    | ascii_general_ci    | 1      |
| ujis     | EUC-JP Japanese             | ujis_japanese_ci    | 3      |
| sjis     | Shift-JIS Japanese          | sjis_japanese_ci    | 2      |
| hebrew   | ISO 8859-8 Hebrew           | hebrew_general_ci   | 1      |
| tis620   | TIS620 Thai                 | tis620_thai_ci      | 1      |
| euckr    | EUC-KR Korean               | euckr_korean_ci     | 2      |
| koi8u    | KOI8-U Ukrainian            | koi8u_general_ci    | 1      |
| gb2312   | GB2312 Simplified Chinese   | gb2312_chinese_ci   | 2      |
| greek    | ISO 8859-7 Greek            | greek_general_ci    | 1      |
| cp1250   | Windows Central European    | cp1250_general_ci   | 1      |
| gbk      | GBK Simplified Chinese      | gbk_chinese_ci      | 2      |
| latin5   | ISO 8859-9 Turkish          | latin5_turkish_ci   | 1      |
| armscii8 | ARMSCII-8 Armenian          | armscii8_general_ci | 1      |
| utf8     | UTF-8 Unicode               | utf8_general_ci     | 3      |
```

```
| ucs2     | UCS-2 Unicode              | ucs2_general_ci     | 2 |
| cp866    | DOS Russian               | cp866_general_ci    | 1 |
| keybcs2  | DOS Kamenicky Czech-Slovak | keybcs2_general_ci  | 1 |
| macce    | Mac Central European       | macce_general_ci    | 1 |
| macroman | Mac West European          | macroman_general_ci | 1 |
| cp852    | DOS Central European       | cp852_general_ci    | 1 |
| latin7   | ISO 8859-13 Baltic         | latin7_general_ci   | 1 |
| cp1251   | Windows Cyrillic           | cp1251_general_ci   | 1 |
| cp1256   | Windows Arabic             | cp1256_general_ci   | 1 |
| cp1257   | Windows Baltic             | cp1257_general_ci   | 1 |
| binary   | Binary pseudo charset      | binary              | 1 |
| geostd8  | GEOSTD8 Georgian           | geostd8_general_ci  | 1 |
| cp932    | SJIS for Windows Japanese  | cp932_japanese_ci   | 2 |
| eucjpms  | UJIS for Windows Japanese  | eucjpms_japanese_ci | 3 |
+----------+----------------------------+---------------------+--------+
36 rows in set (0.30 sec)
```

For example, the `latin1` character set is actually the Windows code page 1252 that supports West European languages. The default collation for this character set is `latin1_swedish_ci`, which follows Swedish conventions to sort accented characters (English is handled as you'd expect). This collation is case-insensitive, as indicated by the letters `ci`. Finally, each character takes up one byte. By comparison, if you use the `ucs2` character set, each character would take up to two bytes of storage.

Similarly, you can list the collation orders and the character sets they apply to:

```
mysql> SHOW COLLATION;
+---------------------+----------+-----+---------+----------+---------+
| Collation           | Charset  | Id  | Default | Compiled | Sortlen |
+---------------------+----------+-----+---------+----------+---------+
| big5_chinese_ci     | big5     | 1   | Yes     | Yes      | 1       |
...
| latin1_german1_ci   | latin1   | 5   |         |          | 0       |
| latin1_swedish_ci   | latin1   | 8   | Yes     | Yes      | 1       |
| latin1_danish_ci    | latin1   | 15  |         |          | 0       |
| latin1_german2_ci   | latin1   | 31  |         | Yes      | 2       |
| latin1_bin          | latin1   | 47  |         | Yes      | 1       |
| latin1_general_ci   | latin1   | 48  |         |          | 0       |
| latin1_general_cs   | latin1   | 49  |         |          | 0       |
..
| hebrew_general_ci   | hebrew   | 16  | Yes     |          | 0       |
...
| gb2312_chinese_ci   | gb2312   | 24  | Yes     | Yes      | 1       |
...
| utf8_persian_ci     | utf8     | 208 |         | Yes      | 8       |
| utf8_esperanto_ci   | utf8     | 209 |         | Yes      | 8       |
...
| eucjpms_japanese_ci | eucjpms  | 97  | Yes     | Yes      | 1       |
| eucjpms_bin         | eucjpms  | 98  |         | Yes      | 1       |
+---------------------+----------+-----+---------+----------+---------+
126 rows in set (0.02 sec)
```

You can see the current defaults on your server as follows:

```
mysql> SHOW VARIABLES LIKE 'c%';
+--------------------------+----------------------------+
| Variable_name            | Value                      |
+--------------------------+----------------------------+
| character_set_client     | latin1                     |
| character_set_connection | latin1                     |
| character_set_database   | latin1                     |
| character_set_filesystem | binary                     |
| character_set_results    | latin1                     |
| character_set_server     | latin1                     |
| character_set_system     | utf8                       |
| character_sets_dir       | /usr/share/mysql/charsets/ |
| collation_connection     | latin1_swedish_ci          |
| collation_database       | latin1_swedish_ci          |
| collation_server         | latin1_swedish_ci          |
...
+--------------------------+----------------------------+
14 rows in set (0.00 sec)
```

When you're creating a database, you can set the default character set and sort order for the database and its tables. For example, if you want to use the latin1 character set and the latin1_swedish_cs (case-sensitive) collation order, you would write:

```
mysql> CREATE DATABASE rose DEFAULT CHARACTER SET latin1 COLLATE latin1_swedish_cs;
Query OK, 1 row affected (0.00 sec)
```

As we've previously discussed, there's no need to do this if you've installed your MySQL correctly for your language and region, and if you're not planning on internationalizing your application. You can also control the character set and collation for individual tables or columns, but we won't go into the detail of how to do that here.

Other Features

This section briefly describes other features of the MySQL CREATE TABLE statement. It includes an example using the IF NOT EXISTS feature, and a list of advanced features and where to find more about them in this book.

You can use the IF NOT EXISTS keyword phrase when creating a table, and it works much as it does for databases. Here's an example that won't report an error even when the artist table exists:

```
mysql> CREATE TABLE IF NOT EXISTS artist (
    -> artist_id SMALLINT(5) NOT NULL DEFAULT 0,
    -> artist_name CHAR(128) DEFAULT NULL,
    -> PRIMARY KEY (artist_id)
    -> );

Query OK, 0 rows affected (0.00 sec)
```

It's actually hard to tell success from failure here: zero rows are affected whether or not the table exists, and no warning is reported when the table does exist.

There are a wide range of additional features you can add to a CREATE TABLE statement. Many of these are advanced and aren't discussed in this book, but you can find more information in the MySQL manual under the heading "CREATE TABLE syntax." These additional features include:

The AUTO_INCREMENT *feature for numeric columns*
> This feature allows you to automatically create unique identifiers for a table. We discuss it in detail later in this chapter in "The AUTO_INCREMENT Feature."

Column comments
> You can add a comment to a column; this is displayed when you use the SHOW CREATE TABLE command that we discuss later in this section.

Foreign key constraints
> You can tell MySQL to check whether data in one or more columns matches data in another table. For example, you might want to prevent an album from being added to the music database unless there's a matching artist in the artist table. As we explain in "Table Types," we don't recommend using foreign key constraints for most applications. This feature is currently supported for only the InnoDB table type.

Creating temporary tables
> If you create a table using the keyword phrase CREATE TEMPORARY TABLE, it'll be removed (*dropped*) when the monitor connection is closed. This is useful for copying and reformatting data because you don't have to remember to clean up.

Advanced table options
> You can control a wide range of features of the table using table options. These include the starting value of AUTO_INCREMENT, the way indexes and rows are stored, and options to override the information that the MySQL query optimizer gathers from the table.

Control over index structures
> Since MySQL 4.1, for some table types, you've been able to control what type of internal structure—such as a B-tree or hash table—MySQL uses for its indexes. You can also tell MySQL that you want a full text or spatial data index on a column, allowing special types of search.

You can check the CREATE TABLE statement for a table using the SHOW CREATE TABLE statement introduced in Chapter 5. This often shows you output that includes some of the advanced features we've just discussed; the output rarely matches what you actually typed to create the table. Here's an example for the artist table:

```
mysql> SHOW CREATE TABLE artist;
+--------+---------------------------------------------------+
| Table  | Create Table                                      |
+--------+---------------------------------------------------+
| artist | CREATE TABLE `artist` (
           `artist_id` smallint(5) NOT NULL default '0',
           `artist_name` char(128) default NULL,
```

```
        PRIMARY KEY (`artist_id`)
        ) ENGINE=MyISAM DEFAULT CHARSET=latin1         |
+--------+----------------------------------------------------+
1 row in set (0.08 sec)
```

We've reformatted the output slightly to fit better in this book. You'll notice that the output includes content added by MySQL that wasn't in our original CREATE TABLE statement:

- The names of the table and columns are enclosed in backticks. This isn't necessary, but it does avoid any parsing problems that can occur through using reserved words and special characters, as discussed previously

- An additional default ENGINE clause is included, which explicitly states the *table type* that should be used. The setting in a default installation of MySQL is MyISAM, so it has no effect in this example

- An additional DEFAULT CHARSET=latin1 clause is included, which tells MySQL what character set is used by the columns in the table. Again, this has no effect in a default, Latin-character-set-based installation

Column Types

This section describes the column types you can use in MySQL. It explains when each should be used and any limitations it has. We've ordered the choices in two sections: first, the commonly used, and, second, the less frequently used choices. Skip the second part if you want to and revisit it when one of the common choices doesn't fit your needs; it's certainly worth reviewing when you're tackling the exercises at the end of this chapter.

Common column types

The following are the six commonly used column types in MySQL tables:

INT[(*width*)] [UNSIGNED] [ZEROFILL]
 The most commonly used numeric type. Stores integer (whole number) values in the range –2,147,483,648 to 2,147,483,647. If the optional UNSIGNED keyword is added, the range is 0 to 4,294,967,295. The keyword INT is short for INTEGER, and they can be used interchangeably. An INT column requires four bytes of storage space.

 You can also include optional *width* and ZEROFILL arguments to left-pad the values with zeros up to the specified length. The maximum *width* is 255. The *width* parameter has no effect on what is stored. If you store a value wider than the *width*, the *width* value is ignored. Consider this example:

```
mysql> CREATE TABLE numbers (my_number INT(4) ZEROFILL );
Query OK, 0 rows affected (0.01 sec)

mysql> INSERT INTO numbers VALUES(3),(33),(333),(3333),(33333),(333333);
```

```
Query OK, 6 rows affected (0.00 sec)
Records: 6  Duplicates: 0  Warnings: 0

mysql> SELECT * FROM numbers;
+-----------+
| my_number |
+-----------+
| 0003      |
| 0033      |
| 0333      |
| 3333      |
| 33333     |
| 333333    |
+-----------+
6 rows in set (0.00 sec)
```

You can see that numbers shorter than four digits wide are zero-padded to four digits; once the numbers are longer than four digits long, they are shown unaffected by the width and the ZEROFILL parameters.

If you use ZEROFILL, MySQL automatically adds UNSIGNED to the declaration (since zero filling makes sense only in the context of positive numbers).

DECIMAL[(*width*[,*decimals*])] [UNSIGNED] [ZEROFILL]

A commonly used numeric type. Stores a fixed-point number such as a salary or distance, with a total of *width* digits of which some smaller number are *decimals* that follow a decimal point. For example, a column declared as price DECI MAL(4,2) should be used to store values in the range –99.99 to 99.99. If you try to store a value that's outside this range, it will be stored as the closest value in the allowed range. For example, 100 would be stored as 99.99, and –100 would be stored as –99.99. Note that MySQL versions before 5.03 would allow an extra digit for positive values (numbers from –99.99 to 999.99 could be stored). The *width* is optional, and a value of 10 is assumed when this is omitted. The maximum value of *width* is 255.

The number of *decimals* is optional and, when omitted, a value of 0 is assumed; the maximum value of *decimals* should be two less than the value of *width*. If you're storing only positive values, use the UNSIGNED keyword as described for INT. If you want zero padding, use the ZEROFILL keyword for the same behavior as described for INT. The keyword DECIMAL has three identical, interchangeable alternatives: DEC, NUMERIC, and FIXED.

Prior to MySQL version 5.0.3, a DECIMAL column was stored as a string, and so required exactly the number of bytes of storage space as the length of the value (plus up to two bytes for a minus sign and a decimal point if required). Beginning with version 5.0.3, a binary format was introduced that uses four bytes for every nine digits. Under both approaches, the value retrieved is identical to the value stored; this isn't always the case with other types that contain decimal points, such as the FLOAT and DOUBLE types described later.

DATE

Stores and displays a date in the format *YYYY-MM-DD* for the range 1000-01-01 to 9999-12-31. Dates must always be input as year, month, and day triples, but the format of the input can vary, as shown in the following examples:

YYYY-MM-DD or *YY-MM-DD*

It's optional whether you provide two-digit or four-digit years. We strongly recommend that you use the four-digit version to avoid confusion about the century. In practice, if you use the two-digit version, you'll find that 70 to 99 are interpreted as 1970 to 1999, and 00 to 69 are interpreted as 2000 to 2069.

YYYY/MM/DD, *YYYY:MM:DD*, *YY/MM/DD*, or other punctuated formats

MySQL allows any punctuation characters to separate the components of a date. We recommend using dashes and, again, avoiding the two-digit years.

YYYY-M-D, *YYYY-MM-D*, or *YYYY-M-DD*

When punctuation is used (again, any punctuation character is allowed), single-digit days and months can be specified as such. For example, February 2, 2006, can be specified as `2006-2-2`. The two-digit year equivalent is available, but not recommended.

YYYYMMDD or *YYMMDD*

Punctuation can be omitted in both date styles, but the digit sequences must be six or eight digits in length.

You can also input a date by providing both a date and time in the formats described later for `DATETIME` and `TIMESTAMP`, but only the date component is stored in a `DATE` type column. Regardless of the input type, the storage and display type is always *YYYY-MM-DD*. The *zero date* 0000-00-00 is allowed in all versions and can be used to represent an unknown or dummy value. If an input date is out of range, the zero date 0000-00-00 is stored. By default, from MySQL 5.0.2 onward, the zero date is stored when you insert an invalid date such as `2007-02-31`. Prior to that version, invalid dates are stored provided the month is in the range 0 to 12, and the day is in the range 0 to 31. Consider this example:

```
mysql> CREATE TABLE testdate (mydate DATE);
Query OK, 0 rows affected (0.00 sec)

mysql> INSERT INTO testdate VALUES ('2007/02/0');
Query OK, 1 row affected (0.00 sec)

mysql> INSERT INTO testdate VALUES ('2007/02/1');
Query OK, 1 row affected (0.00 sec)

mysql> INSERT INTO testdate VALUES ('2007/02/31');
Query OK, 1 row affected (0.00 sec)

mysql> INSERT INTO testdate VALUES ('2007/02/100');
Query OK, 1 row affected, 1 warning (0.00 sec)
```

With a version of MySQL older than 5.0.2, we would have:

```
mysql> SELECT * FROM testdate;
+------------+
| mydate     |
+------------+
| 2007-02-00 |
| 2007-02-01 |
| 2007-02-31 |
| 0000-00-00 |
+------------+
4 rows in set (0.00 sec)
```

while with version 5.0.2 onwards, we have:

```
mysql> SELECT * FROM testdate;
+------------+
| mydate     |
+------------+
| 2007-02-00 |
| 2007-02-01 |
| 0000-00-00 |
| 0000-00-00 |
+------------+
4 rows in set (0.01 sec)
```

Note also that the date is displayed in the *YYYY-MM-DD* format, regardless of how it was input.

TIME

Stores a time in the format *HHH:MM:SS* for the range -838:59:59 to 838:59:59. The values that can be stored are outside the range of the 24-hour clock to allow large differences between time values (up to 34 days, 22 hours, 59 minutes, and 59 seconds) to be computed and stored. Times must always be input in the order *days*, *hours*, *minutes*, and *seconds*, using the following formats:

DD HH:MM:SS, *HH:MM:SS*, *DD HH:MM*, *HH:MM*, *DD HH*, or *SS*

The *DD* represents a one-digit or two-digit value of days in the range 0 to 34. The *DD* value is separated from the hour value, *HH*, by a space, while the other components are separated by a colon. Note that *MM:SS* is not a valid combination, since it cannot be disambiguated from *HH:MM*.

For example, if you insert 2 13:25:59 into a TIME type column, the value 61:25:59 is stored, since the sum of 2 days (48 hours) and 13 hours is 61 hours. If you try inserting a value that's out of bounds, a warning is generated, and the value is limited to the maximum time available. Similarly, if you try inserting an incorrect value, a warning is generated and the value is set to zero. You can use the SHOW WARNINGS command to reports the details of the warning generated by the previous SQL statement.

Let's try all these out in practice:

```
mysql  CREATE TABLE test_time(id SMALLINT, mytime TIME);
Query OK, 0 rows affected (0.00 sec)

mysql  INSERT INTO test_time VALUES(1, "2 13:25:59");
```

```
Query OK, 1 row affected (0.00 sec)

mysql  INSERT INTO test_time VALUES(2, "35 13:25:59");
Query OK, 1 row affected, 1 warning (0.00 sec)

mysql  SHOW WARNINGS;
+---------+------+---------------------------------------------------------------+
| Level   | Code | Message                                                       |
+---------+------+---------------------------------------------------------------+
| Warning | 1264 | Out of range value adjusted for column 'mytime' at row 1 |
+---------+------+---------------------------------------------------------------+
1 row in set (0.00 sec)

mysql  INSERT INTO test_time VALUES(3, "-35 13:25:59");
Query OK, 1 row affected, 1 warning (0.00 sec)

mysql  INSERT INTO test_time VALUES(4, "35 13:25:69");
Query OK, 1 row affected, 1 warning (0.00 sec)

mysql  SHOW WARNINGS;
+---------+------+-------------------------------------------------+
| Level   | Code | Message                                         |
+---------+------+-------------------------------------------------+
| Warning | 1265 | Data truncated for column 'mytime' at row 1 |
+---------+------+-------------------------------------------------+
1 row in set (0.00 sec)

mysql  SELECT * FROM test_time;
+----+------------+
| id | mytime     |
+----+------------+
| 1  | 61:25:59   |
| 2  | 838:59:59  |
| 3  | -838:59:59 |
| 4  | 00:00:00   |
+----+------------+
4 rows in set (0.00 sec)
```

Note how the out-of-range and invalid times are stored.

H:M:S, and single-, double-, and triple-digit combinations

You can use different combinations of digits when inserting or updating data; MySQL converts them into the internal time format and displays them consistently. For example, 1:1:3 is equivalent to 01:01:03. Different numbers of digits can be mixed; for example, 1:12:3 is equivalent to 01:12:03. Consider these examples:

```
mysql> CREATE TABLE mytime (testtime TIME);
Query OK, 0 rows affected (0.12 sec)

mysql> INSERT INTO mytime VALUES
    -> ('-1:1:1'), ('1:1:1'),
    -> ('1:23:45'), ('123:4:5'),
    -> ('123:45:6'), ('-123:45:6');
Query OK, 4 rows affected (0.00 sec)
```

```
Records: 4  Duplicates: 0  Warnings: 0

mysql> SELECT * FROM mytime;
+------------+
| testtime   |
+------------+
| -01:01:01  |
| 01:01:01   |
| 01:23:45   |
| 123:04:05  |
| 123:45:06  |
| -123:45:06 |
+------------+
5 rows in set (0.01 sec)
```

Note that hours are shown with two digits for values within the range –99 to +99.

HHMMSS, *MMSS*, and *SS*

Punctuation can be omitted, but the digit sequences must be two, four, or six digits in length. Note that the rightmost pair of digits is always interpreted as a *SS* (seconds) value, the second next rightmost pair (if present) as *MM* (minutes), and the third rightmost pair (if present) as *HH* (hours). The result is that a value such as 1222 is interpreted as 12 minutes and 22 seconds, not 12 hours and 22 minutes.

You can also input a time by providing both a date and time in the formats described for DATETIME and TIMESTAMP, but only the time component is stored in a TIME type column. Regardless of the input type, the storage and display type is always *HH:MM:SS*. The *zero time* 00:00:00 can be used to represent an unknown or dummy value. If an input date is invalid or out of range, the zero time 00:00:00 is stored. The TIME type has an additional *fraction* component for storing fractions of seconds, but, while a time value can be input with a fractional component, it is presently truncated before storage by MySQL; we've therefore omitted it from our discussions.

TIMESTAMP

Stores and displays a date and time pair in the format *YYYY-MM-DD HH:MM:SS* for the range 1970-01-01 00:00:00 to sometime in 2037. The behavior of this type has varied over the life of MySQL (and continues to do so!), and this section describes only the version implemented since MySQL 4.1. The key features of a TIMESTAMP column are twofold. First, if you assign NULL to it, it's set to the current date and time. Second, a developer-selected TIMESTAMP column in a table can be automatically updated to the current date and time when a row is inserted or updated. You can always explicitly set a column to a value you want by assigning that value to the column, regardless of whether it's the automatically updating column. The automatic update feature is discussed later in this section. A nonupdating near-equivalent is the DATETIME type described later in this section.

The value stored always matches the template *YYYY-MM-DD HH:MM:SS*, but the value can be provided in a wide range of formats:

YYYY-MM-DD HH:MM:SS or *YY-MM-DD HH:MM:SS*

The date and time components follow the same relaxed restrictions as the `DATE` and `TIME` components described previously (however, as of MySQL 5.0.2, zero values aren't permitted). This includes allowance for any punctuation characters, including (unlike `TIME`) flexibility in the punctuation used in the time component. For example, 2005/02/15 12+22+23 is valid.

YYYYMMDDHHMMSS or *YYMMDDHHMMSS*

Punctuation can be omitted, but the string should be either 12 or 14 digits in length. We recommend only the unambiguous 14-digit version, for the reasons discussed for the `DATE` type. You can specify values with other lengths without providing separators, but we don't recommend doing so.

Let's discuss the automatic-update feature in detail. Only one `TIMESTAMP` column per table can be automatically set to the current date and time on insert or update. You control this by following these steps when creating a table:

1. Choose the column you want to be automatically updated.

2. If you have other `TIMESTAMP` columns in the table, set the ones that precede the selected column in the `CREATE TABLE` statement to have a constant default (such as `DEFAULT 0`).

3. For the automatically updating column, decide which behavior you want:

   a. If you want the timestamp to be set only when a new row is inserted into the table, add `DEFAULT CURRENT_TIMESTAMP` to the end of the column declaration.

   b. If you don't want a default timestamp but want the current time to be used whenever the data in a row is updated, add `ON UPDATE CURRENT_TIMESTAMP` to the end of the column declaration.

   c. If you want both of the above—that is, you want the timestamp to be set to the current time in each new row or whenever an existing row is modified— add `DEFAULT CURRENT_TIMESTAMP ON UPDATE CURRENT_TIMESTAMP` to the end of the column declaration.

If you specify `DEFAULT NULL` for a `TIMESTAMP` column, it will be interpreted differently depending on whether there are any other `TIMESTAMP` columns before it in the table. `DEFAULT NULL` is handled as `DEFAULT CURRENT_TIMESTAMP` for the first timestamp column, but as `DEFAULT 0` for any subsequent ones.

Consider this example:

```
mysql> CREATE TABLE mytime(id INT NOT NULL,
    -> changetime TIMESTAMP DEFAULT CURRENT_TIMESTAMP ON UPDATE CURRENT_TIMESTAMP);
Query OK, 0 rows affected (0.00 sec)

mysql> INSERT INTO mytime VALUES(1,''),(2,'2006-07-16 1:2:3'),(3,NULL);
Query OK, 3 rows affected, 2 warnings (0.01 sec)
```

```
Records: 3  Duplicates: 0  Warnings: 2

mysql> SELECT * FROM mytime;
+----+---------------------+
| id | changetime          |
+----+---------------------+
| 1  | 0000-00-00 00:00:00 |
| 2  | 2006-07-16 01:02:03 |
| 3  | 2006-07-16 01:05:24 |
+----+---------------------+
3 rows in set (0.00 sec)
```

Note how the current time is stored when we ask to insert a NULL value. Now, let's change the id for the first row:

```
mysql> UPDATE mytime SET id=4 WHERE id=1;
Query OK, 1 row affected (0.08 sec)
Rows matched: 1  Changed: 1  Warnings: 0

mysql> SELECT * FROM mytime;
+----+---------------------+
| id | changetime          |
+----+---------------------+
| 4  | 2006-07-16 01:05:42 |
| 2  | 2006-07-16 01:02:03 |
| 3  | 2006-07-16 01:05:24 |
+----+---------------------+
3 rows in set (0.00 sec)
```

As you can see, the timestamp is updated to the current timestamp.

There are other variations on how you can control which column updates automatically, but if you stick to the previous steps, you'll get the behavior you want. You can find more examples of using timestamps later in "The Sample Music Database."

CHAR[(width)]

The most commonly used string type. CHAR stores a fixed-length string (such as a name, address, or city) of length width. If a width is not provided, CHAR(1) is assumed. The maximum value of width is 255. With MySQL versions between 4.1.0 and 5.0.2, MySQL accepts values greater than 255 and silently changes the CHAR type to the smallest TEXT type that is suitable; we discuss the TEXT type later in this section.

You can in fact define a special CHAR(0) NULL column that takes up only one bit of storage. This provides two handy features. First, it allows you to include a dummy column in a table that doesn't do anything (which might be useful as a placeholder for a future feature, or to be backward-compatible with an old application). Second, it allows you to store one of two values: NULL or the empty string '', giving you very compact storage of binary (Boolean) values. To help you understand this better, let's create a table with a CHAR(0) field, and an id field to help differentiate between entries:

```
mysql> CREATE TABLE bool(id INT, bit CHAR(0) NULL);
Query OK, 0 rows affected (0.02 sec)
```

Now, let's add three values: an empty string '', NULL, and the character 1:

```
mysql> INSERT INTO bool VALUES (1,''), (2,NULL), (3,'1');
Query OK, 3 rows affected, 1 warning (0.01 sec)
Records: 3  Duplicates: 0  Warnings: 1
```

These all look the same:

```
mysql> SELECT * FROM bool;
+----+------+
| id | bit  |
+----+------+
|  1 |      |
|  2 |      |
|  3 |      |
+----+------+
3 rows in set (0.00 sec)
```

However, one is NULL:

```
mysql> SELECT * FROM bool WHERE bit IS NULL;
+----+------+
| id | bit  |
+----+------+
|  2 |      |
+----+------+
1 row in set (0.00 sec)
```

and the other two aren't:

```
mysql> SELECT * FROM bool WHERE bit IS NOT NULL;
+----+------+
| id | bit  |
+----+------+
|  1 |      |
|  3 |      |
+----+------+
2 rows in set (0.01 sec)
```

In all other cases, the CHAR type takes exactly the number of bytes in storage space as the width of the column (assuming your chosen character set uses one byte per character). Values that are less than *width* characters in length are stored left-aligned in the allocated space, with space character padding on the right side. All trailing spaces are ignored when retrieving and displaying values, as in this example:

```
mysql> CREATE TABLE show_padding(mystring CHAR(10));
Query OK, 0 rows affected (0.01 sec)

mysql> INSERT INTO show_padding VALUES ('a'),('abc'),('abcde'),('abcdefg   ');
Query OK, 4 rows affected (0.00 sec)
Records: 4  Duplicates: 0  Warnings: 0
```

```
mysql> SELECT * FROM show_padding;
+----------+
| mystring |
+----------+
| a        |
| abc      |
| abcde    |
| abcdefg  |
+----------+
4 rows in set (0.01 sec)
```

As you can see, the trailing spaces aren't shown in the last row. They're also ignored if you try to find strings that have a trailing space:

```
mysql> SELECT * FROM show_padding WHERE mystring LIKE '% ';
Empty set (0.00 sec)
```

Since trailing spaces are ignored, no matches are reported.

Note that this has an interesting side effect: you can't differentiate between strings of spaces alone; the strings " " and "   " are considered to be the same thing. Consequently, you can't use one value in the primary key if you've already got the other. Consider an example; we can create a table to store names and email addresses, with the email address as the primary key:

```
mysql> CREATE TABLE contacts (name CHAR(40), email CHAR(40) PRIMARY KEY);
Query OK, 0 rows affected (0.01 sec)

mysql> INSERT INTO contacts VALUES('Sarah', 'sarah@learningmysql.com');
Query OK, 1 row affected (0.01 sec)
```

So far, so good. Now, if we don't know someone's email address, we can store an empty string:

```
mysql> INSERT INTO contacts VALUES('Zahra', '');
Query OK, 1 row affected (0.00 sec)
```

Note that an empty string is not NULL, so MySQL doesn't complain; however, since the email address is the primary key, we can't store another empty string. Let's try storing a single space:

```
mysql> INSERT INTO Contacts VALUES('Samaneh', ' ');
ERROR 1062 (23000): Duplicate entry '' for key 1
```

MySQL complains about a duplicate key, since the single space is treated as an empty string. Trying to insert the string "not sure" works, but then "not sure " (with a trailing space) doesn't work:

```
mysql> INSERT INTO Contacts VALUES('Samaneh', 'not sure');
Query OK, 1 row affected (0.00 sec)

mysql> INSERT INTO Contacts VALUES('Sadri', 'not sure ');
ERROR 1062 (23000): Duplicate entry 'not sure' for key 1
```

Leading spaces don't cause any problems:

```
mysql> INSERT INTO Contacts VALUES('Saleh', ' not sure');
Query OK, 1 row affected (0.00 sec)

mysql> INSERT INTO Contacts VALUES('Susan', '  not sure');
Query OK, 1 row affected (0.00 sec)
```

You should use the BLOB or TEXT types described later if you don't want this behavior.

That concludes our discussion of the six common column types used in MySQL. You'll find examples using some of these types in "The Sample Music Database," later in this chapter. The remainder of this section covers the other type choices available in MySQL, beginning with the other choices for numeric values.

Other integer types

In "Common column types," we saw the INT type for storing integer numbers. In this section, we'll look at a few other integer types that you can use. We recommend that you always choose the smallest possible type to store values. For example, if you're storing age values, choose TINYINT instead of the regular INT. Smaller types require less storage space; this reduces disk and memory requirements and speeds up the retrieval of data from disk. Indeed, column type tuning is a key step that professional database tuners use in optimizing database applications.

Here is the list of the integer types—besides INT—that you can choose from. Be aware that the general issues described for INT apply to these types as well:

BOOLEAN
> A type introduced in MySQL 4.1 that stores a Boolean value of false (zero) or true (nonzero). For example, it might be used to store whether a person is alive (true) or dead (false), a customer is active (true) or inactive (false), or whether a customer wants to receive emails (true) or not (false). The BOOLEAN type has the synonyms BOOL and BIT. It is equivalent to TINYINT(1), and so requires one byte of storage space; you can achieve more compact, one-bit Boolean values by using CHAR(0), as described previously.

TINYINT[(*width*)] [UNSIGNED] [ZEROFILL]
> Stores integer (whole number) values in the range −128 to 127. The *width*, UNSIGNED, and ZEROFILL options behave as for INT. When UNSIGNED is used, a column can store values in the range 0 to 255. A TINYINT column requires one byte of storage space.

SMALLINT[(*width*)] [UNSIGNED] [ZEROFILL]
> Stores integer (whole number) values in the range −32,768 to 32,767. The *width*, UNSIGNED, and ZEROFILL options behave as for INT. When UNSIGNED is used, a column can store values in the range 0 to 65,535. A SMALLINT column requires two bytes of storage space.

MEDIUMINT[(*width*)] [UNSIGNED] [ZEROFILL]

> Stores integer (whole number) values in the range –8,388,608 to 8,388,607. The *width*, UNSIGNED, and ZEROFILL options behave as for INT. When UNSIGNED is used, a column can store values in the range 0 to 16,777,215. A MEDIUMINT column requires three bytes of storage space.

BIGINT[(*width*)] [UNSIGNED] [ZEROFILL]

> Stores integer (whole number) values in the range –9,223,372,036,854,775,808 to 9,223,372,036,854,775,807. The *width*, UNSIGNED, and ZEROFILL options behave as for INT. When UNSIGNED is used, a column can store values in the range 0 to 18,446,744,073,709,551,615. A BIGINT column requires eight bytes of storage space.

Other rational number types

In "Common column types," we discussed the fixed-point DECIMAL type. There are two other types that support decimal points: DOUBLE (also known as REAL) and FLOAT. They're designed to store approximate numeric values rather than the exact values stored by DECIMAL. Why would you want approximate values? The answer is that many numbers with a decimal point are approximations of real quantities. For example, suppose you earn $50,000 per annum and you want to store it as a monthly wage. When you convert it to a per-month amount, it's $4,166 plus 66 and 2/3rds cents. If you store this as $4,166.67, it's not exact enough to convert to a yearly wage (since 12 multiplied by $4,166.67 is $50,000.04). However, if you store 2/3rds with enough decimal places, it's a closer approximation, and you'll find that it is accurate enough to correctly multiply to obtain the original value in a high-precision environment such as MySQL. That's where DOUBLE and FLOAT are useful: they let you store values such as 2/3rds or pi with a large number of decimal places, allowing accurate approximate representations of exact quantities.

Let's continue the previous example using DOUBLE. Suppose you create a table as follows:

```
mysql> CREATE TABLE wage (monthly DOUBLE);
Query OK, 0 rows affected (0.09 sec)
```

You can now insert the monthly wage using:

```
mysql> INSERT INTO wage VALUES (50000/12);
Query OK, 1 row affected (0.00 sec)
```

When you multiply it to a yearly value, you get an accurate approximation:

```
mysql> SELECT monthly*12 FROM wage;
+------------+
| monthly*12 |
+------------+
|      50000 |
+------------+
1 row in set (0.00 sec)
```

Here are the details of the DOUBLE and FLOAT types:

FLOAT[(width, decimals)] [UNSIGNED] [ZEROFILL] or FLOAT[(precision)] [UNSIGNED] [ZEROFILL]

> Stores floating-point numbers. It has two optional syntaxes: the first allows an optional number of *decimals* and an optional display *width*, and the second allows an optional *precision* that controls the accuracy of the approximation measured in bits. Without parameters, the type stores small, four-byte, single-precision floating-point values; usually, you use it without providing any parameters. When *precision* is between 0 and 24, the default behavior occurs. When *precision* is between 25 and 53, the type behaves as for DOUBLE. The *width* has no effect on what is stored, only on what is displayed. The UNSIGNED and ZEROFILL options behave as for INT.

DOUBLE[(*width, decimals*)] [UNSIGNED] [ZEROFILL]

> Stores floating-point numbers. It has one optional syntax: it allows an optional number of *decimals* and an optional display *width*. Without parameters, the type stores normal, eight-byte, double-precision floating point values; usually, you use it without providing any parameters. The *width* has no effect on what is stored, only on what is displayed. The UNSIGNED and ZEROFILL options behave as for INT. The DOUBLE type has two identical synonyms: REAL and DOUBLE PRECISION. The REAL alternative can be made to behave as FLOAT using a nondefault parameter to the MySQL server, but this is not discussed here.

Other date and time types

We discussed the DATE, TIME, and TIMESTAMP types in "Common column types." There are two more date and time types: YEAR for storing only year values, and DATETIME for storing date and time combinations without the automatic-update feature of TIMESTAMP. These work as follows:

YEAR[(*digits*)]

> Stores a two- or four-digit year, depending on whether 2 or 4 is passed as the optional digits parameter. Without the parameter, four digits is the default. The two-digit version stores values from 70 to 69, representing 1970 to 2069; again, we caution against using two-digit dates. The four-digit version stores values in the range 1901 to 2155, as well as the *zero year*, 0000. Illegal values are converted to the zero date. You can input year values as either strings (such as '2005') or integers (such as 2005). The YEAR type requires one byte of storage space.

DATETIME

> Stores and displays a date and time pair in the format *YYYY-MM-DD HH:MM:SS* for the range 1000-01-01 00:00:00 to 9999-12-31 23:59:59. As for TIMESTAMP, the value stored always matches the template *YYYY-MM-DD HH:MM:SS*, but the value can be input in the same formats listed for the TIMESTAMP description. If you assign only a date to a DATETIME column, the zero time 00:00:00 is assumed. If you assign only a time to a DATETIME column, the zero date 0000-00-00 is assumed. This type does not have the automatic update features of TIMESTAMP.

Other string types

The remaining types in MySQL are variants of the string type; here's a list that you can choose from—excepting CHAR, which was described in "Common column types":

VARCHAR(*width*)
> A commonly used string type. Stores variable-length strings (such as names, addresses, or cities) up to a maximum *width*. The maximum value of *width* is 65,535 characters.
>
> Prior to MySQL version 5.0.3, the maximum length was 255 characters. Trying to specify a longer length would cause an error in versions up to 4.1.0. Between versions 4.1.0 and 5.0.3, the server would silently change the column type to the smallest TEXT type that would hold values of that length
>
> A VARCHAR type incurs one or two extra bytes of overhead to store the length of the string, depending on whether the string is shorter than or longer than 255 characters.
>
> Trailing spaces are removed when a value is stored; you can use TEXT or BLOB types to avoid this behavior.

BINARY(width) and VARBINARY(width)
> Available since MySQL 4.1.2, these are equivalent to CHAR and VARCHAR but allow you to store binary strings. Binary strings have no character set, and sorting them is case-sensitive. Read the descriptions of CHAR and VARCHAR for other details. If you're using a MySQL version earlier than 4.1.2, you can create the same behavior by adding the keyword BINARY after the CHAR or VARCHAR declaration, as in CHAR(12) BINARY.

BLOB
> The commonly used type for storing large data. Stores a variable amount of data (such as an image, video, or other nontext file) up to 65,535 bytes in length. The data is treated as binary—that is, no character set is assumed, and comparisons and sorts are case-sensitive. There is no trailing-space-removal behavior as for the CHAR or VARCHAR types. In addition, a DEFAULT clause is not permitted, and you must take a prefix of the value when using it in an index (this is discussed in the next section).

TEXT
> A commonly used type for storing large string data objects. Stores a variable amount of data (such as a document or other text file) up to 65,535 bytes in length. It is identical to BLOB, except that the data is treated as belonging to a character set. Since MySQL 4.1, the character set can be set for each column, and prior to that the character set of the server was assumed. Comparisons and sorts are case-*insensitive*.

TINYBLOB and TINYTEXT
> Identical to BLOB and TEXT, respectively, except that a maximum of 255 bytes can be stored.

MEDIUMBLOB and MEDIUMTEXT

Identical to BLOB and TEXT, respectively, except that a maximum of 16,777,215 bytes can be stored.

LONGBLOB and LONGTEXT

Identical to BLOB and TEXT, respectively, except that a maximum of four gigabytes of data can be stored. The effective maximum can vary depending on the memory available on the server and its configuration.

ENUM('value1'[,'value2'[, ...]])

A list, or *enumeration* of string values. A column of type ENUM can be set to a value from the list *value1*, *value2*, and so on, up to a maximum of 65,535 different values. While the values are stored and retrieved as strings, what's stored in the database is an integer representation. The enumerated column can contain NULL (stored as NULL), the empty string '' (stored as 0), or any of the valid elements (stored as 1, 2, 3, and so on). You can prevent NULL values from being accepted by declaring the column as NOT NULL when creating the table.

This type is a compact way of storing values from a list of predefined values, such as state or country names. Consider this example using fruit names; the name can be any one of the predefined values Apple, Orange, or Pear (in addition to NULL and the empty string):

```
mysql> CREATE TABLE fruits_enum ( fruit_name ENUM('Apple', 'Orange', 'Pear') );
Query OK, 0 rows affected (0.00 sec)

mysql> INSERT INTO fruits_enum VALUES ('Apple');
Query OK, 1 row affected (0.00 sec)
```

If you try inserting a value that's not in the list, MySQL warns you that it didn't store the data you asked:

```
mysql> INSERT INTO fruits_enum VALUES ('Banana');
Query OK, 1 row affected, 1 warning (0.00 sec)

mysql> SHOW WARNINGS;
+---------+------+------------------------------------------------+
| Level   | Code | Message                                        |
+---------+------+------------------------------------------------+
| Warning | 1265 | Data truncated for column 'fruit_name' at row 1 |
+---------+------+------------------------------------------------+
1 row in set (0.00 sec)
```

Similarly, a list of several allowed values isn't accepted either:

```
mysql> INSERT INTO fruits_enum VALUES ('Apple,Orange');
Query OK, 1 row affected, 1 warning (0.00 sec)

mysql> SHOW WARNINGS;
+---------+------+------------------------------------------------+
| Level   | Code | Message                                        |
+---------+------+------------------------------------------------+
| Warning | 1265 | Data truncated for column 'fruit_name' at row 1 |
```

```
+---------+------+-------------------------------------------------+
1 row in set (0.00 sec)
```

Displaying the contents of the table, you can see that when you try to store anything that's not in the valid values, an empty string is stored instead:

```
mysql> SELECT * FROM fruits_enum;
+------------+
| fruit_name |
+------------+
| Apple      |
|            |
|            |
+------------+
3 rows in set (0.00 sec)
```

You can also specify a default value other than the empty string:

```
mysql> CREATE TABLE new_fruits_enum ( fruit_name ENUM('Apple', 'Orange', 'Pear')
    -> DEFAULT 'Pear');
Query OK, 0 rows affected (0.01 sec)

mysql> INSERT INTO new_fruits_enum VALUES();
Query OK, 1 row affected (0.00 sec)

mysql> SELECT * FROM new_fruits_enum;
+------------+
| fruit_name |
+------------+
| Pear       |
+------------+
1 row in set (0.00 sec)
```

Here, not specifying a value results in the default value Pear being stored.

SET('*value1*'[,'*value2*'[, ...]])

A set of string values. A column of type SET can be set to zero or more values from the list *value1*, *value2*, and so on, up to a maximum of 64 different values. While the values are strings, what's stored in the database is an integer representation. SET differs from ENUM in that each row can store only one ENUM value in a column, but can store multiple SET values. This type is useful for storing a selection of choices from a list, such as user preferences. Consider this example using fruit names; the name can be any combination of the predefined values:

```
mysql> CREATE TABLE fruits_set ( fruit_name SET('Apple', 'Orange', 'Pear') );
Query OK, 0 rows affected (0.01 sec)

mysql> INSERT INTO fruits_set VALUES ('Apple');
Query OK, 1 row affected (0.00 sec)

mysql> INSERT INTO fruits_set VALUES ('Banana');
Query OK, 1 row affected, 1 warning (0.00 sec)

mysql> SHOW WARNINGS;
+---------+------+-------------------------------------------------+
```

```
| Level   | Code | Message                                            |
+---------+------+----------------------------------------------------+
| Warning | 1265 | Data truncated for column 'fruit_name' at row 1 |
+---------+------+----------------------------------------------------+
1 row in set (0.00 sec)

mysql> INSERT INTO fruits_set VALUES ('Apple,Orange');
Query OK, 1 row affected (0.00 sec)

mysql> SELECT * FROM fruits_set;
+--------------+
| fruit_name   |
+--------------+
| Apple        |
|              |
| Apple,Orange |
+--------------+
3 rows in set (0.01 sec)
```

Again, note that we can store multiple values from the set in a single field, and that an empty string is stored for invalid input.

As with numeric types, we recommend that you always choose the smallest possible type to store values. For example, if you're storing a city name, use CHAR or VARCHAR, rather than, say, the TEXT type. Having shorter columns helps keep your table size down, which in turns helps performance when the server has to search through a table.

Using a fixed size with the CHAR type is often faster than using a variable size with VARCHAR, since the MySQL server knows where each row starts and ends, and can quickly skip over rows to find the one it needs. However, with fixed-length fields, any space that you don't use is wasted. For example, if you allow up to 40 characters in a city name, then CHAR(40) will always use up 40 characters, no matter how long the city name actually is. If you declare the city name to be VARCHAR(40), then you'll use up only as much space as you need, plus one byte to store the name length. If the average city name is 10 characters long, this means that using a variable length field will take up 29 fewer bytes per entry; this can make a big difference if you're storing millions of addresses.

In general, if storage space is at a premium or you expect large variations in the length of strings that are to be stored, use a variable-length field; if performance is a priority, use a fixed length.

Keys and Indexes

You'll find that almost all tables you use will have a PRIMARY KEY clause declared in their CREATE TABLE statement. The reasons why you need a primary key are discussed in Chapter 4. This section discusses how primary keys are declared, what happens behind the scenes when you do so, and why you might want to also create other keys and indexes on your data.

A *primary key* uniquely identifies each row in a table. When you declare one to MySQL, it creates a new file on disk that stores information about where the data from each row in the table is stored. This information is called an *index*, and its purpose is to speed up searches that use the primary key. For example, when you declare PRIMARY KEY (artist_id) in the artist table in the music database, MySQL creates a structure that allows it to find rows that match a specific artist_id (or a range of identifiers) extremely quickly. This is very useful to match artists to albums, tracks, and playlist information. You can display the indexes available on a table using the SHOW INDEX command:

```
mysql> SHOW INDEX FROM artist;
+--------+------------+----------+--------------+-------------+-----------+...
| Table  | Non_unique | Key_name | Seq_in_index | Column_name | Collation |...
+--------+------------+----------+--------------+-------------+-----------+...
| artist | 0          | PRIMARY  | 1            | artist_id   | A         |...
+--------+------------+----------+--------------+-------------+-----------+...

... +-------------+----------+--------+------+------------+---------+
... | Cardinality | Sub_part | Packed | Null | Index_type | Comment |
... +-------------+----------+--------+------+------------+---------+
... | 6           | NULL     |        |      | BTREE      |         |
... +-------------+----------+--------+------+------------+---------+
1 row in set (0.00 sec)
```

We've wrapped the output here so that it would fit on the page. The *cardinality* is the number of unique values in the index; for an index on a primary key, this is the same as the number of rows in the table.

Note that all columns that are part of a primary key must be declared as NOT NULL, since they must have a value for the row to be valid. Without the index, the only way to find rows in the table is to read each one from disk and check whether it matches the artist_id you're searching for. For tables with many rows, this exhaustive, sequential searching is extremely slow. However, you can't just index everything; we'll come back to this point at the end of this section.

You can create other indexes on the data in a table. You do this so that other searches —on other columns or combinations of columns—are extremely fast and in order to avoid sequential scans. For example, suppose you often want to search by artist_name. You can drop the table and modify the CREATE TABLE definition to add an extra index:

```
mysql> DROP TABLE artist;
Query OK, 0 rows affected (0.01 sec)

mysql> CREATE TABLE artist (
    -> artist_id SMALLINT(5) NOT NULL DEFAULT 0,
    -> artist_name CHAR(128) DEFAULT NULL,
    -> PRIMARY KEY (artist_id),
    -> KEY artist_name (artist_name)
    -> );
Query OK, 0 rows affected (0.06 sec)
```

You can see we've used the keyword KEY to tell MySQL that we want an extra index; you can use the word INDEX in place of KEY. Following this, we've named the index—in this example, we've named it after the column name—and then we've included the column to index in parentheses. You can also add indexes after tables are created—in fact, you can pretty much change anything about a table after its creation—and this is discussed in "Altering Structures."

You can build an index on more than one column. For example, consider the following customer table:

```
mysql> CREATE TABLE customer (
    -> cust_id INT(4) NOT NULL DEFAULT 0,
    -> firstname CHAR(50),
    -> secondname CHAR(50),
    -> surname CHAR(50),
    -> PRIMARY KEY (cust_id),
    -> KEY names (firstname, secondname, surname));
Query OK, 0 rows affected (0.01 sec)
```

You can see that we've added a primary key index on the cust_id identifier column, and we've also added another index—called names—that includes the firstname, secondname, and surname columns in this order. Let's now consider how you can use that extra index.

You can use the names index for fast searching by combinations of the three name columns. For example, it's useful in the following query:

```
mysql> SELECT * FROM customer WHERE
    -> firstname = "Rose" AND
    -> secondname = "Elizabeth" AND
    -> surname = "Williams";
```

We know it helps the search, because all columns listed in the index are used in the query. You can use the EXPLAIN statement to check whether what you think should happen is in fact happening:

```
mysql> EXPLAIN SELECT * FROM customer WHERE
    -> firstname = "Rose" AND
    -> secondname = "Elizabeth" AND
    -> surname = "Williams";
+----+-------------+----------+------+---------------+...
| id | select_type | table    | type | possible_keys |...
+----+-------------+----------+------+---------------+...
|  1 | SIMPLE      | customer | ref  | names         |...
+----+-------------+----------+------+---------------+...

...+-------+---------+-------------------+------+-------------+
...| key   | key_len | ref               | rows | Extra       |
...+-------+---------+-------------------+------+-------------+
...| names |     153 | const,const,const |    1 | Using where |
...+-------+---------+-------------------+------+-------------+
1 row in set (0.00 sec)
```

We've reformatted the output slightly to fit better in the book. You can see that MySQL reports that the possible_keys are names (meaning that the index could be used for this query) and that the key that it's decided to use is names. So, what you expect and what is happening are the same, and that's good news! You'll find out more about the EXPLAIN statement in Chapter 7.

The index we've created is also useful for queries on only the firstname column. For example, it can be used by the following query:

```
mysql> SELECT * FROM customer WHERE
    -> firstname = "Rose";
```

You can use EXPLAIN to check whether the index is being used. The reason it can be used is because the firstname column is the first listed in the index. In practice, this means that the index *clusters*, or stores together, information about rows for all people with the same first name, and so the index can be used to find anyone with a matching first name.

The index can also be used for searches involving combinations of first name and second name, for exactly the same reasons we've just discussed. The index clusters together people with the same first name, and within that it clusters people with identical first names ordered by second name. So, it can be used for this query:

```
mysql> SELECT * FROM customer WHERE
    -> firstname = "Rose" AND
    -> secondname = "Elizabeth";
```

However, the index can't be used for this query because the leftmost column in the index, firstname, does not appear in the query:

```
mysql> SELECT * FROM customer WHERE
    -> surname = "Williams" AND
    -> secondname = "Elizabeth";
```

The index should help narrow down the set of rows to a smaller set of possible answers. For MySQL to be able to use an index, the query needs to meet both the following conditions:

1. The leftmost column listed in the KEY (or PRIMARY KEY) clause must be in the query.
2. The query must contain no OR clauses for columns that aren't indexed.

Again, you can always use the EXPLAIN statement to check whether an index can be used for a particular query.

Before we finish this section, here are a few ideas on how to choose and design indexes. When you're considering adding an index, think about the following:

- Indexes cost space on disk, and they need to be updated whenever data changes. If your data changes frequently, or lots of data changes when you do make a change, indexes will slow the process down. However, in practice, since SELECT statements (data reads) are usually much more common than other statements (data modifications), indexes are usually beneficial.

- Only add an index that'll be used frequently. Don't bother indexing columns before you see what queries your users and your applications need. You can always add indexes afterward.

- If all columns in an index are used in all queries, list the column with the highest number of duplicates at the left of the KEY clause. This minimizes index size.

- The smaller the index, the faster it'll be. If you index large columns, you'll get a larger index. This is a good reason to ensure your columns are as small as possible when you design your tables.

- For long columns, you can use only a prefix of the values from a column to create the index. You can do this by adding a value in parentheses after the column definition, such as KEY names (firstname(3), secondname(2), surname(10)). This means that only the first three characters of firstname are indexed, then the first two characters of secondname, and then 10 characters from surname. This is a significant saving over indexing 50 characters from each of the 3 columns! When you do this, your index will be less able to uniquely identify rows, but it'll be much smaller and still reasonably good at finding matching rows.

The AUTO_INCREMENT Feature

MySQL's proprietary AUTO_INCREMENT feature allows you to create a unique identifier for a row without running a SELECT query. Here's how it works. Suppose you drop and re-create the artist table as follows:

```
mysql> DROP TABLE artist;
Query OK, 0 rows affected (0.01 sec)

mysql> CREATE TABLE artist (
    -> artist_id SMALLINT(5) NOT NULL AUTO_INCREMENT,
    -> artist_name CHAR(128) DEFAULT NULL,
    -> PRIMARY KEY (artist_id)
    -> );

Query OK, 0 rows affected (0.06 sec)
```

You can now insert rows, without providing an artist_id:

```
mysql> INSERT INTO artist VALUES (NULL, "The Shamen");
Query OK, 1 row affected (0.06 sec)

mysql> INSERT INTO artist VALUES (NULL, "Probot");
Query OK, 1 row affected (0.00 sec)

mysql> INSERT INTO artist VALUES (NULL, "The Cult");
Query OK, 1 row affected (0.00 sec)
```

When you view the data in this table you can see that each artist has a meaningful artist_id:

```
mysql> SELECT * FROM artist;
+-----------+-------------+
| artist_id | artist_name |
+-----------+-------------+
|         1 | The Shamen  |
|         2 | Probot      |
|         3 | The Cult    |
+-----------+-------------+
3 rows in set (0.01 sec)
```

Each time an artist is inserted, a unique artist_id is created for the new row.

Let's consider how the new feature works. You can see that the artist_id column is declared as an integer with the clauses NOT NULL AUTO_INCREMENT. The AUTO_INCREMENT keyword tells MySQL that when a value isn't provided for this column, the value allocated should be one more than the maximum currently stored in the table. The AUTO_INCREMENT sequence begins at 1 for an empty table.

The NOT NULL is required for AUTO_INCREMENT columns; when you insert NULL (or 0, though this isn't recommended), the MySQL server automatically finds the next available identifier and assigns it to the new row. You can manually insert negative values if the column was not defined as UNSIGNED; however, for the next automatic increment, MySQL will simply use the largest (most positive) value in the column, or start from 1 if there are no positive values.

The AUTO_INCREMENT feature has the following requirements:

- The column it is used on must be indexed.
- The column that is it used on cannot have a DEFAULT value.
- There can be only one AUTO_INCREMENT column per table.

MySQL supports different table types; we'll learn more about these in "Table Types" in Chapter 7. When you're using the default MyISAM table type, you can use the AUTO_INCREMENT feature on keys that comprise multiple columns. In our music database example, we could create the album table as follows:

```
mysql> CREATE TABLE album (
    -> artist_id INT(5) NOT NULL,
    -> album_id INT(4) NOT NULL AUTO_INCREMENT,
    -> album_name CHAR(128) DEFAULT NULL,
    -> PRIMARY KEY (artist_id, album_id)
    -> );

Query OK, 0 rows affected (0.00 sec)
```

You can see that the primary key is on two columns—artist_id and album_id—and that the AUTO_INCREMENT feature is applied to the album_id column.

Suppose you want to insert two albums for The Shamen, the artist we added earlier with an `artist_id` of 1. Here's how you do it:

```
mysql> INSERT INTO album VALUES (1, NULL, "Boss Drum");
Query OK, 1 row affected (0.00 sec)

mysql> INSERT INTO album VALUES (1, NULL, "Entact");
Query OK, 1 row affected (0.00 sec)
```

Now, let's inspect the results:

```
mysql> SELECT * FROM album WHERE artist_id = 1;
+-----------+----------+------------+
| artist_id | album_id | album_name |
+-----------+----------+------------+
|         1 |        1 | Boss Drum  |
|         1 |        2 | Entact     |
+-----------+----------+------------+
2 rows in set (0.00 sec)
```

You can see that the correct `album_id` values are assigned; this is just as we'd expect. Now, consider what happens when we add two albums for the artist "The Cult":

```
mysql> INSERT INTO album VALUES (3, NULL, "Electric");
Query OK, 1 row affected (0.01 sec)

mysql> INSERT INTO album VALUES (3, NULL, "Sonic Temple");
Query OK, 1 row affected (0.00 sec)
```

Here are the results:

```
mysql> SELECT * FROM album WHERE artist_id = 3;
+-----------+----------+--------------+
| artist_id | album_id | album_name   |
+-----------+----------+--------------+
|         3 |        1 | Electric     |
|         3 |        2 | Sonic Temple |
+-----------+----------+--------------+
2 rows in set (0.00 sec)
```

You can see how the feature works with two columns in the primary key: it's reused the `artist_id` value that was used for The Cult, and the weak key (`album_id`) is incremented automatically. This ensures that the album primary key (the combination of `artist_id` and `album_id`) is unique for each album. We now have albums 1 and 2 for The Shamen (with an `artist_id` of 1), and albums 1 and 2 for The Cult (with an `artist_id` of 3).

While the `AUTO_INCREMENT` feature is useful, it isn't portable to other database environments, and it hides the logical steps to creating new identifiers. It can also lead to ambiguity; for example, dropping or truncating a table will reset the counter, but deleting selected rows (with a `WHERE` clause) doesn't reset the counter. Consider an example; let's create the table count that contains an auto-incrementing field counter:

```
mysql> CREATE TABLE count (counter INT AUTO_INCREMENT KEY);
Query OK, 0 rows affected (0.13 sec)
```

```
mysql> INSERT INTO count VALUES (),(),(),(),(),();
Query OK, 6 rows affected (0.01 sec)
Records: 6  Duplicates: 0  Warnings: 0

mysql> SELECT * FROM count;
+---------+
| counter |
+---------+
| 1       |
| 2       |
| 3       |
| 4       |
| 5       |
| 6       |
+---------+
6 rows in set (0.00 sec)
```

Inserting several values works as expected. Now, let's delete a few rows and then add six new rows:

```
mysql> DELETE FROM count WHERE counter > 4;
Query OK, 2 rows affected (0.00 sec)

mysql> INSERT INTO count VALUES (),(),(),(),(),();
Query OK, 6 rows affected (0.00 sec)
Records: 6  Duplicates: 0  Warnings: 0

mysql> SELECT * FROM count;
+---------+
| counter |
+---------+
| 1       |
| 2       |
| 3       |
| 4       |
| 7       |
| 8       |
| 9       |
| 10      |
| 11      |
| 12      |
+---------+
10 rows in set (0.00 sec)
```

Here, we see that the counter is not reset, and continues from 7. If, however, we delete all the data in the table, the counter is reset to 1:

```
mysql> TRUNCATE TABLE count;
Query OK, 0 rows affected (0.00 sec)

mysql> INSERT INTO count VALUES (),(),(),(),(),();
Query OK, 6 rows affected (0.01 sec)
Records: 6  Duplicates: 0  Warnings: 0

mysql> SELECT * FROM count;
```

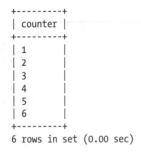

```
+---------+
| counter |
+---------+
| 1       |
| 2       |
| 3       |
| 4       |
| 5       |
| 6       |
+---------+
6 rows in set (0.00 sec)
```

Instead of relying on MySQL to handle incrementing fields as you hope, you can manage the process in program code that you write to interact with the database. We don't use an auto-incrementing field in the final music database specification, described fully in the next section. However, we do use one in our wedding gift registry in Chapter 15.

The Sample Music Database

We've used the music database extensively in this and the previous chapter, so you're already familiar with its structure. This section explains the steps we took to express our sample music database as SQL statements for loading into MySQL. It also lists the complete SQL statements used to create the structures, which you'll find a useful reference for discussions in later chapters.

Let's begin by discussing how we structured the file that contains the SQL statements. You can download the file *music.sql* from the book's web site. We created the table using the monitor, and created the file from the output of one of MySQL's commands for dumping SQL, and then edited it for readability. You'll find more about how to dump SQL statements to a file in Chapter 10.

The *music.sql* file is structured as follows:

1. Drop the database if it exists, and then create it.
2. Use the database.
3. Create the tables.
4. Insert the data.

This structure allows you to reload the database—using the SOURCE command discussed in Chapter 3—at any time without having to worry about whether the database, tables, or data exist. Loading the file just wipes the database and starts again. Of course, in a production environment, always ensure your backups are reasonably up-to-date before commencing a restore operation that involves dropping tables or deleting existing data.

The first three lines of the file carry out the first two steps:

```
DROP DATABASE IF EXISTS music;
CREATE DATABASE music;
USE music;
```

The next section of the file creates the tables (the third step), and that's the focus of this section; we don't list the insert statements in this book, but they're easily viewed in *music.sql*. Let's start by looking at how we created the **artist** table:

```
CREATE TABLE artist (
  artist_id SMALLINT(5) NOT NULL DEFAULT 0,
  artist_name CHAR(128) DEFAULT NULL,
  PRIMARY KEY (artist_id)
  );
```

The table has a structure that's derived from the design in Chapter 4. The **artist_id** is the primary key; because of this, and as required by MySQL, we've added a **NOT NULL** clause. The **DEFAULT** clause inserts a default value for the column if we don't provide one. If a field doesn't have a default value, MySQL reports an error if a value isn't provided for it during an insert operation. In the **artist** table, the **artist_id** will be set to 0 if we don't provide an **artist_id** ourselves. MySQL will complain the second time we try to do this, since **artist_id** is the primary key of the **artist** table, and we can't have two rows with the same primary key.

We've used the **SMALLINT** type for the **artist_id** because it's a numeric identifier, and a **SMALLINT** allows us to have around 65,000 artists; we've limited its display width to 5 characters.

We've decided that 128 characters is more than we'd need for any likely **artist_name**. We use the **CHAR** type instead of the **VARCHAR** type so that each row has an fixed, predictable size; this allows MySQL to better optimize the retrieval of rows from its files, typically making the application faster despite the files being typically larger than if **VARCHAR** was used. We haven't added a **NOT NULL** clause to the **artist_name**, and have instead assumed that whatever application we build will do the checking for us. In general, the fewer the constraints and conditions that are built into the database, the faster it is for MySQL to work with. However, MySQL now optimizes for NOT NULL columns, so it is better to declare NOT NULL where the data will never be NULL. See the "Data Size" section of the MySQL manual for details.

The **album** table follows a similar rationale:

```
CREATE TABLE album (
  artist_id SMALLINT(5) NOT NULL DEFAULT 0,
  album_id SMALLINT(4) NOT NULL DEFAULT 0,
  album_name CHAR(128) DEFAULT NULL,
  PRIMARY KEY (artist_id,album_id)
  );
```

We've declared the **artist_id** to be the same type as in **artist**. This is important as otherwise MySQL couldn't use indexes to join tables together to resolve queries (which is a very common cause of odd results in **EXPLAIN** output). We've used **SMALLINT** for the **album_id**, since we don't expect more than 65,000 albums per artist! We define **album_name** as a **CHAR(128)** because 128 characters seems long enough for album titles.

Again, we've added `NOT NULL` for the primary key, added `DEFAULT` clauses to make the behavior predictable, and gone with only fixed-length types to improve performance.

The `track` table is created as follows:

```
CREATE TABLE track (
  track_id SMALLINT(3) NOT NULL DEFAULT 0,
  track_name CHAR(128) DEFAULT NULL,
  artist_id SMALLINT(5) NOT NULL DEFAULT 0,
  album_id SMALLINT(4) NOT NULL DEFAULT 0,
  time TIME DEFAULT NULL,
  PRIMARY KEY (artist_id,album_id,track_id)
  );
```

The reasoning behind the choices for the first four columns is the same as for the other tables. The `time` column stores the duration of each track, and we've chosen to use the `TIME` type to store this. Using the `TIME` type—in preference to a numeric type such as `DECIMAL`—makes it easy to do math such as summing values to find the running time for an album. It also gives you flexibility in formats for the time data, as discussed previously. Despite this, you'll see that in *music.sql* we use the format *HH:MM:SS* because we prefer to keep SQL queries readable and unambiguous.

The final table is `played`:

```
CREATE TABLE played (
  artist_id SMALLINT(5) NOT NULL DEFAULT 0,
  album_id SMALLINT(4) NOT NULL DEFAULT 0,
  track_id SMALLINT(3) NOT NULL DEFAULT 0,
  played TIMESTAMP NOT NULL DEFAULT CURRENT_TIMESTAMP on update CURRENT_TIMESTAMP,
  PRIMARY KEY (artist_id,album_id,track_id,played)
  );
```

The choices for the first three columns are again as previously described. The `played` column makes use of the `TIMESTAMP` type and its automatic-update feature: we want the value to be set to the current date and time whenever a row is inserted (and, for good measure, whenever it's updated, which we don't plan to do). To use the feature, whenever we play a track, we create a new row with the `artist_id`, `album_id`, and `track_id`, and set the `played` column to `NULL`. Since all columns form the primary key, it's acceptable to have more than one entry for a specific combination of artist, album, and track, as long as the timestamps aren't the same. We can reasonably assume that two tracks won't be played at the same time in a single-user application, and can also add instructions to enforce this in any application that uses this database.

Altering Structures

We've shown you all the basics you need for creating databases, tables, indexes, and columns. In this section, you'll learn how to add, remove, and change columns, databases, tables, and indexes in structures that already exist.

Adding, Removing, and Changing Columns

You can use the ALTER TABLE statement to add new columns to a table, remove existing columns, and change column names, types, and lengths.

Let's begin by considering how you modify existing columns. Consider an example in which we rename a table column. The played table has a column—also called played —that contains the time the track was played. To change the name of this column to last_played, you would write:

```
mysql> ALTER TABLE played CHANGE played last_played TIMESTAMP;
Query OK, 12 rows affected (0.03 sec)
Records: 12  Duplicates: 0  Warnings: 0
```

You can see that MySQL processes and alters each row. What actually happens behind the scenes is that MySQL creates a new table with the new structure, copies the data into that table, removes the original played table, and renames the table to played. You can check the result with the SHOW COLUMNS statement:

```
mysql> SHOW COLUMNS FROM played;
+-------------+-------------+------+-----+-------------------+-------+
| Field       | Type        | Null | Key | Default           | Extra |
+-------------+-------------+------+-----+-------------------+-------+
| artist_id   | smallint(5) |      | PRI | 0                 |       |
| album_id    | smallint(4) |      | PRI | 0                 |       |
| track_id    | smallint(3) |      | PRI | 0                 |       |
| last_played | timestamp   | YES  | PRI | CURRENT_TIMESTAMP |       |
+-------------+-------------+------+-----+-------------------+-------+
4 rows in set (0.01 sec)
```

In the previous example, you can see that we provided four parameters to the ALTER TABLE statement with the CHANGE keyword:

1. The table name, played
2. The original column name, played
3. The new column name, last_played
4. The column type, TIMESTAMP

You must provide all four; that means you need to respecify the type and any clauses that go with it. In the previous example, it just happens that the TIMESTAMP type defaults to:

```
DEFAULT CURRENT_TIMESTAMP ON UPDATE CURRENT_TIMESTAMP
```

If you want to rename the artist_name column to artist-name, you would write:

```
ALTER TABLE artist CHANGE artist_name artist-name CHAR(128) DEFAULT NULL;
```

If you want to modify the type and clauses of a column, but not its name, you can use the MODIFY keyword:

```
mysql> ALTER TABLE artist MODIFY artist_name CHAR(64) DEFAULT "Unknown";
Query OK, 6 rows affected (0.01 sec)
Records: 6  Duplicates: 0  Warnings: 0
```

You can also do this with the CHANGE keyword, but by specifying the same column name twice:

```
mysql> ALTER TABLE artist CHANGE artist_name artist_name CHAR(64) DEFAULT "Unknown";
Query OK, 6 rows affected (0.03 sec)
Records: 6  Duplicates: 0  Warnings: 0
```

Be careful when you're modifying types:

- Don't use incompatible types, since you're relying on MySQL to successfully convert data from one format to another (for example, converting an INT column to a DATETIME column isn't likely to do what you hoped).

- Don't truncate the data unless that's what you want. If you reduce the size of a type, the values will be edited to match the new width, and you can lose data.

Suppose you want to add an extra column to an existing table. Here's how to do it with the ALTER TABLE statement:

```
mysql> ALTER TABLE artist ADD formed YEAR;
Query OK, 6 rows affected (0.02 sec)
Records: 6  Duplicates: 0  Warnings: 0
```

You must supply the ADD keyword, the new column name, and the column type and clauses. This example adds the new column, formed, as the last column in the table, as shown with the SHOW COLUMNS statement:

```
mysql> SHOW COLUMNS FROM artist;
+-------------+-------------+------+-----+---------+-------+
| Field       | Type        | Null | Key | Default | Extra |
+-------------+-------------+------+-----+---------+-------+
| artist_id   | smallint(5) |      | PRI | 0       |       |
| artist_name | char(64)    | YES  |     | Unknown |       |
| formed      | year(4)     | YES  |     | NULL    |       |
+-------------+-------------+------+-----+---------+-------+
3 rows in set (0.02 sec)
```

If you want it to instead be the first column, use the FIRST keyword as follows:

```
mysql> ALTER TABLE artist ADD formed YEAR FIRST;
Query OK, 6 rows affected (0.04 sec)
Records: 6  Duplicates: 0  Warnings: 0

mysql> SHOW COLUMNS FROM artist;
+-------------+-------------+------+-----+---------+-------+
| Field       | Type        | Null | Key | Default | Extra |
+-------------+-------------+------+-----+---------+-------+
| formed      | year(4)     | YES  |     | NULL    |       |
| artist_id   | smallint(5) |      | PRI | 0       |       |
| artist_name | char(64)    | YES  |     | Unknown |       |
+-------------+-------------+------+-----+---------+-------+
3 rows in set (0.01 sec)
```

If you want it added in a specific position, use the AFTER keyword:

```
mysql> ALTER TABLE artist ADD formed YEAR AFTER artist_id;
Query OK, 6 rows affected (0.03 sec)
Records: 6  Duplicates: 0  Warnings: 0

mysql> SHOW COLUMNS FROM artist;
+-------------+-------------+------+-----+---------+-------+
| Field       | Type        | Null | Key | Default | Extra |
+-------------+-------------+------+-----+---------+-------+
| artist_id   | smallint(5) |      | PRI | 0       |       |
| formed      | year(4)     | YES  |     | NULL    |       |
| artist_name | char(64)    | YES  |     | Unknown |       |
+-------------+-------------+------+-----+---------+-------+
3 rows in set (0.01 sec)
```

To remove a column, use the DROP keyword followed by the column name. Here's how to get rid of the newly added formed column:

```
mysql> ALTER TABLE artist DROP formed;
Query OK, 6 rows affected (0.02 sec)
Records: 6  Duplicates: 0  Warnings: 0
```

This removes both the column structure and any data contained in that column. It also removes the column from any index it was in; if it's the only column in the index, the index is dropped, too. You can't remove a column if it's the only one in a table; to do this, you drop the table instead as explained later in "Deleting Structures." Be careful when dropping columns; you discard both the data and the structure of your table. When the structure of a table changes, you will generally have to modify any INSERT statements that you use to insert values in a particular order. We described INSERT statements in "The INSERT Statement" in Chapter 5.

MySQL allows you to specify multiple alterations in a single ALTER TABLE statement by separating them with commas. Here's an example that adds a new column and adjusts another:

```
mysql> ALTER TABLE artist ADD formed YEAR, MODIFY artist_name char(256);
Query OK, 6 rows affected, 1 warning (0.08 sec)
Records: 6  Duplicates: 0  Warnings: 0
```

It's very efficient to join multiple modifications in a single operation, as it potentially saves the cost of creating a new table, copying data from the old table to the new table, dropping the old table, and renaming the new table with the name of the old table for each modification individually.

Adding, Removing, and Changing Indexes

As we discussed previously, it's often hard to know what indexes are useful before the application you're building is used. You might find that a particular feature of the application is much more popular than you expected, causing you to evaluate how to improve performance for the associated queries. You'll therefore find it useful to be able to add, alter, and remove indexes on the fly after your application is deployed. This section shows you how. Modifying indexes does not affect the data stored in the table.

We'll start with adding a new index. Imagine that the artist table is frequently queried using a WHERE clause that specifies an artist_name. To speed this query, you've decided to add a new index, which you've named by_name. Here's how you add it after the table is created:

```
mysql> ALTER TABLE artist ADD INDEX by_name (artist_name);
Query OK, 6 rows affected (0.02 sec)
Records: 6  Duplicates: 0  Warnings: 0
```

Again, you can use the terms KEY and INDEX interchangeably. You can check the results with the SHOW CREATE TABLE statement:

```
mysql> SHOW CREATE TABLE artist;
+--------+--------------------------------------------------+
| Table  | Create Table                                     |
+--------+--------------------------------------------------+
| artist | CREATE TABLE `artist` (                          |
|        |   `artist_id` smallint(5) NOT NULL default '0',  |
|        |   `artist_name` char(128) default NULL,          |
|        |   PRIMARY KEY (`artist_id`),                     |
|        |   KEY `by_name` (`artist_name`)                  |
|        | ) ENGINE=MyISAM DEFAULT CHARSET=latin1           |
+--------+--------------------------------------------------+
```

As expected, the new index forms part of the table structure. You can also specify a primary key for a table after it's created:

```
mysql> ALTER TABLE artist ADD PRIMARY KEY (artist_id);
```

Now let's consider how to remove an index. To remove a non-primary-key index, you do the following:

```
mysql> ALTER TABLE artist DROP INDEX by_name;
Query OK, 6 rows affected (0.01 sec)
Records: 6  Duplicates: 0  Warnings: 0
```

You can drop a primary-key index as follows:

```
mysql> ALTER TABLE artist DROP PRIMARY KEY;
```

MySQL won't allow you to have multiple primary keys in a table. If you want to change the primary key, you'll have to remove the existing index before adding the new one. Consider this example:

```
mysql> CREATE TABLE staff (staff_id INT, name CHAR(40));
Query OK, 0 rows affected (0.01 sec)

mysql> ALTER TABLE staff ADD PRIMARY KEY (staff_id);
Query OK, 0 rows affected (0.00 sec)
Records: 0  Duplicates: 0  Warnings: 0
```

```
mysql> ALTER TABLE staff ADD PRIMARY KEY (name);
ERROR 1068 (42000): Multiple primary key defined

mysql> ALTER TABLE staff DROP PRIMARY KEY;
Query OK, 0 rows affected (0.00 sec)
Records: 0  Duplicates: 0  Warnings: 0

mysql> ALTER TABLE staff ADD PRIMARY KEY (name);
Query OK, 0 rows affected (0.00 sec)
Records: 0  Duplicates: 0  Warnings: 0
```

MySQL complains when we try to add the second primary key on name; we have to drop the existing primary key on staff_id, and then add one on name.

You can't modify an index once it's been created. However, sometimes you'll want to; for example, you might want to reduce the number of characters indexed from a column or add another column to the index. The best method to do this is to drop the index and then create it again with the new specification. For example, suppose you decide that you want the by_name index to include only the first 10 characters of the artist_name. Simply do the following:

```
mysql> ALTER TABLE artist DROP INDEX by_name;
Query OK, 6 rows affected (0.02 sec)
Records: 6  Duplicates: 0  Warnings: 0

mysql> ALTER TABLE artist ADD INDEX by_name (artist_name(10));
Query OK, 6 rows affected (0.03 sec)
Records: 6  Duplicates: 0  Warnings: 0
```

Renaming Tables and Altering Other Structures

We've seen how to modify columns and indexes in a table; now let's see how to modify tables themselves. It's easy to rename a table. Suppose you want to rename played to playlist. Use the following command:

```
mysql> ALTER TABLE played RENAME TO playlist;
Query OK, 0 rows affected (0.00 sec)
```

The TO keyword is optional.

There are several other things you can do with ALTER statements:

- Change the default character set and collation order for a database, a table, or a column.

- Change the order of the rows in a table. This is useful only if you know you want to access the rows in a particular order and you want to help get the data into or near that order.

- Manage and change constraints. For example, you can add and remove foreign keys.

You can find more about these operations in the MySQL manual under the "ALTER DATABASE" and "ALTER TABLE" headings.

Beginning with MySQL 5.1, you can also change the name of a database using the new RENAME DATABASE command:

```
mysql> RENAME DATABASE old_database_name new_database_name;
Query OK, 0 rows affected (0.01 sec)
```

Deleting Structures

In the previous section, we showed how you can delete columns and rows from a database; now we'll describe how to remove databases and tables.

Dropping Databases

Removing, or *dropping*, a database is straightforward. Here's how you drop the music database:

```
mysql> DROP DATABASE music;
Query OK, 4 rows affected (0.01 sec)
```

The number of rows returned in the response is the number of tables removed. You should take care when dropping a database, since all its tables, indexes, and columns are deleted, as are all the associated disk-based files and directories that MySQL uses to maintain them.

If a database doesn't exist, trying to drop it causes MySQL to report an error. Let's try dropping the music database again:

```
mysql> DROP DATABASE music;
ERROR 1008 (HY000): Can't drop database 'music'; database doesn't exist
```

You can avoid the error, which is useful when including the statement in a script, by using the IF EXISTS phrase:

```
mysql> DROP DATABASE IF EXISTS music;
Query OK, 0 rows affected, 1 warning (0.00 sec)
```

You can see that a warning is reported, since the music database has already been dropped. You can always check what the warning was with the SHOW WARNINGS statement, which has been available since MySQL 4.1.0:

```
mysql> SHOW WARNINGS;
+-------+------+------------------------------------------------------+
| Level | Code | Message                                              |
+-------+------+------------------------------------------------------+
| Note  | 1008 | Can't drop database 'music'; database doesn't exist  |
+-------+------+------------------------------------------------------+
1 row in set (0.00 sec)
```

The warning is also generated with the error if you leave out the IF EXISTS clause.

Removing Tables

Removing tables is as easy as removing a database. Let's create and remove a table from the `music` database:

```
mysql> CREATE TABLE temp (temp INT(3), PRIMARY KEY (temp));
Query OK, 0 rows affected (0.00 sec)

mysql> DROP TABLE temp;
Query OK, 0 rows affected (0.00 sec)
```

Don't worry: the `0 rows affected` message is misleading. You'll find the table is definitely gone.

You can use the `IF EXISTS` phrase to prevent errors. Let's try dropping the `temp` table again:

```
mysql> DROP TABLE IF EXISTS temp;
Query OK, 0 rows affected, 1 warning (0.00 sec)
```

Again, you can investigate the warning indicates with the `SHOW WARNINGS` statement:

```
mysql> SHOW WARNINGS;
+-------+------+----------------------+
| Level | Code | Message              |
+-------+------+----------------------+
| Note  | 1051 | Unknown table 'temp' |
+-------+------+----------------------+
1 row in set (0.00 sec)
```

You can drop more than one table in a single statement by separating table names with commas:

```
mysql> DROP TABLE IF EXISTS temp, temp1, temp2;
Query OK, 0 rows affected, 3 warnings (0.00 sec)
```

You can see three warnings because none of these tables existed.

Exercises

All exercises here concern the `music` database. You'll find that the `CREATE TABLE` statements in "The Sample Music Database" are a useful reference.

1. You've decided to store more information about artists and albums. Specifically, for artists, you want to store the names of people who have worked with the artist (for example, vocalists, guitarists, trumpeters, and drummers), when they began working with the artist, and when they stopped working with the artist (if they have done so).

   For albums, you want to store the name of the album producer, when the album was released, and where the album was recorded. Design tables or columns that can store this information, and explain the advantages and disadvantages of your design. Choose the column types you need, explaining the advantages and disadvantages of your choices.

2. There are five types for storing temporal data: DATETIME, DATE, TIME, YEAR, and TIMESTAMP. Explain what each is used for, and give an example of a situation in which you would choose to use it.

3. You've decided to use the AUTO_INCREMENT feature. List the three requirements that must be met by the column you're applying it to.

4. Why can only one column in a table have the AUTO_INCREMENT feature?

5. Using the monitor, create a table with the following statement:

```
mysql> CREATE TABLE exercise (field1 INT(3));
```

Using the ALTER TABLE statement, make field1 the primary key, carrying out any additional steps you need to make this possible. Add a second column, field2, of type CHAR(64) with a DEFAULT 5 clause. Create an index on a prefix of 10 characters from field2.

## CHAPTER 7

Advanced Querying

Over the previous two chapters, you've completed an introduction to the basic features of querying and modifying databases with SQL. You should now be able to create, modify, and remove database structures, as well as work with data as you read, insert, delete, and update entries. Over the next three chapters, we'll look at more advanced concepts. You can skim these chapters and return to read them thoroughly when you're comfortable with using MySQL.

This chapter teaches you more about querying, giving you skills to answer complex information needs. You'll learn how to:

- Use nicknames, or *aliases*, in queries to save typing and allow a table to be used more than once in a query
- Aggregate data into groups so you can discover sums, averages, and counts
- Join tables in different ways
- Use nested queries
- Save query results in variables so they can be reused in other queries
- Understand why MySQL supports several table types

Aliases

Aliases are nicknames. They give you a shorthand way of expressing a column, table, or function name, allowing you to:

- Write shorter queries
- Express your queries more clearly
- Use one table in two or more ways in a single query
- Access data more easily from programs (for example, from PHP scripts, as discussed in Chapter 14)

- Use special types of nested queries; these are the subject of "Nested Queries," discussed later in this chapter

Column Aliases

Column aliases are useful for improving the expression of your queries, reducing the number of characters you need to type, and making it easier to work with languages such as PHP. Consider a simple, not-very-useful example:

```
mysql> SELECT artist_name AS artists FROM artist;
+--------------------------+
| artists                  |
+--------------------------+
| New Order                |
| Nick Cave & The Bad Seeds |
| Miles Davis              |
| The Rolling Stones       |
| The Stone Roses          |
| Kylie Minogue            |
+--------------------------+
6 rows in set (0.00 sec)
```

The column artist_name is aliased as artists. You can see that in the output, the usual column heading, artist_name, is replaced by the alias artists. The advantage is that the alias artists might be more meaningful to users. Other than that, it's not very useful, but it does illustrate the idea: for a column, you add the keyword AS and then a string that represents what you'd like the column to be known as.

Now let's see column aliases doing something useful. Here's an example that uses a MySQL function and an ORDER BY clause:

```
mysql> SELECT CONCAT(artist_name, " recorded ", album_name) AS recording
    -> FROM artist INNER JOIN album USING (artist_id)
    -> ORDER BY recording;
+----------------------------------------------------------------+
| recording                                                      |
+----------------------------------------------------------------+
| Kylie Minogue recorded Light Years                             |
| Miles Davis recorded In A Silent Way                           |
| Miles Davis recorded Live Around The World                     |
| New Order recorded Brotherhood                                 |
| New Order recorded Power, Corruption & Lies                    |
| New Order recorded Retro - John McCready FAN                   |
| New Order recorded Retro - Miranda Sawyer POP                  |
| New Order recorded Retro - New Order / Bobby Gillespie LIVE    |
| New Order recorded Substance (Disc 2)                          |
| New Order recorded Substance 1987 (Disc 1)                     |
| Nick Cave & The Bad Seeds recorded Let Love In                 |
| The Rolling Stones recorded Exile On Main Street               |
| The Stone Roses recorded Second Coming                         |
+----------------------------------------------------------------+
13 rows in set (0.03 sec)
```

The MySQL function `CONCAT( )` *concatenates* together the strings that are parameters —in this case, the `artist_name`, a constant string `recorded`, and the `album_name` to give output such as `New Order recorded Brotherhood`. We've added an alias to the function, `AS recording`, so that we can refer to it easily as `recording` throughout the query. You can see that we do this in the `ORDER BY` clause, where we ask MySQL to sort the output by ascending `recording` value. This is much better than the unaliased alternative, which requires you to write out the `CONCAT( )` function again:

```
mysql> SELECT CONCAT(artist_name, " recorded ", album_name)
    -> FROM artist INNER JOIN album USING (artist_id)
    -> ORDER BY CONCAT(artist_name, " recorded ", album_name);
+--------------------------------------------------------------+
| recording                                                    |
+--------------------------------------------------------------+
| Kylie Minogue recorded Light Years                           |
| Miles Davis recorded In A Silent Way                         |
| Miles Davis recorded Live Around The World                   |
| New Order recorded Brotherhood                               |
| New Order recorded Power, Corruption & Lies                  |
| New Order recorded Retro - John McCready FAN                 |
| New Order recorded Retro - Miranda Sawyer POP                |
| New Order recorded Retro - New Order / Bobby Gillespie LIVE  |
| New Order recorded Substance (Disc 2)                        |
| New Order recorded Substance 1987 (Disc 1)                   |
| Nick Cave & The Bad Seeds recorded Let Love In               |
| The Rolling Stones recorded Exile On Main Street             |
| The Stone Roses recorded Second Coming                       |
+--------------------------------------------------------------+
13 rows in set (0.21 sec)
```

The alternative is unwieldy, and worse, you risk mistyping some part of the `ORDER BY` clause and getting a result different from what you expect. (Note that we've used `as recording` on the first line so that the displayed column has the label `recording`.)

There are restrictions on where you can use column aliases. You can't use them in a `WHERE` clause, or in the `USING` and `ON` clauses that we discuss later in this chapter. This means you can't write a query such as:

```
mysql> SELECT artist_name AS a FROM artist WHERE a = "New Order";
ERROR 1054 (42S22): Unknown column 'a' in 'where clause'
```

You can't do this because MySQL doesn't always know the column values before it executes the `WHERE` clause. However, you can use column aliases in the `ORDER BY` clause, and in the `GROUP BY` and `HAVING` clauses discussed later in this chapter.

The `AS` keyword is optional. Because of this, the following two queries are equivalent:

```
mysql> SELECT artist_id AS id FROM artist WHERE artist_name = "New Order";
+----+
| id |
+----+
|  1 |
+----+
1 row in set (0.05 sec)
```

```
mysql> SELECT artist_id id FROM artist WHERE artist_name = "New Order";
+----+
| id |
+----+
|  1 |
+----+
1 row in set (0.00 sec)
```

We recommend using the AS keyword, since it helps to clearly distinguish an aliased column, especially where you're selecting multiple columns from a list of columns separated by commas.

Alias names have few restrictions. They can be at most 255 characters in length and can contain any character. If you plan to use characters that might confuse the MySQL parser—such as periods, commas, or semicolons—make sure you enclose the alias name in backticks. We recommend using lowercase alphanumeric strings for alias names and using a consistent character choice—such as an underscore—to separate words. Aliases are case-insensitive on all platforms.

Table Aliases

Table aliases are useful for the same reasons as column aliases, but they are also sometimes the only way to express a query. This section shows you how to use table aliases, and "Nested Queries," later in this chapter, shows you other sample queries where table aliases are essential.

Here's a basic table-alias example that shows you how to save some typing:

```
mysql> SELECT ar.artist_id, al.album_name, ar.artist_name FROM
    -> album AS al INNER JOIN artist AS ar
    -> USING (artist_id) WHERE al.album_name = "Brotherhood";
+-----------+-------------+-------------+
| artist_id | album_name  | artist_name |
+-----------+-------------+-------------+
|         1 | Brotherhood | New Order   |
+-----------+-------------+-------------+
1 row in set (0.00 sec)
```

You can see that the album and artist tables are aliased as al and ar, respectively, using the AS keyword. This allows you to express column names more compactly, such as ar.artist_id. Notice also that you can use table aliases in the WHERE clause; unlike column aliases, there are no restrictions on where table aliases can be used in queries. From our example, you can see that we're referring to the table aliases before they have been defined.

As with column aliases, the AS keyword is optional. This means that:

```
album AS al INNER JOIN artist AS ar
```

is the same as:

```
album al INNER JOIN artist ar
```

Again, we prefer the **AS** style, as it's clearer to anyone looking at your queries than the alternative. The restrictions on table-alias-name characters and lengths are the same as column aliases, and our recommendations on choosing them are the same, too.

As discussed in the introduction to this section, table aliases allow you to write queries that you can't otherwise easily express. Consider an example: suppose you want to know whether two or more artists have released an album of the same name and, if so, what the identifiers for those artists are. Let's think about the basic requirement: you want to know if two albums have the same name. To do this, you might try a query like this:

```
mysql> SELECT * FROM album WHERE album_name = album_name;
```

But that doesn't make sense: an album has the same name as itself, and so it just produces all albums as output:

```
+-----------+----------+-------------------------------------------+
| artist_id | album_id | album_name                                |
+-----------+----------+-------------------------------------------+
|         2 |        1 | Let Love In                               |
|         1 |        1 | Retro - John McCready FAN                 |
|         1 |        2 | Substance (Disc 2)                        |
|         1 |        3 | Retro - Miranda Sawyer POP                |
|         1 |        4 | Retro - New Order / Bobby Gillespie LIVE  |
|         3 |        1 | Live Around The World                     |
|         3 |        2 | In A Silent Way                           |
|         1 |        5 | Power, Corruption & Lies                  |
|         4 |        1 | Exile On Main Street                      |
|         1 |        6 | Substance 1987 (Disc 1)                   |
|         5 |        1 | Second Coming                             |
|         6 |        1 | Light Years                               |
|         1 |        7 | Brotherhood                               |
+-----------+----------+-------------------------------------------+
13 rows in set (0.01 sec)
```

What you really want is to know if two different albums from the album table have the same name. But how can you do that in a single query? The answer is to give the table two different aliases; you then check if one row in the first aliased table matches a row in the second:

```
mysql> SELECT a1.artist_id, a2.album_id
    -> FROM album AS a1, album AS a2 WHERE
    -> a1.album_name = a2.album_name;
+-----------+----------+
| artist_id | album_id |
+-----------+----------+
|         2 |        1 |
|         1 |        1 |
|         1 |        2 |
|         1 |        3 |
|         1 |        4 |
|         3 |        1 |
```

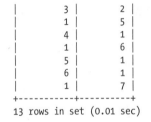

```
|          3 |        2 |
|          1 |        5 |
|          4 |        1 |
|          1 |        6 |
|          5 |        1 |
|          6 |        1 |
|          1 |        7 |
+-----------+----------+
13 rows in set (0.01 sec)
```

But it still doesn't work! We get all 13 albums as answers. The reason is that an album still matches itself because it occurs in both aliased tables.

To get the query to work, we need to make sure an album from one aliased table doesn't match itself in the other aliased table. The way to do so is to specify that the albums in each table shouldn't have the same artist:

```
mysql> SELECT a1.artist_id, a2.album_id
    -> FROM album AS a1, album AS a2
    -> WHERE a1.album_name = a2.album_name
    -> AND a1.artist_id != a2.artist_id;
Empty set (0.00 sec)
```

You can now see that there aren't two albums in the database with the same name but by different artists. The additional `AND a1.artist_id != a2.artist_id` stops answers from being reported where the artist is the same in both tables.

Table aliases are also useful in nested queries that use the `EXISTS` and `ON` clauses. We show you examples later in this chapter when we introduce nested techniques.

Aggregating Data

Aggregate functions allow you to discover the properties of a group of rows. You use them for purposes such as discovering how many rows there are in a table, how many rows in a table share a property (such as having the same name or date of birth), finding averages (such as the average temperature in November), or finding the maximum or minimum values of rows that meet some condition (such as finding the coldest day in August).

This section explains the `GROUP BY` and `HAVING` clauses, the two most commonly used SQL statements for aggregation. But first, it explains the `DISTINCT` clause, which is used to report unique results for the output of a query. When neither the `DISTINCT` nor the `GROUP BY` clause is specified, the returned raw data can still be processed using the aggregate functions that we describe in this section.

The DISTINCT Clause

To begin our discussion on aggregate functions, we'll focus on the `DISTINCT` clause. This isn't really an aggregate function, but more of a post-processing filter that allows you to remove duplicates. We've added it into this section because, like aggregate functions, it's concerned with picking examples from the output of a query, rather than processing individual rows.

An example is the best way to understand DISTINCT. Consider this query:

```
mysql> SELECT DISTINCT artist_name FROM
    -> artist INNER JOIN album USING (artist_id);
+---------------------------+
| artist_name               |
+---------------------------+
| New Order                 |
| Nick Cave & The Bad Seeds |
| Miles Davis               |
| The Rolling Stones        |
| The Stone Roses           |
| Kylie Minogue             |
+---------------------------+
6 rows in set (0.03 sec)
```

The query finds artists who have made albums—by joining together **artist** and **album** with an INNER JOIN clause—and reports one example of each artist. You can see that we have six artists in our database for whom we own albums. If you remove the DISTINCT clause, you get one row of output for each album we own:

```
mysql> SELECT artist_name FROM
    -> artist INNER JOIN album USING (artist_id);
+---------------------------+
| artist_name               |
+---------------------------+
| New Order                 |
| New Order                 |
| New Order                 |
| New Order                 |
| New Order                 |
| New Order                 |
| New Order                 |
| Nick Cave & The Bad Seeds |
| Miles Davis               |
| Miles Davis               |
| The Rolling Stones        |
| The Stone Roses           |
| Kylie Minogue             |
+---------------------------+
13 rows in set (0.00 sec)
```

So, the DISTINCT clause helps get a summary.

The DISTINCT clause applies to the query output and removes rows that have identical values in the columns selected for output in the query. If you rephrase the previous query to output both artist_name and album_name (but otherwise don't change the JOIN clause and still use DISTINCT), you'll get all 13 rows in the output:

```
mysql> SELECT DISTINCT artist_name, album_name FROM
    -> artist INNER JOIN album USING (artist_id);
```

```
+-----------------------------+----------------------------------------+
| artist_name                 | album_name                             |
+-----------------------------+----------------------------------------+
| New Order                   | Retro - John McCready FAN              |
| New Order                   | Substance (Disc 2)                     |
| New Order                   | Retro - Miranda Sawyer POP             |
| New Order                   | Retro - New Order / Bobby Gillespie LIVE |
| New Order                   | Power, Corruption & Lies               |
| New Order                   | Substance 1987 (Disc 1)                |
| New Order                   | Brotherhood                            |
| Nick Cave & The Bad Seeds   | Let Love In                            |
| Miles Davis                 | Live Around The World                  |
| Miles Davis                 | In A Silent Way                        |
| The Rolling Stones          | Exile On Main Street                   |
| The Stone Roses             | Second Coming                          |
| Kylie Minogue               | Light Years                            |
+-----------------------------+----------------------------------------+
13 rows in set (0.00 sec)
```

Because none of the rows are identical, no duplicates are removed using `DISTINCT`. You can check this by rephrasing the query to omit the `DISTINCT` clause; you'll get the same output.

To remove duplicates, MySQL needs to sort the output. If indexes are available that are in the same order as required for the sort—or the data itself is in an order that's useful—this process has very little overhead. However, for large tables and without an easy way of accessing the data in the right order, sorting can be very slow. You should use `DISTINCT` (and other aggregate functions) with caution on large data sets. If you do use it, you can check its behavior using the `EXPLAIN` statement discussed in Chapter 8.

The GROUP BY Clause

The `GROUP BY` clause sorts data into groups for the purpose of aggregation. It's similar to `ORDER BY`, but it occurs much earlier in the query process: `GROUP BY` is used to organize the data before other clauses—such as `WHERE`, `ORDER BY`, and functions—are applied. In contrast, `ORDER BY` is applied last—after the query has been resolved—to reorganize the query output for display.

An example will help you understand what `GROUP BY` is used for. Suppose you want to know how many albums we own by each artist. Using the techniques you've learned so far, you could perform an `INNER JOIN` between `artist` and `album`, and use an `ORDER BY artist_name` clause to organize the artists into an order to make it easy for you to count. Here's the query that you'd use:

```
mysql> SELECT artist_name FROM
    -> artist INNER JOIN album USING (artist_id)
    -> ORDER BY artist_name;
+---------------------------+
| artist_name               |
+---------------------------+
| Kylie Minogue             |
```

```
| Miles Davis              |
| Miles Davis              |
| New Order                |
| New Order                |
| New Order                |
| New Order                |
| New Order                |
| New Order                |
| New Order                |
| Nick Cave & The Bad Seeds |
| The Rolling Stones       |
| The Stone Roses          |
+--------------------------+
13 rows in set (0.00 sec)
```

By running down the list, it's easy to count off how many albums we've got by each artist: one by Kylie Minogue, two by Miles Davis, seven by New Order, and so on.

The GROUP BY clause can help automate this process by grouping the albums by artist; we can then use the COUNT( ) function to count off the number of albums in each group. Here's the query that does what we want:

```
mysql> SELECT artist_name, COUNT(artist_name) FROM
    -> artist INNER JOIN album USING (artist_id)
    -> GROUP BY artist_name;
+--------------------------+--------------------+
| artist_name              | COUNT(artist_name) |
+--------------------------+--------------------+
| Kylie Minogue            |                  1 |
| Miles Davis              |                  2 |
| New Order                |                  7 |
| Nick Cave & The Bad Seeds |                 1 |
| The Rolling Stones       |                  1 |
| The Stone Roses          |                  1 |
+--------------------------+--------------------+
6 rows in set (0.01 sec)
```

You can see that the output we've asked for is artist_name, COUNT(artist_name), and this tells us exactly what we wanted to know. Notice also that we've used GROUP BY artist_name to sort early for aggregation, rather than using ORDER BY artist_name later for presentation.

Let's consider the query further. We'll start with the GROUP BY clause. This tells us how to put rows together into groups: in this example, we're telling MySQL that the way to group rows is by artist_name. The result is that rows for artists with the same name form a cluster—that is, each distinct name becomes one group. Once the rows are grouped, they're treated in the rest of the query as if they're one row. So, for example, when we write SELECT artist_name, we get just one row for each group. This is exactly the same as DISTINCT, which performs the same function as grouping by a column name and then selecting that column for display. The COUNT( ) function tells us about the properties of the group. More specifically, it tells us the number of rows that form each group; you can count any column in a group, and you'll get the same answer, so

COUNT(artist_name) is the same as COUNT(*) or COUNT(artist_id). Of course, you can use a column alias for the COUNT( ) column.

Let's try another example. Suppose you want to know how many tracks are on each album, along with the artist and album name. Here's the query:

```
mysql> SELECT artist_name, album_name, COUNT(*) FROM
    -> artist INNER JOIN album USING (artist_id)
    -> INNER JOIN track USING (artist_id, album_id)
    -> GROUP BY artist.artist_id, album.album_id;
+--------------------------+------------------------------------+----------+
| artist_name              | album_name                         | COUNT(*) |
+--------------------------+------------------------------------+----------+
| New Order                | Retro - John McCready FAN          |       15 |
| New Order                | Substance (Disc 2)                 |       12 |
| New Order                | Retro - Miranda Sawyer POP         |       14 |
| New Order                | Retro - New Order / Bobby Gillespie|       15 |
| New Order                | Power, Corruption & Lies           |        8 |
| New Order                | Substance 1987 (Disc 1)            |       12 |
| New Order                | Brotherhood                        |       10 |
| Nick Cave & The Bad Seeds| Let Love In                        |       10 |
| Miles Davis              | Live Around The World              |       11 |
| Miles Davis              | In A Silent Way                    |        2 |
| The Rolling Stones       | Exile On Main Street               |       18 |
| The Stone Roses          | Second Coming                      |       13 |
| Kylie Minogue            | Light Years                        |       13 |
+--------------------------+------------------------------------+----------+
13 rows in set (0.12 sec)
```

Before we discuss what's new, think about the general function of the query: it's an INNER JOIN between artist, album, and track using the primary-key (identifier) columns. Forgetting the aggregation for a moment, the output of this query is one row per track.

The GROUP BY clause puts the rows together into clusters. In this query, we want the tracks grouped together for each album by an artist. So, the GROUP BY clause uses artist_id and album_id to do that. You can use the artist_id from any of the three tables; artist.artist_id, album.artist_id, or track.artist_id are the same for this purpose. It doesn't matter since the INNER JOIN makes sure they match anyway. The same applies to album_id.

As in the previous example query, we're using the COUNT( ) function to tell us how many rows are in each group. For example, you can see that COUNT(*) tells us that there are 15 tracks on New Order's *Retro - John McReady FAN* album. Again, it doesn't matter what column or columns you count in the query: for example, COUNT(*) has the same effect as COUNT(artist.artist_id) or COUNT(artist_name).

Let's try another example. Say we want to know how many times we've listened to tracks on each album. This query is a little trickier than the previous ones: we need to think carefully about how to group the rows. We want rows for each album grouped together—that is, we want to count the total number of times that any of the tracks on the album have been played. So, we want to group together by artist and by album; we don't want to group by track, since that'd split the tracks from each album into different groups and tell us how many times we'd listened to each track. We also need a four-way join between all four tables in the database, but that isn't hard to do using the skills we've developed so far. Here's the query:

```
mysql> SELECT artist_name, album_name, COUNT(*) FROM
    -> artist INNER JOIN album USING (artist_id)
    -> INNER JOIN track USING (artist_id, album_id)
    -> INNER JOIN played USING (artist_id, album_id, track_id)
    -> GROUP BY album.artist_id, album.album_id;
+-------------+------------------------------+----------+
| artist_name | album_name                   | COUNT(*) |
+-------------+------------------------------+----------+
| New Order   | Retro - Miranda Sawyer POP   |        8 |
| Miles Davis | Live Around The World        |        3 |
+-------------+------------------------------+----------+
2 rows in set (0.11 sec)
```

You can see we've only listened to two albums: we've listened to one or more tracks on New Order's *Retro - Miranda Sawyer POP* eight times, and one or more tracks on the Miles Davis album *Live Around The World* three times. We don't know whether it's the same track we've listened to multiple times, different tracks a few times, or many tracks once: the GROUP BY clause hides the details. Again, we use COUNT(*) to do the counting of rows in the groups, and you can see the INNER JOIN spread over lines 2 to 4 in the query.

Before we end this section, let's consider how results are displayed for a grouping operation. The output rows are grouped together according to the GROUP BY clause, with one row displayed for each group. You will typically not ask for fields that are collected together in the grouping process, since the result will be meaningless. For example, grouping the tracks by artist will produce:

```
mysql> SELECT * FROM track GROUP BY artist_id;
+----------+----------------------+-----------+----------+----------+
| track_id | track_name           | artist_id | album_id | time     |
+----------+----------------------+-----------+----------+----------+
| 0        | Elegia               | 1         | 1        | 00:04:93 |
| 0        | Do You Love Me?      | 2         | 1        | 00:05:95 |
| 0        | In A Silent Way      | 3         | 1        | 00:01:81 |
| 0        | Rocks Off            | 4         | 1        | 00:04:54 |
| 0        | Breaking Into Heaven | 5         | 1        | 00:11:37 |
| 0        | Spinning Around      | 6         | 1        | 00:03:46 |
+----------+----------------------+-----------+----------+----------+
6 rows in set (0.01 sec)
```

Only the artist_id here is meaningful; the rest of the columns just contain the first-listed entry from each group. To illustrate this point, "Elegia" is the first track that would be listed for artist_id 1 if we hadn't performed any grouping:

```
mysql> SELECT * FROM track WHERE artist_id=1;
+----------+----------------------+-----------+----------+----------+
```

```
| track_id | track_name          | artist_id | album_id | time     |
+----------+---------------------+-----------+----------+----------+
| 0        | Elegia              | 1         | 1        | 00:04:93 |
| 1        | In A Lonely Place   | 1         | 1        | 00:06:26 |
| 2        | Procession          | 1         | 1        | 00:04:28 |
...
+----------+---------------------+-----------+----------+----------+
86 rows in set (0.00 sec)
```

Other aggregate functions

We've seen examples of how the COUNT( ) function can be used to tell how many rows are in a group. Here are other functions commonly used to explore the properties of aggregated rows:

AVG( )

Returns the average (mean) of the values in the specified column for all rows in a group. For example, you could use it to find the average cost of a house in a city, when the houses are grouped by city:

```
SELECT AVG(cost) FROM house_prices GROUP BY city;
```

MAX( )

Returns the maximum value from rows in a group. For example, you could use it to find the warmest day in a month, when the rows are grouped by month.

MIN( )

Returns the minimum value from rows in a group. For example, you could use it to find the youngest student in a class, when the rows are grouped by class.

STD( ) or STDDEV( )

Returns the standard deviation of values from rows in a group. For example, you could use it to understand the spread of test scores, when rows are grouped by university course.

SUM( )

Returns the sum of values from rows in a group. For example, you could use it to compute the dollar amount of sales in a given month, when rows are grouped by month.

There are other functions available for use with GROUP BY; they're less frequently used than the ones we've introduced. You can find more details on them in the MySQL manual under the heading "GROUP BY (Aggregate) Functions."

The HAVING Clause

You're now familiar with the GROUP BY clause, which allows you to sort and cluster data. You should now be able to use it find out about counts, averages, minimums, and maximums. This section shows how you can use the HAVING clause to add additional control to the aggregation of rows in a GROUP BY operation.

Suppose you want to know how many times you've listened to tracks on popular albums. You've decided to define an album as popular if you've listened to one or more of its tracks at least five times. In the previous section, we tried an almost identical query but without the popularity limitation. Here's the new query, with an additional HAVING clause that adds the constraint:

```
mysql> SELECT artist_name, album_name, COUNT(*) FROM
    -> artist INNER JOIN album USING (artist_id)
    -> INNER JOIN track USING (artist_id, album_id)
    -> INNER JOIN played USING (artist_id, album_id, track_id)
    -> GROUP BY album.artist_id, album.album_id
    -> HAVING COUNT(*) >= 5;
+-------------+---------------------------+----------+
| artist_name | album_name                | COUNT(*) |
+-------------+---------------------------+----------+
| New Order   | Retro - Miranda Sawyer POP |       8 |
+-------------+---------------------------+----------+
1 row in set (0.01 sec)
```

You can see there's only one album that meets the new criteria.

The HAVING clause must contain an expression or column that's listed in the SELECT clause. In this example, we've used HAVING COUNT(*) >= 5, and you can see that COUNT(*) is part of the SELECT clause. Typically, the expression in the HAVING clause uses an aggregate function such as COUNT( ), SUM( ), MIN( ), or MAX( ). If you find yourself wanting to write a HAVING clause that uses a column or expression that isn't in the SELECT clause, chances are you should be using a WHERE clause instead. The HAVING clause is only for deciding how to form each group or cluster, not for choosing rows in the output. We'll show you an example later that illustrates when not to use HAVING.

Let's try another example. Suppose you want a list of albums that have more than 10 tracks, together with the number of tracks they contain. Here's the query you'd use:

```
mysql> SELECT artist_name, album_name, COUNT(*) FROM
    -> artist INNER JOIN album USING (artist_id)
    -> INNER JOIN track USING (artist_id, album_id)
    -> GROUP BY artist.artist_id, album.album_id
    -> HAVING COUNT(*) > 10;
+-------------------+------------------------------------------+----------+
| artist_name       | album_name                               | COUNT(*) |
+-------------------+------------------------------------------+----------+
| New Order         | Retro - John McCready FAN                |       15 |
| New Order         | Substance (Disc 2)                       |       12 |
| New Order         | Retro - Miranda Sawyer POP               |       14 |
| New Order         | Retro - New Order / Bobby Gillespie LIVE |       15 |
| New Order         | Substance 1987 (Disc 1)                  |       12 |
| Miles Davis       | Live Around The World                    |       11 |
| The Rolling Stones | Exile On Main Street                     |       18 |
| The Stone Roses   | Second Coming                            |       13 |
| Kylie Minogue     | Light Years                              |       13 |
+-------------------+------------------------------------------+----------+
9 rows in set (0.00 sec)
```

You can again see that the expression `COUNT(*)` is used in both the `SELECT` and `HAVING` clauses.

Now let's consider an example where you shouldn't use `HAVING`. You want to know how many tracks are on albums by New Order. Here's the query you shouldn't use:

```
mysql> SELECT artist_name, album_name, COUNT(*) FROM
    -> artist INNER JOIN album USING (artist_id)
    -> INNER JOIN track USING (artist_id, album_id)
    -> GROUP BY artist.artist_id, album.album_id
    -> HAVING artist_name = "New Order";
+-------------+----------------------------------------+----------+
| artist_name | album_name                             | COUNT(*) |
+-------------+----------------------------------------+----------+
| New Order   | Retro - John McCready FAN              |       15 |
| New Order   | Substance (Disc 2)                     |       12 |
| New Order   | Retro - Miranda Sawyer POP             |       14 |
| New Order   | Retro - New Order / Bobby Gillespie LIVE |     15 |
| New Order   | Power, Corruption & Lies               |        8 |
| New Order   | Substance 1987 (Disc 1)                |       12 |
| New Order   | Brotherhood                            |       10 |
+-------------+----------------------------------------+----------+
7 rows in set (0.00 sec)
```

It gets the right answer, but in the wrong—and, for large amounts of data, much slower—way. It's not the correct way to write the query because the `HAVING` clause isn't being used to decide what rows should form each group, but is instead being incorrectly used to filter the answers to display. For this query, we should really use a `WHERE` clause as follows:

```
mysql> SELECT artist_name, album_name, COUNT(*) FROM
    -> artist INNER JOIN album USING (artist_id)
    -> INNER JOIN track USING (artist_id, album_id)
    -> WHERE artist_name = "New Order"
    -> GROUP BY artist.artist_id, album.album_id;
+-------------+----------------------------------------+----------+
| artist_name | album_name                             | COUNT(*) |
+-------------+----------------------------------------+----------+
| New Order   | Retro - John McCready FAN              |       15 |
| New Order   | Substance (Disc 2)                     |       12 |
| New Order   | Retro - Miranda Sawyer POP             |       14 |
| New Order   | Retro - New Order / Bobby Gillespie LIVE |     15 |
| New Order   | Power, Corruption & Lies               |        8 |
| New Order   | Substance 1987 (Disc 1)                |       12 |
| New Order   | Brotherhood                            |       10 |
+-------------+----------------------------------------+----------+
7 rows in set (0.00 sec)
```

This correct query forms the groups, and then picks which groups to display based on the `WHERE` clause.

Advanced Joins

So far in the book, we've used the INNER JOIN clause to bring together rows from two or more tables. We'll explain the inner join in more detail in this section, contrasting it with the other join types we explain: the union, left and right joins, and natural joins. At the conclusion of this section, you'll be able to answer difficult information needs and be familiar with the correct choice of join for the task.

The Inner Join

The INNER JOIN clause matches rows between two tables based on the criteria you provide in the USING clause. For example, you're very familiar now with an inner join of the artist and album tables:

```
mysql> SELECT artist_name, album_name FROM
    -> artist INNER JOIN album USING (artist_id);
+--------------------------+------------------------------------------+
| artist_name              | album_name                               |
+--------------------------+------------------------------------------+
| New Order                | Retro - John McCready FAN                 |
| New Order                | Substance (Disc 2)                        |
| New Order                | Retro - Miranda Sawyer POP                |
| New Order                | Retro - New Order / Bobby Gillespie LIVE |
| New Order                | Power, Corruption & Lies                  |
| New Order                | Substance 1987 (Disc 1)                   |
| New Order                | Brotherhood                               |
| Nick Cave & The Bad Seeds | Let Love In                              |
| Miles Davis              | Live Around The World                     |
| Miles Davis              | In A Silent Way                           |
| The Rolling Stones       | Exile On Main Street                      |
| The Stone Roses          | Second Coming                             |
| Kylie Minogue            | Light Years                               |
+--------------------------+------------------------------------------+
13 rows in set (0.00 sec)
```

Let's review the key features of an INNER JOIN:

- Two tables (or results of a previous join) are listed on either side of the INNER JOIN keyphrase.

- The USING clause defines one or more columns that are in both tables or results, and used to join or match rows.

- Rows that don't match aren't returned. For example, if you have a row in the artist table that doesn't have any matching albums in the album table, it won't be included in the output.

You can actually write inner-join queries with the WHERE clause without using the INNER JOIN keyphrase. Here's a rewritten version of the previous query that produces the same result:

```
mysql> SELECT artist_name, album_name FROM artist, album
    -> WHERE artist.artist_id = album.artist_id;
+---------------------------+-------------------------------------------+
| artist_name               | album_name                                |
+---------------------------+-------------------------------------------+
| New Order                 | Retro - John McCready FAN                 |
| New Order                 | Substance (Disc 2)                        |
| New Order                 | Retro - Miranda Sawyer POP                |
| New Order                 | Retro - New Order / Bobby Gillespie LIVE  |
| New Order                 | Power, Corruption & Lies                  |
| New Order                 | Substance 1987 (Disc 1)                   |
| New Order                 | Brotherhood                               |
| Nick Cave & The Bad Seeds | Let Love In                               |
| Miles Davis               | Live Around The World                     |
| Miles Davis               | In A Silent Way                           |
| The Rolling Stones        | Exile On Main Street                      |
| The Stone Roses           | Second Coming                             |
| Kylie Minogue             | Light Years                               |
+---------------------------+-------------------------------------------+
13 rows in set (0.00 sec)
```

You can see that we've spelled out the inner join: we're selecting from the **artist** and **album** tables the rows where the identifiers match between the tables.

You can modify the INNER JOIN syntax to express the join criteria in a way that's similar to using a WHERE clause. This is useful if the names of the identifiers don't match between the tables. Here's the previous query, rewritten in this style:

```
mysql> SELECT artist_name, album_name FROM
    -> artist INNER JOIN album ON artist.artist_id = album.artist_id;
+---------------------------+-------------------------------------------+
| artist_name               | album_name                                |
+---------------------------+-------------------------------------------+
| New Order                 | Retro - John McCready FAN                 |
| New Order                 | Substance (Disc 2)                        |
| New Order                 | Retro - Miranda Sawyer POP                |
| New Order                 | Retro - New Order / Bobby Gillespie LIVE  |
| New Order                 | Power, Corruption & Lies                  |
| New Order                 | Substance 1987 (Disc 1)                   |
| New Order                 | Brotherhood                               |
| Nick Cave & The Bad Seeds | Let Love In                               |
| Miles Davis               | Live Around The World                     |
| Miles Davis               | In A Silent Way                           |
| The Rolling Stones        | Exile On Main Street                      |
| The Stone Roses           | Second Coming                             |
| Kylie Minogue             | Light Years                               |
+---------------------------+-------------------------------------------+
13 rows in set (0.00 sec)
```

You can see that the ON clause replaces the USING clause, and that the columns that follow are fully specified to include the table and column names. There's no real advantage or disadvantage in using ON or a WHERE clause; it's just a matter of taste. Typically, you'll find most SQL professionals use the WHERE clause in preference to INNER JOIN, most likely because it's the technique they learned first.

Before we move on, let's consider what purpose the WHERE, ON, and USING clauses serve. If you omit the WHERE clause from the query we showed you, you get a very different result. Here's the query, and the first few lines of output:

```
mysql> SELECT artist_name, album_name FROM artist, album;
+--------------------------+------------------------------------------+
| artist_name              | album_name                               |
+--------------------------+------------------------------------------+
| New Order                | Let Love In                              |
| Nick Cave & The Bad Seeds | Let Love In                             |
| Miles Davis              | Let Love In                              |
| The Rolling Stones       | Let Love In                              |
| The Stone Roses          | Let Love In                              |
| Kylie Minogue            | Let Love In                              |
| New Order                | Retro - John McCready FAN                |
| Nick Cave & The Bad Seeds | Retro - John McCready FAN               |
| Miles Davis              | Retro - John McCready FAN                |
| The Rolling Stones       | Retro - John McCready FAN                |
| The Stone Roses          | Retro - John McCready FAN                |
| Kylie Minogue            | Retro - John McCready FAN                |
...
```

The output is nonsensical: what's happened is that each row from the artist table has been output alongside each row from the album table, for all possible combinations. Since there are 6 artists and 13 albums, there are 6 × 13 = 78 rows of output, and we know that only 13 of those combinations actually make sense (there are only 13 albums). This type of query, without a clause that matches rows, is known as a *Cartesian product*. Incidentally, you also get the Cartesian product if you perform an inner join without specifying a column with a USING or ON clause, as in the query:

```
SELECT artist_name, album_name FROM artist INNER JOIN album;
```

Later in "The Natural Join," we'll introduce the natural join, which is an inner join on identically named columns. While the natural join doesn't use explicitly specified columns, it still produces an inner join, rather than a Cartesian product.

The keyphrase INNER JOIN can be replaced with JOIN or STRAIGHT JOIN; they all do the same thing. However, STRAIGHT JOIN forces MySQL to always read the table on the left before it reads the table on the right. We'll have a look at how MySQL processes queries behind the scenes in Chapter 8. The keyphrase INNER JOIN is the one you'll see most commonly used: it's used by many other database systems besides MySQL, and we use it in all our inner-join examples.

The Union

The UNION statement isn't really a join operator. Rather, it allows you to combine the output of more than one SELECT statement to give a consolidated result set. It's useful in cases where you want to produce a single list from more than one source, or you want to create lists from a single source that are difficult to express in a single query.

Let's look at an example. If you wanted to output all of the text in the music database, you could do this with a UNION statement. It's a contrived example, but you might want to do this just to list all of the text fragments, rather than to meaningfully present the relationships between the data. There's text in the artist_name, album_name, and track_name columns in the artist, album, and track tables, respectively. Here's how to display it:

```
mysql> SELECT artist_name FROM artist
    -> UNION
    -> SELECT album_name FROM album
    -> UNION
    -> SELECT track_name FROM track;
+------------------------------------------+
| artist_name                              |
+------------------------------------------+
| New Order                                |
| Nick Cave & The Bad Seeds                |
| Miles Davis                              |
| The Rolling Stones                       |
| The Stone Roses                          |
| Kylie Minogue                            |
| Let Love In                              |
| Retro - John McCready FAN                |
| Substance (Disc 2)                       |
| Retro - Miranda Sawyer POP               |
| Retro - New Order / Bobby Gillespie LIVE |
| Live Around The World                    |
| In A Silent Way                          |
| Power, Corruption & Lies                 |
| Exile On Main Street                     |
| Substance 1987 (Disc 1)                  |
| Second Coming                            |
| Light Years                              |
| Brotherhood                              |
| Do You Love Me?                          |
...
```

We've only shown the first 20 of 153 rows. The UNION statement outputs all results from all queries together, under a heading appropriate to the first query.

A slightly less contrived example is to create a list of the first five and last five tracks you've played. You can do this easily with the UNION operator:

```
mysql> (SELECT track_name FROM
    -> track INNER JOIN played USING (artist_id, album_id, track_id)
    -> ORDER BY played ASC LIMIT 5)
    -> UNION
    -> (SELECT track_name FROM
    -> track INNER JOIN played USING (artist_id, album_id, track_id)
    -> ORDER BY played DESC LIMIT 5);
+-----------------------+
| track_name            |
+-----------------------+
| Fine Time             |
```

```
| Temptation            |
| True Faith            |
| The Perfect Kiss      |
| Ceremony              |
| New Blues             |
| Intruder              |
| In A Silent Way       |
| Bizarre Love Triangle |
| Crystal               |
+-----------------------+
10 rows in set (0.09 sec)
```

The first query uses ORDER BY with the ASC (ascending) modifier and a LIMIT 5 clause to find the first five tracks played. The second query uses ORDER BY with the DESC (descending) modifier and a LIMIT 5 clause to find the last five tracks played. The UNION combines the result sets.

The UNION operator has several limitations:

- The output is labeled with the names of the columns or expressions from the first query. Use column aliases to change this behavior.

- The queries should output the same number of columns. If you try using different numbers of columns, MySQL will report an error.

- All matching columns should have the same type. So, for example, if the first column output from the first query is a date, the first column output from any other query must be a date.

- The results returned are unique, as if you'd applied a DISTINCT to the overall result set. To see this in action, let's add a new row for the track "Fine Time" to the played table. This has artist_id 1, album_id 3, and track_id 0:

  ```
  mysql> INSERT INTO played SET
      -> artist_id = 1,
      -> album_id = 3,
      -> track_id = 0,
      -> played='2006-08-14 10:27:03';
  Query OK, 1 row affected (0.02 sec)
  ```

  We've used the more verbose INSERT format to clarify what we're inserting.

  Now, if you run the previous SELECT query again, you'll see 9 rows instead of 10, since "Fine Time" appears twice in the first 5 tracks placed, but the implicit DISTINCT operation means it's shown only once:

  ```
  mysql> (SELECT track_name FROM
      -> track INNER JOIN played USING (artist_id, album_id, track_id)
      -> ORDER BY played ASC LIMIT 5)
      -> UNION
      -> (SELECT track_name FROM
      -> track INNER JOIN played USING (artist_id, album_id, track_id)
      -> ORDER BY played DESC LIMIT 5);
  +-----------------------+
  | track_name            |
  ```

```
+-----------------------+
| Fine Time             |
| Temptation            |
| True Faith            |
| The Perfect Kiss      |
| New Blues             |
| Intruder              |
| In A Silent Way       |
| Bizarre Love Triangle |
| Crystal               |
+-----------------------+
9 rows in set (0.01 sec)
```

If you want to show any duplicates, replace UNION with UNION ALL:

```
mysql> (SELECT track_name FROM
    -> track INNER JOIN played USING (artist_id, album_id, track_id)
    -> ORDER BY played ASC LIMIT 5)
    -> UNION ALL
    -> (SELECT track_name FROM
    -> track INNER JOIN played USING (artist_id, album_id, track_id)
    -> ORDER BY played DESC LIMIT 5);
+-----------------------+
| track_name            |
+-----------------------+
| Fine Time             |
| Temptation            |
| Fine Time             |
| True Faith            |
| The Perfect Kiss      |
| New Blues             |
| Intruder              |
| In A Silent Way       |
| Bizarre Love Triangle |
| Crystal               |
+-----------------------+
10 rows in set (0.00 sec)
```

Here, "Fine Time" appears twice.

- If you want to apply LIMIT or ORDER BY to an individual query that is part of a UNION statement, enclose that query in parentheses (as shown in the previous example). It's useful to use parentheses anyway to keep the query easy to understand.

The UNION operation simply concatenates the results of the component queries with no attention to order, so there's not much point in using ORDER BY within one of the subqueries. The only time that it makes sense to order a subquery in a UNION operation is when you want to select a subset of results. In our example, we've ordered the tracks by the time they were played, and then selected only the first five (in the first subquery) and the last five (in the second subquery).

For efficiency, MySQL will actually ignore an ORDER BY clause within a subquery if it's used without LIMIT. Let's look at some examples to see exactly how this works.

First, let's run a simple query to list the tracks that have been played, along with the time each track was played. We've enclosed the query in parentheses for consistency with our other examples—the parentheses don't actually have any effect here—and haven't used an ORDER BY or LIMIT clause:

```
mysql> (SELECT track_name, played
    -> FROM track INNER JOIN played USING (artist_id, album_id, track_id)
    -> );
+----------------------+---------------------+
| track_name           | played              |
+----------------------+---------------------+
| Fine Time            | 2006-08-14 10:21:03 |
| Fine Time            | 2006-08-14 10:27:03 |
| Temptation           | 2006-08-14 10:25:22 |
| True Faith           | 2006-08-14 10:30:25 |
| The Perfect Kiss     | 2006-08-14 10:36:54 |
| Ceremony             | 2006-08-14 10:41:43 |
| Regret               | 2006-08-14 10:43:37 |
| Crystal              | 2006-08-14 10:47:21 |
| Bizarre Love Triangle| 2006-08-14 10:54:02 |
| In A Silent Way      | 2006-08-15 14:00:03 |
| Intruder             | 2006-08-15 14:26:12 |
| New Blues            | 2006-08-15 14:33:57 |
+----------------------+---------------------+
12 rows in set (0.00 sec)
```

The query returns all the played tracks, in no particular order (see the second and third entries).

Now, let's add an ORDER BY clause to this query:

```
mysql> (SELECT track_name, played
    -> FROM track INNER JOIN played USING (artist_id, album_id, track_id)
    -> ORDER BY played ASC);
+----------------------+---------------------+
| track_name           | played              |
+----------------------+---------------------+
| Fine Time            | 2006-08-14 10:21:03 |
| Temptation           | 2006-08-14 10:25:22 |
| Fine Time            | 2006-08-14 10:27:03 |
| True Faith           | 2006-08-14 10:30:25 |
| The Perfect Kiss     | 2006-08-14 10:36:54 |
| Ceremony             | 2006-08-14 10:41:43 |
| Regret               | 2006-08-14 10:43:37 |
| Crystal              | 2006-08-14 10:47:21 |
| Bizarre Love Triangle| 2006-08-14 10:54:02 |
| In A Silent Way      | 2006-08-15 14:00:03 |
| Intruder             | 2006-08-15 14:26:12 |
| New Blues            | 2006-08-15 14:33:57 |
+----------------------+---------------------+
12 rows in set (0.03 sec)
```

As expected, we get all the played tracks, in the order that they've been played.

Adding a LIMIT clause to the previous query selects the first five tracks played, in chronological order—no surprises here:

```
mysql> (SELECT track_name, played
    -> FROM track INNER JOIN played USING (artist_id, album_id, track_id)
    -> ORDER BY played ASC LIMIT 5);
+------------------+---------------------+
| track_name       | played              |
+------------------+---------------------+
| Fine Time        | 2006-08-14 10:21:03 |
| Temptation       | 2006-08-14 10:25:22 |
| Fine Time        | 2006-08-14 10:27:03 |
| True Faith       | 2006-08-14 10:30:25 |
| The Perfect Kiss | 2006-08-14 10:36:54 |
+------------------+---------------------+
5 rows in set (0.00 sec)
```

Now, let's see what happens when we perform a UNION operation. In this example, we're using two subqueries, each with an ORDER BY clause. We've used a LIMIT clause for the second subquery, but not for the first:

```
mysql> (SELECT track_name, played
    -> FROM track INNER JOIN played USING (artist_id, album_id, track_id)
    -> ORDER BY played ASC)
    -> UNION ALL
    -> (SELECT track_name,played
    -> FROM track INNER JOIN played USING (artist_id, album_id, track_id)
    -> ORDER BY played DESC LIMIT 5);
+----------------------+---------------------+
| track_name           | played              |
+----------------------+---------------------+
| Fine Time            | 2006-08-14 10:21:03 |
| Fine Time            | 2006-08-14 10:27:03 |
| Temptation           | 2006-08-14 10:25:22 |
| True Faith           | 2006-08-14 10:30:25 |
| The Perfect Kiss     | 2006-08-14 10:36:54 |
| Ceremony             | 2006-08-14 10:41:43 |
| Regret               | 2006-08-14 10:43:37 |
| Crystal              | 2006-08-14 10:47:21 |
| Bizarre Love Triangle | 2006-08-14 10:54:02 |
| In A Silent Way      | 2006-08-15 14:00:03 |
| Intruder             | 2006-08-15 14:26:12 |
| New Blues            | 2006-08-15 14:33:57 |
| New Blues            | 2006-08-15 14:33:57 |
| Intruder             | 2006-08-15 14:26:12 |
| In A Silent Way      | 2006-08-15 14:00:03 |
| Bizarre Love Triangle | 2006-08-14 10:54:02 |
| Crystal              | 2006-08-14 10:47:21 |
+----------------------+---------------------+
17 rows in set (0.00 sec)
```

As expected, the first subquery returns all the played tracks (the first 12 rows of this output), and the second subquery returns the last 5 tracks (the last 5 rows of this output). Notice how the first 12 rows are not in order (see the second and third rows), even though the first subquery does have a `ORDER BY` clause. Since we're performing a `UNION` operation, the MySQL server has decided that there's no point sorting the result of the subquery. The second subquery includes a `LIMIT` operation, so the results of that subquery are sorted.

The output of a `UNION` operation isn't guaranteed to be ordered, even if the subqueries are ordered, so if you want the final output to be ordered, you should add an `ORDER BY` clause at the end of the whole query:

```
mysql> (SELECT track_name, played
    -> FROM track INNER JOIN played USING (artist_id, album_id, track_id)
    -> ORDER BY played ASC)
    -> UNION ALL
    -> (SELECT track_name, played
    -> FROM track INNER JOIN played USING (artist_id, album_id, track_id)
    -> ORDER BY played DESC LIMIT 5)
    -> ORDER BY played;
+----------------------+---------------------+
| track_name           | played              |
+----------------------+---------------------+
| Fine Time            | 2006-08-14 10:21:03 |
| Temptation           | 2006-08-14 10:25:22 |
| Fine Time            | 2006-08-14 10:27:03 |
| True Faith           | 2006-08-14 10:30:25 |
| The Perfect Kiss     | 2006-08-14 10:36:54 |
| Ceremony             | 2006-08-14 10:41:43 |
| Regret               | 2006-08-14 10:43:37 |
| Crystal              | 2006-08-14 10:47:21 |
| Crystal              | 2006-08-14 10:47:21 |
| Bizarre Love Triangle| 2006-08-14 10:54:02 |
| Bizarre Love Triangle| 2006-08-14 10:54:02 |
| In A Silent Way      | 2006-08-15 14:00:03 |
| In A Silent Way      | 2006-08-15 14:00:03 |
| Intruder             | 2006-08-15 14:26:12 |
| Intruder             | 2006-08-15 14:26:12 |
| New Blues            | 2006-08-15 14:33:57 |
| New Blues            | 2006-08-15 14:33:57 |
+----------------------+---------------------+
17 rows in set (0.00 sec)
```

Here's another example of sorting the final results, including a limit on the number of returned results:

```
mysql> (SELECT artist_name FROM artist WHERE artist_id < 5)
    -> UNION
    -> (SELECT artist_name FROM artist WHERE artist_id > 7)
    -> ORDER BY artist_name LIMIT 4;
+---------------------------+
| artist_name               |
+---------------------------+
| Miles Davis               |
| New Order                 |
| Nick Cave & The Bad Seeds |
| The Rolling Stones        |
```

```
+---------------------------+
4 rows in set (0.01 sec)
```

The UNION operation is somewhat unwieldy, and there are generally alternative ways of getting the same result. For example, the previous query could have been written more simply as:

```
mysql> SELECT artist_name FROM artist WHERE
    -> artist_id < 3 OR artist_id > 5
    -> ORDER BY artist_name LIMIT 4;
+---------------------------+
| artist_name               |
+---------------------------+
| Kylie Minogue             |
| New Order                 |
| Nick Cave & The Bad Seeds |
+---------------------------+
3 rows in set (0.00 sec)
```

The Left and Right Joins

The joins we've discussed so far output only rows that match between tables. For example, when you join the track and played tables, you see only the tracks that have been played. Therefore, rows for tracks that haven't been played are ignored and—if they existed—would play data for tracks that don't exist. This makes sense in many cases, but it isn't the only way to join data. This section explains other options you have.

Suppose you did want a comprehensive list of all albums and the number of times you've played tracks from them. Unlike the example earlier in this chapter, included in the list you want to see a zero next to albums that haven't been played. You can do this with a *left join*, a different type of join that's driven by one of the two tables participating in the join. A left join works like this: each row in the left table—the one that's doing the driving—is processed and output, with the matching data from the second table if it exists and NULL values if there is no matching data in the second table. We'll show you how to write this type of query later in this section, but we'll start with a simpler example.

Here's a simple LEFT JOIN example. You want to list all tracks, and next to each track you want to show when it was played. If a track has been never been played, you want to see that. If it's been played many times, you want to see that too. Here's the query:

```
mysql> SELECT track_name, played FROM
    -> track LEFT JOIN played USING (artist_id, album_id, track_id)
    -> ORDER BY played DESC;
+---------------------------+---------------------+
| track_name                | played              |
+---------------------------+---------------------+
| New Blues                 | 2006-08-15 14:33:57 |
| Intruder                  | 2006-08-15 14:26:12 |
| In A Silent Way           | 2006-08-15 14:00:03 |
| Bizarre Love Triangle     | 2006-08-14 10:54:02 |
```

```
| Crystal         | 2006-08-14 10:47:21 |
| Regret          | 2006-08-14 10:43:37 |
| Ceremony        | 2006-08-14 10:41:43 |
| The Perfect Kiss | 2006-08-14 10:36:54 |
| True Faith      | 2006-08-14 10:30:25 |
| Temptation      | 2006-08-14 10:25:22 |
| Fine Time       | 2006-08-14 10:21:03 |
| Do You Love Me? |                NULL |
| Nobody's Baby Now |              NULL |
| Loverman        |                NULL |
| Jangling Jack   |                NULL |
| Red Right Hand  |                NULL |
| I Let Love In   |                NULL |
...
```

You can see what happens: tracks that have been played have dates and times, and those that haven't don't (the played value is NULL). We've added an ORDER BY played DESC to display the output from most to least recently played, where "never played" (NULL) is the smallest possible value.

The order of the tables in the LEFT JOIN is important. If you reverse the order in the previous query, you get very different output:

```
mysql> SELECT track_name, played FROM
    -> played LEFT JOIN track USING (artist_id, album_id, track_id)
    -> ORDER BY played DESC;
+----------------------+---------------------+
| track_name           | played              |
+----------------------+---------------------+
| New Blues            | 2006-08-15 14:33:57 |
| Intruder             | 2006-08-15 14:26:12 |
| In A Silent Way      | 2006-08-15 14:00:03 |
| Bizarre Love Triangle | 2006-08-14 10:54:02 |
| Crystal              | 2006-08-14 10:47:21 |
| Regret               | 2006-08-14 10:43:37 |
| Ceremony             | 2006-08-14 10:41:43 |
| The Perfect Kiss     | 2006-08-14 10:36:54 |
| True Faith           | 2006-08-14 10:30:25 |
| Temptation           | 2006-08-14 10:25:22 |
| Fine Time            | 2006-08-14 10:21:03 |
+----------------------+---------------------+
11 rows in set (0.18 sec)
```

In this, the query is driven by the played table, and so all rows from it are output matched against track values if they exist and NULL otherwise. Since all rows in the played table have matching tracks, no NULL values are shown. Importantly, because the played table drives the process, you don't see all the rows from the track table (because not all tracks have been played).

In the introduction to this section, we motivated left joins with the example of listing all albums and the number of times they've been played, regardless of whether that value is zero. You'll recall from "The GROUP BY Clause" the following query that shows you that information, but only for albums you've played:

```
mysql> SELECT artist_name, album_name, COUNT(*) FROM
    -> artist INNER JOIN album USING (artist_id)
    -> INNER JOIN track USING (artist_id, album_id)
    -> INNER JOIN played USING (artist_id, album_id, track_id)
    -> GROUP BY album.artist_id, album.album_id;
+-------------+---------------------------+----------+
| artist_name | album_name                | COUNT(*) |
+-------------+---------------------------+----------+
| New Order   | Retro - Miranda Sawyer POP |       8 |
| Miles Davis | Live Around The World     |        3 |
+-------------+---------------------------+----------+
2 rows in set (0.11 sec)
```

Here's how you modify that query to use a left join to list all albums, even those that have never been played:

```
mysql> SELECT artist_name, album_name, COUNT(played) FROM
    -> artist INNER JOIN album USING (artist_id)
    -> INNER JOIN track USING (artist_id, album_id)
    -> LEFT JOIN played USING (artist_id, album_id, track_id)
    -> GROUP BY album.artist_id, album.album_id;
+-------------------------+-----------------------------------------+----------+
| artist_name             | album_name                              | COUNT(*) |
+-------------------------+-----------------------------------------+----------+
| New Order               | Retro - John McCready FAN               |        0 |
| New Order               | Substance (Disc 2)                      |        0 |
| New Order               | Retro - Miranda Sawyer POP              |        8 |
| New Order               | Retro - New Order / Bobby Gillespie LIVE |       0 |
| New Order               | Power, Corruption & Lies                |        0 |
| New Order               | Substance 1987 (Disc 1)                 |        0 |
| New Order               | Brotherhood                             |        0 |
| Nick Cave & The Bad Seeds | Let Love In                           |        0 |
| Miles Davis             | Live Around The World                   |        3 |
| Miles Davis             | In A Silent Way                         |        0 |
| The Rolling Stones      | Exile On Main Street                    |        0 |
| The Stone Roses         | Second Coming                           |        0 |
| Kylie Minogue           | Light Years                             |        0 |
+-------------------------+-----------------------------------------+----------+
13 rows in set (0.18 sec)
```

The only difference is that the final INNER JOIN is replaced by a LEFT JOIN, which means that the data from the first two inner joins—of artist and album—drives the process. The result is that all albums and their artists are displayed, along with the count of the number of matching rows in the played table. You can see we haven't listened to the majority of the albums.

We've shown you that it matters what comes before and after the LEFT JOIN statement. Whatever is on the left drives the process, hence the name "left join." If you really don't want to reorganize your query so it matches that template, you can use rollRIGHT JOIN. It's exactly the same, except whatever is on the right drives the process. Here's our earlier played and track example written as a right join:

```
mysql> SELECT track_name, played FROM
    -> played RIGHT JOIN track USING (artist_id, album_id, track_id)
```

```
        -> ORDER BY played DESC;
+----------------------+----------------------+
| track_name           | played               |
+----------------------+----------------------+
| New Blues            | 2006-08-15 14:33:57  |
| Intruder             | 2006-08-15 14:26:12  |
| In A Silent Way      | 2006-08-15 14:00:03  |
| Bizarre Love Triangle| 2006-08-14 10:54:02  |
| Crystal              | 2006-08-14 10:47:21  |
| Regret               | 2006-08-14 10:43:37  |
| Ceremony             | 2006-08-14 10:41:43  |
| The Perfect Kiss     | 2006-08-14 10:36:54  |
| True Faith           | 2006-08-14 10:30:25  |
| Temptation           | 2006-08-14 10:25:22  |
| Fine Time            | 2006-08-14 10:21:03  |
| Do You Love Me?      |                 NULL |
| Nobody's Baby Now    |                 NULL |
| Loverman             |                 NULL |
| Jangling Jack        |                 NULL |
+----------------------+----------------------+
```

The right join is useful sometimes because it allows you to write a query more naturally, expressing it in a way that's more intuitive. However, you won't often see it used, and we'd recommend avoiding it where possible.

Both the LEFT JOIN and RIGHT JOIN can use either the USING or ON clauses discussed for the INNER JOIN earlier in this chapter in "The Inner Join." You should use one or the other: without them, you'll get the Cartesian product discussed in "The Inner Join."

There's an extra OUTER keyword that you can optionally use in left and right joins, to make them read as LEFT OUTER JOIN and RIGHT OUTER JOIN. It's just an alternative syntax that doesn't do anything different, and you won't often see it used. We stick to the basic versions in this book.

The Natural Join

We're not big fans of the natural join that we're about to describe in this section. It's in here only for completeness and because you'll see it used sometimes in SQL statements you'll encounter. Our advice is to avoid using it where possible.

A natural join is, well, supposed to be magically natural. This means that you tell MySQL what tables you want to join, and it figures out how to do it and gives you an INNER JOIN result set. Here's an example for the artist and album tables:

```
mysql> SELECT artist_name, album_name FROM artist NATURAL JOIN album;
+-------------------------+-------------------------------------------+
| artist_name             | album_name                                |
+-------------------------+-------------------------------------------+
| New Order               | Retro - John McCready FAN                 |
| New Order               | Substance (Disc 2)                        |
| New Order               | Retro - Miranda Sawyer POP                |
| New Order               | Retro - New Order / Bobby Gillespie LIVE  |
| New Order               | Power, Corruption & Lies                  |
```

```
| New Order                 | Substance 1987 (Disc 1)   |
| New Order                 | Brotherhood               |
| Nick Cave & The Bad Seeds | Let Love In               |
| Miles Davis               | Live Around The World     |
| Miles Davis               | In A Silent Way           |
| The Rolling Stones        | Exile On Main Street      |
| The Stone Roses           | Second Coming             |
| Kylie Minogue             | Light Years               |
+---------------------------+---------------------------------------------+
13 rows in set (0.03 sec)
```

In reality, it's not quite magical: all MySQL does is look for columns with the same names and, behind the scenes, adds these silently into an inner join with a USING clause. So, the above query is actually translated into:

```
mysql> SELECT artist_name, album_name FROM
    -> artist INNER JOIN album USING (artist_id);
```

If identifier columns don't share the same name, natural joins won't work. Also, more dangerously, if columns that do share the same names aren't identifiers, they'll get thrown into the behind-the-scenes USING clause anyway. For example, if you had name columns in the artist and album tables (instead of artist_name and album_name), you'd get USING (artist_id, name) and some unpredictable results. The magic and mystery makes natural joins worth avoiding; spell out queries using an inner join or a WHERE clause instead.

You'll sometimes see the natural join mixed with left and right joins. The following are valid join syntaxes: NATURAL LEFT JOIN, NATURAL LEFT OUTER JOIN, NATURAL RIGHT JOIN, and NATURAL RIGHT OUTER JOIN. The former two are left joins without ON or USING clauses, and the latter two are right joins. Again, avoid writing them when you can, but you should understand what they mean if you see them used.

Nested Queries

Nested queries—supported by MySQL since version 4.1—are the most difficult to learn. However, they provide a powerful, useful, and concise way of expressing difficult information needs in short SQL statements. This section explains them, beginning with simple examples and leading to the more complex features of the EXISTS and IN statements. At the conclusion of this section, you'll have completed everything this book contains about querying data, and you should be comfortable understanding almost any SQL query you encounter.

Nested Query Basics

You know how to find the name of an artist who made a particular album using an INNER JOIN:

```
mysql> SELECT artist_name FROM
    -> artist INNER JOIN album USING (artist_id)
```

```
    -> WHERE album_name = "In A Silent Way";
+--------------+
| artist_name |
+--------------+
| Miles Davis |
+--------------+
1 row in set (0.14 sec)
```

But there's another way, using a *nested query*:

```
mysql> SELECT artist_name FROM artist WHERE artist_id =
    -> (SELECT artist_id FROM album WHERE album_name = "In A Silent Way");
+--------------+
| artist_name |
+--------------+
| Miles Davis |
+--------------+
1 row in set (0.28 sec)
```

It's called a nested query because one query is inside another. The *inner query*, or *subquery*—the one that is nested—is written in parentheses, and you can see that it determines the `artist_id` for the album with the name `In A Silent Way`. The parentheses are required for inner queries. The *outer query* is the one that's listed first and isn't parenthesized here: you can see that it finds the `artist_name` of the the artist with an `artist_id` that matches the result of the subquery. So, overall, the inner query finds the `artist_id`, and the outer query uses it to find the artist's name.

So, which approach is preferable: nested or not nested? The answer isn't easy. In terms of performance, the answer is usually not: nested queries are hard to optimize, and so they're almost always slower to run than the unnested alternative. Does this mean you should avoid nesting? The answer is no: sometimes it's your only choice if you want to write a single query, and sometimes nested queries can answer information needs that can't be easily solved otherwise. What's more, nested queries are expressive. Once you're comfortable with the idea, they're a very readable way to show how a query is evaluated. In fact, many SQL designers advocate teaching nested queries before the join-based alternatives we've shown you in the past few chapters. We'll show you examples of where nesting is readable and powerful throughout this section.

Before we begin to cover the keywords that can be used in nested queries, let's visit an example that can't be done easily in a single query—at least, not without MySQL's proprietary `LIMIT` clause! Suppose you want to know which track you listened to most recently. To do this, following the methods we've learned previously, you could find the date and time of the most recently stored row in the `played` table:

```
mysql> SELECT MAX(played) FROM played;
+---------------------+
| MAX(played)         |
+---------------------+
| 2006-08-15 14:33:57 |
+---------------------+
1 row in set (0.00 sec)
```

You can then use the output as input to another query to find the track name:

```
mysql> SELECT track_name FROM track INNER JOIN played
    -> USING (artist_id, album_id, track_id)
    -> WHERE played = "2006-08-15 14:33:57";
+------------+
| track_name |
+------------+
| New Blues  |
+------------+
1 row in set (0.31 sec)
```

In "User Variables," later in this chapter, we'll show how you can use variables to avoid having to type in the value in the second query.

With a nested query, you can do both steps in one shot:

```
mysql> SELECT track_name FROM track INNER JOIN played
    -> USING (artist_id, album_id, track_id)
    -> WHERE played = (SELECT MAX(played) FROM played);
+------------+
| track_name |
+------------+
| New Blues  |
+------------+
1 row in set (0.28 sec)
```

You can see the nested query combines the two previous queries. Rather than using the constant date and time value discovered from a previous query, it executes the query directly as a subquery. This is the simplest type of nested query, one that returns a *scalar operand*—that is, a single value.

The previous example used the equality operator, the equals sign, =. You can use all types of comparison operators: < (less than), <= (less than or equal to), > (greater than), >= (greater than or equal to), and != (not equals) or <> (not equals).

The ANY, SOME, ALL, IN, and NOT IN Clauses

Before we start to show some more advanced features of nested queries, we need to create two new tables to use in our examples. Unfortunately, our music database is a little too simple to effectively demonstrate the full power of nested querying. So, let's extend the database to give us something to play with.

We'll create two new tables that share common data, but store different types of facts. The first table we'll create contains information about producers—that is, the people who oversee the music recording process. Here's the structure and some data:

```
mysql> CREATE TABLE producer (
    -> producer_id SMALLINT(4) NOT NULL DEFAULT 0,
    -> producer_name CHAR(128) DEFAULT NULL,
    -> years SMALLINT(3) DEFAULT 0,
    -> PRIMARY KEY (producer_id));
```

```
Query OK, 0 rows affected (1.03 sec)

mysql> INSERT INTO producer VALUES
    -> (1, "Phil Spector", 36),
    -> (2, "George Martin", 40),
    -> (3, "Tina Weymouth", 20),
    -> (4, "Chris Frantz", 20),
    -> (5, "Ed Kuepper", 15);

Query OK, 5 rows affected (0.50 sec)
Records: 5  Duplicates: 0  Warnings: 0
```

You can download these instructions from the book's web site in the file *producer.sql*, and run them in the same way you ran the *music.sql* file.

You can see it's a fairly simple table: an identifier column, a textual name, and an integer value of the number of years they've been producing. The second table is almost identical, but stores information about engineers—that is, the people who work the mixing desks and other equipment that's used in the music recording process. Here's the table and its data:

```
mysql> CREATE TABLE engineer (
    -> engineer_id SMALLINT(4) NOT NULL DEFAULT 0,
    -> engineer_name CHAR(128) DEFAULT NULL,
    -> years SMALLINT(3) DEFAULT 0,
    -> PRIMARY KEY (engineer_id));
Query OK, 0 rows affected (0.04 sec)

mysql> INSERT INTO engineer VALUES
    -> (1, "George Martin", 40),
    -> (2, "Eddie Kramer", 38),
    -> (3, "Jeff Jarratt", 40),
    -> (4, "Ed Stasium", 25);
Query OK, 4 rows affected (0.14 sec)
Records: 4  Duplicates: 0  Warnings: 0
```

You can download these instructions from the book's web site in the file *engineer.sql*.

Using ANY and IN

Now that you've created the sample tables, you can try an example using ANY. Suppose you're looking to find engineers who've been working longer than the least experienced producer. You can express this information need as follows:

```
mysql> SELECT engineer_name, years
    -> FROM engineer WHERE years > ANY
    -> (SELECT years FROM producer);
+---------------+-------+
| engineer_name | years |
+---------------+-------+
| George Martin |    40 |
| Eddie Kramer  |    38 |
| Jeff Jarratt  |    40 |
| Ed Stasium    |    25 |
```

```
+---------------+-------+
```
4 rows in set (0.08 sec)

The subquery finds the years that the producers have worked:

```
mysql> SELECT years FROM producer;
+-------+
| years |
+-------+
| 36    |
| 40    |
| 20    |
| 20    |
| 15    |
+-------+
5 rows in set (0.00 sec)
```

The outer query goes through each engineer, returning the engineer if their number of years is greater than any of the values in the set returned by the subquery. So, for example, Eddie Kramer is output because 38 is greater than at least one value in the set (36, 40, 20, 15). The ANY keyword means just that: it's true if the column or expression preceding it is true for *any* of the values in the set returned by the subquery. Used in this way, ANY has the alias SOME, which was included so that some queries can be read more clearly as English expressions; it doesn't do anything different and you'll rarely see it used.

The ANY keyword gives you more power in expressing nested queries. Indeed, the previous query is the first nested query in this section with a *column subquery*—that is, the results returned by the subquery are one or more values from a column, instead of a single scalar value as in the previous section. With this, you can now compare a column value from an outer query to a set of values returned from a subquery.

Consider another example using ANY. Suppose you want to know the producers who are also engineers. You can do this with the following nested query:

```
mysql> SELECT producer_name FROM producer WHERE
    -> producer_name = ANY
    -> (SELECT engineer_name FROM engineer);
+---------------+
| producer_name |
+---------------+
| George Martin |
+---------------+
1 row in set (0.04 sec)
```

The = ANY causes the outer query to return a producer when the producer_name is equal to any of the engineer names returned by the subquery. The = ANY keyphrase has the alias IN, which you'll see commonly used in nested queries. Using IN, the previous example can be rewritten:

```
mysql> SELECT producer_name FROM producer WHERE producer_name
    -> IN (SELECT engineer_name FROM engineer);
+---------------+
```

```
| producer_name |
+----------------+
| George Martin |
+----------------+
1 row in set (0.06 sec)
```

Of course, for this particular example, you could also have used a join query:

```
mysql> SELECT producer_name FROM producer INNER JOIN engineer
    -> ON (producer_name = engineer_name);
+----------------+
| producer_name |
+----------------+
| George Martin |
+----------------+
1 row in set (0.17 sec)
```

Again, nested queries are expressive but typically slow in MySQL, so use a join where you can.

Using ALL

Suppose you want to find engineers who are more experienced than all of the producers —that is, more experienced than the most experienced producer. You can do this with the ALL keyword in place of ANY:

```
mysql> SELECT engineer_name, years FROM engineer
    -> WHERE years > ALL (SELECT years FROM producer);
Empty set (0.00 sec)
```

You can see that there are no answers: looking at the data, we see that George Martin has been a producer for 40 years, equal to or longer than the time any engineer has been engineering. While the ANY keyword returns values that satisfy at least one condition (Boolean OR), the ALL keyword returns values when all the conditions are satisfied (Boolean AND).

We can use the alias NOT IN in place of <> ANY or != ANY. Let's find all the engineers who aren't producers:

```
mysql> SELECT engineer_name FROM engineer WHERE
    -> engineer_name NOT IN
    -> (SELECT producer_name FROM producer);
+----------------+
| engineer_name |
+----------------+
| Eddie Kramer  |
| Jeff Jarratt  |
| Ed Stasium    |
+----------------+
3 rows in set (0.25 sec)
```

As an exercise, try writing the above query using the ANY syntax and in at least two ways as a join query.

The ALL keyword has a few tricks and traps:

- If it's false for any value, it's false. Suppose that table a contains a row with the value 14. Suppose table b contains the values 16, 1, and NULL. If you check whether the value in a is greater than ALL values in b, you'll get false, since 14 isn't greater than 16. It doesn't matter that the other values are 1 and NULL.

- If it isn't false for any value, it isn't true unless it's true for all values. Suppose that table a again contains 14, and suppose b contains 1 and NULL. If you check whether the value in a is greater than ALL values in b, you'll get UNKNOWN (neither true or false) because it can't be determined whether NULL is greater than or less than 14.

- If the table in the subquery is empty, the result is always true. Hence, if a contains 14 and b is empty, you'll get true when you check if the value in a is greater than ALL values in b.

When using the ALL keyword, be very careful with tables that can have NULL values in columns; consider disallowing NULL values in such cases. Also, be careful with empty tables.

Writing row subqueries

In the previous examples, the subquery returned a single, scalar value (such as an artist_id) or a set of values from one column (such as all of the engineer_name values). This section describes another type of subquery, the *row subquery* that works with multiple columns from multiple rows.

Suppose you're interested in whether an engineer has been a producer for the same length of time. To answer this need, you must match both names and years. You can easily write this as a join query:

```
mysql> SELECT producer_name, producer.years FROM
    -> producer, engineer WHERE producer_name = engineer_name AND
    -> producer.years = engineer.years;
+---------------+-------+
| producer_name | years |
+---------------+-------+
| George Martin |    40 |
+---------------+-------+
1 row in set (0.30 sec)
```

But you can also write it as a nested query:

```
mysql> SELECT producer_name, years FROM producer WHERE
    -> (producer_name, years) IN
    -> (SELECT engineer_name, years FROM engineer);
+---------------+-------+
| producer_name | years |
+---------------+-------+
| George Martin |    40 |
+---------------+-------+
1 row in set (0.17 sec)
```

You can see there's a different syntax being used in this nested query: a list of two column names in parentheses follows the WHERE statement, and the inner query returns two columns. We'll explain this syntax next.

The row subquery syntax allows you to compare multiple values per row. The expression (producer_name, years) means two values per row are compared to the output of the subquery. You can see following the IN keyword that the subquery returns two values, engineer_name and years. So, the fragment:

```
(producer_name, years) IN (SELECT engineer_name, years FROM engineer)
```

matches producer names and years to engineer names and years, and returns a true value when a match is found. The result is that if a matching pair is found, the overall query outputs a result. This is a typical row subquery: it finds rows that exist in two tables.

To explain the syntax further, let's consider another example. Suppose you want to see if you own the *Brotherhood* album by New Order. You can do this with the following query:

```
mysql> SELECT artist_name, album_name FROM artist, album WHERE
    -> (artist.artist_id, artist_name, album_name) =
    -> (album.artist_id, "New Order", "Brotherhood");
+-------------+-------------+
| artist_name | album_name  |
+-------------+-------------+
| New Order   | Brotherhood |
+-------------+-------------+
1 row in set (0.16 sec)
```

It's not a nested query, but it shows you how the new row subquery syntax works. You can see that the query matches the list of columns before the equals sign, (artist.artist_id, artist_name, album_name), to the list of columns and values after the equals sign, (album.artist_id, "New Order", "Brotherhood"). So, when the artist_id values match, the artist is New Order, and the album is *Brotherhood*, we get output from the query. We don't recommend writing queries like this—use a WHERE clause instead—but it does illustrate exactly what's going on. For an exercise, try writing this query using a join.

Row subqueries require that the number, order, and type of values in the columns match. So, for example, our previous example matches a SMALLINT to a SMALLINT, and two character strings to two character strings.

The EXISTS and NOT EXISTS Clauses

You've now seen three types of subquery: scalar subqueries, column subqueries, and row subqueries. In this section, you'll learn about a fourth type, the *correlated subquery*, where a table used in the outer query is referenced in the subquery. Correlated subqueries are often used with the `IN` statement we've already discussed, and almost always used with the `EXISTS` and `NOT EXISTS` clauses that are the focus of this section.

EXISTS and NOT EXISTS basics

Before we start on our discussion of correlated subqueries, let's investigate what the `EXISTS` clause does. We'll need a simple but strange example to introduce the clause, since we're not discussing correlated subqueries just yet. So, here goes: suppose you want to find a list of all artists in the database, but only if the database is active (which you've defined to mean only if at least one track from any album by any artist has been played). Here's the query that does it:

```
mysql> SELECT * FROM artist WHERE EXISTS
    -> (SELECT * FROM played);
+-----------+---------------------------+
| artist_id | artist_name               |
+-----------+---------------------------+
|         1 | New Order                 |
|         2 | Nick Cave & The Bad Seeds |
|         3 | Miles Davis               |
|         4 | The Rolling Stones        |
|         5 | The Stone Roses           |
|         6 | Kylie Minogue             |
+-----------+---------------------------+
6 rows in set (0.18 sec)
```

The subquery returns all rows from the `played` table. However, what's important is that it returns at least one row; it doesn't matter what's in the row, how many rows there are, or whether the row contains only `NULL` values. So, you can think of the subquery as being true or false, and in this case it's true because it produces some output. When the subquery is true, the outer query that uses the `EXISTS` clause returns a row. The overall result is that all rows in the `artist` table are displayed because, for each one, the subquery is true.

Let's try a query where the subquery isn't true. Again, let's contrive a query: this time, we'll output the names of all albums in the database, but only if we own at least one album by John Coltrane. Here's the query:

```
mysql> SELECT album_name FROM album WHERE EXISTS
    -> (SELECT * FROM artist WHERE artist_name = "John Coltrane");
Empty set (0.10 sec)
```

Since the subquery isn't true—no rows are returned because John Coltrane isn't in our database—no results are returned by the outer query.

The `NOT EXISTS` clause does the opposite. Imagine you want a list of all producers if you don't have an artist called New Order in the database. Here it is:

```
mysql> SELECT * FROM producer WHERE NOT EXISTS
    -> (SELECT * FROM artist WHERE artist_name = "New Order");
Empty set (0.16 sec)
```

This time, the inner query is true but the NOT EXISTS clause negates it to give false. Since it's false, the outer query doesn't produce results.

You'll notice that the subquery begins with SELECT * FROM artist. It doesn't actually matter what you select in an inner query when you're using the EXISTS clause, since it's not used by the outer query anyway. You can select one column, everything, or even a constant (as in SELECT "cat" from artist), and it'll have the same effect. Traditionally, though, you'll see most SQL authors write SELECT * by convention.

Correlated subqueries

So far, it's difficult to imagine what you'd do with the EXISTS or NOT EXISTS clauses. This section shows you how they're really used, illustrating the most advanced type of nested query that you'll typically see in action.

Let's think about a realistic information need you might want to answer from the music database. Suppose you want a list of all artists who've produced a self-titled album. You can do this easily with a join query, which we recommend you try to think about before you continue. You can also do it with the following nested query that uses a *correlated subquery*:

```
mysql> SELECT artist_name FROM artist WHERE EXISTS
    -> (SELECT * FROM album WHERE album_name = artist_name);
Empty set (0.28 sec)
```

There's no output because there are no self-titled albums. Let's add an artist with a self-titled album and try again:

```
mysql> INSERT INTO artist VALUES (7, "The Beatles");
Query OK, 1 row affected (0.13 sec)

mysql> INSERT INTO album VALUES (7, 1, "The Beatles");
Query OK, 1 row affected (0.14 sec)
```

Now the query:

```
mysql> SELECT artist_name FROM artist WHERE EXISTS
    -> (SELECT * FROM album WHERE album_name = artist_name);
+-------------+
| artist_name |
+-------------+
| The Beatles |
+-------------+
1 row in set (0.17 sec)
```

So, the query works; now, we just need to understand how!

Let's examine the subquery in our previous example. You can see that it lists only the album table in the FROM clause, but it uses a column from the artist table in the WHERE clause. If you run it in isolation, you'll see this isn't allowed:

```
mysql> SELECT * FROM album WHERE album_name = artist_name;
ERROR 1054 (42S22): Unknown column 'artist_name' in 'where clause'
```

However, it's legal when executed as a subquery because tables listed in the outer query are allowed to be accessed in the subquery. So, in this example, the current value of `artist_name` in the outer query is supplied to the subquery as a constant, scalar value and compared to the album name. If the album name matches the artist name, the subquery is true, and so the outer query outputs a row. Consider two cases that illustrate this more clearly:

- When the `artist_name` being processed by the outer query is `New Order`, the subquery is false because `SELECT * FROM album WHERE album_name = "New Order"` doesn't return any rows, and so the artist row for New Order isn't output as an answer.

- When the `artist_name` being processed by the outer query is `The Beatles`, the subquery is true because `SELECT * FROM album WHERE album_name = "The Beatles"` returns at least one row. Overall, the artist row for The Beatles is output as an answer.

Can you see the power of correlated subqueries? You can use values from the outer query in the inner query to evaluate complex information needs.

We'll now explore another example using `EXISTS`. Let's try to find all artists from whom we own at least two albums. To do this with `EXISTS`, we need to think through what the inner and outer queries should do. The inner query should produce a result only when the condition we're checking is true; in this case, it should produce output when the artist has at least two albums in the database. The outer query should produce the artist name whenever the inner query is true. Here's the query:

```
mysql> SELECT artist_name FROM artist WHERE EXISTS
    -> (SELECT * FROM album WHERE artist.artist_id = album.artist_id
    -> GROUP BY artist.artist_id HAVING COUNT(*) >= 2);
+-------------+
| artist_name |
+-------------+
| New Order   |
| Miles Davis |
+-------------+
2 rows in set (0.12 sec)
```

This is yet another query where nesting isn't necessary and a join would suffice, but let's stick with this version for the purpose of explanation. Have a look at the inner query: you can see that the `WHERE` clause ensures only album rows for the artist being referenced by the outer query—the current artist—are considered by the subquery. The `GROUP BY` clause clusters the rows for that artist, but only if there are at least two albums. Therefore, the inner query only produces output when there are at least two albums for the current artist. The outer query is straightforward: it outputs an artist's name when the subquery produces output.

Here's one more example before we move on and discuss other issues. We've already shown you a query that uses `IN` and finds producers who are also engineers:

```
mysql> SELECT producer_name FROM producer WHERE producer_name
    -> IN (SELECT engineer_name FROM engineer);
+---------------+
| producer_name |
+---------------+
| George Martin |
+---------------+
1 row in set (0.06 sec)
```

Let's rewrite the query to use EXISTS. First, think about the subquery: it should produce output when there's an engineer with the same name as a producer.

Second, think about the outer query: it should return the producer's name when the inner query produces output. Here's the rewritten query:

```
mysql> SELECT producer_name FROM producer WHERE EXISTS
    -> (SELECT * FROM engineer WHERE producer_name = engineer_name);
+---------------+
| producer_name |
+---------------+
| George Martin |
+---------------+
1 row in set (0.06 sec)
```

Again, you can see that the subquery references the producer_name column, which comes from the outer query.

Correlated subqueries can be used with any nested query type. Here's the previous IN query rewritten with an outer reference:

```
mysql> SELECT producer_name FROM producer WHERE producer_name
    -> IN (SELECT engineer_name FROM engineer WHERE
    -> engineer_name = producer_name);
+---------------+
| producer_name |
+---------------+
| George Martin |
+---------------+
1 row in set (0.14 sec)
```

The query is more convoluted than it needs to be, but it illustrates the idea. You can see that the producer_name in the subquery references the producer table from the outer query. This query can also be rewritten to use an equals instead of IN:

```
mysql> SELECT producer_name FROM producer WHERE producer_name
    -> = (SELECT engineer_name FROM engineer WHERE
    -> engineer_name = producer_name);
+---------------+
| producer_name |
+---------------+
| George Martin |
+---------------+
1 row in set (0.01 sec)
```

This works because the subquery returns one scalar value—there's only one engineer and producer with each name—and so the column subquery operator IN isn't necessary. Of course, if names are duplicated, you'd need to use IN, ANY, or ALL instead.

Nested Queries in the FROM Clause

The techniques we've shown all use nested queries in the WHERE clause. This section shows you how they can alternatively be used in the FROM clause. This is useful when you want to manipulate the source of the data you're using in a query.

The producer and engineer tables store the number of years that a person has been producing and engineering, respectively. If you want that value in months, there are several ways you can obtain it. One way—which we'll show you in Chapter 8—is to use a date and time function to do the conversion. Another way is to do some math in the query; one option in this class is to do it with a subquery:

```
mysql> SELECT producer_name, months FROM
    -> (SELECT producer_name, years*12 AS months FROM producer) AS prod;
+---------------+--------+
| producer_name | months |
+---------------+--------+
| Phil Spector  |    432 |
| George Martin |    480 |
| Tina Weymouth |    240 |
| Chris Frantz  |    240 |
| Ed Kuepper    |    180 |
+---------------+--------+
5 rows in set (0.05 sec)
```

Focus on what follows the FROM clause: the subquery uses the producer table and returns two columns. The first column is the producer_name; the second column is aliased as months, and is the years value multiplied by 12. The outer query is straightforward: it just returns the producer_name and the month value created through the subquery. Note that we've added the table alias as prod for the subquery. When we use a subquery as a table, that is, we use a SELECT FROM operation on it—this "derived table" must have an alias—even if we don't use the alias in our query. MySQL complains if we omit the alias:

```
mysql> SELECT producer_name, months FROM
    -> (SELECT producer_name, years*12 AS months FROM producer);
ERROR 1248 (42000): Every derived table must have its own alias
```

Here's another example, where we'll find out the average number of albums that we own by each artist. Let's begin by thinking through the subquery. It should return the number of albums that we own by each artist. Then, the outer query should average the values to give the answer. Here's the query:

```
mysql> SELECT AVG(albums) FROM
    -> (SELECT COUNT(*) AS albums FROM artist INNER JOIN album
    -> USING (artist_id) GROUP BY artist.artist_id) AS alb;
+-------------+
```

```
| AVG(albums) |
+-------------+
|      2.0000 |
+-------------+
1 row in set (0.00 sec)
```

You can see that the inner query joins together `artist` and `album`, and groups the albums together by artist so you can get a count for each artist. If you run it in isolation, here's what happens:

```
mysql> SELECT COUNT(*) AS albums FROM artist INNER JOIN album
    -> USING (artist_id) GROUP BY artist.artist_id;
+--------+
| albums |
+--------+
|      7 |
|      1 |
|      2 |
|      1 |
|      1 |
|      1 |
|      1 |
+--------+
7 rows in set (0.00 sec)
```

Now, the outer query takes these counts—which are aliased as `albums`—and averages them to give the final result. This query is the typical way that you apply two aggregate functions to one set of data. You can't apply aggregate functions in cascade, as in `AVG(COUNT(*))`; it won't work:

```
mysql> SELECT AVG(COUNT(*)) FROM album INNER JOIN artist
    -> USING (artist_id) GROUP BY artist.artist_id;
ERROR 1111 (HY000): Invalid use of group function
```

With subqueries in `FROM` clauses, you can return a scalar value, a set of column values, more than one row, or even a whole table. However, you can't use correlated subqueries, meaning that you can't reference tables or columns from tables that aren't explicitly listed in the subquery. Note also that you must alias the whole subquery using the `AS` keyword and give it a name, even if you don't use that name anywhere in the query.

User Variables

Often you'll want to save values that are returned from queries. You might want to do this so that you can easily use a value in a later query. You might also simply want to save a result for later display. In both cases, user variables solve the problem: they allow you to store a result and use it later.

Let's illustrate user variables with a simple example. The following query finds the name of an artist and saves the result in a user variable:

```
mysql> SELECT @artist:=artist_name FROM artist WHERE artist_id = 1;
+----------------------+
| @artist:=artist_name |
+----------------------+
| New Order            |
+----------------------+
1 row in set (0.05 sec)
```

The user variable is named artist, and it's denoted as a user variable by the @ character that precedes it. The value is assigned using the := operator. You can print out the contents of the user variable with the following very short query:

```
mysql> SELECT @artist;
+-----------+
| @artist   |
+-----------+
| New Order |
+-----------+
1 row in set (0.00 sec)
```

You can explicitly set a variable using the SET statement without a SELECT. Suppose you want to initialize a counter to 0:

```
mysql> SET @counter := 0;
Query OK, 0 rows affected (0.11 sec)
```

You should separate several assignments with a comma, or put each in a statement of its own:

```
mysql> SET @counter := 0, @age:=23;
Query OK, 0 rows affected (0.00 sec)
```

The most common use of user variables is to save a result and use it later. You'll recall the following example from earlier in the chapter, which we used to motivate nested queries (which are certainly a better solution for this problem). We want to find the name of the track that was played most recently:

```
mysql> SELECT MAX(played) FROM played;
+---------------------+
| max(played)         |
+---------------------+
| 2006-08-15 14:33:57 |
+---------------------+
1 row in set (0.00 sec)

mysql> SELECT track_name FROM track INNER JOIN played
    -> USING (artist_id, album_id, track_id)
    -> WHERE played = "2006-08-15 14:33:57";
+------------+
| track_name |
+------------+
| New Blues  |
+------------+
1 row in set (0.31 sec)
```

You can use a user variable to save the result for input into the following query. Here's the same query pair rewritten using this approach:

```
mysql> SELECT @recent :=  MAX(played) FROM played;
+-------------------------+
| @recent :=  MAX(played) |
+-------------------------+
| 2006-08-15 14:33:57     |
+-------------------------+
1 row in set (0.00 sec)

mysql> SELECT track_name FROM track INNER JOIN played
    -> USING (artist_id, album_id, track_id)
    -> WHERE played = @recent;
+------------+
| track_name |
+------------+
| New Blues  |
+------------+
1 row in set (0.44 sec)
```

This can save you cutting and pasting, and it certainly helps you avoid typing errors.

Here are some guidelines on using user variables:

- User variables are unique to a connection: variables that you create can't be seen by anyone else, and two different connections can have two different variables with the same name.

- The variable names can be alphanumeric strings and can also include the period (.), underscore (_), and dollar ($) characters.

- Variable names are case-sensitive in MySQL versions earlier than version 5, and case-insensitive from version 5 onward.

- Any variable that isn't initialized has the value NULL; you can also manually set a variable to be NULL.

- Variables are destroyed when a connection closes.

- You should avoid trying to both assign a value to a variable and use the variable as part of a SELECT query. Two reasons for this are that the new value may not be available for use immediately in the same statement, and a variable's type is set when it's first assigned in a query; trying to use it later as a different type in the same SQL statement can lead to unexpected results.

  Let's look at the first issue in more detail using the new variable @aid. Since we haven't used this variable before, it's empty. Now, let's show the artist_id for artists who have an entry in the album table. Instead of showing it directly, we'll assign the artist_id to the @aid variable. Our query will show the variable twice: once before the assignment operation, once as part of the assignment operation, and once afterwards:

```
mysql> SELECT @aid, @aid:=artist.artist_id, @aid FROM artist,album
    -> WHERE album.artist_id=@aid;
Empty set (0.00 sec)
```

This returns nothing; since there's nothing in the variable to start with, the WHERE clause tries to look for empty artist_id values. If we modify the query to use artist.artist_id as part of the WHERE clause, things work as expected:

```
mysql> SELECT @aid, @aid:=artist.artist_id, @aid FROM artist,album
    -> WHERE album.artist_id=artist.artist_id;
+------+------------------------+------+
| @aid | @aid:=artist.artist_id | @aid |
+------+------------------------+------+
|      | 1                      | 1    |
| 1    | 1                      | 1    |
| 1    | 1                      | 1    |
| 1    | 1                      | 1    |
| 1    | 1                      | 1    |
| 1    | 1                      | 1    |
| 1    | 1                      | 1    |
| 1    | 2                      | 2    |
| 2    | 3                      | 3    |
| 3    | 3                      | 3    |
| 3    | 4                      | 4    |
| 4    | 5                      | 5    |
| 5    | 6                      | 6    |
+------+------------------------+------+
13 rows in set (0.01 sec)
```

Now that @aid isn't empty, the initial query will produce some results:

```
mysql> SELECT @aid, @aid:=artist.artist_id, @aid FROM artist,album
    -> WHERE album.artist_id=@aid;
+------+------------------------+------+
| @aid | @aid:=artist.artist_id | @aid |
+------+------------------------+------+
| 6    | 1                      | 1    |
| 1    | 1                      | 1    |
| 1    | 2                      | 2    |
+------+------------------------+------+
3 rows in set (0.01 sec)
```

It's best to avoid such circumstances where the behavior is not guaranteed and is hence unpredictable.

Transactions and Locking

When a database is concurrently accessed by several users, you have to consider how you may be affected if other users change the data that you're accessing, and how changes you make may affect other users. For example, you might get the wrong value for the total sales so far this year if new sales are being added to the database while you're adding up the sales figures.

Locks can be applied to prevent concurrent users from interacting destructively with one other's data. A *read lock* allows you to prevent other users from changing data while you're reading and processing the data, while a *write lock* tells other users that the data is being changed and that they should not read or modify it. For example, you need locks to avoid problems with reports when one user is trying to produce a report while another user changes the data the report is derived from.

In some cases, you want all or none of a series of operations to succeed. For example, if you want to travel from Melbourne to Seattle via Los Angeles, you need to have a seat on the flight from Melbourne to Los Angeles, and a seat on the connecting flight from Los Angeles to Seattle. Having a confirmed seat on just one leg of the route is no use to you; you can't fly without confirmed seats on both legs.

Transactions allow you to batch together SQL statements as an indivisible set that either succeeds or has no effect on the database. This means you can start a transaction and then issue a series of SQL statements. At the conclusion, you have the option of *committing* (saving) the transaction to the database or *rolling back* (canceling) the transaction.

By default, MySQL operates in `AUTOCOMMIT` mode, where each update is treated as an atomic transaction of its own, and changes are automatically committed. If this mode is disabled, or a transaction is explicitly started, changes aren't commited to the database unless you execute a `COMMIT` or `ROLLBACK` instruction.

Locking and transaction support is complex, and you need to make choices about the degree of isolation needed between users and the trade-offs involved in implementing them for your application. This is a difficult and advanced topic that's mostly outside the scope of this book, but in the next section we discuss how the main table types supported by MySQL allow locking and transactions. We also include a simple transaction example in "Transaction examples," and we describe how simple locking can be used—and avoided—for our PHP wedding-registry application in "Selecting and Deselecting Gifts" in Chapter 15.

Table Types

In the book so far, we've used only the default MyISAM table type. There's a good reason behind this: you very rarely need to make any other choice in small- to medium-size applications because it's a very fast, reliable table type for most tasks. However, at the time of writing, there are at least nine other choices you can make. This section gives you an insight into these choices, explaining briefly the pros and cons of the alternatives to MyISAM.

You can divide the MySQL table types up into two sets using a few different criteria. The most common division is transaction-safe (TST) versus non-transaction-safe (NTST):

transaction-safe tables (TSTs)

These include the InnoDB and the (no longer supported) Berkeley Database (BDB) table types. TSTs support transactions and have advanced features that allow you safely restore and recover from database failures.

Non-transaction-safe tables (NTSTs)

These include the MyISAM, Merge, and Memory (also called Heap) types described in this section. They're less advanced than the TSTs, but that isn't always bad. They're typically much faster to query because there's less overhead, and they use much less disk and memory space. They're also much easier to understand.

We've avoided TSTs in this book, because you're unlikely to need to configure, set parameters for, and use such tables for most applications.

Another consideration when choosing a table type is whether it supports foreign key constraints. With foreign-key support, you can tell MySQL that a row in a table shouldn't exist without another matching row in another table. For example, you could use it to stop you from adding a new album for an artist who doesn't exist. We don't use foreign-key constraints, and instead rely on the application to do the checking, not the database. Doing the checking in the database slows everything down because MySQL needs to verify the foreign-key constraints before it modifies anything. It also prevents you from ignoring the rules for good reasons—such as improved performance —when you want to. Currently, only the InnoDB table type supports foreign-key constraints, although support is planned for MyISAM. If you're not using the InnoDB table type and specify foreign-key constraints for a field, MySQL won't complain, but won't actually do anything, either. We won't discuss foreign key constraints in further detail.

You can use the SHOW TABLE STATUS command to display technical information about how your tables are stored:

```
mysql> USE music
mysql> SHOW TABLE STATUS;
+--------+--------+---------+------------+------+----------------+-------------+...
| Name   | Engine | Version | Row_format | Rows | Avg_row_length | Data_length |...
+--------+--------+---------+------------+------+----------------+-------------+...
| album  | MyISAM | 10      | Fixed      | 13   | 133            | 1729        |...
| artist | MyISAM | 10      | Fixed      | 6    | 131            | 786         |...
| played | MyISAM | 10      | Fixed      | 11   | 11             | 121         |...
| track  | MyISAM | 10      | Fixed      | 153  | 138            | 21114       |...
+--------+--------+---------+------------+------+----------------+-------------+...

... +------------------+--------------+-----------+----------------+...
... | Max_data_length  | Index_length | Data_free | Auto_increment |...
... +------------------+--------------+-----------+----------------+...
... | 374436171902517247 | 2048       | 0         | NULL           |...
... | 368873221949095935 | 2048       | 0         | NULL           |...
... | 3096224743817215   | 2048       | 0         | NULL           |...
... | 38843546786070527  | 5120       | 0         | NULL           |...
... +------------------+--------------+-----------+----------------+...
... +---------------------+---------------------+------------+-------------------+...
... | Create_time         | Update_time         | Check_time | Collation         |...
... +---------------------+---------------------+------------+-------------------+...
```

```
... | 2006-06-12 07:17:06 | 2006-06-12 07:17:06 |           | latin1_swedish_ci |...
... | 2006-06-12 07:17:06 | 2006-06-12 07:17:06 |           | latin1_swedish_ci |...
... | 2006-06-12 07:17:06 | 2006-06-12 07:17:06 |           | latin1_swedish_ci |...
... | 2006-06-12 07:17:06 | 2006-06-12 07:17:06 |           | latin1_swedish_ci |...
... +--------------------+--------------------+----------+-------------------+...
... +--------------------+--------------------+----------+-------------------+...
... | Update_time         | Check_time | Collation         | Checksum |...
... +--------------------+------------+-------------------+----------+...
... | 2006-06-12 07:17:06 |            | latin1_swedish_ci | NULL     |...
... | 2006-06-12 07:17:06 |            | latin1_swedish_ci | NULL     |...
... | 2006-06-12 07:17:06 |            | latin1_swedish_ci | NULL     |...
... | 2006-06-12 07:17:06 |            | latin1_swedish_ci | NULL     |...
... +--------------------+------------+-------------------+----------+...
... +----------------+---------+
... | Create_options | Comment |
... +----------------+---------+
... |                |         |
... |                |         |
... |                |         |
... |                |         |
... +----------------+---------+
4 rows in set (0.00 sec)
```

The SHOW ENGINES command displays a list of all table types and indicates whether
they're available for use on your MySQL installation:

```
mysql> SHOW ENGINES;
+------------+---------+----------------------------------------------------------+
| Engine     | Support | Comment                                                  |
+------------+---------+----------------------------------------------------------+
| MyISAM     | DEFAULT | Default engine as of MySQL 3.23 with great performance   |
| MEMORY     | YES     | Hash based, stored in memory, useful for temporary tables|
| InnoDB     | YES     | Supports transactions, row-level locking, and foreign keys|
| BerkeleyDB | NO      | Supports transactions and page-level locking             |
| BLACKHOLE  | NO      | /dev/null storage engine (anything you write disappears) |
| EXAMPLE    | NO      | Example storage engine                                   |
| ARCHIVE    | NO      | Archive storage engine                                   |
| CSV        | NO      | CSV storage engine                                       |
| ndbcluster | NO      | Clustered, fault-tolerant, memory-based tables           |
| FEDERATED  | NO      | Federated MySQL storage engine                           |
| MRG_MYISAM | YES     | Collection of identical MyISAM tables                    |
| ISAM       | NO      | Obsolete storage engine                                  |
+------------+---------+----------------------------------------------------------+
12 rows in set (0.00 sec)
```

For example, if we need a transaction-safe table on this server, we can use the InnoDB
table type.

If you decide you want to use a different table type, there are two ways to exercise your
choice. One way to do it is in the CREATE TABLE statement. For example, you can create
a new Memory table mytable as follows:

```
mysql> CREATE TABLE mytable (field INT(2)) type=Memory;
Query OK, 0 rows affected, 1 warning (0.08 sec)
```

Alternatively, you can use ALTER TABLE to adjust the type after it's created. For example, you could convert the artist table to the InnoDB type:

```
mysql> ALTER TABLE artist type = InnoDB;
```

In both examples, you can substitute the alias ENGINE for TYPE. Of course, much like every other ALTER TABLE statement, the overhead of changing your choice can be high for large tables.

Note that there are several, rarely used table types we don't discuss at all in this book. These include Merge (which is a variant of MyISAM used in large distributed installations), Example (a nonfunctioning type used to illustrate ideas for programmers), NDB Cluster (a high-performance type used to partition tables across many computers), Archive (a high-performance, index-free table type used for very large data collections), CSV (a table type for working with data stored as comma-separated values in text files), and Federated (a very new engine—added in MySQL 5.0.3—that's used to store data in remote databases). You can find out more about these under "Storage Engines and Table Types" in the MySQL manual.

MyISAM

Before we discuss the alternatives, let's focus on the default MyISAM type. It's an all-around performer that's designed for typical applications; it supports very fast querying and has very low overhead for changes to data. It's also very flexible: underneath; it adapts how it stores data, depending on the structure of the tables you ask it to create. You'll recall from Chapter 6 that we encouraged you to consider using fixed-length column types in preference to variable-length types. It was with MyISAM in mind that we made the recommendation: when you use fixed-length fields, MySQL adapts its disk-storage structures for fast data access and modification; it's also easier to recover data from a corrupted table file if it uses fixed-length fields.

One of the key features of MyISAM is its unique way of *locking* tables. In brief, MyISAM locks are whole-table locks. This means that when you decide to lock a table, other users can have no access to the table at all. While this seems heavy-handed, it works fine for most typical applications, and management of the locks in this way costs very little memory and computational overhead. We'll contrast this with other locking schemes later when we describe InnoDB and BDB tables.

Unless you can see a good reason, stick with MyISAM while you're learning MySQL.

Memory or Heap

Prior to MySQL 4.1, the Memory table type was known as the Heap table type. Both keywords are supported, but the MySQL designers now prefer the term *Memory*. We'll use the new term here, but they're interchangeable.

The Memory table type is useful when you want to force data to be in main memory and not on disk. You do this when you want very fast access to a typically small set of data. It's ideal, for example, for storing and finding country names, lists of states or cities, or salutations. Don't use it for large files, as you need main memory for other tasks, such as SQL query evaluation and whatever other tasks your computer performs. Choose it when speed is essential for small tables with data that doesn't change.

There are serious disadvantages to the Memory type that can make it annoying. The most serious is that when you stop and restart a MySQL server, the data stored in a Memory table is lost. This means you need to restore it each time you start the MySQL server, which you might do by using the SOURCE statement or by using the init-file option to cause it to load a file on startup; the former is discussed in "Running the Monitor in Batch Mode" in Chapter 3 and the latter in "Resetting Forgotten MySQL Passwords" in Chapter 9. This is also a good reason to ensure the data doesn't change: use it for tasks where you have a fixed set of choices, not for tasks where you're dynamically updating those choices. Remember that if your MySQL server goes down, you'll lose any changes you've made if you've haven't explicitly dumped them to a disk file.

The Memory type has one significant advantage: it's an extremely fast environment for searching for exact matches (for example, checking if a country entered by a user matches a list of valid countries). Its list of disadvantages and limitations is longer:

- As discussed, data is lost when the server stops. You need to reload it each time the server starts.
- It doesn't support TEXT or BLOB type columns, or any of their variants.
- Prior to MySQL 4.0.2, it doesn't support indexes on columns that contain NULL values.
- Prior to MySQL 4.1.0, the AUTO_INCREMENT feature isn't supported.
- The tables are stored exclusively in memory. While this is what makes them fast, it's a disadvantage if there are many memory-based tables, if the memory-based tables are large, or if the server needs the memory for other tasks.

InnoDB

The InnoDB type is the heavyweight, reliable, high-performance choice for large-scale, highly reliable applications. It's similar to MyISAM but includes extra features that make it transaction-safe, reliable, and flexible for high-end applications. Choose it if you're building an application that needs features MyISAM doesn't have. In this book, we don't discuss those features in detail, so it's unlikely you'll need to use it while you're learning MySQL. However, note that with MySQL 4.1.5 and later, InnoDB is the default table type in Windows when you download and install a binary package from the MySQL AB web site; in practice, this has no impact on you, so don't be too concerned whether the default is MyISAM or InnoDB while using this book.

The InnoDB table type includes the following features:

Support for transactions
> This is discussed at the start of this section.

Advanced crash recovery features
> The InnoDB table type uses logs, which are files that contain the actions that MySQL has taken to change the database. With the combination of a log and the database, MySQL can recover effectively from power losses, crashes, and other basic database failures. Of course, nothing can help you recover from loss of a machine, failure of a disk drive, or other catastrophic failures. For these, you need offsite backups and new hardware.

Row-level locking
> We've explained how MyISAM locks at the table level, and the advantages and disadvantages of this. InnoDB locks at the row level, meaning that only the rows of data that are affected are unavailable to other users, which promotes better concurrency (sharing) of resources in certain circumstances. For applications that write more data than they read, or for applications that change large amounts of data when they do, InnoDB may be a better choice than MyISAM.

Foreign-key support
> InnoDB is currently the only MySQL table type that supports foreign keys.

Fast, flexible indexing
> The InnoDB type chooses the right data structure for the task when you create an index. It can switch from the fast, exact-match *hash index* to the fast, all-around *B-tree* index as the need arises, giving you fast searching for most applications without you having to explicitly set the index type.

The InnoDB type has the following limitations:

More features means more to understand
> You need to know about transactions, foreign keys, data versioning, and other features to use it effectively.

It's difficult to set up
> It has tens of startup parameters and options, and to use it effectively, you need to understand and tune these. If you're planning on using it, you need to know its details because that's why you've chosen it over MyISAM. Tuning InnoDB requires a book of its own!

It's disk-hungry
> To support its transaction-safe and robust behavior, InnoDB needs extra disk space. MyISAM is much more compact because it doesn't have these features.

Locking overheads
> Row locking is more complex than table locking, and so it's slower and takes more memory.

Transaction examples

Because transactions are the key feature that make InnoDB different from MyISAM, we'll conclude this section with an introductory example that shows how they work.

Suppose you decide you want to add a new artist and album to the database. You want to ensure that either both actions succeed or neither do, and you want to carry out the process in complete isolation from other users; you don't want to insert tracks for a peculiar artist ID if the `artist_id` values is already taken for another artist, or other people using your data until it's finalized. To do this with a transaction, we need to first, change the table type for `artist` and `album` to InnoDB:

```
mysql> ALTER TABLE artist type = InnoDB;
Query OK, 7 rows affected, 1 warning (0.54 sec)
Records: 7  Duplicates: 0  Warnings: 0

mysql> ALTER TABLE album type = InnoDB;
Query OK, 14 rows affected, 1 warning (0.01 sec)
Records: 14  Duplicates: 0  Warnings: 0
```

With the InnoDB tables, we can now perform the following transaction:

```
mysql> START TRANSACTION;
Query OK, 0 rows affected (0.01 sec)

mysql> INSERT INTO artist VALUES (8, "The Cure");
Query OK, 1 row affected (0.04 sec)

mysql> INSERT INTO album VALUES (8, 1, "Disintegration");
Query OK, 1 row affected (0.00 sec)

mysql> COMMIT;
Query OK, 0 rows affected (0.00 sec)
```

The first statement, `START TRANSACTION`, tells MySQL that you're beginning a set of statements you want in isolation and to be treated as a block or *atomic entity*. You then execute the two statements that modify the database. At the conclusion, you tell MySQL to `COMMIT`—that is, end the transaction and make the changes to the database.

Transactions also allow you to abort or rollback—that is, undo everything that's in the transaction. Let's try an example where we do just that:

```
mysql> START TRANSACTION;
Query OK, 0 rows affected (0.00 sec)

mysql> INSERT INTO artist VALUES (9, "The Wh");
Query OK, 1 row affected (0.01 sec)

mysql> ROLLBACK;
Query OK, 0 rows affected (0.04 sec)

mysql> SELECT * FROM artist;
+-----------+--------------------------+
| artist_id | artist_name              |
```

```
+-----------+---------------------------+
|         1 | New Order                 |
|         2 | Nick Cave & The Bad Seeds |
|         3 | Miles Davis               |
|         4 | The Rolling Stones        |
|         5 | The Stone Roses           |
|         6 | Kylie Minogue             |
|         7 | The Beatles               |
|         8 | The Cure                  |
+-----------+---------------------------+
8 rows in set (0.06 sec)
```

You can see in the second statement that we've misspelled the name of the band The Who, so we've decided to ROLLBACK the transaction. You can see that the rollback was successful, since the SELECT statement shows the artist wasn't added.

BDB

The Berkeley Database (BDB) table type can survive the same types of database crashes as the InnoDB table type, and also has the COMMIT and ROLLBACK functionality we showed you in the previous section. The Berkeley DB software itself is developed by Sleepycat Software (*http://www.sleepycat.com*) and is modified to work with MySQL. While Berkeley DB is very stable and is used by over 200 million installations in a very wide range of products, the interface between MySQL and Berkeley DB is still under development —and so the MySQL BDB table type is not yet widely used. Inbuilt support for this table type was dropped from MySQL version 5.1.12 onward. If you really need to use this table type, you can add support for it as a plug-in storage table, but that's outside the scope of this book.

This table type includes the following features:

Transaction support
 See our earlier description of transactions in "Transactions and Locking."

Advanced crash-recovery features
 See our earlier description in "InnoDB" for a discussion of logging and recovery.

Page-level locking
 We've explained how MyISAM and InnoDB lock at the table and row levels, respectively. The BDB locking philosophy lies somewhere between the two, locking typically a block of rows that reside in a physical disk-drive block.

Fast primary-key indexing
 The primary key index is stored with the data, and MySQL can avoid accessing the data itself if you require only columns that are part of the primary key. However, this also means that you must have a primary-key index. MySQL will automatically create a hidden five-byte primary key if you don't specify one. It's also slower to scan all rows in a table if required for a query.

The BDB type has the following limitations:

Gamma-quality interface and limited support

The Berkeley DB engine never became a fully integrated and supported part of MySQL, and it could not be used on some non-Intel architectures. As mentioned earlier, inbuilt support for the BDB engine was officially dropped from MySQL version 5.1.12.

It's disk-hungry, like InnoDB

With the features that make it transaction safe and robust to recover comes the cost of extra disk space for storing the information that's needed. MyISAM is much more compact because it doesn't have those features.

It's difficult to set up

You generally need a compiler to generate the required program files from source code. There are plenty of startup parameters and options, and you need to understand and tune these to make effective use of the BDB engine. This is a good enough reason not to use it, unless you really know what you're doing and why you want it.

Exercises

Selected exercises in this section concern the `music` database. You'll find that the description of table structures in "The Music Database" in Chapter 4 is a useful reference:

1. Write a join query that displays the name of each artist and the albums they've made. Alongside the album, display the number of tracks on the album.

2. Repeat Question 1, but now display only those albums that have more than 10 tracks.

3. Repeat Question 1, but write it as a nested query.

4. What are the four types of nested queries? For each type, write a sample query on the `music` database. Try to use different keywords in each query, selecting from `ANY`, `ALL`, `EXISTS` (or `NOT EXISTS`), and `IN` (or `NOT IN`).

5. What is the difference between an `INNER JOIN`, a `LEFT JOIN`, and a `RIGHT JOIN`? Does the order of tables matter in an `INNER JOIN`?

## CHAPTER 8

Doing More with MySQL

MySQL is feature-rich. Over the past three chapters, you've seen the wide variety of techniques that can be used to query, modify, and manage data. However, there's still much more that MySQL can do, and some of those additional features are the subject of this chapter.

In this chapter, you'll learn how to:

- Insert data into a database from other sources, including with queries and from text files
- Perform updates and deletes using multiple tables in a single statement
- Replace data
- Use MySQL functions in queries to meet more complex information needs
- Analyze queries using the EXPLAIN statement and then improve their performance with simple optimization techniques

Inserting Data Using Queries

Much of the time, you'll create tables using data from another source. The examples you've seen so far in Chapter 5 therefore illustrate only part of the problem: they show you how to insert data that's already in the form you want—that is, formatted as an SQL INSERT statement. The other ways to insert data include using SQL SELECT statements on other tables or databases, and reading in files from other sources. This section shows you how to tackle the former method of inserting data; you'll learn how to insert data from a file of comma-separated values in the next section, "Loading Data from Comma-Delimited Files."

Suppose you've decided to create a new table in the music database. It's going to store a shuffle list, tracks that are randomly selected from your music collection, put into a list, and played to you in that order. It's a way of tasting part of the collection, rediscovering some old favorites and learning about hidden treasures in those albums you haven't explored. We've decided to structure the table as follows:

```
mysql> CREATE TABLE shuffle (
    -> artist_id SMALLINT(5) NOT NULL DEFAULT 0,
    -> album_id SMALLINT(4) NOT NULL DEFAULT 0,
    -> track_id SMALLINT(3) NOT NULL DEFAULT 0,
    -> sequence_id SMALLINT(3) AUTO_INCREMENT NOT NULL,
    -> PRIMARY KEY (sequence_id));
Query OK, 0 rows affected (0.01 sec)
```

You can download these instructions from the the file *shuffle.sql* on the book's web site. This table stores the details of the track, allowing you to find the artist, album, and track names using simple queries on the other tables. It also stores a `sequence_id`, which is a unique number that enumerates where the track is in your playlist. When you first start using the shuffle feature, you'll listen to the track with a `sequence_id` of 1, then track 2, and so on. When we get to track 999, we can have our application reset the counter and table so it starts again at 1. Our reasoning is that after you've heard 999 tracks, it doesn't matter if you start hearing the same ones again. You can see that we're using the MySQL `auto_increment` feature to allocate the `sequence_id` values.

Now we need to fill up our new `shuffle` table with a random selection of tracks. Importantly, we're going to do the SELECT and INSERT together in one statement. Here we go:

```
mysql> INSERT INTO shuffle (artist_id, album_id, track_id)
    -> SELECT artist_id, album_id, track_id FROM
    -> track ORDER BY RAND() LIMIT 10;
Query OK, 10 rows affected (0.07 sec)
Records: 10  Duplicates: 0  Warnings: 0
```

Now, let's investigate what happened before we explain how this command works:

```
mysql> SELECT * FROM shuffle;
+-----------+----------+----------+-------------+
| artist_id | album_id | track_id | sequence_id |
+-----------+----------+----------+-------------+
|         1 |        7 |        0 |           1 |
|         3 |        1 |        3 |           2 |
|         1 |        3 |       10 |           3 |
|         6 |        1 |        1 |           4 |
|         4 |        1 |        8 |           5 |
|         1 |        7 |        1 |           6 |
|         1 |        1 |        4 |           7 |
|         2 |        1 |        6 |           8 |
|         1 |        6 |        0 |           9 |
|         4 |        1 |        1 |          10 |
+-----------+----------+----------+-------------+
10 rows in set (0.00 sec)
```

You can see that we got 10 tracks into our shuffle playlist, numbered with `sequence_id` values from 1 to 10. We're ready to start playing the shuffled tracks!

Let's discuss how the command works. There are two parts to the SQL statement: an INSERT INTO and a SELECT. The INSERT INTO statement lists the destination table into which the data will be stored, followed by an optional list of column names in

---

parentheses; if you omit the column names, all columns in the destination table are assumed in the order they appear in a DESCRIBE TABLE or SHOW CREATE TABLE statement. The SELECT statement outputs a list of columns that must match the type and order of the list provided for the INSERT INTO statement (or the implicit, complete list if one isn't provided). The overall effect is that the rows output from the SELECT statement are inserted into the destination table by the INSERT INTO statement. In our example, artist_id, album_id, and track_id values from the track table are inserted into the three columns with the same names and types in the shuffle table; the sequence_id is automatically created using MySQL's AUTO_INCREMENT feature, and so isn't specified in the statements.

Our example includes the clause ORDER BY RAND( ); this orders the results according to the MySQL function RAND( ). The RAND( ) function returns a pseudorandom number in the range 0 to 1:

```
mysql> SELECT RAND();
+-------------------+
| RAND()            |
+-------------------+
| 0.34423927529178 |
+-------------------+
1 row in set (0.00 sec)
```

A pseudorandom number generator doesn't generate truly random numbers, but rather generates numbers based on some property of the system, such as the time of day; this is sufficiently random for most applications. A notable exception is cryptography applications that depend on the true randomness of numbers for security.

If you ask for the RAND( ) value in a SELECT operation, you'll get a random value for each returned row:

```
mysql> SELECT *, RAND() FROM artist;
+-----------+--------------------------+-------------------+
| artist_id | artist_name              | RAND()            |
+-----------+--------------------------+-------------------+
| 1         | New Order                | 0.866806439       |
| 2         | Nick Cave & The Bad Seeds | 0.66403617492322 |
| 3         | Miles Davis              | 0.71976158834972 |
| 4         | The Rolling Stones       | 0.60669944771258 |
| 5         | The Stone Roses          | 0.8742125042474  |
| 6         | Kylie Minogue            | 0.55096420883291 |
+-----------+--------------------------+-------------------+
6 rows in set (0.00 sec)
```

Since the values are effectively random, you'll almost certainly see different results than we've shown here. Let's return to the INSERT operation. When we ask that the results be ordered by RAND( ), the results of the SELECT statement are sorted in a pseudorandom order.

The `LIMIT 10` is there to limit the number of rows returned by the `SELECT`; we've limited in this example simply for readability, but in practice you'd limit it to 999 because that's the maximum `sequence_id` you want to use.

The `SELECT` statement in an `INSERT INTO` statement can use all of the features of `SELECT` statements. You can use joins, aggregation, functions, and any other features you choose. You can also query data from one database into another, by prefacing the table names with the database name followed by a period (`.`) character. For example, if you wanted to insert the `artist` table from the `music` database into a new `art` database, you could do the following:

```
mysql> CREATE DATABASE art;
Query OK, 1 row affected (0.01 sec)

mysql> USE art;
Database changed
mysql> CREATE TABLE people (
    -> people_id SMALLINT(4) NOT NULL,
    -> name CHAR(128) NOT NULL,
    -> PRIMARY KEY (people_id));
Query OK, 0 rows affected (0.00 sec)

mysql> INSERT INTO art.people (people_id, name)
    -> SELECT artist_id, artist_name FROM music.artist;
Query OK, 8 rows affected (0.00 sec)
Records: 8  Duplicates: 0  Warnings: 0
```

You can see that the new `people` table is referred to as `art.people` (though it doesn't need to be, since `art` is the database that's currently in use), and the `artist` table is referred to as `music.artist` (which it needs to be, since it isn't the database being used). Note also that the column names don't need to be the same for the `SELECT` and the `INSERT`.

Sometimes, you'll encounter duplication issues when inserting with a `SELECT` statement. This occurs if you try to insert the same primary key value twice; it won't happen in the `shuffle` table, as long as you automatically allocate a new `sequence_id` using the `auto_increment` feature. However, when you try to insert duplicate key values, MySQL will abort. Let's force a duplicate into the `shuffle` table to show the behavior:

```
mysql> USE music;
Database changed

mysql> INSERT INTO shuffle (artist_id, album_id, track_id, sequence_id)
    -> SELECT artist_id, album_id, track_id, 1 FROM track LIMIT 1;
ERROR 1062 (23000): Duplicate entry '1' for key 1
```

If you want MySQL to ignore this and keep going, add an `IGNORE` keyword after the `INSERT`:

```
mysql> INSERT IGNORE INTO shuffle (artist_id, album_id, track_id, sequence_id)
    -> SELECT artist_id, album_id, track_id, 1 FROM track LIMIT 1;
```

```
Query OK, 0 rows affected (0.00 sec)
Records: 1  Duplicates: 1  Warnings: 0
```

MySQL doesn't complain, but it does report that it encountered a duplicate. Prior to MySQL 4.0.1, the IGNORE mode was the default behavior, but for later versions, you have to add the keyword if you want duplicates to be ignored.

Finally, note that for versions of MySQL older than 4.0.14, you couldn't insert into a table that's listed in the SELECT statement, since the SELECT would find the newly inserted rows and try to insert them again. On newer systems, you still need to avoid duplicate primary keys:

```
mysql> INSERT INTO artist SELECT artist_id,artist_name FROM artist;
ERROR 1062 (23000): Duplicate entry '1' for key 1
```

but you can modify values in the SELECT statement to get a different primary key value and insert it back into the same table:

```
mysql> INSERT INTO artist SELECT 10*artist_id,artist_name FROM artist;
Query OK, 6 rows affected (0.00 sec)
Records: 6  Duplicates: 0  Warnings: 0
```

Here, we're copying the rows but multiplying their artist_ids by 10 before we insert them. This is the result:

```
mysql> SELECT * FROM artist;
+-----------+---------------------------+
| artist_id | artist_name               |
+-----------+---------------------------+
|         1 | New Order                 |
|         2 | Nick Cave & The Bad Seeds |
|         3 | Miles Davis               |
|         4 | The Rolling Stones        |
|         5 | The Stone Roses           |
|         6 | Kylie Minogue             |
|        60 | Kylie Minogue             |
|        50 | The Stone Roses           |
|        40 | The Rolling Stones        |
|        30 | Miles Davis               |
|        20 | Nick Cave & The Bad Seeds |
|        10 | New Order                 |
+-----------+---------------------------+
12 rows in set (0.01 sec)
```

Loading Data from Comma-Delimited Files

Databases are sometimes an afterthought. In fact, a staggeringly large amount of time spent by IT professionals is devoted to reformatting data from one application to suit another. It's very common, for example, to store data using a spreadsheet program such as Microsoft Excel or OpenOffice Calc, only to realize later—when you're swamped with data—that a relational database would have been a better choice. Most spreadsheet programs allow you to export data as rows of *comma-separated values* (CSV),

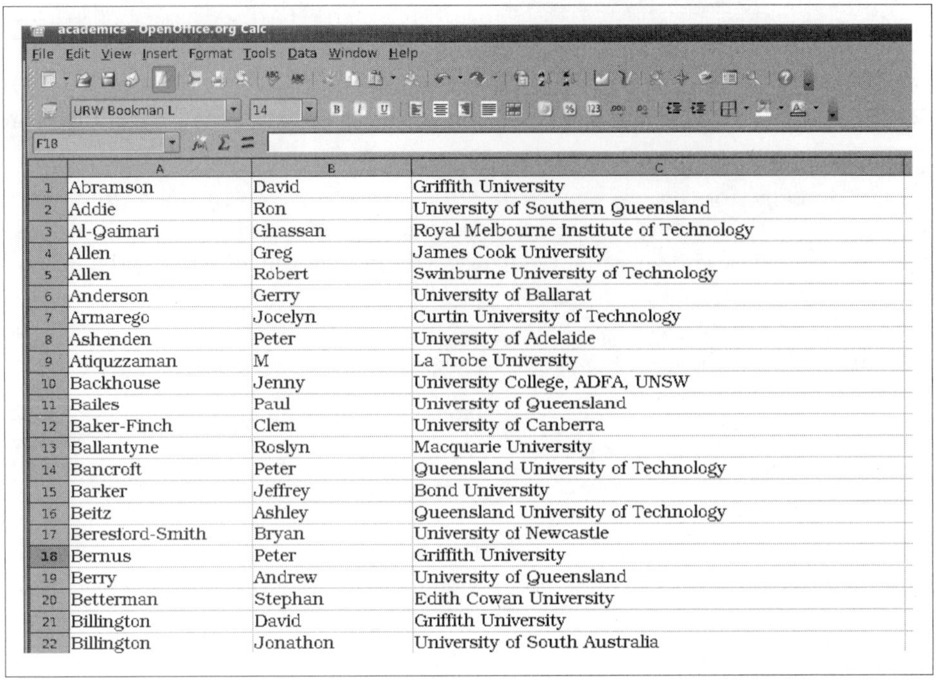

Figure 8-1. List of Australian academics stored in a spreadsheet file

often also referred to as *comma-delimited format* (CDF). You can then import the data with a little effort into MySQL.

If you need to import large numbers of spreadsheet files, you could use the *xls2csv* script (*http://search.cpan.org/~ken/xls2csv*) to automate the conversion from the Excel spreadsheet files to text files of comma-separated values.

If you're not using a spreadsheet program, you can still often use tools such as sed and awk to convert text data into a CSV format suitable for import by MySQL. This section shows you the basics of how to import CSV data into MySQL.

Let's work through an example. We have a list of Australian academics with their university affiliation that we want to store in a database. At present, it's stored in a spreadsheet workbook file named *academics.xls* and has the format shown in Figure 8-1. You can see that the surname is stored in the first column, one or more given names and initials in the second column, and their affiliation in the third column. This example is formulated from a file that is publicly available at *http://www.cs.jcu.edu.au/acsadb/nameonly_db.html*, and the workbook format example is available from the book's web site.

Saving the *academics.xls* file as values with a comma or other character as a delimiter is easy in most spreadsheet programs. In most versions of Microsoft Excel, you click on the File menu, then select Save As, and then choose "CSV (Comma delimited)" for the "Save as type" field. If you're using OpenOffice or StarOffice, follow the same steps, but choose "Text CSV (.csv)" for the "File type" field. When you save the file, you'll find it has the same name as the workbook (in this case, *academics*) but with the extension *.csv*.

If you open the file using a text editor (we discussed how to use a text editor in "Using a Text Editor" in Chapter 2), you'll see the result: the file has one line per spreadsheet row, with the value for each column separated by a comma. If you're on a non-Windows platform, you may find each line terminated with a ^M, but don't worry about this; it's an artifact of the origins of Windows. Data in this format is often referred to as *DOS format*, and most software applications can handle it without problem. Here are a few lines selected from *academics.csv*:

```
Abramson,David,Griffith University
Addie,Ron,University of Southern Queensland
Al-Qaimari,Ghassan,Royal Melbourne Institute of Technology
Allen,Greg,James Cook University
Allen,Robert,Swinburne University of Technology
Anderson,Gerry,University of Ballarat
Armarego,Jocelyn,Curtin University of Technology
Ashenden,Peter,University of Adelaide
Atiquzzaman,M,La Trobe University
Backhouse,Jenny,"University College, ADFA, UNSW"
```

If there are commas within values, the whole value is enclosed in quotes, as in the last line shown here.

Let's import this data into MySQL. First, create the new `academics` database:

```
mysql> CREATE DATABASE academics;
```

and choose this as the active database:

```
mysql> USE academics;
```

Now, create the `details` table to store the data. This needs to handle three fields: the surname, the given names, and the institution:

```
mysql> CREATE TABLE details (surname CHAR(40), given_names CHAR(40),
       institution CHAR(40));
```

We've allocated 40 characters for each field.

Now that we've set up the database table, we can import the data from the file using the `LOAD DATA INFILE` command:

```
mysql> LOAD DATA INFILE 'academics.csv' INTO TABLE details FIELDS TERMINATED BY ',';
```

If the *academics.csv* file isn't in the current directory, you'll need to specify the full path —for example, `/home/adam/academics.csv` or `C:\academics.csv`. The MySQL server must have permission to read this file; for example, if the server is running as the user `mysql` on a Linux or Mac OS X system, the datafile must have its permissions set such that this user can read it.

The clause `FIELDS TERMINATED BY ','` specifies the character that delimits the field values in the text file. For example, if you have a file called *academics.colon_sv* with values separated by colons, you can import it by specifying the colon as the field terminator:

```
mysql> LOAD DATA INFILE 'academics.colon_sv' INTO
    -> TABLE details FIELDS TERMINATED BY ':';
```

Writing Data into Comma-Delimited Files

You can use the `SELECT INTO OUTFILE` statement to write out the result of a query into a comma-separated values (CSV) file that can be opened by a spreadsheet or other program.

Let's export the list of artists from our music database into a CSV file. The query used to list all the artists is shown below:

```
mysql> USE music;
Database changed

mysql> SELECT artist_name, album_name FROM
    -> artist, album WHERE artist.artist_id=album.artist_id;
+--------------------------+-------------------------------------------+
| artist_name              | album_name                                |
+--------------------------+-------------------------------------------+
| New Order                | Retro - John McCready FAN                 |
| New Order                | Substance (Disc 2)                        |
| New Order                | Retro - Miranda Sawyer POP                |
| New Order                | Retro - New Order / Bobby Gillespie LIVE  |
| New Order                | Power, Corruption & Lies                  |
| New Order                | Substance 1987 (Disc 1)                   |
| New Order                | Brotherhood                               |
| Nick Cave & The Bad Seeds| Let Love In                               |
| Miles Davis              | Live Around The World                     |
| Miles Davis              | In A Silent Way                           |
| The Rolling Stones       | Exile On Main Street                      |
| The Stone Roses          | Second Coming                             |
| Kylie Minogue            | Light Years                               |
+--------------------------+-------------------------------------------+
13 rows in set (0.10 sec)
```

We can change this `SELECT` query slightly to write this data into an output file as comma-separated values:

```
mysql> SELECT artist_name, album_name FROM
    -> artist, album WHERE artist.artist_id=album.artist_id
    -> INTO OUTFILE '/tmp/artists_and_albums.csv' FIELDS TERMINATED BY ',';

Query OK, 13 rows affected (0.02 sec)
```

Here, we've saved the results into the file *artists_and_albums.csv* in the */tmp* directory; the MySQL server must be able to write to the directory that you specify. On a Windows system, specify a path such as *C:\artists_and_albums.csv* instead. If you omit the `FIELDS`

TERMINATED BY clause, the server will use tabs as the default separator between the data values.

You can view the contents of the file *artists_and_albums.csv* in a text editor, or import it into a spreadsheet program:

```
New Order,Retro - John McCready FAN
New Order,Substance (Disc 2)
New Order,Retro - Miranda Sawyer POP
New Order,Retro - New Order / Bobby Gillespie LIVE
New Order,Power\, Corruption & Lies
New Order,Substance 1987 (Disc 1)
New Order,Brotherhood
Nick Cave & The Bad Seeds,Let Love In
Miles Davis,Live Around The World
Miles Davis,In A Silent Way
The Rolling Stones,Exile On Main Street
The Stone Roses,Second Coming
Kylie Minogue,Light Years
```

Notice how the comma in `Power, Corruption & Lies` has been automatically escaped with a backslash to distinguish it from the separator. Spreadsheet programs understand this and remove the backslash when importing the file.

Creating Tables with Queries

You can create a table or easily create a copy of a table using a query. This is useful when you want to build a new database using existing data—for example, you might want to copy across a list of countries—or when you want to reorganize data for some reason. Data reorganization is common for producing reports, merging data from two or more tables, and redesigning on the fly. This short section shows you how it's done.

From MySQL 4.1 onward, you can easily duplicate the structure of a table using a variant of the `CREATE TABLE` syntax:

```
mysql> CREATE TABLE artist_2 LIKE artist;
Query OK, 0 rows affected (0.24 sec)

mysql> DESCRIBE artist_2;
+-------------+-------------+------+-----+---------+-------+
| Field       | Type        | Null | Key | Default | Extra |
+-------------+-------------+------+-----+---------+-------+
| artist_id   | smallint(5) |      | PRI | 0       |       |
| artist_name | char(128)   | YES  |     | NULL    |       |
+-------------+-------------+------+-----+---------+-------+
2 rows in set (0.09 sec)

mysql> SELECT * FROM artist_2;
Empty set (0.30 sec)
```

The LIKE syntax allows you to create a new table with exactly the same structure as another, including keys. You can see that it doesn't copy the data across. You can also use the IF NOT EXISTS and TEMPORARY features with this syntax.

If you want to create a table and copy some data, you can do that with a combination of the CREATE TABLE and SELECT statements. Let's remove the artist_2 table and re-create it using this new approach:

```
mysql> DROP TABLE artist_2;
Query OK, 0 rows affected (0.08 sec)

mysql> CREATE TABLE artist_2 SELECT * from artist;
Query OK, 7 rows affected (0.02 sec)
Records: 7  Duplicates: 0  Warnings: 0

mysql> SELECT * FROM artist_2;
+-----------+----------------------------+
| artist_id | artist_name                |
+-----------+----------------------------+
|         1 | New Order                  |
|         2 | Nick Cave and The Bad Seeds |
|         3 | Miles Dewey Davis          |
|         4 | The Rolling Stones         |
|         5 | The Stone Roses            |
|         6 | Kylie Minogue              |
|        10 | Jane's Addiction           |
+-----------+----------------------------+
7 rows in set (0.01 sec)
```

An identical table artist_2 is created, and all of the data is copied across by the SELECT statement.

This technique is powerful. You can create new tables with new structures and use powerful queries to populate them with data. For example, here's a report table that's created to contain the names of artists and albums in our database:

```
mysql> CREATE TABLE report (artist_name CHAR(128), album_name CHAR(128))
    -> SELECT artist_name, album_name FROM artist INNER JOIN album
    -> USING (artist_id);
Query OK, 13 rows affected (0.45 sec)
Records: 13  Duplicates: 0  Warnings: 0
```

You can see that the syntax is a little different from the previous example. In this example, the new table name, report, is followed by a list of column names and types in parentheses; this is necessary because we're not duplicating the structure of an existing table. Then, the SELECT statement follows, with its output matching the new columns in the new table. You can check the contents of the new table:

```
mysql> SELECT * FROM report;
+------------------------+----------------------------------------+
| artist_name            | album_name                             |
+------------------------+----------------------------------------+
| New Order              | Retro - John McCready FAN              |
| New Order              | Substance (Disc 2)                     |
```

```
| New Order                  | RETRO - MIRANDA SAWYER POP             |
| New Order                  | Retro - New Order / Bobby Gillespie LIVE |
| New Order                  | Power, Corruption & Lies               |
| New Order                  | Substance 1987 (Disc 1)                |
| New Order                  | Brotherhood                            |
| Nick Cave and The Bad Seeds | Let Love In                           |
| Miles Dewey Davis          | LIVE AROUND THE WORLD                  |
| Miles Dewey Davis          | In A Silent Way                        |
| The Rolling Stones         | Exile On Main Street                   |
| The Stone Roses            | Second Coming                          |
| Kylie Minogue              | Light Years                            |
+----------------------------+----------------------------------------+
13 rows in set (0.00 sec)
```

So, in this example, the `artist_name` and `album_name` values from the `SELECT` statement are used to populate the new `artist_name` and `album_name` columns in the `report` table.

Creating tables with a query has a major caveat that you need to be careful about. It doesn't copy the indexes (or foreign keys, if you use them); this is a feature, since it gives you a lot of flexibility, but it can be a catch if you forget. Have a look at our `artist_2` example:

```
mysql> DESCRIBE artist_2;
+-------------+-------------+------+-----+---------+-------+
| Field       | Type        | Null | Key | Default | Extra |
+-------------+-------------+------+-----+---------+-------+
| artist_id   | smallint(5) |      |     | 0       |       |
| artist_name | char(128)   | YES  |     | NULL    |       |
+-------------+-------------+------+-----+---------+-------+
2 rows in set (0.31 sec)

mysql> SHOW CREATE TABLE artist_2;
+----------+------------------------------------------------------+
| Table    | Create Table                                         |
+----------+------------------------------------------------------+
| artist_2 | CREATE TABLE `artist_2` (                            |
|            `artist_id` smallint(5) NOT NULL default '0',       |
|            `artist_name` char(128) default NULL)              |
|            ENGINE=MyISAM DEFAULT CHARSET=latin1               |
+----------+------------------------------------------------------+
1 row in set (0.33 sec)
```

You can see that there's no primary key; if there had been other keys, they'd be missing too.

To copy indexes across to the new table, there are at least three things you can do. The first is to use the `LIKE` statement to create the empty table with the indexes, as described earlier and then copy the data across using an `INSERT` with a `SELECT` statement as described earlier in this chapter in "Inserting Data Using Queries."

The second thing you can do is to use `CREATE TABLE` with a `SELECT` statement, and then add indexes using `ALTER TABLE` as described in Chapter 6.

The third way is to use the UNIQUE (or PRIMARY KEY or KEY) keyword in combination with the CREATE TABLE and SELECT to add a primary-key index. Here's an example of this approach:

```
mysql> CREATE TABLE artist_2 (UNIQUE(artist_id))
    -> SELECT * FROM artist;
Query OK, 7 rows affected (0.27 sec)
Records: 7  Duplicates: 0  Warnings: 0

mysql> DESCRIBE artist_2;
+-------------+-------------+------+-----+---------+-------+
| Field       | Type        | Null | Key | Default | Extra |
+-------------+-------------+------+-----+---------+-------+
| artist_id   | smallint(5) |      | PRI | 0       |       |
| artist_name | char(128)   | YES  |     | NULL    |       |
+-------------+-------------+------+-----+---------+-------+
2 rows in set (0.26 sec)
```

The UNIQUE keyword is applied to the artist_id column, making it the primary key in the newly created table. The keywords UNIQUE and PRIMARY KEY can be interchanged.

You can use different modifiers when you're creating tables using these techniques. For example, here's a table created with defaults and other settings:

```
mysql> CREATE TABLE artist_3
    -> (artist_id SMALLINT(5) NOT NULL AUTO_INCREMENT,
    -> artist_name CHAR(128) NOT NULL DEFAULT "New Order",
    -> PRIMARY KEY (artist_id), KEY (artist_name))
    -> SELECT * FROM artist;
Query OK, 7 rows affected (0.31 sec)
Records: 7  Duplicates: 0  Warnings: 0
```

Here, we've set NOT NULL for the new columns, used the AUTO_INCREMENT feature on artist_id, and created two keys. Anything you can do in a regular CREATE TABLE statement can be done in this variant; just remember to add those indexes explicitly!

Updates and Deletes with Multiple Tables

In Chapter 5, we showed you how to update and delete data. In the examples there, each update and delete affected one table and used properties of that table to decide what to modify. This section shows you more complex updates and deletes, with which you can delete or update rows from more than one table in one statement and can use those or other tables to decide what rows to change.

Deletion

Imagine you've just run out of disk space or you're sick of browsing unwanted data in your music collection. One way to solve this problem is to remove some data, and it'd make sense to remove tracks you've never listened to. Unfortunately, this means you need to remove data from the track table using information from the played table.

With the techniques we've described so far in the book, there's no way of doing this without creating a table that combines the two tables (perhaps using INSERT with SELECT), removing unwanted rows, and copying the data back to its source. In fact, this is exactly what you had to do prior to MySQL 4.0. This section shows you how you can perform this procedure and other more advanced types of deletion in recent versions of MySQL.

Consider the query you need to write to find tracks you've never played. One way to do it is to use a nested query—following the techniques we showed you in Chapter 7 —with the NOT EXISTS clause. Here's the query:

```
mysql> SELECT track_name FROM track WHERE NOT EXISTS
    -> (SELECT * FROM played WHERE
    -> track.artist_id = played.artist_id AND
    -> track.album_id = played.album_id AND
    -> track.track_id = played.track_id);
+---------------------------+
| track_name                |
+---------------------------+
| Do You Love Me?           |
| Nobody's Baby Now         |
| Loverman                  |
| Jangling Jack             |
| Red Right Hand            |
| I Let Love In             |
| Thirsty Dog               |
| Ain't Gonna Rain Anymore  |
| Lay Me Low                |
| Do You Love Me? (Part Two)|
...
+---------------------------+
```

We've shown only 10 tracks from the output, but there are actually 142 tracks we've never listened to. You can probably see how the query works, but let's briefly discuss it anyway before we move on. You can see it uses a correlated subquery, where the current row being processed in the outer query is referenced by the subquery; you can tell this because three columns from track are referenced, but the track table isn't listed in the FROM clause of the subquery. The subquery produces output when there's a row in the played table that matches the current row in the outer query (and so there's a track that's been played). However, since the query uses NOT EXISTS, the outer query doesn't produce output when this is the case, and so the overall result is that rows are output for tracks that haven't been played.

Now let's take our query and turn it into a DELETE statement. Here it is:

```
mysql> DELETE track FROM track WHERE NOT EXISTS
    -> (SELECT * FROM played WHERE track.artist_id = played.artist_id AND
    -> track.album_id = played.album_id AND
    -> track.track_id = played.track_id);
Query OK, 142 rows affected (0.01 sec)
```

You can see that the subquery remains the same, but the outer SELECT query is replaced by a DELETE statement. The DELETE statement syntax is as follows: first, the keyword DELETE is followed by the table or tables from which rows should be removed; second, the keyword FROM is followed by the table or tables that should be queried to determine which rows to delete; and, last, a WHERE clause (and any other query clauses, such as GROUP BY or HAVING) follow. In this query, rows are deleted from the track table using the track table in the query along with the played table in the nested subquery.

As another example, let's clean up our database to remove albums and tracks by the band New Order:

```
mysql> DELETE FROM track, album USING artist, album, track WHERE
    -> artist_name = "New Order" AND
    -> artist.artist_id = album.artist_id AND
    -> artist.artist_id = track.artist_id AND
    -> album.album_id = track.album_id;
Query OK, 93 rows affected (0.00 sec)
```

This query deletes rows from track and album, based on a query that involves artist, album, and track. You can see the result is that 93 rows are removed: 7 albums and 86 tracks.

In this syntax, the keywords DELETE FROM are followed by the table or tables from which you want to delete rows. The keyword USING then follows with a list of tables that are used in the query part of the statement (and then the WHERE clause or other associated query mechanisms).

With MySQL versions between 4.0 and 4.02, you had to use the following syntax:

```
mysql> DELETE track, album FROM artist, album, track WHERE
    -> artist_name = "New Order" AND
    -> artist.artist_id = album.artist_id AND
    -> artist.artist_id = track.artist_id AND
    -> album.album_id = track.album_id;
Query OK, 93 rows affected (0.10 sec)
```

The query identifies the artist_id of "New Order" and performs a join between the tables.

We prefer the newer syntax because it is clearer: DELETE FROM some tables USING other tables to drive the querying process.

Note that you can use clauses such as LEFT JOIN and INNER JOIN in DELETE statements. However, you can't delete from a table that's read from in a nested subquery, such as in the following line:

```
mysql> DELETE FROM artist WHERE artist_id IN (SELECT artist_id FROM artist);
ERROR 1093 (HY000): You can't specify target table 'artist' for update in
                    FROM clause
```

In multiple table deletes, you can't use ORDER BY or LIMIT clauses.

Updates

Now we'll contrive an example using the `music` database to illustrate multiple-table updates. We've decided to highlight albums we've played. Our method of highlighting is to change the album's name to all capital letters. To begin, let's display albums we've played:

```
mysql> SELECT DISTINCT album_name FROM
    -> album INNER JOIN track USING (artist_id, album_id)
    -> INNER JOIN played USING (artist_id, album_id, track_id);
+----------------------------+
| album_name                 |
+----------------------------+
| Retro - Miranda Sawyer POP |
| Live Around The World      |
+----------------------------+
2 rows in set (0.00 sec)
```

Now, let's put that query into an `UPDATE` statement:

```
mysql> UPDATE album INNER JOIN track USING (artist_id, album_id)
    -> INNER JOIN played USING (artist_id, album_id, track_id)
    -> SET album_name = UPPER(album_name);
Query OK, 2 rows affected (0.01 sec)
Rows matched: 11  Changed: 2  Warnings: 0
```

Let's look at the syntax: a multiple-table update looks similar to a `SELECT` query. The `UPDATE` statement is followed by a list of tables that incorporates whatever join clauses you need or prefer; in this example, we've used `INNER JOIN` to bring together the `artist`, `album`, and `track` tables. This is followed by the keyword `SET`, with assignments to individual columns; in this example, you can see that only one column is modified (to put the album name in uppercase), so columns in all other tables besides `album` aren't modified. An optional `WHERE` may in turn follow (but doesn't in this example, since the `USING` clause does it for us).

To illustrate using a `WHERE` clause, here's the previous query rewritten with the join expressed using `WHERE`:

```
mysql> UPDATE artist, album, track, played
    -> SET album_name = UPPER(album_name)
    -> WHERE artist.artist_id = album.artist_id AND
    -> album.artist_id = track.artist_id AND
    -> album.album_id = track.album_id AND
    -> track.artist_id = played.artist_id AND
    -> track.album_id = played.album_id AND
    -> track.track_id = played.track_id;
Query OK, 2 rows affected (0.00 sec)
Rows matched: 11  Changed: 2  Warnings: 0
```

The method that you choose to use is just personal preference, and that might be driven by the amount of typing you're prepared to do!

As with multiple-table deletes, there are some limitations on updates:

- You can't use `ORDER BY`.
- You can't use `LIMIT`.
- You can't update a table that's read from in a nested subquery.

Other than that, multiple-table updates are much the same as single-table ones.

Replacing Data

You'll sometimes want to overwrite data. You can do this in two ways using the techniques we've shown previously:

- Delete an existing row using its primary key and then insert a new replacement with the same primary key.
- Update a row using its primary key, replacing some or all of the values (except the primary key).

The `REPLACE` statement gives you a third, convenient way to change data. This section explains how it works.

The `REPLACE` statement is just like `INSERT`, but with one difference. You can't `INSERT` a new row if there is an existing row in the table with the same primary key, You can get around this problem with a `REPLACE` query, which first removes any existing row with the same primary key and then inserts the new one.

Let's try an example, where we'll replace the row for `"Nick Cave & The Bad Seeds"`:

```
mysql> REPLACE artist VALUES (2, "Nick Cave and The Bad Seeds");
Query OK, 2 rows affected (0.02 sec)
```

You can see that MySQL reports that two rows were affected: first, the old row was deleted, and, second, the new row was inserted. You can see that the change we made was minor—we just changed the & to an "and"—and therefore, it could easily have been accomplished with an `UPDATE`. Because the tables in the `music` database contain few columns, it's difficult to illustrate an example in which `REPLACE` looks simpler than `UPDATE`.

You can use the different `INSERT` syntaxes with `REPLACE`, including using `SELECT` queries. Here are some examples:

```
mysql> REPLACE INTO artist VALUES (2, "Nick Cave and The Bad Seeds");
Query OK, 2 rows affected (0.00 sec)

mysql> REPLACE INTO artist (artist_id, artist_name)
    -> VALUES (2, "Nick Cave and The Bad Seeds");
Query OK, 2 rows affected (0.00 sec)

mysql> REPLACE artist (artist_id, artist_name)
    -> VALUES (2, "Nick Cave and The Bad Seeds");
Query OK, 2 rows affected (0.01 sec)
```

```
mysql> REPLACE artist SET artist_id = 2,
    -> artist_name = "Nick Cave and The Bad Seeds";
Query OK, 2 rows affected (0.00 sec)
```

The first variant is almost identical to our previous example, except it includes the optional INTO keyword (which, arguably, improves the readability of the statement). The second variant explicitly lists the column names that the matching values should be inserted into. The third variant is the same as the second, without the optional INTO keyword. The final variant uses the SET syntax; you can add the optional keyword INTO to this variant if you want. Note that if you don't specify a value for a column, it's set to its default value, just like for INSERT.

You can also bulk-replace into a table, removing and inserting more than one row. Here's an example:

```
mysql> REPLACE artist (artist_id, artist_name)
    -> VALUES (2, "Nick Cave and The Bad Seeds"),
    -> (3, "Miles Dewey Davis");
Query OK, 4 rows affected (0.00 sec)
Records: 2  Duplicates: 2  Warnings: 0
```

Note that four rows are affected: two deletions and two insertions. You can also see that two duplicates were found, meaning the replacement of existing rows succeeded. In contrast, if there isn't a matching row in a REPLACE statement, it acts just like an INSERT:

```
mysql> REPLACE INTO artist VALUES (10, "Jane's Addiction");
Query OK, 1 row affected (0.22 sec)
```

You can tell that only the insert occurred, since only one row was affected.

Replacing also works with a SELECT statement. Recall the shuffle table from "Inserting Data Using Queries," at the beginning of this chapter. Suppose you've added 10 tracks to it, but you don't like the choice of the seventh track in the playlist. Here's how you can replace it with a random choice of another track:

```
mysql> REPLACE INTO shuffle (artist_id, album_id, track_id, sequence_id)
    -> SELECT artist_id, album_id, track_id, 7 FROM
    -> track ORDER BY RAND() LIMIT 1;
Query OK, 2 rows affected (0.01 sec)
Records: 1  Duplicates: 1  Warnings: 0
```

Again, the syntax is the same as with INSERT, but a deletion is attempted (and succeeds!) before the insertion. Note that we keep the value of the sequence_id as 7.

If a table doesn't have a primary key, replacing doesn't make sense. This is because there's no way of uniquely identifying a matching row in order to delete it. When you use REPLACE on such a table, its behavior is identical to INSERT. Also, as with INSERT, you can't replace rows in a table that's used in a subquery. Finally, note the difference between INSERT IGNORE and REPLACE: the first keeps the existing data with the duplicate key and does not insert the new row, while the second deletes the existing row and replaces it with the new one.

The EXPLAIN Statement

You'll sometimes find that MySQL doesn't run queries as quickly as you expect. For example, you'll often find that a nested query runs slowly. You might also find—or, at least, suspect—that MySQL isn't doing what you hoped, because you know an index exists but the query still seems slow. You can diagnose and solve query optimization problems using the EXPLAIN statement.

The EXPLAIN statement helps you learn about a SELECT query. Specifically, it tells you how MySQL is going to do the job in terms of the indexes, keys, and steps it'll take if you ask it to resolve a query. Let's try a simple example that illustrates the idea:

```
mysql> EXPLAIN SELECT * FROM artist;
+---+------------+-------+-----+---------------+-----+--------+-----+-----+------+
|id |select_type |table  |type |possible_keys  |key  |key_len |ref  |rows |Extra |
+---+------------+-------+-----+---------------+-----+--------+-----+-----+------+
| 1 |SIMPLE      |artist |ALL  |NULL           |NULL |   NULL |NULL |  6  |      |
+---+------------+-------+-----+---------------+-----+--------+-----+-----+------+
1 row in set (0.10 sec)
```

The statement gives you lots of information. It tells you in this example that:

- The id is 1, meaning the row in the output refers to the first (and only!) SELECT statement in this query. In the query:

    SELECT * FROM artist WHERE artist_id in (SELECT artist_id FROM played);

    each SELECT statement will have a different id in the EXPLAIN output.
- The select_type is SIMPLE, meaning it doesn't use a UNION or subqueries.
- The table that this row is referring to is **artist.**
- The type of join is ALL, meaning all rows in the table are processed by this SELECT statement. This is often bad—but not in this case—and we'll explain why later.
- The possible_keys that could be used are listed. In this case, no index will help find all rows in a table, so NULL is reported.
- The key that is actually used is listed, taken from the list of possible_keys. In this case, since no key is available, none is used.
- The key_len (key length) of the key MySQL plans to use is listed. Again, no key means a NULL key_len is reported.
- The ref (reference) columns or constants that are used with the key is listed. Again, none in this example.
- The rows that MySQL thinks it needs to process to get an answer are listed.
- Any Extra information about the query resolution is listed. Here, there's none.

In summary, the output tells you that all rows from the **artist** table will be processed (there are six of them), and no indexes will be used to resolve the query. This makes sense and is probably exactly what you expected would happen.

We'll now give the EXPLAIN statement some work to do. Let's ask it to explain an INNER JOIN between artist and album:

```
mysql> EXPLAIN SELECT * FROM artist INNER JOIN album USING (artist_id);
+----+-------------+--------+------+---------------+...
| id | select_type | table  | type | possible_keys |...
+----+-------------+--------+------+---------------+...
| 1  | SIMPLE      | artist | ALL  | PRIMARY       |...
| 1  | SIMPLE      | album  | ref  | PRIMARY       |...
+----+-------------+--------+------+---------------+...

...+---------+---------+-----------------------+------+-------+
...| key     | key_len | ref                   | rows | Extra |
...+---------+---------+-----------------------+------+-------+
...|         |         |                       | 6    |       |
...| PRIMARY | 2       | music.artist.artist_id | 1   |       |
...+---------+---------+-----------------------+------+-------+
2 rows in set (0.01 sec)
```

Before we discuss the output, think about how the query could be evaluated. MySQL could go through each row in the artist table and look up the album table to see what rows match. Or it could go through each row in the album table and look up the artist table to see what rows match. Let's see what MySQL has decided to do. This time, there are two rows because there are two tables in the join. Let's run through this, focusing on those things that are different from the previous example:

- The first row is basically identical to the previous example. All rows in the artist table are processed, so MySQL has decided that the same method of solving the query is its preferred way here, too.

- The join type for the album table is ref, meaning that all rows in the album table that match rows in the artist table will be read. In practice, this means one or more rows from the album table will be read for each artist_id.

- The possible_keys for artist and album are both only the PRIMARY key. A key isn't used in artist (because we're scanning the whole table), but the key used for album is that table's PRIMARY key

- The primary key used to search album has a key_len of 2 and is searched using the music.artist.artist_id value from the artist table

Again, this seems like a sensible strategy, and it fits with what we thought about in our design of the database.

Exercises

1. Write the monitor command to import the file *academics.tsv*, which has its values separated by tabs, into the details table. Hint: the tab character is shown with the \t escape sequence.

2. When would you need to insert data using a query?

3. What's the difference between REPLACE and INSERT IGNORE?

4. What can you tell from this output produced by the EXPLAIN command?

```
+----+-------------+------------+-------+---------------+---------+...
| id | select_type | table      | type  | possible_keys | key     |...
+----+-------------+------------+-------+---------------+---------+...
|  1 | SIMPLE      | supervisor | const | PRIMARY       | PRIMARY |...
|  1 | SIMPLE      | student    | ALL   | NULL          | NULL    |...
|  1 | SIMPLE      | supervises | index | NULL          | PRIMARY |...
+----+-------------+------------+-------+---------------+---------+...

... +---------+-------+------+------------------------------------+
... | key_len | ref   | rows | Extra                              |
... +---------+-------+------+------------------------------------+
... |       4 | const |    1 | Using index; Using temporary       |
... |    NULL | NULL  |   95 |                                    |
... |      12 | NULL  |  570 | Using where; Using index; Distinct |
... +---------+-------+------+------------------------------------+
3 rows in set (0.00 sec)
```

5. What can you tell from this output produced by the EXPLAIN command?

```
+-----+--------------+-----------+--------+---------------+---------+---------+...
| id  | select_type  | table     | type   | possible_keys | key     | key_len |...
+-----+--------------+-----------+--------+---------------+---------+---------+...
|  1  | PRIMARY      | played    | index  | PRIMARY       | PRIMARY | 10      |...
|  1  | PRIMARY      | track     | eq_ref | PRIMARY       | PRIMARY | 6       |...
|  2  | UNION        | played    | index  | PRIMARY       | PRIMARY | 10      |...
|  2  | UNION        | track     | eq_ref | PRIMARY       | PRIMARY | 6       |...
| NULL| UNION RESULT | <union1,2>| ALL    |               |         |         |...
+-----+--------------+-----------+--------+---------------+---------+---------+...

...+-----------------------------------------------------------------+------+...
...| ref                                                             | rows |...
...+-----------------------------------------------------------------+------+...
...|                                                                 | 12   |...
...| music.played.artist_id,music.played.album_id,music.played.track_id | 1    |...
...|                                                                 | 12   |...
...| music.played.artist_id,music.played.album_id,music.played.track_id | 1    |...
...|                                                                 | NULL |...
...+-----------------------------------------------------------------+------+...

...+----------------------------+
...| Extra                      |
...+----------------------------+
...| Using index; Using filesort |
...|                            |
...| Using index; Using filesort |
...|                            |
...|                            |
...+----------------------------+
5 rows in set (0.01 sec)
```

## CHAPTER 9

Managing Users and Privileges

Learning MySQL, developing applications, and deploying finished software are tasks with very different security requirements. While you're learning the basics—especially if you're working on your own machine—it's not usually critical if you accidentally remove databases or tables, change data, or don't carefully limit access to the MySQL server and its databases. However, when you develop and maintain real applications, it's crucial that you secure your server and databases against accidental or deliberate acts that can delete, change, or expose your data. Fortunately, using MySQL's sophisticated user and privilege management tools, you can properly set up and secure access to your database server. This chapter shows you how.

In addition to setting up the MySQL server access privileges, you should separately ensure the physical security of your host computer and backup media, and proper configuration of permissions at the operating system level. We've explained some important aspects of this in Chapters 2 and 10, and we'll also look at this topic briefly in this chapter.

The MySQL server comes with the user **root**, who can do everything on the MySQL server, including creating and deleting users, databases, tables, indexes, and data. Up to this point, we've connected to the server under this superuser account, which is very convenient, but not very secure—remember the saying about how absolute power corrupts absolutely?

Most applications don't need superuser privileges for day-to-day activities. You can define less powerful users who have only the privileges they need to get their jobs done. You may want to prevent users creating or changing indexes, tables, or databases. You may even want to prevent users doing more than simply running SELECT statements on a given database or even particular tables in a database.

For example, you could have a user **allmusic** who can perform any database operation on the **music** database, and the user **partmusic** who can read data from the **music** database but can't change anything.

In this way, if the **allmusic** account is compromised, an attacker can at most delete the **music** database, but nothing else—and, of course, you would have backups, wouldn't you?! Similarly, a manager creating a report of daily sales wouldn't be able to accidentally—or deliberately—change any data.

It's also a good idea to use less privileged accounts yourself wherever possible; if you log in as the MySQL root user for routine tasks, there's a greater likelihood that an unauthorized user will somehow be able to gather enough information to access that account. You might even make a mistake and inadvertently damage your database.

In this chapter, we show you how to:

- Understand MySQL privileges
- Add, remove, and change MySQL users and passwords
- GRANT and REVOKE privileges
- Understand MySQL's default security configuration
- Devise a security policy for your MySQL server
- Manage users and privileges using SQL queries
- Limit server usage by user

Understanding Users and Privileges

MySQL, like most other database servers, has users who have privileges that determine whether they can create, modify, delete, and query databases, and also whether they can modify the privileges and control the server. In practice, this control can be *coarse-grained*—a user may be allowed or prevented from accessing the server—or *fine-grained*, where a user can access only some tables in a database or only some columns in a table. Some database servers support only coarse-grained control, while others such as MySQL allow both coarse-grained and fine-grained control over access.

MySQL allows you to control which users can access the server; the databases, tables, and columns on the server that they can access; and the types of actions that users can carry out on these structures. For example, MySQL allows you to explicitly control whether users can run the SELECT, UPDATE, INSERT, and DELETE statements, as well as whether they can LOCK TABLES, ALTER structures, or create and remove indexes. Most of the time, you'll create users who can access and modify the data in a database but otherwise have no privileges to adjust the server configuration, change the database's structure, or access other databases. We show you how to create different users and list all of the privileges later in this section.

MySQL users are distinct from the operating system users on the server computer. When you set up your machine, you automatically create superuser accounts that allow configuration of the server—the root user on a Linux or Mac OS X server, and the Administrator on Windows—and also one or more user accounts that you use to work with the server. For example, you could have a superuser account that's used only when installing or configuring software such as MySQL or a new word processor, and an ordinary account that you log in to while writing, reading email, web browsing, and doing the other things you normally do.

The ordinary account can't access or modify sensitive system-wide files, such as the system's hardware settings, or the MySQL server logfiles or datafiles. On a single-user system, having a less privileged account for day-to-day use helps reduce the chances of doing silly things such as deleting important system files or installing malware by mistake. On a corporate or university server, this security is essential: it not only helps prevent accidental damage or malicious attack, but also helps protect confidential files and data.

If a system account on your server can access the MySQL configuration, it can bypass the monitor (and every other MySQL client) and carry out actions directly on the server or databases. For example, the system `root` user can manipulate any MySQL instance on the system, while an ordinary user can manipulate any MySQL instance that runs under her account. With this access, you can bypass the MySQL server's authentication and user-management scheme by starting the server with the `skip-grant-tables` option; we discuss this and other ways to get around a forgotten `root` password in "Resetting Forgotten MySQL Passwords," later in this chapter. You can also browse data, indexes, and database structures using a text editor, or just copy the databases elsewhere and access them using another installation of MySQL. Therefore, you should take the usual precautions of maintaining physical security of your server, keeping operating system patches up-to-date, adding a network firewall, using appropriate permission settings on files and directories, and requiring hard-to-guess passwords. Remember, if your server is insecure or compromised, your MySQL server is insecure; it doesn't matter how the MySQL users and privileges are configured. You should be similarly vigilant about access to your database backups.

Creating and Using New Users

To create a new user, you need to have permission to do so; the `root` user has this permission, so connect to the monitor as the `root` user:

```
$ mysql --user=root --password=the_mysql_root_password
```

Now create a new user called `allmusic` who'll connect from the same system as the one the MySQL server is running on (`localhost`). We'll grant this user all privileges on all tables in the `music` database (`music.*`) and assign the password `the_password`:

```
mysql> GRANT ALL ON music.* TO 'allmusic'@'localhost' IDENTIFIED BY 'the_password';
Query OK, 0 rows affected (0.02 sec)
```

This instruction creates the new user and assigns some privileges. Now, let's discuss what we've done in more detail.

The `GRANT` statement gives privileges to users. Immediately following the keyword `GRANT` is the list of privileges that are given, which, in the previous case, is `ALL` (all simple privileges); we discuss the actual privileges later. Following the privilege list is the required keyword ON, and the databases or tables that the privileges are for. In the example, we grant the privileges for music.*, which means the music database and all its tables. If the specified MySQL user account does not exist, it will be created automatically by the GRANT statement.

In the example, we're assigning privileges to 'allmusic'@'localhost', which means the user has the name allmusic and can connect to the server only from the localhost, the machine on which the database server is installed. There's a 16-character limit on usernames. The at symbol (@) implies that the user is trying to connect to the server from the specified host; the MySQL user account doesn't need to correspond to any system user account on that host, and so there is no relation to any email address. The quotes surrounding the username and the client hostname are optional; you need them only if either the username or the hostname has special characters, such as hyphens (-) or wildcard characters. For example, you could write:

```
mysql> GRANT ALL ON music.* TO ali@localhost IDENTIFIED BY 'the_password';
Query OK, 0 rows affected (0.02 sec)
```

However, we recommend that you use the quotes all the time to avoid any surprises.

The optional IDENTIFIED BY 'the_password' component sets the user's password to *the_password*. There's no limit on password length, but we recommend using eight or fewer characters because this avoids problems with system libraries on some platforms.

You'll find many examples using GRANT throughout this chapter.

Let's experiment with our new user. Quit the monitor using the QUIT command. Then run it again and connect as the user allmusic:

```
$ mysql --user=allmusic --password=the_password
```

Note that this time, we've specified the MySQL user allmusic for the user parameter and passed this user's password to the password parameter.

You should see the mysql> prompt again. You will now be able to use the music database by typing USE music; and pressing Enter. Try running a simple query:

```
mysql> SELECT * FROM album;
```

You should see the albums in the database.

So far, we haven't found the limits of our privileges. Let's try using the university database:

```
mysql> USE university;
ERROR 1044 (42000): Access denied for user: 'allmusic'@'localhost' to database
  'university'
```

MySQL complains that our new user doesn't have permission to access the database university. Indeed, if we ask MySQL what databases are available, you'll see that MySQL is secretive:

```
mysql> SHOW DATABASES;
+----------+
| Database |
+----------+
| music    |
| test     |
+----------+
2 rows in set (0.00 sec)
```

A user who doesn't have any privileges for a database can't see or use that database (the exception to this is a user who has the global SHOW DATABASE privilege we discuss later).

Let's try to create a new database:

```
mysql> CREATE DATABASE some_new_database;
ERROR 1044 (42000): Access denied for user 'allmusic'@'localhost' to database
  'some_new_database'
```

We can't; when we were logged in as the MySQL root user, we never granted the allmusic user the privilege to create new databases.

Let's create a second new user who can access only the artist table in the music database (music.artist). Quit the monitor (or start the monitor from another terminal or command prompt window) and connect again as the root user. Then, create this new user:

```
mysql> GRANT ALL ON music.artist TO 'partmusic'@'localhost'
    -> IDENTIFIED BY 'the_password';
Query OK, 0 rows affected (0.01 sec)
```

We've specified the artist table in the music database by using music.artist. If you want to provide access to more than one table (but not all tables) in a database (or tables in different databases), you have to type several GRANT statements. For example, to add access to the album table to our newly created user, type:

```
mysql> GRANT ALL ON music.album TO 'partmusic'@'localhost';
Query OK, 0 rows affected (0.01 sec)
```

Since we're reusing the username and location 'partmusic'@'localhost', there's no need to provide a password in this second statement; the password was set when the user was first created, and it isn't changed by the second statement.

You can also allow a user to access only specific columns in a table. For example, you can allow the partmusic user to have only read (SELECT) access to the title and time columns of the track table:

```
mysql> GRANT SELECT (track_id, time) ON music.track TO 'partmusic'@'localhost';
Query OK, 0 rows affected (0.01 sec)
```

The syntax is different from the previous examples: instead of specifying ALL privileges, we've specified only SELECT, and we've listed the columns to which the privilege applies —track_id and time—in parentheses after it. The remainder of the statement follows the same syntax as the previous examples, including the music.track component that specifies where the columns track-id and `time` are located. Note that you can't grant all privileges at the column level; you must specifically list them.

Before you experiment with your new user, let's summarize what you've done. You've created a new user, `partmusic`, set this user's password to *the_password*, and allowed access to the database server from only the machine on which the server is installed, the `localhost`. The `partmusic` user has access to the `music` database and has all privileges for the `album` and `artist` tables. In addition, this user can run `SELECT` statements that retrieve values from the `track_id` and `time` columns in the `track` table.

Let's test what our new user can do. Start the monitor as the new user by supplying the appropriate `user` and `password` parameters:

```
$ mysql --user=partmusic --password=the_password
```

and connect to the `music` database:

```
mysql> USE music;
```

Now, check what tables this user can access:

```
mysql> SHOW TABLES;
+-----------------+
| Tables_in_music |
+-----------------+
| album           |
| artist          |
| track           |
+-----------------+
3 rows in set (0.00 sec)
```

You can see three of the four tables in the database, but since you (the `partmusic` user) don't have privileges for the `played` table, you can't see it. You do have privileges to do anything you want to the `album` and `artist` tables, so try this out:

```
mysql> INSERT INTO artist VALUES (7, "The Jimi Hendrix Experience");
Query OK, 1 row affected (0.00 sec)

mysql> SELECT album_name FROM album WHERE album_id=4;
+-------------------------------------+
| album_name                          |
+-------------------------------------+
| Retro - New Order / Bobby Gillespie LIVE |
+-------------------------------------+
1 row in set (0.00 sec)
```

Feel free to test your access to these tables further: you'll be able to insert, delete, update, and retrieve all data.

Now, let's test our limited access to the `track` table. First, we'll try to retrieve the values in all columns:

```
mysql> SELECT * FROM track;
ERROR 1143 (42000): select command denied to user:
'partmusic'@'localhost' for column 'track_name' in table 'track'
```

As expected, MySQL complains that you don't have privileges to retrieve values from the columns other than `track_id` and `time`; note that MySQL stops on its first error and doesn't report all the columns you can't access. If you now try to retrieve values for columns you can access, it works as expected:

```
mysql> SELECT time FROM TRACK LIMIT 3;
+------+
| time |
+------+
| 8.10 |
| 5.27 |
| 8.66 |
+------+
3 rows in set (0.00 sec)
```

Notice that, unlike databases and tables, you can see the details of all columns in a table even if you don't have access to them:

```
mysql> DESCRIBE track;
+------------+--------------+------+-----+---------+-------+
| Field      | Type         | Null | Key | Default | Extra |
+------------+--------------+------+-----+---------+-------+
| track_id   | int(3)       |      | PRI | 0       |       |
| track_name | char(128)    | YES  |     | NULL    |       |
| artist_id  | int(5)       |      | PRI | 0       |       |
| album_id   | int(4)       |      | PRI | 0       |       |
| time       | decimal(5,2) | YES  |     | NULL    |       |
+------------+--------------+------+-----+---------+-------+
5 rows in set (0.00 sec
```

Privileges

So far, we've shown you how to add new users and grant privileges for databases, tables, and columns. In this section, we discuss the privileges in more detail and explain which ones are used at the global, database, table, and column level. Then we discuss how the different privilege levels interact.

You can see a list of all available privileges by running the SHOW PRIVILEGES command in the MySQL monitor; Table 9-1 lists some of the more important of these. Each row shows a privilege, followed by a description, and then a list of the four levels at which the privilege can be granted. For example, the second row shows the ALTER privilege that controls whether the ALTER TABLE statement can be used, and shows that it can be controlled at the global, database, and table levels:

Global level
> You can use ON *.* in a GRANT statement to grant a user a particular privilege across all databases on the server.

Database level
> You can use, for example, music.* to grant a privilege for one or more databases.

Table level

> You can use, for example, `music.album` to grant a privilege for one or more tables in a database.

Column level

> Grants access for one or more columns in a table in a database (but isn't available for ALTER). You grant column-level access using a comma-separated list in parentheses after the privilege, as in, for example:
>
> ```
> GRANT SELECT (album_name, album_id) ON music.album
> ```

In this chapter, we explain how to manage privileges using the `GRANT` statement. Many of the statements affected by the privileges are discussed elsewhere as follows:

- The statements `DELETE`, `INSERT`, `SELECT`, `SHOW DATABASES`, and `UPDATE` are introduced in Chapter 5 and discussed further in Chapters 7 and 8.
- The statements `ALTER`, `CREATE`, `DROP`, `LOAD DATA INFILE`, and `SELECT ... INTO` are described in Chapter 6.
- The statements `LOCK TABLES` and `UNLOCK TABLES` are discussed in Chapter 7.

The `EXECUTE`, `PROCESS`, `REPLICATION CLIENT`, `REPLICATION SLAVE`, `CHANGE MASTER`, `KILL`, and `PURGE MASTER LOGS` statements are outside the scope of this book; see the MySQL manual for more on these. We discuss `GRANT OPTION` in the next section.

Table 9-1 shows the levels at which the privileges can be configured: Global (G), Database (D), Table (T), and Column (C). For example, the first row shows that the `ALL` option is available at all levels except for columns.

Table 9-1. Privileges and their levels in MySQL

Privilege	Application	G	D	T	C
ALL	All simple privileges except the ability to grant privileges (GRANT OPTION).	✓	✓	✓	✗
ALTER	The ALTER TABLE statement.	✓	✓	✓	✗
CREATE	The CREATE statement.	✓	✓	✗	✗
CREATE TEMPO RARY TABLES	The CREATE TEMPORARY TABLES statement; user is allowed to create a temporary table in the active database for her own session.	✓	✓	✗	✗
DELETE	The DELETE statement.	✓	✓	✓	✗
DROP	The DROP statement.	✓	✓	✓	✗
EXECUTE	Stored procedures (MySQL version 5 and later only).	✓	✗	✗	✗
FILE	Reading and writing of disk files with SELECT ... INTO and LOAD DATA INFILE.	✓	✗	✗	✗
GRANT OPTION	Ability to grant own privileges to others. For most applications, there is generally no need for this, because the root user decides on access privileges.	✓	✓	✓	✗

Privilege	Application	G	D	T	C
INDEX	The CREATE INDEX and DROP INDEX statements.	✓	✓	✓	✗
INSERT	The INSERT statement.	✓	✓	✓	✓
LOCK TABLES	The use of LOCK TABLES and UNLOCK TABLES. Must have SELECT privilege for the tables. Since this is a database-wide privilege, it can only be granted using the *database_name.** (or *.*) format.	✓	✓	✗	✗
PROCESS	The use of SHOW FULL PROCESSLIST.	✓	✗	✗	✗
RELOAD	The use of FLUSH (discussed later in this chapter in "Managing Privileges with SQL").	✓	✗	✗	✗
REPLICATION CLIENT	Controls whether you can see where master and slave servers are.	✓	✗	✗	✗
REPLICATION SLAVE	Controls whether slaves can read the master binary log.	✓	✗	✗	✗
SELECT	The use of SELECT, allowing data to be read from the specified table(s).	✓	✓	✓	✓
SHOW DATABASES	Controls whether all databases are shown with SHOW DATABASES.	✓	✗	✗	✗
SHUTDOWN	Controls whether the server can be shut down with the mysqladmin shutdown command.	✓	✗	✗	✗
SUPER	The use of the CHANGE MASTER, KILL, PURGE MASTER LOGS, SET GLOBAL, and the mysqladmin debug commands.	✓	✗	✗	✗
UPDATE	The use of UPDATE to modify existing data in the specified table(s).	✓	✓	✓	✓
USAGE	No privileges; not explicitly allowed to do anything other than connect to the server. Used when creating an account or updating details.	✓	✓	✓	✓

Table 9-2 shows what the ALL option means at the global, database, and table levels. For example, the second column shows what happens when you GRANT ALL ON *.* to a user. All privileges listed with a checkmark (✓) are given to the user, and those with a cross (✗) are omitted. The GRANT OPTION—which allows a user to pass on his privileges to another user—isn't available for ALL at any level, and therefore must be granted explicitly. We discuss it next.

Table 9-2. Simple privileges that comprise the ALL privilege at different levels

Privilege	Global	Database	Table
ALTER	✓	✓	✓
CREATE	✓	✓	✗
CREATE TEMPORARY TABLES	✓	✓	✗
DELETE	✓	✓	✓

Privilege	Global	Database	Table
DROP	✓	✓	✓
EXECUTE	✓	✗	✗
FILE	✓	✗	✗
GRANT OPTION	✗	✗	✗
INDEX	✓	✓	✓
INSERT	✓	✓	✓
LOCK TABLES	✓	✓	✗
PROCESS	✓	✗	✗
RELOAD	✓	✗	✗
REPLICATION CLIENT	✓	✗	✗
REPLICATION SLAVE	✓	✗	✗
SELECT	✓	✓	✓
SHOW DATABASES	✓	✗	✗
SHUTDOWN	✓	✗	✗
SUPER	✓	✗	✗
UPDATE	✓	✓	✓

The GRANT OPTION Privilege

The GRANT OPTION privilege allows a user to pass on any privileges she has to other users. Consider an example, which we've run when connected to the monitor as the root user:

```
mysql> GRANT ALL ON music.* TO 'hugh'@'localhost';
Query OK, 0 rows affected (0.00 sec)

mysql>  GRANT GRANT OPTION ON music.* TO 'hugh'@'localhost';
Query OK, 0 rows affected (0.00 sec)
```

This creates a MySQL user hugh (with no password!) and allows him to pass on his privileges for the music database to other users. Since the GRANT OPTION is given at the database level (to music.*), hugh can pass on his privileges on that database, or on any of the tables or columns in that database. GRANT OPTION always allows a user to pass on his privileges at the level which they're given, or any lower level, and it also allows him to pass on any future privileges he's given. We explain this hierarchy more in the next section.

Let's test our new privilege using the user hugh. Quit the monitor, and then reconnect as the MySQL user hugh:

```
$ mysql --user=hugh
```

Now, let's give our privileges to another user:

```
mysql> GRANT ALL ON music.* TO 'selina'@'localhost';
Query OK, 0 rows affected (0.00 sec)
```

This passes on all privileges to a new user, selina (with no password). It doesn't pass on the GRANT OPTION privilege, but you can do this if you want to:

```
mysql> GRANT GRANT OPTION ON music.* TO 'selina'@'localhost';
Query OK, 0 rows affected (0.00 sec)
```

Now selina can do the same things hugh can on the music database.

You can also pass on the GRANT OPTION privilege in a single SQL statement that also grants other privileges. Here's an example using an alternative syntax:

```
mysql> GRANT ALL ON music.* to 'lucy'@'localhost' WITH GRANT OPTION;
Query OK, 0 rows affected (0.00 sec)
```

This has exactly the same effect as the previous two-step example that created the user selina.

As discussed previously, users can pass on privileges at the same or lower levels. Consider an example that's executed when we're connected as hugh:

```
mysql> GRANT ALL ON music.artist TO 'rose'@'localhost';
Query OK, 0 rows affected (0.00 sec)
```

Since hugh has all privileges for all tables in the music database, he can pass all privileges for only the artist table to a new user, rose.

Be careful with GRANT OPTION; users with this privilege can share other privileges in ways you may not anticipate. We discuss this further later in this chapter in "More Security Tips."

How Privileges Interact

In the previous section, we explained how the GRANT OPTION privilege is used to pass privileges to other users and how it allows privileges at lower levels in the privilege hierarchy to be granted. In this section, we explore the privilege hierarchy further and explain how MySQL allows or denies access to resources.

Figure 9-1 shows an example of the MySQL privilege hierarchy. There are four levels; reading from highest to lowest, these are global, database, table, and column. In Figure 9-1, the global level contains the MySQL server system and three databases: music, university, and flight. Each database contains tables; the figure shows the tables in the music database. Each table in turn contains columns, and the figure shows the columns in the artist table.

When you grant privileges at a level, those privileges are available at that and all lower levels. In Figure 9-1, if you grant privileges at the global level, those privileges are available for MySQL server functions and throughout the databases, tables, and columns. For example, if you have the UPDATE privilege at the global level, you can execute the

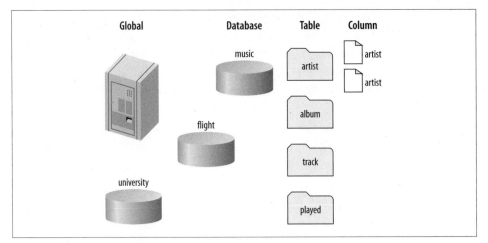

Figure 9-1. The privilege hierarchy

UPDATE statement on any table or column in any database. If you grant privileges for only the music database, the privileges are available for just it and its tables and columns. Privileges never propagate up the hierarchy; for example, if you grant privileges for only a column, those privileges don't apply for the table, database, or server.

When you run a statement, your privileges to run that statement are determined using a logical OR operation. The operation checks whether you have any of the following for the statement:

- Global privileges
- Database privileges
- Table privileges
- Column privileges

If any of these permit the statement, it proceeds. This has an important consequence: if you allow a privilege for a statement at a level, it doesn't matter if it's allowed or disallowed at another level. This can lead to unexpected behavior. For example, if you revoke a previously granted permission to SELECT from the artist table, access will not be revoked if the user still has the SELECT privilege to the music database or at the global level. "Users and Hosts" discusses how users are allowed or disallowed server connections, and "Revoking Privileges" explains how to revoke privileges.

Users and Hosts

So far, we've discussed the steps to grant privileges, as well as how these privileges interact in a hierarchy. However, we've skipped over the basic principles of connecting to the server and explaining how MySQL validates a connection. This section covers these topics and helps you understand how you connect to a MySQL server.

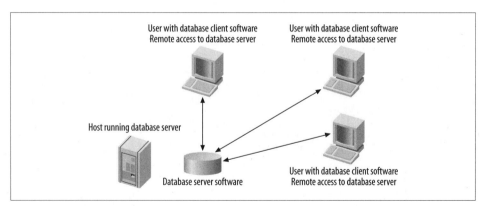

Figure 9-2. Database server, with managers' computers configured for remote access to the database server

Local and Remote Users

MySQL supports both local and remote users. A *local user* connects to the server and accesses the databases from the same computer that the MySQL server is running on (`localhost`). All our examples so far have been for a local user. In contrast, a *remote user* connects to the server and accesses the databases from another computer.

For each application, you must decide how the database will be used and apply the most restrictive set of access privileges needed to get the job done. There are performance as well as security issues to be considered when doing this. MySQL actually treats local connections differently; if the client is local, the connection is made internally through a Unix socket (for Linux and Mac OS X) or through a named pipe (for Windows). This is generally much faster than the TCP/IP network connection used for remote access.

You should be careful not to give remote access to the database when you can avoid it. Consider the case where three different managers need to see how many items of each title there are in stock. You could give each manager an account on the MySQL server and allow remote access so that they can connect to the database from their own computers and run queries to view the data. This is shown in Figure 9-2.

Since there are a limited number of queries needed to generate standard reports for the managers, you could instead create a password-protected dynamic web page that displays the output of the necessary reporting queries; managers would still access the reports from their own computers, but through a web browser rather than a MySQL client. This approach has several security benefits: you don't have to give database server accounts to other users, you don't have to allow remote access, only your own client programs can run queries on the database server, and only the limited set of queries supported by your client program will be executed. Figure 9-3 shows how this could be configured.

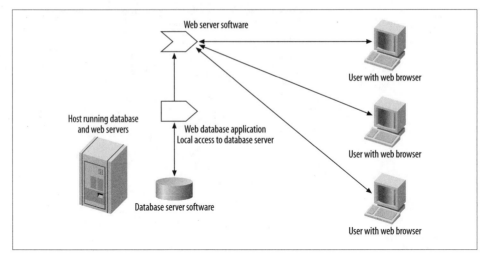

Figure 9-3. Database server and web application; the web application has local access to the database server, and the managers' computers interact with the database through the web application

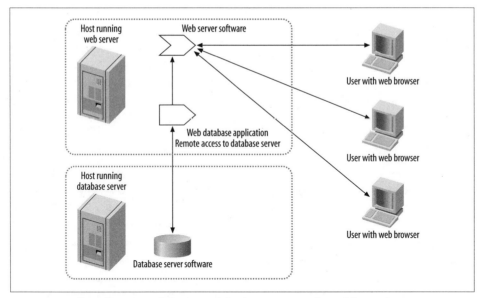

Figure 9-4. Web application, web server, and database server configured for remote access

If the web server and the database server are on different computers, you have to allow the web application on the web server to connect remotely to the database server, as shown in Figure 9-4.

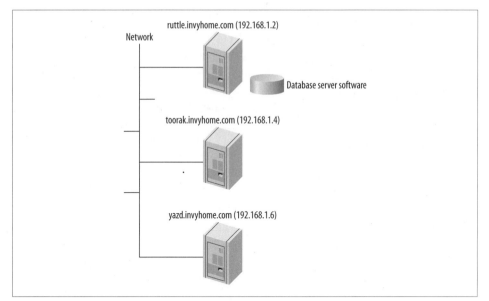

Figure 9-5. A simple home network with three computers, and one MySQL server

Creating a New Remote User

If you want to allow a user to connect to the server from another computer, you must specify the host from which they can do so (the remote client). Suppose that you have a home network, that your machine has the private IP address 192.168.1.2, that your home domain is *invyhome.com*, and that your machine is named `ruttle` (that is, its complete name is `ruttle.invyhome.com`). Let's also assume that you're running a MySQL server on `ruttle`, and that there are two other machines on the network: `toorak.invyhome.com` with the IP address 192.168.1.4 and `yazd.invyhome.com` with IP address 192.168.1.6.

Figure 9-5 illustrates this setup. Again, we differentiate between user accounts on the MySQL server (*MySQL users* or *MySQL accounts*) and user accounts on the host machines (*system users* or *system accounts*).

Now, let's consider the MySQL setup on `ruttle`. Let's assume you've previously logged in to the MySQL server on `ruttle` as the `root` user and created the user `hugh` with the statement:

```
mysql> GRANT ALL on *.* TO 'hugh'@'localhost' IDENTIFIED BY 'the_password';
Query OK, 0 rows affected (0.00 sec)
```

If you're logged in to your system account on `ruttle`, you can connect to the MySQL server on `ruttle` using the following:

```
$ mysql --host=localhost --user=hugh --password=the_password
```

Including the `--host=localhost` actually has no effect, since `localhost` is the default anyway. Now, let's try specifying the IP address for `localhost`; this is always 127.0.0.1:

```
$ mysql --user=hugh --host=127.0.0.1 --password=the_password
Welcome to the MySQL monitor.  Commands end with ; or \g.
Your MySQL connection id is 47 to server version: 5.0.22-standard-log

Type 'help;' or '\h' for help. Type '\c' to clear the buffer.

mysql>
```

The result is another successful connection, since `localhost` and 127.0.0.1 are the same system, and MySQL matches the request for host 127.0.0.1 against the privileges for `localhost`.

Now, let's try connecting to the MySQL server on `ruttle` from `ruttle` by using its IP address:

```
$ mysql --user=hugh --host=192.168.1.2 --password=the_password
ERROR 1130 (): #HY000Host '192.168.1.2' is not allowed to connect to this
                MySQL server
```

This time, the connection isn't successful. If you replace `192.168.1.2` with `ruttle.invy home.com`, you'll see the same problem. Let's explore why we can't connect.

At the beginning of this section, we allowed access to the user `'hugh'@'localhost'`. That's exactly what the MySQL server is enforcing: we can only connect from the `localhost`, and not from anywhere else, including from the actual IP address or domain of the `localhost` machine. If you want to allow access from 192.168.1.2 (and its equivalent domain name `ruttle.invyhome.com`), you need to grant those privileges by creating a new user with the username hugh and the host 192.168.1.2. Note that each username and host pair is treated as a separate user and has its own password.

Log in to the monitor as the root user, and type:

```
mysql> GRANT ALL ON *.* TO 'hugh'@'192.168.1.2' IDENTIFIED BY 'the_password';
Query OK, 0 rows affected (0.00 sec)
```

Now, quit the monitor and try connecting as the user hugh:

```
$ mysql --user=hugh --host=192.168.1.2 --password=the_password
Welcome to the MySQL monitor.  Commands end with ; or \g.
Your MySQL connection id is 50 to server version: 5.0.22-standard-log

Type 'help;' or '\h' for help. Type '\c' to clear the buffer.

mysql>
```

You'll also find you can now connect using `ruttle.invyhome.com` in place of 192.168.1.2, as long as you've got a correctly configured domain nameserver (DNS) setup. If you have trouble connecting to the MySQL server, refer to the checklist in "Client Programs Can't Connect to the Server" in Chapter 2.

Suppose now that you want to allow **toorak** to access the MySQL server that's running on **ruttle**. There are several different ways to do this, some more flexible than others. The simplest approach is to connect to the MySQL server on **ruttle** as the **root** user and grant privileges to a new user **'hugh'@'toorak.invyhome.com'** using the following statement:

```
mysql> GRANT ALL ON *.* TO 'hugh'@'toorak.invyhome.com' IDENTIFIED BY 'the_password';
Query OK, 0 rows affected (0.00 sec)
```

You'll now find that you can run a MySQL monitor on **toorak** and connect to **ruttle** using the following command:

```
$ mysql --user=hugh --host=ruttle.invyhome.com --password=the_password
Welcome to the MySQL monitor.  Commands end with ; or \g.
Your MySQL connection id is 52 to server version: 5.0.22-standard-log

Type 'help;' or '\h' for help. Type '\c' to clear the buffer.

mysql>
```

Using the IP addresses 192.168.1.2 for **ruttle.invyhome.com** and 192.168.1.4 for **toorak.invyhome.com** should work too, and it's more secure, as IP addresses are harder to spoof than domain names.

Our approach so far has been to create new users for each IP address. We now have three users with the name **hugh**, one each for the **localhost**, 192.168.1.2, and 192.168.1.4. This isn't always a good approach: we now have to remember to maintain all three users and keep their privileges synchronized if we want the same access level from all three locations. However, it's also flexible: it allows you to differentiate between different remote users with the same username, or offer a flexible, customized security policy when a user connects from different locations.

Let's consider other ways to allow the same user to connect from several locations. You can allow a user to connect from all computers on a network subnet by using one or more wildcards in the **GRANT** statement. Suppose you want to allow **jill** to connect from any of the machines in the domain **invyhome.com**. You can do this with:

```
mysql> GRANT ALL ON *.* TO 'jill'@'%.invyhome.com' IDENTIFIED BY 'the_password';
Query OK, 0 rows affected (0.01 sec)
```

As in the SQL **LIKE** clause, the wildcard character % matches any string, and so this entry now matches any domain name with the suffix *invyhome.com*. The outcome is that connections as **jill** from **ruttle.invyhome.com** and **toorak.invyhome.com** are allowed; **jill** can also connect from any other machine that joins the network.

You can also use wildcards in IP addresses. For example, you can allow connections from all machines on the **invyhome.com** subnet by allowing access to machines matching the IP address range **192.168.1.%**.

To do this, run the following:

```
mysql> GRANT ALL ON *.* TO 'harry'@'192.168.1.%' IDENTIFIED BY 'the_password';
Query OK, 0 rows affected (0.01 sec)
```

Again, connections as harry from ruttle and toorak (and any other machines on the local network) are allowed.

Table 9-3 shows different specifications of network addresses that use wildcards and gives examples of where the user lloyd could connect from. The entry in the final row allows lloyd to connect from anywhere and should be used with caution.

Table 9-3. Host specifications and their meanings in GRANT statements

Host specification	Example	Effect
Hostname	'lloyd'@'lloyd.lloydhouse.com'	1
Domain name	'lloyd'@'%.lloydhouse.com'	2
IP address	'lloyd'@'192.168.1.2'	3
IP address range	'lloyd'@'192.168.1.0/255.255.255.0'	4
Any machine	'lloyd'@'%' or 'lloyd'	5

The effect of each of these settings is as follows:

1. Connections are allowed only from the machine lloyd.lloydhouse.com.

2. Connections are allowed from any machine in the lloydhouse.com domain.

3. Connections are allowed only from the machine with the IP address 192.168.1.2.

4. The address range is specified as an IP address and a netmask. The current standard IPv4 addresses are 32 bits long and are commonly shown in the dotted decimal notation as 4 decimal numbers, each corresponding to 8 bits of the IP address or netmask. For example, the IP address:

   11000000101010000000000100000001

   is shown as:

   192.168.1.1

   which is much easier to read!

   The *netmask* specifies how many of these bits (from left) identify the network; the remaining bits identify the hosts on that network. The smaller the netmask, the more bits remain for the hosts, and so the greater number of hosts that fall into the specified range. The sample specification 192.168.1.0/255.255.255.0 says that the first 24 bits of the host IP address must match the first 24 bits of the address 192.168.1.0, so any address that starts with 192.168.1. is accepted. The netmask specified to MySQL can only be 8, 16, 24, or 32 bits in length.

5. Connections are allowed from any machine. If you omit the host specification, % is assumed.

The wildcard approach typically removes the need to create multiple users, as a given user can connect from more than one machine. However, consider the case where the user steph wants to connect from the client hosts localhost, steph.lloydhouse.com, and steph.hughwilliams.com. Using the techniques we've discussed so far, you have two choices: have three users, one for each host; or allow access from any host using 'steph'@'%'. Neither solution is ideal. Fortunately, MySQL supports yet another way to create one user for different hosts, but this requires knowledge of the structure of the database tables used to manage the privilege system. We present this later in the chapter in "Managing Privileges with SQL."

Anonymous Users

We've previously seen how we can use wildcard specifications for hosts, but wildcard characters aren't allowed in usernames; you can't, for example, specify 'fred%'@'localhost'. However, you can have a user with an empty username that allows anonymous connections and matches all usernames.

You can create an anonymous local user who can read data from the music database as follows:

```
mysql> GRANT SELECT ON music.* TO ''@'localhost';
Query OK, 0 rows affected (0.00 sec)
```

Note that the username is specified as two single quotes, with nothing between them. This user allows you to connect without a username or password from the localhost:

```
$ mysql
Welcome to the MySQL monitor.  Commands end with ; or \g.
Your MySQL connection id is 55 to server version: 5.0.22-standard-log

Type 'help;' or '\h' for help. Type '\c' to clear the buffer.

mysql>
```

You can use the CURRENT_USER( ) function to check which user you're logged in as:

```
mysql> SELECT CURRENT_USER();
+----------------+
| CURRENT_USER() |
+----------------+
| @localhost     |
+----------------+
1 row in set (0.00 sec)
```

Here, there is nothing before the @ symbol, indicating that you're logged in as the anonymous user ''@localhost. The MySQL server decides which user to log you in as based on a checklist we describe in the next section.

Which User Is Connected?

So far, we have created several users and deliberately chosen a different name for each. We did this to avoid discussing an important issue: what happens if more than one user and host combination matches when a connection is attempted?

To understand how MySQL allows connections, connect as the MySQL user root and create two users with the same name and different host specifications:

```
mysql> GRANT SELECT ON music.* TO 'dave'@'%' IDENTIFIED BY 'the_password';
Query OK, 0 rows affected (0.06 sec)

mysql> GRANT ALL ON music.* TO 'dave'@'localhost' IDENTIFIED BY 'the_password';
Query OK, 0 rows affected (0.01 sec)
```

The first user dave can now connect from any host and run only SELECT statements on the music database. The second user dave is specific to the localhost and is allowed all privileges on music. The host specifications of the two users overlap: '%' means all hosts, and so includes localhost as one of the allowed hosts. Now, let's experiment with dave.

Let's connect to the server using the monitor installed on localhost:

```
$ mysql --user=dave --password=the_password
Welcome to the MySQL monitor.  Commands end with ; or \g.
Your MySQL connection id is 57 to server version: 5.0.22-standard-log

Type 'help;' or '\h' for help. Type '\c' to clear the buffer.

mysql>
```

Now, let's try to do more than just SELECT data:

```
mysql> USE music;
Database changed

mysql> INSERT INTO artist VALUES (8, "The Psychedelic Furs");
Query OK, 1 row affected (0.06 sec)
```

That worked, so we must be logged in as the user 'dave'@'localhost' and not 'dave'@'%'.

Here's what the CURRENT_USER( ) function reports for the connection we've just used:

```
mysql> SELECT CURRENT_USER();
+----------------+
| CURRENT_USER() |
+----------------+
| dave@localhost |
+----------------+
1 row in set (0.00 sec)
```

This confirms we're logged in as 'dave'@'localhost', and not through the more general host specification 'dave'@'%'.

How does MySQL decide which user to use when you establish a connection? The answer has two parts: first, MySQL sorts the user entries by host from most to least specific and, for duplicate hosts, any anonymous user entry appears last. Consider an example. Suppose you have four user and host combinations:

- `'dave'@'localhost'`
- `'dave'@'%'`
- `''@'localhost'`
- `'hugh'@'192.168.1.%'`

From most specific to least, the hosts are `localhost`, then `192.168.1.%`, and finally `%`. There are two entries for users on the `localhost`, and, since one is anonymous, the one with a name (`dave`) is more specific. Overall, this leads to the following sort order:

- `'dave'@'localhost'`
- `''@'localhost'`
- `'hugh'@'192.168.1.%'`
- `'dave'@'%'`

The second step in establishing a connection is matching your connection request against the sorted list. The first entry that matches your connection requirements is used; if none match, you're denied access. Suppose you try to connect from the local host using the username `dave`. The first entry in the list, `'dave'@'localhost'` matches, and so you're authenticated and given the privileges of that user. Suppose now you try to connect from the `localhost` using the username `hugh`. Here's a surprise: MySQL ignores the username you provide, and you're connected as `''@'localhost'` because, as discussed in the previous section, the anonymous username is a wildcard that matches all usernames! You might find this annoying, but some argue it's a feature that can be used to ensure users from particular hosts get at least a minimal set of privileges.

Consider a final example, where you try to connect from the network machine `yazd` (192.168.1.6) as `dave`. The first two entries are for the `localhost` and so don't match. The third entry has a host specification that matches, but the username `hugh` does not. The final entry's host specification matches, and so does the username, and therefore the connection is established with the privileges of the user `'dave'@'%'`.

Checking Privileges

We've explained how to grant privileges and how to understand the scope of those privileges. This section explains how to identify the privileges that a user has, and how to revoke those privileges.

If you've been following our examples, you have created more than 10 users so far in this chapter, and you probably can't remember all of them. It's important to know the users you have defined and the privileges that these users have, and that you understand how connections are verified: without careful management, you can accidentally allow more privileges than you planned, or allow connections by users you didn't want to grant access to. Fortunately, there are a few tools available to help you explore access privileges.

The simplest method to check the privileges of a user is to use the SHOW GRANTS statement. You can execute this statement to check the privileges of other users only if you have access to the mysql database; however, you can always check your own privileges. If you want to experiment, it's best to log in now as the root user or another user with sufficient global privileges. We explain the role of the mysql database in privilege management later in "Managing Privileges with SQL."

After logging in to the monitor, you can check the current user's privileges with:

```
mysql> SHOW GRANTS;
+----------------------------------------------------------------------+
| Grants for root@localhost                                            |
+----------------------------------------------------------------------+
| GRANT ALL PRIVILEGES ON *.* TO 'root'@'localhost' WITH GRANT OPTION |
+----------------------------------------------------------------------+
1 row in set (0.00 sec)
```

MySQL reports the privileges as one or more GRANT statements. Not surprisingly, 'root'@'localhost' has all privileges, including GRANT OPTION.

Now let's check the privileges of the user 'selina'@'localhost' we created earlier in this chapter:

```
mysql> SHOW GRANTS FOR 'selina'@'localhost';
+---------------------------------------------------------------------------+
| Grants for selina@localhost                                               |
+---------------------------------------------------------------------------+
| GRANT USAGE ON *.* TO 'selina'@'localhost'                                |
| GRANT ALL PRIVILEGES ON `music`.* TO 'selina'@'localhost' WITH GRANT OPTION |
+---------------------------------------------------------------------------+
2 rows in set (0.00 sec)
```

This syntax works on MySQL versions later than 4.1.2. The first GRANT statement is a default privilege that creates the user with no privileges (yes, USAGE implies no privileges!). The second statement gives all privileges for the music database.

Let's also check the user 'partmusic'@'localhost':

```
mysql> SHOW GRANTS FOR 'partmusic'@'localhost';
+-------------------------------------------------------------------------+
| Grants for partmusic@localhost                                          |
+-------------------------------------------------------------------------+
| GRANT USAGE ON *.* TO 'partmusic'@'localhost' IDENTIFIED BY             |
|    PASSWORD '*14E65567ABDB5135D0CFD9A70B3032C179A49EE7'                 |
| GRANT ALL PRIVILEGES ON `music`.`album` TO 'partmusic'@'localhost'      |
| GRANT ALL PRIVILEGES ON `music`.`artist` TO 'partmusic'@'localhost'     |
| GRANT SELECT (track_id, time) ON `music`.`track` TO 'partmusic'@'localhost' |
+-------------------------------------------------------------------------+
4 rows in set (0.00 sec)
```

Again, the first statement creates a user with no privileges, and later statements add the privileges. The first statement also serves another purpose: it sets the password for the user. Since the password has been hashed with a one-way encryption function, it can't be decrypted, and so we repeat the encrypted password string with the statement `IDENTIFIED BY PASSWORD`. We discuss passwords in detail later in this chapter.

The `SHOW GRANTS` statement works only for exploring exactly one user that matches the string you provide. For example, if you've previously created a user `'fred'@'%'`, you can list the privileges of that user with:

```
mysql> SHOW GRANTS FOR 'fred'@'%';
```

This statement doesn't check for all users with the name fred, however. Each username and host pair is treated separately; for example, we could have the user `'ali'@'sadri.invyhome.com'` with all privileges on the test database, and the user `'ali'@'saleh.invyhome.com'` with all privileges on the music database:

```
mysql> GRANT ALL ON test.* TO 'ali'@'sadri.invyhome.com'
    -> IDENTIFIED BY 'a_password';
Query OK, 0 rows affected (0.00 sec)

mysql> GRANT ALL ON music.* TO 'ali'@'saleh.invyhome.com'
IDENTIFIED BY 'another_password';
Query OK, 0 rows affected (0.00 sec)
```

If you check the privileges with the `SHOW GRANTS` statement, you'll see that the access privileges and the stored password are different for each username and host pair:

```
mysql> SHOW GRANTS FOR 'ali'@'sadri.invyhome.com';
+-------------------------------------------------------------------+
| Grants for ali@sadri.invyhome.com                                 |
+-------------------------------------------------------------------+
| GRANT USAGE ON *.* TO 'ali'@'sadri.invyhome.com'                  |
| IDENTIFIED BY PASSWORD '*5DC1D11F45824A9DD613961F05C1EC1E7A1601AA' |
| GRANT ALL PRIVILEGES ON `test`.* TO 'ali'@'sadri.invyhome.com'    |
+-------------------------------------------------------------------+
2 rows in set (0.00 sec)

mysql> SHOW GRANTS FOR 'ali'@'saleh.invyhome.com';
+-------------------------------------------------------------------+
| Grants for ali@saleh.invyhome.com                                 |
+-------------------------------------------------------------------+
| GRANT USAGE ON *.* TO 'ali'@'saleh.invyhome.com'                  |
| IDENTIFIED BY PASSWORD '*A5CF560EBFDD483CD4162DD31FBA6AF8F5586069' |
| GRANT ALL PRIVILEGES ON `music`.* TO 'ali'@'saleh.invyhome.com'   |
+-------------------------------------------------------------------+
2 rows in set (0.00 sec)
```

As you can see, a connection by ali is allowed different privileges and uses a different password according to the host the connection is coming from.

To explore all of the users available on your MySQL server, you can use the command-line `mysqlaccess` utility that we describe in the next section.

Another method to check current privileges is to use SQL to explore the mysql database that manages the privileges. If you're experienced with SQL, this is perhaps the easiest approach, and it's the one we usually use. We describe this approach later in "Managing Privileges with SQL."

mysqlaccess

To quickly see what level of access a particular user has for a particular database, you can use the mysqlaccess script from a terminal or command prompt. Let's see what level of access the user partmusic has for the database music. We'll need to specify the MySQL superuser name (root) and password to access the information:

```
$ mysqlaccess --user=root --password=the_mysql_root_password partmusic music
mysqlaccess Version 2.06, 20 Dec 2000
By RUG-AIV, by Yves Carlier (Yves.Carlier@rug.ac.be)
Changes by Steve Harvey (sgh@vex.net)
This software comes with ABSOLUTELY NO WARRANTY.

Access-rights
for USER 'partmusic', from HOST 'localhost', to DB 'music'
    +----------------------+---+ +----------------------+---+
    | Select_priv          | N | | Lock_tables_priv     | N |
    | Insert_priv          | N | | Execute_priv         | N |
    | Update_priv          | N | | Repl_slave_priv      | N |
    | Delete_priv          | N | | Repl_client_priv     | N |
    | Create_priv          | N | | Create_view_priv     | N |
    | Drop_priv            | N | | Show_view_priv       | N |
    | Reload_priv          | N | | Create_routine_priv  | N |
    | Shutdown_priv        | N | | Alter_routine_priv   | N |
    | Process_priv         | N | | Create_user_priv     | N |
    | File_priv            | N | | Ssl_type             | ? |
    | Grant_priv           | N | | Ssl_cipher           | ? |
    | References_priv      | N | | X509_issuer          | ? |
    | Index_priv           | N | | X509_subject         | ? |
    | Alter_priv           | N | | Max_questions        | 0 |
    | Show_db_priv         | N | | Max_updates          | 0 |
    | Super_priv           | N | | Max_connections      | 0 |
    | Create_tmp_table_priv| N | | Max_user_connections | 0 |
    +----------------------+---+ +----------------------+---+
NOTE:    A password is required for user `partmusic' :-(

The following rules are used:
 db   : 'No matching rule'
 host : 'Not processed: host-field is not empty in db-table.'
 user : 'localhost','partmusic','652f9c175d1914f9',
  'N','N','N','N','N','N','N','N','N','N','N','N','N','N','N','N','N',
  'N','N','N','N','N','N','N','N','N','','','','','0','0','0','0'

BUGs can be reported by email to bugs@mysql.com
```

If you specify the wildcard character '*' in place of music, the access privileges for all databases will be shown. Similarly, you can specify the wildcard character '*' in place of `partmusic` to see the access privileges for all users: if you specify both, you can exhaustively explore all users of all databases:

```
$ mysqlaccess --user=root --password=the_mysql_root_password '*' '*'
```

A particularly useful feature of `mysqlaccess` is that it shows what privileges a current user would have for any new database that is created. For example, part of the output of the previous command is:

```
Access-rights
for USER 'partmusic', from HOST 'localhost', to DB 'ANY_NEW_DB'
    +----------------------+---+ +----------------------+---+
    | Select_priv          | N | | Lock_tables_priv     | N |
    | Insert_priv          | N | | Execute_priv         | N |
    | Update_priv          | N | | Repl_slave_priv      | N |
    | Delete_priv          | N | | Repl_client_priv     | N |
    | Create_priv          | N | | Create_view_priv     | N |
    | Drop_priv            | N | | Show_view_priv       | N |
    | Reload_priv          | N | | Create_routine_priv  | N |
    | Shutdown_priv        | N | | Alter_routine_priv   | N |
    | Process_priv         | N | | Create_user_priv     | N |
    | File_priv            | N | | Ssl_type             | ? |
    | Grant_priv           | N | | Ssl_cipher           | ? |
    | References_priv      | N | | X509_issuer          | ? |
    | Index_priv           | N | | X509_subject         | ? |
    | Alter_priv           | N | | Max_questions        | 0 |
    | Show_db_priv         | N | | Max_updates          | 0 |
    | Super_priv           | N | | Max_connections      | 0 |
    | Create_tmp_table_priv | N | | Max_user_connections | 0 |
    +----------------------+---+ +----------------------+---+
NOTE:    A password is required for user `partmusic' :-(

The following rules are used:
 db     : 'No matching rule'
 host   : 'Not processed: host-field is not empty in db-table.'
 user   : 'localhost','partmusic','652f9c175d1914f9','N','N','N','N',
   'N','N','N','N','N','N','N','N','N','N','N','N','N','N','N','N',
   'N','N','N','N','N','N','N','','','','','0','0','0','0'
```

It also shows what privileges an anonymous user has for all current databases:

```
Access-rights
for USER 'ANY_NEW_USER', from HOST 'localhost', to DB 'ANY_NEW_DB'
    +----------------------+---+ +----------------------+---+
    | Select_priv          | N | | Lock_tables_priv     | N |
    | Insert_priv          | N | | Execute_priv         | N |
    | Update_priv          | N | | Repl_slave_priv      | N |
    | Delete_priv          | N | | Repl_client_priv     | N |
    | Create_priv          | N | | Create_view_priv     | N |
    | Drop_priv            | N | | Show_view_priv       | N |
    | Reload_priv          | N | | Create_routine_priv  | N |
    | Shutdown_priv        | N | | Alter_routine_priv   | N |
    | Process_priv         | N | | Create_user_priv     | N |
    | File_priv            | N | | Ssl_type             | ? |
    | Grant_priv           | N | | Ssl_cipher           | ? |
    | References_priv      | N | | X509_issuer          | ? |
```

```
| Index_priv            | N | | X509_subject         | ? |
| Alter_priv            | N | | Max_questions        | 0 |
| Show_db_priv          | N | | Max_updates          | 0 |
| Super_priv            | N | | Max_connections      | 0 |
| Create_tmp_table_priv | N | | Max_user_connections | 0 |
+-----------------------+---+ +----------------------+---+
BEWARE:  Everybody can access your DB as user `ANY_NEW_USER' from host `localhost'
    :  WITHOUT supplying a password.
    :  Be very careful about it!!
BEWARE:  Accessing the db as an anonymous user.
    :  Your username has no relevance

The following rules are used:
 db    : 'No matching rule'
 host  : 'Not processed: host-field is not empty in db-table.'
 user  : 'localhost','','','N','N','N','N','N','N','N','N','N','N','N',
  'N','N','N','N','N','N','N','N','N','N','N','N','N','N','N','',
  '','','','0','0','0','0'

    BUGs can be reported by email to bugs@mysql.com
```

You can also check the results for all hosts by executing `mysqlaccess '*' '*' '*'`. Note that `mysqlaccess` shows only database-level access and not finer-grained privileges such as table- or column-level access. For this level of information, you must use SHOW GRANTS or direct SQL access to the `mysql` database.

Configuring mysqlaccess

The `mysqlaccess` program is a Perl script; if you're using Windows, you'll need to follow the instructions in "Installing Perl modules under Windows" in Chapter 2 to be able to use Perl scripts.

A common problem occurs when `mysqlaccess` doesn't know where to find your MySQL directories. If you've installed MySQL in a nonstandard location, you may get an error message saying that the script couldn't find the MySQL client program. To resolve this problem, you'll need to provide the correct path to the `mysql` executable. Find the `mysqlaccess` file in the MySQL `bin` directory, open it in a text editor, find the line that sets the `$MYSQL` variable, and modify it to specify the correct path for your MySQL installation.

For example, you might find the path set to **/usr/bin/mysql** as below:

```
$MYSQL    = '/usr/bin/mysql';    # path to mysql executable
```

If you've installed MySQL in **/usr/local/mysql**, you would change this to:

```
$MYSQL    = '/usr/local/mysql/bin/mysql';    # path to mysql executable
```

Now save the file and exit the editor; hopefully, everything should work now.

Revoking Privileges

You can selectively revoke privileges with the REVOKE statement, which essentially has the same syntax as GRANT. Consider a simple example, in which we remove the SELECT privilege from the user 'partmusic'@'localhost' for the time column in the track table in the music database. Here's the statement, which we've run when logged in as 'root'@'localhost':

```
mysql> REVOKE SELECT (time) ON music.track FROM 'partmusic'@'localhost';
Query OK, 0 rows affected (0.06 sec)
```

The format of REVOKE is straightforward when you understand GRANT. Following the keyword REVOKE is one or more comma-separated privileges, and these are optionally followed by column names, comma-separated in braces; this is the same as GRANT. The ON keyword has the same function as in GRANT and is followed by a database and table name, both of which can be wildcards. The FROM keyword is followed by the user and host from which the privileges are to be revoked, and the host can include wildcards.

Removing privileges using the basic syntax is laborious, since it requires that you remove the privileges in the same way they are granted. For example, to remove all privileges of 'partmusic'@'localhost', you would use the following steps:

```
mysql> REVOKE SELECT (track_id) ON music.track FROM 'partmusic'@'localhost';
Query OK, 0 rows affected (0.00 sec)

mysql> REVOKE ALL PRIVILEGES ON music.artist FROM 'partmusic'@'localhost';
Query OK, 0 rows affected (0.00 sec)

mysql> REVOKE ALL PRIVILEGES ON music.album FROM 'partmusic'@'localhost';
Query OK, 0 rows affected (0.00 sec)
```

You can remove all database-, table-, and column-level privileges of a user at once using one of the following two methods. If you're using a version of MySQL earlier than 4.1.2, use:

```
mysql> REVOKE ALL PRIVILEGES FROM 'partmusic'@'localhost';
Query OK, 0 rows affected (0.00 sec)

mysql> REVOKE GRANT OPTION FROM 'partmusic'@'localhost';
Query OK, 0 rows affected (0.00 sec)
```

From MySQL version 4.1.2 onward, you can combine these into a single statement:

```
mysql> REVOKE ALL PRIVILEGES, GRANT OPTION FROM 'partmusic'@'localhost';
Query OK, 0 rows affected (0.00 sec)
```

You could get a similar result using:

```
mysql> REVOKE ALL PRIVILEGES ON *.* FROM 'allmusic'@'localhost';
```

but this would not revoke any GRANT OPTION privileges that the user might have. To limit the revocation to the music database, you would write **music.*** rather than ***.***.

Removing Users

The previous section explained how to remove privileges, but the user is not actually deleted from the server; you can check this using the `SHOW GRANTS` statement:

```
mysql> SHOW GRANTS FOR 'partmusic'@'localhost';
+------------------------------------------------------------+
| Grants for partmusic@localhost                             |
+------------------------------------------------------------+
| GRANT USAGE ON *.* TO 'partmusic'@'localhost' IDENTIFIED BY |
|     PASSWORD '*14E65567ABDB5135D0CFD9A70B3032C179A49EE7'    |
+------------------------------------------------------------+
1 row in set (0.00 sec)
```

This means the user can still connect, but has no privileges when she does.

You can remove access to the MySQL server by removing a user. The `DROP USER` statement (available since MySQL 4.1.1) removes a user who has no privileges. Here's an example that completes the removal of `'partmusic'@'localhost'` that we began in the previous section:

```
mysql> DROP USER 'partmusic'@'localhost';
Query OK, 0 rows affected (0.00 sec)
```

Prior to MySQL version 5.02, the `DROP USER` statement reported an error if any privileges remained for a user:

```
mysql> DROP USER 'selina'@'localhost';
ERROR 1268 (HY000): Can't drop one or more of the requested users
```

In such a case, you must first revoke all privileges for a user before trying to `DROP` them.

Prior to MySQL version 4.1.1, you needed to use the SQL `DELETE` statement to remove a user. Here's how you remove the user `'partmusic'@'localhost'` in these versions:

```
mysql> DELETE FROM mysql.user WHERE User='partmusic' and Host='localhost';
Query OK, 1 row affected (0.00 sec)
```

Whenever you update the grant tables in the `mysql` database directly, you have to use the `FLUSH PRIVILEGES` instruction to tell the server to read in the updated data:

```
mysql> FLUSH PRIVILEGES;
Query OK, 0 rows affected (0.00 sec)
```

The structure of the `mysql` database and the `FLUSH PRIVILEGES` statement are explained later in "Managing Privileges with SQL."

Understanding and Changing Passwords

This section explains how user passwords work in MySQL and how they can be set, changed, and removed. Passwords can be of any length, though practical limitations in some operating systems necessitate that they be no longer than eight characters. When assigning passwords, we recommend that you follow the same principles that you would with any other password-protected system: choose passwords that have a mix of uppercase, lowercase, numeric, and special characters; avoid using dictionary words; and avoid recording your password anywhere it can be easily found. We use no passwords and simple passwords—such as *the_password*—in this chapter to demonstrate concepts, but we recommend that in practice you use a more complex password that incorporates a mix of letters, numbers, and punctuation symbols (for example, 1n1T?s313Y0). Of course, choose a password that you can remember without having to write it down somewhere; pieces of paper often turn up in the wrong hands!

The simplest method to set a password is to use the IDENTIFIED BY clause when you create or modify the privileges of a user. You've seen several examples of this so far in this chapter. Here's one reproduced from a previous section:

```
mysql> GRANT ALL ON music.* TO 'allmusic'@'localhost' IDENTIFIED BY 'the_password';
Query OK, 0 rows affected (0.06 sec)
```

This process takes the plain-text string *the_password*, hashes it using the MySQL PASSWORD( ) function, and stores the hashed string in the user table in the mysql database. Later, when a client wants a connection as this user, the plain-text password supplied by the client is hashed with the PASSWORD( ) function and compared to the string in the database. If it matches, the client is authenticated; otherwise, not. Prior to MySQL 4.1.0, the hashed string was 16 characters in length, and since 4.1.1 it has been 41 characters; don't use MySQL 4.1.0, which has an incompatible 45-character password and a different PASSWORD( ) function.

You can experiment with the PASSWORD( ) function to examine the strings produced from a plain-text password. With a server older than 4.1.1, or with a new server configured with the old_passwords option, you would see:

```
mysql> SELECT PASSWORD('the_password');
+--------------------------+
| PASSWORD('the_password') |
+--------------------------+
| 268f5b591007a24f         |
+--------------------------+
1 row in set (0.07 sec)
```

Using exactly the same command on a MySQL server that is newer than version 4.1.1 (and that has not been configured with the old_passwords option), we get:

```
mysql> SELECT PASSWORD('the_password');
+-------------------------------------------+
| PASSWORD('the_password')                  |
+-------------------------------------------+
| *201716EF6717C367868F777B9C6E17796F19F379 |
+-------------------------------------------+
1 row in set (0.02 sec)
```

You can still list the old-format password using the OLD_PASSWORD( ) function:

```
mysql> SELECT OLD_PASSWORD('the_password');
+--------------------------+
```

```
| PASSWORD('the_password') |
+---------------------------+
| 268f5b591007a24f          |
+---------------------------+
1 row in set (0.07 sec)
```

It's not possible to reverse the hashing process to derive the plain-text password from the hashed string, so the actual passwords cannot be deduced even if you have access to the hashed passwords in the mysql database. However, this scheme is still susceptible to dictionary and brute-force attacks, and allowing access to any user details can have security implications. Hence, you shouldn't allow users to access the mysql database unless they have administrator privileges.

There are three ways to set or change a password. One way is to issue a GRANT statement and include the IDENTIFIED BY clause. Suppose you've already created the user 'selina'@'localhost' using this statement:

```
mysql> GRANT ALL ON music.* TO 'selina'@'localhost' IDENTIFIED BY 'the_password';
Query OK, 0 rows affected (0.00 sec)
```

If the user exists, you can change the password while you're granting new privileges, or simply by granting no further privileges as follows:

```
mysql> GRANT USAGE ON *.* TO 'selina'@'localhost' IDENTIFIED BY 'another_password';
Query OK, 0 rows affected (0.00 sec)
```

This statement changes the password but has no effect on the current privileges.

Another way to change a password is to use the SET PASSWORD statement. Here's an example:

```
mysql> SET PASSWORD FOR 'selina'@'localhost' = PASSWORD('another_password');
Query OK, 0 rows affected (0.00 sec)
```

You can set the password for the user you're logged in as by using:

```
mysql> SET PASSWORD=PASSWORD('the_password');
Query OK, 0 rows affected (0.00 sec)
```

In both cases, remember to include the PASSWORD( ) function in the statement; if you leave it out, the server will store the plain-text password instead of the hashed string. When authenticating a user, MySQL compares the hash of the user's input to the stored string; if the stored string isn't already hashed, these won't match, and the server will refuse access.

You can also use the mysqladmin password command to change your own password from the command line. For example, you can change the password for the user *your_mysql_username* from *your_old_mysql_password* to *your new mysql password* by typing:

```
$ mysqladmin \
  --user=your_mysql_username \
  --password=your_old_mysql_password \
  password "your new mysql password"
```

Notice that since the new password contains spaces, we've enclosed it in quotes.

The user and host options are for the user you want to connect as and the server you want to connect to, respectively. You can use mysqladmin to change the password for only your own username on localhost. For example, if your MySQL username is sarah, you can change the password only for 'sarah'@'localhost'. Or if you want to change the password for another username and host pair, such as 'sarah'@'sadri.invy home.com' or 'susan'@'localhost', you'll need to use the MySQL monitor or another more flexible MySQL client.

If you're running MySQL for the first time, or if your MySQL user doesn't have a password already set, you don't need to specify the current password—that is, you can omit the password option.

You can also remove a user's password. Here's an example using the SET PASSWORD statement:

```
mysql> SET PASSWORD FOR 'selina'@'localhost' = '';
Query OK, 0 rows affected (0.00 sec)
```

This stores the empty string as the password, allowing connections without a pass word parameter. Again, it's important to always use passwords for any production server.

Sometimes, you'll want to create a new user with the same password as another, or you'll want to re-create or migrate users from one installation to another. In these cases, you may not know the plain-text password of all users, but if you have access to the SHOW GRANTS statement or the mysql database, you can discover the hashed values. If you want to create a user using a hashed password instead of asking MySQL to hash the password for you, use the PASSWORD keyword as follows:

```
mysql> GRANT USAGE ON *.* TO 'partmusic'@'localhost'
    -> IDENTIFIED BY PASSWORD '*14E65567ABDB5135D0CFD9A70B3032C179A49EE7';
Query OK, 0 rows affected (0.00 sec)
```

The PASSWORD keyword stores the hashed string directly, rather than passing it through the PASSWORD( ) function. You'll recall from earlier that the plain-text password was actually *the_password*, and you'll find you can now connect using it:

```
$ mysql --user=partmusic --password=the_password
Welcome to the MySQL monitor.  Commands end with ; or \g.
Your MySQL connection id is 60 to server version: 5.0.22-standard-log

Type 'help;' or '\h' for help. Type '\c' to clear the buffer.

mysql>
```

You can also manually set a password to its hashed version by using the SET PASS WORD statement without the PASSWORD( ) function as follows:

```
mysql> SET PASSWORD FOR 'partmusic'@'localhost' =
    '*14E65567ABDB5135D0CFD9A70B3032C179A49EE7'
Query OK, 0 rows affected (0.00 sec)
```

Again, you can now connect using the plain-text password *the_password*.

The Default Users

This section explains the user accounts that are created when MySQL is installed and shows you how to secure your installation by making important changes to these default settings. The next section explains how to put together the things you've learned to develop a complete user security policy.

When you install your MySQL server, it comes preconfigured with one or two default users. The privileges of these users and the locations vary between operating systems, but you must ensure that their privileges match your requirements, and make decisions about the machines that connections to your database server can come from; you might also decide to remove one or more of the default users. Before we explain how to make these decisions, let's discuss the users and how they access the server.

On all platforms, MySQL may come installed with two users:

root
> This is the superuser, who can do anything to the server, users, databases, and data. The superuser usually creates new users who have authority to access and manipulate specific databases. Once you've installed MySQL, you must configure the root user, and we show you how to do this later in this section.

anonymous
> This user has no username; you can use it to connect to the server without supplying any credentials. Also, as described earlier in "Anonymous Users," it is used when host credentials match but the requested username doesn't. The anonymous user has very limited privileges by default; in the next section, we'll explain what these are.

Both users have no password by default. With the anonymous user, this means you can connect to the database server without a username and password. For the root user, you supply the username root, but there's no password. Again, these are user accounts on the MySQL server, not on the operating system (Linux, Windows, or Mac OS X).

Default User Configuration

The default installation allows the default users to access the server, but the machines they can connect from depend on whether you're using Windows or a Unix-like system, such as Linux or Mac OS X. This section shows you the GRANT statements used to create the default users and explains what they mean in practice.

Linux and Mac OS X

For Linux, Mac OS X, and other Unix variants, the **root** user can access the server from only the computer hosting the server, specified using the mnemonic `localhost`, using the IP address 127.0.0.1, or by providing its actual IP address or hostname.

You can see the default configuration by listing the user- and hostnames in the **user** table of the **mysql** database:

```
mysql> SELECT User,Host FROM mysql.user;
+------+--------------------+
| User | Host               |
+------+--------------------+
|      | localhost          |
| root | localhost          |
|      | ruttle.invyhome.com |
| root | ruttle.invyhome.com |
+------+--------------------+
4 rows in set (0.00 sec)
```

When the MySQL server is installed, the **root** user is automatically created with the following **GRANT** statements:

```
mysql> SHOW GRANTS for 'root'@'localhost';
+-----------------------------------------------------------------------+
| Grants for root@localhost                                             |
+-----------------------------------------------------------------------+
| GRANT ALL PRIVILEGES ON *.* TO 'root'@'localhost' WITH GRANT OPTION |
+-----------------------------------------------------------------------+
1 row in set (0.01 sec)

mysql> SHOW GRANTS for 'root'@'ruttle.invyhome.com';
+--------------------------------------------------------------------------------+
| Grants for root@ruttle.invyhome.com                                           |
+--------------------------------------------------------------------------------+
| GRANT ALL PRIVILEGES ON *.* TO 'root'@'ruttle.invyhome.com' WITH GRANT OPTION |
+--------------------------------------------------------------------------------+
1 row in set (0.00 sec)
```

Here, `ruttle.invyhome.com` is the network name of the `localhost` system.

The anonymous user can access the server from only the `localhost`, specified using the mnemonic `localhost`, using the IP address 127.0.0.1, or by providing the actual IP address or hostname of that machine. The anonymous user has default access to only the **test** database and those databases beginning with the string **test_**.

When the MySQL server is installed, the anonymous user is automatically created with the following **GRANT** statements:

```
mysql> SHOW GRANTS for ''@'localhost';
+-------------------------------------+
| Grants for @localhost               |
+-------------------------------------+
| GRANT USAGE ON *.* TO ''@'localhost' |
+-------------------------------------+
```

```
1 row in set (0.00 sec)

mysql> SHOW GRANTS for ''@'ruttle.invyhome.com';
+------------------------------------------------+
| Grants for @hugh.local                         |
+------------------------------------------------+
| GRANT USAGE ON *.* TO ''@'ruttle.invyhome.com' |
+------------------------------------------------+
1 row in set (0.00 sec)
```

The anonymous user also has permission to access the **test** database and databases beginning with **test_**, effectively as though you'd executed these statements:

```
mysql> GRANT ALL ON test.* TO ''@'%';
Query OK, 0 rows affected (0.00 sec)

mysql> GRANT ALL ON `test\_%`.* TO ''@'%';
Query OK, 0 rows affected (0.06 sec)
```

Note that we've used backtick symbols (`` ` ``) on the second line to enclose the table name to prevent the backslash, underscore, and percentage symbols from confusing MySQL.

You can verify that these privileges are in effect by running a `SELECT * FROM db;` query. However, you can't explore these privileges with the `SHOW GRANTS` statement because there's no matching user `''@'%'`. It would be more secure for the default installation to grant privileges for the **test** databases to only the local anonymous users `''@'localhost'` and `''@'ruttle.invyhome.com'`, rather than to `''@'%'`.

Windows

Current versions of MySQL for Windows come with only the **root** user defined. You can allow anonymous access by asking the MySQL Windows installer program to create anonymous users. Again, we recommend that you don't do this.

The **root** user has permission to access the server only from the `localhost` machine:

```
mysql> SELECT User,Host from mysql.user;
+------+-----------+
| User | Host      |
+------+-----------+
| root | localhost |
+------+-----------+
1 row in set (0.01 sec)
```

When the MySQL server is installed, the **root** user is automatically created with the following `GRANT` statements:

```
mysql> SHOW GRANTS for 'root'@'localhost';
+----------------------------------------------------------------+
| Grants for root@localhost                                      |
+----------------------------------------------------------------+
| GRANT ALL PRIVILEGES ON *.* TO 'root'@'localhost' WITH GRANT OPTION |
+----------------------------------------------------------------+
1 row in set (0.01 sec)
```

You can explicitly allow access to other specific users; for example, you can create an anonymous user and allow anonymous access from any host by typing:

```
mysql> GRANT USAGE on *.* to ''@'';
```

Securing the Default Users

Now that you understand the default users and from which locations they can access the database server, let's take steps to secure the users. We recommend that you do the following:

Always set a password for the root *user*
> Choosing and setting a strong password for your administrator user is essential, except in the case where you're the only user of a machine that is unconnected to a network and contains no valuable information.

Remove privileges for the test *databases*
> Allowing any user to work with the test database and any database beginning with the string test_ is insecure.

Remove anonymous access
> Unless you want anyone to be able to connect to your MySQL server, it's better to allow access only by named users. We therefore recommend that you remove the anonymous users. If you understand and want anonymous access, read the next section, "Devising a User Security Policy," to devise an appropriate access policy.

Remove remote access
> Unless there's a requirement for the server to allow client connections from other machines, it's better to allow access from only the localhost. If you need remote access, read "Devising a User Security Policy" to devise an appropriate access policy.

To perform our recommended steps to secure your server, you need to log in to the monitor as the root user:

```
$ mysql --user=root --password=the_mysql_root_password
```

Having connected, set a password for the root user connecting from localhost:

```
mysql> SET PASSWORD FOR 'root'@'localhost' = password('the_mysql_root_password');
Query OK, 0 rows affected (0.22 sec)
```

If you've already set a password for the root user, this will update it. If you plan to keep other root users who can access the server from other hosts, make sure you add passwords for these, too. If you don't plan to keep them, don't worry; our later steps will remove them anyway.

To remove access to the test databases, type the following:

```
mysql> REVOKE ALL ON test.* FROM ''@'%';
Query OK, 0 rows affected (0.28 sec)
```

```
mysql> REVOKE ALL ON `test\_%`.* FROM ''@'%';
Query OK, 0 rows affected (0.16 sec)
```

You might also want to remove the test database; you'll almost never need to use it, and removing it leaves one less thing to worry about:

```
mysql> DROP DATABASE test;
Query OK, 0 rows affected (0.18 sec)
```

That's the test issue dealt with.

The next step is to remove anonymous access. You can do this by deleting the accounts that have no username:

```
mysql> DROP USER ''@'localhost';
Query OK, 0 rows affected (0.27 sec)

mysql> DROP USER ''@'host.domain'

Query OK, 0 rows affected (0.00 sec)
```

Replace *host.domain* with the server's fully qualified domain name, such as `ruttle.invy home.com`.

Alternatively, you can manually update the grant tables:

```
mysql> DELETE FROM mysql.user WHERE User = '';
Query OK, 2 rows affected (0.26 sec)

mysql> FLUSH PRIVILEGES;
Query OK, 0 rows affected (0.20 sec)
```

We discuss managing privileges with SQL, including the FLUSH PRIVILEGES syntax, later in "Managing Privileges with SQL."

Instead of deleting the anonymous accounts, you can disable unauthenticated access to the server by setting passwords for these accounts:

```
mysql> UPDATE mysql.user SET Password = PASSWORD('the_new_anonymous_user_password')
    -> WHERE User = '';
mysql> FLUSH PRIVILEGES;
```

This allows authenticated, minimally privileged access to the MySQL server from any host, allowing access to test databases but nothing else. It's rare for such a setup to be needed, so we recommend you simply remove any anonymous accounts.

The final step we recommend is to remove remote access unless you really need it. Allowing only local connections is more secure. As we explained in "Configuring Access to the MySQL Server," you can increase security even further by telling the server to not accept incoming network connections, and to communicate with clients only through TCP sockets (Linux and Mac OS X) or named pipes (Windows).

Since we've removed the anonymous user, the only remaining user is root; we can remove remote access for root with:

```
mysql> DROP USER 'root'@'host.domain'
Query OK, 0 rows affected (0.00 sec)
```

Replace *host.domain* with the server's fully qualified domain name. For example, if your host was called `ruttle.invyhome.com`, you would write:

```
mysql> DROP USER 'root'@'ruttle.invyhome.com'
```

Again, you can instead manually modify the grant tables; here, you can delete all accounts that have a host other then `localhost`:

```
mysql> DELETE FROM mysql.user WHERE Host <> 'localhost';
Query OK, 1 row affected (0.26 sec)

mysql> FLUSH PRIVILEGES;
Query OK, 0 rows affected (0.20 sec)
```

Removing users makes us nervous, especially when a wrong keystroke in a `DELETE` statement can remove all your users; you can even remove the `root` account! If you make a mistake, you should restore the files for the `mysql` database (in the `mysql` directory of the data directory) from your backups. On a Linux or Mac OS X system, you can also restore the default users with the `mysql_install_db` script; simply run this command the same way you ran it in Chapter 2. We look at backups and recovery in Chapter 10.

Devising a User Security Policy

You now understand the principles of creating, maintaining, and removing users and their privileges. In this section, we show you how to take those basics and put them together to develop a security policy and a maintainable, flexible, secure MySQL installation. Importantly, we also show you how to balance server performance against security, and develop the thinking that'll allow you to effectively manage your MySQL server.

Flexibility and security are enemies. The most secure MySQL installation has no users with no privileges. The most flexible installation lets everyone in as `root`, in case they need to administer or change the server or its databases. Balancing security and flexibility is important: you should have sufficient users and privileges to permit the user requirements of the applications you develop, but you should constrain those users and privileges to the minimal set that's needed. The next section walks you through a checklist of decisions you should make in setting up your users and their privileges.

Choosing Users and Privileges

To begin, you should decide whether you'll have a "default allow" or "default deny" philosophy. In the "default allow" philosophy, you decide on all of the users you might need and grant them all privileges. You then explicitly revoke any privileges they don't need. In the "default deny" philosophy, you decide on the users you must have and create them with no privileges. You then explicitly grant the privileges that these users need. Security experts prefer the "default deny" approach over the "default allow" one, since there's a smaller chance that you'll create users or privileges that make your server insecure. Developers tend to prefer the "default allow" approach, since you only need to think about the few things that you don't want to happen, rather than the larger set of things you do want to allow. We recommend that you use the "default deny" approach during production, but the "default allow" approach is acceptable if you're just experimenting on noncritical data in a relatively secure environment. We now consider the issues you need to consider when creating users and assigning privileges using the "default deny" philosophy:

Clients

> From what computers does the database server need to be accessed? Typically, the answer is at least the localhost, where the machine's security protects accounts that are used to access the database server; if you are authenticated to access the localhost, you must have access to an account on the host, and so must have passed an important security check. What other clients need access? Be as explicit as possible, listing client machines by their IP addresses or full domain names; avoid using the wildcard % where possible. Avoid listing clients that *may* want access, and limit your choices to only those that *must have* access; you can always add clients later when you're sure they're needed.

Users

> Who needs access to the database server? The answer always includes the **root** user who administers the server. You'll also need at least one other user who—as we discuss in the next step—has the smallest set of privileges required to work with your database. If possible, partition your database users into those that need more privileges and those that need fewer. For example, can you divide the users into a database administrator user, and then others who need fewer privileges to use the database?

> Can you separate the database users from the application users? For example, in a web application, it's typical that the server scripts manage the users of the application and always access MySQL as a single user themselves. If you have more than one application, we recommend having a different user for each application.

Privileges

> What needs to be done? The section "Privileges" at the beginning of this chapter lists all of the privileges that are available. The **root** user has all of the privileges for all databases and the server. Consider which privileges are needed for your database, and what components of the database each is needed for. Are the privileges needed for columns, tables, or for the database? Don't add any privileges you don't need, avoid adding privileges you only think you might want, and avoid privileges for parts of the database that you don't need to access. Try to avoid using the asterisk * wildcard, and, in particular, avoid assigning global privileges with *.* where possible.

Now that you've made it through the checklist, you need to consider how the issues are related. For each user, consider which client hosts the user must be able to access the server from. For example, you might decide that root needs access from only local host, while the user working with the music database needs access from localhost and ruttle.invyhome.com. For each user and host combination, determine the minimal set of privileges that you need.

Let's try a simple example. Suppose you're setting up a database server that will manage the music database and be accessed by PHP scripts that run on a web server on the localhost. Let's run through the checklist:

Clients

Only the localhost needs access.

Users

We need the root user, and one other user that we'll name musicuser to use in the PHP script.

Privileges

After examining the list at the beginning of the chapter in "Privileges," we identify that the PHP scripts need the following privileges: DELETE, INSERT, SELECT, UPDATE, and LOCK TABLES. We identify that they are needed for all tables in the database.

Now we're ready to create musicuser.

The first step in setting up our user is to remove all other non-root users and ensure root is allowed access from only the localhost; the steps for this were described earlier in "Securing the Default Users." Then, create musicuser with the following statement (we're setting the password as 'MiSeCr8'):

```
mysql> GRANT DELETE, INSERT, SELECT, UPDATE, LOCK TABLES ON music.*
    -> TO 'musicuser'@'localhost' IDENTIFIED BY 'MiSeCr8';
Query OK, 0 rows affected (0.28 sec)
```

Your PHP scripts now have sufficient privileges to access the database.

More Security Tips

The previous section explained a simple philosophy for creating users and privileges. This section lists some basic tips to consider when creating users and privileges. Think very carefully before granting these privileges:

ALTER

The ALTER privilege allows the user to change the structure of databases, permitting operations such as renaming tables, adding and removing columns, and creating and deleting indexes. This can allow the user to change or destroy data; for example, reducing the size of an INT(5) column to an INT(1) destroys four digits of integer precision. Importantly, if you grant ALTER as a global privilege, the user can subvert the privilege-checking process by renaming the mysql database or its tables.

FILE

The FILE privilege allows the user to use statements that read and write disk files, permitting access to potentially sensitive information on the server and allowing the user to write large files. In practice, the user can only read and write files to which the server has access; this includes all world-readable files and any file in the database directories. Fortunately, existing files can't be overwritten, but this is still a powerful privilege.

CREATE, DROP, and INDEX

The CREATE and DROP privileges allow the user to create and delete databases, tables, and indexes. At a global level, these privileges pose the same security problems as ALTER. At a database and table level, they allow destruction of data and indexes. The INDEX privilege is a subset of CREATE, allowing only the key-creation feature; you should limit access to this privilege too, since a user could add unnecessary indexes that slow down the operation of your database server.

GRANT OPTION

This privilege allows one user to pass on privileges to another. In practice, only administrators should grant privileges, and you should avoid allowing other users to do so. A particular problem can occur if one user shares his privileges with another; the user receiving additional privileges will obviously end up with more than he was initially granted—and perhaps more than he's supposed to have.

PROCESS

This allows the user to view current processes, including the statements that started them. In practice, this means that the user can view databases and tables being created and changed and, importantly, statements that create users and their passwords.

SHUTDOWN

This allows a user to stop the server.

You should avoid granting any privileges on the special mysql database. This is a default part of any MySQL installation that stores user privileges. Nobody other than the MySQL root user should be able to be read, change, or delete information in this database.

Avoid granting access to anonymous users. You should instead require that all users be explicitly identified, along with the hosts they can connect from and the databases that they can access.

Choose good passwords: always specify passwords when creating users, and ensure these passwords meet the basic criteria of being hard to guess while remaining straightforward to remember.

Finally, use secure remote connections: if you allow remote access to the MySQL server, require that these connections be encrypted. We don't discuss how to do this, but you'll find more detail under the heading "Using Secure Connections" in the MySQL manual.

Resource-Limit Controls

MySQL 4.0.2 added new resource-limit controls for users. These are maintained along with the global privileges, and affect users rather than client connections. With these controls, you can limit:

- The number of SQL statements per hour, using the `MAX_QUERIES_PER_HOUR` clause. All statements executed by a user are counted toward this limit.
- The number of updates per hour, using the `MAX_UPDATES_PER_HOUR` clause. Any statement that modifies a database or its tables counts toward this limit.
- The number of connections per hour, using the `MAX_CONNECTIONS_PER_HOUR` clause. Any connection, from the monitor, a program, or a web script, counts toward this limit.

These clauses can be added to a `GRANT` statement, or you can set them manually using SQL as discussed later in "Managing Privileges with SQL."

For example, to set limits for the existing user `'partmusic'@'localhost'`, giving this user a maximum of 100 queries per hour, 10 updates, and 5 connections, you'd type:

```
mysql> GRANT USAGE ON *.* to 'partmusic'@'localhost' WITH
    -> MAX_QUERIES_PER_HOUR 100
    -> MAX_UPDATES_PER_HOUR 10
    -> MAX_CONNECTIONS_PER_HOUR 5;
Query OK, 0 rows affected (0.06 sec)
```

Since we've used `USAGE`, the privileges aren't affected when the new limits are imposed.

After imposing these limits, you'll find an error message is returned when you exceed them. For example, after running and quitting the monitor five times in succession, you'll see this:

```
$ mysql --user=partmusic
ERROR 1226 (42000): User 'partmusic' has exceeded the 'max_connections'
  resource (current value: 5)
```

Remember, these limits apply per user and not per connection. If you start two separate instances of the MySQL monitor client and log in to the server as the same user, both connections contribute towards reaching the user's hourly limits.

Another useful parameter to manage the MySQL server load is the `MAX_USER_CONNEC` `TIONS` option. This limits the number of simultaneous clients that can access the server and is usually set when you start `mysqld` or in an options file. We discuss options files in Chapter 11.

The mysql_setpermission Program

`mysql_setpermission` is an interactive program that allows you to choose from a menu of routine database and user administration tasks, such as creating a database, setting a user password, and modifying user privileges. The program menu is shown here:

```
$ mysql_setpermission --user=root --password=the_mysql_root_password
####################################################################
## Welcome to the permission setter 1.3 for MySQL.
## made by Luuk de Boer
####################################################################
What would you like to do:
  1. Set password for an existing user.
  2. Create a database + user privilege for that database
     and host combination (user can only do SELECT)
  3. Create/append user privilege for an existing database
     and host combination (user can only do SELECT)
  4. Create/append broader user privileges for an existing
     database and host combination
     (user can do SELECT,INSERT,UPDATE,DELETE)
  5. Create/append quite extended user privileges for an
     existing database and host combination (user can do
     SELECT,INSERT,UPDATE,DELETE,CREATE,DROP,INDEX,
     LOCK TABLES,CREATE TEMPORARY TABLES)
  6. Create/append database administrative privileges for an
     existing database and host combination (user can do
     SELECT,INSERT,UPDATE,DELETE,CREATE,DROP,INDEX,LOCK TABLES,
     CREATE TEMPORARY TABLES,SHOW DATABASES,PROCESS)
  7. Create/append full privileges for an existing database
     and host combination (user has FULL privilege)
  8. Remove all privileges for for an existing database and
     host combination.
     (user will have all permission fields set to N)
  0. exit this program

Make your choice [1,2,3,4,5,6,7,0]:
```

The program's very easy to use; for example, let's choose option number **1** to set the password for the user allmusic connecting from localhost:

```
Setting a (new) password for a user.

For which user do you want to specify a password: allmusic
Username = allmusic
Would you like to set a password for allmusic [y/n]: y
What password do you want to specify for allmusic: the_password
Type the password again: the_password
We now need to know which host for allmusic we have to change.
Choose from the following hosts:
  - localhost
The host please (case sensitive): localhost
The following host will be used: localhost.
####################################################################

That was it ... here is an overview of what you gave to me:
The username          : allmusic
The host              : localhost
####################################################################

Are you pretty sure you would like to implement this [yes/no]: yes
Okay ... let's go then ...
```

```
The password is set for user 'allmusic'.
```

The `mysql_setpermission` program is a Perl script; it should run on a Linux or Mac OS X system, but for a Windows system you will need to follow the instructions of "Installing Perl modules under Windows" in Chapter 2. Using the monitor approach is more portable, since you can use it even when `mysql_setpermission` isn't installed on a system, or where you have limited access to the server, such as on a server run by a hosting company.

Only users who have access to the `mysql` database can use the `mysql_setpermission` command. Usually, only the MySQL `root` user has this access; if you try using the script as a user who doesn't have access privileges for the `mysql` database, you'll get an "Access denied" message:

```
$ mysql_setpermission --user=unprivileged_username
Password for user unprivileged_username to connect to MySQL:
Can't make a connection to the mysql server.
The error: Access denied for user 'unprivileged_username'@'localhost' to
database 'mysql' at /usr/bin/mysql_setpermission line 70, <STDIN> line 1.
```

Managing Privileges with SQL

MySQL privileges are managed in five tables in the `mysql` database. You can manage this database yourself, using queries to manage users and privileges rather than using the `GRANT` and `REVOKE` statements. It's useful to know how to do this, because it can save you time and allow you to access features that aren't available through `GRANT` and `REVOKE`. This section explains how the privileges are managed and shows you how to modify them directly.

The privileges are managed in the `mysql` database. As we've discussed previously, only administrators should have access to this database and, therefore, you'll usually need to log in as the `root` user to follow the steps in this section. In MySQL 5.0, the database contains 17 tables, but only 5 are relevant to privileges: `user`, `db`, `tables_priv`, `columns_priv`, and `host`.

The user Table

The `user` table manages users and global privileges. Its structure is straightforward, even though it has around 30 columns. Each row includes a `User`, `Password`, and `Host` column; these are the credentials that are used to match against connection attempts and authenticate users. All three are optional; the `User` and `Password` values are optional because MySQL includes support for anonymous access and because it's possible for a user to not have a password (although this isn't recommended). We explain why the `Host` value is optional later in this section. Each row also contains a `Y` or `N` for each possible privilege—for example, `Select_priv` and `Alter_priv` might be set to `Y` and `N`, respectively—and other values associated with the user; we explain the other parameters that can be set for users later.

Let's consider an example. Suppose you issue the statement:

```
mysql> GRANT SELECT, INSERT, UPDATE, DELETE, LOCK TABLES ON *.*
    -> TO 'fred'@'localhost' IDENTIFIED BY '4fgh6!aa';
Query OK, 0 rows affected (0.19 sec)
```

This creates a row in the User table of the mysql database. Select this database, and list the table rows for fred; here's the output, modified so that it fits on this page:

```
mysql> USE mysql
Database changed
mysql> SELECT * FROM user WHERE User = 'fred';
+-----------+------+-------------------------------------------+------------+...
| Host      | User | Password                                  | Select_priv|...
+-----------+------+-------------------------------------------+------------+...
| localhost | fred | *8325B39F81993E24AC6802CD33722DB8B1D64C21 | Y          |...
+-----------+------+-------------------------------------------+------------+...

...+-------------+-------------+-------------+-------------+-----------+...
...| Insert_priv | Update_priv | Delete_priv | Create_priv | Drop_priv |...
...+-------------+-------------+-------------+-------------+-----------+...
...| Y           | Y           | Y           | N           | N         |...
...+-------------+-------------+-------------+-------------+-----------+...

...+-------------+---------------+--------------+-----------+------------+...
...| Reload_priv | Shutdown_priv | Process_priv | File_priv | Grant_priv |...
...+-------------+---------------+--------------+-----------+------------+...
...| N           | N             | N            | N         | N          |...
...+-------------+---------------+--------------+-----------+------------+...

...+----------------+------------+------------+-------------+------------+...
...| References_priv | Index_priv | Alter_priv | Show_db_priv | Super_priv |...
...+----------------+------------+------------+-------------+------------+...
...| N              | N          | N          | N           | N          |...
...+----------------+------------+------------+-------------+------------+...

...+----------------------+------------------+--------------+...
...| Create_tmp_table_priv | Lock_tables_priv | Execute_priv |...
...+----------------------+------------------+--------------+...
...| N                    | Y                | N            |...
...+----------------------+------------------+--------------+...

...+-----------------+-----------------+-----------------+----------------+...
...| Repl_slave_priv | Repl_client_priv | Create_view_priv | Show_view_priv |...
...+-----------------+-----------------+-----------------+----------------+...
...| N               | N               | N               | N              |...
...+-----------------+-----------------+-----------------+----------------+...

...+--------------------+-------------------+------------------+----------+...
...| Create_routine_priv | Alter_routine_priv | Create_user_priv | ssl_type |...
...+--------------------+-------------------+------------------+----------+...
...| N                  | N                 | N                |          |...
...+--------------------+-------------------+------------------+----------+...

...+------------+-------------+--------------+---------------+-------------+...
...| ssl_cipher | x509_issuer | x509_subject | max_questions | max_updates |...
...+------------+-------------+--------------+---------------+-------------+...
...|            |             |              | 0             | 0           |...
...+------------+-------------+--------------+---------------+-------------+...
...+-----------------+--------------------+
```

```
...| max_connections | max_user_connections |
...+-----------------+-----------------------+
...| 0               | 0                     |
...+-----------------+-----------------------+
1 row in set (0.00 sec)
```

You can see that the password is encrypted using the PASSWORD( ) function, and that all privileges are N except for the four simple privileges we've granted. If you create a user with no global privileges—because the privileges you grant are for a database, tables, or columns—you'll find that all privileges in the user table are set to N.

The user table is used to authenticate connections, as well as store global privileges. If a connection's parameters—its username, password, and host—don't match an entry in the user table, then the user isn't authenticated and it doesn't matter what privileges are available in the other four tables. If the parameters do match, then the user is allowed access to the MySQL server, and her privileges are a combination of those in the five privilege tables. There's no requirement for an exact match between the parameters and the user table for authentication because a blank username allows anonymous access from a host, and the hostname column can contain wildcards.

The db Table

When you grant privileges for a particular database, they are stored in the db table of the mysql database. The table is similar to the user table but stores privilege values for Host, Db, and User combinations. Consider what happens when you grant 'bob'@'localhost' privileges for the music database:

```
mysql> GRANT SELECT, INSERT, DELETE on music.*
    -> TO 'bob'@'localhost';
Query OK, 0 rows affected (0.00 sec)
```

You'll now see these privileges in the db table:

```
mysql> SELECT * FROM db WHERE User = 'bob';
+-----------+-------+------+-------------+-------------+-------------+...
| Host      | Db    | User | Select_priv | Insert_priv | Update_priv |...
+-----------+-------+------+-------------+-------------+-------------+...
| localhost | music | bob  | Y           | Y           | N           |...
+-----------+-------+------+-------------+-------------+-------------+...

...+-------------+-------------+-----------+------------+-----------------+...
...| Delete_priv | Create_priv | Drop_priv | Grant_priv | References_priv |...
...+-------------+-------------+-----------+------------+-----------------+...
...| Y           | N           | N         | N          | N               |...
...+-------------+-------------+-----------+------------+-----------------+...

...+------------+------------+----------------------+-------------------+...
...| Index_priv | Alter_priv | Create_tmp_table_priv | Lock_tables_priv |...
...+------------+------------+----------------------+-------------------+...
...| N          | N          | N                     | N                |...
...+------------+------------+----------------------+-------------------+...

...+-----------------+----------------+---------------------+...
...| Create_view_priv | Show_view_priv | Create_routine_priv |...
...+-----------------+----------------+---------------------+...
```

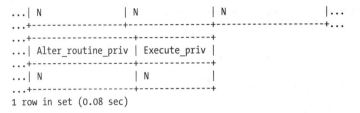

```
...| N               | N               | N                    |...
...+-----------------+-----------------+----------------------+...
...+-------------------+--------------+
...| Alter_routine_priv | Execute_priv |
...+-------------------+--------------+
...| N               | N            |
...+-------------------+--------------+
1 row in set (0.08 sec)
```

Again, we've modified the output so it fits in the book.

The tables_priv Table

The tables_priv table stores privileges for the table level. This is similar to the db table but holds privilege values for Host, Db, User, and Table_name combinations. Consider what happens when you grant 'bob'@'localhost' the INDEX privilege for the artist table in the music database:

```
mysql> GRANT INDEX on music.artist TO 'bob'@'localhost';
Query OK, 0 rows affected (0.00 sec)
```

A SELECT statement shows the effect:

```
mysql> SELECT * FROM tables_priv WHERE User = 'bob';
+-----------+-------+------+------------+----------------+...
| Host      | Db    | User | Table_name | Grantor        |...
+-----------+-------+------+------------+----------------+...
| localhost | music | bob  | artist     | root@localhost |...
+-----------+-------+------+------------+----------------+...

... +---------------------+------------+-------------+
... | Timestamp           | Table_priv | Column_priv |
... +---------------------+------------+-------------+
... | 2006-08-21 10:03:18 | Index      |             |
... +---------------------+------------+-------------+
1 row in set (0.16 sec)
```

The structure is a little different from the other tables: the tables_priv table includes who granted the privilege and when it was granted, and it explicitly lists the table privileges in the Table_priv column.

The Column_priv column in the tables_priv table lists privileges that are available only at column level for the user. Consider what happens if we grant 'bob'@'localhost' the UPDATE privilege for the album_name column on the album table:

```
mysql> GRANT UPDATE (album_name) ON music.album TO 'bob'@'localhost';
Query OK, 0 rows affected (0.12 sec)
```

Here's the result:

```
mysql> SELECT * FROM tables_priv WHERE User = 'bob';
+-----------+-------+------+------------+----------------+...
| Host      | Db    | User | Table_name | Grantor        |...
+-----------+-------+------+------------+----------------+...
| localhost | music | bob  | artist     | root@localhost |...
| localhost | music | bob  | album      | root@localhost |...
```

```
+-----------+-------+------+------------+---------------+...
...  +--------------------+------------+------------+
...  | Timestamp          | Table_priv | Column_priv |
...  +--------------------+------------+------------+
...  | 2006-08-21 10:03:18 | Index      |            |
...  | 2006-08-21 10:12:36 |            | Update     |
...  +--------------------+------------+------------+
2 rows in set (0.25 sec)
```

You can see that that the Update privilege is now available on at least one of the columns of the album table, but the tables_priv table doesn't show which column or columns.

The columns_priv Table

The columns_priv table lists which privileges are available for which columns. It's only accessed if the tables_priv table says that a privilege is available for one or more columns in a table and that privilege isn't already available at the table level. We've granted UPDATE to 'bob'@'localhost' for the album_name column in the album table. Here's what's stored:

```
mysql> SELECT * FROM columns_priv WHERE User = 'bob';
+-----------+-------+------+------------+-------------+...
| Host      | Db    | User | Table_name | Column_name |...
+-----------+-------+------+------------+-------------+...
| localhost | music | bob  | album      | album_name  |...
+-----------+-------+------+------------+-------------+...
...  +--------------------+------------+
...  | Timestamp          | Column_priv |
...  +--------------------+------------+
...  | 2006-08-21 10:12:36 | Update     |
...  +--------------------+------------+
1 row in set (0.07 sec)
```

The table structure is much the same as tables_priv, except that it includes the Column_name but no table privileges.

The host Table

The remaining privilege table is host. This table isn't modified or accessed by the GRANT and REVOKE statements. Therefore, it can be maintained only by SQL queries, and so remains unused in most MySQL installations. Indeed, you can skip this advanced section if you want.

The server verifies that users have authorization to perform an operation by checking the global privileges listed for them in the user table. If they don't have the required privilege for all databases, then the server checks the db table to see whether they have that privilege for the active database. If the Host field in the db table is blank, the user's privileges for the database vary depending on the host they're connecting from. These privileges are stored in the host table and are verified against the global settings in the db table to determine the privileges for a database when it's accessed from a client or range of clients. For example, you could specify that users connecting from outside the company network do not have the privilege to delete data or drop tables.

We'll explain how the host table works through an example. Suppose you've decided to create a MySQL user for Sam (with the username sam), but you want to allow him to access the music database from different locations, but with different privileges. Assume there are three scenarios you want to implement. First, when sam accesses the server from the localhost, you want him to have all privileges for the database except GRANT OPTION. Second, when he accesses the server from anywhere else on your network subnet—which is all machines matching 192.168.1.%—you want him to have all simple non-administrator privileges. Last, when he connects from anywhere else, you want him to have the SELECT privilege only. You know how to do this by creating three users that that have access to music.*: 'sam'@'localhost', 'sam'@'192.168.1.%', and 'sam'@'%'. However, using the host table, you can instead create just one user.

Here's how you create one user with two or more host specifications. First, you add the user account with a superset of the privileges you want on music.*:

```
mysql> GRANT ALL ON music.* TO 'sam'@'' IDENTIFIED BY 'p^R5wrD';
```

Notice that we've given the privileges to 'sam'@'', which sets the Host column value to the empty string; don't use just 'sam' because this is the same as 'sam'@'%'. We've also set this user's password to 'p^R5wrD'.

We've created an account that allows Sam to log in to the MySQL server from any host, and he now has all privileges for the music database. Let's now create the entries in the host database that allow and restrict his access depending on the client from which he connects. To begin, let's create an entry for the localhost that doesn't restrict his privileges at all. To do this, you need to understand the structure of the host table:

```
mysql> DESCRIBE host;
+----------------------+---------------+------+-----+---------+-------+
| Field                | Type          | Null | Key | Default | Extra |
+----------------------+---------------+------+-----+---------+-------+
| Host                 | char(60)      |      | PRI |         |       |
| Db                   | char(64)      |      | PRI |         |       |
| Select_priv          | enum('N','Y') |      |     | N       |       |
| Insert_priv          | enum('N','Y') |      |     | N       |       |
| Update_priv          | enum('N','Y') |      |     | N       |       |
| Delete_priv          | enum('N','Y') |      |     | N       |       |
| Create_priv          | enum('N','Y') |      |     | N       |       |
| Drop_priv            | enum('N','Y') |      |     | N       |       |
| Grant_priv           | enum('N','Y') |      |     | N       |       |
| References_priv      | enum('N','Y') |      |     | N       |       |
| Index_priv           | enum('N','Y') |      |     | N       |       |
| Alter_priv           | enum('N','Y') |      |     | N       |       |
| Create_tmp_table_priv| enum('N','Y') |      |     | N       |       |
| Lock_tables_priv     | enum('N','Y') |      |     | N       |       |
+----------------------+---------------+------+-----+---------+-------+
14 rows in set (0.21 sec)
```

You can see it has an entry for a Host and a Db, as well as the usual table-level privileges. Now, let's add an entry for localhost that allows all privileges:

```
mysql> INSERT INTO host VALUES ('localhost', 'music',
    -> 'Y','Y','Y','Y','Y','Y','Y','Y','Y','Y','Y','Y');
Query OK, 1 row affected (0.00 sec)

mysql> FLUSH PRIVILEGES;
Query OK, 0 rows affected (0.29 sec)
```

From now on, Sam can access the server as 'sam'@'localhost' and have all privileges for the music database. We explain how this works next.

When Sam connects as 'sam'@'localhost', the following steps occur:

1. The row in the user table for Sam is matched against the user and password credentials, giving him access to the server.

2. Global privileges are added to Sam's permissions.

3. The db table is searched for entries that match the user sam; there's one matching entry for the music database that has a blank Host column.

4. The host table is searched for any specific entries for the database music; in this case, there's one row with a Host value of localhost. We now have two sets of privileges for the music database: privileges for Sam, and privileges for localhost.

5. Last, the intersection—the logical AND—of the privileges is computed, and these are added to the global permissions for Sam's connection; if either or both rows have an N for a privilege, then that privilege is denied unless it was granted globally. In this case, since Sam has all privileges in both rows except GRANT OPTIONS (he doesn't have it for the db table row), then Sam has those privileges for accessing the music database.

We still need to configure access so that Sam has the appropriate access privileges from other machines on our network subnet and from the Internet. To configure for the network subnet, we add the following entry to the host table:

```
mysql> INSERT INTO host VALUES ('192.168.1.%','music',
    -> 'Y','Y','Y','Y','N','N','N','N','N','N','N','Y');
Query OK, 1 row affected (0.21 sec)

mysql> FLUSH PRIVILEGES;
Query OK, 0 rows affected (0.29 sec)
```

When Sam connects from the local network, he has only the SELECT, INSERT, UPDATE, DELETE, and LOCK TABLES privileges, since the intersection of this row and his row in the db table yields a Y for only those privileges.

To configure his access for elsewhere on the Internet, we add:

```
mysql> INSERT INTO host VALUES ('%', 'music',
    -> 'Y','N','N','N','N','N','N','N','N','N','N','N');
Query OK, 1 row affected (0.20 sec)
```

```
mysql> FLUSH PRIVILEGES;
Query OK, 0 rows affected (0.29 sec)
```

This limits Sam's access to the SELECT privilege when he accesses the server from any-where but localhost and our local subnet.

The host table allows you to configure client access controls. For example, using the wildcard % in the Db column, you can control access for a client to all databases on the server. Suppose you want to forbid access from your web server machine, 192.168.1.200. To do this, you add this entry to the host table:

```
mysql> INSERT INTO host VALUES ('192.168.1.200', '%',
    -> 'N','N','N','N','N','N','N','N','N','N','N','N');
Query OK, 1 row affected (0.20 sec)

mysql> FLUSH PRIVILEGES;
Query OK, 0 rows affected (0.29 sec)
```

All database privileges are denied to connections from the web server, as long as no db table rows specify it as a valid host, and global privileges are not granted.

Activating Privileges

We've used SQL statements to manipulate the host table in the previous section, and prior to that in "The Default Users" as a shortcut for removing users. You'll find this is useful: it's sometimes easier to apply an SQL statement to all rows in a table, or join tables, rather than apply successive GRANT and REVOKE statements.

You've also seen that whenever we manipulate the mysql database with SQL statements, we run the FLUSH PRIVILEGES statement afterward. This clears MySQL's internal priv-ilege cache, causing it to reread the current privileges and cache any recent updates. If you don't do this, your privilege changes won't appear until you restart the server or carry out a GRANT or REVOKE statement that affects the same privilege table. You must remember to run FLUSH PRIVILEGES after any privilege or user modifications are per-formed with SQL statements; you don't need to use FLUSH PRIVILEGES with GRANT or REVOKE, as the server does this for you automatically.

You may also have wondered when exactly privilege changes with GRANT and REVOKE take effect on a current connection. Any change you make at the column or table level takes effect when you run the next statement. Changes at the database level take effect when you next choose a database. Changes at the global level—including password changes—take effect when the specified user next connects. Finally, all changes take effect immediately if you stop and restart the server.

Privileges and Performance

MySQL's user and privilege management gives you fine-grain control over who has access to which parts of the server and its databases, as well as what that access allows.

However, this fine-grained control comes at a price: when you implement complex user and privilege settings, checking these for each SQL statement you execute adds a performance penalty.

When you choose your users and their privileges, you should strive to balance control and performance. Here are some basic tips:

- Keep it simple. If you follow the "default deny" philosophy, you'll create only the users you need; avoid creating users whom you only *think* you might want in the future.

- Grant the privilege as high up the hierarchy as possible. For example, if you want to grant a privilege for all tables in a database, grant it for the database instead. Avoid using column and table privileges unless you really need them.

- Minimize your use of the host table.

Remember, the more comparisons required to determine permissions, the slower each query will run on your server. However, don't compromise your security policy for the sake of performance; a server that has been rendered unusable by an attack has zero performance!

Resetting Forgotten MySQL Passwords

If you've forgotten a MySQL user password, you can log in to the server as the MySQL root user and update the password manually. If you've forgotten the root password, you'll need to stop the server and restart it in a special way to allow you to change the root password.

The server is normally stopped with the `mysqladmin shutdown` command, but you can't use this command if you've forgotten the MySQL root user password. Instead, you'll need to use the */etc/init.d/mysql* or */etc/init.d/mysqld* script under Linux, the *MySQL_Directory/scripts/mysql.server* under Linux or Mac OS X, the MySQL preferences pane under Mac OS X, or the Windows Services window to shut down the server. If none of these are available, you can forcibly end or "kill" the server process, though this is not recommended since it can lead to data loss. You will need to have sufficient authorization to kill the server process, so you should be logged in under the same username the server is running under—for example, `mysql`, or your own account if the server is running under your username—or as a superuser (system root or Windows administrator).

To kill the server under Linux or Mac OS X, you should first determine the *process identifier* (or PID) of the server process. The PID is normally stored under the server data directory in a file with the extension *.pid*. You can list the contents of this file using the `cat` command and enclose the command in backtick symbols (`` ` ``) to pass the output directly to the `kill` command:

```
$ kill `cat MySQL_Directory/data/your_host_name.pid`
```

An example of a command to kill a server running from the */usr/local/mysql* directory would be:

```
$ kill `cat /usr/local/mysql/data/localhost.pid`
```

If you specified a custom PID file location with the `pid-file` option, you'll need to specify the same location here.

To kill the server under Windows, press the Ctrl-Alt-Del keys together to open the Task Manager, select the *mysqld-nt.exe* entry under the Processes tab, and click on the End Process button.

Once the server is stopped, you need to restart it and change the database **root** user password. There are two approaches that you can use. First, you can open a text editor and create a text file containing an SQL command to update the database **root** user password:

```
SET PASSWORD FOR 'root'@'localhost' = PASSWORD('the_mysql_root_password');
```

Save this file under the name *reset_root_password.sql*. Now, you need to start the MySQL server with the `init-file` option, telling the server to execute the commands in this file:

```
$ mysqld_safe --init-file=path_to_the_init_file &
```

For example, on a Linux or Mac OS X system, with the file in the *~/tmp* directory, you would write:

```
$ mysqld_safe --init-file=~/tmp/reset_root_password.sql &
```

while on a Windows system with the file in the *C:* directory, you would write:

```
C:\> mysqld-nt --init-file=C:\reset_root_password.sql &
```

Note that the server should have permission to access and read this file. If the server can't access the file, it will refuse to start and write a message such as this one in the server log:

```
051009 22:12:01 [ERROR] /usr/sbin/mysqld: File '/home/adam/tmp/reset_root_passwrd.sql'
   not found (Errcode: 13)
```

Here, the name of the initialization file has been mistyped. Once you've started the server successfully, you should shut it down and start it again normally without the `init-file` option. You should then carefully delete the text file containing the password. If you drag and drop the file to the system Trash can or Recycle Bin, empty this so that the file can't be easily recovered. Even better, you should use a file-wiping tool such as `shred` (under Linux and Mac OS X) or Eraser (under Windows) that ensures that sensitive files—and any temporary or backup files created by your text editor—are destroyed when they are deleted.

An alternative approach is to start the server using the `skip-grant-tables` option. This tells the server not to check user passwords and access levels:

```
$ mysqld_safe --skip-grant-tables
```

Now, anyone can have access to the server with maximum privileges and without a password. Be very careful—it's wise to disconnect your system from the network while you're doing this! Connect to the server with the MySQL monitor program:

```
$ mysql
```

(You don't need to specify any user or password, since without the grant tables, MySQL can't enforce any authentication). Then immediately re-enable the grant tables so that the authentication details will be checked if anyone else tries to connect to the server:

```
mysql> FLUSH PRIVILEGES;
```

You can then reset the root user password using the SQL query:

```
mysql> UPDATE mysql.user SET Password = PASSWORD('new_password') WHERE User = 'root';
```

or alternatively:

```
mysql> SET PASSWORD for 'root'@'localhost'=PASSWORD('the_new_mysql_root_password');
```

Now, tell MySQL to put the new privileges into effect:

```
mysql> FLUSH PRIVILEGES;
```

and exit the monitor:

```
mysql> QUIT
```

You can now restart the server normally.

Exercises

1. What's the difference between a local and a remote user?

2. When would you grant only read access to a user?

3. Write a GRANT statement to create a user, rowena, who has privileges to execute SELECT, UPDATE, and INSERT statements on the contacts and appointment databases. The user should be allowed to access the server from machines in the domain *invyhome.com*.

4. Write a GRANT statement that modifies the privileges of the user rowena created in Question 3. Add privileges to SELECT from the customer table in the sales database, and to SELECT the debtor column from the invoice table in the accounts database.

5. Three GRANT statements have been issued on your MySQL server:

```
GRANT ALL ON *.* TO 'hugh'@'hugh.invyhome.com';
GRANT SELECT, UPDATE, INSERT, DELETE ON *.* TO 'hugh'@'*.invyhome.com';
GRANT SELECT ON *.* TO ''@'localhost';
```

For each of the following attempts to connect to the server, state whether the connection is allowed and, if so, which user the client is connected as. Assume all connections are attempted from localhost:

- `mysql --user=hugh --host=localhost`
- `mysql --user=fred`
- `mysql`

6. You've been employed to evaluate the security of a MySQL installation. Assuming that you're already satisfied with the security configuration from the physical and operating system perspective, list four things that you'd check about the MySQL server. For each item, explain why you would check it and what you would expect the outcome to be.

7. You've recently installed a wireless access point for visitors to your office and configured it so that machines that connect through it have IP addresses in the range 192.168.1.1 to 192.168.1.254. You've decided you want users who connect to your MySQL server from those IP addresses to have only the SELECT privilege on the contacts database. What steps do you take in your MySQL privilege tables to set this up?

## PART III

Advanced Topics

## CHAPTER 10

Backups and Recovery

If you suffer a crippling attack, or your server has technical problems, you should have backups that allow you to quickly get a server up and running with relatively up-to-date data. The simplest way to create backups is to shut down the MySQL server and make a copy of the data directory (we listed common locations for the data directory in "Server Doesn't Start" in Chapter 2) to a secure location, and copy it back if required.

With a Windows system, you can right-click on the data directory folder and select the menu option to create a compressed folder. On a Linux or Mac OS X system, you can make a compressed package of all the databases on the server by typing:

```
# tar zcf /tmp/`date +"%Y.%m.%d.%H.%M"`.MySQL_Backup.tgz mysql_data_directory
```

The backup file is created in the */tmp* directory. The segment `date +"%Y.%m.%d.%H.%M"` is a trick to include a timestamp in the filename. The resulting compressed file will have a name like *2006.08.16.06.08.MySQL_Backup.tgz*; an explicit record of the backup date and time is very useful when you need to recover data from a particular point in time.

The MySQL server must be stopped when you make a backup in this way, since you want the files on disk to be up-to-date and consistent. For a home user, this is inconvenient; for a production database, such downtime can be very disruptive and should be avoided when possible.

In this chapter, we explain alternative approaches to backing up and restoring your MySQL databases, and how to configure regular automatic backups. We also explain how to check and repair damaged database tables. Finally, we show how you can re-create a damaged `mysql` database.

Dumping a Database as SQL Statements

You can make a database backup by generating a file of all the SQL commands necessary to re-create the existing database structure from scratch, and (if you want) the SQL commands to insert all the data. Note that this is different from exporting table contents using the `SELECT INTO OUTFILE` syntax that we saw in "Writing Data into Comma-

Delimited Files" in Chapter 8 since we get the actual SQL INSERT statements, rather than just the raw values.

SQL statements are an excellent form of backup. One of the easiest ways to safely back up your data is to export it from MySQL, write it to stable media (such as a high-quality recordable CD or DVD), and store it in a safe location. Since the file of SQL statements contains just text, it can be compressed to a fraction of its original size using a compression program. Suitable compression programs on Linux or Mac OS X are gzip, bzip2, or zip; you can also use the StuffIt program under Mac OS X. Under Windows, you can compress a file by right-clicking on the file icon and selecting "Send To" and then "Compressed (zipped) Folder." You can also use third-party tools such as WinZip and PKZIP.

Let's try a simple example to back up the music database. To do this, we'll run the mysqldump utility and save the output to the file *music.sql*:

```
$ mysqldump --user=root --password=the_mysql_root_password \
--result-file=music.sql music
```

This tries to create the file *music.sql* in the current directory. If you don't have permission to write to the current directory, specify a path to another location—for example, */tmp/music.sql* under Linux or Mac OS X, or *C:\music.sql* under Windows.

Now open this *music.sql* file using a text editor; if you're unsure about how to do this, see the instructions in "Using a Text Editor." In the file, you'll see something like this:

```
-- MySQL dump 10.10
--
-- Host: localhost    Database: music
-- ------------------------------------------------------
-- Server version    5.0.22

/*!40101 SET @OLD_CHARACTER_SET_CLIENT=@@CHARACTER_SET_CLIENT */;
/*!40101 SET @OLD_CHARACTER_SET_RESULTS=@@CHARACTER_SET_RESULTS */;
/*!40101 SET @OLD_COLLATION_CONNECTION=@@COLLATION_CONNECTION */;
/*!40101 SET NAMES utf8 */;
/*!40103 SET @OLD_TIME_ZONE=@@TIME_ZONE */;
/*!40103 SET TIME_ZONE='+00:00' */;
/*!40014 SET @OLD_UNIQUE_CHECKS=@@UNIQUE_CHECKS, UNIQUE_CHECKS=0 */;
/*!40014 SET @OLD_FOREIGN_KEY_CHECKS=@@FOREIGN_KEY_CHECKS, FOREIGN_KEY_CHECKS=0 */;
/*!40101 SET @OLD_SQL_MODE=@@SQL_MODE, SQL_MODE='NO_AUTO_VALUE_ON_ZERO' */;
/*!40111 SET @OLD_SQL_NOTES=@@SQL_NOTES, SQL_NOTES=0 */;


--
-- Table structure for table `album`
--

DROP TABLE IF EXISTS `album`;
CREATE TABLE `album` (
  `artist_id` smallint(5) NOT NULL default '0',
  `album_id` smallint(4) NOT NULL default '0',
  `album_name` char(128) default NULL,
  PRIMARY KEY (`artist_id`,`album_id`)
```

```
) ENGINE=MyISAM DEFAULT CHARSET=latin1;

--
-- Dumping data for table `album`
--


/*!40000 ALTER TABLE `album` DISABLE KEYS */;
LOCK TABLES `album` WRITE;
INSERT INTO `album` VALUES (2,1,'Let Love In'),(1,1,'Retro - John McCready FAN'),
  (1,2,'Substance (Disc 2)'),(1,3,'Retro - Miranda Sawyer POP'),
  (1,4,'Retro - New Order / Bobby Gillespie LIVE'),(3,1,'Live Around The World'),
  (3,2,'In A Silent Way'),(1,5,'Power, Corruption & Lies'),
  (4,1,'Exile On Main Street'),(1,6,'Substance 1987 (Disc 1)'),
  (5,1,'Second Coming'),(6,1,'Light Years'),(1,7,'Brotherhood');
UNLOCK TABLES;
/*!40000 ALTER TABLE `album` ENABLE KEYS */;

--
-- Table structure for table `artist`
--

DROP TABLE IF EXISTS `artist`;
CREATE TABLE `artist` (
  `artist_id` smallint(5) NOT NULL default '0',
  `artist_name` char(128) default NULL,
  PRIMARY KEY  (`artist_id`)
) ENGINE=MyISAM DEFAULT CHARSET=latin1;

--
-- Dumping data for table `artist`
--


/*!40000 ALTER TABLE `artist` DISABLE KEYS */;
LOCK TABLES `artist` WRITE;
INSERT INTO `artist` VALUES (1,'New Order'),(2,'Nick Cave & The Bad Seeds'),
  (3,'Miles Davis'),(4,'The Rolling Stones'),(5,'The Stone Roses'),
  (6,'Kylie Minogue');
UNLOCK TABLES;
/*!40000 ALTER TABLE `artist` ENABLE KEYS */;

--
-- Table structure for table `played`
--

DROP TABLE IF EXISTS `played`;
CREATE TABLE `played` (
  `artist_id` smallint(5) NOT NULL default '0',
  `album_id` smallint(4) NOT NULL default '0',
  `track_id` smallint(3) NOT NULL default '0',
  `played` timestamp NOT NULL default CURRENT_TIMESTAMP on update
  CURRENT_TIMESTAMP,
  PRIMARY KEY  (`artist_id`,`album_id`,`track_id`,`played`)
) ENGINE=MyISAM DEFAULT CHARSET=latin1;
```

```
--
-- Dumping data for table `played`
--


/*!40000 ALTER TABLE `played` DISABLE KEYS */;
LOCK TABLES `played` WRITE;
INSERT INTO `played` VALUES
  (1,3,0,'2006-08-14 00:21:03'),(1,3,1,'2006-08-14 00:25:22'),
  (1,3,2,'2006-08-14 00:30:25'),(1,3,3,'2006-08-14 00:36:54'),
  (1,3,4,'2006-08-14 00:41:43'),(1,3,5,'2006-08-14 00:43:37'),
  (1,3,6,'2006-08-14 00:47:21'),(1,3,7,'2006-08-14 00:54:02'),
  (3,1,0,'2006-08-15 04:00:03'),(3,1,1,'2006-08-15 04:26:12'),
  (3,1,2,'2006-08-15 04:33:57');
UNLOCK TABLES;
/*!40000 ALTER TABLE `played` ENABLE KEYS */;


--
-- Table structure for table `track`
--

DROP TABLE IF EXISTS `track`;
CREATE TABLE `track` (
  `track_id` smallint(3) NOT NULL default '0',
  `track_name` char(128) default NULL,
  `artist_id` smallint(5) NOT NULL default '0',
  `album_id` smallint(4) NOT NULL default '0',
  `time` time default NULL,
  PRIMARY KEY  (`artist_id`,`album_id`,`track_id`)
) ENGINE=MyISAM DEFAULT CHARSET=latin1;


--
-- Dumping data for table `track`
--


/*!40000 ALTER TABLE `track` DISABLE KEYS */;
LOCK TABLES `track` WRITE;
INSERT INTO `track` VALUES (0,'Do You Love Me?',2,1,'00:05:95'),
  (1,'Nobody''s Baby Now',2,1,'00:03:87'),(2,'Loverman',2,1,'00:06:37'),
  (3,'Jangling Jack',2,1,'00:02:78'),(4,'Red Right Hand',2,1,'00:06:18'),
  (5,'I Let Love In',2,1,'00:04:25'),(6,'Thirsty Dog',2,1,'00:03:81'),
  ...
UNLOCK TABLES;
/*!40000 ALTER TABLE `track` ENABLE KEYS */;
/*!40103 SET TIME_ZONE=@OLD_TIME_ZONE */;

/*!40101 SET SQL_MODE=@OLD_SQL_MODE */;
/*!40014 SET FOREIGN_KEY_CHECKS=@OLD_FOREIGN_KEY_CHECKS */;
/*!40014 SET UNIQUE_CHECKS=@OLD_UNIQUE_CHECKS */;
/*!40101 SET CHARACTER_SET_CLIENT=@OLD_CHARACTER_SET_CLIENT */;
/*!40101 SET CHARACTER_SET_RESULTS=@OLD_CHARACTER_SET_RESULTS */;
/*!40101 SET COLLATION_CONNECTION=@OLD_COLLATION_CONNECTION */;
/*!40111 SET SQL_NOTES=@OLD_SQL_NOTES */;
```

As we explained in Chapter 5 in "Exploring Databases and Tables with SHOW and mysqlshow," the text between the /*! ... */ symbols contains MySQL-specific instructions. Notice several features in this dump file:

- CREATE TABLE statements for all tables in the database that are identical to the output of SHOW CREATE TABLE.
- DROP TABLE statements that precede each CREATE TABLE statement. These allow you to load the file into your MySQL database without error, even when the tables already exist; of course, you'll lose any data that may already be on the server in this table of the database.
- INSERT statements that add all of the data to the tables. There's only such statement per table, that is, the rows are each parenthesized and comma-separated.
- LOCK TABLES and UNLOCK TABLES statements. These ensure that you're the only user modifying or using a table when you're inserting the data, and they also speed up the inserts. We discuss locking briefly in "Transactions and Locking" in Chapter 7.

You'll also notice two missing features:

- There's no CREATE DATABASE statement to set up the database.
- There's no USE statement that selects the database.

Fortunately, you can use command-line parameters to customize what mysqldump does. We'll show you some examples next. You might find that your mysqldump output doesn't exactly match what we've stated here, but don't worry; the defaults change over time, and everything can be customized.

mysqldump Options

The mysqldump program has options to control whether tables should be locked when making the dump, whether restoring a dump should overwrite any existing tables, and so on. These options can be appended as parameters, just like the user and password options for the username and password, respectively. Here's a list of the most useful options, but the default settings should be sufficient for most cases:

add-drop-table
  Includes a DROP TABLE statement for each table, ensuring that any existing table data is removed before the dump is restored.

add-locks
  Includes a LOCK TABLES statement before each data INSERT statement, and a corresponding UNLOCK TABLES statement afterward. Helps speed up data restoration from the dump file.

all-databases
> Creates a dump of all databases on the server. This means you don't have to supply any database names on the command line. We'll show you an example of this later in this section.

create-options
> Includes MySQL-specific information such as ENGINE and CHARSET in the table creation statements.

databases
> Create a dump of the specified databases. This also ensures—even if you list only one database—that CREATE DATABASE and USE statements are added to the output.

disable-keys
> Tells MySQL to disable index updates during the INSERT operations for MyISAM tables; the index is created after all the data has been loaded, which is more efficient.

extended-insert
> Combines INSERT statements so that each statement inserts multiple table rows; this helps speed up data restoration.

flush-logs
> Flushes the server logs before dumping the data. This is useful in conjunction with incremental backups, as described later in "The Binary Log."

lock-tables
> Locks all the tables in a database for the duration of the dump so that the dump is a consistent snapshot.

no-data
> Dumps only the information necessary to re-create the database structure and leaves out the data; the dump file will have no INSERT statements.

opt
> This option, which is enabled by default from MySQL version 4.1 onwards, enables the options add-drop-table, add-locks, create-options, disable-keys, extended-insert, lock-tables, quick, and set-charset. You can disable all these by using the skip-opt option, or you can disable individual options by adding the prefix skip- in front of them; for example, to disable add-locks, you'd write skip-add-locks. However, they're all sensible defaults that you're likely to want in most cases.

quick
> Prevents mysqldump from buffering tables in memory before writing to the file; this speeds up dumps from large tables.

result-file
> Specifies the name of the output dump file, where the SQL commands are stored.

set-charset
> Specifies the character set—for example, latin1 or utf8—used by the database.

`tables`
> Creates a dump of the specified database tables.

`where`
> Dumps only records meeting a specified `WHERE` clause.

You can use `mysqldump` in four main ways (assume you want to get the database dump in the file *outputfile.sql*):

- To make a backup of all the databases on a MySQL server, use the command:

```
$ mysqldump --user=root --password=the_mysql_root_password \
  --result-file=outputfile.sql --all-databases
```

This dumps `CREATE DATABASE`, `USE`, `CREATE TABLE`, and `INSERT` statements for all data in all databases that are accessible by the user `root`. If you specify a user other than `root`, the output is affected by the privileges of that user.

- To make a backup of specific databases, use the command:

```
$ mysqldump --user=root --password=the_mysql_root_password \
  --result-file=outputfile.sql --databases database_name
```

This dumps `CREATE DATABASE`, `CREATE TABLE`, and `INSERT` statements for only the specified databases. Use this if you want a `CREATE DATABASE` statement, in preference to the variant we showed you at the beginning of this section.

You can list several databases one after the other in the command. For example, to dump the `music` and `wedding` databases, you would type:

```
$ mysqldump --user=root --password=the_mysql_root_password \
  --result-file=outputfile.sql --databases music wedding
```

- To make a backup of specific tables from a database, use the command:

```
$ mysqldump --user=root --password=the_mysql_root_password \
  --result-file=outputfile.sql database_name table_name
```

You can list several tables, one after the other, in the command.

- To make a backup of specific data from a table in a database, use the command:

```
$ mysqldump --user=root --password=the_mysql_root_password \
  --result-file=outputfile.sql database_name table_name where=where_clause
```

For example, to use the `artist` table of the `music` database, and dump SQL statements for all the artists having a name beginning with "N", you would write:

```
$ mysqldump --user=root --password=the_mysql_root_password \
  --result-file=outputfile.sql \
  --where="artist_name like 'N%'" \
  music artist
```

Loading Data from an SQL Dump File

The previous section showed you how to back up your databases. Let's see how to restore them from those backups.

To load the structures and data in a dump file, you can tell the MySQL monitor to read in the SQL commands from the file:

```
mysql> SOURCE dumpfile.sql
```

Alternatively, you can simply run the MySQL monitor in batch mode and execute the instructions in the dump file:

```
$ mysql mysql_options < dumpfile.sql
```

We don't recommend this approach, as it's a little less portable than the SOURCE command; more importantly, it doesn't show you any error and warning messages as the SQL statements are processed.

If the backup file doesn't have CREATE DATABASE and USE statements, you'll need to type these into the monitor before you read in the dump file, or add them to the dump file if you want to run the monitor in batch mode. A good step prior to carrying out a restore operation is to inspect the backup file with a text editor. Once you've inspected the file, you can decide whether you need to drop and re-create databases, use databases whether you need to take any other steps prior to a restore operation. Of course, you can use the mysqldump options to control what's written to the dump file when it's created.

You previously backed up the music database to the file *music.sql*. The way you did this didn't include any CREATE DATABASE and USE statements in the dump file, so you need to use the monitor to enter these yourself.

Start the monitor as the root user:

```
$ mysql --user=root --password=the_mysql_root_password
```

Now, drop the existing music database:

```
mysql> DROP DATABASE music;
```

and create a new (empty) database with the same name:

```
mysql> CREATE DATABASE music;
```

Then select the music database as the active database:

```
mysql> USE music;
```

Now you can restore the data by reading in the *music.sql* dump file:

```
mysql> SOURCE music.sql;
```

If your *music.sql* file isn't in the current directory, you should specify the full path. If you used our earlier suggestions in "Dumping a Database as SQL Statements," this

---

path would be */tmp/music.sql* under Linux or Mac OS X, and *C:\music.sql* under Windows.

mysqlhotcopy

If you want to create a copy of a database on the same host as the server, and all the tables in your database are of the MyISAM (or the older ISAM) type, then you may find `mysqlhotcopy` handy. This is a Perl script file that's in the *scripts* directory, and differs from `mysqldump` in that it's a *binary* copy, so you get the MySQL database files, not a text file of SQL statements, after copying. It's also faster.

You may wonder why you need a special command to copy the database files. After all, they're already there in the `data` directory, and you could use the operating system copy command (e.g., `cp` or `copy`) to copy them. The problem is that if the server is running, what you have on disk is not always consistent with the status according to the MySQL server. The `mysqlhotcopy` command takes care of the locking needed to ensure that the copies are consistent, even if the server is running.

Let's look at an example that copies the database `music` to the database `music_bak`:

```
# mysqlhotcopy --user=root --password=the_mysql_root_password music music_bak
Locked 4 tables in 0 seconds.
Flushed tables (`music`.`album`, `music`.`artist`, `music`.`played`, `music`.`track`)
  in 0 seconds.
Copying 13 files...
Copying indices for 0 files...
Unlocked tables.
mysqlhotcopy copied 4 tables (13 files) in 1 second (1 seconds overall).
```

There are two things worth mentioning here. First, the server has to be running when you run `mysqlhotcopy`. Second, you must have operating-system-level access to the database files. For example, you would need to be logged in as the user who owns the MySQL *data* directory (this could be you, or the `mysql` user), or as the system root user.

Note that `mysqlhotcopy` is a Perl script, and you'll need to follow the instructions in "Installing Perl modules under Windows" in Chapter 2 to use this on Windows. Linux and Mac OS X users should be able to use this script without problems.

To restore a database from the backup copy, you should stop the server, copy the backup directory to the MySQL data directory, and restart the server. To restore all databases on a server, you'll need backups of all the individual databases, as well as the `mysql` grants database.

Scheduling Backups

We all forget to do backups, and as Murphy's Law would have it: "The hard drive on your computer will crash only when it contains vital information that has not been backed up" (for this and other interesting variations on Murphy's Law, see *http://www*

.murphys-laws.com). In this section, we'll describe how you can configure automatic, regular backups using `mysqldump`; you can also use `mysqlhotcopy` if you wish.

Linux and Mac OS X

Under Linux and Mac OS X, you can list the commands you want to be executed in a *crontab* file; commands in the *crontab* file are run at the times you specify. First, you have to edit a *crontab* file:

```
$ crontab -e
```

This opens the crontab file for the current user for editing; the default editor on most systems is `vi`. If you're not comfortable with this editor, you can specify your preferred editor by setting the `EDITOR` variable to the name of your favorite editor. For example, many novice users find the `pico` editor somewhat easier to use:

```
$ export EDITOR=pico
$ crontab -e
```

The general format of a *crontab* entry is:

```
MINUTE  HOUR  DAY  MONTH  DAYOFTHEWEEK  COMMAND
```

If you want a dump to be created from a particular database using the `mysqldump` command at 4:45 A.M. every Sunday, you can add the line:

```
45 4  *  *  sun /usr/local/mysql/bin/mysqldump \
  --user=root \
  --password=the_mysql_root_password \
  --result-file=path_to_backup_file \
  database_to_dump
```

Note that each entry must be on one line, and you must specify full paths to executables; the cron program might not inherit your path settings.

SQL files have a lot of repeating information that can be highly compressed. You can create compressed SQL files by passing the `mysqldump` output to the `gzip` compression program:

```
45 4  *  *  sun /usr/local/mysql/bin/mysqldump \
  --user=root \
  --password=the_mysql_root_password \
  database_to_dump \
  | gzip --best --to-stdout \
  > dump_directory/`date +"%Y.%m.%d.%H.%M"`.MySQL_Backup.sql.gz
```

Here, we've left out the `result-file` option so that the `mysqldump` output is passed directly to the standard output (normally the screen), rather than to a file. The pipe symbol (|) then sends this output to the `gzip` compression program. The `best` option tells `gzip` to compress the data as much as possible, while the `to-stdout` option tells `gzip` to pass its own output to the standard output. Finally, the greater-than symbol (>) redirects this compressed data into a file. We've included the string:

```
`date +"%Y.%m.%d.%H.%M"`
```

as part of the result filename so that the filename includes a timestamp. The resulting compressed SQL dump file will be given a name like *2006.08.16.06.08.MySQL_Backup.sql.gz*;

Check that your changes have been saved by typing **crontab -l** (the "l" stands for list). It's also useful to first test the command yourself from the shell prompt. When entering the command in the *crontab* file, use a time that's near so that you can monitor that things are working as you expect. There are few things more depressing than finding that your regular backups weren't being done properly, and that you can't recover your lost data. You can edit the file again later and set the regular backup times you actually require.

Any output messages from the automatic execution are generally emailed to the *cron tab* owner; you can specify a different address by defining the `MAILTO` variable at the top of your *crontab* file:

```
MAILTO=your_email_address
```

Windows XP

Under Windows XP, you can add a scheduled task by selecting Scheduled Tasks by opening the Windows Control Panel, selecting the "Performance and Maintenance" entry, and choosing Scheduled Tasks. If you have Classic View enabled, you can choose Scheduled Tasks directly from the Windows Control Panel. Select Add Scheduled Task, browse to the MySQL *bin* directory, and select *mysqldump.exe*. Select how frequently you want to run this program; at the end of the configuration process, select the check-box for "Open advanced properties for this task when I click Finish," and then click the Finish button. In the Run tab, type in the full command below. When prompted to specify your password, enter your Windows password. Note that scheduled tasks don't run if you don't have a password set for your Windows account:

```
"C:\Program Files\MySQL\MySQL Server 5.0\bin\mysqldump.exe" \
--user=root \
--password=the_mysql_root_password \
--result-file=C:\outputfile.sql \
database_name
```

Under Windows Vista, take the following steps. Open the Windows Control Panel, and select the "System and Maintenance" entry, and then select the Administrative Tools. If you have Classic View enabled, choose Administrative Tools directly from the Control Panel. From the Administrative Tools, choose the Task Scheduler entry. Windows may prompt you for authorization—click Continue.

From the Task Schedule window, choose the Create Task entry from the Actions menu on the right. A dialog box will open with several tabs at the top. On the first tab (General), enter a name for the new task—for example, "MySQL daily dumps."

Select the next tab (Triggers); click the "New..." button, and select the backup schedule you want—for example, "Daily at 3.20 AM"—and click the OK button. Select the next tab (Actions); click the "New..." button, and ensure that the Action drop-down list is set to "Start a program." In the "Program/script" text box, type in the full command from before; you can use the Browse button to find select the *mysqldump.exe* program, and then you can add the user, password, database, and result-file options yourself. Click the OK button to close the New Action dialog box, and then again to close the Create Task window. Your new task should now appear in the list of Active Tasks.

General Backup Tips

The frequency of your backups depends on how often data updates occur in your application, and how valuable those updates are to your organization. For example, you might be able to absorb the loss of some or all user comments on your hobby blog, but not the sales data for your high-throughput online store, or a university student-marks database.

When you're backing up a database, it's wise to ensure that MySQL isn't being used by other users. This allows you to get a consistent backup, where all operations that have been intended to run have completed. You can ensure single-user access by having `mysqldump` lock the tables using the `lock-tables` or the `opt` option. If for some reason you can't lock the database, don't be overly concerned: having a near-perfect backup is usually much better than no backup at all.

Make sure that the backup ends up on stable media—such as flash memory or a high-quality writable CD or DVD—and that the stable media isn't stored with the computer. There's little point in storing a backup on the same disk as the MySQL databases, since the backup would disappear with the databases in case of a disk failure. There's also little point in storing the backup on a computer, CD, or flash memory device nearby, since theft or destruction would result in the loss of everything. Get in the habit of storing your backup offsite; we sometimes swap backups with family members who live nearby, and often leave a home backup at work. Alternatively, copy your backups to a trustworthy online storage site; a simple web search for "online storage service" turns up many low-cost and free services.

Take care to regularly check that your backups are occurring correctly and are usable. Often, the only time people look at their backups is when they need them, and there are few things as frustrating as finding that the backups you desperately need have not been generated correctly due to a problem such as a full backup device.

Finally, remember to treat the security of your backups with the same seriousness as you do the server; an attacker could get access to your company's sensitive data by simply stealing a backup DVD from your home. Think carefully before you trust any person or organization with your valuable data.

The Binary Log

An update log contains all the information needed to re-create any changes to the database since the server was started or the logs were flushed; this feature allows you to always have an up-to-date backup of your database. You can keep a list of every SQL query that changes data on the server by passing the `log-bin` option to the MySQL server (`mysqld_safe`, `mysqld-nt.exe`, or `mysqld`).

If no preferred name and directory is specified for the logfile, the server will use the file *<hostname>-bin* in the MySQL data directory. Individual logfiles will have the extensions *.000001*, *.000002*, and so on; any extensions you specify to the `log-bin` option are ignored. For example, on a machine with the hostname `eden`, the binary logfiles are typically named *eden-bin.000001*, *eden-bin.000002*, and so on. It's also common to see the word *mysql* used in place of the hostname. The update log is saved in a compact binary format; prior to MySQL version 5.0, the `log-update` option would save an update log in text format. However, the text format is deprecated and is treated the same as `log-bin` in MySQL 5.0 and later.

When the server is shut down, it ensures that all modifications to data have been written (*flushed*) to the binary log. The next time the server is started, it opens a new logfile alongside the old one with an incremented number in the extension. For example, the current binary logfile might be called *eden-bin.000012*; after the server is restarted, it creates the new logfile *eden-bin.000013* to log all modifications to the database since the restart. The logs can be manually flushed at any time using the `FLUSH LOGS` command in the monitor, or the `mysqladmin flush-logs` command from the command line.

You can view the SQL statements in the binary log by using the `msqlbinlog` command and specifying the full path to the binary logfile. For example, if on this system the MySQL data directory is */usr/lib/mysql/data*, you can view the contents of the binary logfile *eden-bin.000002* by typing:

```
# mysqlbinlog /usr/lib/mysql/data/eden-bin.000002
```

You'll need to have the necessary permissions to access the MySQL data directory and to read the binary logfile on your host system. You might see something like this when you open a logfile:

```
...
use music;
SET TIMESTAMP=1151221361;
SET @@session.foreign_key_checks=0, @@session.unique_checks=0;
SET @@session.sql_mode=524288;
/*!\C utf8 */;
SET @@session.character_set_client=33,@@session.collation_connection=33,
  @@session.collation_server=8;
DROP TABLE IF EXISTS `artist`;
# at 30551
#060625 17:42:41 server id 1  end_log_pos 30794          Query    thread_id=168
  exec_time=0      error_code=0
SET TIMESTAMP=1151221361;
```

```
CREATE TABLE `artist` (
`artist_id` smallint(5) NOT NULL default '0',
`artist_name` char(128) default NULL,
PRIMARY KEY (`artist_id`)
) ENGINE=MyISAM DEFAULT CHARSET=latin1;
# at 30794
#060625 17:42:41 server id 1  end_log_pos 30903          Query    thread_id=168
  exec_time=0      error_code=0
SET TIMESTAMP=1151221361;
...
```

Note that the text between the /*! ... */ symbols contains MySQL-specific instructions, as described in "Exploring Databases and Tables with SHOW and mysqlshow" in Chapter 5.

You should create regular dumps of the database using `mysqldump` with the `flush-logs` option. In the event of a disaster, you can follow the instructions described earlier in "Loading Data from an SQL Dump File" to restore the database to the state it was at the time you generated the dump file. You can then use `mysqlbinlog` to extract the SQL statements from all the binary logs, and the pipe symbol (|) to pass them to the monitor in batch mode:

```
# mysqlbinlog hostname-bin.* | mysql
```

The asterisk wildcard character (*) tells the operating system to read all the files that have names starting with *<hostname-bin>*.

Checking and Repairing Corrupted Tables

Problems such as running out of disk space or a power failure could cause your databases files to be corrupted; in these cases, the server will often not have written all transactions to disk. It's a good idea to check the tables before you start to use them again. Repairing tables will not guarantee that no data will be lost, but it does allow you to use the database again without losing any more data.

One way to check and repair tables is to use the CHECK TABLE and REPAIR TABLE commands from the monitor. For example, to check the `artist` table in the `music` database, you would write:

```
mysql> CHECK TABLE music.artist;
+--------------+-------+----------+------------------------------+
| Table        | Op    | Msg_type | Msg_text                     |
+--------------+-------+----------+------------------------------+
| music.artist | check | error    | Checksum for key:  1 doesn't |
|              |       |          |    match checksum for records|
| music.artist | check | error    | Corrupt                      |
+--------------+-------+----------+------------------------------+
2 rows in set (0.00 sec)
```

In this example, the table is damaged; you can repair it using the REPAIR TABLE command:

```
mysql> REPAIR TABLE music.artist;
+--------------+--------+-----------+----------+
| Table        | Op     | Msg_type  | Msg_text |
+--------------+--------+-----------+----------+
| music.artist | repair | status    | OK       |
+--------------+--------+-----------+----------+
1 row in set (0.00 sec)
```

If the music database was previously selected with the USE music command, you can write artist instead of music.artist.

The mysqlcheck and mysqlisamchk programs allow you to check and repair tables from the command line.

mysqlcheck

mysqlcheck allows you to check and repair tables from the command line. In practice, the most important options you'll need are:

all-databases
> Performs operation on all tables in all databases on the server.

repair
> Tries to repair any corrupted tables.

extended
> Tries harder to repair any corrupted tables (slower than just repair).

For example, to check and repair all tables in the music database, you would write:

```
$ mysqlcheck --user=root --password=the_mysql_root_password --repair music
music.album                                         OK
music.artist
warning  : Number of rows changed from 1 to 0
status   : OK
music.played                                        OK
music.track                                         OK
```

To check and attempt to repair all databases on the server, you would write:

```
$ mysqlcheck --user=root --password=the_mysql_root_password --extended --all-databases
```

myisamchk

This tool operates directly on the MyISAM database files, and so does not require the server to be shut down. However, you need to ensure that the server is not using the tables while you're trying to repair them; if you can't stop queries to the server, it's probably a good idea to shut down the server before using myisamchk.

To use this utility, you need to specify the table or index file you want to check or repair. For example, to check the artist table in the music database, give the path to the *artist.MYI* file:

```
$ myisamchk --check /var/lib/mysql/music/artist.MYI
Checking MyISAM  /var/lib/mysql/music/artist.MYI
Data records:       87   Deleted blocks:      0
- check file-size
- check record delete-chain
- check key delete-chain
- check index reference
- check data record references index: 1
myisamchk: error: Can't read indexpage from filepos: 1024
- check record links
myisamchk: error: Found wrong record at 0
MyISAM-table '/var/lib/mysql/music/artist.MYI' is corrupted
Fix it using switch "-r" or "-o"
```

Let's try to repair the table:

```
$ myisamchk --recover /var/lib/mysql/music/artist.MYI
- recovering (with sort) MyISAM-table '/var/lib/mysql/music/artist.MYI'
Data records: 87
- Fixing index 1
Key 1 - Found wrong stored record at 0
Found block with too small length at 3060; Skipped
Found block that points outside data file at 19024
Found block that points outside data file at 19824
Found block with too small length at 20052; Skipped
Found block with too small length at 20636; Skipped
Found block that points outside data file at 22860
Found block that points outside data file at 23344
Found block that points outside data file at 30836
Found block with too small length at 30980; Skipped
Found block that points outside data file at 32628
Found block that points outside data file at 32868
Found block that points outside data file at 33660
Found block that points outside data file at 33752
Data records: 0
```

Now, let's see if this had the desired effect:

```
$ myisamchk --check /var/lib/mysql/music/artist.MYI
Checking MyISAM  /var/lib/mysql/music/artist.MYI
Data records:        0   Deleted blocks:       0
- check file-size
- check record delete-chain
- check key delete-chain
- check index reference
- check data record references index: 1
- check record links
```

The error has been fixed, but, of course, some data could have been lost as a result of
the problem.

Re-Creating Damaged Grant Tables

If you cannot restore your `mysql` grants database from backup, you will need to create a fresh one. With Windows, you can extract the `mysql` directory from the installation package and place it under the MySQL *data* directory.

Under Linux or Mac OS X, you can use the *mysql_install_db* script to regenerate the `mysql` database and the privilege tables in it. This is particularly handy if your `mysql` database has somehow become corrupted. Note that if the `user` table has to be created, the `root` password for the server will be reset to the default value (blank).

If *mysql_install_db* isn't already in your system path, you can generally find it in the *scripts* directory under your MySQL installation directory. Run *mysql_install_db* the same way you ran it in Chapter 2. If you're not sure how to run the script, try logging in as the system superuser and running it with no parameters:

```
# mysql_install_db
```

or optionally with the `user=mysql` parameter so that MySQL is configured to run under the `mysql` system user account:

```
# mysql_install_db --user=mysql
```

Resources

To learn more about backing up MySQL databases, see the "Database Backups" section of the MySQL manual (*http://dev.mysql.com/doc/mysql/en/backup.html*).

Exercises

1. SQL dump files are often very large; why is this generally not a cause for worry?
2. Set up a weekly backup of all databases on your server.
3. For a production server, what time would you choose for your regular backups?
4. How can you recover modifications that have been made to your data since the last dump?
5. For an application where any loss of data is unacceptable, how would you choose the location of your binary logfile?

## CHAPTER 11

Using an Options File

Over the course of this book, you've seen that you can pass options to many of the programs and scripts that are part of the MySQL distribution. For example, you can pass the user and password options to the MySQL monitor. If you don't specify a value for an option, the default options are used. For example, most client programs try to use the default values localhost and 3306 for the server host and port options, respectively.

If you need to use an option value that's not the default, you have to specify it each time you run a program that needs that option; this is tedious and prone to errors. Fortunately, you can save option values to an *options file*, also sometimes called a *configuration file*, that most of the key MySQL programs and scripts can read. The programs that read options files include: myisamchk, myisampack, mysql, mysqladmin, mysqlbinlog, mysqlcc, mysqlcheck, mysqld, mysqld_safe, mysqldump, mysqlhotcopy, mysqlimport, mysql.server, and mysqlshow.

We'll start our tour of options files with an example using the MySQL monitor.

Configuring Options for the MySQL Monitor

Throughout this book, you've specified the user and password options when starting the monitor program:

```
$ mysql --user=root --password=the_mysql_root_password
Welcome to the MySQL monitor.  Commands end with ; or \g.
Your MySQL connection id is 486 to server version: 5.0.22

Type 'help;' or '\h' for help. Type '\c' to clear the buffer.

mysql>
```

You can save yourself some typing by storing the username and password in an options file and placing it in a location where the monitor will look. The monitor will automatically read in the option values from the file instead of asking you.

In the options file, we specify the program that we're interested in—here, it's `mysql` for the MySQL monitor—and then list each option on a line of its own:

```
[mysql]
user=root
password=the_mysql_root_password
```

If you're using a Linux or Mac OS X system, type these lines using a text editor and save it with the name *.my.cnf* in your home directory (*~/.my.cnf*). Under Windows, save this file with the name *my.cnf* in the root of the *C:* drive (*C:\my.cnf*). You can now start the monitor without providing the username and password options; the values are read in automatically from the options file:

```
$ mysql
Welcome to the MySQL monitor.  Commands end with ; or \g.
Your MySQL connection id is 486 to server version: 5.0.22

Type 'help;' or '\h' for help. Type '\c' to clear the buffer.

mysql>
```

This is very convenient! Unfortunately, we now have to spoil the fun and note that it's generally not a good idea to store passwords unencrypted (in *plain-text*); at the very least, you should ensure that only you can read (and write) the file. On a Linux or Mac OS X server, you can use the `chmod` command to do this:

```
$ chmod u=rw,g=,o= ~/.my.cnf
```

We discuss permission settings in "Restricting access to files and directories" in Chapter 2. The trade-off between convenience and security is a recurring theme in discussions of protection of systems and data. You need to assess the requirements of each individual application.

Let's look at another example. Say you want to use the MySQL monitor to connect to a MySQL server running on port 57777 of the host *sadri.learningmysql.com*, and wish to use the `music` database on this server. For this database, we have the MySQL account name `allmusic` and the password *the_password*. The command to start the monitor would be (all on one line):

```
$ mysql \
  --host=sadri.learningmysql.com \
  --port=57777 \
  --user=allmusic \
  --password=the_password \
  --database=music
```

This can be tiresome to type all the time, so you could save these values in the options file as:

```
[mysql]
host=sadri.learningmysql.com
port=57777
user=allmusic
```

```
password=the_password
database=music
```

If you're concerned about security, you can omit specifying a password and simply write the option password:

```
[mysql]
host=sadri.learningmysql.com
port=57777
user=allmusic
password
database=music
```

This way, the monitor knows that you want to use a password, and it'll prompt you for the password before trying to connect to the server.

Structure of the Options File

We saw in the last section how you can specify options for the MySQL monitor. An options file can have a section for each program that uses it. For example, you can have a [mysql] section for the mysql program and a [mysqldump] section for the mysqldump program. Similarly, you can have a [mysqld] section for the MySQL server daemons mysqld, mysqld_safe, and mysqld-nt.

Where options are common to all client programs, they can be consolidated under a [client] section. Similarly, options common to all server programs can be listed under a [server] section.

Be careful not to make program options too generic. For example, the mysql program is a client and takes a database option. However, mysqladmin and mysqlshow are examples of client programs that don't understand this option. If you include the database option in the [client] section, like this:

```
[client]
database=music
```

these programs will just complain and quit, as below:

```
$ mysqladmin status
mysqladmin: unknown variable 'database=music'
```

You should include the database option in a separate group for the [mysql] program, rather than including it in the [client] group.

Let's look at a more interesting options file:

```
[server]
user=mysql
port=57777

basedir=/usr/local/mysql-standard-5.0.22-linux-i686

socket=/home/mysql/server1.sock
```

```
datadir=/home/mysql/data
tmpdir=/home/mysql/tmp
pid_file=/home/mysql/logs/server1.pid

# log server messages to:
log=/home/mysql/logs/server1.main.log

# log errors to this
log_error=/home/mysql/logs/server1.error.log

# log updates to this binary logfile
log_bin=/home/mysql/logs/server1_updates.bin

[client]
socket=/home/mysql/server1.sock

[mysql]
database=mysql

[mysqldump]
all-databases
result_file=/tmp/dump.sql
```

There are four groups here: one for the server, one for all clients, one for the `mysql` program, and one for the `mysqldump` program. The latter two are both clients, but the options we want to list in the file aren't common to all clients, so we list them separately.

If an option appears for two applicable groups (for example `[client]` and `[mysql]`), the more specific setting (here, for `[mysql]`) takes precedence.

Lines starting with the hash or pound symbol (#) are ignored; this allows you to add comments to the configuration file to explain entries. Blank lines are also ignored.

Scope of Options

The directives in an options file can apply at different levels depending on where the options file is located:

System-wide

Settings apply for all MySQL programs on the system.

The default location for a system-wide options file is */etc/my.cnf* for Linux or Mac OS X systems. Under Linux and Mac OS X, the MySQL server and client programs automatically read in an options file at the default location.

For a Windows system, the possible configuration file paths are *<Windows_Directory>\my.ini*, *<Windows_Directory>\my.cnf*, *C:\my.ini*, and *C:\my.cnf*. The *<Windows_Directory>* is the directory Windows is installed in, typically *C:\Windows*. Under Windows, current versions of the MySQL server (version 4.1.5 and above) don't actually read in an options file by default, so you should always specify one as we discuss in the section on server-wide options. Note that Windows *client* programs do read in any existing options files.

Server-specific
Settings apply for the MySQL programs in a particular installation.

The default location for a server-specific options file is *<MySQL_directory>/ my.cnf* for Linux and Mac OS X, and *<MySQL_directory>\my.ini* for Windows.

The options file is sometimes placed in the data directory, but this is not recommended for two reasons: first, it won't work if you don't use the default location of data directory specified when the MySQL installation was compiled. Second, the data directory must be readable by any client programs (and therefore by other users on the system) that need to see the options file. It's better that access to the data directory be limited to only the server, so it's best to keep the options file elsewhere.

Under Windows, the MySQL installation process places a *my.ini* options file in the MySQL directory. When MySQL is installed as a Windows service, the location of this options file is also specified; a typical service entry is:

```
"C:\Program Files\MySQL\MySQL Server 5.0\bin\mysqld-nt"
 --defaults-file="C:\Program Files\MySQL\MySQL Server 5.0\my.ini"
```

If you want to use a different options file location, you'll need to change the service entry. For example, you could ask your server to read in the options file *C:\my.cnf* by specifying the service as:

```
"C:\Program Files\MySQL\MySQL Server 5.0\bin\mysqld-nt"
 --defaults-file="C:\my.cnf"
```

If you want to start the server from the command line instead of using the Windows service, you'll need to specify the path to the options file; you can use the same file or a different one. For example, you could ask your server to read in the options file *C:\my.cnf* as follows:

```
C:\> mysqld-nt --defaults-file="C:\my.cnf"
```

User-specific
Settings apply for the MySQL programs run by a particular user.

The default location of a user-specific options file on a Linux or Mac OS X system is the file *.my.cnf* located in the user's home directory—that is, *~/.my.cnf*. There is currently no support for user-specific options files under Windows.

Search Order for Options Files

The MySQL server and client programs look for options files in the standard locations and read them in order; values from later files take precedence over earlier ones. Options specified on the command line override values from options files.

You can tell a MySQL program to ignore the default options files by telling it to read a specific file at a location given with the `defaults-file` option. For example, you can write:

```
$ mysql --defaults-file=path_to_options_file
```

If you'd like to use an options file *alongside* the default files, you can specify it using the `defaults-extra-file` option:

```
$ mysql --defaults-extra-file=path_to_local_options_file
```

Finally, you can prevent programs from reading in any options files by adding the `no-defaults` option:

```
$ mysql --no-defaults
```

On a Linux or Mac OS X system, the search order is */etc/my.cnf*, then *<MySQL_Directory>/my.cnf*, `defaults-extra-file`, and finally *~/.my.cnf*. Note that for security reasons, files that are world-writable are ignored. A generally appropriate permission setting is for the file owner (user) to be able to read and write the file, but for the group and others to be able to only read the file. You can set this level of access by opening a terminal window and typing:

```
$ chmod u=rw,g=r,o=r configuration_file
```

Note that if you're trying to change the permissions of a file owned by the system root user, you'll need to run the `chmod` command when logged in as the system root user, or prefix the command with the `sudo` keyword.

On a Windows system, clients try to access options files in this order: first *<Windows_Directory>\my.ini*, then *<Windows_Directory>\my.cnf*, *C:\my.ini*, *C:\my.cnf*, *<MySQL_directory>\my.ini*, *<MySQL_directory>\my.cnf* and then `defaults-extra-file`. Again, under Windows, the server doesn't read in the options file automatically, and you need to tell it to do so using the `defaults-file` option.

Determining the Options in Effect

It can sometimes be unclear which options are in effect for a given program, particularly if you've got several options files with overlapping directives. You can use the `print-defaults` option to most MySQL programs to see the options in effect. For example, to see the active options for `mysqldump`, you can type:

```
$ mysqldump --print-defaults
mysqldump would have been started with the following arguments:
--socket=/home/mysql/server1.sock
--all-databases
--result_file=/tmp/dump.sql
--host=localhost
--port=3306
--database=Music
--result_file=/home/saied/dump.sql
```

You can get a similar effect using the `my_print_defaults` program and specifying the command groups you're interested in. For example, to see the settings for all clients and for the `mysqldump` program, you can type:

```
$ my_print_defaults client mysqldump
--socket=/home/mysql/server1.sock
--all-databases
--result_file=/tmp/dump.sql
--host=localhost
--port=3306
--database=Music
--result_file=/home/saied/dump.sql
```

Exercises

1. What issues would you consider before storing your password in an options file?

2. On a Linux or Mac OS X system, under what circumstances would the [`server`] section of the *~/.my.cnf* options file be read?

3. How can you tell what options a program uses by default?

## CHAPTER 12

Configuring and Tuning the Server

The MySQL server has many features that can be configured to best fit the needs of your system hardware and application. The default settings are fine for most applications, but there are a few that you should be aware of. In this chapter, we look at how you can modify server configuration to suit your setup and for improved overall performance.

There are two types of MySQL program settings: options, which dictate what a program should do, and variables, which dictate the amount of resources that should be set aside for different tasks. Options and variables can be server-wide (global) or limited to a single client session. Some variables apply to the server, while others apply to individual processes, or *threads*, that handle queries. Resources are generally allocated to a thread only if it requires them. Options and variables can be specified in an options file, or from the command line when starting a program.

You don't have to come up with optimal settings for each setting on your server. There are ready-to-use configuration files in the *support-files* directory under the MySQL directory. The *my-medium.conf* file includes recommended settings for most applications and server configurations; other distributed configuration file variants are tailored for "small," "large," and "huge" installations. You can use one of these files as a starting point for your customizations. On a Linux or Mac OS X system, you can copy the file you want to a standard location so that it will be read by the server; on a Windows system, you will have to explicitly tell the server to read in the file. Let's look at the server options in more detail.

The MySQL Server Daemon

The main MySQL server program, or *MySQL server daemon*, is called `mysqld`. Under Windows, there are two main programs you can use: *mysqld-nt.exe*—which is optimized for Windows XP, 2000, and NT (and probably soon, for Vista)—and *mysqld.exe*, which can work on older versions of Windows.

On Linux or Mac OS X, the recommended way to start the `mysqld` program is by calling the `mysqld_safe` script. This in turn starts `mysqld` or, if it's available, `mysqld-max`—a variant of the MySQL server that includes some more cutting-edge (and less commonly used) features. It also turns on server error logging, which you'd otherwise need to specify as an option to `mysqld`, and automatically restarts the server if it crashes. Prior to MySQL version 4, this was called `safe_mysqld`. On a Linux or OS X installation, you will still find a symbolic link called `safe_mysqld` pointing to `mysqld_safe`.

MySQL Server Options

The MySQL server is a complex piece of software and has many settings that you can tweak to make it better fit your needs. We'll discuss some of the more useful server options here. `mysqld_safe` accepts a number of options of its own and passes on any options it doesn't handle to `mysqld`. The options specific to `mysqld_safe` are probably not of interest to most readers of this book; you can find these by typing `mysqld_safe --help` at the command line:

basedir
> This tells `mysqld` where MySQL is installed on the system. If you don't specify this option, the program will try to use the location specified when the program was compiled.

datadir
> This tells `mysqld` where the database files are stored.

defaults-file
> This specifies the location of the options file to read; this is particularly useful if you want the server to read in options from a nondefault location.

enable-named-pipe
> Allows a server running under Windows to use a named pipe. See `skip-networking` for more information.

init-file
> This specifies a text file containing SQL commands that the server must execute when starting up. This is commonly used to reset a forgotten MySQL root password as discussed in "Resetting Forgotten MySQL Passwords" in Chapter 9.

log
> This tells `mysqld` to use the specified file to log every client connection and query.

log-bin
> This specifies where you want the binary log of commands that attempt to modify data on the server.

log-error
> This tells `mysqld` to use the specified file to log server startup, shutdown, and errors. By default, this is the file *<hostname>.err* in the data directory. For example, the log might show that we've run out of disk space:

```
060514 12:39:11 [ERROR] /usr/local/mysql/bin/mysqld: Disk is full writing
'/usr/local/mysql/data/Moodle/mdl_user.MYI' (Errcode: 49).
Waiting for someone to free space... Retry in 60 secs
```

log-slow-queries

> This tells mysqld to log queries that take an unusually long time to process. You can use this information together with the EXPLAIN command to determine how best to tune the server or optimize the tables. Queries that take a time longer than the value of the long_query_time server variable are logged.

pid-file

> For servers running on Linux and Mac OS X, this tells mysqld to save its process ID to the specified file; by default, this is *<hostname>.pid* (for Linux systems) or *<hostname>.local.pid* (for Mac OS X systems) and located in the MySQL data directory.

port

> This is the port the MySQL server should listen to for incoming connections. The default MySQL port is 3306. If there's already a server listening on that port, you'll need to specify a different port. We described how to do this in Chapter 2. On a Linux or Mac OS X system, connections from a client on the same system go through a Unix socket file rather than through this TCP port.

shared-memory-base-name

> For servers running on Windows, this tells mysqld to use the specified shared memory name. The default value is MYSQL. If you want to run multiple MySQL servers on a single Windows host, you'll need to specify a different value for each server.

skip-networking

> With this option, you can ask the server to not listen to a TCP port for incoming connections. This is more secure, as only connections from clients on the same system as the server (localhost) will be accepted. On a Linux or Mac OS X system, clients connect through the Unix socket file (described next). Under Windows, clients need to connect through a named pipe, so you'll need to set the enable-named-pipe option for this to work.

socket

> The absolute path to the Unix socket file on Linux and Mac OS X, or the named pipe under Windows, that the server uses for incoming connections from the local host. The default path is */tmp/mysql.sock* for the Unix socket, and *MYSQL* for the Windows named pipe. You generally need to specify a different value only if there's already a server using the default socket.

tmpdir

> This tells mysqld where to store its temporary files.

user

> On Linux and Mac OS X, the server tries to run under your account; if you start the server from the root account, the server will run with all the privileges of this

superuser, which is dangerous. The user option tells mysqld what user account to run under. It's a good idea to create an account with the name mysql, with access permissions for only the MySQL directories, and set the server to run under that username. Don't forget that this user should be able to read and write files in the MySQL data and temporary directories. If you don't specify the username, most MySQL scripts will automatically try to use your operating system account name as the value for the username.

Examples

Let's look at how you might use these options in practice. Consider the case where we need to run multiple servers on a single host; each server must have a different port, socket, and process ID file. If we want the servers to keep logs, the logfiles for each server should be different as well. For example, if we've installed MySQL under Linux or Mac OS X in the directory */usr/local/mysql* and want to run the server under the mysql account—with the database, log, and temporary files under the */tmp/mysql* directory—we could start the server with the command (all on one line):

```
$ mysqld_safe \
  --user=mysql \
  --port=57777 \
  --socket=/tmp/mysql/server1.sock \
  --basedir=/usr/local/mysql \
  --datadir=/tmp/mysql/data \
  --tmpdir=/tmp/mysql/tmp \
  --log=/tmp/mysql/logs/server1.main.log \
  --log-error=/tmp/mysql/logs/server1.error.log \
  --pid-file=/tmp/mysql/logs/server1.pid
```

Instead of typing in the settings at the command line, we can specify the required values in an options file as:

```
[mysqld]
user=     mysql
port=     57777
socket=   /tmp/mysql/server1.sock
basedir=  /usr/local/mysql
datadir=  /tmp/mysql/data
tmpdir=   /tmp/mysql/tmp

# log server messages to:
log=      /tmp/mysql/logs/server1.main.log

# log errors to this file:
log-error=/tmp/mysql/logs/server1.error.log

pid-file= /tmp/mysql/logs/server1.pid
```

We described how to use options files in Chapter 11. Note that since these are really options to the mysqld program, these options are listed under the mysqld group. Options specific to mysqld_safe can be listed under the mysqld_safe group.

Now consider the case where MySQL has been installed to the directory */home/adam/ mysql-5.0.22*. You can imagine the directory */Users/adam/mysql-5.0.22* being used for Mac OS X. For nonstandard installations, the `mysqld_safe` program should be called from the MySQL installation directory, so we first change to that directory:

```
$ cd /home/adam/mysql-5.0.22
```

and then start the server by typing (all on one line):

```
$ bin/mysqld_safe \
  --port=57777 \
  --socket=/home/adam/mysql-5.0.22/logs/mysqld-new.sock.file \
  --basedir=/home/adam/mysql-5.0.22 \
  --datadir=/home/adam/mysql-5.0.22/data \
  --log=/home/adam/mysql-5.0.22/logs/main.log \
  --log-error=/home/adam/mysql-5.0.22/logs/error.log \
  --pid-file=/home/adam/mysql-5.0.22/logs/zahra.pid
```

The corresponding options file entries would be:

```
[mysqld]
port=      57777
socket=    /home/adam/mysql-5.0.22/logs/mysqld-new.sock.file
basedir=   /home/adam/mysql-5.0.22
datadir=   /home/adam/mysql-5.0.22/data
log=       /home/adam/mysql-5.0.22/logs/main.log
log-error=/home/adam/mysql-5.0.22/logs/error.log
pid-file= /home/adam/mysql-5.0.22/logs/zahra.pid
```

Finally, let's look at an example for Windows, where we have MySQL installed in the directory *C:\mysql-5.0.22-win32*. We want to have the MySQL datafiles placed in *C:\mysql\data*, we want the logfiles placed in *C:\mysql\logs*, and we want the server to listen on port 13306. So we type (all on one line):

```
C:\>mysqld-net.exe \
  --port=13306 \
  --basedir=C:\mysql-5.0.22-win32 \
  --datadir=C:\mysql\data \
  --log-bin=C:\mysql\logs\mysql-binary.log
```

Note that the specified directories must exist, and the data directory must contain the `mysql` database files (the privilege tables); otherwise, MySQL will complain and abort.

Server Variables

Variables configure server resources and can be used to optimize the server settings to suit the hardware of the host computer, and to allocate resources for improved performance. For example, the variable `max_connections` specifies the maximum number of clients that can be connected to the server at any one time.

When choosing a value for a server variable, you need to think carefully about the nature of your application and your clients. For example, when setting the `max_connections` variable, you need to remember that clients can include application web pages that interact with the database. This variable affects the number of people who can concurrently load the database-enabled web pages; each request to load such a page counts as a separate connection. Of course, these connections are short, typically lasting only a few seconds while the page is generated and served to the web browser.

Some of the more important variables control how memory and files are managed. MySQL databases are stored in files in the data directory, and the server needs to open and close these files. However, opening and closing files is a relatively slow operation, so the fewer times we need to do this, the better. The MySQL server variable `table_cache` specifies the maximum number of tables that can be open at once. The larger this number, the fewer times we need to close open files and open closed ones.

You also need to consider how the `max_connections` value influences the value you choose for `table_cache`. If you allow 100 concurrent connections, and your application has queries that perform join operations on three tables, then your `table_cache` should be at least 300. Note that operating systems impose their own limitations on the maximum number of files that can be held open by any program, as well as for the whole system overall, so you may run into operating system limits if you set some MySQL variable values too high.

We mentioned earlier that opening and closing files is a relatively costly process. It's also far more costly to access files on disk than to access memory; if the server can keep most of what it needs handy in memory, things will generally be much faster. In "Keys and Indexes" in Chapter 6, we explored how an index can help MySQL to quickly find data in a large table, just as an index page allows us to quickly find text in a book. When data is requested from a database table that has an index, the server first looks up the data location using the index file, then reads the data from the appropriate location in the table file. This means that the server has to access the disk twice; if it can keep the index file in memory, it has to read the disk only once to fetch the data, which is much more efficient.

The MySQL server variable `key_buffer_size` controls the amount of memory set aside for MyISAM table indexes. The default value is 8 MB, but you can set it to any value up to 4 GB. Of course, you should actually have the required amount of memory on your system, and you should leave enough memory for the operating system and other processes. If you're using a dedicated MySQL server, you might want to set this value as high as 20 to 40 percent of total system memory.

Some queries can't use an existing index. For example, entries in a telephone directory are typically sorted by surname, then by given name. We can easily find all the people with a surname starting with the letter "S," but to find all the people with a first name starting with "S," we'd need to look at every entry in the directory. For such operations, a thread needs to read through all the data in a database table, which involves lots of disk reads. It's faster to read a small number of large data chunks, so it's good to allocate a large value for the `read_buffer_size` for such whole-of-table operations. Similarly, the `sort_buffer_size` variable controls the amount of memory available for queries that have an `ORDER BY` clause. The `read_buffer_size` and `sort_buffer_size` variables operate on a per-thread basis.

As with options, variables can be specified on the command line or in an options file. For example, the variable `max_connections` can be specified from the command line as:

```
$ mysqld --max_connections=200
```

or in an options file as:

```
[server]
max_connections=200
```

Some variables can also be set from within a client using the `SET` command; for example, you could write:

```
mysql> SET sort_buffer_size=2000000;
Query OK, 0 rows affected (0.00 sec)
```

To set a variable to apply across the server, rather than to the current client session, you need to add the GLOBAL keyword:

```
mysql> SET GLOBAL sort_buffer_size=2000000;
Query OK, 0 rows affected (0.01 sec)
```

To set `GLOBAL` variables, you need to have superuser privileges (in practice, you need to be logged in as the user root):

```
mysql> SET max_connections=200;
ERROR 1227 (HY000): Access denied; you need the SUPER privilege for this operation
```

Some variables are inherently related to the server, rather than to an individual session. MySQL will complain if you try to set a value for such variables without using the `GLOBAL` keyword:

```
mysql> SET max_connections=200;
ERROR 1229 (HY000): Variable 'max_connections' is a GLOBAL variable and should be
                    set with SET GLOBAL
```

The Slow Query Log

To determine what you should optimize, you should identify the frequently used queries that take a long time to complete. If you start the server with the `log-slow-queries` option, any queries that take more than 10 seconds to complete will be logged. You can change this duration by modifying the value of the `long_query_time` variable. You can add the `log-queries-not-using-indexes` option to ask the server to also log queries that don't use an index. The default location of the slow queries log is in the data directory, with a name in the form *<hostname>-slow.log*.

Let's look at an excerpt from a slow query log:

```
# Time: 060630 22:51:32
# User@Host: root[root] @ localhost []
```

```
# Query_time: 65  Lock_time: 0  Rows_sent: 8228  Rows_examined: 16577
USE LinkTracktclick;
SELECT DISTINCT * FROM Countries, clicktable ORDER BY CLICKS DESC;
```

This SELECT query took 65 seconds; if it's a query that's used often, we should add indexes to improve the query speed, or perhaps redesign the query in a manner that takes less time.

It can be hard to understand the entries in the slow-query logfile; you can use the mysqldumpslow script from the MySQL scripts directory to help summarize and organize this information. For example, we can ask for the two queries that took the longest time using the -t option:

```
$ scripts/mysqldumpslow -t 2
Reading mysql slow query log from ./log-slow.log
Count: 1 Time=65.00s (565s) Lock=0.00s (0s) Rows=8228.0 (8228), root[root]@localhost
  select distinct * from tmpCountries, clicktable order by clicks desc

Count: 35  Time=12.00s (0s)  Lock=0.00s (0s)  Rows=3.8 (132),
  RPUser[RPUser]@redback.cs.rmit.edu.au
select distinct id, surname, firstname, position_id from
student st, supervises s where st.id = s.student_id and s.status=N
and st.active=N and st.visible=N and supervisor_id = N
```

The Count is the number of queries that have been executed; from this, it would probably be better to focus on optimizing the second query, since it's been run 35 times, rather than the top query, which has been run only once.

The script tries to process the slow-query logfile at the default location; if you're using a nonstandard location, you should specify the logfile location:

```
$ mysqldumpslow path_to_your_slow_query_log_file
```

If you're using Windows, you will need to follow the steps in "Installing Perl modules under Windows" in Chapter 2 to use this Perl script.

Query Caching

Some applications require the database to repeatedly look up and return specific data. For example, the front page of an online store application might display all the products in stock that have been marked as being on sale. Every visitor to the online store will load this front page, and every page load will require the database server to look up all the products that are on sale.

It's much more efficient for the database server to store, or *cache*, the result of this query, and simply return the cached result every time it sees the same query. If the data is changed, the database considers the cached result to be *stale* and runs the query again (and caches the new result). Query caching can have a huge effect on performance; the MySQL manual describes a speedup of more than two times as being typical.

You can configure the size of the server's query cache by modifying the `query_cache_size` variable. The larger the cache, the more queries that can be cached. Like most other buffers, this follows the law of diminishing returns; doubling the query cache size is unlikely to double the effectiveness of the cache. You can check the server's cache settings as follows:

```
mysql> SHOW VARIABLES LIKE '%query_cache%';
+------------------------------+---------+
| Variable_name                | Value   |
+------------------------------+---------+
| have_query_cache             | YES     |
| query_cache_limit            | 1048576 |
| query_cache_min_res_unit     | 4096    |
| query_cache_size             | 3999744 |
| query_cache_type             | ON      |
| query_cache_wlock_invalidate | OFF     |
+------------------------------+---------+
6 rows in set (0.00 sec)
```

Here, caching is available (`have_query_cache` is YES), and the query cache size is 399,360 KB. When the query cache size is nonzero, the `query_cache_type` setting determines which queries should be cached; with this set to ON, almost all SELECT queries are cached. There are main two exceptions: queries that explicitly disable caching with the `SQL_NO_CACHE` keyword immediately after the SELECT, and queries that use functions that vary with time and user—for example, queries that include the function `CURRENT_TIMESTAMP( )`.

The `query_cache_limit` variable indicates the largest result to store for any given query, while `query_cache_min_res_unit` specifies the allocation units in the cache (the default is generally fine). Finally, `query_cache_wlock_invalidate` determines whether an active write lock granted to one client will prevent other clients from reading cached results.

Of these settings, you will typically only need to ensure that caching is available (`query_cache_type` is ON) and set an appropriate value for `query_cache_size`:

```
mysql> SET query_cache_type = ON;
Query OK, 0 rows affected (0.00 sec)

mysql> SET GLOBAL query_cache_size = 40000000;
Query OK, 0 rows affected (0.01 sec)
```

You can then check on how queries are being read from the cache:

```
mysql> SHOW STATUS LIKE 'qcache%';
+-------------------------+----------+
| Variable_name           | Value    |
+-------------------------+----------+
| Qcache_free_blocks      | 1        |
| Qcache_free_memory      | 39826928 |
| Qcache_hits             | 7        |
| Qcache_inserts          | 128      |
| Qcache_lowmem_prunes    | 0        |
| Qcache_not_cached       | 10       |
```

```
| Qcache_queries_in_cache | 73     |
| Qcache_total_blocks     | 178    |
+-------------------------+--------+
8 rows in set (0.00 sec)
```

Qcache_hits indicates how many queries have been answered directly from the cache. Over time, you should see a fair number of hits.

The Old Variables Format

You may encounter an older way of specifying variable values from the command line and in the options file. Under the old way, you'd use the set-variable= option from the command line, as in:

```
$ mysqld_safe --set-variable=sort-buffer-size=1048576
```

or in an options file, as in:

```
set-variable=sort_buffer_size=1048576
```

This format still works but has been deprecated since MySQL version 4.1. In the new format, you omit the set-variable=; we recommend you use the new method where possible.

Checking Server Settings

The SHOW VARIABLES command lists detailed server configuration settings, including things like the server version, paths to the different directories and files used by the server, and maximum concurrent connections. We'll show only a few of them here; try them on your own server:

```
mysql> SHOW VARIABLES;
+-------------------------------+-----------------------------------------------+
| Variable_name                 | Value                                         |
+-------------------------------+-----------------------------------------------+
| auto_increment_increment      | 1                                             |
| auto_increment_offset         | 1                                             |
| automatic_sp_privileges       | ON                                            |
| back_log                      | 50                                            |
| basedir                       | /                                             |
| binlog_cache_size             | 32768                                         |
| bulk_insert_buffer_size       | 8388608                                       |
| character_set_client          | latin1                                        |
| version_compile_os            | mandriva-linux-gnu                            |
...
| wait_timeout                  | 28800                                         |
+-------------------------------+-----------------------------------------------+
185 rows in set (0.01 sec)
```

The mysqladmin variables command produces the same result from the command line:

```
$ mysqladmin --user=root --password=the_mysql_root_password  variables
+-------------------------------+-----------------------------------------------------+
| Variable_name                 | Value                                               |
+-------------------------------+-----------------------------------------------------+
| auto_increment_increment      | 1                                                   |
...
| wait_timeout                  | 28800                                               |
+-------------------------------+-----------------------------------------------------+
```

From the monitor, you can view a subset of the variables by adding a LIKE clause:

```
mysql> SHOW VARIABLES LIKE 'k%';
+--------------------------+----------+
| Variable_name            | Value    |
+--------------------------+----------+
| key_buffer_size          | 16777216 |
| key_cache_age_threshold  | 300      |
| key_cache_block_size     | 1024     |
| key_cache_division_limit | 100      |
+--------------------------+----------+
4 rows in set (0.00 sec)
```

The SHOW STATUS command shows you MySQL server status information:

```
mysql> SHOW STATUS;
+---------------------------+------------+
| Variable_name             | Value      |
+---------------------------+------------+
| Aborted_clients           | 8          |
| Aborted_connects          | 0          |
| Binlog_cache_disk_use     | 0          |
| Binlog_cache_use          | 0          |
| Bytes_received            | 858887090  |
| Bytes_sent                | 8535929437 |
...
| Com_insert                | 318046     |
...
| Com_lock_tables           | 126        |
...
| Com_select                | 4541404    |
..
| Com_unlock_tables         | 126        |
| Com_update                | 153656     |
| Connections               | 238544     |
| Created_tmp_disk_tables   | 83154      |
| Created_tmp_files         | 47         |
| Created_tmp_tables        | 128857     |
...
| Key_blocks_not_flushed    | 0          |
| Key_blocks_unused         | 6119       |
| Key_blocks_used           | 6698       |
| Key_read_requests         | 45921497   |
| Key_reads                 | 35348      |
| Key_write_requests        | 1612717    |
| Key_writes                | 986186     |
| Max_used_connections      | 15         |
```

```
...
| Open_files                   | 128       |
| Slave_retried_transactions   | 0         |
| Slow_launch_threads          | 0         |
| Slow_queries                 | 21        |
...
| Sort_scan                    | 212588    |
| Table_locks_immediate        | 5831792   |
| Table_locks_waited           | 185       |
| Threads_cached               | 0         |
| Threads_connected            | 1         |
| Threads_created              | 238543    |
| Threads_running              | 1         |
| Uptime                       | 1786334   |
+------------------------------+-----------+
157 rows in set (0.00 sec)
```

We've omitted most of the rows here for space considerations; your instance may well show over 250 variable values.

You can also display the server status using `mysqladmin status` or `mysqladmin extended-status` commands:

```
$ mysqladmin --user=root --password=the_mysql_root_password status
Uptime: 12093  Threads: 1  Questions: 7160  Slow queries: 0  Opens: 76
Flush tables: 1  Open tables: 60  Queries per second avg: 0.592
```

The `extended-status` command produces the same output as the monitor's `SHOW STATUS` command.

The `SHOW PROCESSLIST` command displays all running threads on the MySQL server and is a useful tool for diagnosing problems or understanding what users are doing. Try it on your server when you're logged in as the **root** user:

```
mysql> SHOW PROCESSLIST;
+-------+------------+-----------------------------+--------+...
| Id    | User       | Host                        | db     |...
+-------+------------+-----------------------------+--------+...
| 26533 | moodleuser | zahra.learningmysql.com:63593| Moodle |...
| 26534 | root       | localhost                   |        |...
+-------+------------+-----------------------------+--------+...
... +---------+------+-------+------------------+
... | Command | Time | State | Info             |
... +---------+------+-------+------------------+
... | Sleep   | 1    |       |                  |
... | Query   | 0    |       | show processlist |
... +---------+------+-------+------------------+
2 rows in set (0.00 sec)
```

The output is fairly self-explanatory, and details are in the "SHOW syntax" section of the MySQL manual. The `mysqladmin processlist` command produces the same output:

```
$ mysqladmin --user=root --password=the_mysql_root_password processlist
+-------+------------+-----------------------------+--------+...
| Id    | User       | Host                        | db     |...
+-------+------------+-----------------------------+--------+...
```

```
| 26533 | moodleuser | zahra.learningmysql.com:63593| Moodle |...
| 26534 | root       | localhost             |          |...
+-------+------------+----------------------------------+--------+...

... +---------+------+-------+-----------------+
... | Command | Time | State | Info            |
... +---------+------+-------+-----------------+
... | Sleep   | 1    |       |                 |
... | Query   | 0    |       | show processlist|
... +---------+------+-------+-----------------+
```

You can end a problematic process using the `KILL` command with the number of the process. If you somehow kill your own connection, the monitor will establish a new connection to the server, resulting in a new process number. Here, we kill our own (the `root` user's) connection — see how the new process number (26535) is different?:

```
mysql> KILL 26534;
Query OK, 0 rows affected (0.02 sec)

mysql> SHOW PROCESSLIST;
ERROR 2006 (HY000): MySQL server has gone away
No connection. Trying to reconnect...
Connection id:    26535
Current database: *** NONE ***

+-------+------------+----------------------------------+--------+...
| Id    | User       | Host                             | db     |...
+-------+------------+----------------------------------+--------+...
| 26533 | moodleuser | zahra.learningmysql.com:63593| Moodle |...
| 26535 | root       | localhost             |          |...
+-------+------------+----------------------------------+--------+...

... +---------+------+-------+-----------------+
... | Command | Time | State | Info            |
... +---------+------+-------+-----------------+
... | Sleep   | 1    |       |                 |
... | Query   | 0    |       | show processlist|
... +---------+------+-------+-----------------+
2 rows in set (0.00 sec)
```

The `mysqladmin kill` command does the same thing:

```
$ mysqladmin --user=root --password=the_mysql_root_password kill 26534
```

Other Things to Consider

There are many other aspects of database and application design that you can look at when considering performance. For example, if you make large-scale changes to a table (for example, by deleting many entries), you are likely to get better performance if you run the `OPTIMIZE TABLE` command to reorganize the table file on disk. This is especially true if the table contains variable length fields:

```
mysql> OPTIMIZE TABLE artist;
+--------------+----------+----------+----------+
| Table        | Op       | Msg_type | Msg_text |
```

```
+--------------+----------+----------+----------+
| music.artist | optimize | status   | OK       |
+--------------+----------+----------+----------+
1 row in set (0.06 sec)
```

In most cases, the MySQL server handles this adequately, so you won't need to use this command often, if at all.

Careful design of tables and indexes can also help improve performance. In "Transactions and Locking" in Chapter 7, we saw how transaction support can be useful for some applications. However, transaction support adds overhead to database operations. If you need transaction support in some tables, but not in others, you can use different table types within a single database. In "The EXPLAIN Statement" in Chapter 8, we saw how indexes can help increase the speed of queries. Try to minimize operations that scan all rows in a table, and try to add indexes that can be used by frequent queries. Shorter keys are generally faster to use, so try to keep the length of primary keys down.

We won't discuss performance any further in this book, but if you're setting up a production database site, it's definitely worth looking at the resources listed in the next section.

Resources

Database server tuning is a complex art, and is largely beyond the scope of this book To learn more about tuning MySQL, we recommend the following resources:

- The MySQL Manual: Optimization (*http://dev.mysql.com/doc/refman/5.1/en/optimization.html*)
- *MySQL Database Design and Tuning* by Robert D. Schneider (MySQL Press)
- *High Performance MySQL* by Jeremy D. Zawodny and Derek J. Balling (O'Reilly)

Exercises

1. Why is it important to allocate a large value to read_buffer_size?
2. What is the advantage of caching query results?
3. What does the OPTIMIZE TABLE command do?

## PART IV

Web Database Applications with PHP

## CHAPTER 13

Web Database Applications

MySQL's most common use is in wePHPMyb database applications. It's often teamed with PHP—a web-enabled scripting language—and the Apache web server to develop powerful applications including online shopping, news, sports, and blogs. Indeed, the Apache web server, MySQL, and PHP together form three of the four components of the most popular of all web development platforms, LAMP. The "L" stands for Linux, but the material we cover here works with all three operating systems we look at in this book: Linux, Windows, and Mac OS X.

The LAMP acronym is increasingly interpreted rather loosely as representing any open source development platform for web database applications. The "P" is alternatively taken to stand for Perl, which we introduce in Chapter 16; Python; or another of the popular web programming languages. Similarly, MySQL can be replaced by another open source database system, PostgreSQL (*http://www.postgresql.org*). PostgreSQL is less popular than MySQL, but it has strong standards compliance, is rich in features, and has looser licensing conditions, making it more appropriate for some applications.

We introduce the following concepts in this chapter:

- Components of a web database application
- An overview of the Apache web server
- An overview of the PHP language, including short examples

The final section of this chapter lists resources where you can find out more about Apache and PHP. We'll look at several PHP examples but will leave detailed explanation of using PHP and MySQL to Chapter 14, and will build a complete application with these in Chapter 15.

Building a Web Database Application

This section gives an overview of web database applications, drawing analogies and contrasts to the conventional software that you use on your computer. As an overview, it doesn't discuss technical details in depth; we get to the details later. "How Web

Software Works" briefly explains how web software works and shows you the steps that occur when a user clicks on a link in his web browser. In "Three-Tier Architectures," we discuss web database applications more formally, describing the three-tier architecture model and how MySQL, PHP, and Apache fit that model.

We'll assume in this and the next two chapters that you're familiar with basic programming concepts, including loops, conditionals, and expressions. We'll also assume you're familiar with the Web and, in particular, that you understand the basic principles of HTML markup. It doesn't matter if you don't know the details of the HTML standard, but we expect you'll understand HTML when it's shown to you. If you've never programmed or don't know HTML, then we advise you to use one of the resources listed in "Resources" at the end of this chapter before reading this and the next two chapters.

How Web Software Works

Web software is very different from a conventional application. To understand, consider the word processing software on your computer, an example of a traditional, conventional tool. You start the program, then interact with it: you move between typing, clicking on menus and widgets, and between open windows. When you're finished, you save your files and close the application. The software is an integrated, interactive package: you work with your documents, surrounded by the application's tools and windows. The software developer has customized the environment to support only word processing, and the tool is tailored carefully to that need; it has special-purpose tools—such as floating toolbars—that are designed to help you when you're editing a document. Also, usually, you're the only person using your word processor on your computer.

The interface to most web software isn't specialized in the same way as a word processor. Instead, you use a conventional web browser—probably Mozilla Firefox, Internet Explorer, or Safari—that sends requests and receive responses from standardized, distributed web servers. The web servers process your requests, run scripts, and return the output to your browser; they serve the many users that are authorized to use the software. The interface environment is constrained: you usually move back and forward through HTML documents—much like using a setup wizard—entering data into HTML forms or clicking on HTML widgets. The tools you use are general-purpose browser tools—such as the Back, Forward, Refresh, and Home buttons, and the Bookmarks or Favorites menu—that don't vary with the application.

Web software itself is also different. It's distributed: a small part of it—the simple web browser interface with its limited capabilities—resides on the user's computer, while the majority of the application logic is captured in scripts that are on a remote web server. The scripts aren't an integrated, large package: they are simple parts—each performs a specific function—that together provide the application functionality when the user follows a series of steps. Because of this, web software is limited. It isn't very

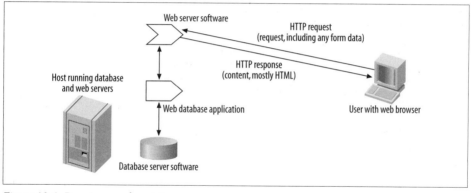

Figure 13-1. Running a web script

interactive, it must be fault-tolerant, it's limited by network speed bottlenecks, and it must work with generic browsers. The relatively recent Ajax technique relies heavily on client-side programming to deliver a more customized user interface. However, the basic building blocks remain the same.

The advantage of web software is its flexibility. Any user, anywhere, with almost any browser on any platform, can use the software. Importantly, no configuration is required, and training isn't usually needed. Web software is predictable: there are a limited number of ways you can build an application, and most users have seen the paradigms before and know where to start. With web software, deployment is as simple as setting up your web server, installing scripts on it, and publishing the address of your web application page.

Figure 13-1 shows how web software works. When a user clicks on a link (or submits a form, or types a URL), a request is sent from her web browser to a web server identified by the URL. The web server extracts path, resource, and other information from the URL and uses this to identify what script to run and what parameters to give it. The script is then executed and its output sent to the browser, along with a status message that indicates whether the operation was successful. If the request was successful, then (usually) an HTML resource is displayed, and the request process starts again when the user makes her next click in their browser.

Consider an example. You've decided to build an online store and have started to write the scripts that compose the application. Suppose you've authored one script, *shop.php*, which allows a user to add an item to his shopping cart. The script expects two parameters to capture what the user wants to purchase: a `productID` number that identifies the product, and a `quantity` value that is the amount of the product. The script outputs a success message in HTML when everything works, and an error message in HTML when it doesn't.

To test your *shop.php* script, you can save it in a directory from which your Apache web server serves scripts (the document root). If you're using a Linux or Mac OS X system, you also need to make sure that the file can be read by everyone, since the web

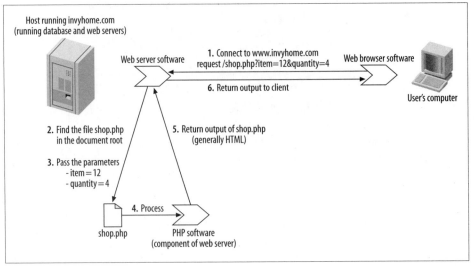

Figure 13-2. The steps to run shop.php

server is generally configured as a minimally privileged user who can access only those files that everyone else can access. (We explained how to find the document root in "The Apache Document Root" and how to set the correct file permissions in "Checking Whether Your Apache Installation Supports PHP," both in Chapter 2.

Now, you're ready to test the script by requesting it with a web browser. Suppose the web server serves pages for the domain *http://www.invyhome.com*. You can request *shop.php* by loading the URL *http://www.invyhome.com/shop.php* with your web browser. If you're trying things out on your own development system (`localhost`), you can use *http://localhost/shop.php*.

To supply the required parameters, you (or typically, another script) can add them after a question-mark character in the URL, as in *http://www.invyhome.com/ shop.php?productID=12&quantity=4* and send a request for this address to the server. The request asks for 4 units of `productID` 12 to be added to the cart. When you request the URL, the web server looks in the directory */var/www/html/*, finds the script *shop.php*, starts the PHP script processor, runs the script and supplies the parameters, and captures the output. The output is then sent to the browser, which displays the response: in this case, an HTML success message that shows 4 units of `productID` 12 have been successfully added to the cart. Figure 13-2 illustrates these steps.

Three-Tier Architectures

Figure 13-3 shows the architecture of a typical web database application. The web browser is the *client tier*, providing the interface to the application but very little of the application logic itself. The *middle tier* is the web server, the script processor, and the scripts; most of the application logic resides here, typically including user authentica-

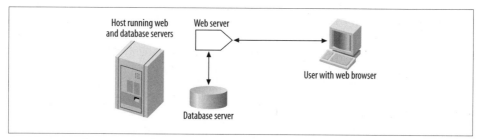

Figure 13-3. A three-tiered web database application

tion, security features, input validation, user session management, the database access library, SQL queries, and other functionality. The *database tier* is the database server itself, along with its databases, indexes, and utilities. For the applications we discuss in this chapter, the MySQL server is the database tier, and the Apache web server and PHP are the middle tier. Any popular browser can be used as a client.

We've previously broadly discussed what makes three-tier-architecture software—that is, web database applications—different from conventional software. In the context of a three-tier architecture, the browser is a very *thin client*—that is, very little of the application logic resides there. Instead, the middle tier carries out almost all of the application functions, and the browser usually displays only static HTML content. The exception is when the HTML page contains embedded JavaScript—or scripts written in another client-side language—that adds basic interactive features to the web pages; for example, JavaScript is often used to animate menus, highlight options as the mouse passes over them, alert the user with pop-up windows, and perform other simple tasks. We don't discuss client-side scripting further in this book; there are several good resources listed on the topic at the end of this chapter.

Most of the application logic is captured in PHP scripts in the middle tier. These are invoked when a user requests a resource from the web server, and the web server calls the PHP engine that runs the script. Of course, because all the scripts are accessible with a web browser, users can request any script, any time, from anywhere. This creates unique problems. Web database applications must robustly handle users making unexpected requests; bookmarking and returning to pages later; reloading or refreshing pages when they shouldn't; or simply disappearing, never to be seen again. Applications must also protect against the threat of accidental damage or malicious attacks. All this is made more difficult by the HTTP protocol that's used for communication between web browsers and servers. HTTP has no high-level concept of *state*. Every request from a browser must contain all information needed to answer the request, since the server forgets all about it once the request is answered. We explain solutions to some of these problems in Chapter 14.

The database tier is very similar to that in nonweb applications. The MySQL server listens for connections from clients, such as the MySQL monitor, and authenticates users when they connect. Once the connection is established, the user can run queries, disconnecting when she's finished. Using MySQL from a PHP script is conceptually similar to using it through the MySQL monitor. The key difference is that you don't type queries into an interface but instead use PHP library functions to carry out actions such as connecting to the database server, choosing a database, running a query, and retrieving the results. We show you an example later in this chapter.

The Apache Web Server

The LAMP platform includes the Apache web server. While it isn't necessary to use Apache—PHP and MySQL can be used with other web servers—it's our server of choice in this book. There are several reasons for this: it's free in a monetary and open source sense, it's the most popular server on the Web, it's robust and scalable, it is the web server most commonly used with PHP, and it works on all popular platforms, including Linux, Windows, and Mac OS X. This section briefly explains web servers and Apache. We discussed how to configure Apache in Chapter 2.

Web servers are also known as HTTP servers. This describes their function: a web browser or other web client makes a request for a web resource to a web server using the HTTP protocol; the web server then serves this request and sends an HTTP response to the browser. There are essentially two classes of request that web servers can handle: first, requests for static resources, such as HTML, XML, or PDF documents, and, second, requests to run a script—often with parameters provided by the browser request —and return the output in a response. The latter class is central to web database applications.

Web browsers send textual requests to web servers. An HTTP request is a text description of a required resource. For example, the following is what the Lynx browser sends as a request for the resource *http://www.invyhome.com/artist.php* on the web server:

```
GET /artist.php HTTP/1.0
Host: www.invyhome.com
Accept: text/html, text/plain, audio/mod, image/*, video/*, video/mpeg,
application/pgp, application/pgp, application/pdf, message/partial,
message/external-body, application/postscript, x-be2,
application/andrew-inset, text/richtext, text/enriched
Accept: x-sun-attachment, audio-file, postscript-file, default, mail-file,
sun-deskset-message, application/x-metamail-patch, application/msword,
text/sgml, */*;q=0.01
Accept-Encoding: gzip, compress
Accept-Language: en
User-Agent: Lynx/2.8.4dev.16 libwww-FM/2.14 SSL-MM/1.4.1 OpenSSL/0.9.6
```

The request lists all information required to serve the request: a *method* to use (GET), the required resource, the HTTP version, the host server, and details of the browser and what types of responses it can receive.

In response, the web server returns an HTTP header, and then the requested resource if the request is satisfied. Continuing the example, the server looking after *http://www .invyhome.com* returns the following response:

```
HTTP/1.1 200 OK
Date: Wed, 02 Aug 2006 14:55:15 GMT
Server: Apache/2.2.3 (Mandriva Linux/PREFORK-1mdv2007.0)
Last-Modified: Tue, 27 Jul 2006 18:27:45 GMT
ETag: "3fc424-1e5-be72aa40"
Accept-Ranges: bytes
Content-Length: 1485
Content-Type: text/html
X-Pad: avoid browser bug


<!DOCTYPE HTML PUBLIC
 "-//W3C//DTD HTML 4.01 Transitional//EN"
 "http://www.w3.org/TR/html401/loose.dtd">
<html>
 <head>
  <meta http-equiv="Content-Type" content="text/html; charset=iso-8859-1" />
  <title>Artists</title>
 </head>
 <body>
  <h1>Artists</h1>

  <table>
   <tr>
    <th>artist_id</th>
    <th>artist_name</th>
   </tr>
...
  </table>
 </body>
</html>
```

As with a request, the response includes the HTTP standard version, whether the request was satisfied (200 OK), server details, the response type, and then the response itself.

A key feature of HTTP is that each request and response is self-contained. You'll notice that the request includes all the information needed to respond to the request, and the response includes all information needed for the browser to process it. If a browser makes subsequent requests to the same server, it will again provide all of the information. The process is unlike traditional communications protocols where a *handshaking* phase establishes the credentials and then communication takes place until the line is closed. When we talk about HTTP lacking *state*, this is what we mean: nothing is assumed when a browser and server communicate, each exchange is separate, and everything is specified exhaustively each time.

Lack of state means speed. Since servers don't have to remember anything, they can process a request and respond immediately without having to restore information about the client. This means they adapt to changes in load and can handle very large numbers of requests on modest hardware. The stateless model is ideal for fast, one-off communications where you want to retrieve a document or run one script.

At the same time, lack of state makes application development harder. If you need state, then you have to add it programmatically so that it can be restored with subsequent requests. For example, if you want to lead a user through a series of steps, ensure they don't access certain parts of the web site without logging in, or make sure they only run a script once, then you need state. PHP provides tools for this purpose—embedded in the *sessions* functions and features discussed in Chapter 14—but they need to be used carefully. Adding state to web database applications isn't straightforward, and it must carefully follow rules so that it's robust and secure.

Web Server Index Files

The browser may simply request a directory rather than a specific filename. For example, the address *http://www.invyhome.com/* corresponds to the document root directory, while the address *http://www.invyhome.com/shop/* corresponds to the the *shop* directory under the document root. When the web server receives such a request, it searches for an *index* file in the directory. The index file is typically used as the starting point for a web site or web application and has the filename *index.html* (for plain HTML), *index.php* (for a PHP script), or *index.pl* (for a Perl script). If there is no index file present in the directory, the web server returns a listing of all files in the directory, or, if the server has been configured for greater security, tells the browser that access to the directory contents is denied.

You can check what filenames your Apache server treats as index files by looking inside the Apache configuration file and searching for the `DirectoryIndex` directive. For example, you might see:

```
DirectoryIndex default.htm Default.htm index.cgi index.htm index.html index.php
    index.php3 index.php4 index.php5 index.phtml index.pl index.xml
```

If there are multiple index files in a directory, the server will use the one that appears first in its `DirectoryIndex` list.

If the requested address doesn't end with a forward slash symbol (/), the web server has to first check if the address corresponds to a file or a directory. For example, for the address *http://www.invyhome.com/shop*, the server needs to check whether it should return the file *shop* in the document root, or the index file in the *shop* directory under the document root.

Introducing PHP

PHP is a scripting language that is designed to be embedded into the HTML markup used for web pages; it can be used for other purposes, but that's outside the scope of our discussions. It works on almost all Unix platforms—including Linux and Mac OS X—and with Windows 32-bit environments, such as Windows 2000, XP, and Vista. Web pages that contain PHP scripts are preprocessed by the PHP scripting engine, and the source code is replaced with the output of the script. Indeed, the acronym PHP obliquely suggests just that—*PHP: Hypertext Preprocessor*.

PHP is extremely popular for several reasons: it's easy to include PHP scripts in HTML documents, PHP is free in a monetary and open source sense, it has a large number of powerful but easy-to-use function libraries, and it shares syntax with C or Perl-like languages. PHP is also widely supported; there are a very large number of books, web sites, and add-on products available. You'll find that moving from simple examples to advanced material is made easy by this wide-ranging support.

Example 13-1 shows simple PHP script embedded in an HTML document:

Example 13-1. PHP Script to say "Hello, world!"

```
<!DOCTYPE HTML PUBLIC
"-//W3C//DTD HTML 4.0 Transitional//EN"
"http://www.w3.org/TR/html4/loose.dtd" >
<html>
  <head>
    <title>Hello, world</title>
  </head>
  <body>
    <?php echo "Hello, world"; ?>
  </body>
</html>
```

When preprocessed by the PHP scripting engine, the short (and not very useful) script:

```
<?php echo "Hello, world"; ?>
```

is replaced with its output:

```
Hello, world
```

The text before and after the script is HTML; the first three lines define that HTML version 4 is being used. Any number of PHP scripts can be embedded in an HTML document, as long as each PHP script is surrounded by the begin tag <?php and the end tag ?>. Other tags can also be used to delimit PHP scripts, but the tags we use are the most common and reliable.

One of the best language features of PHP is how it decodes user data and automatically initializes variables. Consider a sample script stored in the file *printuser.php*:

```
<!DOCTYPE HTML PUBLIC
"-//W3C//DTD HTML 4.0 Transitional//EN"
"http://www.w3.org/TR/html4/loose.dtd" >
<html>
  <head>
    <title>Saying hello</title>
  </head>
```

```
  <body>
    <?php
      echo "Hello, {$_GET["username"]}";
    ?>
  </body>
</html>
```

Let's assume that the file is stored on the web server in the document root of the web server. The script can be retrieved using a web browser—in the case where it is running on the same machine as the web server (localhost)—by requesting the URL *http://localhost/printuser.php?username=Selina*. In response to the request, the PHP engine replaces the script:

```
<?php
  echo "Hello, {$_GET["username"]}";
?>
```

with the output:

```
Hello, Selina
```

In this example, the URL is automatically decoded and an array variable $_GET initialized. The array contains an element username, which matches the name of the attribute in the URL, and its value is set to the value in the URL, Selina. This automatic registration of variables is an excellent feature; we explain how to use it securely in "Untainting User Data" in Chapter 14, and we revisit the issue of how to pass information to scripts using the URL in "Passing a Message to a Script" in Chapter 15. Don't worry too much now about arrays, elements, and the PHP syntax; we'll return to the details in the next two chapters.

Files that contain PHP scripts usually have the extension *.php* instead of the HTML file extension of *.html* or *.htm*. The *.php* extension is the trigger for the web server to invoke the PHP scripting engine to preprocess the file. This is controlled by a directive in the web server's configuration file, which we discussed briefly in "Configuring and Controlling the Apache Web Server" in Chapter 2.

Passing variables and values using a URL is one way of transferring data from a web browser to a web server. However, the most common technique is to use an HTML form such as the following:

```
<!DOCTYPE HTML PUBLIC
"-//W3C//DTD HTML 4.0 Transitional//EN"
"http://www.w3.org/TR/html4/loose.dtd" >

<html>
  <head>
    <title>Saying hello</title>
  </head>

  <body>
    <form method="GET" action="printuser.php" />
      Enter your name: <input type="text" name="username" />
      <br /><input type="submit" value="Show it!" />
```

Figure 13-4. A form that requests the script printuser.php

```
        </form>
    </body>
</html>
```

When this HTML document is rendered by a web browser, as shown in Figure 13-4, the user is able to enter their name into an input widget. Below the widget is a button labeled "Show it!". When the user presses the button, the script listed as the `action` attribute of the form element is requested, and the data in the input widget is sent to the server as part of the URL.

For example, if the user enters the name **Selina** into the input widget and presses the "Show it!" button, then the URL *http://localhost/printuser.php?username=Selina* is requested. The web server runs the script *printuser.php* and passes the submitted data to it. This script takes the submitted name and uses the `echo` statement to generate the message "Hello," followed by the text typed into the form. The web server returns any output produced by the PHP script to the user's browser, which then displays it. In our example, the user would see the message:

```
Hello, Selina
```

Example: Displaying the Artists from the Music Collection

We now look at another example that illustrates how you can use a PHP script, which is accessible with a web browser, to run a query on a MySQL server and return a list of artists from the `music` database; the script then formats this list as an HTML table for display on the browser. We don't discuss the details of the process here, or the syntax of the language; these are covered in the next two chapters. The aim of this section is to give you a taste for how PHP and the web environment fit together with MySQL to build a web database application.

You used the MySQL monitor in Chapter 5 to run basic queries on the `music` database. Using it, you know how to display all artists:

```
mysql> USE music;
Database changed
mysql> SELECT * FROM artist;
```

```
+-----------+--------------------------+
| artist_id | artist_name              |
+-----------+--------------------------+
|         1 | New Order                |
|         2 | Nick Cave & The Bad Seeds |
|         3 | Miles Davis              |
|         4 | The Rolling Stones       |
|         5 | The Stone Roses          |
|         6 | Kylie Minogue            |
+-----------+--------------------------+
6 rows in set (0.00 sec)
```

Example 13-2 uses PHP to do the same thing: use the `music` database, run the `SELECT` query, and display the results formatted in a table.

Example 13-2. Querying the music database with PHP

```
<!DOCTYPE HTML PUBLIC
"-//W3C//DTD HTML 4.01 Transitional//EN"
"http://www.w3.org/TR/html401/loose.dtd">
<html>
 <head>
  <meta http-equiv="Content-Type" content="text/html;
    charset=iso-8859-1" />
  <title>Artists</title>
 </head>
 <body>
  <h1>Artists</h1>

  <table>
   <tr>
    <th>artist_id</th>
    <th>artist_name</th>
   </tr>
   <?php
   // Connect to the MySQL server
   if (!($connection = @ mysql_connect("localhost", "root",

     "the_mysql_root_password")))

     die("Cannot connect");

   if (!(mysql_select_db("music", $connection)))
    die("Couldn't select music database");

   // Run the query on the connection
   if (!($result = @ mysql_query("SELECT * FROM artist", $connection)))
    die("Couldn't run query");

   // Until there are no rows in the result set, fetch a row into
   // the $row array and ...
   while ($row = @ mysql_fetch_array($result, MYSQL_ASSOC))
   {
    // Start a table row
    print "<tr>\n";
```

Figure 13-5. Output of query_artists.php shown in a web browser

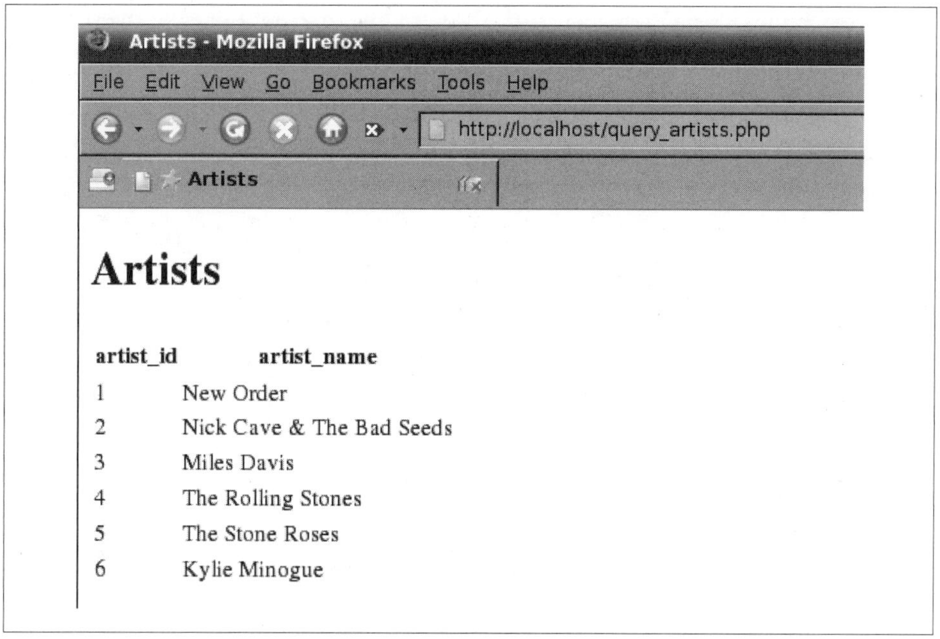

```
// ... and print out each of the columns
foreach($row as $data)
 print "\t<td>{$data}</td>\n";

// Finish the row
print "</tr>\n";
}
?>
</table>
</body>
</html>
```

This script doesn't take parameters, and so returns the same results every time unless you change the data. Its output is shown in Figure 13-5.

To edit the file, you can use any text editor. See "Using a Text Editor" in Chapter 2 for a discussion of text editors for different operating systems. Once you've typed in the contents and saved this as the file *query_artists.php* in the document root of our Apache web server installation, you can test that it works by loading the URL *http://localhost/ query_artists.php* in a web browser.

If you do so and get a message like:

```
Fatal error: Call to undefined function mysql_connect()
```

you should ensure that your installation of PHP has the MySQL libraries installed. If you're using RPMs, the libraries are typically in the *php-mysql* package.

The first 16 lines of the file are HTML. Of these, the first eight lines of the script are the preamble, which starts an HTML document, defines the content type, and sets the page title. The following eight lines start a table, displaying column headings for the data that follows. The final three lines of the file close the HTML document. The remainder of the file—producing the content inside the HTML table—is the PHP script.

The PHP script is encapsulated in the `<?php` and `?>` tags. The script itself carries out four main steps:

1. Connect to MySQL, using the `mysql_connect( )` MySQL library function
2. Select the database, using the `mysql_select_db( )` MySQL library function
3. Run the SQL query, using the `mysql_query( )` MySQL library function
4. Retrieve and display the data, using a `while` loop, the `mysql_fetch_array( )` MySQL library function, the `print` statement, and a `foreach` loop

With the exception of the last step, you already know how to carry out these steps using the MySQL monitor.

The first step in the PHP script is to connect to MySQL. This is performed with the following fragment:

```
if (!($connection = @ mysql_connect("localhost", "root", "the_mysql_root_password")))
  die("Cannot connect");
```

The function `mysql_connect( )` opens a connection, and the three parameters to the function—`"localhost"`, `"root"`, and `"the_mysql_root_password"`—are the hostname of the server, the MySQL user, and the user's password, respectively. The function does the same thing as running the MySQL monitor: it authenticates you, giving you access to the MySQL server so that you can run SQL statements. The other important feature is that a connection *resource handle* is returned and saved in a PHP variable `$connection`; this is used in the following two steps. The at symbol (@) tells PHP not to display its own error messages. If we discover a critical error, we call the `die( )` function to display an error message and stop processing the script. We look at error handling in detail in "Handling MySQL Errors" in Chapter 4.

The second step is to use a database. This occurs through this fragment:

```
if (!(mysql_select_db("music", $connection)))
  die("Couldn't select music database");
```

The function `mysql_select_db( )` is the PHP library equivalent of the USE command. In this fragment, the `music` database is selected as the current database. The second parameter to the function, `$connection`, is the database connection resource handle returned from the first step; it's used to identify the connection to the database server.

The third step runs the query. It performs the same function as typing it into the MySQL monitor does, but it doesn't retrieve or display the results. Here's the code fragment:

```
if (!($result = @ mysql_query("SELECT * FROM artist", $connection)))
  die("Couldn't run query");
```

The function that does the actual work is mysql_query( ), and it takes two parameters: first, the SQL query, and, second, the database connection resource handle that identifies the connection to use. It returns a database *result resource* that is used to identify the rows to be retrieved in the next step; in this example, it's saved in the variable $result. Unlike with the MySQL monitor, there's no need to add a semicolon symbol (;) at the end of the query.

The fourth step retrieves and displays the results; it's the most complicated step and spans 14 lines in the script:

```
// Until there are no rows in the result set, fetch a row into
// the $row array and ...
while ($row = @ mysql_fetch_array($result))
{
 // Start a table row
 print "<tr>\n";

 // ... and print out each of the columns
 foreach($row as $data)
  print "\t<td>{$data}</td>\n";

 // Finish the row
 print "</tr>\n";
}
```

It works as follows:

- The while loop fetches each result row, one by one, from the MySQL server using mysql_fetch_array( ). The parameter to the function is $result, which references the results from the query that was executed in the third step. Each row returned by the function is saved in the variable $row and then processed in the loop body as detailed next. The loop stops when there are no more rows to retrieve.

- Inside the body of the while loop, three steps occur for each retrieved row:

  1. The first print statement produces an HTML <tr> tag to start a new table row.

  2. The foreach loop processes each column value for the row and uses a print statement to surround each column value with <td> and </td> tags.

  3. The last print statement produces an HTML </tr> tag to end the row.

Because there are always two columns in every row of output—and they're always in the same order—the artist_id and artist_name column values line up with the headings, as shown in Figure 13-5. When all of the artists have been printed, the while loop ends, and the script finishes.

We haven't discussed many of the features of PHP that we've used. For example, the script has error-handling capabilities, so it'll report a message to the user when something goes wrong. Statements such as foreach require some explanation, but don't worry about the details for now. The next two chapters explain all you need to build a basic application.

Using a PHP-Enabled Web Hosting Site

There are a large number of companies that offer low-cost or free web hosting packages with PHP and MySQL support. To start looking for one, perform a web search for "php mysql web hosting." These hosting packages usually include FTP access to copy files to your web directory, and a web-based MySQL client such as phpMyAdmin.

To get your site up and running on such a site, first copy your files across to the server using FTP. Under Linux, the KDE Konqueror and GNOME Nautilus file managers both support FTP. Under Mac OS X, select "Connect to Server" from the Finder Go menu; you can also use the free Cyberduck program. Under Windows, you'll need to download an FTP tool such as FileZilla (*http://sourceforge.net/projects/filezilla*).

To connect to the server, enter your username and the name of your FTP server—for example, *ftp://adam@isp_ftp_server.net*. If you're a power user and want command-line control, including possibly scripting file transfers, you can use the `ncftp` tool set (*http://www.ncftp.com/ncftp*), especially the `ncftpput` program. This is the tool we use ourselves, and is available for Linux, Windows, and Mac OS X.

Now, how do you set up the database? Well, there are two ways. You could create the database on the web host; this is likely to be tedious. A better solution is to create the database on your own machine and then *export* it to the web host.

You can export data from a database into an SQL dump file using the `mysqldump` command discussed in Chapter 10. Once you have the dump file, you can upload it to the server as an SQL query text file. The server will run all the SQL queries in the file and re-create the database.

Hosting companies generally don't give subscribers access to the MySQL server `root` account and instead allocate each subscriber a non-`root` username and password. You'll need to modify your scripts to use the authentication details provided to you.

Most web-hosting packages with MySQL support allow you to access the MySQL server using the phpMyAdmin web-based MySQL administration tool. As you can see from Figure 13-6, phpMyAdmin allows you to perform common operations such as creating, browsing, editing, and dropping database tables by clicking on links in your browser. You can run SQL queries on the database by typing them into the phpMyAdmin text box or by uploading a text file that contains the query. You can upload a complete database in this way by telling phpMyAdmin to run the queries in a database dump file created using `mysqldump`.

Similarly, you can download a dump file of selected tables or the complete database by selecting the "Save as file" option under the "View dump" section.

The XAMPP integrated package includes an installation of phpMyAdmin. Note that if you configure web tools such as phpMyAdmin to access the server, you should take great care to authenticate users, since you are effectively publishing your database on the Web.

PhpMyAdmin - Deer Park Alpha 2

File   Edit   View   Go   Bookmarks   Tools   Help

http://my.hosting_site.net/?php4uadmin=RandomIVK%1EE%B2%EEt9   Go

LYCOS   *tripod*

asip_uk_db (89)
nuke_authors
nuke_autonews
nuke_banned_ip
nuke_banner
nuke_bannerclient
nuke_bbauth_access
nuke_bbbanlist
nuke_bbcategories
nuke_bbconfig
nuke_bbdisallow
nuke_bbforum_prune
nuke_bbforums
nuke_bbgroups
nuke_bbposts
nuke_bbposts_text
nuke_bbprivmsgs
nuke_bbprivmsgs_text
nuke_bbranks
nuke_bbsearch_results
nuke_bbsearch_wordlist
nuke_bbsearch_wordmatch
nuke_bbsessions
nuke_bbsmilies
nuke_bbthemes
nuke_bbthemes_name
nuke_bbtopics
nuke_bbtopics_watch
nuke_bbuser_group
nuke_bbvote_desc
nuke_bbvote_results
nuke_bbvote_voters
nuke_bbwords
nuke_blocks
nuke_comments
nuke_config
nuke_confirm
nuke_counter
nuke_downloads_categories
nuke_downloads_downloads
nuke_downloads_editorials
nuke_downloads_modreque
nuke_downloads_newdownl
nuke_downloads_votedata
nuke_encyclopedia
nuke_encyclopedia_text
nuke_faqanswer
nuke_faqcategories
nuke_groups
nuke_groups_points
nuke_headlines
nuke_journal
nuke_journal_comments
nuke_journal_stats
nuke_links_categories
nuke_links_editorials
nuke_links_links
nuke_links_modrequest
nuke_links_newlink
nuke_links_votedata
nuke_main

nuke_stories_cat	Browse	Select	Insert	Properties	Drop	Empty	1	MyISAM	3.0 KB
nuke_subscriptions	Browse	Select	Insert	Properties	Drop	Empty	0	MyISAM	1.0 KB
nuke_topics	Browse	Select	Insert	Properties	Drop	Empty	2	MyISAM	3.1 KB
nuke_users	Browse	Select	Insert	Properties	Drop	Empty	26	MyISAM	10.5 KB
nuke_users_temp	Browse	Select	Insert	Properties	Drop	Empty	14	MyISAM	3.8 KB
89 table(s)				Sum			7,735	–	331.2 KB

With checked: Drop   Or   Empty

- Print view

- Run SQL query/queries on database asip_uk_db [Documentation] :

☑ Show this query here again

Or Location of the textfile :
                    Browse...
Go

- Query by Example

- View dump (schema) of database

nuke_authors
nuke_autonews
nuke_banned_ip
nuke_banner
nuke_bannerclient

(• Structure only
(○ Structure and data
(○ Data only

☐ Add 'drop table'
☐ Complete inserts
☐ Extended inserts
☐ Use backquotes with tables and fields' names
☐ Save as file (☐ "gzipped")
Go

- Create new table on database asip_uk_db :
Name :
Fields :   Go

PhpMyAdmin   Search

Stopped

Figure 13-6. The phpMyAdmin graphical MySQL administration tool

Resources

To learn more about the origins of LAMP, and related technologies, visit the *http://www.onlamp.com* web site run by O'Reilly Media.

To learn more about PHP and PHP programming, we recommend the following books:

- *Learning PHP 5* by David Sklar (O'Reilly). This is an excellent introductory book.

- *Programming PHP* by Rasmus Lerdorf et al. (O'Reilly). A reference-style book that covers the core libraries.
- *PHP Pocket Reference* by Rasmus Lerdorf (O'Reilly).
- *PHP Cookbook* by David Sklar and Adam Trachtenberg (O'Reilly). This contains solutions to tricky PHP problems.
- *PHP Essentials* by Julie Meloni (Premier Press). A good introductory book covering programming basics.

Other books are listed on the *http://www.php.net/books.php* web page.

To learn more about Apache, we recommend:

- The Apache web site (*http://httpd.apache.org*).
- *Apache: The Definitive Guide* by Ben Laurie and Peter Laurie (O'Reilly). This really is the definitive guide to Apache configuration.
- *Apache Cookbook* by Ken Coar and Rich Bowen (O'Reilly). Solutions to problems with Apache.

To learn more about building web database applications that use PHP, Apache, and MySQL, read Hugh's other book:

- *Web Database Applications with PHP and MySQL* by Hugh E. Williams and David Lane (O'Reilly).

You might also find it interesting to learn about the relatively new Ajax programming paradigm, which relies heavily on client-side processing: (*http://en.wikipedia.org/wiki/AJAX*)

To learn more about client-side programming with JavaScript, see:

- The W3Schools JavaScript tutorial at *http://www.w3schools.com/js*.
- *JavaScript: The Definitive Guide* by David Flanagan (O'Reilly).

To learn more about phpMyAdmin, see the program's web site at *http://www.phpmyadmin.net*.

You might also be interested in Ruby on Rails, which is designed for easy development of web database applications using the Ruby scripting language; to learn more, visit the Ruby on Rails web site at: *http://www.rubyonrails.org*.

Exercises

1. What does the acronym LAMP stand for?
2. Draw a diagram that explains a three-tier architecture. For each tier, list the LAMP components that make up that tier.

3. HTTP is a stateless protocol. What does this mean? What are the advantages and disadvantages of statelessness?

4. How does Apache know when to start the PHP engine? What steps would you take if PHP code itself were displayed in the browser rather than the result of running the PHP code?

## CHAPTER 14

PHP

In Chapter 13, we discussed how the triad of MySQL, PHP, and the Apache web server is one of the most popular web development platforms. In this chapter, we introduce you to building web database applications for this platform. We cover the following topics:

- An introduction to the PHP language
- How the commonly used MySQL library functions are used to access the MySQL DBMS
- How to handle MySQL DBMS errors, use include files to modularize code, and secure user data
- How to write data to databases and manage sessions in applications

PHP has a large set of libraries available that can be used for tasks as diverse as string manipulation, network communications, data compression, and disk access. We can only touch on some of these in this book; you'll find the PHP manual and the resources listed at the end of this chapter invaluable as you learn more about the language.

Language Basics

This section is a short introduction to the basic syntax of PHP. If you're familiar with high-level languages such as C, C++, Java, JavaScript, or Perl, then you'll find PHP very easy to learn. PHP began its life as a simple, procedural language that was designed to be embedded into HTML pages, and that's mostly what we focus on this chapter. More recently, it has become a full-fledged object oriented (OO) language that can be used for nonweb and cross-platform applications, including both scripts that run from the command-line and programs with graphical user interfaces (see the PHP-GTK web site, *http://gtk.php.net*). You'll find pointers to comprehensive PHP resources in "Resources" at the end of this chapter.

As discussed previously, PHP scripts are surrounded by the PHP start tag `<?php` and the PHP end tag `?>`. You'll sometimes see the start tag abbreviated to `<?`, but this conflicts

with the XHTML standard and should be avoided. Statements in a script are terminated with a semicolon. Statements can be formatted for readability by including any amount of whitespace—such as space characters, tab characters,or blank lines—in a script.

Comments can be included in a PHP script using the following styles:

```
// One-line comment

#  Another one-line comment

/* A
multiple-line
comment */
```

Anything that appears after the // or #, or between the /* and */ characters, is ignored.

Variables are prefixed with a dollar sign ($) and variable names are case-sensitive. PHP has several variable types. *Scalar* variables contain one value; scalar types are integer, Boolean, string, and float (floating-point number). There are two *compound* types of variable, array and object, that themselves contain scalar variables—possibly of different types.

Variables are automatically declared and given a type when they're first used. You don't have to declare them beforehand; the type of a variable can change in a script. Values are assigned to variables with a single = character:

```
// $x is an integer with the value 4
$x = 4;

// Now $x is a float
$x = 3.142;

// Now $x is a string
$x = "Selina";

// Now $x is a Boolean
$x = true;

// $y is an array of integers, strings, and Booleans
$y = array("hello", 1, 2, true, false, "cat");
```

Strings

PHP Strings are enclosed in double or single quotes. The following are identical:

```
$string = "Hello world";
$string = 'Hello world';
```

You can switch between quote styles for the convenience of including the other type of quote in the string:

```
$string = "This string includes a single ' quote";
$string = 'This string includes a double " quote';
```

You can also include quotes using the backslash character as an escape code:

```
$string = "This string includes a double \" quote";
$string = 'This string includes a single \' quote';
```

To include a backslash character, escape it with a backslash:

```
$string = "Here's a \\ blackslash character";
```

Unlike most other languages, you can incorporate carriage returns and line feeds directly into strings:

```
$string = "Here's a string spread over
  two lines";
```

You can also include carriage return, line feed, and tab characters using the \n, \r, and \t shortcuts, respectively:

```
$string = "This string is spread over\n two lines. And it has a \t tab in it.";
```

Adding newlines and tabs in content sent to the browser makes the HTML source more readable. However, such whitespace has no significance in HTML unless you enclose the text in <pre> tags to mark it as preformatted content. Adding such whitespace characters often comes in handy when developing and debugging an application, but you can also safely omit them in production code.

Arrays

Arrays can be accessed by their numeric or associative index. Numeric indexes are numbered from zero. Consider two sample arrays:

```
// This is an associative array
$x = array("one" => 1,
           "two" => 2,
           "three" => 3);

// The value 1 from the array $x is placed into the variable $y
$y = $x["one"];

// This is a numerically indexed array
$a = array(10, 20, 30);

// This places the value 20 from the array $a in the variable $b
// (since arrays begin with an index of 0)
$b = $a[1];
```

You can create and manipulate arrays using the indexes. For example, in addition to using the array( ) syntax:

```
$x = array(10, 20, 30);
```

you can access the elements directly and get the same result by writing:

```
$x[0] = 10;
$x[1] = 20;
$x[2] = 30;
```

The style you use is a personal preference; the former style is compact and simple, while the second style is familiar to most programmers.

Manipulating Variables

You can manipulate variables to modify the values they contain. For example, you can add the values in two variables and place this value in a third variable:

```
$x = 4;
$y = 7;
$z = $x + $y;
```

You could in fact place the sum into an existing variable, such as **$x**:

```
$x = $x + $y;
```

Of course, this would overwrite the previous value (4) with the sum (11).

The arithmetic shortcuts that work in many other languages also work in PHP:

```
$x = 4;

// add one to $x in three different ways
$x = $x + 1;
$x++;
$x += 1;

// subtract one from $x in three different ways
$x = $x - 1;
$x--;
$x -= 1;

// Multiply $x by two in two ways
$x = $x * 2;
$x *= 2;

// Divide $x by three in two ways
$x = $x / 3;
$x /= 3;
```

To concatenate strings, use the . operator:

```
$x = "Hello";
$y = "world";

// $z contains "Hello world";
$z = $x . " " . $y;
```

Displaying Information

To display information, we can use the PHP statements `print`, `echo`, or `printf`. The first two are interchangeable; the third is for more complex output, and its use is identical to that in programming languages such as C, and in scripting languages such as awk. Consider a few examples:

```
// These are the same; all display the text: [This is output]
echo   "This is output";
print  "This is output";
printf("This is output");
```

The `printf` command can be used with placeholders, or *format specifiers*. For example, `%d` represents an integer number, `%f` represents a floating-point (decimal) number, and `%s` represents a string of characters:

```
// This displays: [6 inches x 2.540000 = 15.240000 centimeters]
printf("%d %s x %f = %f %s", 6, "inches", 2.54, 6*2.54, "centimeters");
```

We can modify the format specifiers to control formatting; for example, we can space values out and limit the number of decimal digits displayed:

```
// This displays: [          6 inches x        2.54 = 15.2                centimeters]
printf("%10d %s x %10.2f = %-10.1f %20s", 6, "inches", 2.54, 6*2.54, "centimeters");
```

The `%10d` specifies that 10 characters should be set aside for displaying the integer value —in this case, 6; since the number is only one character long, there are nine blank spaces to the left of the displayed value. If you add a minus sign just after the percent symbol, the spaces appear to the right of the value. With floating-point numbers, we can control the number of decimal places to be displayed; here, we're limiting the first floating-point number (2.54) to two digits, and the second floating point number (6*2.54) to one decimal place. You can learn more about format specifiers from *http://www.php.net/manual/en/function.sprintf.php*.

You can print variables using `print` or `echo` using several styles. The most convenient is to incorporate the variable into a string enclosed in double quotes:

```
$x = 4;

// Prints "x is 4";
echo "x is {$x}";
```

The braces, { and }, form an escape sequence that tells PHP to process the enclosed value as a variable expression. You don't always need to use the braces; the following works equally well:

```
$x = 4;

// Prints "x is 4";
echo "x is $x";
```

However, using braces is useful to avoid ambiguity, and you can even display values from an associative array without needing to escape the double quotes:

```
// This is an associative array
$x = array("one" => 1,
           "two" => 2,
           "three" => 3);

// This prints "x is 1"
echo "x is {$x["one"]}";
```

Adding braces allows all variables to be included directly into strings that are delimited by double quotation marks. If a variable can be unambiguously parsed from within a double-quoted string, then the braces can be omitted. Here, the double quotes around the array index ("one") can be confused with the double quotes surrounding the complete string, and so the braces are necessary; you can also include braces to help make your code more readable, even when they're not strictly needed.

If you wanted to avoid using braces, you would need to append the associative array value to the string with the period symbol (.):

```
echo "x is ".$x["one"];
```

If you actually want to display a brace, you need to escape it with the backslash symbol (\):

```
echo "A left brace: \{";
```

Variable substitution in strings doesn't work with single-quoted strings: whatever is included in a single-quoted string is printed out literally:

```
// Doesn't work as expected. It prints: ["x is {$x}"]
echo 'x is {$x}';
```

Conditional Statements

You can have parts of a PHP script executed only if certain conditions are met. The most frequently used conditional statement in PHP is if:

```
if ($x < 5)
  echo "x is less than 5";
```

Frequently used expressions are less-than (<); greater-than (>); less-than-or-equals (<=); greater-than-or-equals (>=); and not-equals (!=).

You can implement more complex conditions using the else keyword:

```
if ($x < 5)
  echo "x is less than 5";
else if ($x > 5)
  echo "x is greater than 5";
else
  echo "x is equal to 5";
```

You can write else if as one word, elseif.

The `switch...case` construct allows you to easily select between several possible values, as in the following example:

```
switch ($x)
{
 case 1:
  echo "x is 1";
  break;
 case 2:
  echo "x is 2";
  break;
 case 3:
  echo "x is 3";
  break;
 default:
  echo "x is not 1, 2, or 3";
}
```

The `default` section is executed if the `switch` value doesn't match any of the `case` values. The `break` keyword tells PHP to leave the `switch` construct; if you leave it out, processing will drop through to the next `case` condition, and the statements there will also be executed. For example, if $x is one, and the first break is missing, the program would print "x is 1", and then continue into the next case, and also print "x is 2".

Equality is tested with the double-equals (==) syntax:

```
$x = 4;

if ($x == 4)
 echo "x is four!";
```

It's a very common mistake to forget to write the second equals symbol (=) in an equality test. PHP considers a variable assignment operation to have a **true** value, so the test will always succeed. For instance, the test below will always succeed, and so the message "x is four!" will be printed whatever the value of x—for example, 3:

```
$x = 3;

if ($x = 4)
 echo "x is four!";
```

A triple-equals operator (===) can also be used to test if the parameters are both equal and of the same type:

```
$x = 0;

// This prints, since 0 and false are the same value
if ($x == false)
 echo "$x is false";

// This doesn't print, because 0 and false aren't the same type
if ($x === false)
 echo "$x is false";
```

The not-equals operator (!=) is the opposite of the equality operator (==). Similarly, the !== operator is a type-sensitive not-equals and is the opposite of ===.

There are two handy functions—isset( ) and empty( )—for checking the state of a variable:

```
// Has the variable been declared?
if (isset($x))
 echo "x is set";

// Is the variable empty?
if (empty($x))
 echo "x is empty";
```

A variable that doesn't exist (is not set) is always empty. However, a variable that's empty may or may not exist, but if it does, it has a NULL value. A third function, unset( ), can be used to destroy a variable:

```
$x = 5;

unset($x);

// Prints "not set"
if (isset($x))
 echo $x;
else
 echo "not set";
```

Loops

The standard loop constructs are for, while, and do...while. Let's look at different ways to print out the integers 0 to 9 using these constructs.

The for statement has three parameters: an instruction to initialize any variables, a condition that must be met for the loop to continue, and an instruction that is executed after each round of the loop. To count from 0 to 9, we can start by setting the variable $x to 0 ($x=0). We increment $x one by one ($x++) as long as it is less than 10 ($x<10):

```
for ($x=0; $x<10; $x++)
 echo "$x\n";
```

The while loop can take the same parameters, but here they are placed at different locations in the code:

```
$x = 0;
while ($x < 10)
{
 echo "$x\n";
 $x++;
}
```

Notice that when more than one statement forms the body of the loop, the statements are enclosed in braces. Braces are also used with the conditional if when there's more than one statement you want to execute.

The do...while loop is almost identical to the while loop:

```php
$x = 0;
do
{
 echo "$x\n";
 $x++;
} while ($x < 10);
```

However, there is one important difference between while and do...while: in the latter construct, the condition is checked *after* the body of the loop, so the instructions between the braces are always executed at least once; if the condition is false, the loop is not repeated.

The foreach statement is a different type of loop construct that is used to simplify iteration through an array:

```php
// $x is an array of strings
$x = array("one", "two", "three", "four", "five");

// This prints out each element of the array
foreach ($x as $element)
 echo $element;
```

Functions

PHP has a large number of built-in functions that you can use to perform common tasks. A function call is followed by parentheses that contain zero or more arguments to the function. The following fragment uses the library function count( ) to display the number of elements in an array:

```php
// $x is an array of strings
$x = array("one", "two", "three", "four", "five");

// Displays 5
print count($x);
```

The count( ) function takes one parameter, which should be an array type. Functions can return nothing or a value of any type; the previous example returns an integer value, which is then output using print. When a value is returned, the function can be used in an expression. For example, the following uses count( ) in an if statement:

```php
// $x is an array of strings
$x = array("one", "two", "three", "four", "five");

if (count($x) >= 3)
 echo "This array has several elements";
else
 echo "This array contains less than three elements";
```

The PHP manual web site (*http://www.php.net/manual*) has excellent search and browse features for locating details on functions. When you visit this page, you'll see a search box at the top right. By default, if you type text and press Enter (or click the small right-arrow icon), you'll search the function library names for exact or near matches. For example, if you type **print** and press Enter, you'll be taken directly to the manual page for the print statement. If instead you type **prin**, you'll be taken to a page of near matches, including links to print, printf, sprintf, and related entries. Very close matches are shown in bold, while less likely matches are shown without bold (and, in this example, include functions such as phpinfo, phpinfo, and pi that make passing reference to printing in their descriptions).

You can also define your own functions. User-defined functions are created with the keyword function and enclosed in braces. Here's an example of a user-defined function do-math( ) that itself calls PHP math library functions to output interesting values:

```
function do-math($x)
{
 if ($x > 0)
 {
  print "log10(x) = " . log($x,10);
  print "logN(x) = "  . log($x);
  print "sqrt(x) = "  . sqrt($x);
  print "x^2 = "      . pow($x, 2);
  return true;
 }
 else
  return false;
}

// Print out interesting math for the value 10
$ret = do-math(10);

// This test should fail, since the function should return true for 10
if ($ret == false)
 print "Can't do math for <=0";

// Now, try to print out interesting math for the value 0
$ret = do-math(0);

// This test should succeed and print the error message,
// since the function should return false for 0
if ($ret == false)
 print "Can't do math for <=0";
```

The function returns true when the parameter is greater than 0, and false otherwise. In the example, the return value is assigned to $ret and used in the subsequent if test.

Passing variables by reference

If you add the ampersand symbol (&) before the name of a variable in a function declaration, a *reference* to the variable will be passed to the function, rather than the variable value itself. This allows the function to change the variable, and the main program can use the new value. Consider Example 14-1.

Example 14-1. Passing variables to function by value and by reference

```
<!DOCTYPE HTML PUBLIC
  "-//W3C//DTD HTML 4.01 Transitional//EN"
  "http://www.w3.org/TR/html401/loose.dtd">
<html>
    <head>
    <title>Passing variables to a function by value or by reference</title>
  </head>
  <body>
  <table border='1'>
    <tr>
      <th>
        Step
      </th>
      <th>
        Variable Value
      </th>
    </tr>
    <?php
    // Set initial value for the variable
    $Variable=110;

    // Display the initial variable value.
    echo "<tr>
        <td>Initial value</td>
        <td align='right'>$Variable</td>
      </tr>";

    // Pass the variable by value to the AddNineteen_value() function.
    AddNineteen_value($Variable);

    // Display the variable value after passing it by value.
    echo "<tr>
        <td>After passing by value</td>
        <td align='right'>$Variable</td>
      </tr>";

    // Pass the variable by reference to the AddNineteen_reference() function.
    AddNineteen_reference($Variable);

    // Display the variable value after passing it by reference.
    echo "<tr>
        <td>After passing by reference</td>
        <td align='right'>$Variable</td>
      </tr>";

    // Function to add 19 to the received variable;
    // the function receives the variable value.
    function AddNineteen_value($MyVariable)
    {
      $MyVariable+=19;
```

Step	Variable Value
Initial values	110
After passing by value	110
After passing by reference	129

Figure 14-1. Web page produced when running Example 14-1

```
    }

    // Function to add 19 to the received variable;
    // the function receives a reference to the variable
    // (note the ampersand before the variable name).
    function AddNineteen_reference(&$MyVariable)
    {
      $MyVariable+=19;
    }
    ?>
    </table>
  </body>
</html>
```

The output of the program is shown in Figure 14-1.

When the variable is passed by value, the function makes its own copy, and any operations it performs on the variable are limited to the function itself. When the variable is passed by reference, any changes that the function makes (in this case, adding 19 to the value) are seen by the main program. Note that the name of the variable used by the function can be different from the name used by the main program when calling the function; here, the `AddNineteen_value( )` and `AddNineteen_reference( )` functions use the name `$MyVariable` internally.

Handling Errors in PHP

Sadly, every programmer—however experienced—makes mistakes. PHP tries to help in finding and rectifying these mistakes by providing detailed error messages when it detects a problem. It's useful to have PHP report detailed information on all errors during development, but it's best to avoid displaying much of this information to the end user in a production system. This will reduce the amount of confusion and also hide information that an attacker could find useful.

PHP is configured through a *php.ini* configuration file that includes two important directives that affect error reporting: `error_reporting` and `display_errors`. The former controls what types of errors are trapped, and the latter controls whether error messages are reported. When PHP is configured, `display_errors` is set to `On` and `error_reporting` lists selected errors that can occur; by default, in PHP4 and PHP5, it reports all errors except those in the insignificant NOTICE class. Your PHP installation may be configured differently.

If you find that you're not seeing PHP error messages, you can find the php.ini file and ensure that it contains the line:

```
display_errors = On
```

Add this line if necessary. Whenever you make a change to the *php.ini* file, you should restart the Apache web server to put the changes into effect. To ensure that all errors are reported, make sure the error_reporting line in *php.ini* file is set to:

```
error_reporting = E_ALL
```

and restart Apache.

If you don't have control of the web server (for example, on a web-hosting site), you won't be able to modify the *php.ini* file. You can instead enable error reporting by adding the two lines:

```
ini_set("display_errors", true);
error_reporting(E_ALL);
```

to the top of each PHP file, just after the PHP opening tag (<?php). There's no harm in doing this even if the PHP configuration is suitable, and it allows your scripts to be portable independent of the PHP settings on the web server.

When you're ready to deploy, turn off display_errors or change error_reporting to a setting that won't show the user minor (or perhaps, at your discretion, any) internal error messages. For example, you can use:

```
error_reporting(E_ALL & ~E_NOTICE & ~E_WARNING);
```

to force PHP to display only critical error messages. You'll find a description of the error-setting choices at *http://www.php.net/error_reporting*.

Throughout the rest of this book, we assume your PHP installation is configured to report all errors, or at least everything more serious than a notice.

Accessing MySQL Using PHP

Because this book is about MySQL, this chapter focuses on how to use PHP to access a MySQL database. Since the release of MySQL 4.1, there have been two PHP libraries that you can use: the original MySQL library and the MySQL Improved (MySQLi) library.

This creates a dilemma: which library should you use? If you're working on legacy code or a MySQL server older than version 4.1, you may not have a choice and will need to use the original library. If you're developing new code, you do have a choice: you can go with the original MySQL library that most developers still understand and use, or the MySQLi library that has additional features and better performance. We recom-

mend that you use the new library for new code, but you should also learn about the
older library because you're likely to encounter it as you develop and modify PHP code.

The Original PHP MySQL Library

This section describes the original PHP library designed for MySQL versions earlier
than 4.1. In most PHP installations, it works with later versions, although you can't
take advantage of some newer MySQL features.

In Chapter 13, we showed you a simple PHP code example that uses the original MySQL
library. It's reproduced in Example 14-2.

Example 14-2. Querying the music database with PHP

```
<!DOCTYPE HTML PUBLIC
"-//W3C//DTD HTML 4.01 Transitional//EN"
"http://www.w3.org/TR/html401/loose.dtd">
<html>
 <head>
  <meta http-equiv="Content-Type" content="text/html;
    charset=iso-8859-1" />
  <title>Artists</title>
 </head>
 <body>
  <h1>Artists</h1>

  <table>
   <tr>
    <th>artist_id</th>
    <th>artist_name</th>
   </tr>
   <?php
   // Connect to the MySQL server
   if (!($connection = @ mysql_connect("localhost", "root",

     "the_mysql_root_password")))

     die("Cannot connect");

   if (!(mysql_select_db("music", $connection)))
     die("Couldn't select music database");

   // Run the query on the connection
   if (!($result = @ mysql_query("SELECT * FROM artist",
     $connection)))
     die("Couldn't run query");

   // Until there are no rows in the result set, fetch a row into
   // the $row array and ...
   while ($row = @ mysql_fetch_array($result, MYSQL_ASSOC))
   {
    // Start a table row
    print "<tr>\n";
```

```
    // ... and print out each of the columns
    foreach($row as $data)
     print "\t<td>{$data}</td>\n";

    // Finish the row
    print "</tr>\n";
  }
  ?>
  </table>
 </body>
</html>
```

This example uses four key MySQL functions that we'll describe here. Each function takes one or more arguments and returns a value when it's completed the required operation. In the list below, we've adhered to convention by writing the return type first, and then the function name, which is followed by parentheses enclosing the arguments that can be passed to the function:

`resource mysql_connect(string hostname, string username, string password)`
Opens a connection to the MySQL server. Conceptually, this is the same as running the MySQL monitor, and it requires the same parameters: a *hostname* that identifies the server machine, a *username* of a MySQL user, and a *password* for the MySQL user. The hostname can be an IP address, the mnemonic `localhost`, or a fully qualified machine and domain, such as `ruttle.invyhome.com`.

By default, a MySQL server listens for incoming connections on port 3306; if your MySQL server has been configured to use a different port, you can append this to the hostname as *hostname:port*.

If the hostname is `localhost`, PHP makes a fast direct connection through a Unix socket (under Linux or Mac OS X) or a named pipe (under Windows) rather than through the network. If your server has been configured with a nonstandard socket path, you can also append this to the hostname parameter after the port, as in `localhost:port:path_to_socket`. We discussed sockets and named pipes briefly in "Configuring Access to the MySQL Server" in Chapter 2.

The return value of the function is a *resource handle* that is usually stored in a variable. The variable is then passed as a parameter to other MySQL functions—such as `mysql_query( )`—to identify the connection to use. If the function fails, it returns `false` instead of a connection handle.

`Boolean mysql_select_db(string database, resource connection)`
Selects a database to use. This is conceptually identical to typing the `USE` command in the MySQL monitor. The first parameter is a *database* name to use, and the second is the MySQL server *connection* to use. The *connection* is the return value from a previous call to the `mysql_connect( )` function. The function returns `true` on success and `false` on failure.

```
mixed mysql_query(string query, resource connection)
```
Executes an SQL query on a connection. This is conceptually the same as typing an SQL query into the MySQL monitor and pressing the Enter key. The first parameter is an SQL *query*, and the second is a connection resource handle that was returned from `mysql_connect( )`.

The function does not return or display the results. Instead, for `SELECT`, `SHOW`, `EXPLAIN`, or `DESCRIBE` queries, it returns a *resource handle* that can be assigned to a variable and used to access the results. The `mysql_fetch_array( )` function discussed next is usually used for this task. For `UPDATE`, `INSERT`, `DELETE`, and other queries that do not produce output, the return value is either `true` (indicating success) or `false` (indicating failure). Note that you don't need to include a semicolon (;) at the end of the query string, though there are no problems if you do. In the MySQLi library, the order of the parameters is reversed.

```
array mysql_fetch_array(resource result[, int type])
```
Returns an array containing one row of results from a previously executed query. The *result* handle parameter is the return value from a previously executed `mysql_query( )` function, and the optional *type* controls what type of array is returned; this is discussed later in this chapter in "Accessing Query Results with mysql_fetch_array() and mysqli_fetch_array()." Each call to the function returns the next available row of results as an array, with `false` returned when no further rows are available.

The four previous functions are sufficient to build simple applications. The three functions discussed next are also important, and you'll find them helpful in all but the most basic applications.

When you run queries, the MySQL monitor reports useful information that helps you make decisions about what to do next. To access this information from PHP scripts, you need to use functions. Three functions you'll find useful are:

```
int mysql_insert_id(resource connection)
```
If you use the `AUTO_INCREMENT` feature, this function allows you to access the unique identifier value associated with the most recent `INSERT` statement on a connection. The database *connection* is passed as a parameter, and the return value is an integer that uniquely identifies the new row. A value of 0 is returned if `AUTO_INCREMENT` wasn't used by the most recent query.

```
int mysql_affected_rows(resource connection)
```
Reports the number of rows that were modified by the last query on the connection identified by the resource handle *connection*. We describe this function in more detail later in "Finding the Number of Changed Rows Using mysql_affected_rows and mysqli_affected_rows."

```
int mysql_num_rows(resource result)
```
Reports the number of rows returned by a SELECT query identified by a *result* resource handle. The function doesn't work for queries that modify the database; mysql_affected_rows( ) should be used there instead.

The PHP Improved MySQL Library

This section discusses the Improved MySQL library, which we refer to as MySQLi. This library was introduced with PHP 5 and is designed to work with MySQL version 4.1.3 and above. We use the same conventions in this section as in the last one so that you can use them as independent references.

Example 14-3 rewrites Example 14-2 to use the new MySQLi library.

Example 14-3. Querying the music database with the MySQLi library

```
<!DOCTYPE HTML PUBLIC
"-//W3C//DTD HTML 4.01 Transitional//EN"
"http://www.w3.org/TR/html401/loose.dtd">
<html>
  <head>
    <meta http-equiv="Content-Type" content="text/html;
        charset=iso-8859-1" />
    <title>Artists</title>
  </head>
  <body>
    <h1>Artists</h1>

    <table>
      <tr>
        <th>artist_id</th>
        <th>artist_name</th>
      </tr>
      <?php
      // Connect to the MySQL server
      if (!($connection = @ mysqli_connect("localhost", "root",

        "the_mysql_root_password")))

        die("Cannot connect");

      if (!(mysqli_select_db($connection, "music")))
        die("Couldn't select music database");

      // Run the query on the connection
      if (!($result = @ mysqli_query($connection, "SELECT * FROM artist")))
        die("Couldn't run query");

      // Until there are no rows in the result set, fetch a row into
      // the $row array and ...
      while ($row = @ mysqli_fetch_array($result, MYSQL_ASSOC))
      {
        // Start a table row
```

```
        print "<tr>\n";

        // ... and print out each of the columns
        foreach($row as $data)
          print "\t<td>{$data}</td>\n";

        // Finish the row
        print "</tr>\n";
      }
      ?>
    </table>
  </body>
</html>
```

The example uses three key MySQLi functions, described next in a simplified form. As with the standard MySQL library, each function takes one or more arguments and returns a value when it's completed the required operation. Again, we follow convention and write the return type first, then the function name, and, in parentheses, the list of arguments that can be passed to the function:

resource mysqli_connect(string *hostname,* string *username,* string *password,* string *database*)

> Opens a connection to the MySQL server and uses a database. Conceptually, this is the same as running the MySQL monitor and issuing a USE command. It requires the same parameters and input: a *hostname* that identifies the server machine, a *username* of a MySQL user, a *password* for the MySQL user, and the database to use. The hostname can be an IP address, the mnemonic localhost, or a fully qualified machine and domain such as ruttle.invyhome.com.

> By default, a MySQL server listens for incoming connections on port 3306; if your MySQL server has been configured to use a different port, you can specify this as an additional parameter to mysqli_connect( ) after the database name. If the hostname is localhost, PHP makes a fast direct connection through a Unix socket (under Linux or Mac OS X) or a named pipe (under Windows) rather than through the network. If your server has been configured with a nonstandard socket path, you can also append this as an additional parameter after the port. We discussed sockets and named pipes briefly in "Configuring Access to the MySQL Server" in Chapter 2.

> The return value of the function is a *resource handle* that is usually stored in a variable. The variable is passed as a parameter to other MySQL functions—such as mysqli_query( )—to identify the connection to use. If the function fails, it returns false instead of a connection handle.

> The database is selected when the connection is established. You can change the active database using the mysqli_select_db( ) function, but you normally just use the database that you activated in the call to mysqli_connect( ).

```
mixed mysqli_query(resource connection, string query)
```
Executes an SQL query on a connection. This is conceptually the same as typing an SQL query into the MySQL monitor and pressing the Enter key. The first parameter is a *connection* resource handle that was returned from `mysqli_connect( )` and the second is an SQL *query*; note that the parameter order is the opposite of the original MySQL library's `mysql_query( )` function.

The function does not return or display the results. Instead, for `SELECT`, `SHOW`, `EXPLAIN`, or `DESCRIBE` queries, it returns a *resource handle* that can be assigned to a variable and used to access the results. The `mysqli_fetch_array( )` function discussed next is usually used for this task. For `UPDATE`, `INSERT`, `DELETE`, and other queries that do not produce output, the return value is either `true` (indicating success) or `false` (indicating failure). Note that you don't need to include a semicolon (`;`) at the end of the query string, though there are no problems if you do.

```
array mysqli_fetch_array(resource result[, int type])
```
Returns an array containing one row of results from a previously executed query. The *result* handle parameter is the return value from a previously-executed `mysqli_query( )` function. Each call to the function returns the next available row of results as an array, with `false` returned when no further rows are available. This function is explained in detail later in "Accessing Query Results with mysql_fetch_array( ) and mysqli_fetch_array( )."

The three previous functions are sufficient to build simple applications. The three functions discussed next are also important, and you'll find them helpful in all but the most basic applications.

When you run queries, the MySQL monitor reports useful information that helps you make decisions about what to do next. To access this information from PHP scripts, you need to use functions. Three functions you'll find useful are:

```
int mysqli_insert_id(resource connection)
```
If you use the `AUTO_INCREMENT` feature, this function allows you to access the unique identifier value associated with the most recent `INSERT` statement on a connection. The database *connection* is passed as a parameter, and the return value is an integer that uniquely identifies the new row. A value of 0 is returned if `AUTO_INCREMENT` wasn't used by the most recent query.

```
int mysqli_affected_rows(resource connection)
```
Reports the number of rows that were modified by the last query on the connection identified by the resource handle *connection*. We describe this function in more detail later in "Finding the Number of Changed Rows Using mysql_affected_rows and mysqli_affected_rows."

```
int mysqli_num_rows(resource result)
```
Reports the number of rows returned by a `SELECT` query identified by a *result* resource handle. The function doesn't work for queries that modify the database; `mysqli_affected_rows( )` should be used there instead.

The descriptions in this section are simplified. We've omitted function parameters that are rarely used, avoided some of the details of how the functions are used, and shown some optional parameters as mandatory. We've also shown only the *procedural* style for the library, which means we've shown the features of the library as functions; you can also use the new library in an object-oriented programming style, but that's outside the scope of this book. You'll find more detail on MySQLi functions in the PHP manual at *http://www.php.net/manual/en/ref.mysqli.php* and in the resources listed in "Resources" at the end of this chapter.

What's New in MySQLi

The examples and functions we've discussed don't show the differences between the MySQL and MySQLi libraries; let's look at these now. The most significant difference between the libraries is under the hood. The MySQLi library is a complete rewrite of the MySQL library, designed to offer better performance. This means that even if you're not using the advanced features it offers, it's always better to use MySQLi when you're not constrained by other issues (such as maintaining legacy code). Other features of MySQLi include:

Support for encrypted and compressed connections
These allow faster, secure connections between PHP and MySQL over a network. Encryption using SSL is highly secure and ensures that hackers can't eavesdrop on your data as it is being transmitted. Compression means that less data is transferred between the web server and the MySQL server, which for moderate or high rates of data transfer means that communications are faster.

Prepared statements
These allow you to prepare (parse, optimize, and plan) an SQL statement once and reuse it many times, saving that cost each time you use it. This is useful if you want to repeat a query with different parameters—for example, when bulk inserting data.

Object-oriented methods
As discussed previously, you can now use an object-oriented style with the MySQLi library in addition to the procedural style shown in this section.

Transaction control
Transactions are discussed in "Transactions and Locking" in Chapter 7. The MySQLi library gives you functions to turn the autocommit feature on or off, and also start, commit, and roll back transactions.

Profiling
Allows you to view statistics and debugging information from your MySQL server. This includes timing details for function calls, the output of the EXPLAIN statement that describes how the queries are evaluated, and so on.

Distribution and replication functions
> Many new functions have been added to allow you to manage many MySQL servers that perform the same tasks. This allows you to build highly scalable systems that can handle hundreds of thousands or millions of requests each day.

We don't discuss these features in detail as they're outside the scope of this book.

Accessing Query Results with mysql_fetch_array( ) and mysqli_fetch_array( )

The mysql_fetch_array( ) and mysqli_fetch_array( ) functions retrieve result rows from queries that produce output. These functions are typically used to retrieve the results output by an SQL SELECT statement. This section uses examples to show how. To keep our description simple, we'll use the standard MySQL library, but our explanations apply to mysqli_fetch_array( ) as well.

As with the array examples described previously, you can access elements returned with mysql_fetch_array( ) using either *numeric* or *associative* access. For numeric access, attributes are numbered in the order they are specified in the SQL statement. If you use a SELECT * FROM *table* statement, then the attributes are ordered first by the table names and then by the order they were created with the CREATE TABLE statement (which is as listed by the output of the DESCRIBE or SHOW statements). Let's explore three examples of numeric access that illustrate these ideas.

We'll begin with a simple example that uses the music database. Suppose you want to output the artist_id column and then the artist_name column for all rows from the artist table. You can do this with the following PHP fragment:

```
// Tell the browser to expect preformatted text
print "<pre>";

// Run the query on the connection
if (!($result = @ mysql_query("SELECT artist_id, artist_name FROM artist",
  $connection)))
  die("Couldn't run query");

// Until there are no rows in the result set, fetch a row into
// the $row array.
while ($row = @ mysql_fetch_array($result))
{
 // Start a new line
 print "\n";

 // Print out the columns
 print "{$row[0]} {$row[1]}";
}

// Tell the browser that the preformatted text has ended
print "</pre>";
```

This produces the following output:

```
1 New Order
2 Nick Cave & The Bad Seeds
3 Miles Davis
4 The Rolling Stones
5 The Stone Roses
6 Kylie Minogue
```

You can see that the `artist_id` column is output by printing the first element of the array `$row` by referencing `$row[0]`. The `artist_name` is output by referencing `$row[1]`.

Note that we enclosed the output in HTML `<pre>` tags; if we hadn't, the browser would have ignored the newline (\n) character during display. You could still have used your browser's View Source option to see the lines as they were sent to the browser by the PHP script.

Consider another example from the music database. This time, let's examine the structure of the artist table:

```
mysql> DESCRIBE artist;
+-------------+-----------+------+-----+---------+-------+
| Field       | Type      | Null | Key | Default | Extra |
+-------------+-----------+------+-----+---------+-------+
| artist_id   | int(5)    |      | PRI | 0       |       |
| artist_name | char(128) | YES  |     | NULL    |       |
+-------------+-----------+------+-----+---------+-------+
2 rows in set (0.00 sec)
```

The following code fragment selects all rows from the artist table and prints the columns after a call to `mysql_fetch_array( )`. In this example, rather than explicitly printing the individual elements, we print all elements of the row starting with the first:

```php
// Tell the browser to expect preformatted text
print "<pre>";

// Run the query on the connection
if (!($result = @ mysql_query("SELECT * FROM artist", $connection)))
  die("Couldn't run query");

// Count the number of columns in the results
$count = @ mysql_num_fields($result);

// Until there are no rows in the result set, fetch a row into
// the $row array.
while ($row = @ mysql_fetch_array($result))
{
 print "\n";
 // Print out the columns
 for($x=0; $x<$len; $x++)
  print "{$row[$x]} ";
}

// Tell the browser that the preformatted text has ended
print "</pre>";
```

The output looks identical to the previous example:

```
1 New Order
2 Nick Cave & The Bad Seeds
3 Miles Davis
4 The Rolling Stones
5 The Stone Roses
6 Kylie Minogue
```

You can see that the columns appear in the order they do in the table—that is, the `artist_id` appears before the `artist_name`. Notice also that we used the `mysql_num_fields( )` function described in the previous example to figure out how many columns there were in the results.

Suppose that you want to to run the following query that uses two tables:

```
SELECT * FROM artist, album WHERE artist.artist_id = album.artist_id
```

With the monitor, you'd get:

```
mysql> SELECT * FROM artist, album WHERE artist.artist_id = album.artist_id;
+-----------+---------------------------+-----------+----------+...
| artist_id | artist_name               | artist_id | album_id |...
+-----------+---------------------------+-----------+----------+...
| 1         | New Order                 | 1         | 1        |...
| 1         | New Order                 | 1         | 2        |...
| 1         | New Order                 | 1         | 3        |...
| 1         | New Order                 | 1         | 4        |...
| 1         | New Order                 | 1         | 5        |...
| 1         | New Order                 | 1         | 6        |...
| 1         | New Order                 | 1         | 7        |...
| 2         | Nick Cave & The Bad Seeds | 2         | 1        |...
| 3         | Miles Davis               | 3         | 1        |...
| 3         | Miles Davis               | 3         | 2        |...
| 4         | The Rolling Stones        | 4         | 1        |...
| 5         | The Stone Roses           | 5         | 1        |...
| 6         | Kylie Minogue             | 6         | 1        |...
+-----------+---------------------------+-----------+----------+...
...+----------------------------------------+
...| album_name                             |
...+----------------------------------------+
...| Retro - John McCready FAN              |
...| Substance (Disc 2)                     |
...| Retro - Miranda Sawyer POP             |
...| Retro - New Order / Bobby Gillespie LIVE |
...| Power, Corruption & Lies               |
...| Substance 1987 (Disc 1)                |
...| Brotherhood                            |
...| Let Love In                            |
...| Live Around The World                  |
...| In A Silent Way                        |
...| Exile On Main Street                   |
...| Second Coming                          |
...| Light Years                            |
...+----------------------------------------+
13 rows in set (0.01 sec)
```

The PHP code you'd write to run this query would be as follows:

```
// Run the query on the connection
if (!($result = @ mysql_query(
  "SELECT * FROM artist, album WHERE artist.artist_id = album.artist_id",
  $connection)))
    die("Couldn't run query");

// Count the number of columns in the results
$count = @ mysql_num_fields($result);

// Until there are no rows in the result set, fetch a row into
// the $row array.
while ($row = @ mysql_fetch_array($result))
{
 print "\n";
 // Print out the columns
 for ($x=0;$x<$count;$x++)
  print "{$row[$x]} ";
}
```

We've used nested loops here; the outer while loop iterates over each result row, while the inner for loop iterates over each column in the row. The output you get is as follows:

```
1 New Order 1 1 Retro - John McCready FAN
1 New Order 1 2 Substance (Disc 2)
1 New Order 1 3 Retro - Miranda Sawyer POP
1 New Order 1 4 Retro - New Order / Bobby Gillespie LIVE
1 New Order 1 5 Power, Corruption & Lies
1 New Order 1 6 Substance 1987 (Disc 1)
1 New Order 1 7 Brotherhood
2 Nick Cave & The Bad Seeds 2 1 Let Love In
3 Miles Davis 3 1 Live Around The World
3 Miles Davis 3 2 In A Silent Way
4 The Rolling Stones 4 1 Exile On Main Street
5 The Stone Roses 5 1 Second Coming
6 Kylie Minogue 6 1 Light Years
```

You can see that the two columns from artist appear before the three columns from album, since artist is listed before album in the SELECT statement.

Numeric access is clumsy when you want to print out columns in nonsequential order. For example, continuing the previous example, if you want to print the artist_name and album_name columns, then you need to know they're referenced as $row[1] and $row[4], respectively. If you change the SQL query or change the table structure, then you also need to modify the PHP code that works with the array. A better approach is to access the columns using their names, but this has a few catches as we show you in the next few examples.

Let's start with a simple associative access example. Suppose you want to do what we just discussed: print the artist_name and album_name columns after a join between the artist and album tables. Here's the code fragment you need:

```
// Run the query on the connection
if (!($result = @ mysql_query(
 "SELECT * FROM artist, album WHERE artist.artist_id = album.artist_id",
 $connection)))
  die("Couldn't run query");

// Until there are no rows in the result set, fetch a row into
// the $row array.
while ($row = @ mysql_fetch_array($result))
{
 print "\n";
 // Print out the columns
 print "{$row["artist_name"]} {$row["album_name"]}";
}
```

You can see that to access the artist_name column, you provide the column name as an associative key into the $row array as $row["artist_name"]. As you'd expect, the code outputs the following:

```
New Order Retro - John McCready FAN
New Order Substance (Disc 2)
New Order Retro - Miranda Sawyer POP
New Order Retro - New Order / Bobby Gillespie LIVE
New Order Power, Corruption & Lies
New Order Substance 1987 (Disc 1)
New Order Brotherhood
Nick Cave & The Bad Seeds Let Love In
Miles Davis Live Around The World
Miles Davis In A Silent Way
The Rolling Stones Exile On Main Street
The Stone Roses Second Coming
Kylie Minogue Light Years
```

This is a flexible, powerful method: you use the database column names directly, and it makes your code readable and robust to most database and SQL query changes.

However, there are some cases where associative access is tricky. If both a table and attribute name are used in a SELECT statement, only the attribute name is used to access the data associatively. For example, if two or more tables contain columns with the same name, only the one that occurs last in the query result can be accessed associatively. You can get around this problem by using aliases as described in Chapter 7. For example, to access the artist_id columns from both the artist and album tables, you'd write:

```
// Run the query on the connection
if (!($result = @ mysql_query(
 "SELECT artist.artist_id AS id1,
 album.artist_id AS id2
 FROM artist, album
 WHERE artist.artist_id = album.artist_id",
 $connection)))
  die("Couldn't run query");

// Until there are no rows in the result set, fetch a row into
```

```
// the $row array.
while ($row = @ mysql_fetch_array($result))
{
 print "\n";
 // Print out the columns
 print "{$row["id1"]} {$row["id2"]}";
}
```

You can see that the columns are accessed in the $row array using their aliases, id1 and id2.

You can't solve the name-clash problem using table or database names as prefixes. For example, suppose you run the following query:

```
if (!($result = @ mysql_query(
 "SELECT artist.artist_id,
 album.artist_id
 FROM artist, album
 WHERE artist.artist_id = album.artist_id",
 $connection)))
   die("Couldn't run query");
```

If you try to access the column with the table name:

```
print "{$row["artist.artist_id"]}";
```

you'll get a PHP notice telling you that you're using an undefined index. If you omit the table name, like this:

```
print "{$row["artist_id"]}";
```

you'll see the value for the last artist_id returned by the query, which is album.artist_id. The best solution is to use aliases; you could design tables that avoid duplicate names for columns you want to retrieve, but this could lead to a more convoluted design that's less clear and could lead to other problems.

The array returned by mysql_fetch_array( ) contains two elements for each column, one each for numeric and associative access. You can see this when you use the foreach statement to output data:

```
// Run the query on the connection
if (!($result = @ mysql_query(
 "SELECT * FROM artist, album
 WHERE artist.artist_id = album.artist_id",
 $connection)))
   die("Couldn't run query");

// Until there are no rows in the result set, fetch a row into
// the $row array.
while ($row = @ mysql_fetch_array($result))
{
 print "\n";
 // Print out the columns
 foreach($row as $element)
```

```
    print $element;
}
```

In part, this displays:

```
11New OrderNew Order111Retro - John McCready FANRetro - John McCready FAN
11New OrderNew Order122Substance (Disc 2)Substance (Disc 2)
11New OrderNew Order133Retro - Miranda Sawyer POPRetro - Miranda Sawyer POP
```

Each column value is printed twice. If you want to use foreach or you have another reason for wanting only one copy, you can force mysql_fetch_array( ) to return one copy by passing a second parameter to the function. If you want only associatively accessed elements, you use:

```
while ($row = @ mysql_fetch_array($result, MYSQL_ASSOC))
```

For numeric access, you use:

```
while ($row = @ mysql_fetch_array($result, MYSQL_NUM))
```

The same problem occurs with other array functions such as count( ). If you try count($row) on a row returned from mysql_fetch_array( ) without the second parameter, you'll get twice the number of columns that were returned by the query—that is, twice the value reported by mysql_num_fields( ).

MySQL function values can be accessed associatively. Suppose you want to count the number of rows returned by a SELECT statement:

```
// Run the query on the connection
if (!($result = @ mysql_query(
  "SELECT count(*) FROM artist",
  $connection)))
    die("Couldn't run query");

// There is only one row to fetch
$row = @ mysql_fetch_array($result);

print "There are {$row["count(*)"]} rows.";
```

This outputs:

```
There are 6 rows.
```

You can obtain the same result using SELECT * FROM artist and then using the mysql_num_rows( ) function. However, for large result sets, it's more efficient to use the MySQL function count( ) instead, since it doesn't buffer an entire result set that you're not using.

Finding the Number of Changed Rows Using mysql_affected_rows and mysqli_affected_rows

We've seen how the mysql_num_rows( ) and mysqli_num_rows( ) return the number of rows retrieved by a SELECT query. However, some operations, such as UPDATE, DELETE, or INSERT, do not return a result set. For these, we have another pair of functions that we can use.

The mysql_affected_rows( ) and mysqli_affected_rows( ) functions report the number of rows affected by queries that change data, such as INSERT, UPDATE, and DELETE. If no rows were actually changed by a query, these functions return zero, but this doesn't mean an error has occurred. For example, a zero is returned if a DELETE query with a WHERE clause doesn't match any rows, or if an UPDATE doesn't require any values to be changed. If an error does occur, the function returns the value −1. You can add code to check for these return values and handle any problems.

A REPLACE query updates an existing row or inserts a new row in a table. If there is an existing row in the table with the same key, that row is deleted before the new row is inserted. The insertion counts as one row affected, and a deletion would count as another affected row. Hence, a REPLACE query may be reported as affecting one or two rows.

Handling MySQL Errors

We provided an introductory discussion of PHP error handling earlier in "Handling Errors in PHP." In this section, we take a detailed look at the classes of problems that can occur when you're developing a script that works with MySQL. Errors that occur in PHP scripts could be related to general PHP issues, the PHP MySQL functions, or MySQL data:

General PHP issues

These include syntax errors in scripts, problems with the script engine, runtime errors, and programmer-triggered errors. In turn, these are divided into the insignificant NOTICE class, the significant WARNING class, and the critical ERROR class.

For example, if you leave out a quote in a PHP statement:

```
echo   "This is output;
```

a PHP error message such as:

```
Parse error: syntax error, unexpected T_STRING, expecting ',' or ';' in
    /var/www/html/test.php on line 22
```

is displayed when the page is loaded in a web browser. These problems aren't related to MySQL and are usually related to mistyped statements or flawed program logic.

PHP MySQL functions

These errors can occur during many operations; for example, the MySQL server might be unavailable, it might not be possible to establish a connection because the authentication credentials are incorrect, or an SQL query might be incorrectly formed. These are not PHP errors, but PHP can report them.

For example, if an attempt to connect to the MySQL server fails, the `mysqli_connect( )` function returns `FALSE` and displays an error message, as below:

```
Warning: mysqli_connect() [function.mysqli-connect.html]: (28000/1045):
Access denied for user 'fred'@'localhost' (using password: YES)
in /var/www/html/wedding/index.php on line 68
```

MySQL data

These are error conditions that are detected programmatically, but are neither PHP nor MySQL problems. For example, deleting rows that don't exist, returning incorrect numbers of rows, and concurrency-related problems fall into this class. Typically, these are design problems that are common to any database system.

You can use PHP to handle MySQL errors by testing for a `FALSE` return value from calls to functions such as `mysqli_connect( )` and `mysqli_query( )`:

```
if(!($connection=@mysqli_connect
  ($DB_hostname, $DB_username, $DB_password, $DB_databasename)))
    die("Failed while trying to connect to the database.");
```

Here, we've used the PHP `die( )` function to display an error message and stop the program if `mysqli_connect( )` returns `FALSE`. It's common to suppress the default PHP error messages by adding the at symbol (@) just before the call to MySQL functions; without it, you'll get both a message from PHP's own error handler, which is cryptic to a user, and your message from the `die( )` function. Here's another example:

```
// Run the query on the connection
if (!($result = @ mysqli_query($connection, "SELECT * FROM artist")))
  die("Couldn't run query");
```

Handling errors using the MySQLi library

PHP provides error-reporting functions that provide the text error message and the numeric error code for a MySQL error that has occurred. Error numbers make it easier to look up information in the MySQL manual list of error codes and messages at *http://dev.mysql.com/doc/mysql/en/Error-handling.html*

The functions `mysqli_connect_error( )` and `mysqli_connect_errno( )` provide the error message and numeric code corresponding to the latest error that occurred while trying to initialize a given MySQL connection. If no error has occurred, `mysqli_connect_error( )` returns an empty string (""), and `mysqli_connect_errno( )` returns 0.

Similarly, the PHP functions `mysqli_error( )` and `mysqli_errno( )` provide the error message and numeric code corresponding to the latest error on an active connection. They do not report connection errors; the previous two functions do that instead.

Together, these can be used to report errors to the programmer, or to trigger code that displays useful messages to the user. You could use these error-handling functions in your own custom function; for example, you could display the error number and the error message:

```
// Custom error handler function
function showerror($connection)
{
  // Was there an error during connection?
  if(mysqli_connect_errno())
    // Yes;  display information about the connection error
    die("Error " .
      mysqli_connect_errno($connection) . " : ".
      mysqli_connect_error($connection));
  else
    // No;  display the error information for the active connection
    die("Error " .
      mysqli_errno($connection) . " : ".
      mysqli_error($connection));
}
```

You could then call the `showerror( )` function whenever you encounter a database error:

```
if(!($connection= @ mysqli_connect
  ($DB_hostname, $DB_username, $DB_password, $DB_databasename)))
    showerror($connection);
```

This would display a message such as:

```
Error 1146 : Table 'music.art' doesn't exist
```

Consider the following code fragment that uses the MySQLi error functions.

```
// Connect to the MySQL server
$connection = @ mysqli_connect("localhost", "root",
    "the_mysql_root_password", "vapor");

if (mysqli_connect_errno() != 0)
  die("Connection problem: " .
      mysqli_connect_error() . " (" .
      mysqli_connect_errno() . ")");

$result = @ mysqli_query($connection, "SELECT * FROM artis");

if (mysqli_errno($connection) != 0)
  die("Query problem: " .
      mysqli_error($connection) . " (" .
      mysqli_errno($connection) . ")");
```

If the `mysqli_connect` statement fails—as it will in this example, because the database vapor doesn't exist—then `mysqli_connect_errno( )` reports a nonzero value and you see:

```
Connection problem: Unknown database 'vapor' (1049)
```

If the database did exist, the `mysqli_query( )` statement would fail because the table artis doesn't exist, and the code would report:

```
Query problem: Table 'vapor.artis' doesn't exist (1146)
```

Handling errors using the older MySQL library

The default MySQL (as opposed to MySQLi) library has two similar error-handling functions that you can use to check for problems. The function `mysql_errno( )` returns an error number for the most recent MySQL function that used the specified connection; if no error occurred, it returns 0. Similarly, the function `mysql_error( )` returns a string describing an error for the most recent MySQL function that used the specified connection; if no error occurred, it returns the empty string "". Note that neither works for the `mysql_connect( )` function; both need a working connection as a parameter to interrogate the MySQL server about the error. The old MySQL function library doesn't have any equivalents for the MySQLi functions `mysqli_connect_error( )` and `mysqli_connect_errno( )`, so you need to check for a failed connection yourself, perhaps by calling the `die( )` function to print an error message and stop processing.

Let's look at an example. Suppose you have the following fragment that tries to use the nonexistent **vapor** database:

```
// Connect to the MySQL server
if (!($connection = @ mysql_connect("localhost", "root",
    "the_mysql_root_password")))
  die("Cannot connect");

if (!(@ mysql_select_db("vapor", $connection)))
  die(mysql_error($connection) . " (" . mysql_errno($connection) . ")");
```

The final line of the fragment concatenates a string that describes the error using `mysql_error( )` and then includes in parentheses the error number using `mysql_errno( )`. When you run the fragment, you get the output:

```
Unknown database 'vapor' (1049)
```

As with the MySQLi library, you could write a simple function to handle MySQL errors:

```
// Custom error handler function
function showerror($connection)
{
  die(mysql_error($connection) . " (" . mysql_errno($connection) . ")");
}
```

You could then call this function instead of the `die( )` function and pass it the `$connection` parameter:

```
// Connect to the MySQL server
if (!($connection = @ mysql_connect("localhost", "root",
    "the_mysql_root_password")))
  die("Cannot connect");

if (!(@ mysql_select_db("vapor", $connection)))
  showerror($connection);
```

Handling errors in production code

Production code needs to handle errors gracefully. As mentioned earlier, it's very useful to allow PHP error messages to be displayed while you're developing and debugging your code. However, when you're ready to deploy your application, we recommend that you customize the messages that are displayed so that they're more polite and also give away fewer details about your system to potential attackers.

We can have our `showerror( )` function simply display a generic message as follows:

```
// Custom error handler function
function showerror($connection)
{
 // Display a message to the user
 echo "<h3>Failure</h3>
  Unfortunately we're having technical difficulties.
  Please try again later.";
}
```

However, as the administrator, you won't know anything about the error unless your users complain.

You can configure PHP to record errors to a logfile. To do this, you'll need to edit the *php.ini* configuration file and enable the `log_errors` option:

```
log_errors = On
```

You should also specify the location of the logfile with the `error_log` option. The web server should be able to write to this file, so you should check the permission settings of the directory you use. For example, we can specify the file */tmp/php_errors.log* for a Linux or Mac OS X system:

```
error_log = /tmp/php_errors.log
```

On a Windows system, use a path such as *C:\php_errors.log*. If you modify the PHP configuration, you will need to restart the web server to activate the changes.

You can also log errors using the PHP `error_log( )` function; let's modify our `showerror( )` function to log errors:

```
// Custom error handler function
function showerror($connection)
{
 // Display a message to the user
 echo "<h3>Failure</h3>
  Unfortunately we're having technical difficulties; this has been logged.
  Please try again later.";

 // Create message with the current timestamp and the MySQL error.
 $sMessage= date("Y.m.d_H:i:s")."."." ".mysqli_error($connection)."\n";

 // Log the timestamp and error description to the file /tmp/php_errors.log
 error_log(
 $sMessage,
 3,
```

```
    "/tmp/php_errors.log");
  exit;
}
```

The first parameter to the error_log( ) function is the message string. The second parameter is the type of logging we want; 3 means write to the specified file. The last parameter is the path to the logfile. In building up the message, we've used the date( ) function to get the current timestamp (for example, 2006.07.17_04:34:27) and then append the error message to this. The logfile would contain error messages like this:

```
2006.07.17_04:38:00: Can't connect to local MySQL server through socket
             '/var/lib/mysql/mysql.sock' (2)
2006.08.05_11:52:37: Unknown column 'artist' in 'where clause'
```

Ideally, you wouldn't want to regularly check the logfile to learn about problems. You can ask the error_log( ) function to send you an email for each error:

```php
// Define the email address separately from the code, making it easier to maintain.
// This line can be placed in a separate configuration file.
define("ADMINISTRATOR_EMAIL_ADDRESS", "support@learningmysql.com");

// Custom error handler function
function showerror($connection)
{
 // Display a message to the user
 echo "<h3>Failure</h3>
  Unfortunately we're having technical difficulties; this has been logged.
  Please try again later.";

 // Create message with the current timestamp and the MySQL error.
 $sMessage= date("Y.m.d_H:i:s").": ".mysqli_error($connection)."\n";

 // Log the timestamp and error description to the specified email address
 error_log(
  $sMessage,
  1,
  ADMINISTRATOR_EMAIL_ADDRESS);
 exit;
}
```

Here, the second parameter is set to 1, indicating that we want to send an email, and the third parameter is the destination email address. In case you were wondering, using 0 for the second parameter writes the message to the default log specified in the *php.ini* file, while using 2 writes the message to a TCP port for use with a PHP debugging tool. We don't think either of these options is particularly useful for you at this stage. Note that we've used the define( ) function to define the constant ADMINISTRA TOR_EMAIL_ADDRESS outside the body of the function. This allows us to specify the email address somewhere easy to access and modify (perhaps in a header file), rather than having to search complex code for the email address.

Writing files and sending emails using PHP

We've just seen how the error_log( ) function can be used to write messages to a logfile or to email them to a specified address. This is a good time to look at how PHP generally accesses files and sends emails.

To write to a file, we first need to use the fopen( ) function to open the file for writing; this function returns a file pointer that we use for all further access to the file. We write the data using the fwrite( ) function, and then close the file using the fclose( ) function. Consider how we can use the PHP file-access functions to write error messages to file:

```php
function showerror($connection)
{
 // Display a message to the user
 echo "<h3>Failure</h3>
  Unfortunately we're having technical difficulties; this has been logged.
  Please try again later.";

 // Create message with the current timestamp and the MySQL error.
 $sMessage= date("Y.m.d_H:i:s").": ".mysqli_error($connection)."\n";

 // Save the message to the logfile
 // Open the file php_errors.log in the /tmp directory for appending:
 $fp=fopen("/tmp/php_errors.log", "a+");
 // Write the message out, up to a maximum of 10000 bytes
 fwrite($fp, $sMessage, 10000);
 // Close the file
 fclose($fp);
}
```

PHP has a mail( ) function that allows you to send emails with a configurable message and using different addresses. You can add a few more lines to the showerror( ) function to also send you an email:

```php
...
 // Assign the target email address and subject
 $ToAddress     = "System administrator <".ADMINISTRATOR_EMAIL_ADDRESS.">";
 $Subject       = "System error";

 // Assign extra headers to improve appearance and handling in email programs.
 $From          = "From: System <".ADMINISTRATOR_EMAIL_ADDRESS.">\n";
 $ReplyTo       = "Reply-To: System <".ADMINISTRATOR_EMAIL_ADDRESS.">";
 $Sender        = "Sender: System <".ADMINISTRATOR_EMAIL_ADDRESS.">\n";
 $ExtraHeaders  = "$From$ReplyTo$Sender";

 // Send the message
 if(!mail($ToAddress, $Subject, wordwrap($sMessage, 78), $ExtraHeaders))
  // If we couldn't send the message, tell the user to contact
  // the administrator himself
  die("Problems sending email - please send an email to the system administrator: ".
   ADMINISTRATOR_EMAIL_ADDRESS);
}
```

The $ExtraHeaders string configures who the email appears to be coming from and where replies to the email will go. If you're using the error_log( ) function to send emails, you can pass this same string as an optional fourth parameter.

Modularizing Code

A common requirement in PHP development is to reuse parameters and functions across many scripts. For example, you might want to use the username and password credentials many times to connect to the MySQL server, or you might have a function such as showerror( ) (described earlier in "Handling MySQL Errors") that you want to call from many different places. This section shows you how to do this effectively.

PHP has four built-in functions for including scripts in other scripts. These allow you to share variables and functions between those scripts without duplicating them, making it much easier to maintain code and decreasing the chance of bugs through duplication and redundancy. The functions are include( ), require( ), require_once( ), and include_once( ). We discuss the two require variants here, which are identical to the include variants in every way, except what happens when an error occurs: include( ) triggers a PHP WARNING (which, by default, doesn't stop the script), while require( ) triggers a fatal ERROR that stops script execution.

Suppose you have the following code that you want to reuse across several scripts:

```php
<?php
$username = "root";
$password = "the_mysql_root_password";
$database = "music";
$host = "localhost";

// Custom error handler function
function showerror($connection)
{
  die(mysqli_error($connection) . " (" . mysqli_errno($connection) . ")");
}
?>
```

It's stored in the file db.php. You can reuse it with the require( ) directive. Here's an example, in which the file *artists.php* reads in and uses the contents of the *db.php* file:

```php
<?php
require "db.php";

// Connect to the MySQL server
if (!($connection = @ mysql_connect($host, $username, $password)))
  die("Cannot connect");

if (!(mysql_select_db($database, $connection)))
  showerror($connection);

// Run the query on the connection
if (!($result = @ mysql_query("SELECT * FROM artist", $connection)))
```

```
  showerror($connection);
  ...
?>
```

The code in *db.php* can be used as if it were incorporated directly in *artists.php*, and the showerror( ) function is accessible to the code in *artist.php*.

The difference between require( ) and require_once( ) is what happens when a file is incorporated twice. Suppose you decide to create a new file, *musicheader.php*, that has a function to connect to the MySQL server:

```php
<?php
 require "db.php";

 function musicconnect()
 {
  // Connect to the MySQL server
  if (!($connection = @ mysql_connect($host, $username, $password)))
   die("Cannot connect");

  if (!(mysql_select_db($database, $connection)))
   showerror($connection);

  return $connection;
 }
?>
```

The function allows you to establish a connection, and it makes uses of the parameters and functions in *db.php*. Suppose you then write a script that uses *musicheader.php* but also uses require( ) to incorporate *db.php*:

```php
<?php
 require "db.php";
 require "musicheader.php";

 $conn = musicconnect();


 ...
?>
```

When you execute the script, you see the following error message:

```
Fatal error: Cannot redeclare showerror() (previously declared in
/Library/WebServer/Documents/mysql/db.php:7) in
/Library/WebServer/Documents/mysql/db.php on line 10
```

This occurs since the *db.php* file is included twice, once by the script and again by *musicheader.php*; this means that the function showerror( ) is defined twice, which causes PHP to stop processing.

Unfortunately, it's sometimes difficult to ensure you avoid doing this; for example, it's common that you want to include two header files in a script, and that those header files include the contents of a third because it's needed in both. Fortunately, there's an easy way around this with require_once( ): you can use it as many times as you like for a particular file; the file will only be read in once. Here's how you'd rewrite the previous examples with `require_once( )`. First, there's `musicheader.php`:

```php
<?php
require_once "db.php";

function musicconnect()
{
 // Connect to the MySQL server
 if (!($connection = @ mysql_connect($host, $username, $password)))
  die("Cannot connect");

 if (!(mysql_select_db($database, $connection)))
  showerror($connection);

 return $connection;
}
?>
```

Second, there's the script:

```php
<?php
require_once "db.php";
require_once "musicheader.php";

$conn = musicconnect();

...
?>
```

The script now works as desired. We use `require_once( )` in preference to `require( )` because it automatically looks after the problem we've shown, and we recommend you do the same.

There are rare cases where you do actually want a header file to be included and processed multiple times; for example, you could have a set of statements that are loaded and run in the body of a loop, as in:

```php
for($i=0; $i<10; $i++)
{
 // Load the header file
 require("myfile.php");
}
```

However, this code isn't efficient (a custom function would be faster), so you're generally better off avoiding `require( )`.

Protecting Script and Header Files

Web database applications need to store the database user credentials in the PHP program code. Users with accounts on your web server can access script and header files directly from disk, so you should set the file permissions such that only the web server has permission to read any files that contain sensitive information, such as the database server password.

PHP scripts are executed by the server before content is sent to a requesting web browser, so people won't see the password when they load a PHP page. However, included files are sometimes given names with the *.inc* extension. The web server only processes files with the *.php* extension, and sends other text files untouched to the web browser. This presents a worrisome security problem if the file contains sensitive information; if a user correctly types in the URL of a header file, she'll be able to see its contents.

We recommend that you always use the *.php* extension for header files. The web server will provide the output produced by running this script, and since the script doesn't actually print anything, a user who directly requests the include file will see only a blank page.

If you choose to use an extension other than *.php*, you should place the include files outside the web server document tree, so that the web server does not serve the file to users; this can lead to difficulties with maintenance because the application files won't all be located together. Alternatively, you can tell the web server to refuse access to files with that particular extension. For the Apache web server, you can do this by adding the following directives to the httpd.conf configuration file and restarting the server:

```
<Files ~ "\.inc$">
 Order allow,deny
 Deny from all
 Satisfy All
</Files>
```

Processing and Using User Data

Up to this point, we've shown you how to query and return results from MySQL. However, all our examples are simple because they don't take user input and use it in the querying process. Indeed, unless you change the data in the database, the queries we've shown produce the same results each time. This section shows you the basics of securely and effectively including user data in the process to customize your query input and output.

Consider an example of an HTML page. Example 14-4 contains a form that's designed to capture details about a new artist and album to add to the music database.

Example 14-4. A simple HTML form

```
<!DOCTYPE HTML PUBLIC
"-//W3C//DTD HTML 4.01 Transitional//EN"
"http://www.w3.org/TR/html401/loose.dtd">
<html>
  <head>
    <meta http-equiv="Content-Type" content="text/html; charset=iso-8859-1" />
```

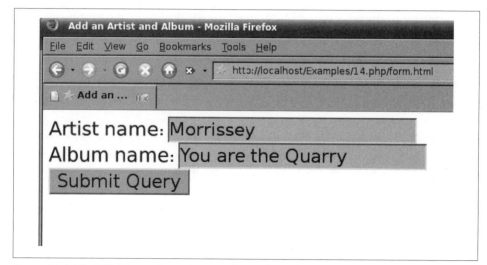

Figure 14-2. The HTML entry form shown in the Firefox web browser

```
    <title>Add an Artist and Album</title>
  </head>
  <body>
    <form action="add.php" method="GET">
      Artist name: <input type="text" name="artist" />
      <br />
      Album name: <input type="text" name="album" />
      <br />
      <input type="submit" />
    </form>
  </body>
</html>
```

When it's rendered in the Firefox web browser, the HTML page looks as shown in Figure 14-2. You can see we've entered the artist name Morrissey and the album You are the Quarry in the fields.

In our HTML example, the <form> tag has two attributes, action and method. The action attribute tells the browser what resource to request when the user submits the form. In this example, it's *add.php*. The method attribute tells the browser how to send the data entered into the form to the web server. With the GET method that's used in the example, the data is appended to the URL. For example, if the user types Morrissey and You are the Quarry in the fields and the web server runs at the address localhost, the URL that's requested when the form submits is:

```
http://localhost/add.php?artist=Morrissey&album=You+are+the+Quarry
```

Notice that the name attributes of the <input> elements, artist and album, are paired with the values that the user typed in the fields. You can also see that the space characters in You are the Quarry are translated into + characters, since the HTTP standard doesn't allow spaces in URLs.

The alternative to the GET method is POST. You should always use the POST method to submit confidential information from forms. If you use the GET method, any information typed into the form—including passwords—will appear in plain view in the browser's address bar, and in any bookmarks of pages that receive the submitted data.

In the target PHP script, submitted form data is placed in the predefined $_GET or $_POST array variable, depending on the method that was used to submit the form. For example, the form variable artist would be accessible as $_GET['artist'] with a form submitted using the GET method, and as $_POST['artist'] with a form submitted using the POST method. The type of quotes—single or double—does not matter. The $_GET and $_POST arrays are *superglobal* variables, meaning that they're automatically created and accessible anywhere in your PHP script.

Let's now consider how *add.php*—the script that's requested—accesses and uses the values from the form. You can display the values of the artist and album elements with the following short script stored in the file *add.php*:

```
<html>
  <body>
    <pre>
      <?php
        print $_GET["artist"] . "\n";
        print $_GET["album"];
      ?>
    </pre>
  </body>
</html>
```

When run, this displays the text:

```
Morrissey
You are the Quarry
```

Our add.php script isn't very useful because it doesn't access the database to add the form data to it. Here's a new version that does what we want:

```
<?php
// Connect to the MySQL server
if (!($connection = @ mysql_connect("localhost", "root",
    "the_mysql_root_password")))
  die("Cannot connect");

if (!(mysql_select_db("music", $connection)))
  die("Couldn't select music database");

// Add the artist, using the next available artist_id
if (! @ mysql_query(
    "INSERT INTO artist (artist_id, artist_name)
    SELECT MAX(artist_id)+1, \"{$_GET["artist"]}\" FROM artist",
    $connection))
        die("Couldn't add artist");

// Discover the artist_id of the row we added
if (!($result = @ mysql_query(
```

```
                 "SELECT artist_id FROM artist WHERE
                 artist_name = \"{$_GET["artist"]}\"",
                 $connection)))
                        die("Couldn't find artist");

        $row = @ mysql_fetch_array($result);

        $artist_id = $row["artist_id"];

        // Add the album, setting album_id to 1 and using the $artist_id
        if (! @ mysql_query(
            "INSERT INTO album (artist_id, album_id, album_name)
            VALUES ({$artist_id}, 1, \"{$_GET["album"]}\")",
            $connection))
                    die("Couldn't add album");

        print "Added artist: {$_GET["artist"]}, with album: {$_GET["album"]}.";

    ?>
```

The script adds a new row to the **artist** table using an **INSERT ... SELECT** statement and the **MAX( )** function described in Chapter 8. The **artist** value entered by the user is stored in **$_GET["artist"]**. It then uses **SELECT** to find the **artist_id** of the newly added row. The final step is to insert a row into the **album** table, using the new **artist_id** and the album name stored in **$_GET["album"]**, and setting the **album_id** to **1** (since this is the first album for the artist). Finally, the script displays a success message or an error message depending on how things went.

The script has three serious problems. First, it's not secure: no steps are taken to ensure that users pass sensible parameters to the script, and this can have serious consequences for some scripts; we show you basic steps to guard against this next. Second, it suffers from the *reload problem* that's discussed in "The Reload Problem," later in this chapter. When you request the *add.php* script a second time, it adds the same information to the database again. Last, it doesn't have validation or error handling; for example, you can insert the same artist more than once, each will be allocated a new **artist_id**, and you won't see an error message. In Chapter 15, we'll look at examples of how to handle such errors.

The PHP Predefined Superglobal Variables

Superglobal variables are automatically created and initialized by the PHP engine, and are accessible throughout the script. We've already seen the **$_GET** and **$_POST** associative arrays that contain data passed to the script from a form using the **GET** or **POST** method, respectively.

The array **$_SESSION** contains data related to a user's interaction with a web application within a single session; we describe sessions and this variable in "Sessions," later in this chapter.

The `$_COOKIE` array contains cookie data provided by the user's browser. *Cookies* are strings that are passed back and forth between the web server and browser to maintain a unique key. They are useful for storing information on a user on the user's computer; you can use the PHP `set_cookie( )` function to send a cookie to the user's browser. Each subsequent time the user visits your site, his browser automatically provides the cookie data. Cookies can be set to expire once the user closes their browser, at a later date, or never. A good use for cookies is to remember what news articles users have read and to show them new articles that they haven't read yet. Note that cookies should never be used to store confidential information, as they are not secure. In addition, they shouldn't be used to store information critical to your application, since users can move among computers, or modify or delete cookies at any time. Cookies have been widely abused by companies trying to track user web surfing and shopping habits, and so informed users tend to treat them with suspicion and often block them. For these reasons, we recommend you don't make extensive use of cookies, and we don't go into details of cookies in this book.

There's one more superglobal array that you should know about. The `$_SERVER` array contains information on the server configuration and the currently executing script. In this book, we use one item from this array: the `$_SERVER["PHP_SELF"]` variable, which contains the relative path from the document root to the currently executing script. For example, the `$_SERVER["PHP_SELF"]` value for the script *http://www.invyhome.com/shop/process.php* will be `/shop/process.php`. You can find a full list of PHP variables in the output of the *phpinfo.php* page that you created in "Checking Whether Your Apache Installation Supports PHP" in Chapter 2.

Untainting User Data

When you make scripts accessible from the Web, they are vulnerable to security problems caused by deliberate or accidental abuse from users all over the world. When your scripts process input provided by users, you must be even more vigilant and validate the data to ensure that it is in the format and size your scripts expect and must handle. Let's look at three issues.

Limiting the Size and Type of Input Data

Many problems are caused by the system encountering data that it can't handle; for example, a user may try to log in to the system with a login name that is longer than the database can handle, resulting in unexpected behavior. An attacker may try to overload your script with more data than it can handle and in this way cause something to break. You should limit the amount of data that you accept and process. There are server variables that you can configure to do this, but we won't look at those. Instead, we'll look at how your script can reject excess data.

The PHP `substr( )` function returns a specified portion of a string. You can limit the data passed from a form using this function; for example, you can choose to use just the first 15 characters:

```
// Reduce the length of the artist name to at most 15 characters
$_GET["artist"] = substr($_GET["artist"], 0, 15);
```

The 0 indicates that the returned substring should start from the initial character (character 0), and the 15 specifies the maximum number of characters to be returned.

Before processing input data, you should check that some data has in fact been passed to you:

```
// Check that an artist name has been passed to us
if(empty($_GET["artist"]))
 die("You should have entered an artist name.");
```

When data has a specific type, you should consider adding extra steps in the validation process. For example, suppose you're expecting a user to type in a currency amount in dollars and cents, and this is available as $_GET["money"] in your script. You can validate it by checking that the data isn't longer than expected and also that it contains only digits and period characters. There are many ways to do this, but let's use one with the techniques we've shown in this chapter:

```
$len = strlen($_GET["money"]);

for($x=0; $x&<$len; $x++)
{
 if (
  (
   ($_GET["money"][$x] < "0" || $_GET["money"][$x] > "9")
   &&
   ($_GET["money"][$x] != ".")
  )
  ||
  ($x > 6)
  )
   die("Invalid parameter: {$_GET["money"]}");
}
```

The `strlen( )` function is a string library function that reports the length of a string as an integer value. The `for` loop goes through each character in the input, which is accessed as $_GET["money"][$x]. If the character is less than 0 or greater than 9 and isn't a period character, an error is generated. Also, if the loop is repeated more than six times, an error is generated because the input is too long.

Another common way to validate data is to use regular expressions; we won't go into the detail of that approach here.

Abusing Calls to Shell Commands

Another way attackers can compromise your server is by adding extra parameters to scripts that run programs on the web server. For example, the semicolon character is used to separate commands on Unix-like operating systems such as Linux and Mac OS X. If a script passes user input directly to a shell command, it's easy to manipulate the script using this character.

Consider this example: the system( ) function runs a program on the server host and returns the resulting text. For example, the following line runs the fortune program from the */usr/games/* directory and displays the result:

```
system("/usr/games/fortune");
```

The fortune program displays random quotes and jokes; if you loaded this script in your browser, you might see something like:

```
Rudeness is a weak man's imitation of strength.
```

You might decide to have a script that is more useful. For example, you might write a script that allows users to enter mathematical queries; the script passes the query to the bc program and displays the answer:

```
system("/bin/echo {$_GET['query']} | /usr/bin/bc");
```

Let's say your script is called calculate.php; a user could load the page:

```
http://somehost.net/calculate.php?query=3*2
```

Not surprisingly, the server will display the answer 6.

What would happen if a user used the semicolon character as part of the query, followed by a command to list all accounts on the server?

```
http://somehost.net/calculate.php?query=3*2;/bin/cat%20/etc/passwd;echo%201
```

The system( ) function would execute the command:

```
/bin/echo 3*2;/bin/cat /etc/passwd;echo 1 | /usr/bin/bc
```

which is actually three commands. The first just prints 3*2, the second displays the contents of the */etc/passwd* file, while the third passes the dummy value 1 to the bc program for it to calculate.

The simplest way to prevent this type of attack is to ensure that the semicolon and other special characters aren't passed directly to the system( ) function but are escaped by adding a backslash in front of them so that they are interpreted differently. The escapeshellcmd( ) function does this for you:

```
// Escape any characters that could be used to trick a shell command
$query = escapeshellcmd($_GET["query"]);
system("/bin/echo {$query} | /usr/bin/bc");
```

In this way, the previous query would become:

```
/bin/echo 3*2\;/bin/cat /etc/passwd\;echo 1 | /usr/bin/bc
```

which is an incorrectly formed shell command that won't be executed properly, so the attack will fail. We recommend that you completely avoid using any shell commands if possible, as the risk to security is relatively high.

Preventing SQL Injection Attacks

Another type of problem to protect against is the *SQL injection attack*, where a malicious user tries to insert additional SQL fragments into your SQL statements, and in this way cause the script to add, update, delete, or expose data that shouldn't be modified or seen. Consider a PHP script that authenticates the user by verifying that the username and password entered by the user exist in the database users; the script might execute the following SQL query:

```
$query="SELECT * FROM USERS WHERE username='{$_POST["username"]}' AND
    password='{$_POST["password"]}'";
```

The PHP script replaces the placeholders `{$_POST["username"]}` and `{$_POST["password"]}'` with the contents of the username and password fields entered in the form. If the query returns any matching rows, the user is authenticated.

Now, imagine if a malicious user enters:

```
' OR '' = '
```

for both the username and password. The SQL query composed by the PHP program would then be:

```
$query="SELECT * FROM users WHERE username='' OR '' = '' AND password='' OR '' = ''";
```

Since this is always true, the attacker will be authenticated and granted access to the system.

The attacker could likewise specify the username as:

```
testusername'; DELETE FROM users
```

The statement would then be:

```
$query="SELECT * FROM users WHERE username='testusername'; DELETE FROM users";
```

which would delete all entries in the users table!

To prevent this type of attack, we must ensure that characters that have special meaning in SQL, such as the single quote (') or the semicolon (;), are neutralized by adding a backslash before them.

We can use the PHP `mysqli_real_escape_string( )` function to do this for us:

```
$input=mysqli_real_escape_string($connection, $_POST["username"])
```

The equivalent function in the old MySQL library is `mysql_real_escape_string( )`, which doesn't require the connection parameter:

```
$input=mysql_real_escape_string($_POST["username"])
```

Consider how each of the sample input strings is processed. Without the escaping step, the input:

```
' OR '' = '
```

for both username and password produces the SQL query:

```
SELECT * FROM users WHERE username='' OR '' = '' AND password='' OR '' = ''
```

but after the escaping step, we get the query:

```
SELECT * FROM users WHERE username='\' OR \'\' = \'' AND password='\' OR \'\' = \''
```

Similarly, the input string:

```
testusername'; DELETE FROM users;
```

results in the SQL query:

```
SELECT * FROM users WHERE username='testusername'; DELETE FROM users;'
   AND password='testusername'; DELETE FROM users;'
```

without escaping, but:

```
SELECT * FROM users WHERE username='testusername\'; DELETE FROM users;'
   AND password='testusername\'; DELETE FROM users;'
```

after it.

Note that the escaping step also helps avoid problems with input strings that legitimately have an apostrophe in them; for example, if we have an SQL query to select users by surname, the surname "D'Arcy" would result in an invalid query:

```
SELECT * FROM users WHERE surname='D'Arcy'
```

Escaping the backslash before the apostrophe solves the problem.

```
SELECT * FROM users WHERE surname='D\'Arcy'
```

PHP has a `magic_quotes_gpc` directive that, if set in the *php.ini* configuration file, automatically escapes single quotes and double quotes in data sent from the client's browser from web forms or cookies. However, this in turn causes other problems and is disabled in the upcoming PHP version 6.

We can write a function to limit the length of the input data, and escape semicolons and, if needed, single and double quotes. This function—let's call it `clean( )`—takes two arguments—the input data to be cleaned, and the maximum length the data is allowed to have:

```
// Secure the user data by escaping characters and shortening the
// input string
function clean($input, $maxlength)
{
    // Access the MySQL connection from outside this function.
    global $connection;
```

```
// Limit the length of the string
$input = substr($input, 0, $maxlength);

// Escape semicolons and (if magic quotes are off) single and
// double quotes
if(get_magic_quotes_gpc())
    $input = stripslashes($input);

$input = mysqli_real_escape_string($connection, $input);

return $input;
}
```

We can pass the input string and the maximum permissible length to the function, and obtain the processed string as the return value, for example:

```
$username = clean($_POST["username"], 30);
```

Remember that there must be an active connection to the MySQL server for `mysqli_real_escape_string( )` to work, and so we must connect to the MySQL server before we ever use the **clean( )** function. On a high-volume application, you can avoid unnecessary connections to the MySQL server by validating the input in two steps. First, the script can perform simple checks that don't use `mysqli_real_escape_string( )`. Then, the script can connect to the MySQL server, escape the input using `mysqli_real_escape_string( )`, and then continue with other database operations.

The `global` keyword tells PHP to use the `$connection` variable from outside the clean( ) function; without it, PHP would create a new, completely different variable with the name `$connection` that would be in effect inside the function, which would be useless for our function. We could instead have defined the function as:

```
function clean($input, $maxlength, $connection)
{
...
}
```

so that the value of the `$connection` variable is passed to the function as part of the function call, for example:

```
$username = clean($_POST["username"], 30, $connection);
```

Using Data from the Client

You should also be careful how you use data that is received from the browser. For example, it is unwise to use the price of an item from a form widget to calculate an invoice; even if the price is hidden or read-only, the user can still change it by modifying the form or the URL. The correct approach is to verify the price against the database before calculating the invoice. Similarly, don't embed SQL in HTML—even if it is hidden—as the user can browse the HTML source, understand the database structure, and then modify the statements. This may sound silly, but several companies have actually made such mistakes—and lost a lot of money as a result!

Validation, error checking, and security are large topics. Resources that discuss them in more detail can be found in "Resources," at the end of this chapter.

Sessions

The Web was designed for browsing documents, where each request from a web browser to a web server was intended to be independent of each other interaction. To develop applications for the Web, additional logic is required so that different requests can be related. For example, code is required to allow a user to log in, use the application, and log out when she's finished. In PHP, this logic is provided by the sessions library. Sessions allow variables to be stored on the server, so that these variables can be restored each time a user requests a script. Consider a short example:

```php
<?php
// Initialize the session
session_start();

// If there is no "count" session variable, create one, and welcome
// the user.
if (!isset($_SESSION["count"]))
{
  $_SESSION["count"] = 0;
  echo "Welcome new user!";
}
// Otherwise, increment the number of visits and display a message.
else
{
  $_SESSION["count"]++;
  echo "Hello! You've visited this page {$_SESSION["count"]} times before.";
}
?>
```

The session_start function activates an existing session or, if none exists, creates a new one. When the user requests the script for the first time, the $_SESSION["count"] variable does not exist, so the isset( ) function returns the value FALSE. A new session is created, and a new session variable count is defined in the $_SESSION superglobal array, with its value set to 0. Session variables are stored on the web server; when the user next requests the script, the isset( ) function returns TRUE, the $_SESSION["count"] variable is automatically restored by the PHP engine, and the count incremented. For example, on the fifth request of the script, the output is:

```
Hello!
You've visited this page 4 times before.
```

With its default configuration, the sessions library relies on cookies to maintain a unique key. This key is used on the server to locate the variables associated with the session. If cookies are disabled or unsupported by the browser, sessions won't work;

this problem can be solved by storing the session key in the URL, but we don't discuss that here.

Sessions can be destroyed by calling the `session_destroy( )` function. This is typically done to end a user's session in an application:

```php
<?php
  // Logout of the system
  session_start();
  session_destroy();

  print "You've logged out!";
?>
```

Note that a session must be started before it can be destroyed.

In a web environment, there is no guarantee that users will actually log out. They may forget to log out of an application, leaving the session active, and thus allow another person using the same browser to access the restricted sections of the application. Moreover, since the browser is tied to the session data on the server through a cookie value, an attacker could fake the cookie information to gain access to the target session.

To reduce the risk of unauthorized users gaining access to a session, PHP sessions have a timeout. This means that if a user doesn't access the web server within a predetermined period, the session is destroyed. By default, the timeout is set to 1,440 seconds or 24 minutes, after which time the session is a candidate for being cleaned up. This can be adjusted—along with other session parameters—through the *php.ini* configuration file.

The Reload Problem

In "Processing and Using User Data," earlier in this chapter, we showed you an example that writes data to the music database. This section briefly discusses a common problem that can arise when writing to web databases and shows you a simple way to avoid it.

Consider a simple script, *process.php*, that writes an artist to the music database:

```php
<?php
if(!empty($_GET))
{
  // Include database parameters and related functions
  require_once("../db.php");
  $DB_databasename='music';
  // Connect to the MySQL DBMS and use the wedding database - credentials are
  // in the file db.php
  if(!($connection= mysqli_connect($DB_hostname, $DB_username, $DB_password,
    $DB_databasename)))
    showerror($connection);

  // Untaint the artist name, and use at most 15 characters
  $artist_name = clean($_GET["artist_name"], 15);
```

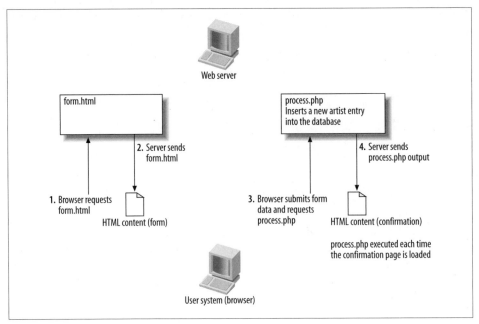

Figure 14-3. The reload problem

```
    // Add the artist, using the next available artist_id
    $query="INSERT INTO artist (artist_id, artist_name) ".
      "SELECT MAX(artist_id)+1, '$artist_name' FROM artist";
    if (! @ mysqli_query($connection, $query))
      die("Couldn't add artist");

    print "Added artist: ".$_GET['artist_name'];
  }
  else
  {
    print "No artist name was provided";
  }
  ?>
```

Note that we've included the *db.php* file for the database parameters and the definition of the clean( ) function to untaint data from the user.

Figure 14-3 shows what happens when the user submits the form we described earlier in "Processing and Using User Data." The web browser submits the artist name and the album name provided by the user, and requests the *process.php* script. A new artist row is added to the database each time the *process.php* script runs, which is each time the PHP page is requested by a web browser. There are many ways that the page can be requested by a web browser. The user can press the Refresh or Reload button; type in the URL and press the Enter key; print the page; visit the page again using the Back or Forward buttons or browser history; or resize the browser window.

This is a common problem in web applications, known as the *reload problem*; it affects not only writing to databases, but also tasks such as registering session variables, charging credit cards, logging data, and every other situation in which an action has a lasting effect. Fortunately, it's easy to avoid by not sending any content to the browser from the script that actually performs the action, but to instead produce the output from a different script.

Here's the previous script, rewritten to avoid the reload problem:

```php
<?php
if(!empty($_GET))
{
  // Include database parameters and related functions
  require_once("../db.php");
  $DB_databasename='music';
  // Connect to the MySQL DBMS and use the wedding database
  // - credentials are in the file db.php
  if(!($connection= mysqli_connect($DB_hostname, $DB_username, $DB_password,
    $DB_databasename)))
    showerror($connection);

  // Untaint the artist name, and use at most 15 characters
  $artist_name = clean($_GET["artist_name"], 15);

  // Add the artist, using the next available artist_id
  $query="INSERT INTO artist (artist_id, artist_name) ".
    "SELECT MAX(artist_id)+1, '$artist_name' FROM artist";
  if (! @ mysqli_query($connection, $query))
    die("Couldn't add artist");

  // Silently send the browser to the receipt page
  header("Location: receipt.php?Status=OK&artist_name=$artist_name");
}
else
{
  print "No artist name was provided";
}
?>
```

This modified script adds the artist but doesn't produce HTML output. Instead, it sends an HTTP header to the web browser using the PHP library `header( )` function:

```php
header("Location: receipt.php?Status=OK&artist_name=$artist_name");
```

The `Location` HTTP header instructs the web browser to go to another page, in this case `receipt.php`. The `receipt.php` script performs no database activity, but simply displays a confirmation message:

```php
<?php
  print "Added artist: ".$_GET['artist_name'];
?>
```

Figure 14-4 illustrates how the modified script works. Reloading this receipt page has no effect on the database; users can reload it as many times as they wish.

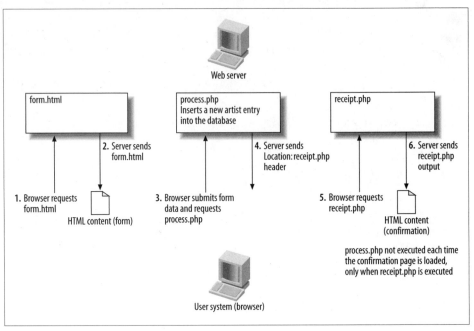

Figure 14-4. A solution to the reload problem

Before we end this section, we should point out that the header( ) function is associated with the very common error in which the PHP engine complains that it cannot send any header information:

```
Warning: Cannot modify header information
 - headers already sent by (output started at logout.php:2)
```

This error occurs because the web server sends headers as soon as any output is sent to the browser. If you generate any output, or even accidentally leave a blank line or even a single space character before the PHP start tag, the server treats this output as content, and sends it to the browser along with the HTTP headers. You must ensure you don't generate any output before the call to the header( ) function. The session_start( ) function sends its own headers to the browser, and so you'll run into the same problem if you have any output before a call to this function.

Using PHP for Command-Line Scripts

PHP scripts don't need to be run from a web server—although that's how the majority of PHP scripts are deployed. In this section, we'll briefly look at how you can run PHP scripts from the command line. This allows you to query the MySQL server from the command line to generate reports and to import or export data.

Consider Example 14-5, which simply says "Hello, world!".

Example 14-5. A PHP script to say hello

```
<?php
echo "Hello, world\n";
?>
```

Type this in an editor and save it to a file called *hello.cl.php*.

You can run PHP scripts from the shell prompt or command window by running the PHP executable and passing the name of the script to it:

```
$ php hello.cl.php
Hello, world
```

If the operating system can't find the php executable, you'll need to specify the full path to the file. On a Linux or Mac OS X system, this may be available as the file */usr/bin/ php*. If you've installed XAMPP, you can use the program */opt/lampp/bin/php* on Linux, */Applications/xampp/xamppfiles/bin/php* on Mac OS X, and *C:\Program Files \xampp\php\php.exe* on Windows.

You can also have the operating system call the PHP program automatically when you run a PHP script from the command line. To do this on a Linux or Mac OS X system, you need to add this line to the top of each script to specify the PHP program to use:

```
#!path_to_the_php_executable
```

For example, you could specify the */usr/bin/php* program in the *hello.cl.pl* script as follows:

```
#!/usr/bin/php
<?php
echo "Hello, world\n";
?>
```

You must add the "executable" permission to the file so that the operating system can execute this script:

```
$ chmod u=rwx,g=,o= hello.cl.php
```

We explained permission settings in "Restricting access to files and directories" in Chapter 2.

You can now run the script by just typing in its name:

```
$ ./hello.cl.php
Hello, world
```

The initial ./ tells the operating system that the file is in the current working directory. If the script is in a directory that's also listed in your system PATH, you can omit these characters. See "Error Message About MySQL Executable Programs Not Being Found or Recognized" in Chapter 2 for details on setting the system PATH.

For a Windows system, you should associate PHP files with the PHP program. Open a command-prompt window and type in these two lines:

```
C:\> ASSOC .php=PHPScript
C:\> FTYPE PHPScript=C:\Program Files\xampp\php\php.exe %1 %*
```

You can now type in the name of the script, and it should run automatically:

```
C:\> hello.cl.php
Hello, world
```

You can run almost any PHP script from the command line, although some functionality, such as sessions, is useful only in the context of web applications. Let's try running
the scripts of Examples 14-2 or 14-3 from the command line; these connect to the
music database and display the artist_id and artist_name:

```
$ php query_artists.php
```

```
<!DOCTYPE HTML PUBLIC
"-//W3C//DTD HTML 4.01 Transitional//EN"
"http://www.w3.org/TR/html401/loose.dtd">
<html>
  <head>
    <meta http-equiv="Content-Type" content="text/html;
      charset=iso-8859-1" />
    <title>Artists</title>
  </head>
  <body>
    <h1>Artists</h1>

    <table>
      <tr>
        <th>artist_id</th>
        <th>artist_name</th>
      </tr>
      <tr>
        <td>1</td>
        <td>New Order</td>
      </tr>
      <tr>
        <td>2</td>
        <td>Nick Cave & The Bad Seeds</td>
      </tr>
      <tr>
        <td>3</td>
        <td>Miles Davis</td>
      </tr>
      <tr>
        <td>4</td>
        <td>The Rolling Stones</td>
      </tr>
      <tr>
        <td>5</td>
        <td>The Stone Roses</td>
      </tr>
      <tr>
        <td>6</td>
        <td>Kylie Minogue</td>
      </tr>
```

```
            </tr>
          </table>
        </body>
      </html>
```

We get the output, but it's HTML code that's not very useful from the command line. If you want to run PHP scripts from the command line, you don't need to include HTML tags in the output, but you should make good use of the \n newline character.

Example 14-6 rewrites Example 14-3 without the HTML tags.

Example 14-6. Querying the music database from the command line

```php
<?php
print "Artists\n=======\n";

printf("%-40s %-40s\n".
       "---------------------------------------- ".
       "----------------------------------------\n",
       "artist_id", "artist_name");

// Connect to the MySQL server
if (!($connection = @ mysqli_connect("localhost", "root",
    "")))
    die("Cannot connect");

if (!(mysqli_select_db($connection, "music")))
    die("Couldn't select music database");

// Run the query on the connection
if (!($result = @ mysqli_query($connection, "SELECT * FROM artist")))
    die("Couldn't run query");

// Until there are no rows in the result set, fetch a row into
// the $row array and ...
while ($row = @ mysqli_fetch_array($result, MYSQL_ASSOC))
{
// print out each of the columns
    foreach($row as $data)
        printf("%-40s ", $data);

    // Start a new line
    print "\n";
}
?>
```

This will produce output as shown below:

```
    Artists
    =======
    artist_id                                artist_name
    ---------------------------------------- ----------------------------------------
    1                                        New Order
    2                                        Nick Cave & The Bad Seeds
    3                                        Miles Davis
    4                                        The Rolling Stones
```

```
5       The Stone Roses
6       Kylie Minogue
```

Using Command-Line Arguments

You can pass arguments to PHP scripts from the command line. You can use command-line arguments to modify the behavior of a program, or to provide information. The $argc variable indicates the count of the arguments passed, and the $argv array contains the argument values. The first entry in the $argv array ($argv[0]) is always the command that was used to run the script. The second entry in this array ($argv[1]) is the first argument typed in after the command name. The third entry ($argv[2]) is the second argument, and so on. This means that the the number of values in the $argv array will always be one more than the number of arguments typed after the command. If one argument is entered, the count will be 2.

Let's modify our *hello.cl.php* script to use command-line arguments, as shown in Example 14-7.

Example 14-7. PHP command-line program that prints a message using the first command-line argument

```
#!/usr/bin/php
<?php
if($argc==2)
  echo "Hello, {$argv[1]}!\n";
else
  echo "Syntax: {$argv[0]} [Your First Name]\n";
?>
```

To use any number of entered arguments rather than just one, Example 14-8 uses the foreach( ) function to iterate over every argument. For each entry in the $argv array, the $index => $argument construct places the entry index (also known as the key) in the $index variable, and the entry value in the $argument variable. If the index is not zero, we print out the value. We don't print the value for index zero, as that is the name of the command itself. Notice how we've included a space before each argument, and how we add an exclamation mark and newline after all the arguments have been printed.

Example 14-8. PHP command-line program that prints a message using all the provided command-line arguments.

```
#!/usr/bin/php
<?php
if($argc==1)
  echo "Syntax: {$argv[0]} [Your Name]\n";
else
{
  echo "Hello";
  foreach($argv as $index => $argument)
    if($index!=0)
```

```
        echo " $argument";
    echo "!\n";
}
?>
```

Now when you type in any number of arguments after the command name, they will be displayed as part of the greeting:

```
$ ./hello.cl.all_args.php
Syntax: ./hello.cl.args.php [Your Name]
$ ./hello.cl.all_args.php Somayyeh
Hello, Somayyeh!
$ ./hello.cl.all_args.php Somayyeh Sadat Sabet
Hello, Somayyeh Sadat Sabet!
```

Resources

We listed several resources on web database applications and PHP at the end of Chapter 13. This section lists resources you can read that contain more about using PHP with MySQL.

The descriptions we've provided in this chapter are simplified: we've omitted function parameters that are rarely used, avoided some of the details of how the functions are used, and shown some optional parameters as mandatory. See the MySQL manual (*http://www.php.net/manual/en/ref.mysql.php*) for more detail on MySQL functions.

There are also many useful web sites that include tutorials, sample code, online discussion forums, and links to sample PHP applications. The official PHP site links page (*http://www.php.net/links.php*) points to most of these sites. These include:

http://dev.mysql.com/usingmysql/php
> The MySQL AB web page on using PHP with MySQL

http://php.net/manual/en/ref.mysql.php
> The PHP manual section on MySQL

Exercises

1. In a PHP script, how can we access data entered by a user in an HTML form?
2. Why is it important to untaint information that arrives from the client?
3. What is the difference between the PHP library functions `mysqli_num_rows( )` and `mysqli_affected_rows( )`?
4. When would you pass a variable to a function by reference rather than by value?
5. What does this program do?

   ```
   #!/usr/bin/php
   <?php
     $Time="2006-06-20 19:00:00";
   ```

```
        TimeDifference($Time, $seconds, $hours, $minutes, $days);
        echo "\n".sprintf("%3d days, %2d hours, %2d minutes, and %2d seconds",
            $days, $hours, $minutes, $seconds);
        echo " since you left ... :(";

        $Time="2006-11-15 20:00:00";
        TimeDifference($Time, $seconds, $hours, $minutes, $days);
        echo "\n".sprintf("%3d days, %2d hours, %2d minutes, and %2d seconds",
            $days, $hours, $minutes, $seconds);
        echo " till I see you again... :)";

        echo "\n";

        function TimeDifference($ReferenceTime, &$seconds, &$hours, &$minutes, &$days)
        {
          $seconds=abs(strtotime($ReferenceTime) - mktime());
          $days =intval(($seconds)                              /( 24*60*60));
          $hours =intval(($seconds-($days*24*60*60))            /(   60*60));
          $minutes=intval(($seconds-($days*24*60*60)-($hours*60*60)) /(    60));
          $seconds=intval(($seconds-($days*24*60*60)-($hours*60*60)-($minutes*60)));
        }
      ?>
```

You should use the PHP manual at *http://www.php.net/manual/* to look up information on new functions. To get you started, here are some short explanations:

abs( )

> Returns the absolute value of a number passed to it (it removes the minus sign for negative numbers).

intval( )

> Converts a floating number into an integer.

mktime( )

> Returns the current time in the Unix timestamp format.

sprintf( )

> Creates a string from the values passed to it using the format specifiers.

strtotime( )

> Converts a string into the Unix timestamp format.

What does the line at the top of the file indicate? What would happen if you tried to run this program from a web server?

## CHAPTER 15

A PHP Application: The Wedding Gift Registry

In the previous chapter, we looked at the basics of the PHP language and how it can interact with a MySQL database. In this chapter, we explore how to access and exchange information with a MySQL server from within a practical PHP application. As a running example, we present a simple wedding gift registry application that allows wedding guests to log in, view a list of gifts wanted by the bride and groom, and reserve gifts that they plan to purchase by putting them on a shopping list.

In the process, we show how the common database functions are used in practice, including how to:

- Call PHP library functions to connect to the MySQL DBMS and handle MySQL errors with PHP
- Manage DBMS credentials with include files
- Execute queries through the DBMS connection, and retrieve query result sets
- Present query results using HTML
- Create HTML form environments using PHP
- Interact with the user and preprocess user data to minimize security risks
- Add session support to an application so that a user can log in and log out
- Pass data between scripts by creating embedded hypertext links in HTML
- Use HTTP headers

The database and script files for this example are available from the book's web site; we recommend you download these and look at them while reading through this chapter. Even better, set up the application on your system and try it out. The program source code is also listed in the Appendix.

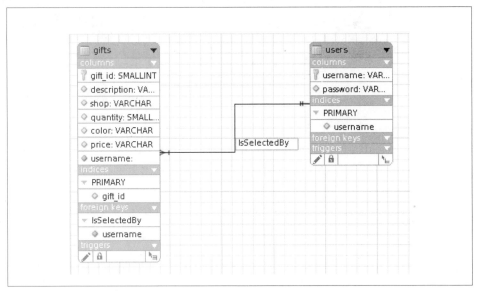

Figure 15-1. The wedding registry ER model using the MySQL Workbench

Designing and Creating the Wedding Database

Let's say Jack and Jill are getting married and would rather not receive the traditional 7 toasters and 11 electric kettles. Instead, they've decided to lists things they actually do want on a web site and let wedding guests select something useful to buy from the list.

Thinking about the problem carefully, we come across several requirements. Our application should:

- Allow Jack and Jill to add to or modify the list of required gifts
- Allow users to view the gifts that can be selected
- Allow users to select gifts to buy, or to deselect gifts they have previously reserved
- Not allow users to select gifts that are already reserved
- Authenticate users to identify them and prevent one user modifying the selections of another

There are two entities here: users and gifts. Each user has a unique username and password, while each gift has a unique gift ID number, a description, desired quantity, color, place of purchase, and price. A gift may be reserved by a user, so each gift record can have a username associated with it. A one-to-many relationship is maintained between the two tables: each gift can be reserved by only one user; each user can reserve zero or more gifts. Figure 15-1 shows the ER model in the MySQL Workbench. Our database needs to contains only two tables—**users**, which stores a unique username and password for each wedding guest:

```
CREATE TABLE `users` (
 `username` VARCHAR(30) NOT NULL,
 `password` VARCHAR(30) NOT NULL,
 PRIMARY KEY (`username`)
);
```

and `gifts`, which stores data about gifts:

```
CREATE TABLE `gifts` (
 `gift_id` SMALLINT NOT NULL AUTO_INCREMENT,
 `description` VARCHAR(255) NOT NULL,
 `shop` VARCHAR(100) NOT NULL,
 `quantity` SMALLINT NOT NULL,
 `color` VARCHAR(30) DEFAULT NULL,
 `price` VARCHAR(30) DEFAULT NULL,
 `username` VARCHAR(30) DEFAULT NULL,
 PRIMARY KEY (`gift_id`)
);
```

The `username` is unique for each user and is used as a foreign key in the `gifts` table. Since this is a relatively simple application, we won't use a separate user ID field; for a complex application with heavy usage, it would be more efficient to have a small user ID field in the declaration, as shown here:

```
CREATE TABLE `users` (
 `username` VARCHAR(30) NOT NULL,
 `password` VARCHAR(30) NOT NULL,
 `user_id` INT NOT NULL AUTO_INCREMENT,
 PRIMARY KEY (`user_id`)
);
```

and use the `user_id` field as a foreign key in other tables.

Instead of typing in the CREATE statements, you can conveniently create the database by running the *create_wedding_database.sql* file, which you can download from the book's home page:

```
$ mysql --user=root --password=the_mysql_root_password \
< create_wedding_database.sql
```

You'll find these lines near the beginning of the file:

```
DROP DATABASE IF EXISTS wedding;
CREATE DATABASE wedding;
USE wedding;
```

These delete any existing wedding database before creating the new one from scratch.

We should also allow access to the database from a client; in our application, the client is primarily the PHP engine that executes our code. We can create the MySQL user `fred` who has a password `shhh`. This user is set up using the following SQL GRANT statement:

```
GRANT SELECT, INSERT, DELETE, UPDATE
 ON wedding.*
```

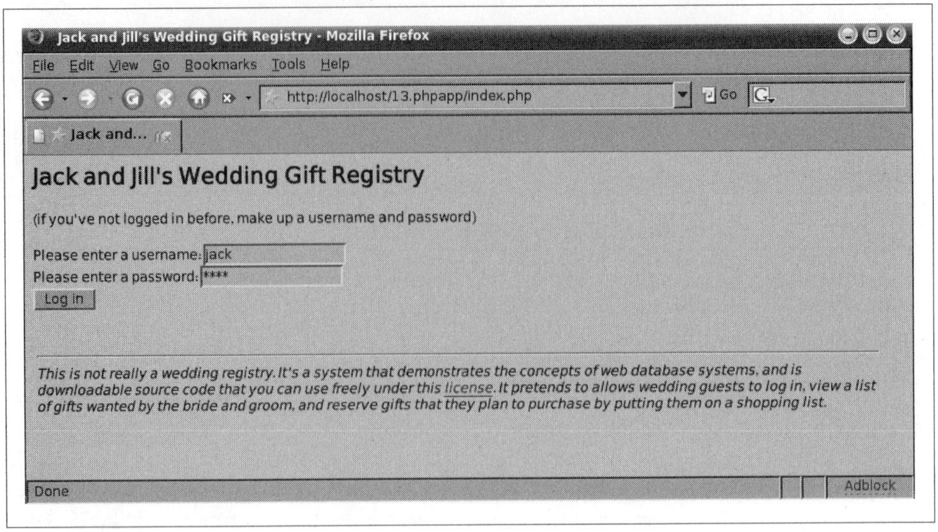

Figure 15-2. The wedding registry login page

```
TO fred@localhost
IDENTIFIED by 'shhh';
```

You can enter this statement in the MySQL monitor, or download the *grant_privi
leges.sql* from the book's home page and run it:

```
$ mysql --user=root --password=the_mysql_root_password < grant_privileges.sql
```

The Login Form

As the start page for our application, we will show a login form asking users for their
username and password. The HTML source for the login form is show below, and
Figure 15-2 shows the page rendered in a web browser:

```html
<html>
 <head>
  <title>Jack and Jill's Wedding Gift Registry</title>
 </head>
 <body bgcolor='LIGHTBLUE'>
  <h2>Jack and Jill's Wedding Gift Registry</h2>
  (if you've not logged in before, make up a username and password)
   <form action="process.php" method="POST">
    <br />Please enter a username: <input type="text"     name="username" />
    <br />Please enter a password: <input type="password" name="password" />
    <br /><input type="submit" value="Log in" />
   </form>
 </body>
</html>
```

When the user types in information and clicks the Submit button, the form passes the data to the script specified in the form `action` attribute; in our example, the data is sent to the script *process.php*.

Our form has three input fields: `username`, `password`, and `submit`. Since the form submits the data using the `POST` method, we can look inside the `$_POST` superglobal array in `process.php` to access the corresponding values as `$_POST["username"]`, `$_POST["password"]`, and `$_POST["submit"]`. The data from the submit field will just be `Log In` (as specified in the form), and this field isn't very useful; however, it's important to know that it exists.

Using One Script for the Form and for Processing

It's common to use a single PHP script to both generate the HTML form and to receive the submitted form data. When the user submits the form, the browser sends the user data along with the request. The script can decide what to do by checking for the user data: if there's no user data, it generates and sends the HTML login form; if there is some user data, it processes it. We can use the `count( )` function to count the number of entries in the `$_POST` array. If the count is nonzero, we know that some data has been submitted using the `POST` method:

```
// If the number of elements in the $_POST array is nonzero...
if(count($_POST))
{
  // Process form data
}
// otherwise...
else
{
  // Generate HTML form
}
?>
```

We can improve this code a bit. If a user clicks the Submit button without typing in a username or password, the `$_POST` array will still contain one item: the data from the Submit button itself (`$_POST["submit"]`). We can try to read the username and password from the `$_POST` array; if the form has not been submitted, this array will be uninitialized, and so the username and password entries will be empty. The username and password can also be left blank by the user. In either case, our script will detect an empty username or password, and will show the form. If the username and password aren't empty, the script will process the data and try to log the user in to the application:

```
// Pre-process the authentication data from the form for security
// and assign the username and password to local variables
if(count($_POST))
{
  $username = clean($_POST["username"], 30);
  $password = clean($_POST["password"], 30);
}
```

```
// If no username or password has been entered,
// show the login page
if(empty($username) ||
    empty($password) )
{
  // Generate HTML form
}
else
{
  // Process form data
}
?>
```

In script files that both generate the form and process the submitted data, the form action is set to the name of the script file itself. As our login form is the start page of our application, we'll call the script *index.php* so that it's the index file. We described index files in "Web Server Index Files" in Chapter 13. The form action in the *index.php* script is then also *index.php*:

```
<form action="index.php" method="POST">
```

Instead of typing the name of the script into the form action field, we can simply access the PHP_SELF entry from the $_SERVER superglobal array that we first saw in "The PHP Predefined Superglobal Variables" in Chapter 14:

```
<form action="<?php echo $_SERVER["PHP_SELF"];?>" method="POST">
```

When the PHP script is processed, the form action is set to the address of the script before the HTML is sent to the browser.

Passing a Message to a Script

If the user submits the form without providing any authentication details, or submits details that are incorrect, we should display the form again with an appropriate error message. We can modify our *index.php* script to display the login form if a message has been passed to it for display, in addition to the previous check for an empty username or password:

```
// If no username or password has been entered, or there's a message
// to display, show the login page
if(empty($username) || empty($password) || isset($message) )
{
  // Display the message (if any), and the login form
}
else
{
  // Try to authenticate the user against the database
  ...
  // If unsuccessful, pass an error message and call the form again.
}
?>
```

Here, we've used the `empty( )` function to ensure that the `$username` and `$password` variables are not empty, and the `isset( )` function to check whether the `$message` variable has been initialized. Note that these functions are slightly different: a variable can be initialized (set) to an empty string. Since we set the first two variables earlier in the script, they will always be initialized, so we need to check whether their contents are empty or not. The `$message` variable will be initialized if a message has been passed to us for display; let's see how this is done.

To pass nonsensitive information from one script to another, we can create our own `GET` request by adding a *query string* to the name of the target script. The query string consists of list of value assignments separated by ampersands, and is separated from the address of the script by a question mark symbol (?). For example, we can pass the value `Problem` to the script `index.php` by assigning it to the variable `message` in this way:

```
index.php?message=Problem
```

We can call this URL using the `header( )` function we first saw in "The Reload Problem" in Chapter 14.

In the target script, we can then access these values through the `$_GET` superglobal array. Even though we're creating this message, we depend on the browser to send it to us. Since it arrives from the client, it can be manipulated, and so we must treat it with caution and should apply the `clean( )` function before using it:

```
// Pre-process the message data for security
if(count($_GET))
{
 $message  = clean($_GET["message"], 128);
 echo "The message is: ".$message;
}
```

To avoid confusing the browser with symbols such as spaces and tabs that have special meaning in URL strings, we can process messages with the PHP `urlencode( )` function before appending them to the requested URL. The encoded string can then be safely used as part of a URL string. For example, the following two lines:

```
$message="Please choose a username and password that are ".
         "at least four characters long";
$target_URL="index.php?message=".urlencode($message);
```

produce the `$target_URL` variable with the value:

```
index.php?message=Please+choose+a+username+and+password+that+are+
                at+least+four+characters+long
```

If we want to pass multiple values, we can use the ampersand symbol (&) as a separator between each variable name and value pair, as in this example:

```
search.php?search_term=truth&display_results=50&language=english
```

Most web search engines use this technique as part of their Previous and Next links in the search results page.

Logging Users In and Out

In our application, we can check the username and password obtained from the login form against the authentication details in the database; if we find a matching row, the user is authorized to access the system. Given the limited need for security in our application, we can reasonably have it automatically register new users the first time they enter their authentication details. The next time they visit, the application will authenticate them against the stored data.

Before trying to authenticate the user, we can check to ensure that the entered username and password aren't too short; in general, the longer the authentication strings, the harder they are to subvert by a malicious user. If either the username or the password are less than four characters long, we redirect the browser to the login page with an appropriate error message:

```
// Check that the username and password are each at least three
// characters long.
if( (strlen($username)<4) ||
  (strlen($password)<4) )
{
 // No, they're not; create an error message and redirect
 // the browser to the index page to display the message
 $message = "Please choose a username and password that are " .
  "at least four characters long";
 header("Location: index.php?message=" . urlencode($message));
 exit;
}
```

Once we're happy with the length of the username and password, we can check whether the username already exists in the database; if it does, we check to see whether the provided password is correct. If no such username exists, we add the new username and password pair to the database.

To access the database using PHP, we first set up a connection to the MySQL server using the `mysqli_connect( )` function. This takes four arguments: the name of the host the MySQL server is running on, the username and password to use to connect to the server (these are the same username and password that are used to access the DBMS though the command-line monitor), and the database to use:

```
$DB_hostname     = "localhost";
$DB_username     = "fred";
$DB_password     = "shhh";
$DB_databasename = "wedding";

$connection=mysqli_connect($DB_hostname, $DB_username, $DB_password,
  $DB_databasename);
```

As described in "Accessing MySQL Using PHP" in Chapter 14, the `mysqli_connect( )` function can additionally take parameters that specify the port number and socket path to use.

In our environment, the web server and the MySQL DBMS are running on the same host machine, so the user needs access only from `localhost`. Having the DBMS and web server on the same machine is a good decision for small- to medium-size web database applications because there is no network communications overhead between the DBMS and the web server. For high-traffic or complex web database applications, it may be desirable to have dedicated hardware for each application.

Verifying New Users

In our simple application, we've allowed users to create new accounts for themselves. For applications where security is more important, new accounts might need to be added or approved by the system administrator. To ensure that the email address is valid and owned by the person requesting the account, you can also ask new users to authenticate themselves through an email verification step. For each new account request, you can generate and store a random verification key, and then send an email with a verification link, specifying the user and key:

```
http://www.invyhome.com/verify.php?user_id=313&key=b114bcf8e4a110a786f19f5
```

When the user reads the email and opens this address in their browser, the application can check that the key matches the one stored in the database for this user; if so, the account can be activated. This is still vulnerable to a *brute-force* attack, where an attacker tries all possible permutations of characters to find the correct one—rather like trying all possibilities on a combination lock. For added security, you can count how many times you receive verification attempts for a particular user and block the account (and notify the administrator) if there are more than, say, 10 attempts.

Authenticating the User

Once we have successfully created an active connection to the MySQL server, we can use it in conjunction with other PHP functions to run queries on the database and retrieve data. We can execute an SQL query on the MySQL server using the `mysqli_query( )` function. This function takes two parameters: the DBMS connection to use and the query to execute.

The query does not need to be terminated with a semicolon. For a successful query that returns no answer rows, it returns TRUE; for a successful SELECT, SHOW, DESCRIBE, or EXPLAIN query, it returns the query results for later processing. For an unsuccessful query, it returns FALSE:

```php
// Create a query to find any rows that match the provided username
$query = "SELECT username, password FROM users WHERE username = '$username'";

// Run the query through the connection
if (($result = @ mysqli_query($connection, $query))==FALSE)
  showerror($connection);
```

An SQL query may be successful but return no matching rows. The `mysqli_num_rows( )` function returns the number of rows that have been returned by a `SELECT` query; we can use this to test whether our search for the specified username returned any rows:

```
// Were there any matching rows?
if (mysqli_num_rows($result) == 0)
{
 // No, so insert the new username and password into the table
 ...
}
else
{
 // Yes, so check that the supplied password is correct
 ...
}
```

We store the username and password pair in the `users` table, but with a twist; instead of storing the actual password, we store the result of passing the password through the `crypt( )` one-way encryption function. It's impossible to reverse the one-way encryption function to recover the password from the stored encrypted data.

This approach is more secure, as an attacker who gets hold of the database will not be able to determine what the passwords are and will need to try encrypting different possible passwords—perhaps using a "dictionary" of words—to find ones that appear in the table. We can further complicate any attack by using a variety of ways to encrypt the passwords; the attacker would then need to encrypt the dictionary as many times as the number of encryption methods used.

To add some variation to the one-way encryption, we use a salt in conjunction with the `crypt( )` function. The *salt* is a parameter to the encryption routine that modifies the encryption behavior; we can use the first two characters from the username to obtain a reasonable number of variations to make it more difficult to use a dictionary attack on all the passwords. For example:

```
echo crypt("My secret password", "ss");
```

returns `sstCejlom2fqI`, while:

```
echo crypt("My secret password", "st");
```

returns `steYkLCBz8Ir`.. Note that the salt is prepended to the start of the encrypted string returned by the `crypt( )` function.

To verify that the user has provided the correct password, we take the password, apply the same one-way encryption, and compare the result with the encrypted password stored in the database; if they match, we know that the user has provided the correct password—even though we don't know what the correct password is. This is similar to the way MySQL stores passwords for its own users.

Encrypted passwords on the server are only part of the overall security picture. With an ordinary web server, usernames and passwords are transferred between the web browser and web server as unencrypted text, so it's trivial for an attacker to listen in on the communications to determine the authentication details—without the need to grapple with the encrypted passwords. For an application that has higher security requirements, communications should be encrypted by requiring a Secure Sockets Layer (SSL) connection between the web browser and web server.

To implement this authentication process with PHP, we use the `mysqli_fetch_array( )` function to retrieve the rows of data one at a time from the result-set handle returned by the `mysqli_query( )` function. The function returns `false` when there are no more rows to fetch. Since the username field is the primary key of the `users` table, we expect at most one matching row, and so need to call the `mysqli_fetch_array( )` function only once. We place the retrieved row data in a variable —here we use the variable `$row`—and access the fields associatively using the field names. For example, the `username` field can be accessed through the variable `$row["username"]`.

If the authentication step fails, we redirect the browser to the same login page but ask PHP to display the error message we pass using the query string:

```
// Were there any matching rows?
if (mysqli_num_rows($result) == 0)
{
 // No, so insert the new username and password into the table
 $query = "INSERT INTO users SET username =".
   "'$username', password='".crypt($password, substr($username, 0, 2))."'";

 // Run the query through the connection
 if (($result = @ mysqli_query($connection, $query))==FALSE)
   showerror($connection);
}
else
{
 // Yes, so check that the supplied password is correct

 // Fetch the matching row
 // If we don't get exactly one answer, then we have a problem
 $matchedrows=0;
 while($row = @ mysqli_fetch_array($result))
  $matchedrows++;
 if($matchedrows!=1)
  die("We've just experienced a technical problem - ".
  "please notify the administrator.");

 // Does the user-supplied password match the password in the table?
 if (crypt($password, substr($username, 0, 2)) != $row["password"])
 {
  // No, so redirect the browser to the login page with a
```

```
  // message
  $message = "This user exists, but the password is incorrect. ".
    " Choose another username, or fix the password.";
  header("Location: index.php?message=" . urlencode($message));
  exit;
  }
}
```

We can be pretty certain that we'll get only a single match when we search for the user and password pair, since `username` is the primary key of the `users` table. However, we add an extra check to count the number of rows retrieved; if we get more than one, something odd has happened, and we stop processing. This is an example of defensive programming—thinking through all the possibilities that can occur and trying to ensure that your code can handle problems gracefully. The more effort you put into inserting checks into your code, the easier it will be to identify problems before they cause irretrievable damage to your data or your relationship with your customers!

Incidentally, you could rewrite these three lines:

```
$matchedrows=0;
while($row = @ mysqli_fetch_array($result))
  $matchedrows++;
```

in a `for` loop with an empty body (but note the semicolon at the end):

```
for($matchedrows=0; ($row = @ mysqli_fetch_array($result)) ; $matchedrows++);
```

In this loop, `$matchedrows` is initialized to `0`, and the loop is repeated as long as the condition:

```
($row = @ mysqli_fetch_array($result))
```

is true (not zero). This will be the case as long as `mysqli_fetch_array( )` finds another row to fetch from the results. Each time the loop iterates, the value of `matchedrows` is incremented by one. This code is more compact, but is also slightly harder to understand. Try to avoid writing code that's too difficult to understand, and *always* add clear comments to explain what the code is doing. It's very hard to understand badly commented code, even if you wrote the code yourself.

Starting the User Session

After inserting a new username and password pair into the `users` table, or after verifying that the provided username and password pair is correct, we know that the user is authorized to access the system. We start a new session with the `session_start( )` function and store the username in a session variable. We then redirect the browser to the gift list page with a welcome message:

```
// Everything went OK. Start a session, store the username in a session variable,
// and redirect the browser to the gift list page with a welcome message.
session_start();
$_SESSION['username']=$username;
$message = "Welcome {$_SESSION['username']}! ".
```

```
"Please select gift suggestions from the list to add to your shopping list!";
header("Location: list.php?message=" . urlencode($message));
exit;
```

We can use the $_SESSION['username'] variable to determine whether the guest is logged in and, if so, what their username is. Since we'd like to check that the user is authorized to check each page, we can define a PHP function logincheck( ) to verify that the user is logged in, and redirect the user to the login page if they are attempting to access a page without being logged in, or after their session has expired:

```php
// Check if the user is logged in. If not, send them to the login
// page
function logincheck()
{
  session_start();

  if (empty($_SESSION["username"]))
  {
   // redirect to the login page
   header("Location: index.php");
   exit;
  }
}
```

We call this function near the beginning of each script in our application to prevent people from sidestepping the authentication process; we could include an error message saying something like "You must log in to access that page."

Logging the User Out

To end a user's session with our gift registry application, we can have a "log out" link that calls the *logout.php* script. This script initializes the session and then destroys it. It then redirects the browser to the application main page:

```php
<?php
// Log out of the system by ending the session and load the main
// page

session_start();
session_destroy();

// Redirect to the main page
header("Location: index.php");
?>
```

As you can see, the script doesn't produce any HTML output. Instead, it uses the header( ) function to send a Location header line to the browser. When the browser receives this, it loads the specified web page—in this case, the *index.php* file in the same directory as the *logout.php* script.

The db.php Include File

As discussed in Chapter 14 in "Modularizing Code," include files can be used to provide a single definition for variable values or function declarations used by multiple scripts in an application. In our application, all our scripts need to use the same connection and authentication credentials to communicate with the database. We have previously described the custom `clean( )` and `logincheck( )` functions in "Untainting User Data," in Chapter 14 and "Authenticating the User," earlier in this chapter, and before that we wrote the `showerror( )` function in "Handling MySQL Errors" in Chapter 14. Since these functions are used across several PHP scripts, we can place the function definitions in a common include file that is loaded by the scripts that need it. This helps to keep code easy to maintain; any change to data or definitions in an include file is automatically in effect for the scripts that use it.

We can place the function definitions, along with the database connection details, in the file *db.php*:

```php
<?php
  // These are the DBMS credentials and the database name
  $DB_hostname = "localhost";
  $DB_username = "fred";
  $DB_password = "shhh";
  $DB_databasename = "wedding";

  // Show an error and stop the script
  function showerror($connection)
  {
     // Was there an error during connection?
     if(mysqli_connect_errno())
        // Yes; display information about the connection error
        die("Error " . mysqli_connect_errno($connection) .
          " : " .mysqli_connect_error($connection));
     else
        // No; display the error information for the active connection
        die("Error ".mysqli_errno($connection) . " : "
                   .mysqli_error($connection));
  }

  // Secure the user data by escaping characters and shortening the
  // input string
  function clean($input, $maxlength)
  {
     // Access the MySQL connection from outside this function.
     global $connection;

     // Limit the length of the string
     $input = substr($input, 0, $maxlength);

     // Escape semicolons and (if magic quotes are off) single and
     // double quotes
     if(get_magic_quotes_gpc())
        $input = stripslashes($input);
```

```
    $input = mysqli_real_escape_string($connection, $input);

    return $input;
}

// Check if the user is logged in. If not, send them to the login
// page
function logincheck()
{
    session_start();

    if (empty($_SESSION["username"]))
    {
        // redirect to the login page
        header("Location: index.php");
        exit;
    }
}
?>
```

We can incorporate this file as required using the `require_once( )` directive; for example, we can add the line:

```
require_once("db.php");
```

in the file *index.php* to have the *db.php* file included in it.

Editing the List of Gifts

Jack and Jill, our bride and groom, need to set up the list of gifts for wedding guests to choose from. Our application includes an *edit.php* file that allows the user to add or remove gifts, or modify existing gifts. In this section, we describe how we can prevent users other than Jack and Jill from accessing the editing page, and how the script enables gifts to be added, updated, and deleted.

Restricting Edit Access

To prevent unauthorized access, we ensure that only the users `jack` and `jill` can access this file; other users attempting to access this page are redirected to the gift list page *list.php*:

```
<?php
// edit.php: Show the user the available gifts and the gifts in
// their shopping list

// Include database parameters and related functions
require_once('db.php');

// Check if the user is logged in
// (this also starts the session)
logincheck();
```

```
// Check that the user is Jack or Jill (username is 'jack' or
// 'jill');  other users are not allowed to edit the gifts.
if($_SESSION['username']!="jack" && $_SESSION['username']!="jill")
{
  $message = "You are not authorized to edit the gift details. ".
   " Please select gift suggestions from the list to add to your shopping list!";
  header("Location: list.php?message=".urlencode($message));
  exit;
}

// Other code to display and edit the gifts
...
?>
```

Note that our application automatically creates an account and grants access the first time a user registers a particular username. It's technically possible for a user other than the real Jack or Jill to access the application first and create an account with the username jack or jill, and so gain access to the edit page. Since the username is the primary key to the users table, new accounts can't be added with the privileged usernames jack and jill once both these accounts have been created. If the user provides a username that already exists, our code assumes that they are trying to log in and checks whether the provided password matches the stored password for that username. Obviously, this is not particularly secure but is probably sufficient for the level of security our application requires.

Role-Based Authentication

We've hardcoded the usernames jack and jill into the script; if, for example, we wanted to grant edit access to another user, we would need to modify the code in the *edit.php* file. A more scalable solution is to authorize users according to their roles; for example, users who have an administrator role could be allowed to edit the gifts, while users who have a normal_user role could be allowed only to choose gifts for the couple. This would require us to add an extra role field to the users table and to modify *edit.php* to allow access to users who are administrators.

Role-based authentication helps maintainability, since we don't have to change program code according to individual users. In a large organization with people frequently changing roles or perhaps leaving the organization altogether, we need only to change the role of a particular user to change the level of access. For our application, we can consider two roles: *administrator* and *guest*. Jack and Jill are administrators, and everyone else is a guest. In role-based authentication, the test for the users jack and jill:

```
// Check that the user is Jack or Jill (username is 'jack' or
// 'jill');  other users are not allowed to edit the gifts.
if($_SESSION['username']!="jack" && $_SESSION['username']!="jill")
  ...
```

would instead be something like this:

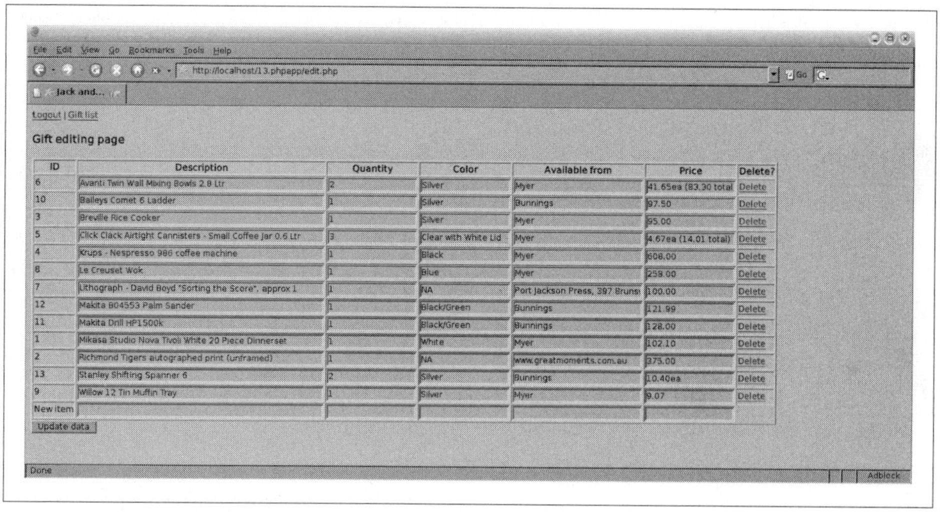

Figure 15-3. The wedding registry gift editing page

```
// Look up this user's role in the database
$query="SELECT role FROM users WHERE username=".$_SESSION['username'];
if (($result = @ mysqli_query($connection, $query))==FALSE)
  showerror($connection);

// Fetch the matching row
// If we don't get exactly one answer, then we have a problem
for($matchedrows=0; ($row = @ mysqli_fetch_array($result)); $matchedrows++);
if($matchedrows!=1)
  die("We've just experienced a technical problem - ".
      "please notify the administrator.");

// Save the role into a session variable for use
// in other parts of the application
$_SESSION['role']=$row['role'];

// Check that the user is an administrator;
// other users are not allowed to edit the gifts.
if($_SESSION['role']!="administrator")
  ...
```

In this example, we've assumed that the users table has a role column. Role-based authentication is probably overkill for our simple wedding gift registry, but it's a good approach for most other applications.

The Gift Editing Form

edit.php The *edit.php* script displays a list of the gifts in the system for editing or deletion, and a blank gift entry to allow a new gift item to be added. Figure 15-3 shows the application gift editing page loaded in a web browser. The HTML source of the file includes a link to the *logout.php* script that ends the user session and a link to the application main page. The form then incorporates the output of the showgiftsforedit( ) function that we describe next:

```
<!DOCTYPE HTML PUBLIC
  "-//W3C//DTD HTML 4.0 Transitional//EN"
  "http://www.w3.org/TR/html4/loose.dtd">
<html>
 <head>
  <title>Jack and Jill's Wedding Gift Registry</title>
 </head>
 <body bgcolor="LIGHTBLUE">
  <?php
    // Show a logout link and a link to the main page
    echo "<a href='logout.php'>Logout</a> | <a href='list.php'>Gift list</a>";

    echo "\n<h3>Gift editing page</h3>";

    // Show the existing gifts for editing
    showgiftsforedit($connection);
  ?>
 </body>
</html>
```

Note the \n in the HTML <h3> header string; this adds a newline in the HTML source to help when developing the application, but you can safely omit it.

The core text of the edit page is produced by the **showgiftsforedit( )** function. This generates an HTML form with an action set to $_SERVER["PHP_SELF"]; this means that the form data is passed back to the *edit.php* script, which must then process it:

```
// Create an HTML form pointing back to this script
echo "\n<form action='{$_SERVER["PHP_SELF"]}' method='POST'>";
...
echo "</form>";
```

The form input fields are prefilled with the gift details retrieved from the database; for neatness, we create an HTML table and arrange the form fields in the table.

```
// Create an HTML table to neatly arrange the form inputs
echo "\n<table border='1'>";

// Create the table headings
echo "\n<tr>" .
  "\n\t<th bgcolor='LIGHTGREEN'>ID</th>" .
  "\n\t<th bgcolor='LIGHTGREEN'>Description</th>" .
  "\n\t<th bgcolor='LIGHTGREEN'>Quantity</th>" .
  "\n\t<th bgcolor='LIGHTGREEN'>Color</th>" .
  "\n\t<th bgcolor='LIGHTGREEN'>Available from</th>" .
  "\n\t<th bgcolor='LIGHTGREEN'>Price</th>" .
  "\n\t<th bgcolor='LIGHTGREEN'>Delete?</th>" .
  "\n</tr>";
...
echo "</table>";
```

Once we've created the table, we run an SQL query to list all the gifts in the `gifts` table, and order the results by the alphabetical order of the gift descriptions. If no gifts are found, we display a suitable message; if any gifts are found, we display them for editing:

```
// Create an SQL query to list the gifts in the database
$query = "SELECT * FROM gifts ORDER BY description";

// Run the query through the connection
if (($result = @ mysqli_query($connection, $query))==FALSE)
  showerror($connection);

// Check whether we found any gifts
if(!mysqli_num_rows($result))
 // No;  display a notice
 echo "\n\t<tr><td colspan='7' align='center'>".
  "There are no gifts in the database</td></tr>";
else
 // Display the results for editing...
```

To display the results, we execute a `while( )` loop that repeatedly calls the `mysqli_fetch_array( )` function to fetch the results a row at a time as an associative array. We assign this array to the `$row` variable, allowing us to access the result fields by using the field name as the array index. For example, we can access the `description` field data for a gift row as `$row["description"]`. When no more rows are available, the function returns `FALSE`; when our `while` loop encounters this value, it ends the loop.

For each gift item, we compose an HTML table row with form input fields, and prefill the fields with the gift data from the database. We have multiple gifts, each with a description, quantity, and so on; we could create the HTML as below:

```
<tr>
<td>6</td>
<td><input name='description' value='Avanti Twin Wall Mixing Bowls 2.8 Ltr'
                             size='60' /></td>
<td><input name='quantity'    value='2'                /></td>
<td><input name='color'       value='Silver'           /></td>
<td><input name='shop'        value='Myer'       size='30' /></td>
<td><input name='price'       value='41.65ea (83.30 total)' /></td>
</tr>
<tr>
<td>10</td>
<td><input name='description' value='Baileys Comet 6 Ladder' size='60' /></td>
<td><input name='quantity'    value='1'                /></td>
<td><input name='color'       value='Silver'           /></td>
<td><input name='shop'        value='Bunnings'  size='30' /></td>
<td><input name='price'       value='97.50'            /></td>
</tr>
```

This form contains as many `description`, `quantity`, `color`, `shop`, and `price` fields as there are gifts. However, we can access only one set through `$_POST["description"]`, `$_POST["quantity"]`, and so on. An easy way to resolve this problem is to name the form fields as arrays, with the ID of each gift used as the index of the array. Thus, for example, the form input for the description of gift 6 is named `description[6]`.

This is the PHP code to generate the HTML form:

```
// Yes; fetch the gift details a row at a time
while($row = @ mysqli_fetch_array($result))
  // Compose the data for this gift into a row of form inputs in the table.
  // Add a delete link in the last column of the row.
  echo "\n<tr>" .
    "\n\t<td>{$row["gift_id"]}</td>".
    "\n\t<td><input name='description[{$row['gift_id']}]' ".
            "value='{$row["description"]}' size='60' /></td>".
    "\n\t<td><input name='quantity[{$row['gift_id']}]'    ".
            "value='{$row["quantity"]}'               /></td>".
    "\n\t<td><input name='color[{$row['gift_id']}]'       ".
            "value='{$row["color"]}'                  /></td>".
    "\n\t<td><input name='shop[{$row['gift_id']}]'        ".
            "value='{$row["shop"]}'        size='30' /></td>".
    "\n\t<td><input name='price[{$row['gift_id']}]'       ".
            "value='{$row["price"]}'                  /></td>".
    "\n\t<td><a href='{$_SERVER['PHP_SELF']}?action=delete&".
            "gift_id={$row["gift_id"]}'>Delete</a></td>".
    "\n</tr>";
```

In the last column of each table row, we create an HTML link to the same script with a query string containing values for two variables: the `action` is set to `delete`, and the `gift_id` is set to the ID of the gift displayed in the current row. Clicking on this link will cause the script to delete the gift with that ID; we describe how this is done later in this chapter.

A sample output of the `while` loop for two gifts—with IDs 6 and 10—is shown below:

```
<tr>
<td>6</td>
<td><input name='description[6]'
  value='Avanti Twin Wall Mixing Bowls 2.8 Ltr' size='60' /></td>
<td><input name='quantity[6]'
  value='2'            /></td>
<td><input name='color[6]'
  value='Silver'               /></td>
<td><input name='shop[6]'
  value='Myer'      size='30' /></td>
<td><input name='price[6]'
  value='41.65ea (83.30 total)'            /></td>
<td><a href='edit.php?action=delete&gift_id=6'>Delete</a></td>
</tr>
<tr>
<td>10</td>
<td><input name='description[10]'
  value='Baileys Comet 6 Ladder' size='60' /></td>
<td><input name='quantity[10]'
  value='1'            /></td>
<td><input name='color[10]'
  value='Silver'               /></td>
<td><input name='shop[10]'
  value='Bunnings'      size='30' /></td>
<td><input name='price[10]'
```

```
          value='97.50'                  /></td>
        <td><a href='edit.php?action=delete&gift_id=10'>Delete</a></td>
      </tr>
```

Note that the whitespace we added to make the source code more readable doesn't affect the formatting of the output. We've also shown each value starting on a new line for readability.

After displaying all the existing gifts, we add a row of empty form input fields to the table; Jack or Jill can enter gift attributes into these fields and submit the form to add a new gift to the database. Since the gift_id field in our database is an auto-incremented field that starts from 1, we can conveniently use the index 0 to identify fields for the new gift. We could use a different name for the new gift fields—for example, newgift_description, newgift_quantity, and so on, but we'd then need to add more code to process these additional variables on the action page. Once we've printed this last table row, we end the table, add a Submit button, and end the form. This ends our showgiftsforedit( ) function:

```
...
echo "\n<table border='1'>";
...

// Display a row with blank form inputs to allow a gift to be added
echo "\n<tr><td></td>" .
  "\n\t<td><input name='description[0]' size='60' /></td>".
  "\n\t<td><input name='quantity[0]'   /></td>".
  "\n\t<td><input name='color[0]'      /></td>".
  "\n\t<td><input name='shop[0]'       size='30' /></td>".
  "\n\t<td><input name='price[0]'      /></td>".
 "\n</tr>";

// End the table
echo "\n</table>";

// Display a submit button and end the form.
echo "\n<input name='update' type='submit' value='Update data' />";
echo "</form>";
```

Deleting a Gift

If the user clicks on a Delete link for a form, the same *edit.php* script is called with the query string action=delete&gift_id=*the_gift_id*; the script must detect that some data has been passed to it to process. As we mentioned earlier in "Logging Users In and Out," the query-string attribute and value pairs are available in the called script as elements in the $_GET superglobal array. The *edit.php* script checks whether the $_GET array contains any data; if it does, the script creates and executes an SQL query to delete the corresponding gift from the database. Once the query has been executed, the program proceeds to display the existing gifts for editing as before:

```
// See if we've arrived here after clicking the delete link
if(count($_GET) && (clean($_GET['action'], 10)=='delete'))
```

```
{
  // Yes; compose a query to delete the specified gift from the gifts table
  $query = "DELETE FROM gifts WHERE gift_id=".clean($_GET['gift_id'], 10);

  // Run the query through the connection
  if (($result = @ mysqli_query($connection, $query))==FALSE)
    showerror($connection);
}
```

We must also call the logincheck( ) function at the top of the *edit.php* script to identify the user and use this information to prevent anybody but Jack or Jill from deleting gifts.

Processing the Submitted Form

When the user clicks on the "Update data" button to submit the gift editing form, the data is sent by the POST method to the same *edit.php* script. The form data is accessible through the $_POST superglobal array. For example, the Submit button was created in the HTML form as:

```
<input name='update' type='submit' value='Update data' />
```

When the form is submitted, this is available as the variable $_POST["update"], which has the value Update data. We can assume that when the $_POST["update"] variable exists (is set), the user has just submitted the HTML form. If this is the case, we can try to update the information in the gifts table. The script iterates through all existing gift IDs in the database and checks whether there's any corresponding data in the $_POST array. If there is any submitted data for a given gift ID, we call the update_or_insert_gift( ) function to update the database.

Normally, each existing gift ID will have a corresponding entry in the HTML form, and so there will be data for it in the $_POST array. However, we have to check for this; we should ensure we don't run into problems if no data is submitted for a particular gift.

This might happen if you add a new gift and submit the form, then make your browser resubmit the original form data again by reloading the form action page (most browsers warn you if you try to do this with a POST form); the ID of the new gift will not be in the submitted form data. It could also happen if another user adds a new gift between the time that you load the form and the time that you submit it.

To avoid problems, we use the isset( ) function on each of the POST fields for each of the gift IDs that appear in the database. Since we've named the form fields as array elements with the gift ID as the array index, the data items we obtain from the $_POST array are themselves arrays. For example, to access the quantity entered for the gift with ID 7, we would use the variable $_POST["quantity"][7].

After updating the existing gifts, we can call the update_or_insert_gift( ) function with the fake gift ID of 0 to read any entered information for a new gift and add it to the database:

```
// See if we've arrived here after clicking the update button;
// if so, update the gift details.
if(isset($_POST['update']))
{
 // Define an SQL query to list the gift IDs in the database
 $query = "SELECT gift_id FROM gifts";

 // Run the query through the connection
 if (($result = @ mysqli_query($connection, $query))==FALSE)
     showerror($connection);

 // Process the submitted data for each gift ID in the database
 while($row = @ mysqli_fetch_array($result))
 {
     $gift_id=$row["gift_id"];

     // Update an existing gift if there is corresponding data
     // submitted from the form
     if(
             isset($_POST["quantity"    ][$gift_id]) &&
             isset($_POST["description"][$gift_id]) &&
             isset($_POST["color"       ][$gift_id]) &&
             isset($_POST["shop"        ][$gift_id]) &&
             isset($_POST["price"       ][$gift_id])
         )
           update_or_insert_gift_data($connection, $gift_id);
 }

 // Process the data submitted in the form fields for the new
 // gift;  we had assigned this the index 0 in the HTML form.
 update_or_insert_gift_data($connection, 0);
}
```

Now let's look at update_or_insert_gift( ). This function extracts and cleans the data of the various form fields from the $_POST array. It then verifies that all the fields contain some data; if any field is empty, an error message is displayed, and the database is not updated. The error message is not displayed if the data items belong to the last table row—which is a blank row allowing the user to optionally enter data for a new gift—and *all* the fields are empty. We check for this by concatenating all the fields with the period or dot symbol (.). We display the message if we're processing any row but the last one, and one of the fields is empty, or if it is the last row and the combined length of all the concatenated strings is not zero.

If some data is available for each gift attribute, the script runs a REPLACE INTO query to update the database. A REPLACE INTO query replaces any existing data for a given key, or automatically creates a new entry if no data already exists for that key:

```
// Update the data for a gift with the specified gift ID; for a
// gift ID of 0, add a new gift to the database.
function update_or_insert_gift_data($connection, $gift_id)
{
 // Extract the data items for the gift attributes from the $_POST array
 $quantity   =clean($_POST["quantity"    ][$gift_id],    5);
```

```php
$description=clean($_POST["description"][$gift_id], 255);
$color      =clean($_POST["color"      ][$gift_id],  30);
$shop       =clean($_POST["shop"       ][$gift_id], 100);
$price      =clean($_POST["price"      ][$gift_id],  30);

// If the gift_id is 0, this is a new gift, so set the
// gift_id to be empty; MySQL will automatically assign a
// unique gift_id to the new gift.
if($gift_id==0)
 $gift_id='';

// If any of the attributes are empty, don't update the database.
if(
 !strlen($quantity    ) ||
 !strlen($description) ||
 !strlen($color       ) ||
 !strlen($shop        ) ||
 !strlen($price       )
 )
{
 // If this isn't the blank row for optionally adding a new gift,
 // or if it is the blank row and the user has actually typed something in,
 // display an error message.
 if(!empty($gift_id)
    ||
   strlen(
     $quantity.
     $description.
     $color.
     $shop.
     $price)
   )
   echo "<font color='red'>There must be no empty fields - not updating:<br />".
      "([$quantity], [$description], [$color], [$shop], [$price]</font><br />";
}
else
{
 // Add or update the gifts table
 $query = "REPLACE INTO gifts ".
   "(gift_id, description,shop,quantity,color,price,username)".
   " values ('$gift_id', '$description', '$shop', $quantity,
      '$color', '$price', NULL)";

 // Run the query through the connection
 if (@ mysqli_query($connection, $query)==FALSE)
   showerror($connection);
 }
}
```

Notice that in our SQL query, we explicitly list field names before specifying the values. The order of the values must match the order that the field names are listed in, but these don't need to match the order of the fields in the database table; if we had omitted the initial list of field names, the field values would need to be in the same order as the fields in the table. Note also that we haven't stored the result of the REPLACE INTO query as we would have done for a SELECT query, since only SELECT queries return an answer set.

Loading Sample Gifts

Earlier in "Editing the List of Gifts," we saw how the administrator can manually add gifts to the database. You can, of course, add gifts by running SQL INSERT queries using the MySQL monitor. For example, you can type:

```
mysql> INSERT INTO gifts VALUES
    -> (NULL,'Acme 48-piece dinner set','SomeShop',1,'White','102.10',NULL);
```

Specifying a NULL value for the first field, gift_id, lets the MySQL server automatically assign an auto-incremented ID; the first gift inserted into the table will have a gift_id of 1, the next one will have a gift_id of 2, and so on.

We also specify a NULL value for the last field, username, since gifts newly loaded in the database are not reserved by any user. When a user reserves a gift, her username is stored in the username field for that gift.

To help save you some typing, we've generated a few sample gifts that you can load into your database by running the SQL queries in the *populate_wedding_database.sql* file that you can download from the book's home page:

```
$ mysql --user=fred --password=shhh < populate_wedding_database.sql
```

Note that this file includes the statement:

```
DELETE FROM gifts;
```

to first delete any existing gift entries from the database.

Listing Gifts for Selection

After logging in to the application, users are sent to the *list.php* page that displays all the gifts that are still available (not yet reserved by a wedding guest). The page also displays the gifts that the user has already reserved.

As with the gift editing page, we create the outline of an HTML page and call on a custom function—in this case, the function showgifts( )—to read the gift information from the database and generate the required HTML:

```
<!DOCTYPE HTML PUBLIC
"-//W3C//DTD HTML 4.0 Transitional//EN"
"http://www.w3.org/TR/html4/loose.dtd">
<html>
 <head>
  <title>Jack and Jill's Wedding Gift Registry</title>
 </head>
 <body bgcolor='LIGHTBLUE'>
  <?php
```

```php
    // Show a logout link
    echo "<a href='logout.php'>Logout</a>";

    // Check whether the user is Jack or Jill (username is 'jack' or
    // 'jill'); if so, show a link to the gift editing page.
    if($_SESSION['username']=="jack" || $_SESSION['username']=="jill")
        echo " | <a href='edit.php'>Edit gifts</a>";

    // Connect to the MySQL DBMS and use the wedding database -
    // credentials are in the file db.php

    if(!($connection= @ mysqli_connect(
        $DB_hostname, $DB_username, $DB_password, $DB_databasename)))
        showerror($connection);

    // Pre-process the message data for security
    if(count($_GET))
        $message = clean($_GET["message"], 128);

    // If there's a message to show, output it
    if (!empty($message))
        echo "\n<h3><font color=\"red\"><em>".
          urldecode($message)."</em></font></h3>";

    echo "\n<h3>Here are some gift suggestions</h3>";

    // Show the gifts that are still unreserved
    showgifts($connection, SHOW_UNRESERVED_GIFTS);

    echo "\n<h3>Your Shopping List</h3>";

    // Show the gifts that have been reserved by this user
    showgifts($connection, SHOW_GIFTS_RESERVED_BY_THIS_USER);
  ?>
  </body>
</html>
```

The showgifts( ) function is defined as:

```php
// Show the user the gifts
//
// Parameters:
// (1) An open connection to the DBMS
// (2) Whether to show the available gifts or the current user's
//     shopping list.
function showgifts($connection, $show_user_selection)
{
  // Show the gifts...
}
```

and takes two arguments: an open connection to the MySQL server, and a value to indicate whether to show available gifts (these can be added to the user's selection) or the gifts reserved by this user (these can be removed from the user's selection). We could use 0 and 1 for this indicator value. However, these values are not meaningful in this context; does 0 mean we want to show reserved gifts or unreserved gifts? You might be tempted to use the constants FALSE and TRUE here; this doesn't solve the problem, however, since there's no clear connection between either of these values and the reserved or unreserved status of a gift.

One useful technique in writing code that is *self-documenting*—that is, code that is easy to read and understand on its own—is to define and use constants that have meaningful names. For example, instead of 0 and 1, we can use SHOW_UNRESERVED_GIFTS and SHOW_GIFTS_RESERVED_BY_THIS_USER. In "Handling errors in production code" in Chapter 14, we used the define( ) function to store the administrator's email address in a constant. We can also use this function to define the two constants we need here:

```
define("SHOW_UNRESERVED_GIFTS",              0);
define("SHOW_GIFTS_RESERVED_BY_THIS_USER", 1);
```

To show the gifts that are unreserved, and then the gifts that have been reserved by the current user, we call the function once with the last parameter set to SHOW_UNRESERVED_GIFTS, and once with it set to SHOW_GIFTS_RESERVED_BY_THIS_USER.

The function itself first tests whether there are any gifts in the database and displays an error message if there aren't any:

```
// Show the user the gifts
//
// Parameters:
// (1) An open connection to the DBMS
// (2) Whether to show the available gifts or the current user's
// shopping list.

// Define constants for use when calling showgifts
define("SHOW_GIFTS_RESERVED_BY_THIS_USER", TRUE);
define("SHOW_UNRESERVED_GIFTS", FALSE);

function showgifts($connection, $show_user_selection)
{
    // See whether there are any gifts in the system
    $query = "SELECT * FROM gifts";

    // Run the query through the connection
    if (($result = @ mysqli_query($connection, $query))==FALSE)
        showerror($connection);

    // Check whether any gifts were found
    if (@ mysqli_num_rows($result) == 0)
        // No; print a notice
        echo "\n<h3><font color=\"red\">".
           "There are no gifts described in the system!</font></h3>";
    else
    {
        // Yes; display the gifts
    }
}
```

In normal operation, there will be gift descriptions in the system; depending on how the function was called, we run a query to list all the unreserved gifts (those that have their username field set to NULL), or all the gifts reserved by the current user (those that have their username field set to $_SESSION['username']):

```
// If we're showing the available gifts, then set up
// a query to show all unreserved gifts (where username IS NULL)
if ($show_user_selection == SHOW_UNRESERVED_GIFTS)
    $query = "SELECT * FROM gifts WHERE username IS NULL ORDER BY description";
else
    // Otherwise, set up a query to show all gifts reserved by
    // this user
    $query = "SELECT * FROM gifts WHERE username = '".
        $_SESSION['username']."' ORDER BY description";

// Run the query through the connection
if (($result = @ mysqli_query($connection, $query))==FALSE)
    showerror($connection);
```

If the query doesn't retrieve any results, we display a message indicating that no unreserved gifts are available or that the user has not reserved any gifts, depending on which list we're showing:

```
// Did we get back any rows?
if (@ mysqli_num_rows($result) == 0)
{
    // No data was returned from the query.
    // Show an appropriate message
    if ($show_user_selection == SHOW_UNRESERVED_GIFTS)
        echo "\n<h3><font color=\"red\">No gifts left!</font></h3>";
    else
        echo "\n<h3><font color=\"red\">Your Basket is Empty!</font></h3>";
}
else
{
    // Yes, so show the gifts as a table
}
```

If we do find some gifts to show, we compose an HTML table and iterate through the results to display the gift attributes:

```
echo "\n<table border=1 width=100%>";

// Create some headings for the table
echo "\n<tr>" .
    "\n\t<th>Quantity</th>" .
    "\n\t<th>Gift</th>" .
    "\n\t<th>Colour</th>" .
    "\n\t<th>Available From</th>" .
    "\n\t<th>Price</th>" .
    "\n\t<th>Action</th>" .
    "\n</tr>";

// Fetch each database table row of the results
while($row = @ mysqli_fetch_array($result))
```

```
{
    // Display the gift data as a table row
    echo "\n<tr>" .
        "\n\t<td>{$row["quantity"]}</td>" .
        "\n\t<td>{$row["description"]}</td>" .
        "\n\t<td>{$row["color"]}</td>" .
        "\n\t<td>{$row["shop"]}</td>" .
        "\n\t<td>{$row["price"]}</td>";

    // Display a link to allow an unreserved gift to be added or
    // a reserved gift to be removed...


    echo "\n</tr>";
}
echo "\n</table>";
```

In the last column of each row, we show a link to "Add to Shopping List" if we're displaying unreserved gifts, or a link to "Remove from Shopping List" if we're displaying gifts reserved by the user:

```
// Are we showing the list of gifts reserved by the
// user?
if ($show_user_selection == SHOW_UNRESERVED_GIFTS)
    // No. So set up an embedded link that the user can click
    // to add the gift to their shopping list by running
    // action.php with action=add
    echo "\n\t<td><a href=\"action.php?action=add&" .
        "gift_id={$row["gift_id"]}\">Add to Shopping List</a></td>";
else
    // Yes. So set up an embedded link that the user can click
    // to remove the gift from their shopping list by running
    // action.php with action=remove
    echo "\n\t<td><a href=\"action.php?action=remove&" .
        "gift_id={$row["gift_id"]}\">Remove from Shopping list</a></td>";
```

The links include a query string to specify the action to perform (add an unreserved gift or remove a reserved gift) and the ID of the gift to process; for example, we might have a link:

```
<a href="action.php?action=add&gift_id=10">Add to Shopping List</a>
```

Clicking on the link calls the *action.php* script with this action and gift ID. We describe the operation of this script in the next section.

Selecting and Deselecting Gifts

Users add gifts to their shopping list or remove them by clicking on links in the *list.php* page. The links call the *action.php* script with the gift ID and the **action** parameter set to **add** or **remove**. For **add**, the script attempts to reserve the gift with the specified **gift_id** for the current guest. Similarly, for **remove**, the script attempts to remove the gift with the specified `gift_id` from the current guest's shopping list. The user is identified by the `username` session variable (`$_SESSION['username']`).

The script checks that the user is authenticated using the `logincheck( )` function and that the URL requested by the browser includes attributes and values in a query string. As discussed earlier, the query-string attributes can be accessed as elements of the `$_GET` superglobal array. The *action.php* script first cleans the values in `$_GET['gift_id']` and `$_GET['action']` and assigns them to the variables `$gift_id` and `$action`:

```php
<?php
    // action.php: Add or remove a gift from the user's shopping list

    // Include database parameters and related functions
    require_once("db.php");

    // Check if the user is logged in
    // (this also starts the session)
    logincheck();

    // Secure the user data
    if(count($_GET))
    {
    // Connect to the MySQL DBMS and use the wedding database
    // - credentials are in the file db.php
        if(!($connection= @ mysqli_connect(
            $DB_hostname, $DB_username, $DB_password, $DB_databasename)))
            showerror($connection);

        $gift_id = clean($_GET['gift_id'], 5);
        $action = clean($_GET['action'] , 6);

    // ...
```

The script then checks whether the requested action is either **add** or **remove**. If it isn't, we stop processing to avoid corrupting the database, and also to block an attacker trying to manipulate the behavior of our script. The script will proceed beyond this point only if a valid action has been requested, so we don't need to add an `else` clause to the `if` statement:

```php
    // Is the action something we know about?
    if($action != "add" && $action != "remove")
        // No, it's not; perhaps someone's trying to manipulate the
        // URL query string?
        die("Unknown action: ".$action);

    // The program should reach this point only if the action is add
    // or remove, since otherwise processing stops with the die()
    // instruction.

    // What did the user want us to do?
    if ($action == "add")
    {
```

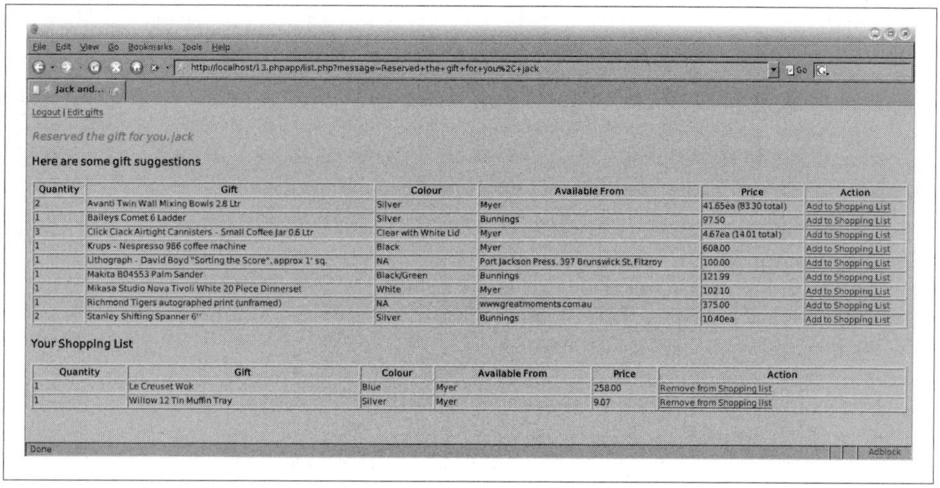

Figure 15-4. The wedding registry list page showing reserved gifts

```
    // The user wants to add a new item to their shopping list.
  ...

  }
else // The action is not add, so it must be remove
{
    // The user wants to remove an existing item from their shopping list.

}

// Redirect the browser back to list.php
header("Location: list.php?message=" . urlencode($message));
exit;
```

At the end of the script, after adding or removing the gift, we redirect the user's browser back to the gift selection page (*list.php*) with the message we prepared earlier indicating the success or failure of the operation. In practice, when the user clicks on the add or remove link in *list.php*, the browser requests the *action.php* script; this quietly performs the update and redirects the browser to the `list.php` page, leaving the user with the impression that they never left the list page:

```
// Redirect the browser back to list.php
header("Location: list.php?message=" . urlencode($message));
exit;
```

Figure 15-4 shows the list of gifts and reserved gifts.

Adding a Gift

If the requested action is to add the gift to the user's shopping list, we should ensure that we reserve the gift only if it is still free. The gift was free when it was listed by the *list.php* script; however, another user could have been viewing the list of gifts at the same time, and they might have selected the same gift first. This gift would then be marked as taken in the database, but the first user wouldn't know this, because the list of gifts they loaded in their browser was generated when the gift was still free. This is another example of where defensive programming is needed; when developing for the Web, each script is independent, and there are no time limits or controls in our application on when a user can request a script.

If we grant the LOCK TABLES privilege to the MySQL user fred, we can use locks for this part of the code:

1. Run a query to apply a write lock to the gifts table; this prevents any changes to the data in this table until we release the write lock:

```
// Lock the gifts table for writing
$query = "LOCK TABLE gifts WRITE";
// Run the query through the connection
if (($result = @ mysqli_query($connection, $query))==FALSE)
    showerror($connection);
```

2. Read the username associated with the specified gift_id:

```
// Create a query to retrieve the gift.
$query = "SELECT * FROM gifts WHERE gift_id = {$gift_id}";
// Run the query through the connection
if (($result = @ mysqli_query($connection, $query))==FALSE)
    showerror($connection);
```

3. If the username associated with the gift is not empty and is not the same as the current user, create a message to tell the user that the gift has just been taken:

```
// Has someone already reserved this? (a race condition)
if (!empty($row["username"]) && $row["username"] != $_SESSION['username'])
    // Yes. So, record a message to show the user
    $message = "Oh dear... Someone just beat you to that gift!";
else
{
    // No...reserve the gift for this user
}
```

4. If the check shows that the gift is still free, we add the current user's username to the gift data to indicate that the gift has been reserved:

```
// No. So, create a query that reserves the gift for this user
$query = "UPDATE gifts SET username = '{$_SESSION['username']}' ".
        "WHERE gift_id = {$gift_id}";

// Run the query through the connection
if (($result = @ mysqli_query($connection, $query))==FALSE)
    showerror($connection);
```

5. Finally, unlock the gifts table:

```
$query = "UNLOCK TABLES";
// Run the query through the connection
if (($result = @ mysqli_query($connection, $query))==FALSE)
    showerror($connection);
```

When developing an application, you should carefully consider whether you can design the process to minimize the duration that locks are held, or avoid locking altogether. This is particularly important if you're using MyISAM tables, since MyISAM locks are table-level. If you apply a write lock to a MyISAM table, nobody else can write to that table or read from it until you release the lock.

In the approach we've just discussed, we lock the `gifts` table, ensure that the specified gift is not reserved, update the `gifts` table to reserve the specified gift, and then unlock the `gifts` table. Thinking through the operation, we realize that we're in fact worried about trying to reserve a gift that is reserved between the time that our application lists it as unreserved and the time that the application tries to reserve it for a particular user. We can design a single SQL query that will only UPDATE the `gifts` table if the gift is not reserved:

```
$query = "UPDATE gifts SET username = '{$_SESSION['username']}' ".
         "WHERE gift_id = {$gift_id} AND username IS NULL";
```

A gift that is reserved by another user—or by the current user—will have a `username` that is not `NULL`. If the MySQL server finds a row with the specified `gift_id` and with no `username`, it will update it to set the `username` to that of the current user.

We can check whether the gift was reserved by examining the number of rows affected by the update. Only one row, the one for the gift with the specified `gift_id`, should be modified. If we identify that the number of affected rows is not `1`, then there are two possibilities: the gift was already reserved by another user or by the current user. We can run an additional query to see which of these it is:

```
// If we found the row and updated it, create a confirmation
// message to show the user
if (mysqli_affected_rows($connection) == 1)
{
    $message = "Reserved the gift for you, {$_SESSION['username']}";
}
else // Couldn't reserve the gift because it wasn't free;
{
    // Check whether it's already booked by someone other
    // than the current user.
    $query = "SELECT * FROM gifts ".
             "WHERE gift_id = {$gift_id} ".
             "AND username = '{$_SESSION['username']}'";
    // Run the query through the connection
    if (($result = @ mysqli_query($connection, $query))==FALSE)
        showerror($connection);

    // Create a message to show the user
    if (mysqli_num_rows($result))
        $message = "The gift is already reserved for you, ".
            "{$_SESSION['username']}";
    else
        $message = "Oh dear... someone just beat you to that gift!";
}
```

Removing a Gift

If the requested action is not **add**, it can only be **remove**, since only these two values are accepted for further processing by our script. The script checks that the gift is actually reserved by the current guest before freeing it; this check should never fail in practice, unless the same user is logged in twice. This is another example of defensive programming.

As with the **add** operation, we prepare a message confirming that the gift has been removed if the number of affected rows is one, and an error message if it isn't:

```
// Create a query to retrieve the gift.
$query = "SELECT * FROM gifts WHERE gift_id = {$gift_id}";

// Run the query through the connection
if (($result = @ mysqli_query($connection, $query))==FALSE)
    showerror($connection);

// Get the matching gift row;
// (there's only one since the gift_id is the primary key)
// If we don't get exactly one answer, then we have a problem
for($matchedrows=0;($row = @ mysqli_fetch_array($result));$matchedrows++);
if($matchedrows!=1)
    die("We've just experienced a technical problem - ".
        "please notify the administrator.");

// Double-check they actually have this gift reserved
if (!empty($row["username"]) && $row["username"] != $_SESSION['username'])
    // They don't, so record a message to show the user
    $message = "That's not your gift, {$_SESSION['username']}!";
else
{
    // They do have it reserved. Create a query to unreserve it.
    $query = "UPDATE gifts SET username = NULL WHERE gift_id = {$gift_id}";

    // Run the query through the connection
    if (($result = @ mysqli_query($connection, $query))==FALSE)
        showerror($connection);

    // Create a message to show the user
    if (mysqli_affected_rows($connection) == 1)
        $message = "Removed the gift from your shopping list, ".
            "{$_SESSION['username']}";
    else
        $message = "There was a problem updating. ".
            "Please contact the administrator.";
}
```

An alternative approach would be to include a check for the username in the UPDATE statement, and to execute this statement first. We could then determine whether the gift was in fact reserved by this user by counting the number of affected rows:

```
// Try to unreserve the gift with the matching username and gift ID
$query = "UPDATE gifts SET username = NULL WHERE gift_id = {$gift_id}".
```

```
                  " AND username='{$_SESSION['username']}'";

// Run the query through the connection
if (($result = @ mysqli_query($connection, $query))==FALSE)
    showerror($connection);

// Create a message to show the user
if (mysqli_affected_rows($connection) == 1)
    $message = "Removed the gift from your shopping list, ".
        "{$_SESSION['username']}";
else
  $message = "Couldn't unreserve the gift - perhaps you hadn't reserved it?";
```

Resources

There are many excellent resources available for you to learn more about PHP, its libraries, web servers, and building web database applications. We have listed several of these resources at the end of the previous two chapters. You might find the following additional resources helpful:

- *Web Database Applications with PHP and MySQL* by Hugh E. Williams and David Lane (O'Reilly)
- *A Programmer's Introduction to PHP 4.0* by W. Jason Gilmore (Apress)
- *PHP Black Book* by Peter Moulding (The Coriolis Group)
- *PHP Functions Essential Reference* by Zak Greant et al. (Sams)
- *PHP and MySQL Web Development* by Luke Welling and Laura Thomson (Sams)
- *Professional PHP4 Programming* by Deepak Thomas et al. (Wrox Press)
- *PHP Developer's Cookbook* by Sterling Hughes and Andrei Zmievski (Sams)

There are also many useful web sites that include tutorials, sample code, online discussion forums, and links to sample PHP applications. The official PHP site has an excellent manual at *http://www.php.net/manual*, and the links page at *http://www.php.net/links.php* points to many of these sites, including:

- *http://www.phpbuilder.com*
- *http://www.devshed.com/Server_Side/PHP*
- *http://www.hotscripts.com/PHP*
- *http://php.resourceindex.com*

Exercises

1. How can you refer to a PHP script file from within itself?
2. Would you use the `urlencode( )` function with data submitted through the POST method?

3. Why is it a good idea to use the `crypt( )` function on user passwords before storing them?

4. Why is it better to avoid locks where possible?

## PART V

Interacting with MySQL Using Perl

## CHAPTER 16

Perl

One of the most useful functions of a database is allowing regular reports to be created that reflect important trends that a user wants to track. For example, a business might be interested in the relative increase in sales that can be directly attributed to a television advertising campain; similarly, a university academic might be interested in identifying the exam questions on which students struggle. Report generation is best automated in a program that issues SQL statements and summarizes and formats the results into something easier to digest. You can create powerful tools that allow users to interact with the data, and also to interchange data with applications such as statistical analysis tools.

A general-purpose client such as the MySQL monitor allows you to execute any SQL query you like. However, most applications use only a limited set of SQL queries to add data to a database, modify existing data, or list data, so you can write a custom client to perform these frequent queries.

Perl has been a hugely popular scripting language since its first release in 1987; while newer languages such as PHP, Python, and Ruby have appeared since then, Perl remains very popular. Perl is very flexible; in fact, the Perl motto is, "There's more than one way to do it," often mentioned as the acronym TMTOWTDI.

Perl is also one of the most portable languages, with support available on a large number of operating systems, including the three that we focus on in this book. This means that you generally don't need to rewrite your Perl scripts if you want to use them on a different operating system.

It also benefits from many function libraries for applications as diverse as data manipulation programs for Personal Digital Assistants (PDAs), word processors and spreadsheet programs, network programming applications, and even full-color graphical games such as Frozen Bubble (*http://www.frozen-bubble.org*). More than 10,500 such libraries are available from the Comprehensive Perl Archive Network (CPAN) (*http://www.cpan.org*).

Perl includes powerful support for data manipulation and interfacing with databases, and is the scripting language most closely linked to MySQL. Most of the scripts that are distributed with MySQL are written in Perl. Over the next three chapters, you'll learn how to write simple Perl scripts that can be run from the command line, such as the Linux or Mac OS X shell, the Windows command prompt, and CGI scripts that run on a web server.

Command-line scripts are typically used to import data from other software or export data from the database. For example, you can import data from a spreadsheet program or export data from the database to a spreadsheet program.

You can also write command-line join applications to run reporting queries. For example, using the GeoIP (*http://www.maxmind.com/app/perl*) database, you can write a script that takes an IP address of a computer and looks up the country the computer is located in.

You'll also see how to use Perl to access to your database from the Web. For example, you can use the techniques you learn to design a music store application in Perl that reads product data from a backend MySQL database and generates a web page containing this information. Note that PHP is a more appropriate choice for new large-scale web database applications.

Writing Your First Perl Program

In this section, we'll take a very quick look at the Perl language. A Perl script is simply a text file containing statements that the Perl interpreter reads and executes. As with most things, the best way to learn is by doing, so we'll walk you through your very first Perl script. Open a text editor following the instructions in "Using a Text Editor" in Chapter 2 and create a text file containing the following lines:

```
#!/usr/bin/perl
print "Hello,\nworld!\n1\t2\t3\n";
```

The first two characters on the first line should be the pound or hash symbol (#) followed by the exclamation mark symbol (!). Together, these two characters form the "shebang" or "hash-bang" marker that tells the shell how to run the script. Immediately after these two characters, specify the path to the location of the Perl interpreter (called perl) on your system. If you're not sure where this is, check the instructions in "Checking Your Existing Setup" in Chapter 2. Save this text file as *HelloWorld.pl* in your current directory; you can exit your editor if you wish.

On a Linux or Mac OS X system, add the executable permission for the user who owns the file (you) using the chmod program. Here, we grant read, write, and executable permissions for the owning user, and no permissions to the group or other users:

```
$ chmod u=rwx,g=,o= HelloWorld.pl
```

You need to do this only once for a file; the permissions don't change if you edit or move the file. We discuss permission settings in "Restricting access to files and directories" in Chapter 2.

You can now run your program from the Linux or Mac OS X command line by typing its name:

```
$ ./HelloWorld.pl
Hello,
world!
1       2       3
```

Most Linux distributions and Mac OS X do not look for programs in the current directory, so the the initial dot and slash (`./`) is needed to tell the operating system where to find the program file. Windows doesn't use the shebang line, but to improve the portability of your scripts, it's good to include a line such as `#!/usr/bin/perl` at the top of any scripts you write. You should follow the instructions of "Installing Perl modules under Windows" in Chapter 2 and associate your Perl interpreter with the *.pl* extension. Windows always looks for the program file in the current directory, so you can simply type:

```
C:\> HelloWorld.pl
Hello,
world!
1       2       3
```

Congratulations! You've just written and executed your first Perl script.

Scripting With Perl

Let's examine the first line of Perl that you wrote earlier:

```
print "Hello, world!\n";
```

The `print` command or *function* takes the text in the quotes (known as a *string* of characters) and displays it. Be sure to put a semicolon at the end of each Perl statement; if you forget one, it gets quite confused and prints error messages that can in turn confuse you!

You've probably noticed already that the \n and \t weren't printed on the screen. The backslash indicates an *escape character* that should be handled in a special way. A \n indicates that a new line should be started at this point. Similarly, a \t tells Perl to jump ahead to the next tab stop, which is useful if you want to show columns of information. Note that the `print` command doesn't insert any line breaks on its own, even when a program finishes; you have to tell it to do so explicitly through \n.

A program that prints out exactly what we've written isn't very exciting. Perl, like most programming languages, allows us to use placeholders, or *variables*, to store values; we can manipulate these variables and then display them. For example, we can define a variable called `$TemperatureToday` to store today's temperature:

```
my $TemperatureToday;
```

The keyword my is used to declare the variable for the first time. Variables that contain a single value are known as *scalar* variables and are identified with a dollar ($) symbol. We'll discuss other types of variables later in this chapter. We can assign a value to this variable; for example, we can set today's temperature to be 33 (Celsius):

```
$TemperatureToday=33;
```

The equals (=) symbol assigns the value on the righthand side (33) to the variable. We can also merge the declaration and the assignment into a single statement:

```
my $TemperatureToday=33;
```

We can define another variable, **$TemperatureYesterday**, to store yesterday's temperature:

```
my $TemperatureYesterday=30;
```

We can use mathematical operations on variables; therefore, to display the difference in temperature between today and yesterday, we can write:

```
print "\nThe temperature difference is: " .
    $TemperatureToday-$TemperatureYesterday. "\n";
```

Here, we've used the concatenation (.) operator to connect several strings of characters together and display the resulting string with a single print statement. We've also used the subtraction (-) operator to find the difference between the two values. Let's have a quick look at some other common mathematical operators.

Mathematical Operators

Mathematical operators can be used to manipulate numbers and variables. There are a few that are easy enough to understand:

=

Assigns the value on the right to the variable on the left, for example:

```
$Today="23rd November";
$Age=33;
```

+

Adds one value to another, for example:

```
$RetailPrice=$CostPrice+$Profit+$Tax;
$Answer=2+2;
```

-

Subtracts one value from another, for example:

```
$Loss=$PriceSold-$PriceBought;
```

*

Multiplies one value by another, for example:

```
$TemperatureInFahrenheit=$TemperatureInCelsius*1.8+32;
```

/

Divides one value by another, for example:

```
$CakePortionSize=1/$NumberOfPeople;
```

%

Calculates the remainder of dividing one number by another, for example:

```
print "Dividing 27 by 4 leaves: ". 27%4;
```

If we want to change the value of a variable based on its existing value, we would use the variable on both the lefthand side and the righthand side of the assignment operator:

```
$CakesLeft=$CakesLeft-$CakesEaten;
$Counter=$Counter+1;
```

This syntax is so common that there's a shorthand way to write it that omits the same variable on the righthand side by merging the two operators:

```
$CakesLeft -= $CakesEaten;
$Counter += 1;
```

It's also very common to increment or decrement a value, so +=1 and -=1 can be written simply as ++ and --, respectively:

++

Increments a number by one, for example:

```
$Counter++;
```

--

Decrements a number by one, for example:

```
$SecondsLeft--;
```

Finally, there are logical operators that are used to compare two values and return true or false depending on the result of the comparison. Perl considers a zero value or empty string to be false, and a nonzero value to be true. If we try to print the result of a comparison, we'll get a 1 for a true outcome, and nothing (an empty string) for a false outcome:

==

Tests whether two values are equal:

```
print "Equal to 33:              [". $TemperatureToday==33. "]\n";
```

produces the result:

```
Equal to 33:              [1]
```

!=

Tests whether two values are unequal:

```
print "Not equal to 33:          [". $TemperatureToday!=33. "]\n";
```

produces the result:

```
Not equal to 33:              []
```

The false result is displayed as an empty string.

<

Tests whether the first value is less than the second:

```
print "Less than 33:              [". $TemperatureToday <33. "]\n";
```

produces the result:

```
Less than 33:              []
```

>

Tests whether the first value is greater than the second:

```
print "Greater than 33:              [". $TemperatureToday >33. "]\n";
```

produces the result:

```
Greater than 33:              []
```

<=

Tests whether the first value is less than or equal to than the second:

```
print "Less than or equal to 33:    [". $TemperatureToday<=33. "]\n";
```

produces the result:

```
Less than or equal to 33:    [1]
```

>=

Tests whether the first value is greater than or equal to the second:

```
print "Greater than or equal to 33: [". $TemperatureToday>=33. "]\n";
```

produces the result:

```
Greater than or equal to 33: [1]
```

Operator precedence

The instructions we've looked at so far have been simple, with only one operator. What happens if we have complex expressions with multiple operators? For example, what's the the value of answer after this statement is executed?

```
$answer=1+2-3*4/5;
```

You may remember from your high school math that mathematical operators have an *order of precedence*: multiplication and division are performed before addition and subtraction. However, relying on the order of precedence can try your memory, and your code will be hard to read. Parentheses override the order of precedence, allowing you to be sure that expressions will be evaluated as you expect. Our example would actually be evaluated as:

```
$answer=(1+2)-(3*4/5);
```

but using parentheses, you could specify that it should be evaluated as:

```
$answer=1+((2-3)*4)/5;
```

We recommend that you make liberal use of parentheses to keep your code readable and to avoid ambiguity.

More on Variables

Variables can be used to store things other than numbers. In Example 16-1, we use variables to store and display text and numbers.

Example 16-1. Perl script to add several variables and display the totals

```perl
#!/usr/bin/perl
use strict;

# Declare variables to store animal names, and assign values to them
my $AnimalNameOne="cats";
my $AnimalNameTwo="dogs";
my $AnimalNameThree="fish";

# Declare variables to store animal counts, and assign values to them
my $AnimalCountOne=3;
my $AnimalCountTwo=7;
my $AnimalCountThree=4;

# Calculate the sum of the animal counts
my $Total=$AnimalCountOne+$AnimalCountTwo+$AnimalCountThree;

# Display the counts and total
print "Pet roll call:\n".
 "===========\n".
 "$AnimalNameOne:\t$AnimalCountOne\n".
 "$AnimalNameTwo:\t$AnimalCountTwo\n".
 "$AnimalNameThree:\t$AnimalCountThree\n".
 "===========\n".
 "Total:\t$Total\n";
```

In this program, we store animal names and counts in variables, and place the total count into the $Total variable. Save this program as *animals.pl* and run it; you'll see the following output:

```
Pet roll call:
===========
cats:   3
dogs:   7
fish:   4
===========
Total:  14
```

The second line of this script is a `use strict;` instruction (also known as a `pragma`) to the Perl interpreter to ensure that all variables are explicitly declared with the `my` keyword before they are used. This helps avoid problems with mistyped variable names. You should try to include this line in all your scripts. Otherwise, if you mistype a variable name in one place, Perl assumes you want to create a new variable and doesn't warn you about the problem, so the program could fail or produce incorrect output that's hard to detect.

Any braces (also known as curly brackets) enclosing the variable declaration limit the *scope* of the declaration. For example, here the `$Time` variable is declared only inside the braces and is not available outside them:

```perl
my $Seconds=97;
{
 my $Time=$Seconds+1;
 print "\nTime: ", $Time;
}
```

However, the variable `$Seconds` is available both outside and inside the braces.

A variable defined inside braces will override any existing variable with the same name outside the braces. For example, we can have two *different* variables called `$counter`:

```perl
#!/usr/bin/perl

my $counter=10;
print "Before braces: $counter\n";
{
 my $counter=33;
 print "Within braces: $counter\n";
}

print "After braces:  $counter\n";
```

This produces the results:

```
Before braces: 10
Within braces: 33
After braces:  10
```

It's generally not good practice to use different variables with the same names, so avoid doing so when you can. We've just shown this here to help you understand existing code and possible causes of problems.

Notice that we've left blank lines between several statements and substrings; Perl ignores such whitespace outside strings. Perl also ignores any lines starting with the hash, or pound, symbol (#); this allows us to write explanatory comments alongside the code. Judicious use of whitespace and comments can help keep your programs readable and easy to understand.

Single and double quotes

Till now, we've used the double-quote (") character to indicate the start and end of a string. We can also enclose strings with the single-quote (') character, but there is an interesting difference. If you run the script:

```
#!/usr/bin/perl
use strict;

my $Answer=42;

print "The answer is: $Answer\n";
print 'The answer is: $Answer\n';
```

you'll see the following output:

```
The answer is: 42
The answer is: $Answer\n
```

When the string is enclosed in single quotes, variables are not replaced by their values, and escape characters are treated as normal text.

You may wonder how we can include one of the quote symbols within a string. For example, you can't have the string:

```
print 'This is Sarah's bag.';
```

since the string would end immediately after "Sarah", and the remainder of the sentence would confuse Perl.

The solution is to enclose one type of quote in a string enclosed by the other type:

```
print "This is Sarah's bag.";
print 'He said, "This is fun!"';
```

or to add a backslash symbol to escape the quote symbol and indicate that it should be processed in a special way:

```
print 'This is Sarah\'s bag.';
print "He said, \"This is fun!\"";
```

There is a third way of creating strings that is peculiar to Perl. The constructs q(*text*) and qq(*text*) have the same effect as enclosing the text in single and double quotes, respectively, but have the advantage that quotes don't need to be escaped. Thus, for example, the following two statements work as expected:

```
print q(This is Sarah's bag.);
print qq(He said, "This is fun!");
```

Arrays and Hashes

Let's look again at our our addition script. We used a different variable to store the name and count of each animal:

```perl
my $AnimalNameOne="cats";
my $AnimalNameTwo="dogs";
my $AnimalNameThree="fish";

my $AnimalCountOne=3;
my $AnimalCountTwo=7;
my $AnimalCountThree=4;
```

Such scalar variables work well enough for three animals but would be difficult to use if we were trying to keep track of the hundreds of species in a zoo. A better way to manage similar values is to store them as a list in a single *array* variable, with the data on each animal stored in a numbered element in the array. Example 16-2 rewrites the script in Example 16-1 accordingly.

Example 16-2. Perl script using array variables

```perl
#!/usr/bin/perl
use strict;

my @AnimalName=("cats", "dogs", "fish");
my @AnimalCount=(3, 7, 4);
my $Total=$AnimalCount[0]+$AnimalCount[1]+$AnimalCount[2];

print "Pet roll call:\n".
 "===========\n".
 "$AnimalName[0]:\t$AnimalCount[0]\n".
 "$AnimalName[1]:\t$AnimalCount[1]\n".
 "$AnimalName[2]:\t$AnimalCount[2]\n".
 "===========\n".
 "Total:\t$Total\n";
```

The @AnimalName array contains three elements with the values cats, dogs, and fish. Elements in the list are labeled starting from zero, so the first element is element 0, the second is element 1, the third is element 2, and so on. Array variables are indicated by the at (@) symbol; the individual elements in the array are scalar variables, so they are indicated with the dollar ($) symbol. For example, the second element in the @AnimalName array is $AnimalName[1], with the value dogs.

Instead of referring to elements by their index number, we can use a third type of variable: the *hash*, that allows us to map elements using a text identifier or *key*. As shown in Example 16-3, we can store the animal counts in a hash called %Animals, with the animal names as the key.

Example 16-3. Perl script using hash variables

```perl
#!/usr/bin/perl
use strict;

print "\nHash:\n";

my %Animals=( cats=>3, dogs=>7, fish=>4);

my $Total= $Animals{cats}+ $Animals{dogs}+ $Animals{fish};
```

```
print "Pet roll call:\n".
 "===========\n".
 "cats:\t$Animals{cats}\n".
 "dogs:\t$Animals{dogs}\n".
 "fish:\t$Animals{fish}\n".
 "===========\n".
 "Total:\t$Total\n";
```

Notice that the hash is indicated by a percentage (%) symbol and that, like for arrays, the individual scalar elements are indicated by a dollar symbol. For example, the number of cats is contained in `$Animals{cats}`; it's common to enclose the identifier in single or double quotes, as in `$Animals{'cats'}` or `$Animals{"cats"}`.

Note that array elements are enclosed in square brackets—`$AnimalName[1]`—whereas hash elements are enclosed in curly braces—`$Animals{'cats'}`.

In this example, we've written the hash keys in the program itself. This is called *hard-coding* and is not good practice. Any change to the keys requires a change to the program. If we don't know the keys, we can still access the elements by first extracting the keys into an array using the **keys** keyword. We can then use the elements in this array to access the hash elements; for example, instead of typing `$Animals{"cats"}`, we can write `$Animals{ $AnimalName[0] }`. This may be hard to read, but think of it this way: Perl looks inside the braces and finds `$AnimalName[0]`. This denotes the first element of the `@AnimalName` array, which is `cats`. Perl then plugs `cats` in where `$AnimalName[0]` was, in order to select the proper value from the `%AnimalName` hash. Using this syntax in a program, we can do calculations and printouts:

```
# Extract the keys of the Animals hash into the AnimalName array
my @AnimalName = keys %Animals;

my $Total=
 $Animals{$AnimalName[0]}+
 $Animals{$AnimalName[1]}+
 $Animals{$AnimalName[2]};

print "Pet roll call:\n".
 "===========\n".
 "$AnimalName[0]:\t$Animals{$AnimalName[0]}\n".
 "$AnimalName[1]:\t$Animals{$AnimalName[1]}\n".
 "$AnimalName[2]:\t$Animals{$AnimalName[2]}\n".
 "===========\n".
 "Total:\t$Total\n";
```

While it's nice to be able to use a single variable to store the data, there's still a lot of ugly manual referencing going on in the **print** statement; if we had a hundred types of animals, we'd need to reference them all individually. If you thought that we don't really have to do this, you're right! In the next section, we'll look at how loops can help simplify processing of arrays.

Before we end our discussion of arrays and hashes, we note that they can also be created with the qw "quote word" construct. For example, the following two statements to create an array are equivalent:

```
my @AnimalName=("cats", "dogs", "fish");
my @AnimalName=qw(cats dogs fish);
```

and the following two statements to create a hash are equivalent:

```
my %Animals=(
 "cats"=>3,
 "dogs"=>7,
 "fish"=>4);

my %Animals=qw(
 cats 3
 dogs 7
 fish 4);
```

You need to be comfortable with only one approach, but it's good to understand what's happening if you see the other format in other people's code.

Control Structures: Loops and Conditionals

We often require computers to do a single task many times; for example, we might write a program to count the number of cars that travel along a particular road, or the number of seconds left till a space rocket blasts off. Instead of writing out statements many times, we can write them out once and use a *loop* construct to repeat them as many times as required.

There are several flavors of loop in Perl; we'll look at these in the context of a simple example: counting from 1 to 10. The simplest is the for loop:

```
for(my $counter=1; $counter<=10; $counter++)
{
 print "\nThe value is: $counter";
}
```

Here, we initialize the $counter variable to 1, then execute the statement between the braces (the *body* of the loop) as long as the counter is less than or equal to 10. Each time we pass through the loop, we increment the counter using the ++ operator. The body of the loop contains a single statement that displays the value of the counter.

In the while loop, the body is executed as long as the condition in the parentheses is true. We can write the previous counter as:

```
my $counter=1;
while($counter<=10)
{
 print "\nThe value is: $counter";
 $counter++;
}
```

Notice that the `while` loop does not include a particular place for initializing or incrementing the counter. In fact, we generally use the `for` loop when we know exactly how many times we want to run the loop, and we use other loop constructs such as the `while` loop when we don't.

The `do...while` loop is almost identical to the `while` loop, with one difference: the condition is first evaluated only *after* the loop body has been executed once. This means that the body is executed even if the condition is not true, which is useful in some circumstances:

```
my $counter=1;
do
{
 print "\nThe value is: $counter";
 $counter++;
}while($counter<=10);
```

Finally, the `until` loop is identical to the `while` loop but inverts the condition; the loop is executed as long as the condition is false:

```
my $counter=1;
until($counter>10)
{
 print "\nThe value is: $counter";
 $counter++;
}
```

Iterating Through Arrays and Hashes

Earlier in "Arrays and Hashes," we accessed the individual scalar elements in the `@Animals` array by their index numbers—for example:

```
my $Total=
$Animals{$AnimalName[0]}+
$Animals{$AnimalName[1]}+
$Animals{$AnimalName[2]};
```

We can use the `foreach` construct to walk through all the keys of the `%Animals` hash (given by `keys %Animals`) and assign each value in turn to the scalar variable `$AnimalName`:

```
my %Animals=( "cats"=>3, "dogs"=>7, "fish"=>4);

my $Total=0;

print "Pet roll call:\n".
      "===========\n";

foreach my $AnimalName (keys %Animals)
{
 $Total+=$Animals{$AnimalName};
 print "$AnimalName:\t$Animals{$AnimalName}\n";
}
```

```
print "===========\n".
      "Total:\t$Total\n";
```

For each value of `$AnimalName`, the statements between the braces are executed. First, the `+=` operator is used to increase the value of the `$Total` variable by the count of that animal, and then the name and count of each animal is printed. Note that we initialized the value of `$Total` to zero before we start adding values to it.

The `foreach` construct shown here extracts the keys of the `%Animals` hash, but we have to use the hash together with the key to find each value. The following `while` statement does the same thing, but in a cleaner way:

```
while( (my $AnimalName, my $Count) = each(%Animals) )
{
 print "$AnimalName:\t$Count\n";
 $Total+=$Count;
}
```

Each time round the loop, the `each` construct assigns the animal name (the key) and count (the value) to the `$AnimalName` and `$Count` variables. The loop is repeated, and the statements within the braces are executed until all the items in the hash are exhausted.

Conditional Statements

Sometimes, we want to execute a statement only if something is true, or only if it's false. The `if` construct allows this:

```
# Numerical comparison

my $var1=786;

if($var1 < 786)
{
    print "The value is less than 786.\n";
}


if($var1 >= 786)
{
    print "The value is greater than or equal to 786.\n";
}

if($var1 == 786)
{
    print "The value is equal to 786.\n";
}
```

If we want to compare strings, rather than numbers, we need to use the string comparison operators. The important ones are eq (equal), lt (alphabetically earlier than), and gt (alphabetically later than):

```
# String comparison

my $username="Ali";

if($username lt "N")
{
    print "The username appears in the first half of the alphabet.\n";
}
```

With the `if...else` construct, we can have some code that is executed when the condition is true, and other code that's executed when the condition is false:

```
if($username eq "Ali")
{
    print "Hi Dad!\n";
}
else
{
    print "Hello!\n";
}
```

If the `$username` variable has the value `"Ali"`, the `"Hi Dad!"` message will be displayed; otherwise, the message "Hello!" is displayed instead.

To handle other possible conditions, we can use the `if...elsif...else` construct. For example:

```
if($username eq "Ali")
{
    print "Hi Dad!\n";
}
elsif($username eq "Sadri")
{
    print "Hi Mom!\n";
}
else
{
    print "Hello!\n";
}
```

If the `$username` variable has the value `"Ali"`, the `"Hi Dad!` message will be displayed (and the later checks will not be performed); if the `$username` variable has the value `"Sadri"`, the `"Hi Mom!"` message will be displayed, and if neither condition is satisfied, the `"Hello!"` message will be displayed.

We can combine conditions using the Boolean operators AND (&&), OR ||(|| OR), and NOT (!). For example, we can print a message if two conditions are met:

```
# Combining conditions
my $temperature=19;

# Boolean AND
if( ($temperature > 18) && ($temperature < 35) )
{
```

```
    print "The weather is fine.\n";
}
```

or if either condition is met:

```
# Boolean OR
if( ($temperature < 18) || ($temperature > 35) )
{
    print "The weather isn't fine.\n";
}
```

or if a condition is not met:

```
# Boolean NOT (negating the condition)
if( !($temperature < 18) )
{
    print "The weather isn't cold.\n";
}
```

You will often see the Boolean operators written in the long form: **and**, **or**, and **not**. For example, you can write:

```
# Symbolic and long form of Boolean expressions
my $value=74;

# A combined expression...
if( ($value > 80) || ( ($value < 75) && ! ($value == 73)) )
{
    print "The value is greater than 80 or less than 75, but is not 73\n";
}
```

as:

```
# ...and the equivalent in long form
if( ($value > 80) or ( ($value < 75) and not ($value == 73)) )
{
    print "The value is greater than 80 or less than 75, but is not 73\n";
}
```

The long forms and and or aren't in fact identical to their symbolic counterparts && and ||. Perl assigns the long forms a very low operator precedence; as we noted earlier in "Operator precedence," it's best to use parentheses to express the precedence you want.

Reading Input from the Command Line and from Files

Consider our sample animals script; the names of the animals and the numbers of each are hardcoded into the program. A better solution is to allow the program to use values provided by the user from the command line or from a file.

Reading in values from the command line

One option is to specify values after the program name on the command line; these values are called *command-line arguments* and are saved in the special ARGV array variable. For example, if we type:

```
$ ./program.pl Argument_1 Argument_2 Argument_3
```

$ARGV[0] will contain *Argument_1*, $ARGV[1] would contain *Argument_2*, and $ARGV[2] would contain *Argument_3*. The number of arguments entered at the command line is the same as the number of elements in the @ARGV array; you can find this number by referring to the name of the array—for example, @ARGV will be 3 if three arguments are typed in at the command line.

Example 16-4 modifies our Animals script to read in the number of cats, dogs, and fish as command-line arguments.

Example 16-4. Reading in numbers from the command line

```perl
#!/usr/bin/perl
use strict;

my %Animals;
# If the user hasn't provided the correct number of command-line
# arguments, provide a helpful error message.
if(@ARGV!=3)
{
 die("Syntax: $0 [count of cats] [count of dogs] [count of fish]\n");
}

# If the user has provided the command-line arguments, fill in the
# Animals hash with the corresponding values.
%Animals=(
 "cats"=>$ARGV[0],
 "dogs"=>$ARGV[1],
 "fish"=>$ARGV[2]);

# Process the data to calculate the total; code beyond this point is
# identical to our previous example, and doesn't deal with the
# command-line arguments.
my $Total=0;
print "Pet roll call:\n".
      "===========\n";
while ((my $Animal, my $Count) = each(%Animals))
{
 print "$Animal:\t$Count\n";
 $Total+=$Count;
}
print "===========\n".
      "Total:\t$Total\n";
```

If an incorrect number of arguments is provided, the **die** statement prints the message string between the parentheses and then stops the program. Since the program will run beyond this point only if a correct number of arguments is provided, there's no need to include an `else` clause to handle such a case.

Save this script as *animals.commandline.pl* and run it with command-line arguments:

```
$ ./animals.commandline.pl 3 7 4
Pet roll call:
===========
cats:   3
dogs:   7
fish:   4
===========
Total:  14
```

As part of the error message, we've used the $0 variable, which is the command used to run the script. If, by mistake, you use too many or too few arguments, you get the helpful error message shown below:

```
$ ./animals.commandline.pl 3 7 4 1
Syntax: ./animals.commandline.pl [count of cats] [count of dogs] [count of fish]
```

Here, $0 is replaced by *./animals.commandline.pl*.

Notice that we still have the animal names hardcoded in the program; each time we want to change the list of animals, we need to change the program code. We can instead change our program to read in both the animal names and counts from the command line, as shown in Example 16-5:

Example 16-5. Reading in both the animal names and counts from the command line

```perl
#!/usr/bin/perl
use strict;

my %Animals;
# If the user hasn't provided a nonzero, even number of command-line
# arguments, provide a helpful error message.
if( (@ARGV==0) || ( (@ARGV%2)!=0) )
{
  die("Syntax: $0 [Animal One Name] [Animal One Count] ".
    "[Animal Two Name] [Animal Two Count] ...\n");
}
# If the user has provided the command-line arguments, fill in the
# Animals hash with the corresponding values.
while(@ARGV)
{
  # Read in an argument and take this as the animal name
  my $AnimalName=shift(@ARGV);

  # Read in another argument and take this as the count for this animal
  my $AnimalCount=shift(@ARGV);

  # Add an entry to the Animals hash for this animal name and
  # count pair:
  $Animals{$AnimalName}=$AnimalCount;
}
```

```
# Process the data to calculate the total; code beyond this point is
# identical to our previous example and doesn't deal with the
# command-line arguments.
my $Total=0;
print "Pet roll call:\n".
      "===========\n";
while ((my $Animal, my $Count) = each(%Animals))
{
 print "$Animal:\t$Count\n";
 $Total+=$Count;
}
print "===========\n".
      "Total:\t$Total\n";
```

This compact program combines many of the features of Perl you've learned so far. Loops allow you to process as many data items as required; when you're writing a program, you generally don't know exactly how many rows of data will be returned by the database. The example also illustrates the `if` control statement, the `||` logical OR operator, and an appropriately used array and hash.

You can also see how the program uses scope to limit the visibility of its variables. The first `while` block defines two variables (`$AnimalName` and `$AnimalCount`) that can be used only within the loop. The second `while` block defines two more variables within the `while` statement itself; these can be used only within that block. Because these variables serve a temporary function inside the loop and aren't needed outside it, defining them within the scope of the block is good coding practice.

In our test for command-line arguments, we print the error message if the user hasn't provided any command-line arguments (the number of arguments is zero), or if there aren't an integer number of animal name and count pairs (which we'll know because there will be a remainder when we divide the number of arguments by two: `@ARGV%2`).

To read in the command-line arguments, we use the `shift` function to pick up one argument from the list. We expect a name and a count, so we call `shift` twice for each animal. The `while` loop continues as long as there are additional arguments, so we can provide data for as many animals as we like.

Let's try the program out:

```
$ ./animals.commandline.types.pl dogs 7 fish 33 elephants 1 giraffes 3
Pet roll call:
===========
giraffes:      3
cats:   4
elephants:     1
dogs:   7
fish:   33
===========
Total:  48
```

Notice that the counts aren't aligned properly; this is because the longer animal names (giraffes and elephants) reach the end of the first tab column, and so the \t in the print statement moves the count into the next tab column.

Reading in values from a file

Instead of typing in the data as command-line arguments, we can ask our program to read in the data from a file. A popular and simple format for data interchange between applications is the comma-separated values (CSV) format. This is a plain-text format with the data separated by commas. Create the following CSV file in a text editor and save it as *animals.csv*:

```
cats,2
dogs,5
fish,3
emus,4
```

Now, let's write a simple program to read in a specified file and print the contents on the screen. Example 16-6 uses the open function to open the file and a while loop to read it in line by line.

Example 16-6. Perl script to read in a text file and display the contents

```
#!/usr/bin/perl
use strict;

# If the user hasn't provided one command-line argument, provide a
# helpful error message.
if(@ARGV!=1)
{
    die("Syntax: $0 [Input file]\n");
}
# Open the file specified on the command line; if we can't open it,
# print an error message and stop.
open(INPUTFILE, $ARGV[0])
    or die("Failed opening $ARGV[0]\n");

# Read in the input file line by line
while(my $Line=<INPUTFILE>)
{
    print $Line;
}
# Close the input file
close(INPUTFILE);
```

Here, we've used the open( ) function to open the file with the name specified on the command line and configure a *file handler* to access this file; in our example, we've used INPUTFILE for the file handler. Note that unlike other types of Perl variables, file handlers don't have a symbol such as the dollar symbol ($) or the at symbol (@) before them.

Every standard Perl function ends by passing back a value to the code that called it. In fact, many functions do nothing *but* return a value. The open( ) function returns a nonzero value to indicate that it succeeded in opening the file, and returns zero if it failed. Common causes of file-access errors include mistyped filenames and insufficient privileges to access a particular file or directory. We can use an if statement to check for a zero value; if the file-open operation failed, we can use the die( ) function to display an error message and stop the script:

```
if(!open(INPUTFILE, $ARGV[0]))
{
  die("Failed opening $ARGV[0]\n");
}
```

This combination of an if statement and an open function is worth noting; we've previously used if on logical tests such as $Username == "Ali", but if is flexible enough to directly test a single value, or the result of a function such as open. We can also use the simpler or construct to call the die( ) function if the open( ) function fails:

```
open(INPUTFILE, $ARGV[0])
  or
  die("Failed opening $ARGV[0]\n");
```

Save this program as *readfile.pl*, and then get it to read in and display the contents of the *animals.csv* file:

```
$ ./readfile.pl animals.csv
cats,2
dogs,5
fish,3
emus,4
```

Instead of simply printing out the file contents, let's load them into our own data structures and process the data. We have to remove the invisible newline at the end of each line of the text file using the chomp( ) function, then load the contents of each line into array elements by the location of the commas using the split( ) function. For convenience, we assign the first value to the scalar variable $AnimalName and the second value to the scalar variable $AnimalCount. We then use these to populate the %Animals hash.

For example, the line:

```
cats,2
```

is split at the comma into the @AnimalData array, with:

```
AnimalsData[0]: cats
AnimalsData[1]: 2
```

and these values are assigned to the variables:

```
AnimalName:  cats
AnimalCount: 2
```

The statement:

```
    $Animals{$AnimalName}=$AnimalCount;
```

is effectively:

```
    $Animals{cats}=2;
```

In this way, we add entries to the %Animals hash for each animal. The complete program code is listed in Example 16-7.

Example 16-7. Perl script to read in data from a CSV file

```
#!/usr/bin/perl
use strict;

# If the user hasn't provided one command-line argument, provide a
# helpful error message.
if(@ARGV!=1)
{
    die("Syntax: $0 [Input file]\n");
}
# Open the file specified on the command line; if we can't open it,
# print an error message and stop.
if(!open(INPUTFILE, $ARGV[0]))
{
    die("Failed opening $ARGV[0]\n");
}

my %Animals;

# Read in from input file line by line; each line is
# automatically placed in $_
while(<INPUTFILE>)
{
    # Remove the newline at the end of the line
    chomp($_);

    # Split the line by commas and load into the AnimalsData array
    my @AnimalsData=split(",", $_);

    # Assign the text before the first comma to the name
    my $AnimalName=$AnimalsData[0];

    # Assign the text between the first comma and the second comma
    # (if any) to the count
    my $AnimalCount=$AnimalsData[1];

    # Add an entry to the Animals hash for this animal name and
    # count pair:
    $Animals{$AnimalName}=$AnimalCount;
}
# Close the input file
close(INPUTFILE);

# Process the data to calculate the total; code beyond this point is
# identical to our previous example and doesn't deal with the
# command-line arguments.
```

```
my $Total=0;
print "Pet roll call:\n".
      "==========\n";
while ((my $Animal, my $Count) = each(%Animals))
{
    print "$Animal:\t$Count\n";
    $Total+=$Count;
}
print "==========\n".
      "Total:\t$Total\n";
```

Reading in values from standard input

The console's standard input is a special file that captures data typed in at the console, sent to the program using a pipe (|), or read from a redirection operator (<). Using the standard input, we can skip the process of opening and closing the file using the file pointer (INPUTFILE in our example), and instead use the built-in Perl STDIN file handle, as shown in Example 16-8.

Example 16-8. Perl script to read in data from a CSV file from standard input

```
#!/usr/bin/perl
use strict;

my %Animals;

# Read in from standard input line by line; each line is
# automatically placed in $_
while(<STDIN>)
{
    # Remove the newline at the end of the line
    chomp($_);

    # Split the line by commas and load it into the AnimalsData array
    my @AnimalsData=split(",", $_);

    # Assign the text before the first comma to the name
    my $AnimalName=$AnimalsData[0];

    # Assign the text between the first comma and the second comma
    # (if any) to the count
    my $AnimalCount=$AnimalsData[1];

    # Add an entry to the Animals hash for this animal name and
    # count pair:
    $Animals{$AnimalName}=$AnimalCount;
}

# Process the data to calculate the total; code beyond this point is
# identical to our previous example and doesn't deal with the
# command-line arguments.
my $Total=0;
print "Pet roll call:\n".
      "==========\n";
```

```
while ((my $Animal, my $Count) = each(%Animals))
{
    print "$Animal:\t$Count\n";
    $Total+=$Count;
}
print "===========\n".
      "Total:\t$Total\n";
```

We can then run this as:

```
$ ./Animals.command_line.tofile.pl < animals.csv
```

or as:

```
$ cat animals.csv | Animals.command_line.tofile.pl
```

on a Linux or Mac OS X system, or as:

```
$ type animals.csv | Animals.command_line.tofile.pl
```

on a system running Windows.

Writing values to a file or standard output

You'll often want to permanently store the output of your program in a file. Example 16-9 modifies the program to take a second command-line argument to specify the name of the output file.

Example 16-9. Perl script to read in data from a CSV file and save results to an output file

```
#!/usr/bin/perl
use strict;

my %Animals;
# If the user hasn't provided any command-line arguments, provide a
# helpful error message.
if(@ARGV!=2)
{
    die("Syntax: $0 [Input file] [Output file]\n");
}
# Open the file specified on the command line; if we can't open it,
# print an error message and stop.
if(!open(INPUTFILE, $ARGV[0]))
{
    die("Failed opening $ARGV[0]\n");
}

# Open the output file specified on the command line; if we can't open it,
# print an error message and stop.
if(!open(OUTPUTFILE, ">$ARGV[1]"))
{
    die("Failed opening $ARGV[1]\n");
}

# Read in from input file line by line; each line is
# automatically placed in $_
```

```
while(<INPUTFILE>)
{
    # Remove the newline at the end of the line
    chomp;

    # Split the line by commas
    my @AnimalsData=split(",", $_);

    # Assign the text before the first comma to the name
    my $AnimalName=@AnimalsData[0];

    # Assign the text between the first comma and the second comma
    # (if any) to the count
    my $AnimalCount=@AnimalsData[1];

    # Add an entry to the Animals hash for this animal name and
    # count pair:
    $Animals{$AnimalName}=$AnimalCount;
}
close(INPUTFILE);

# Process the data to calculate the total, then write to the output file
my $Total=0;
print OUTPUTFILE "Pet roll call:\n".
                 "===========\n";
while ((my $Animal, my $Count) = each(%Animals))
{
    print OUTPUTFILE "$Animal:\t$Count\n";
    $Total+=$Count;
}
print OUTPUTFILE "===========\n".
                 "Total:\t$Total\n";
```

We're providing the name of the output file as the second command-line argument (ARGV[1]). The interesting part of this program starts from the second open( ) statement; since we want to write to the file, we add a greater-than (>) symbol before the name of the output file. We also specify the output file handle OUTPUTFILE immediately after the print command.

If we don't specify an output file handle, program output is sent to the system standard output, known as STDOUT. This is almost always the display screen. As with STDIN, we can use STDOUT without needing to explicitly open and close it. We can also print to standard output by putting STDOUT as the file handle in the print statement:

```
print STDOUT "$Animal:\t$Count\n";
```

Since the program output is sent to standard output by default anyway, STDOUT is assumed when no other file handle is specified, and we can safely omit it (as we have in all our previous scripts):

```
print "$Animal:\t$Count\n";
```

Writing Your Own Perl Functions

As we've seen, a function is a statement such as print( ) or open( ) that performs an operation for your program. Functions can take arguments within parentheses, and can return a value.

You can define your own functions in Perl. Sometimes, you might want to perform a task in several places of your program, such as to repeatedly display messages or perform calculations. You can define your own function to perform the task and then call the function whenever you need the task to be performed.

Example 16-10 is a program with two small functions: one called sum( ) to calculate the sum of a list of numbers, and the other called average( ) to average a list of numbers. The average( ) function uses the sum( ) function in its calculations.

Example 16-10. Perl script with functions to sum and average numbers

```perl
#!/usr/bin/perl
use strict;

print "\nThe total is: ", sum(1, 5, 7);
print "\nThe average is: ", average(1, 5, 7);

# Function to calculate the sum of all the numbers passed to it
sub sum
{
    my $Total=0;
    while(my $value=shift)
    {
        $Total+=$value;
    }
    return $Total;
}

# Function to calculate the average of all the numbers passed to it
# This function calls the sum function internally.
sub average
{
    return sum(@_)/(@_);
}
```

The sum( ) function uses the shift keyword to iterate through the provided values one by one, assigning them in turn to the $value variable. When all the values have been seen and added to the $Total, the function returns the $Total value to the part of the program that called it. This means that sum(1, 5, 7) has the value of $Total, which is 13.

The special array @_ contains all the values passed to the function when it is called. The average( ) function passes this list—in this example 1, 5, 7—to the sum( ) function to get the total, and then divides this total by the number of values in the list, given by the array name @_. Finally, the statement returns the resulting average:

```
    return sum(@_)/(@_);
```

Note that the $Total variable is defined only within the sum( ) function, since it's enclosed by the function braces.

Save this program as *sum_average.floating.pl* and then run it by typing:

```
$ ./sum_average.functions.pl
The total is:    13
The average is: 4.33333333333333
```

Of course, we can use variables instead of hardcoding values in the program. For example, to accept the list of numbers from the command line, we can rewrite the two print lines as:

```
print "\nThe total is:    ", sum(@ARGV);
print "\nThe average is: ", average(@ARGV);
```

allowing us to call this program as:

```
$ ./sum_average.functions.pl 19 313 110
The total is:    442
The average is: 147.33333333333333
```

The value for the average has more precision than we'd generally need, and the numbers aren't aligned. We can use the printf function to format the values using a *format specifier* before printing them. The format specifiers you are most likely to come across are:

%d

> Integer number (decimal)

%f

> Number with a decimal fraction (floating point)

%s

> String of characters

For our example, we could write:

```
printf "\nThe total is:    %10d",   sum(1, 5, 7);
printf "\nThe average is: %10.2f", average(1, 5, 7);
```

The value of sum(1, 5, 7) is mapped to the format specifier %10d, which sets aside 10 decimal places for the sum. Similarly, in the second statement, the value of average(1, 5, 7) is mapped to the format specifier %10.2f, which sets aside 10 characters total for the average and specifies that only 2 decimal places should be displayed. In other words, we leave room for 7 places to the left of the decimal point, 1 character for the decimal point itself, and 2 places for the decimal part of the number. With these statements, the program output would be:

```
The total is:          13
The average is:        4.33
```

which looks much nicer.

Adding a minus (-) symbol immediately after the percentage symbol makes the display left-aligned. For example the statement:

```
printf("\n%15s", "hello");
```

would display:

```
(ten spaces) hello
```

whereas adding the minus symbol as shown here:

```
printf("\n%-15s", "hello");
```

would display:

```
hello (ten spaces)
```

It's typical to display numbers right-aligned, and to display text left-aligned.

Resources

To learn more about Perl, we recommend these resources:

- The Perl.org page for people learning Perl (*http://learn.perl.org*)
- *Learning Perl* by Randal L. Schwartz et al. (O'Reilly)
- The Comprehensive Perl Archive Network web site (*http://www.cpan.org*)

Exercises

1. What are the strengths of Perl?
2. What is the difference between an array and a hash?
3. What does the following Perl script do?

```
#!/usr/bin/perl
use strict;

my $Answer;
while(@ARGV)
{
 $Answer+=shift(@ARGV);
}
print "Answer: $Answer\n"
```

## CHAPTER 17

Using Perl with MySQL

Now that you can find your way about Perl, let's see how you can use it to connect to a MySQL server. In this chapter, we look at how we can use the Perl scripting language to connect to a MySQL database and interchange data with it. We create command-line clients to import data into a database, and to query a database and display results.

The Perl DBI module supports a variety of database drivers. Naturally, we're interested in the MySQL driver for this book, but there are others. Theoretically, you should be able to simply change the driver referenced by your script to get your script to work with another supported database management system, such as Oracle. In practice, however, you'll need to put in some additional thought into writing your scripts so that you don't use MySQL-specific constructs such as `SHOW TABLES` that won't necessarily work on other database servers. Of course, this isn't an issue if you're certain you won't ever change databases, but it's a good idea to think carefully about how your application is likely to be used in a few years' time.

Connecting to the MySQL Server and Database

To access the MySQL server from a Perl script, we need the DBI module discussed in "Setting up Perl" in Chapter 2. In the script, we must tell Perl that we want to use this module:

```
use DBI;
```

Then, we provide connection parameters to the DBI `connect( )` function and store the returned connection in a database handler (`dbh`):

```
my $dbh=DBI->connect("DBI:mysql:host=localhost;database=mysql",
 "the_username",
 "the_password");
```

For a Mac OS X server using the XAMPP Perl installation, you would write:

```
my $dbh=DBI->connect("DBI:mysql:
 host=localhost;mysql_socket=/Applications/xampp/xamppfiles/var/mysql/mysql.sock;
```

```
    database=mysql",
  "the_username",
  "the_password");
```

Don't add a new line before the `database=mysql` parameter; we had to do this so that the instruction would fit on the page. If you followed our XAMPP installation instructions in "Installing Perl modules under Mac OS X" in Chapter 2 to create a symbolic link to the default MySQL socket file location (*/tmp/mysql.sock*), you can omit the `mysql_socket` parameter.

We can follow this with Perl instructions to carry out the main functions of the script. Finally, being good citizens, we disconnect from the server before we end the script:

```
$dbh->disconnect();
```

The arrow (`arrow -> operator`) operator is used to call functions that are associated with a class of objects. In the connection code, we've called on the `connect( )` function of the `DBI` class. We also call on functions associated with the database handler and the statement handler in the same way. We don't describe object-oriented design and programming in detail in this book.

Handling Errors When Interacting with the Database

If the connection to the database fails, the `dbh` variable will contain an undefined (effectively false) value. We should test for this and stop the program if the connection failed; otherwise, we'll run into difficulties once the program tries to use the database, generating unhelpful error messages such as:

```
Can't call method "prepare" on an undefined value at ./select.pl line 9.
```

One way to test for connection failure is simply to check the value of the database handler variable:

```
my $dbh=DBI->connect("DBI:mysql:host=localhost;database=$DB_Database",
 "$DB_Username", "$DB_Password");
if(!$dbh)
{
 die("Failed connecting to the database.");
}
```

If the database handler is not valid, we use the `die( )` function to print an error message and stop the program.

A more compact way is to use the `or` keyword to execute the `die( )` function if the connection failed:

```
my $dbh=DBI->connect("DBI:mysql:host=localhost;database=$DB_Database",
 "$DB_Username", "$DB_Password")
or
 die("Failed connecting to the database.");
```

Finally, we can modify problem-handling behavior by setting the attributes `PrintError` and `RaiseError` in the call to the `connect( )` function. Setting the `PrintError` attribute to 1 displays error messages; setting it to 0 disables this. Similarly, setting the `RaiseError` attribute to 1 displays an error message and stops processing if an error occurs; setting it to 0 disables this. If both are set to 0, no error messages are displayed, and the program tries to continue even if the connection to the MySQL database could not be established. We can use this setting to suppress the default Perl messages and display only our own custom messages:

```
my $dbh=DBI->connect("DBI:mysql:host=localhost;database=mysql", "the_username",
 "the_password", {PrintError=>0, RaiseError=>0})
or
 die("Failed connecting to the database");
```

By default, `PrintError` is 1 and `RaiseError` is 0.

The DBI module includes the special variables `$DBI::err` and `$DBI::errstr` to store information if a problem occurs. These contain, respectively, the error code and human-readable error message returned by the database server. The two colons are a Perl convention for separating the name of a package (in this case, `DBI`) from the name of a variable defined in the package (`err` and `errstr`).

We can use these variables in our own error-handling code. For example, we can write:

```
my $dbh=DBI->connect("DBI:mysql:host=localhost;database=mysql",
 "the_username",
 "the_password", {PrintError=>0, RaiseError=>0})
or
 die("Failed connecting to the database (error number $DBI::err):
 $DBI::errstr\n");
```

If RaiseError is set to 1, a failure to connect to the database might produce the error message:

```
DBI connect('host=localhost;database=mysql','root',...) \
 failed: Can't connect to local MySQL server through socket \
 '/var/lib/mysql/mysql.sock' (2) at ./select.pl line 5
```

whereas our custom error message above would be displayed as:

```
Failed connecting to the database (error number 2002): \
Can't connect to local MySQL server through socket \
'/var/lib/mysql/mysql.sock' (2)
```

While detailed error messages are very useful when debugging code under development, it's generally prudent to hide errors from your users in production code, especially in applications that are published to the Web. Instead, have the program log error messages to a file or email them to you. That way, users aren't exposed to unsightly and possibly confusing error messages, and the internals of your system are not as exposed to potential attackers. When your program does encounter a problem, display a generic error message such as "We are experiencing technical difficulties; please contact the system administrator or try again later."

Using Queries That Return Answer Sets

Most of the queries used for database access—for example, SELECT queries—read information from the database for display or processing. For such queries, you first call the prepare( ) function to set up a *statement handler* and send it to the server, and then call the execute( ) function function to run the query:

```
my $sth=$dbh->prepare("SELECT * FROM artist");
$sth->execute();
```

You can examine the result of a query by using the fetchrow_hashref( ) function to fetch the answer rows one by one and place them in a hash; thus, you can access the individual hash elements for processing, as for the artist_id and artist_name fields below:

```
while(my $val=$sth->fetchrow_hashref())
{
    printf ("%-5s %-128s\n", $ref->{artist_id}, $ref->{artist_name});
}
```

Finally, you deallocate resources assigned to the statement handler:

```
$sth->finish();
```

Example 17-1 lists the artists and their ID numbers from the artist database.

Example 17-1. Perl script to select data from the database

```
#!/usr/bin/perl
use DBI;
use strict;

my $DB_Database="music";
my $DB_Username="root";
my $DB_Password="the_mysql_root_password";
my $dbh=DBI->connect(    "DBI:mysql:host=localhost;database=$DB_Database",
"$DB_Username", "$DB_Password",
{PrintError=>0, RaiseError=>0})
or
    die("Failed connecting to the database ".
        "(error number $DBI::err):$DBI::errstr\n");

my $count=0;

my $Query="SELECT * FROM artist";
my $sth=$dbh->prepare($Query);
$sth->execute();

printf ("%-5s %-30s\n", "ID:", "Name:");
printf ("%-5s %-30s\n", "---", "------------------------");
while(my $ref=$sth->fetchrow_hashref())
{
    printf ("%-5s %-128s\n", $ref->{artist_id}, $ref->{artist_name});
    $count++;
}
```

```
printf ("\nTotal:%d\n", $count);

$sth->finish();
$dbh->disconnect();
```

Save this script as *select.pl* and run it as:

```
$ ./select.pl
```

You should get a display similar to this:

```
ID:    Name:
---    ------------------------
1      New Order
2      Nick Cave & The Bad Seeds
3      Miles Davis
4      The Rolling Stones
5      The Stone Roses
6      Kylie Minogue

Total:6
```

With fetchrow_hashref( ), the example obtains a hash for each row. There are other ways to access the query results. The fetchrow_array( ) function returns an array, where you access elements by index rather than by key. The elements in the array are in the order returned by the SELECT statement. In our example, the SELECT * FROM artist statement returns the artist table fields in the order that they appear in the database; you can find this by running the query from the MySQL monitor or looking at the table description (here it has been truncated to fit the page):

```
mysql> DESCRIBE artist;
+-------------+-------------+------+-----+---------+-------+
| Field       | Type        | Null | Key | Default | Extra |
+-------------+-------------+------+-----+---------+-------+
| artist_id   | smallint(5) | NO   | PRI | 0       |       |
| artist_name | char(128)   | YES  |     |         |       |
+-------------+-------------+------+-----+---------+-------+
2 rows in set (0.22 sec)
```

If we wanted to print the artist name before the artist ID, we would access array element 1 first for the artist name and then array element 0 for the artist ID:

```
while(my @val=$sth->fetchrow_array())
{
    printf ("%-128s %-5s\n", $val[1], $val[0]);
    $count++;
}
```

We can also return a reference to the results array, rather than the array itself, using the fetchrow_arrayref( ) function. Here, we find another application of the arrow operator; the elements in the array can be accessed through the array reference:

```
while(my $ref=$sth->fetchrow_arrayref())
{
```

```
        printf ("%-5s %-128s\n", $ref->[0], $ref->[1]);
        $count++;
    }
```

Both fetchrow_array( ) and fetchrow_arrayref( ) are faster than using fetchrow_hashref( ), but are more prone to problems in mixing up column index numbers. They may also have problems if you alter the order of fields—for example, with an ALTER TABLE statement. We recommend that you use fetchrow_hashref( ) for all but the most time-sensitive applications.

Perl is case-sensitive, so accessing the fetched results using incorrect capitalization won't work. In our example, we're interested in the artist_id and artist_name fields of the music.artist table. If we try to access the results using, say, uppercase names:

```
    printf ("%-5s %-128s\n", $ref->{ARTIST_ID}, $ref->{ARTIST_NAME});
```

blanks will be printed where we expect the field values to be, because ref->{ARTIST_ID} is not the same as ref->{artist_id}. If in doubt, try out a SHOW CREATE TABLE *table_name*; or DESCRIBE *table_name* statement from the MySQL monitor to see exactly how to capitalize field names.

Alternatively, you can use all uppercase or all lowercase field names and ask the fetchrow_hashref( ) function to force all the names to uppercase or lowercase when it retrieves them:

```
    while(my $ref=$sth->fetchrow_hashref("NAME_uc"))
    {
        printf ("%-5s %-128s\n", $ref->{ARTIST_ID}, $ref->{ARTIST_NAME});
        $count++;
    }
```

If you use "NAME_uc", your Perl code should use all uppercase labels; you should use all lowercase labels if you force everything to lowercase with "NAME_lc".

Before we end our discussion on accessing result sets, let's look at a couple of high-level ways of performing all the prepare and execute operations together. The selectall_arrayref( ) function returns a two-dimensional array containing the query results. For example, a query to list the contents of the music.artist table might return the following array:

```
+---+--------------------------+
| 0 | 1                        |
+---+--------------------------+
| 0 | New Order                |
| 1 | Nick Cave & The Bad Seeds |
| 2 | Miles Davis              |
| 3 | The Rolling Stones       |
| 4 | The Stone Roses          |
| 5 | Kylie Minogue            |
+---+--------------------------+
```

Each row of the array is itself an array containing the result fields. The rows and columns can be addressed with an index starting from 0.

The following snippet of code shows how to use the `selectall_arrayref( )` function:

```
print "\n\nselectall_arrayref:\n";
my $ref=$dbh->selectall_arrayref($Query);
while(my $row=shift(@$ref))
{
    printf ("%-5s %-128s\n", $row->[0], $row->[1]);
    $count++;
}
```

We use the `shift( )` function to fetch the rows from the array one at a time and then access the columns by their index—0, 1, 2, and so on. There is a corresponding hash-based `selectall_hashref( )` function that you can also use:

```
my $ref = $dbh->selectall_hashref($Query, 'artist_id');
foreach my $artist_id (keys %$ref)
{
    printf ("%-5s %-128s\n", $artist_id, $ref->{$artist_id}->{artist_name});
    $count++;
}
```

The call to `selectall_hashref( )` specifies the query and the hash key, and returns a reference to a hash. Rows with identical hash keys are overwritten by later rows, so it's important that the hash keys passed to `selectall_hashref( )` be unique.

Using Queries That Don't Return Answer Sets

For queries such as `INSERT`, `UPDATE`, `REPLACE`, and `DELETE` that do not return a result set, we can use the `do( )` function to perform the query without the need for a prior call to `prepare( )`.

The `do( )` function returns the number of rows affected by the query; if the query could not be performed successfully, the function returns zero. If the query was performed successfully but no rows were affected, the function returns the value 0E0, which is 0 times 10 to the power 0 (for instance, 1E3 is 1000). Perl treats 0E0 as having the numerical value zero but the Boolean value true, so if the query returns this value, we know that the operation succeeded (true) but that zero rows were affected:

```
my $rowsaffected=$dbh->do($Query);
if($rowsaffected && $rowsaffected==0E0)
{
 print "Operation was successful but no rows were affected\n";
}
elsif($rowsaffected)
{
 print "Operation was successful ($rowsaffected rows)\n";
}
else
{
 print "Operation failed: $DBI::errstr\n";
}
```

Let's explore this by looking at four possibilities. Imagine you have a database called perltest and it includes a table called testtable with two string columns; these could have been created from the monitor with the following statements:

```
mysql> CREATE DATABASE perltest;
Query OK, 1 row affected (0.23 sec)

mysql> USE perltest;
Database changed
mysql> CREATE TABLE testtable (col1 CHAR(40), col2 CHAR(40));
Query OK, 0 rows affected (0.01 sec)
```

If the query is:

```
my $Query="INSERT INTO testtable (col1, col2) VALUES ('abcd1', 'abcd2')";
```

we'd get the message:

```
Operation was successful (1 rows)
```

reflecting the number of rows inserted.

Deleting matching rows with the query:

```
my $Query="DELETE FROM testtable WHERE col1='abcd1' AND col2='abcd2'";
```

would give us:

```
Operation was successful (1 rows)
```

reflecting the number of rows deleted.

Trying to delete data items that don't exist in the database:

```
my $Query="DELETE FROM testtable WHERE col1='xabcd1' AND col2='abcd2'";
```

would return 0E0, so the success message is printed:

```
Operation was successful but no rows were affected
```

Finally, if the do( ) operation could not be performed for any reason (for example, an incorrect SQL query, duplicate key, or a nonexistent table), the failure message would be printed. If we tried to access the nonexistent table nosuchtable:

```
my $Query="DELETE FROM nosuchtable WHERE col1='abcd1' and col2='abcd2'";
```

This would result in the message:

```
Operation failed: Table 'perltest.nosuchtable' doesn't exist
```

Binding Queries and Variables

The Perl DBI module offers a convenient way to write SQL queries with placeholders that can be replaced by arguments to the execute( ) statement. Similarly, results from a query can be mapped to Perl variables. In this section, we describe how you can use placeholders in your queries.

Binding Variables to a Query

Consider the script we wrote earlier in "Reading in values from a file" in Chapter 16 to read in a list of animals and their counts from the *animals.csv* file of comma-separated values, and load them into the `Animals` hash. We've reproduced the main part of the script in Example 17-2.

Example 17-2. Perl script to load data from a CSV file into the AnimalDB database

```perl
#!/usr/bin/perl
use strict;

# If the user hasn't provided one command-line argument, provide a
# helpful error message.
if(@ARGV!=1)
{
    die("Syntax: $0 [Input file]\n");
}
# Open the file specified on the command line; if we can't open it,
# print an error message and stop.
open(INPUTFILE, $ARGV[0])
or
    die("Failed opening $ARGV[0]\n");

my %Animals;

# Read in from input file line by line; each line is
# automatically placed in $_
while(<INPUTFILE>)
{
    # Remove the newline at the end of the line
    chomp($_);

    # Split the line by commas and load into the AnimalsData array
    my @AnimalsData=split(",", $_);

    # Assign the text before the first comma to the name
    my $AnimalName=$AnimalsData[0];

    # Assign the text between the first comma and the second comma
    # (if any) to the count
    my $AnimalCount=$AnimalsData[1];

    # Add an entry to the Animals hash for this animal name and
    # count pair:
    $Animals{$AnimalName}=$AnimalCount;
}
# Close the input file
close(INPUTFILE);
```

Let's modify the script to load the data into a MySQL table. First, using the MySQL monitor, create a new `AnimalDB` database and a new `Animals` table:

```
mysql> CREATE DATABASE AnimalDB;
Query OK, 1 row affected (0.02 sec)
mysql> USE AnimalDB;
Database changed
mysql> CREATE TABLE Animals (Name CHAR(10), Count SMALLINT);
Query OK, 0 rows affected (0.01 sec)
```

To load the Animals hash into the Animals table in the database, we can create and execute an SQL query for each animal name and count pair:

```
while ((my $Animal, my $Count) = each(%Animals))
{
 my $Query="INSERT INTO Animals (Name, Count) VALUES ($Animal, $Count)";
 my $sth=$dbh->prepare($Query);
 $sth->execute($Animal, $Count);
}
```

This requires us to prepare as many queries as there are data rows, which is inefficient.

A better way is to prepare a single query with placeholders and execute the query in turn with the different parameters:

```
my $Query="INSERT INTO Animals (Name, Count) VALUES (?, ?)";
my $sth=$dbh->prepare($Query);
while ((my $Animal, my $Count) = each(%Animals))
{
 $sth->execute($Animal, $Count);
}
```

Here, the question-mark (?) symbols in the query are placeholders. The placeholders are replaced by the values passed to the execute( ) function. For each iteration of the while loop in our example, the $Animal and $Count values passed to the execute( ) function are plugged into the INSERT query, and the query is executed. This is known as *binding*; besides being more efficient, binding variables to a query in this way helps to prevent some types of security problems.

Binding Query Results to Variables

Binding can work the other way too: we can bind the results of a query to Perl variables. Earlier in this chapter, we saw how we can access the results of a query using fetchrow_hashref( ) and its related functions; for example, to access the Animals table data, we could have a script that uses the fetchrow_arrayref( ) function, as shown in Example 17-3.

Example 17-3. Perl script to read data from the Animals database

```
#!/usr/bin/perl
use DBI;
use strict;

my $DB_Database="AnimalDB";
my $DB_Username="root";
my $DB_Password="the_mysql_root_password";
```

```perl
my $dbh=DBI->connect(     "DBI:mysql:host=localhost;database=$DB_Database",
    "$DB_Username", "$DB_Password", {PrintError=>0, RaiseError=>0})
    or
  die("Failed connecting to the database ".
    "(error number $DBI::err): $DBI::errstr\n");

# Process the data to calculate the total;

my $Animal_Name;
my $Animal_Count;

my $Total=0;
print "Pet roll call:\n".
    "===============\n";

my $Query="SELECT Name, Count FROM Animals";
my $sth = $dbh->prepare($Query);
$sth->execute ();

while(my $ref=$sth->fetchrow_arrayref())
{
    printf("%-10d %-20s\n", $ref->[1], $ref->[0]);
    $Total+=$ref->[0];
}
print "===============\n".
    "Total:\t$Total\n";

$sth->finish();
$dbh->disconnect();
```

Example 17-4 removes the need for the $ref variable by using the bind_columns( ) function to bind the result columns to the Animal_Name and Animal_Count variables.

Example 17-4. Perl fragment to read and display data from the Animals database, using binding

```perl
my $Total=0;
print "Pet roll call:\n",
    "===========\n";

my $Query="SELECT Name, Count from Animals";
my $sth = $dbh->prepare($Query);
$sth->execute ();

my $Animal_Name;
my $Animal_Count;

# Bind query results to variables
$sth->bind_columns(\$Animal_Name, \$Animal_Count);

while($sth->fetchrow_arrayref())
{
    print "$Animal_Name:\t$Animal_Count\n";
    $Total+=$Animal_Count;
}
```

```
print "===========\n",
      "Total:\t$Total\n";
```

The values are assigned to variables in the bind_columns( ) function in the order they appear in the results of the SELECT, so we fetch the query results with the fetchrow_arrayref( ) function, rather than fetchrow_hashref( ). While fetchrow_hashref( ) is often more convenient in other circumstances, there is no advantage to it here, and it would run more slowly. Note that when passing the variable names to the bind_columns( ) function, we add a backslash symbol (\) in front of the dollar symbol so that Perl leaves the variable name intact and doesn't replace it with the value of the variable.

The Complete Script Using Both Types of Binding

For our example of loading data into the database, we can put both parts together to write a single script that loads data into the database and accesses this data, using both types of binding, as shown in Example 17-5.

Example 17-5. Perl script with both types of binding

```perl
#!/usr/bin/perl
use DBI;
use strict;

# If the user hasn't provided any command-line arguments, provide a
# helpful error message.
if(@ARGV!=1)
{
    die("Syntax: $0 [Input file]\n");
}
# If the user has provided the command line arguments, fill in the
# Animals hash with the corresponding values.

# Open the file specified on the command line; if we can't open it,
# print an error message and stop.
open(INPUTFILE, $ARGV[0])
    or die("Failed opening $ARGV[0]\n");

###################################################################
# Load data from the CSV file into the Animals hash
my %Animals;
while(<INPUTFILE>)
{
    # Remove the newline at the end of the line
    chomp;

    # Split the line by commas
    my @AnimalsData=split(",", $_);

    # Assign the text before the first comma to the name
    my $AnimalName=@AnimalsData[0];
```

```perl
    # Assign the text between the first comma and the second comma
    # (if any) to the count
    my $AnimalCount=@AnimalsData[1];

    # Add an entry to the Animals hash for this animal name and
    # count pair:
    $Animals{$AnimalName}=$AnimalCount;
}
close(INPUTFILE);

#################################################################
# Connect to the database
my $DB_Database="AnimalDB";
my $DB_Username="root";
my $DB_Password="the_mysql_root_password";
my $dbh=DBI->connect(    "DBI:mysql:host=localhost;database=$DB_Database",
            "$DB_Username", "$DB_Password", {PrintError=>0, RaiseError=>0})
    or
    die("Failed connecting to the database (error count $DBI::err): $DBI::errstr\n");

#################################################################
# Load the data into the database; variables bound to query
my $Query="INSERT INTO Animals (Name, Count) values (?, ?)";
my $sth=$dbh->prepare($Query);
while ((my $Animal, my $Count) = each(%Animals))
{
    $sth->execute($Animal, $Count);
}

#################################################################
# Read the data from the database; query results bound to variables
my $Total=0;
print "Pet roll call:\n",
      "===========\n";

my $Query="SELECT Name, Count from Animals";
my $sth = $dbh->prepare($Query);
$sth->execute ();

my $Animal_Name;
my $Animal_Count;

# Bind query results to variables
$sth->bind_columns(\$Animal_Name, \$Animal_Count);

while($sth->fetchrow_arrayref())
{
    print "$Animal_Name:\t$Animal_Count\n";
    $Total+=$Animal_Count;
}
print "===========\n",
      "Total:\t$Total\n";

# Free the statement handler and disconnect from the database
```

```
$sth->finish();
$dbh->disconnect();
```

Importing and Exporting Data

From time to time, you may need to transfer data into the database from external sources, or to generate data in a format that other applications can use. A common file format for this is the comma-separated values (CSV) format discussed in "Loading Data from Comma-Delimited Files" in Chapter 8. Data import and export is one of the areas in which Perl is very strong, and programs in Perl can read and write data in a large number of formats. For example, you can generate plain text, HTML, XML, or Rich Text Format (RTF) documents. RTF documents are more complex but can contain formatting instructions that most word processors understand. There are even Perl modules to process binary (nontext) formats, such as the Microsoft Excel spreadsheet file format.

Earlier, in "Binding Variables to a Query," we explained how to import data from a CSV file. Let's now look at an example to export data from our Animals database to a CSV file. All we need to do is to use the print statement to write to the output file, with the data separated by a comma, as shown in Example 17-6.

Example 17-6. Perl script to export data from the Animals database, using binding

```perl
#!/usr/bin/perl
use DBI;
use strict;

# If the user hasn't provided any command-line arguments, provide a
# helpful error message.
if(@ARGV!=1)
{
    die("Syntax: $0 [Output file]\n");
}

my $DB_Database="AnimalDB";
my $DB_Username="root";
my $DB_Password="the_mysql_root_password";
my $dbh=DBI->connect(    "DBI:mysql:host=localhost;database=$DB_Database",
    "$DB_Username", "$DB_Password", {PrintError=>0, RaiseError=>0})
or
    die("Failed connecting to the database ".
      "(error number $DBI::err): $DBI::errstr\n");


my $Query="SELECT Name, SUM(Count) FROM Animals GROUP BY Name";
my $sth = $dbh->prepare($Query);
$sth->execute();

# Bind query results to variables
my $Animal_Name;
my $Animal_Count;
```

```
$sth->bind_columns(\$Animal_Name, \$Animal_Count);

# Open the file specified on the command line; if we can't open it,
# print an error message and stop.
open(OUTPUTFILE, ">$ARGV[0]")
or
    die("Failed opening $ARGV[0]\n");

# Write header row with column names
print OUTPUTFILE "Name,Count\n";

# Iterate through the results and write them as comma-separated values
# to the output file
while($sth->fetchrow_arrayref())
{
    print OUTPUTFILE "$Animal_Name,$Animal_Count\n";
}
$sth->finish();
$dbh->disconnect();

close(OUTPUTFILE);
```

If the data could contain a comma, the resulting file could be unusable. For example, if we want to export names and telephone numbers in the format:

```
Name,Number
```

we'd have difficulty if the data in the MySQL database were allowed to have commas, as it does here:

```
+-----------------+-----------------+
| Name            | Number          |
+-----------------+-----------------+
| Hamzeh Abdollah | +61 3 1234 5678 |
| Bloggs, Fred    | +61 3 8795 4321 |
| ...
+-----------------+-----------------+
```

If we exported this data to a CSV file, we would have:

```
Hamzeh Abdollah,+61 3 1234 5678
Bloggs, Fred,+61 3 8795 4321
```

The spreadsheet program would take the second row to have the name "Bloggs" and the telephone number " Fred". To avoid this problem, we can enclose the data in double quotes when writing it out:

```
print OUTPUTFILE "\"$Name\",\"$Count\"\n";
```

Note that since the text to be written to file is already enclosed in double quotes, we've escaped (placed a backslash symbol before) the quotes surrounding the data. The exported data would be:

```
"Hamzeh Abdollah","+61 3 1234 5678"
"Bloggs, Fred","+61 3 8795 4321"
```

which is handled correctly by most spreadsheet programs.

Handling NULL Values

MySQL operations return undef for fields that have a NULL value; however, Perl handles these values as empty strings, so if we ask it to print the results, we'll simply get blanks for NULL values. Example 17-7 checks whether fields are NULL and handles them, perhaps by setting them to the string "NULL".

Example 17-7. Perl script to handle NULL values

```perl
#!/usr/bin/perl -w
use DBI;
use strict;

my $DB_Database="AnimalDB";
my $DB_Username="root";
my $DB_Password="the_mysql_root_password";
my $dbh=DBI->connect(    "DBI:mysql:host=localhost;database=$DB_Database",
"$DB_Username", "$DB_Password", {PrintError=>0, RaiseError=>0})
    or
    die("Failed connecting to the database ".
      "(error number $DBI::err): $DBI::errstr\n");

my $Query="SELECT Count from Animals";
my $sth=$dbh->prepare($Query);
$sth->execute();
while(my $ref=$sth->fetchrow_hashref("NAME_uc"))
{
    my $Count=$ref->{COUNT};
    if(!defined($Count))
    {
        $Count="NULL";
    }
    print "Count=$Count\n";
}
$sth->finish();
$dbh->disconnect();
```

Resources

See the MySQL AB page (*http://dev.mysql.com/usingmysql/perl*) and the DBI module documentation (*http://search.cpan.org/~timb/DBI/DBI.pm*).

Exercises

1. What does the Perl DBI module do?
2. When would you prefer to use fetchrow_array( ) over fetchrow_hashref( )?

3. What are the advantages of binding variables to a query?

4. How should you handle NULL values in answers returned by MySQL?

## CHAPTER 18

Serving Perl Pages to the Web

In this chapter, we'll see how to write simple web database clients using Perl. Web applications written using Perl can take advantage of the Apache module mod_perl and the HTTP::Mason library for robust and high-performance web sites. We don't discuss these in detail in this book. We should note that unlike Perl, PHP was designed from the start to be used for scripting web pages and is probably a better choice for any major new web application.

In Chapter 2, we saw how to install the Apache web server on a Linux system, and the XAMPP package on Windows and Mac OS X. We can make our Perl scripts accessible from a web server by placing them in a location that the web server can access.

On a Linux system, the scripts should be placed in the *cgi-bin* directory under the web server document root, typically */var/www/cgi-bin* or */usr/local/apache/htdocs/cgi-bin*. For a Windows system, the scripts should be placed in *C:\Program Files\xampp\cgi-bin*. For a Mac OS X system using XAMPP, use */Applications/xampp/htdocs*.

Depending on the system configuration, you may need to have system root or administrator privileges to write files to this location. You can assume these privileges under Linux by typing su -, under Windows by logging in as a user with Windows Administrator privileges, or under Mac OS X prefacing commands with the sudo keyword.

Let's write a small script to generate the following HTML page:

```
<html>
 <head>
  <title>My first Perl CGI script</title>
 </head>
 <body>
  <b>Hello, World!</b><br />
  This is <b>very</b> interesting!
 </body>
</html>
```

We can use the print comand to generate the HTML page. Since the web server sends the script output directly to the browser, we need to add a bit of extra information to tell the web browser to expect HTML text, rather than, say, a JPEG image:

```
    print "Content-type: text/html; charset=UTF-8\n\n";
```

The charset tells the browser that the server will send text using the UTF-8 character set.

Example 18-1 is the complete script to generate the HTML page.

Example 18-1. A first CGI Perl script that just displays some text

```
#!/usr/bin/perl
print "Content-type: text/html; charset=UTF-8\n\n";

print "
<html>
  <title>My first Perl CGI script</title>
  <body>
 <b>Hello, World!</b><br />
 This is <b>very</b> interesting!
  </body>
</html>
";
```

For CGI scripts to work properly, they must print the Content-type line before sending any other data to the browser. Save this file as *HelloWorld.cgi.pl* in the appropriate location under the web server document root as discussed earlier.

The CGI approach requires the web server to execute the program and display the results; this means that the web server should have the necessary access permissions to read and execute the Perl scripts. On Linux or Mac OS X systems, permissions are assigned by three categories:

- The user who owns the file (user)
- Users in the group that the file is in (group)
- Everyone else (other)

The Apache web server typically runs as the user nobody, who isn't in any group, so if you want the web server to be able to run a file, you'll need to give permission for everybody (the o permission, which stands for "other") to read and execute the script.

For example, you can set appropriate permissions for the file *HelloWorld.cgi.pl* by typing the command:

```
$ chmod u=rwx,g=rx,o=rx HelloWorld.cgi.pl
```

We discuss permission settings in "Restricting access to files and directories" in Chapter 2. The permissions for the XAMPP web server directories on Windows are less stringent, and a nonprivileged user can place files in the *cgi-bin* directory for delivery by the server.

Ensure your web server is running, then open the file in a web browser. On a Linux system or a Windows system using XAMPP, the script can be accessed at *http://hostname/cgi-bin/HelloWorld.cgi.pl*, while on a Mac OS X system using XAMPP, the address to use is *http://hostname/xampp/HelloWorld.cgi.pl*. The hostname is the name of the computer containing the scripts. If the web server is on the same computer as your web browser, you can use the value `localhost` for the hostname, so the address to use would be *http://localhost/cgi-bin/HelloWorld.cgi.pl* on a Linux system, and *http://localhost/xampp/HelloWorld.cgi.pl* on a Windows or Mac OS X system using XAMPP.

If your browser reports that you don't have authorization to access the page, you should check the permission settings for the file or the directory it's in. It's often helpful to check the Apache error logfile; we describe how to find this file in "The Apache Error Log" in Chapter 2. Open the error logfile in a text editor and look near the bottom; you might find a line such as this one:

```
[Thu Jun 29 02:26:35 2006] [error] [client 127.0.0.1]
  Options ExecCGI is off in this directory:
  /var/www/cgi-bin/mysql.cgi.animals.popup.pl
```

This means that Apache has not been configured to allow CGI scripts to be run in this directory. The solution is to put the scripts in a directory where CGI scripts are allowed or to configure your server to allow CGI scripts to run in the directory you want. To do the latter, you need to create a new entry in the Apache configuration file; we describe how to locate this file in "The Apache Configuration File" in Chapter 2. For example, to allow CGI scripts to be executed in the directory */var/www/cgi-bin*, you would write:

```
<Directory "/var/www/cgi-bin">
 AllowOverride All
 Options ExecCGI
 Order allow,deny
 Allow from all
 AddHandler cgi-script.pl
</Directory>
```

Back to our script. This first web page was not dynamic; for a slightly more complex example, let's write a CGI script that connects to the MySQL database and lists the animals in our pet database, as shown in Example 18-2.

Example 18-2. A CGI Perl script that lists animals from the MySQL database

```
#!/usr/bin/perl
use strict;

# Connect to the MySQL server, run the query, store the result
use DBI;
my $dbh=DBI->connect("DBI:mysql:host=localhost;database=AnimalDB",
 "the_username",
 "the_password",
 {PrintError=>0, RaiseError=>1});
my $results = $dbh->selectall_hashref('SELECT * FROM Animals', 'Name');
$dbh->disconnect();


my $result=
 "Content-Type: text/html; charset=UTF-8\n\n".
 "<html>".
 "<head>".
```

```
"<title>List of Animals</title>".
"</head><body>".
"<h1>Pet roll call</h1>".
"<table border='true'>".
"<tr align='CENTER' valign='TOP' bgcolor='LIGHTGREEN'>".
 "<th>Name</th><th>Count</th></tr>";

foreach my $Name (keys %$results)
{
 $result.=
 "<tr>".
  "<th align='left' bgcolor='SKYBLUE'>$Name</th>".
  "<td bgcolor='PINK'>".$results->{$Name}->{Count}."</td>".
 "</tr>";
}

$result.=
 "</table>".
 "</body></html>";

print $result;
```

Here, we build up the HTML content as a string in the `$result` variable and print this string out at the end of the script. We've made liberal use of whitespace to help make the script clearer. If it's still daunting to you, try replacing the variable `$Name` with an animal's name, and `$results->{$Name}->{Count}` with a number. The results will then be essentially HTML markup, with some Perl wrapping—for example:

```
<tr>
<th align='left' bgcolor='SKYBLUE'>cats</th>
<td bgcolor='PINK'>2</td>
</tr>
```

The Perl CGI Module

The Perl CGI module has some helpful functions to simplify generating common snippets of HTML. We can enable all these by modifying our **use** statement to:

```
use CGI ':all'
```

We can then generate HTML elements by calling the corresponding function. For example, we can include text within a level-one heading tag pair (`<h1>`*text*`</h1>`) by writing `h1("text")`.

Many of these functions take attributes that are reflected in the generated HTML. For example, to generate the tag `<th align="LEFT" bgcolor="SKYBLUE">`, we would write:

```
th({-align=>"LEFT", -bgcolor=>"SKYBLUE"}, $Name).
```

Example 18-3 rewrites our our previous example using CGI functions.

Example 18-3. The CGI Animal list script rewritten with CGI functions

```perl
#!/usr/bin/perl
use strict;

# Connect to the MySQL server, run the query, store the result
use DBI;
my $dbh=DBI->connect("DBI:mysql:host=localhost;database=AnimalDB",
 "the_username",
 "the_password",
 {PrintError=>0, RaiseError=>1});

my $results = $dbh->selectall_hashref('SELECT * FROM Animals', 'Name');
$dbh->disconnect();

# Prepare and display the results in HTML format
use CGI ':all';

my @AnimalsDataArray;
foreach my $Name (keys %$results)
{
 my $AnimalsDataArrayRow =
  th({-align=>"LEFT", -bgcolor=>"SKYBLUE"}, $Name).
  td({-bgcolor=>"PINK"}, [$results->{$Name}->{Count}]);
 push @AnimalsDataArray, $AnimalsDataArrayRow;
}

my $result=
  header(-type=>"text/html", -charset=>'UTF-8').
  start_html(-title=>"List of Animals", -encoding => 'UTF-8').
  h1("Pet roll call").
  table(
 {-border=>'true'},
 Tr({-align=>"CENTER",-valign=>"TOP", -bgcolor=>"LIGHTGREEN"},
  [th(['Name','Count'])]),
 Tr([@AnimalsDataArray])
  ).
  end_html;
print $result;
```

Instead of printing out the table rows one by one, this example defines the array $AnimalsDataArray, and uses the push command to append each row of data to this array. We build up the $result string using functions provided by the CGI module and place @AnimalsDataArray in a table row. Finally, we print the whole $result string.

The charset parameter of the header( ) function and the encoding parameter of the start_html( ) function are optional, and are used to specify the character encoding that's used in the document. Together, they help the browser determine the appropriate fonts to use to correctly display the page. If you omit these parameters, the default value ISO-8859-1 will be used.

Note that the CGI function to create a table row is Tr( ) rather than tr( ); this is to avoid confusion with a completely different "transliteration replacement" function tr that is available by default in Perl.

Processing User Input

User interaction with a web application is typically a two-way affair; the system displays content to the user, who provides input, such as through a web form, that the system uses in further processing. For example, an online store application displays items for sale; the user chooses items and enters purchase information, and the system displays a receipt.

For our pet roll call example, we could allow the user to enter the name of an animal. The system could then process this information and return the number of animals of that type. This requires two web pages. First, a form is displayed to accept user input. When this form is submitted, a second page is displayed with the query result.

You can generate an HTML form that passes the submitted values to the *process_form.pl* file using the HTTP POST method by writing:

```
print
  start_form(-action=>"process_form.pl", -method=>'POST').
  ...form content....
  end_form;
```

Example 18-4 generates a web form with a simple text input field.

Example 18-4. A CGI Perl script that generates a simple form

```
#!/usr/bin/perl
use strict;
use CGI ':all';

print
  header(-type=>"text/html", -charset=>'UTF-8').
  start_html(-title=>"Search Page", -encoding => 'UTF-8');

if(param())
{
  print "<br />The string you entered was: '".param('query')."'";
  print "<br />Dumping all the submitted data...";
  foreach my $Name (param())
  {
    print "<br /><b>$Name:  $Name);
  }
}
else
{
  #start_form can take -action, -method...
  print
    start_form.
    "Query String: ".
```

```
    textfield(-name=>'query', -value=>'type your query here').
    submit(-name=>'submit_button', -value=>'Submit query').
    end_form;
}
print end_html;
```

The param( ) function can access data submitted through a web form. Our script checks to see whether the param( ) function returns a nonzero value—that is, whether any data has been received. If the function returns a nonzero value, we know that the form has been submitted and can then access the submitted data. Here, we print out the value from the form's query field, which we can access as param('query'). For good measure, we then iterate through each submitted item using the foreach loop and print the name and value of the field.

The generated web page would look something like this (we've added some whitespace for readability):

```
<!DOCTYPE html
  PUBLIC "-//W3C//DTD XHTML 1.0 Transitional//EN"
  "http://www.w3.org/TR/xhtml1/DTD/xhtml1-transitional.dtd">
<html xmlns="http://www.w3.org/1999/xhtml" lang="en-US" xml:lang="en-US">
  <head>
    <title>Search Page</title>
    <meta http-equiv="Content-Type" content="text/html; charset=UTF-8" />
  </head>
  <body>
    <br />The string you entered was: 'type your query here'<br />
    Dumping all the submitted data...<br />
    <b>query:</b> type your query here<br /><b>submit_button:</b> Submit query
  </body>

</html>
```

We've started a new line before Dumping and query: for readability; you won't see these in the output of the program if you run it.

If you have a relatively small number of possible values, it's probably more helpful for the user if you generate a drop-down list populated with values from the database. The CGI module has a useful popup_menu function that generates a drop-down list. To use this, you need to first load the list entries into an array:

```
@results = @{ $dbh->selectcol_arrayref ("SELECT Name FROM Animals")};
```

and then pass this array to the popup_menu function's values parameter:

```
print
  start_form(-action=>"process_form.pl", -method=>'POST').
  "Animal Name: ".
  popup_menu(-name => "Name", -values => \@results).
  submit.
  end_form;
```

The resulting form would look like this:

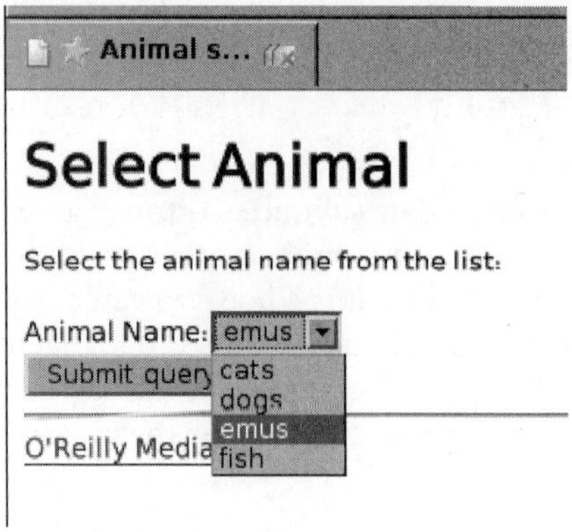

Figure 18-1. The animals form using the CGI pop-up menu

```
<form method="post" action="http://localhost/cgi-bin/mysql.cgi.animals.popup.pl"
  enctype="multipart/form-data">
 Animal Name:
 <select name="Name" tabindex="1">
  <option value="cats">cats</option>
  <option value="dogs">dogs</option>
  <option value="emus">emus</option>
  <option value="fish">fish</option>
 </select>
 <br />
 <input type="submit" tabindex="2" name="submit_button" value="Submit query" />
</form>
```

Figure 18-1 shows a screenshot of this form.

Using One Script for the Form and for Processing

It's convenient to write a single script to generate both the form and the results web pages. The script tests whether there is any form data. If there isn't any form data, the form is displayed; otherwise, the results are shown. In such a script, the value used for the form action field will be the name of the script itself. For example, the script *query.pl* would have:

```
start_form(-action=>"query.pl", -method=>'POST')
```

Rather than hardcoding the filename into the program code, we can use the `url( )` function to automatically provide the address of the current script:

```
start_form(-action=>url(), -method=>'POST')
```

Note that the `url( )` function provides the *absolute URL* of the current script, for example:

```
http://localhost/cgi-bin/query.pl
```

while the related `self_url( )` function returns the URL of the script, together with the query string that preserves entered form information—for example:

```
http://localhost/cgi-bin/popup_menu.pl?Username=saied;Host=wombat.cs.rmit.edu.au
```

Example 18-5 is a single script to display a drop-down list of animal names, and display the count of the animal that the user selects.

Example 18-5. A CGI Perl script that generates a form with a drop-down list

```perl
#!/usr/bin/perl
use strict;

# Connect to the MySQL server, run the query, store the result
use DBI;
my $dbh=DBI->connect("DBI:mysql:host=localhost;database=AnimalDB",
 "the_username",
 "the_password",
 {PrintError=>0, RaiseError=>1});

# Prepare and display the results in HTML format
use CGI ':all';

print header(-type=>"text/html", -charset=>'UTF-8');

my @results;
if(!param())
{
  @results = @{ $dbh->selectcol_arrayref
    ("SELECT Name FROM Animals ORDER BY Name")};

  print
    start_html(-title=>"Animal Selection Page", -encoding => 'UTF-8').
    h1("Select Animal").
    p("Select the animal name from the list: ").
    start_form(-action=>url(), -method=>'POST').
    "Animal Name: ".
    popup_menu(-name => "Name", -values => \@results).
    br().
    submit(-name=>'submit_button', -value=>'Submit query').
    end_form;
}
else
{
  my $Query="SELECT Count FROM Animals where Name='".param("Name")."'";
  @results = @{ $dbh->selectcol_arrayref ($Query)}
    or die("Problem with query $Query: ".$DBI::errstr);
  print
    start_html(-title=>"Animal Counts Page", -encoding => 'UTF-8').
    h1("Query result").
    "The count of ".
    b(param("Name")).
    " is: ".
    @results;
}
```

```
$dbh->disconnect();

print
  hr().
  a({-href=>"http://www.ora.com"}, "O'Reilly Media").
  end_html;
```

The bulk of this script consists of two blocks executed on different runs of the script. The first block follows the if(!param( )) statement; this block runs when the user first calls up the URL without parameters, and it simply displays the form with the initial animal listing. The second block follows the else statement; this block runs after the user has filled out the form and submitted it.

The page includes a horizontal rule (hr) and link to the O'Reilly Media home page at the bottom.

A Note on mod_perl

The mod_perl Apache module moves the processing of Perl scripts into the Apache web server itself. This has two advantages. First, it's more efficient, because the Perl interpreter doesn't need to be started each time a script is called. Second, you don't need to include the path to the Perl interpreter on an initial #! line at the top of each file.

We won't go into the details of mod_perl here, but we recommend you use it for any production site that uses Perl CGI scripts running on an Apache web server. You can find more information on this at *perl.apache.org* and in particular on the *http://perl.apache.org/docs/2.0/user/intro/start_fast.html* web page.

Perl Security

Programmers often assume that their script will be used in a particular way and that users will behave as expected. When writing a script, you should always keep in mind that everybody makes mistakes, and some people deliberately try to break things. For example, if your script expects the number 2 but the user types two, what will happen? This is particularly important if you make your scripts available via the Web. You should never trust user input and use it directly for sensitive operations such as opening files or running commands on the server.

Perl has a *taint mode* that warns you if the script injects user input directly into a sensitive operation. You can turn on the Perl taint mode by adding the -T switch after the path to the Perl interpreter at the top of your script, for example:

```
#!/usr/bin/perl -T
```

Unfortunately, this taint mode does not recognize variables passed to the script from a web form via the param( ) function, so you'll need to manually check that the user

---

input is what you expect. This is typically performed using *regular expressions*, where we match a string against a template.

For example, we can ensure that the form variable Age is a number between 10 and 99:

```
if(param())
{
 if(!(param('Age')=~/^([1-9][0-9])$/))
 {
  print
   font({-color=>'red'}, 'Invalid age:  must be between 10 and 99 inclusive.');
   exit;
 }
 my $user_age = "$1";
 print $user_age;
}
```

Perl offers some cryptic syntax for regular expressions, but they make the expressions very easy to integrate into a program. The =~ operator means "check the item on the left against the regular expression on the right." The regular expression itself is enclosed in forward slashes, although you can choose another character if you find this inconvenient (for instance, if the regular expression itself contains a slash). Thus, the if statement just shown checks whether the Age parameter matches the regular expression /^([1-9][0-9])$/. The expression itself is simpler than it at first appears.

The numbers in the brackets express a range. Here, we want two digits: the first between one and nine, and the second between zero and nine. The parentheses delimit the part of the string that matches these two characters. The caret (^) symbol marks the start of the string, and the dollar ($) symbol marks the end of the string; together, these two *anchors* ensure that there's nothing before or after the two digits. After the regular expression check, the substring enclosed in the first set of parentheses is available as $1, the substring enclosed between the second set of parentheses is available as $2, and so on. We can assign this to a variable and use it; here, we're just printing it on the screen. If the check fails, we print an error message and stop the program with the exit keyword. Note that the die( ) function won't produce the display you want in a web environment because its message is sent to the system standard error location, rather than to standard output.

As another example, we can check that an entered name is less than 10 characters long and that only its first letter is capitalized; we allow an initial character in the range A-Z, and between 0 and 9 characters in the range a-z:

```
if(param())
{
 if(!(param('Name')=~/^([A-Z][a-z]{0,9})$/))
 {
  print
   font({-color=>'red'},
    'Invalid name:  must comprise only letters, '.
    'be at most ten characters long, ',
    'and have only the first letter capitalized.');
```

```
  exit;
  }
my $Name = "$1";
print $Name;
}
```

The square brackets and braces have very different meanings in regular expressions. The square brackets around [a-z] mean "any character in the range from a to z," while the braces around {0,9} means "where the preceding item appears zero to nine times."

Resources

- For more on the CGI module, read the documentation at *http://search.cpan.org/dist/CGI.pm/CGI.pm*.
- For more on web scripting security, read the WWW security FAQ at *http://www.w3.org/Security/faq*.
- Regular expressions are a powerful tool. There are many good books on regular expressions, but try to choose one that focuses on Perl (there are slight variations in the regular expression syntax used in different tools). We recommend you read *Mastering Regular Expressions* by Jeffrey E. F. Friedl (O'Reilly).

Exercises

1. How is a Perl CGI script different from a command-line one?
2. What does the Perl CGI module do?
3. Write a regular expression that matches any word starting with "tele"; the match should not be case-sensitive.

## PART VI

Appendix

The Wedding Registry Code

Overview

In this appendix, we list the complete code of the wedding registry application we developed in Chapter 15. This code is also available for download from the book's web site.

Example A-1 contains the code in *action.php*; Example A-2 contains the code in *db.php*; Example A-3 contains the disclaimer code; Example A-4 contains the code in *edit.php*; Example A-5 contains the code in *index.php*; Example A-6 contains the text in *license.txt*; Example A-7 contains the code in *list.php*; and Example A-8 contains the code in *logout.php*.

Example A-1. action.php

```php
<?php
    // action.php: Add or remove a gift from the user's shopping list

    // Include database parameters and related functions
    require_once("db.php");

    // Check if the user is logged in
    // (this also starts the session)
    logincheck();

    // Secure the user data
    if(count($_GET))
    {
        // Connect to the MySQL DBMS and use the wedding database - credentials are
        // in the file db.php
        if(!($connection= @ mysqli_connect(
            $DB_hostname, $DB_username, $DB_password, $DB_databasename)))
            showerror($connection);

        $gift_id = clean($_GET['gift_id'], 5);
        $action = clean($_GET['action'] , 6);

        // Is the action something we know about?
```

```php
    if($action != "add" && $action != "remove")
        // No, it's not; perhaps someone's trying to manipulate the
        // URL query string?
        die("Unknown action: ".$action);

    // The program should reach this point only if the action is add
    // or remove, since otherwise processing stops with the die()
    // instruction.

    // What did the user want us to do?
    if ($action == "add")
    {
        // The user wants to add a new item to their shopping list.

        // Update the gifts table if we find the gift and it is not
        // taken by any user.
        // This query avoids the need to lock the table.
        $query = "UPDATE gifts SET username = '{$_SESSION['username']}' ".
            "WHERE gift_id = {$gift_id} AND username IS NULL";

        // Run the query through the connection
        if (($result = @ mysqli_query($connection, $query))==FALSE)
            showerror($connection);

        // If we found the row and updated it, create a confirmation
        // message to show the user
        if (mysqli_affected_rows($connection) == 1)
        {
            $message = "Reserved the gift for you, {$_SESSION['username']}";
        }
        else // Couldn't reserve the gift because it wasn't free;
        {
            // Check whether it's booked by someone else
            $query = "SELECT * FROM gifts ".
                "WHERE gift_id = {$gift_id} ".
                "AND username != '{$_SESSION['username']}'";
            // Run the query through the connection
            if (($result = @ mysqli_query($connection, $query))==FALSE)
                showerror($connection);

            // Create a message to show the user
            if (mysqli_num_rows($result))
                $message = "Oh dear... someone just beat you to that gift!";
            else
                $message = "The gift is already reserved for you, ".
                    "{$_SESSION['username']}";
        }
    }
    else // The action is not add, so it must be remove
    {
        // The user wants to remove an existing item from their shopping list.

        // Create a query to retrieve the gift.
        $query = "SELECT * FROM gifts WHERE gift_id = {$gift_id}";
```

```php
        // Run the query through the connection
        if (($result = @ mysqli_query($connection, $query))==FALSE)
            showerror($connection);

        // Get the matching gift row;
        // (there's only one since the gift_id is the primary key)
        // If we don't get exactly one answer, then we have a problem
        for($matchedrows=0;($row = @ mysqli_fetch_array($result));$matchedrows++);
        if($matchedrows!=1)
            die("We've just experienced a technical problem - ".
                "please notify the administrator.");

        // Double-check they actually have this gift reserved
        if (!empty($row["username"]) && $row["username"] != $_SESSION['username'])
            // They don't, so record a message to show the user
            $message = "That's not your gift, {$_SESSION['username']}!";
        else
        {
            // They do have it reserved. Create a query to unreserve it.
            $query = "UPDATE gifts SET username = NULL WHERE gift_id = {$gift_id}";

            // Run the query through the connection
            if (($result = @ mysqli_query($connection, $query))==FALSE)
                showerror($connection);

            // Create a message to show the user
            if (mysqli_affected_rows($connection) == 1)
                $message = "Removed the gift from your shopping list, ".
                    "{$_SESSION['username']}";
            else
                $message = "There was a problem updating. ".
                    "Please contact the administrator.";
        }
    }

    }

    // Redirect the browser back to list.php
    header("Location: list.php?message=" . urlencode($message));
    exit;
?>
```

Example A-2. db.php

```php
<?php
    // These are the DBMS credentials and the database name
    $DB_hostname = "localhost";
    $DB_username    = "fred";
    $DB_password    = "shhh";
    $DB_databasename = "wedding";

    // Show an error and stop the script
    function showerror($connection)
    {
        // Was there an error during connection?
        if(mysqli_connect_errno())
```

```php
        // Yes; display information about the connection error
        die("Error " . mysqli_connect_errno($connection) .
            " : " .mysqli_connect_error($connection));
    else
        // No; display the error information for the active connection
        die("Error " .mysqli_errno($connection) . " : "
                    .mysqli_error($connection));
}

// Secure the user data by escaping characters and shortening the
// input string
function clean($input, $maxlength)
{
    // Access the MySQL connection from outside this function.
    global $connection;

    // Limit the length of the string
    $input = substr($input, 0, $maxlength);

    // Escape semicolons and (if magic quotes are off) single and
    // double quotes
    if(get_magic_quotes_gpc())
        $input = stripslashes($input);

    $input = mysqli_real_escape_string($connection, $input);

    return $input;
}

// Check if the user is logged in. If not, send them to the login
// page
function logincheck()
{
    session_start();

    if (empty($_SESSION["username"]))
    {
        // redirect to the login page
        header("Location: index.php");
        exit;
    }
}
?>
```

Example A-3. disclaimer

```php
<?php
echo "\n<table width=\"60%\">";
echo "\n<tr><td>\n<hr />";
echo "\n<i>This is not really a wedding registry.
    It's a system that demonstrates the concepts of web database systems,
    and is downloadable source code that you can use freely under this
    <A href=\"license.txt\">license</a>. It pretends to
        allows wedding guests to log in, view a list of gifts wanted
        by the bride and groom, and reserve gifts that they plan to
        purchase by putting them on a shopping list.</i>";
```

```php
echo "\n</td>\n</tr>\n</table>\n<br />";
?>
```

Example A-4. edit.php

```php
<?php
    // edit.php: Show the user the available gifts and the gifts in
    // their shopping list

    // Include database parameters and related functions
    require_once("db.php");

    // Check if the user is logged in
    // (this also starts the session)
    logincheck();

    // Check that the user is Jack or Jill (username is 'jack' or
    // 'jill'); other users are not allowed to edit the gifts.
    if($_SESSION['username']!="jack" && $_SESSION['username']!="jill")
    {
        $message = "You are not authorized to edit the gift details. Please ".
            "select gift suggestions from the list to add to your shopping list!";
        header("Location: list.php?message=".urlencode($message));
        exit;
    }

    // Connect to the MySQL DBMS and use the wedding database - credentials are
    // in the file db.php
    if(!($connection= @ mysqli_connect(
        $DB_hostname, $DB_username, $DB_password, $DB_databasename)))
        showerror($connection);

    // See if we've arrived here after clicking the delete link
    if(count($_GET) && (clean($_GET['action'], 10)=='delete'))
    {
        // Yes; compose a query to delete the specified gift from the
        // gifts table
        $query = "DELETE FROM gifts WHERE gift_id=".clean($_GET['gift_id'], 10);

        // Run the query through the connection
        if (($result = @ mysqli_query($connection, $query))==FALSE)
            showerror($connection);
    }
    // See if we've arrived here after clicking the update button; if
    // so, update the gift details.
    elseif(isset($_POST['update']))
    {
        // Define an SQL query to list the gift IDs in the database
        $query = "SELECT gift_id FROM gifts";

        // Run the query through the connection
        if (($result = @ mysqli_query($connection, $query))==FALSE)
            showerror($connection);

        // Process the submitted data for each gift ID in the database
        while($row = @ mysqli_fetch_array($result))
```

```
    {
        $gift_id=$row["gift_id"];

        // Update an existing gift if there is corresponding data
        // submitted from the form
        if(
            isset($_POST["quantity"   ][$gift_id]) &&
            isset($_POST["description"][$gift_id]) &&
            isset($_POST["color"      ][$gift_id]) &&
            isset($_POST["shop"       ][$gift_id]) &&
            isset($_POST["price"      ][$gift_id])
        )
            update_or_insert_gift_data($connection, $gift_id);
    }

    // Process the data submitted in the form fields for the new
    // gift; we had assigned this the index 0 in the HTML form.
    update_or_insert_gift_data($connection, 0);

}

// Update the data for a gift with the specified gift ID; for a
// gift ID of 0, add a new gift to the database.
function update_or_insert_gift_data($connection, $gift_id)
{
    // Extract the data items for the gift attributes from the $_POST array
    $quantity   =clean($_POST["quantity"   ][$gift_id], 5);
    $description=clean($_POST["description"][$gift_id], 255);
    $color      =clean($_POST["color"      ][$gift_id], 30);
    $shop       =clean($_POST["shop"       ][$gift_id], 100);
    $price      =clean($_POST["price"      ][$gift_id], 30);

    // If the gift_id is 0, this is a new gift, so set the
    // gift_id to be empty; MySQL will automatically assign a
    // unique gift_id to the new gift.
    if($gift_id==0)
        $gift_id='';

    // If any of the attributes are empty, don't update the database.
    if(
        !strlen($quantity  ) ||
        !strlen($description) ||
        !strlen($color     ) ||
        !strlen($shop      ) ||
        !strlen($price     )
        )
    {
        // If this isn't the blank row for optionally adding a new gift,
        // or if it is the blank row and the user has actually typed
        // something in, display an error message.
        if(!empty($gift_id)
            ||
            strlen(
                $quantity.
                $description.
```

```
                        $color.
                        $shop.
                        $price)
                )
                echo "<font color='red'>".
                        "There must be no empty fields - not updating:<br />".
                        "([$quantity], [$description], [$color], [$shop], [$price])".
                        "<br /></font>";
        }
        else
        {
            // Add or update the gifts table
            $query = "REPLACE INTO gifts ".
                    "(gift_id, description,shop,quantity,color,price,username) values (".
                    "'$gift_id', '$description', '$shop', $quantity,".
                    "'$color', '$price', NULL)";

            // Run the query through the connection
            if (@ mysqli_query($connection, $query)==FALSE)
                showerror($connection);

        }
    }
}

// Show the user the gifts for editing
//
// Parameters:
// (1) An open $connection to the DBMS
function showgiftsforedit($connection)
{
    // Create an HTML form pointing back to this script
    echo "\n<form action='{$_SERVER["PHP_SELF"]}' method='POST'>";

    // Create an HTML table to neatly arrange the form inputs
    echo "\n<table border='1'>";

    // Create the table headings
    echo "\n<tr>" .
            "\n\t<th bgcolor='LIGHTGREEN'>ID</th>" .
            "\n\t<th bgcolor='LIGHTGREEN'>Description</th>" .
            "\n\t<th bgcolor='LIGHTGREEN'>Quantity</th>" .
            "\n\t<th bgcolor='LIGHTGREEN'>Color</th>" .
            "\n\t<th bgcolor='LIGHTGREEN'>Available from</th>" .
            "\n\t<th bgcolor='LIGHTGREEN'>Price</th>" .
            "\n\t<th bgcolor='LIGHTGREEN'>Delete?</th>" .
        "\n</tr>";

    // Create an SQL query to list the gifts in the database
    $query = "SELECT * FROM gifts ORDER BY description";

    // Run the query through the connection
    if (($result = @ mysqli_query($connection, $query))==FALSE)
        showerror($connection);

    // Check whether we found any gifts
```

```php
    if(!mysqli_num_rows($result))
        // No; display a notice
        echo "\n\t<tr><td colspan='7' align='center'>".
            "There are no gifts in the database</td></tr>";
    else
        // Yes; fetch the gift details a row at a time
        while($row = @ mysqli_fetch_array($result))
            // Compose the data for this gift into a row of form inputs
            // in the table.
            // Add a delete link in the last column of the row.
            echo "\n<tr>" .
                "\n\t<td>{$row["gift_id"]}</td>".
                "\n\t<td><input name='description[{$row['gift_id']}]' ".
                    "value='{$row["description"]}' size='60' /></td>".
                "\n\t<td><input name='quantity[{$row['gift_id']}]' ".
                    "value='{$row["quantity"]}'           /></td>".
                "\n\t<td><input name='color[{$row['gift_id']}]' ".
                    "value='{$row["color"]}'             /></td>".
                "\n\t<td><input name='shop[{$row['gift_id']}]' ".
                    "value='{$row["shop"]}' size='30' /></td>".
                "\n\t<td><input name='price[{$row['gift_id']}]' ".
                    "value='{$row["price"]}'             /></td>".
                "\n\t<td><a href='{$_SERVER['PHP_SELF']}?".
                    "action=delete&gift_id={$row["gift_id"]}'>Delete</a></td>".
                "\n</tr>";

    // Display a row with blank form inputs to allow a gift to be added
        echo "\n<tr><td>New item</td>" .
                "\n\t<td><input name='description[0]' size='60' /></td>".
                "\n\t<td><input name='quantity[0]' /></td>".
                "\n\t<td><input name='color[0]' /></td>".
                "\n\t<td><input name='shop[0]' size='30' /></td>".
                "\n\t<td><input name='price[0]' /></td>".
            "\n</tr>";

    // End the table
    echo "\n</table>";

    // Display a submit button and end the form.
    echo "\n<input name='update' type='submit' value='Update data' />";
    echo "</form>";
    }
?>
<!DOCTYPE HTML PUBLIC
"-//W3C//DTD HTML 4.0 Transitional//EN"
"http://www.w3.org/TR/html4/loose.dtd">
<html>
<head>
<title>Jack and Jill's Wedding Gift Registry</title>
</head>
<body bgcolor="LIGHTBLUE">
<?php
    // Show a logout link and a link to the main page
    echo "<a href='logout.php'>Logout</a> | <a href='list.php'>Gift list</a>";
```

```php
    echo "\n<h3>Gift editing page</h3>";

    // Show the existing gifts for editing
    showgiftsforedit($connection);
?>
</body>
</html>
```

Example A-5. index.php

```php
<?php
    // index.php: Show the user the login screen for the application, or
    // log in a user with correct authentication details.

    // Include database parameters and related functions
    require_once("db.php");

    // Connect to the MySQL DBMS and use the wedding database -
    // credentials are in the file db.php
    if(!($connection= @ mysqli_connect(
        $DB_hostname, $DB_username, $DB_password, $DB_databasename)))
        showerror($connection);

    // Pre-process the authentication data from the form for security
    // and assign the username and password to local variables
    if(count($_POST))
    {
        $username = clean($_POST["username"], 30);
        $password = clean($_POST["password"], 30);
    }

    // Pre-process the message data for security
    if(count($_GET))
    {
        $message = clean($_GET["message"], 128);
    }

    // If no username or password has been entered, or there's a message
    // to display, show the login page
    if(    empty($username) ||
        empty($password) ||
        isset($message) )
    {
        ?>
        <!DOCTYPE HTML PUBLIC "-//W3C//DTD HTML 4.0 Transitional//EN"
            "http://www.w3.org/TR/html4/loose.dtd">
        <html>
            <head>
                <title>Jack and Jill's Wedding Gift Registry</title>
            </head>
            <body bgcolor='LIGHTBLUE'>
                <h2>Jack and Jill's Wedding Gift Registry</h2>
                <?php
                    // If an error message is stored, show it...
                    if (isset($message))
                        echo "<h3><font color=\"red\">{$message}</font></h3>";
```

```
            ?>
            (if you've not logged in before, make up a username and password)
                <form action="<?php echo $_SERVER["PHP_SELF"];?>" method="POST">
                <br />Please enter a username:
                        <input type="text" name="username"
                            value="<?php if(isset($_POST['username']))
                                    echo $_POST['username'];?>" />
                <br />Please enter a password:
                        <input type="password" name="password" />
                <br /><input type="submit" value="Log in">
                </form>
                <br />
        <?php require "disclaimer"; ?>
        </body>
    </html>
    <?php
}
else
{
    // Check that the username and password are each at least four
    // characters long.
    if( (strlen($username)<4) ||
        (strlen($password)<4) )
    {
        // No, they're not; create an error message and redirect
        // the browser to the index page to display the message
        $message = "Please choose a username and password that are ".
            "at least four characters long";
        header("Location: index.php?message=" . urlencode($message));
        exit;
    }

    // Create a query to find any rows that match the provided username
    $query = "SELECT username, password FROM users WHERE username = '$username'";

    // Run the query through the connection
    if (($result = @ mysqli_query($connection, $query))==FALSE)
        showerror($connection);

    // Were there any matching rows?
    if (mysqli_num_rows($result) == 0)
    {
        // No, so insert the new username and password into the table
        $query = "INSERT INTO users SET username = '$username', password='".
            crypt($password, substr($username, 0, 2))."'";

        // Run the query through the connection
        if (($result = @ mysqli_query($connection, $query))==FALSE)
            showerror($connection);
    }
    else
    {
        // Yes, so check that the supplied password is correct

        // Fetch the matching row
```

```php
    // If we don't get exactly one answer, then we have a problem
    for($matchedrows=0;($tmprow = @ mysqli_fetch_array($result));$matchedrows++) $row=$tmprow;
    if($matchedrows!=1)
        die("We've just experienced a technical problem - ".
            "please notify the administrator.");

    // Does the user-supplied password match the password in the table?
    if (crypt($password, substr($username, 0, 2)) != $row["password"])
    {
        // No, so redirect the browser to the login page with a
        // message
        $message = "This user exists, but the password is incorrect. ".
            "Choose another username, or fix the password.";
        header("Location: index.php?message=" . urlencode($message));
        exit;
    }
}

    // Everything went OK. Start a session, store the username in a
    // session variable, and redirect the browser to the gift list
    // page with a welcome message.
    session_start();
    $_SESSION['username']=$username;
    $message = "Welcome {$_SESSION['username']}! Please select gift suggestions".
        " from the list to add to your shopping list!";
    header("Location: list.php?message=" . urlencode($message));
    exit;
}
?>
```

Example A-6. license.txt

```
Source code example for Learning MySQL

Unless otherwise stated, the source code distributed with this book can be
redistributed in source or binary form so long as an acknowledgment appears
in derived source files.
The citation should list that the code comes from
S.M.M. (Saied) Tahaghoghi and Hugh E. Williams,
"Learning MySQL" published by O'Reilly Media.
This code is under copyright and cannot be included in any other book,
publication, or educational product without permission from O'Reilly &
Associates.
No warranty is attached; we cannot take responsibility for errors or fitness
for use.
```

Example A-7. list.php

```php
<?php
    // list.php: Show the user the available gifts and the gifts in
    // their shopping list

    // Include database parameters and related functions
    require_once("db.php");

    // Check if the user is logged in
```

```
    // (this also starts the session)
    logincheck();

    // Show the user the gifts
    //
    // Parameters:
    // (1) An open connection to the DBMS
    // (2) Whether to show the available gifts or the current user's
    // shopping list.

    // Define constants for use when calling showgifts
    define("SHOW_UNRESERVED_GIFTS",             0);
    define("SHOW_GIFTS_RESERVED_BY_THIS_USER", 1);

    function showgifts($connection, $show_user_selection)
    {
        // See whether there are any gifts in the system
        $query = "SELECT * FROM gifts";

        // Run the query through the connection
        if (($result = @ mysqli_query($connection, $query))==FALSE)
            showerror($connection);

        // Check whether any gifts were found
        if (@ mysqli_num_rows($result) == 0)
            // No; print a notice
            echo "\n<h3><font color=\"red\">".
                "There are no gifts described in the system!</font></h3>";
        else
        {
            // Yes; display the gifts

            // If we're showing the available gifts, then set up
            // a query to show all unreserved gifts (where username IS NULL)
            if ($show_user_selection == SHOW_UNRESERVED_GIFTS)
                $query = "SELECT * FROM gifts WHERE username IS NULL ".
                    "ORDER BY description";
            else
                // Otherwise, set up a query to show all gifts reserved by
                // this user
                $query = "SELECT * FROM gifts WHERE username = '".
                    $_SESSION['username']."' ORDER BY description";

            // Run the query through the connection
            if (($result = @ mysqli_query($connection, $query))==FALSE)
                showerror($connection);

            // Did we get back any rows?
            if (@ mysqli_num_rows($result) == 0)
            {
                // No data was returned from the query.
                // Show an appropriate message
                if ($show_user_selection == SHOW_UNRESERVED_GIFTS)
                    echo "\n<h3><font color=\"red\">No gifts left!</font></h3>";
                else
```

```php
            echo "\n<h3><font color=\"red\">Your Basket is Empty!".
                "</font></h3>";
    }
    else
    {
        // Yes, so show the gifts as a table
        echo "\n<table border=1 width=100%>";

        // Create some headings for the table
        echo "\n<tr>" .
            "\n\t<th>Quantity</th>" .
            "\n\t<th>Gift</th>" .
            "\n\t<th>Colour</th>" .
            "\n\t<th>Available From</th>" .
            "\n\t<th>Price</th>" .
            "\n\t<th>Action</th>" .
            "\n</tr>";

        // Fetch each database table row of the results
        while($row = @ mysqli_fetch_array($result))
        {
            // Display the gift data as a table row
            echo "\n<tr>" .
                "\n\t<td>{$row["quantity"]}</td>" .
                "\n\t<td>{$row["description"]}</td>" .
                "\n\t<td>{$row["color"]}</td>" .
                "\n\t<td>{$row["shop"]}</td>" .
                "\n\t<td>{$row["price"]}</td>";

            // Are we showing the list of gifts reserved by the
            // user?
            if ($show_user_selection == SHOW_UNRESERVED_GIFTS)
                // No. So set up an embedded link that the user can click
                // to add the gift to their shopping list by running
                // action.php with action=add
                echo "\n\t<td><a href=\"action.php?action=add&" .
                    "gift_id={$row["gift_id"]}\">".
                    "Add to Shopping List</a></td>";
            else
                // Yes. So set up an embedded link that the user can click
                // to remove the gift to their shopping list by running
                // action.php with action=remove
                echo "\n\t<td><a href=\"action.php?action=remove&" .
                    "gift_id={$row["gift_id"]}\">".
                    "Remove from Shopping list</a></td>";
        }
        echo "\n</table>";
    }
    }
    }
?>
<!DOCTYPE HTML PUBLIC
"-//W3C//DTD HTML 4.0 Transitional//EN"
"http://www.w3.org/TR/html4/loose.dtd">
<html>
```

```
<head>
<title>Jack and Jill's Wedding Gift Registry</title>
</head>
<body bgcolor='LIGHTBLUE'>
<?php
    // Show a logout link
    echo "<a href='logout.php'>Logout</a>";

    // Check whether the user is Jack or Jill (username is 'jack' or
    // 'jill'); if so, show a link to the gift editing page.
    if($_SESSION['username']=="jack" || $_SESSION['username']=="jill")
        echo " | <a href='edit.php'>Edit gifts</a>";

    // Connect to the MySQL DBMS and use the wedding database -
    // credentials are in the file db.php
    if(!($connection= @ mysqli_connect(
        $DB_hostname, $DB_username, $DB_password, $DB_databasename)))
        showerror($connection);

    // Pre-process the message data for security
    if(count($_GET))
        $message = clean($_GET["message"], 128);

    // If there's a message to show, output it
    if (!empty($message))
        echo "\n<h3><font color=\"red\"><em>".
            urldecode($message)."</em></font></h3>";

    echo "\n<h3>Here are some gift suggestions</h3>";

    // Show the gifts that are still unreserved
    showgifts($connection, SHOW_UNRESERVED_GIFTS);

    echo "\n<h3>Your Shopping list</h3>";

    // Show the gifts that have been reserved by this user
    showgifts($connection, SHOW_GIFTS_RESERVED_BY_THIS_USER);
?>
</body>
</html>
```

Example A-8. logout.php

```
<?php
    // Log out of the system by ending the session and load the main
    // page

    session_start();
    session_destroy();

    // Redirect to the main page
    $message = "Thank you for using this system - you have now logged out.";
    header("Location: index.php?message=" . urlencode($message));
?>
```

Index

Symbols

! exclamation mark, 14
! NOT (Perl), 525
!= (Perl), 515
!= (PHP), 420, 422
!== (PHP), 422
$ (PHP), 416
$connection (PHP), 461
$DBI::errstr, 541
$ref, 549
$result string (Perl), 561
$_COOKIE (PHP), 456
$_GET (PHP), 404, 454
$_POST (PHP), 454
$_SERVER (PHP), 456
$_SESSION (PHP), 455
% (Perl), 515, 521
&& (Perl), 525
* (Perl), 514
+ (Perl), 514
++ (Perl), 515, 522
- (Perl), 514
-- (Perl), 515
->, 540
/ (Perl), 515
< (Perl), 516
< (PHP), 420
<= (Perl), 516
<?php (PHP), 403, 415
= (Perl), 514
== (Perl), 515
== (PHP), 421
=== (PHP), 421
> (Perl), 516
> (PHP), 420
>= (Perl), 516
>= (PHP), 420
?> (PHP), 403, 415
@ (Perl), 520
@_ (Perl), 536
\n (Perl), 513
\n (PHP), 469
\t (Perl), 513
|| OR (Perl), 525

A

access privileges, 297–349
action.php, 501, 502
activating privileges, 346
ADD keyword, 216
add.php (PHP), 454
administrator, 12
AFTER keyword, 217
aggregate functions, 228–236, 263
    DISTINCT, 229
    GROUP BY, 230–234
    HAVING, 234
aggregating values, 161
aliases, 223–228
    column, 224
    restrictions, 226
    table, 226
ALL, 255
ALTER, 335
ALTER TABLE statement, 215, 217, 270, 544
AND && (Perl), 525
AND operation, 146
anonymous users, 315, 328
ANY, 253

hash symbol, 20, 374
hash-bang, 512
HAVING, 234
    when not to use, 236
header( ) function (Perl), 561
header( ) function (PHP), 465, 466, 479
host table, 343
HTML, 6
    simple HTML form, 452
HTTP POST method, 562
HTTP request, 400
HTTP servers, 400
HTTP::Mason, 557

I

IBM, 7
IDENTIFIED BY, 325
identifier columns, 250
IF NOT EXISTS, 186, 286
if statement (Perl), 531
if statement (PHP), 420
if...else (Perl), 525
IGNORE, 280
importing and exporting data, 552
IN, 254, 257
.inc files, 452
include (PHP), 449
include directory, 82
index files, web server, 402
INDEX keyword, 206, 336
index.php, 478
indexes, 205, 287
    adding a new, 218
    and keys, 204–208
    modifying once created, 219
    names, 206
    removing, 218
INNER JOIN keywords, 157, 159, 237, 290
inner query, 251
InnoDB, 271
INSERT statement, 278
    basics, 163
    INSERT INTO, 278
inserting data using queries, 277–281
installation, 4, 9–94
    binaries, 9
    choices and platforms, 9–12
    components, 5
    ISP, provided by, 69

Linux, 10, 25–51
Mac OS X, 11, 61–69
source code, 9
troubleshooting, 75–80
Windows, 11, 51–61
INT column type, 188
integer types, alternative, 198
integrity of packages, verifying, 22
interface, 5
intermediate entity, 119
internationalization, 186
Internet Explorer, 396
isset( ) function (PHP), 422, 462, 479, 494

J

joining two tables, 156–162
joins
    inner join, 237–239
    left join, 246–249
    natural join, 249–250
    right join, 246–249
    union, 239–246

K

key constraints, 115
KEY keyword, 206
key, Perl, 520
keys, 113
    candidate, 113
    primary, 113
keys and indexes, 204–208
key_buffer_size, 384
KILL command, 391
Knoppix, 11
konsole, 13

L

LAMP, 6, 395
LEFT JOIN, 246, 290
left joins, 246–249, 246
LEFT OUTER JOIN, 249
lib directory, 82
LIKE statement, 145, 174, 286
LIMIT statement, 155–156, 170, 172, 242, 251, 290
Linux, 10
    Perl, 512
    scheduling backups, 362

ORDER BY RAND( ), 279
OUTER, 249
outer query, 251, 261
overwriting data, 292

P

param( ) function, 563, 566
parentheses, 147
partial participation, 116
participation constraints, 116
PASSWORD keyword, 327
password options, 371
passwords, 324–328
    errors, 103
    hiding, 103
    resetting forgotten, 347
PASSWORD( ) function, 325
performance, 391
    privileges and, 346
Perl, 5, 511–538
    ! NOT, 525
    !=, 515
    $result, 561
    %, 515, 521
    &&, 525
    *, 514
    +, 514
    ++, 515, 522
    -, 514
    --, 515
    /, 515
    <, 516
    <=, 516
    =, 514
    ==, 515
    >, 516
    >=, 516
    @, 520
    @_, 536
    AND &&, 525
    array, 520, 523
    backslash, 513
    braces, 518
    CGI or DBI modules, installing, 89
        error messages, 91
        Linux, 89
        Mac OS X, 91
        Windows, 90
    checking existing setup, 88

Comprehensive Perl Archive Network
    (CPAN), 511
conditional statements, 524–526
curly brackets, 518
do...while loop, 523
double-quote, 519
eq, 524
escape character, 513
for loop, 522
foreach, 524
hash, 520, 523
hash-bang, 512
if...else, 525
installing, 88–92
key, 520
Linux, 512
loop, 522
Mac OS X, 512
mathematical operators, 514–517
MySQL (see Perl and MySQL together)
NOT !, 525
operator precedence, 516
OR ||, 525
print, 537
printf, 537
push command, 561
reading in both animal names and counts
        from the command line, 528
reading in numbers from the command line,
    527
reading in values from a file, 530–533
reading in values from standard input, 533
reading in values from the command line,
    527–530
scalar, 514
scope, 518
script using array variables, 520
script using hash variables, 520
script with both types of binding, 550
scripting, 513–538
security, 566
semicolon, 513
setting up, 88
shebang, 512
shift, 536
single-quote, 519
sum, 536
variables, 513, 517

X

Y

Z

About the Authors

Saied Tahaghoghi is a senior lecturer at the RMIT University School of Computer Science and Information Technology. He has a bachelor's degree in electronics engineering, a master's degree in computer engineering, and a PhD in computer science, and loves tinkering with both hardware and software. Saied is a member of the RMIT Search Engine Group, and supervises research on text, image, video, and code retrieval. He teaches courses on web technologies and security, and is frequently asked to consult on projects by industry. Saied was born in Iran but has spent almost equal parts of his life in Iran, England, Pakistan, and Australia, and is a fervent advocate of dialogue between civilizations. His home page is *http://saied.tahaghoghi.com*.

Hugh E. Williams is a software design engineer at Microsoft's Windows Live Search in Redmond, Washington. Previously, he was an Associate Professor in Information Retrieval at RMIT University in Melbourne, Australia. He's published over 70 research papers and holds around 10 patents, mostly in the search engine area. When not at work, Hugh likes to hang out with his family, exercise, watch Richmond play footy, and learn about baseball. Hugh has a PhD from RMIT University. His home page is *http://hughwilliams.com*.

Colophon

Our look is the result of reader comments, our own experimentation, and feedback from distribution channels. Distinctive covers complement our distinctive approach to technical topics, breathing personality and life into potentially dry subjects.

The type of butterfly on the cover of *Learning MySQL* is the blue spotted crow (*euploea midamus*). One of more than 15,000 species of butterfly, this member of the brush-footed family *Nymphalidae* (which also is home to the Monarch) is native to the Orient and can be found in a region that spreads from Afghanistan to Australia. As its name suggests, the crow is distinguished by its blue tint, as well as a series of white spots that line the hind edge of its large wings.

In the course of their lives, butterflies go through four development stages: egg, larva, pupa, and adult. Butterfly eggs, ovate or spherical in shape, are attached to leaves by a powerful, quickly hardening glue until they hatch. In the larval stage, butterflies are commonly referred to as *caterpillars*, and their bodies are divided into many small segments, each possessing up to four pairs of legs. Caterpillars have insatiable appetites, feeding practically nonstop on plant matter and molting approximately four or five times before becoming pupae. At this third phase, the caterpillar becomes a *chrysalis*, typically cleaving to the underside of a leaf. The chrysalis then consumes foodstuffs that enable it to develop its wing structures and make the metamorphosis into an adult butterfly. In this final stage of development, the butterfly is known as an *imago*, a four-winged creature with six legs. Imagos subsist mainly on flower nectar; some supplement their diets with nutrients from sap, pollen, rotten fruit, or dung.

In Japanese culture, butterflies are somewhat paradoxically mythologized as both harbingers of prosperity and impending doom. One superstition stipulates that a single butterfly flying into one's bedroom presages the arrival of one's dearest love, while an encounter with a swarm of butterflies is thought to be a precursor to ominous events.

The cover image is from Cassell's Natural History. The cover font is Adobe ITC Garamond. The text font is Linotype Birka; the heading font is Adobe Myriad Condensed; and the code font is LucasFont's TheSans Mono Condensed.

Better than e-books

Buy *Learning MySQL* and access the
digital edition FREE on Safari for 45 days.

Go to www.oreilly.com/go/safarienabled
and type in coupon code S5IP-6UBH-WP26-VWHP-QQMV

Search
thousands of
top tech books

Download
whole chapters

Cut and Paste
code examples

Find
answers fast

Search Safari! The premier electronic reference
library for programmers and IT professionals.

Related Titles from O'Reilly

Database

The Art of SQL

Database in Depth

High Performance MySQL

Learning MySQL

Learning PHP and MySQL

Learning SQL

Learning SQL on SQL Server 2005

Managing & Using MySQL, *2nd Edition*

MySQL Cookbook, *2nd Edition*

MySQL in a Nutshell

MySQL Pocket Reference

MySQL Reference Manual

MySQL Stored Procedure Programming

Practical PostgreSQL

Programming SQL Server 2005

The Relational Database Dictionary

SQL Cookbook

SQL in a Nutshell, *2nd Edition*

SQL Pocket Guide, *2nd Edition*

SQL Tuning

Understanding MySQL Internals

Web Database Applications with PHP and MySQL, *2nd Edition*

O'REILLY®

Our books are available at most retail and online bookstores.

To order direct: 1-800-998-9938 • *order@oreilly.com* • *www.oreilly.com*

Online editions of most O'Reilly titles are available by subscription at *safari.oreilly.com*